THE MOST DANGEROUS MAN IN DETROIT

Archives of Labor and Urban Affairs, Wayne State University

THE MOST DANGEROUS MAN IN DETROIT

Walter Reuther and the Fate of American Labor

NELSON LICHTENSTEIN

BasicBooks
A Division of HarperCollins*Publishers*

Designed by Elliott Beard

Library of Congress Cataloging-in-Publication Data
Lichtenstein, Nelson.
    The most dangerous man in Detroit : Walter Reuther and the fate of American Labor / Nelson Lichtenstein.
        p.   cm.
    Includes bibliographical references and index.
    ISBN 0–465–09080–X
    1. Reuther, Walter, 1907–1970.   2. Trade-unions—United States—Officials and employees—Biography.   3. Labor leaders—United States—Biography.   4. Trade-unions—Automobile industry workers—United States—History.   5. International Union, United Automobile, Aerospace, and Agricultural Implement Workers of America—History.   I. Title.
    HD6509.R4L53   1995
    331.88'1292'092—dc20
    [B]   95-16874
                                                                          CIP

96 97 98 ❖/HC 9 8 7 6 5 4 3

To the memory of my parents:
Beryl Rose
and
Theodore Samuel
Lichtenstein

Walter Reuther is the most dangerous man in Detroit because no one is more skillful in bringing about the revolution without seeming to disturb the existing forms of society.

—*George Romney, Automobile Manufacturers' Association, 1945*

CONTENTS

PREFACE

I never met Walter Reuther, but as a youth growing up in the 1950s and
1960s, his name and voice seemed always before me. The content of his
televised speeches and interviews was unexceptional, disappointing in some vague
way, but his words demanded the attention of my parents and myself because we
knew that this man was powerful in a way that other politicians were not. He commanded the big battalions at the very heart of American industry and politics.
Even to small-town liberals in exurban Maryland, the United Automobile, Aircraft, and Agricultural Implement Workers of America (UAW) seemed exciting
and potent allies whose dramatic origins in the great sit-down strikes of the 1930s
reminded us of labor's explosive capacity to reorder the world of work and politics.
Undoubtedly, my very ignorance about what actually happened inside an automobile factory and the considerable distance between Maryland and Detroit made
it easier to put Walter Reuther and his union in a wondrous light.

In graduate school at Berkeley, I learned a lot more about Walter Reuther, but
not inside the classroom. In the New Left and among the older generation of radicals who offered guidance, the contours of his career were given a Talmudic reading. Was he a Communist during his two-year sojourn in Stalin's Russia? When
and why did he abandon the socialist faith? Was the strike he launched against
General Motors in 1945—for wage increases without a rise in the price of cars—
a deployment in the United States of Leon Trotsky's ideas? Why did he not organize a labor party in 1948? Our New Left critique charged him with hypocrisy and
opportunism, but harsh as it was, even this assault on his person and his politics

reflected an understanding that he had once been on our side, and might yet return.

Over the course of a twenty-year career in academe, I've written a good deal about the automobile industry and the American labor movement. Always, I seemed to be writing around or about Walter Reuther. He is an inescapable figure in twentieth-century labor history and midcentury liberalism. His most exciting years were the 1940s, when his power and vision coincided most closely. Inevitably, this book is as much about the UAW as it is about the man who did so much to found it and then spent almost his entire adult life in its governance. "An institution is the lengthened shadow of one man," wrote Ralph Waldo Emerson; during the UAW's brief maturity in the 1950s and 1960s this great union did come to reflect many of the virtues and vanities of Walter Reuther himself. His inner life has been hard to probe, not because he had much to hide, but rather because he so transparently identified himself with the ethos and purpose of the union to which he was wed. Enemies of the labor movement nearly killed Reuther on three occasions, but he never wavered in his chosen vocation. If he experienced any of the self-doubt and turmoil common to the twentieth-century human condition, he left scant record of it, in either private musings or public testimony. The union and its works were his monument, and he would have us judge him by the accomplishments and failures of that cause.

Reuther's UAW helped write this book. In 1962 the union began to deposit its papers at Wayne State University "to insure that future generations in our society will have available an accurate account of the role that the UAW has played in the economic, political and social life of the nation." Four years later it donated money to build the magnificent Walter Reuther Library of Labor and Urban Affairs; I have spent hundreds of pleasant and fruitful hours there. Unless otherwise noted, all reference material in this volume is from the Reuther Library. The staff there is superb. Over the years Patricia Bartkowski, Ray Boryczka, Carolyn Davis, Tom Featherstone, Margery Long, Dione Miles, Warner Pflug, Margaret Raucher, and Kathleen Schmeling have tracked down thousands of documents, newspapers and photographs. In 1990 a Rockefeller Research Fellowship enabled me to spend several continuous months at Wayne State and the Reuther Library.

I am also fortunate to have had support from the National Endowment for the Humanities, the Hagley Museum and Library, the Bankard Fund of the University of Virginia, and the Woodrow Wilson Center. William Cassidy proved a skillful guide at the National Archives, and Michael Nash did much the same at the Hagley Museum. Archivists at the Roosevelt, Truman, Kennedy, and Johnson presidential libraries have aided my work as well.

More than seventy interviews went into the research for this biography. Some were but brief phone calls, others inaugurated friendships of many years' duration. Many of those whom I interviewed have now passed away, including John Anderson, Harry Chester, George Edwards, Henry Kraus, Joseph Rauh, Larry Rogin, Brendan Sexton, Nat Weinberg, and Abe Zwerling. In particular, I want to thank

Irving Bluestone, Lisa Dickmeyer, William Dodds, Walter Dorosh, Douglas Fraser, Martin Gerber, Bill Goode, Herbert Hill, Genora Johnson, Herman Rebban, Linda Reuther, Victor Reuther, Christine Richey, Stephen Schlossberg, Paul Schrade, Carl Shier, Alan Strachan, Shelton Tappes, Saul Wellman, B. J. Widick, and Eleanor Wolf.

Academic life is a village, and I have called upon friends and colleagues without hesitation. Steve Babson, Julian Bond, Ray Borochyka, David Brody, Herbert Hill, Christopher Johnson, Mel Leffler, Dennis MacShane, Ruth Milkman, Bruce Nelson, Judith Stein, and Jonathan Zeitlin have demonstrated wonderful collegiality by reading sections of the manuscript and giving me good advice in return. In addition, conversations with Steven Amberg, Kevin Boyle, Steve Meyer, Tom Segrue, Seth Wigderson, Craig Zabala, and other "autocentric" scholars have proven enormously stimulating. Three individuals, each from a different political generation, have given me much moral support in addition to their sage advice. Saul Wellman shared with me the passions that took him from the Abraham Lincoln Brigade to the New Left and beyond; Mike Parker kept me abreast of contemporary trade union and auto industry affairs; Dana Frank made sure I knew how all this looked to a political generation coming of age years after Walter Reuther passed from the scene. As research assistants, Colleen Doody and Jennifer Klein answered my e-mail queries from faraway Finland when I held a Fulbright Fellowship there in 1993–94. And great thanks to my neighbor William Walsh, who tracked down and obliterated a particularly nasty computer virus when the word processing was at a crucial stage.

Eileen Boris read the earliest and most difficult drafts of the manuscript and offered me the encouragement I craved and the advice I needed to make the leap from writing narrative history to writing political biography. Her loving support and scholarly example never faltered. After a manuscript was completed, Michael Kazin and Joshua Freeman came to my aid with the kind of wise and knowledgeable readings that reduced its bulk, sharpened its point, and saved me from numerous pitfalls. Graduate student Meg Jacobs revealed no less talent and generosity throughout the course of the remarkable editorial commentary she offered on this manuscript. Copy editor Cindy Buck saved me from much embarrassment. And Steve Fraser has again demonstrated his wonderful patience and insight as an editor, guide, and scholar. After writing two books and an article under his editorship, I can safely say, When he offers advice, take it!

My son Daniel knew nothing of Walter Reuther when I began this project. He knows more now, and I look forward to our talk when he decides to read the book. I would also like to have discussed this book with my parents, but they are no longer here. Nevertheless, I feel certain that Theodore and Beryl Lichtenstein would find in the work many of the values and much of the spirit they offered me in my youth.

—*Charlottesville*, VA
June 1995

1

FATHER AND SONS

The workers can be emancipated only by their own collective will . . . and this collective will and conquering power can only be the result of education, enlightenment and self-imposed discipline.
— *Eugene V. Debs, "Sound Socialist Tactics,"* 1912

Late in 1903 the city fathers of Wheeling, West Virginia, asked Andrew Carnegie to build their city a library. The steelmaker turned philanthropist had already funded several hundred all across industrial America, and it seemed certain that their application would meet with success. Wheeling was the largest and most industrialized city in West Virginia, with a diversified manufacturing base that included firms in the iron and steel, pottery, wood, brass, glass, cigarmaking, brewing, and meatpacking industries. This growing community of forty thousand seemed just the sort of deserving place for Carnegie's benevolence. In return, all that Carnegie required was a city commitment, in the form of a $50,000 bond levy, to buy the land and books and staff the building.

The library had all the right supporters: the mayor, the city council, the board of education, the daily newspapers, as well as all the leading businessmen. These were the "go-ahead citizens of this community," asserted Wheeling's *Daily Intelligencer*.[1] And there was Andrew Carnegie himself, who had built his philanthropy on a combination of sincere Christian charity, pious self-justification, and procapitalist propaganda that made him as controversial a figure in retirement as he had been as a captain of industry. The *Daily Intelligencer* captured some of these shadings when it editorialized, "Mr. Carnegie is so situated that any affront to him at

1

this time might in the end prove very disastrous to the physical welfare of Wheeling. . . . We desire Mr. Carnegie's good will. He deserves our good will."[2]

Only the Ohio Valley Trades and Labor Assembly raised its voice against the Carnegie gift. The largest and most vigorous central labor organization in the state, the labor assembly served as the lively political voice for nearly four thousand Wheeling workers organized into more than forty local unions. The labor assembly remembered well the bitter and world-famous Homestead strike of 1892 when Carnegie Steel had used Pinkerton agents and state militia to break its once-powerful unions and open up an era of what even Andrew Carnegie called "prodigious" profits for his billion-dollar corporation. With more than one local of the bloodied Amalgamated Association of Iron, Steel, and Tin Workers represented in its ranks, the Wheeling labor assembly naturally supported the Carnegie Steel strikers, even holding a "Homestead Day" to raise money for the vanquished steelworkers.

Thus Wheeling unionists mobilized quickly, and almost unanimously, against a Carnegie library. The steelworker Mike Mahoney denounced the philanthropist as the "greatest of oppressors," a foe "who gave with one hand and took away with the other." Carnegie's library was nothing more than a "disgraceful monument" to a "cold blooded outrage." Rather than erect such a building, Mahoney asked the citizens of Wheeling to defeat the bond levy, "thereby paying tribute to our murdered comrades, whose ashes repose in the precious soil at Homestead." Wheeling trade unionists took up the challenge: they soapboxed on the street corners, confronted the city council, and put precinct workers at every polling place on election day. The working class must vote no, concluded another Wheeling unionist, so "there will be one place on this great green planet where Andrew Carnegie can't get a monument to his money."[3]

The citywide vote pitted unionist against employer, Wheeling's working-class districts against the civic elite, and a community of German, Scandinavian, Polish, Irish, and Appalachian workers against the economic power and ideological values embodied in giant enterprise. Led by an activist core of Socialists and radicals, many Wheeling workers were persuaded that the fight against the library represented a defense of their dignity and manhood, a declaration of independence cast against the encroaching power of a new feudalism. Throughout the nineteenth century and well into the twentieth, the most active and energetic American workers had framed their struggles in these ethical and moral terms. Such rhetoric reflected a sense of communal citizenship—historians have since labeled it republicanism—that gave to the working-class movement of those years a sense of moral order and transcendent purpose. The fight was waged on many fronts: in the factories and mines, certainly, but also in municipal politics, public education, the construction of parks and playgrounds, even in the shifting character of a city's patriotic rituals. Thus the labor assembly's fight against the Carnegie library was but a skirmish in the larger, protracted struggle waged by so many turn-of-the-century Americans to define and defend a consciously working-class citizenship.[4]

Wheeling unionists cheered the results of the January 1904 vote. A majority of voters had cast ballots for the library, but a three-fifths majority was needed for passage, so the appropriation failed. More important, the working-class districts in South and East Wheeling had voted three-to-one against Carnegie's gift. Wheeling thus became the only city in West Virginia, and one of but a handful in the nation, to spurn the steelmaker's benevolence. The city eventually built its own public library, with its own funds, in the very heart of proletarian South Wheeling.[5]

Among the most active campaigners against the Carnegie library was a twenty-two-year-old German immigrant, a beer wagon driver, who had arrived in Wheeling in the last year of the nineteenth century. Valentine Reuther was typical of the immigrant Socialists who had helped invigorate America's turn-of-the-century labor movement. He was born in 1881 in the Rhineland village of Edigheim. His parents, Jacob and Christina, were peasants, devout, literate Lutherans who set sail for the United States in 1892 in the midst of the last great wave of German immigration to North America. Rhineland farming had become a chronic struggle against poor soil and the international market. But of equal importance, Valentine Reuther's father feared the growing weight of Bismarckian militarism, for which he had a pacifist's disdain. Jacob Reuther arose each morning at 4:00 A.M. to read his Bible, but he rejected much Lutheran doctrine: though not a social democrat, his faith was one of active engagement in the world. The elder Reuther is said to have remarked that churches try to do too much for God and not enough for men.[6]

The Reuther family settled near Effingham on the Illinois prairie, close by one of Jacob's brothers who had come over earlier. Valentine, who was eleven when the family made the move, spent his teenage years in a hard struggle against the land. But he was no more of a farmer than the millions of other young men and women, in both Europe and America, who were determined to free themselves from the stultification of rural life. In the fall of 1899, after the crops were in, Valentine made his leap to the city, to Wheeling, where he joined an older brother, Jake, who had already become part of that city's large and well-organized German community.

He soon wrangled a job in one of Wheeling's ironworks, as a night-shift laborer earning $1.50 a day; within months he made a move to the big money as a "heater" in the rolling mill. As a heater, which was considered skilled work, Val Reuther became eligible to join the Amalgamated Association of Iron, Steel, and Tin Workers, of Homestead fame. He proved a faithful unionist, whose dedication, intelligence, and bilingual fluency made him a natural leader among German workers and their friends. But when the Amalgamated called an unsuccessful strike at the ironworks in 1902, he lost his well-paying job. The strike was hardly as dramatic as Homestead, but the underlying issues were much the same. The Amalgamated, which rejected organization of the many unskilled eastern European laborers in its industry, fought a losing battle to preserve a world in which skilled workmen commanded the respect of their employers and effective control of their work. These workmen, largely of Welsh, German, and Irish extraction,

faced a newly self-conscious management who counterpoised a drive for technological rationalization to their own mastery of the production process.[7] The strike
probably reinforced Valentine Reuther's appreciation of the value of skilled,
autonomous work, an appreciation he would instill in his four sons, all of whom
eventually secured the kind of work he found just beyond his reach.

Like so many other German immigrants, Valentine had been a member of a
German singing society, the Beethoven Gesangverein, which itself was part of the
extraordinarily dense set of German-language cultural associations, including
gymnastic societies, educational circles, and union beer gardens, that sustained
German working-class culture and advanced the political self-confidence of
Valentine's generation of immigrants. Typically, it was through a friend in the
Beethoven Gesangverein that Val got his next job, as a beer wagon driver for the
Schmulbach Brewing Company. Driving a wagon, sometimes in freezing weather,
was "unskilled work," and the wages were far lower than those of a heater or roller
in the ironworks. But the pay was steady, and the job gave Val Reuther the opportunity to play an active role in the leadership of the union movement in Wheeling, his real passion in these years before World War I.

Valentine Reuther helped organize a local of the brewery workers at Schmulbach. In midwestern towns like Wheeling, the brewing trade was heavily German,
both in ownership and workforce, and it was a local market industry that protected
these same owners and workers from the fierce competitive gales that made life so
miserable in the steel mills, coal mines, and railroad yards. The relationship
between the company and the union was therefore a placid one, but this hardly
retarded Valentine Reuther's political development. The International Union of
Brewery Workers was itself an unusual union, industrial in form, largely Socialist in
leadership, one of a handful of well-entrenched, left-wing unions in the nation. Val
also became close friends with a cousin from the old country, Philip Reuther, who
introduced the young unionist to the Socialist movement of the United States.[8]

In the first decade of the twentieth century, socialism was a broad and inclusive
movement in this country, with a place for Marxist intellectuals, Oklahoma pop-
ulists, Jewish bundists, and social gospel ministers. Confident that the growth of
industry, knowledge, and socialist ideas had to go hand in hand, the Socialist Party
(SP) of these prewar years was a school that educated a generation of working-class
youth in economics, science, literature, and philosophy. With thousands of others,
Val Reuther eagerly absorbed the pamphlets and books turned out in cheap edi-
tions by the great Socialist publishing houses of Chicago and Girard, Kansas. He
faithfully read the mass-circulation Socialist weekly, *The Appeal to Reason*, the lectures of the agnostic Robert Ingersoll, and the inspiring speeches of the Socialist
tribune Eugene V. Debs.

Goethe and Schiller, Lincoln and Jefferson, Darwin and Huxley, were all part
of an expansive socialist lexicon studied by self-taught and intellectually hungry
young workers like Val Reuther. Upton Sinclair's 1906 novel, *The Jungle*, a sharply
drawn depiction of capitalist degradation and socialist redemption, won a vast

audience, while the novels and stories of Jack London could be found in almost every schoolboy's bedroom. *The Appeal to Reason* and another Socialist periodical, *Wilshire's* magazine, each averaged 250,000 circulation across the nation. Debsian socialism was therefore very much an organic part of American working-class life—a minority tendency, to be sure, and heavily weighted toward Germans, Jews, Finns, skilled craftsmen in the metal trades, and maritime workers on shore and at sea, but it was hardly the alien, European transplant seen by most of its contemporary foes and even some of its latter-day chroniclers. For many immigrants, Debsian socialism served as an "Americanization" movement that enabled newcomers to retain the cultural and political values of their homelands even as it drew them into the thick of American life.[9]

Val Reuther trod this path. A friendly and energetic young man, he was determined to improve himself as he advanced the Socialist cause in the upper Ohio Valley. The Brewery Workers quickly elected him a delegate to the Ohio Valley Trades and Labor Assembly, where his articulate and bilingual militancy made him a well-known spokesman for Wheeling's organized working class. For more than a decade he defended labor's cause at city hall and before the board of education and legislative committees at the state capital, where he testified often in favor of child labor legislation. He was soon made painfully aware, however, of both his German accent and his limited schooling, which he strove to rectify through a correspondence course in English and spelling.

These were heady days for Ohio Valley Socialists. The state party won support from unions of glassworkers, printers, carpenters, machinists, cigarmakers, and brewery workers; in Wheeling the Socialists generally controlled the Ohio Valley labor assembly and the local labor paper, through both of which they waged a vigorous campaign for independent political action. In 1909, at the age of twenty-seven, Valentine Reuther served a term as president of the Ohio Valley Trades and Labor Assembly. He came to love Eugene V. Debs and campaigned for him throughout the state each time the Socialist leader ran for office. The Socialist Party expanded steadily. The number of Mountain State party branches grew from six to fifty-three in the six years after 1905; likewise, the Socialist vote shot upward to about 6 percent in the statewide poll of 1912, about the national average. In Ohio County (Wheeling) the Debs ticket did even better, capturing 11 percent overall, and more than 42 percent in some working-class wards heavily populated by hard-pressed tobacco and steel workers.[10]

Val Reuther's socialism emphasized political action because strikes and confrontations threatened to disrupt the fragile accommodation that the craft unions of Wheeling had achieved with the local employer class. Moreover, many German Socialists placed a high value on the civic freedom and republican institutions that seemed so advanced in the United States, certainly compared with the German Reich and its inequitable franchise and antisocialist laws. "Ein politisch und sozial befreites Deutschland, das ist unser Amerika" (A politically and socially liberated Germany, that is our America), declared the Berlin *Sozialdemokrat* in an early expression of this sentiment. Although increasingly critical of the great inequalities of wealth in the United States and the manifest exploitation of unskilled labor, German immigrant Socialists considered American citizenship of genuine value and the vote an efficacious weapon against oppression.[11] Upon turning twenty-one, Val Reuther immediately took out his citizenship papers. Thereafter he proved an active campaigner and union lobbyist, especially in the effort to abolish child labor in West Virginia mines. "The ballot is the strongest weapon that working men and women have if you just exercise it," Valentine Reuther told his comrades.[12]

Valentine Reuther stood firmly in the center of the American Socialist Party. He spurned the conservatism of the top leadership of the West Virginia Federation of Labor and sought to win state and local American Federation of Labor (AFL) bodies to the Socialist cause, but along with Debs and most Wheeling Socialists, Valentine rejected the militant syndicalism of the Industrial Workers of the World (IWW), who championed the insurgent coal miners in West Virginia's Kanawha Valley mine wars of 1912 and 1913. IWW talk of social revolution and direct action seemed infantile and self-destructive, and it threatened whatever influence the Socialists had won with the United Mine Workers (UMW) leaders. One can assume that Val Reuther agreed with his good friend Walter Hilton, whose editorials in the *Wheeling Majority* denounced IWW agitation and described the Wobblies as a collection of "every freak and bug" in the labor movement.[13]

These were good years for Val Reuther. In 1904 he married Anna Stocker, the red-haired, twenty-two-year-old daughter of a skilled Swabian wagonmaker who had arrived in Wheeling but twenty months before. The couple met in a workingman's saloon where Val delivered the beer and Anna worked in the kitchen. Anna had fled her native Scharnhausen when a love affair with a local youth was blocked by her mother, but she was far less of a rebel than her new husband. Her family had been more conventionally Lutheran, and in America she insisted upon regular church attendance for herself, for Val, and for their offspring. She loved to dance, cook, and socialize; in later years her outgoing disposition stood in contrast to the more conservative temperament of her husband, whose personal and political rectitude she often considered mere stiff-necked isolation.[14]

Val and Anna had five children: Theodore in 1905, Walter Philip in 1907, Roy Louis in 1909, Victor George in 1912, and Christine in 1922. Walter was born on September 1, Labor Day eve. The family lived in a rough section of Wheeling, Ritchie Town, where railroad tracks and mine shafts commingled with the frame houses occupied by Wheeling's Polish and German laborers. Here the Reuther kids knew all the dangers and pleasures of a poor boy's childhood: second-hand clothes, odd jobs around the neighborhood, chancy swims across the broad Ohio, dangerous experiments with fireworks and gunpowder. In 1926 the family moved to an old but spacious farmhouse surrounded by several acres of land on Bethlehem Hill, two miles outside of town; there Val Reuther's adolescent sons demonstrated a resourcefulness, mechanical aptitude, and fraternal spirit that soon put the house and outlying buildings, including a commercial chicken coop, into good shape. The house remained the elder Reuthers' home for the rest of their lives and served as a warm domestic refuge to which the Reuther sons would return time and again in their adult lives.

Life in the Reuther family was marked by a typically German sense of orderliness. Anna kept close track of the family's sometimes difficult finances, while Val meticulously supervised the education of his sons, political and otherwise. He made his boys understand that ideas and language mattered and that life was to be taken seriously and its difficulties aggressively and purposefully attacked. He gave them all a dramatic demonstration of these values in 1919 when, in the midst of the great postwar strike wave that found Wheeling at its virtual epicenter, a new pastor at the family's Zion Lutheran church attacked trade unionism in a Sunday sermon. Flushed with anger, Val Reuther rose to his feet and, in a booming but measured voice, denounced the minister's opinions and led his family from the church. Val Reuther rarely attended services again, but Anna Reuther insisted that the boys continue; all were confirmed at Zion after a record of perfect attendance at Sunday school. Suspicious as to the content of the Sunday sermons, Val interrogated his sons after the Sabbath services. These dinner table discussions soon turned into set-piece debates on the issues of the day: Prohibition, women's suffrage, capital punishment, the rights of labor. Val assigned the topics, and the boys worked up the arguments. According to Victor, these long-remembered and soon legendary sessions set the style for the Reuther brothers' latter-day oratory: Ted was "the orderly accountant, able to construct a fine column of facts; Walter was contentious and pugnacious; Roy tried to emulate the silver-tongued orators" of the day; Victor described himself as relying "less on logic than on emotional exploitation of the material." The training soon paid off: a schoolmate remembered Victor and Roy as classroom showoffs, their hands eagerly thrust into the air with ready answers for the teacher's queries.[15]

When the U.S. government sent Eugene V. Debs to jail for violation of the Espionage Act during World War I—the Socialist leader had advocated draft resistance—his first prison stop was the Moundsville Penitentiary just south of Wheeling. Debs received scores of visitors there, among them, Val Reuther and other local Socialists. On one occasion in the spring of 1919 Walter and Victor Reuther, then aged eleven and six, were taken along, possibly because their father knew that Debs would soon be transported to the less accessible federal prison in Atlanta. It was a melancholy visit that the boys remembered well. Debs, dressed in prison garb, looked quite gaunt; their father was without words to express his strong feelings, and tears ran down his cheeks as they left the prison. "How can they imprison so kind and gentle a man?" Val repeated again and again on the way back to Wheeling.[16]

Debs's imprisonment was a fitting and heroic climax to the great years of Socialist Party activism before and during World War I, but these years were also the end of the vibrant Socialist labor movement of Val Reuther's youth. As the Reuther boys were emerging from early childhood, their father's life as a union leader and political activist was also drawing to an abrupt and painful end. The tragedy was twofold, involving both personal impoverishment and political isolation. Thus the Reuther boys found themselves divorced from the political culture that had so animated their father's life; when they sought to rejoin and re-create it in the early Depression years, the broad Socialist movement of the early twentieth century, with its sustaining trade unions, publications, and cultural institutions, had become part of a world that was more than half lost.

The first blow struck against Val Reuther came with the rising tide of Prohibitionist sentiment that swept over West Virginia in the years just before World War I. The movement was particularly damaging for brewery workers, for it threatened both to deprive them of their livelihood and to propel them into a politically opportunistic alliance with the brewing companies in a vain effort to reverse the Prohibitionist surge at the polls. In 1912 the Schmulbach Brewing Company gave Val Reuther a three-month leave of absence to campaign all over West Virginia for the Trades Union Liberty League, a group set up by the Brewery Workers to fight Prohibition. The brewery union–industry alliance failed to halt Prohibition, but it did gut much of the German labor movement's historic attachment to radicalism and began the transformation of the Brewery Workers into an organization whose politics was not far different from that of mainstream AFL organizations. The Prohibition fight also opened wide fissures within the Socialist Party, between German and Catholic workers in the North, and many southern and western state organizations that backed the drinking ban.[17]

For Val Reuther, the closure of the Schmulbach Brewing Company in 1914 opened a painful chapter in his life. He had no "trade," and the labor movement, which had been his real career, did not have the resources to offer him full-time employment at a salary adequate to support a family of six. In a pattern typical of working-class families in this era, Val's wife tried to fill the breach. The Reuthers opened a small restaurant near their house, but the project ended in disaster when a warm bottle of ginger ale exploded in Val's hand, blinding him in one eye. For some months he remained despondent, sometimes even suicidal, and when he did finally land other work, it was as an unskilled laborer or factory operative.

Eventually, Val Reuther rescued his family's finances and at least a portion of his dignity by securing a position as an agent of the Metropolitan Life Insurance Company, selling "industrial insurance" to his old comrades and friends in proletarian South Wheeling. Val Reuther knew his clientele: he rarely had to "back the hearse up" to frighten his poor neighbors into signing a contract. Thus he was on his feet again by the mid-1920s, when he also supplemented the family income with the sale and rental of real estate. But the family's newfound financial stability had an ironic edge: the man who had once campaigned so diligently against the imperial outreach of Andrew Carnegie was now the agent within his own working-class community for the financial capitalists of New York and Boston.

Val Reuther's personal travail mirrored the fate of immigrant socialism as a whole. The nativist, xenophobic pressures unleashed by the patriotic mobilizations of World War I virtually suffocated radicalism in provincial towns like Wheeling. German Socialists were particularly hard hit, not only because of the belligerency of their presumptive homeland but because in the postwar era the door to the rapid assimilation of this white, northern European community stood so invitingly open. During World War I there were few arrests or vigilante attacks in the city, but the heavily German representation in the leadership of the labor assembly devastated laborite socialism, even after Wheeling unionists fully endorsed the war in 1917. The next year a can of red paint was splashed across the front door of the Reuther home, and even within the German community some parents told their children to stay away from the "radical" Reuther boys.

With many progressives, the *Wheeling Majority*'s Walter Hilton came to believe that the war could be used to promote social reconstruction; thus, the once fiery editor promoted wartime cooperation between workers and their bosses. The Ohio Valley Trades and Labor Assembly backed government bond drives and escorted military inductees to the railroad station. A prowar lawyer took over leadership of the Socialist Party, after which its meetings and activities nearly ceased. Naturally, the party vote declined as well, from 6 percent in the Ohio County elections of 1914 to 4 percent in 1916, when at least half of all the Socialist sympathizers appear to have voted for President Woodrow Wilson. By 1920 Wheeling Socialists drew only 1 percent of the vote in the presidential election.[18]

Wartime patriotism dealt a body blow to the Socialist Party, but of even greater long-term consequence was the transformation of the industrial and social world upon which Socialist strength had been built. In West Virginia, as in so many other industrial regions, the pre–World War I Socialist Party was almost exclusively composed of skilled workers, whose sense of mastery over their immediate work environment coincided with and reinforced their vision of a society in which the working class itself would master the means of production and the power of the state. But now these skilled workers were coming under sustained attack as the economics and technology of their industries underwent a radical change. The brewery workers union, with its high proportion of skilled German workers, had already been destroyed. In the early 1920s technological erosion of skilled work undermined the pottery and glassmaking trades, two important Ohio Valley centers of radical laborite strength. Technological change also eliminated many of the skilled, male workers from the cigarmaking shops. In coal mining, industrial decay, the defeat of a left-wing insurgency inside the UMW, and the consolidation of John L. Lewis's autocratic regime all sharply reduced the possibility of Socialist agitation in this once-fertile incubator of American labor radicalism. By 1928 dues-paying Socialist Party membership in all of West Virginia had fallen to just eighteen souls.[19]

Val Reuther had become a man without a union and without a party. But he always saw himself as a practical and political man. In 1924, when the Socialists endorsed Robert LaFollette's third-party campaign, Val Reuther cast his ballot for the Wisconsin Progressive as well. Later in the decade, Val, Anna, and Ted (in 1926) registered as Republicans, which in West Virginia appeared less corrupt and more prolabor than the Democratic Party. He still thought socialism "the star of hope that lights the way, leading the workers from wage slavery to social justice," but Valentine Reuther lacked the practical political tools to advance this cause.[20]

Thus the Reuther boys came of age in Wheeling when the social and economic landscape was far bleaker than the one that had faced their father twenty years before. While Anna Reuther was suffering through a lengthy illness after the birth of her only daughter, Christine, in 1922, family meals often consisted of boiled potatoes and perhaps a can of tuna fish. The eldest son Ted left school in 1919, after finishing eighth grade, and took a job in the paymaster's office at the Wheeling Corrugating Company (later Wheeling Steel). It was a lucky break, a first step on the road to white-collar security. A quiet, cautious, and diffident young man, seared more than his brothers by the difficult postwar years, Ted never escaped the parochial world of his youth. Gradually he worked his way up in Wheeling Steel's accounting department, ultimately putting in forty-eight years with the company.[21]

At age fifteen, Walter Reuther left high school before graduation as well, when he learned through Ted of an opening for an apprentice in the toolroom at Wheeling Corrugating. His schoolmates already thought of him as an unusually intense, well-organized, and highly motivated young man. Like his younger brother Roy he had a passion for basketball and a fiercely competitive temperament that soon propelled their church team to a city championship. Like his mother, Anna, Walter had blue-gray eyes and a head of reddish hair, and with Roy he shared her physical vigor and outgoing, optimistic sensibility as well. He respected his father's adventuresome encounters with the world of politics and ideas. Indeed, it was from Valentine Reuther that Walter took his moral, Manichean understanding of class power and economic progress, but unlike his often stiff-necked father Walter never enclosed himself within a virtuous, self-protective isolation. He craved the approval of his mentors and the friendship of his workmates. "I have always been able, wherever I went, to make friends with people," Walter later remarked of his first youthful forays into the world of work.[22]

Walter's entrée into the world of skilled work therefore offered a perfect fit between his growing mechanical aptitude, his search for comradeship, and his youthful quest for self-mastery. Walter had gravitated toward the world of craftsmanship almost from his elementary school days, when he had roamed through a decorative glass factory and watched, fascinated, as the artisans there carefully molded punch bowls laced with intricate figures and lamp shades graced with flowers or the attractive forms of strolling women. The punch bowls were his favorite. "One was a beautiful thing," remembered Reuther some forty-five years later. "The glass was a beautiful crimson color, and it had woven into it a design in gold. The gold had to be added at just the right time, and it was quite a ceremony in the plant when the glass was ready for the gold. Then the president of the company would come by with five or six gold pieces, and he would throw these in to be melted and fused into the glass, reproducing the design."[23]

Intrigued by such wonders, Walter practically lived in the glass factory. By the time he was ten or eleven, he was serving as a "carry boy" who took the glass on a large asbestos paddle from one craftsman to the next. But his real interest lay with the skilled steelworkers who made the molds. This was the heart of the entire enterprise, and these were the men who really created the designs the glass workers reproduced. They were "real artists," remembered Reuther, "and for a time my highest ambition was to work in the glass factory. But the men themselves warned me against it. . . . Machines could stamp out designs much faster and cheaper, and it was becoming obvious that soon there would be no place for the hand craftsman." Indeed, the glassworks soon went out of business, but Reuther had seen a powerful vision of dignity and creativity in the world of work. It was an inspiration from which much of his politics would flow, and it marked the moment from which Reuther dated his determination to become a craftsman in metal.[24]

Walter Reuther had a number of childhood jobs—a paper route, work in a bakery, piece rate work in a Wheeling stove shop—but his aptitude was clearly bent toward the metal trades. Throughout his adolescence, Reuther remained a determined sports enthusiast, but he also spent an increasingly large proportion of his spare time in the high school machine shop. "That's really where my mind and my heart and my soul were at the time," recalled Reuther. He was restless, his grades suffered, and he left school after his sophomore year in 1923. Reuther spent about a year as an eleven-cent-an-hour handyman at Wheeling Corrugating, assigned the dirtiest jobs, before he was transferred to the tool and die department for instruction. Here he thrived. Dies, made from specially hardened metal, were then becoming widely used to stamp out a huge variety of parts and objects. At Wheeling Corrugating, master workmen transformed elaborate floral and geometric designs into the dies that stamped out millions of elaborately ornate ceiling panels and roof ornaments, which graced so many commercial buildings of that era.[25]

Wheeling Corrugating's toolroom was small but full of first-rate craftsmen, so the quick-witted, personable youth had an opportunity to become a good all-around toolmaker. "I learned to do everything," Reuther later remembered. "For example, they would bring us a beat-up piece of metal and say, 'We've got to make this.' We would have to make all the drawings, design the part, make the dies, and finally fashion the piece of machinery that had to be replaced."[26] The machinists and die makers at Corrugating considered Walter Reuther a natural craftsman. Leo Hores, then a few years older than Walter, remembered that the red-haired youth resented sloppy work: "He was neat with his work, he did close work, he could work with anybody and anyone."[27]

The experience at Wheeling Corrugating was preparation for Reuther's entrée into the American industrial aristocracy, but it was still work filled with hazards and happenstance. At age seventeen, Reuther lost his right big toe on a day when a rush order came through to move a heavy die from a press. The die, a single piece of metal weighing about 400 pounds and oiled on its underside, slipped when Walter and two others tried to lift it out of the press. A sharp metal edge sliced through the leather shoe of Walter's right foot as if it were paper. With blood spurting from his foot, he was rushed to the local hospital on a stretcher; in this traumatic moment, he nevertheless demonstrated something of the coolness and foresight under pressure that would sustain him in later years. "I was always the shortest guy on the team, but I always jumped center because I could jump so much higher than anybody else. Now I could see that I wasn't going to be able to jump so high unless I had two big toes." Reuther therefore demanded that his workmates bring the severed toe along in the ambulance, and that his doctor sew it back on in the hospital. The physician knew this to be an impossibility, but Reuther persisted and the doctor finally agreed. Refusing an anesthetic, Reuther watched as his toe was reattached. It turned black and came off within a few days, but Reuther soon learned to walk without a limp and did play center again, for a championship team in a Detroit league.[28]

With both Ted and Walter still living at home and contributing the bulk of their pay packets to the household, and with father Valentine's insurance business steadily expanding, the Reuther family finances could sustain Roy and Victor as full-time high school students. Although both had their share of Reuther family industriousness, neither felt the self-generated pressure that had pushed Walter and Ted out of school. Roy, a slightly stockier, even more athletic version of Walter, was an exceptional basketball player and a great success on the track squad. He was excited by the new field of radio, both as a hobby and as a vocation. Roy had also installed most of the electrical wiring in the Reuther house on Bethlehem Hill. Instead of finishing high school, he took an apprenticeship with a local electrical firm, soon joining the International Brotherhood of Electrical Workers in the same union hall where his father had presided as labor assembly president twenty years before.

By 1927, therefore, Val Reuther's three eldest sons held full-time jobs. But Walter Reuther was restless. After three years at Wheeling Corrugating, he had more than tripled his pay. At nineteen, he still had another year to put in to finish his apprenticeship, yet he had learned all he could at Corrugating, and the family no longer needed all his income. From the conversational buzz in the toolroom, Walter learned that Ford was paying $1.25 an hour for toolmakers' skills; around Wheeling, $.75 was tops for even the most experienced men. Moreover, Reuther disliked the long hours, including occasional Sunday work, that he had to put in at Corrugating; Ford had just advertised its commitment to a five-day workweek. And beyond all this, Reuther was a young man with a young man's dreams who had hardly strayed beyond the hills that enclosed the upper Ohio River. For generations, newly minted tradesmen, in the old country and the new, had sharpened their skills and discovered a broader vision of the world by applying their talents in new workshops, laboring alongside cosmopolitan workmen, in distant cities. In the third decade of the twentieth century, there was no place in the world that a young toolmaker could do so to better advantage than Detroit.

LIFE AT THE ROUGE

It has been asserted that machine production kills the creative ability of the craftsman. This is not true.

—*Henry Ford*, My Philosophy of Industry, 1929

In 1927 Detroit was a boomtown, a city of almost two million restless souls, the fourth largest in the nation. Here was the vital heart of America's greatest industry, a city whose identification with automobile production made it synonymous with speed, innovation, skill, and power. Nothing symbolized the city's new spirit more than the great Ford factories, where Reuther hoped to land a job. The young toolmaker from Wheeling had probably never read *Vanity Fair*, but this chic New York magazine captured something of the awe in which Americans held the Motor City when it put Charles Sheeler's striking photographs of the newly completed Ford River Rouge complex on its February 1928 cover. The magazine proclaimed River Rouge "the most significant public monument in America, throwing its shadow across the land probably more widely and more intimately than the United States Senate, the Metropolitan Museum of Art, the Statue of Liberty. . . . In a landscape where size, quantity and speed are the cardinal virtues, it is natural that the largest factory turning out the most cars in the least time should come to have the quality of America's Mecca, toward which the pious journey for prayer."[1]

Detroit's production lines sucked in a "suitcase brigade" of displaced European peasants, underpaid farmhands, and unemployed coal miners. In 1927 Detroit factories employed 325,000 working men and women; the opportunities offered by

13

this metal-bending capital of the world made it particularly attractive to engineers, machinists, and tool and die makers. Ford laid off sixty thousand production workers when his factories stopped building the Model T in May 1927, but the retooling effort for the new Model A demanded that he deploy some seventeen thousand craftsmen, three or four times the usual complement, to retool his great factories at Highland Park and Dearborn. Other auto manufacturing companies, along with numerous parts and supply firms, were also using more tool and die makers. The segmented product line and the annual model change, both pioneered by General Motors in the mid-1920s, required continual retooling—not so drastic as Ford's retooling for the Model A, but enough to keep the industry on a constant lookout for skilled workers.

A symbiotic relationship existed between the mindless routine of assembly-line operations, where the auto companies assigned the untutored Slavs, Italians, and Appalachian immigrants, and the skilled terrain of the Detroit toolrooms, where the very instruments of mass deskilling were being forged. Mass production, after all, was only feasible once stamping dies and machine tool fixtures made it possible to turn out hundreds of thousands of interchangeable metal parts that required no fitting or fixing to assemble—thus the growing demand for skilled workers. Between 1922 and 1930 workers in Reuther's trade nearly doubled their proportion of the automobile industry labor force, to almost 4 percent. Skilled work in general, which included maintenance and construction, probably accounted for 12–15 percent of all autoworkers. Since Detroit manufacturers were incapable of training such a sizable and mobile group of skilled workmen, they lured workers to the American Midwest from all over the world. The toolrooms of the great auto manufacturing firms were therefore full of Germans, Danes, English, and Scots who had served their apprenticeships in the old country. In the late 1920s perhaps half of all skilled workers were foreign-born.[2]

A second-generation German like Walter Reuther could expect good use of his talents in Detroit. "I hear they need men at Ford's," he told his mother while munching some of her *apfelkuchen*. "I am leaving for Detroit as soon as you can get me packed." Walter had convinced his twenty-five-year-old workmate and sometime instructor, Leo Hores, to give the Motor City a try, and the two piled into Hores's 1924 Studebaker on a cold Saturday morning, February 21, 1927. Reaching Detroit that night, they stayed with friends of the Hores family, then immediately began to look for a boardinghouse and jobs. Their skills served them well, for by Monday afternoon they both had work at Briggs, a body shop notorious for its low wages and difficult conditions.[3] "It was big, rough heavy work," remembered Walter, who ate a lot of emery dust grinding out the big dies for the fenders and roof panels that Briggs sold to Ford and Chrysler. He sometimes worked a thirteen-hour night shift—from 5:30 P.M. until 7:00 A.M., with half an hour for lunch. His pay was $.85 an hour; Hores, a more experienced worker, earned $1.05.[4]

Reuther and Hores were anxious to get out of Briggs. Both preferred the kind of fine, close work on small dies where tolerances were precise. In early April Reuther tried the Burroughs Adding Machine Company, which did a lot of very skilled tool and die work. There were no jobs, but the employment manager, perhaps trying to be helpful, perhaps just having some sport with Walter, suggested that Reuther try Ford's Highland Park factory, where die leaders were being hired for the retooling work on the Model A. After working his usual night shift at Briggs, Reuther took the bus to Highland Park and then stood in wonder and fascination before the birthplace of the Model T, Ford's eight-story, 229-acre manufacturing complex then employing more than forty thousand workers. "I had never seen anything that big before."[5]

Reuther may not have known it then, but this huge assemblage of men, women, and machines was in the midst of a mind-boggling convulsion. Within three weeks Henry Ford would abruptly halt production of the Model T after riding the fifteen-millionth Tin Lizzy off the line. This revolutionary automobile had put America on wheels and captured 50 percent of the entire market in the early 1920s, but it had become outmoded and battered by the competition. The ignition, carburetion, transmission, brake, and suspensions systems, as well as the styling and appointments, were antique. Americans wanted more than basic transportation: by the 1920s the automobile had become an icon, as important as the clothing on their backs or the neighborhoods in which they dwelled in advertising their class, their style, and their aspirations. Ford's competitors had come to understand this. With Alfred Sloan's General Motors in the vanguard, Detroit had begun to offer its customers a carefully differentiated but annually changing product line whose wonders were kept before the public by omnipresent newspaper and magazine advertisements and whose purchase was facilitated by an unparalleled extension of credit that flowed even into the lower reaches of the working class. Not unexpectedly, Model T production had begun to drop: by early 1927 it held little more than one-seventh of the market.[6]

Of course, the Ford organization had the money, the people, the technological resources, and the giant factories to meet this challenge, and as early as 1925 it had begun work on a new car for the mass market. But the Model A was not just a new product: it represented a wrenching and difficult change in the way Ford deployed its mass-production expertise. For almost twenty years the company had grown rich through the total dedication of tools, techniques, and manpower to the production of a single product, unchanging except for its incremental and often unadvertised technical improvements. The company had spared no expense in building or buying thousands of single-purpose machine tools and dies that were suitable only for boring or stamping or turning metal into Model T parts and assemblies. This was classic "Fordism": the production of a sturdy, inexpensive car by tens of thousands of semiskilled workers in scores of manufacturing facilities and assembly plants. But this primitive kind of mass production also fossilized the product, because it made the transition to a new model fantastically disruptive and expensive.[7]

Ford's shift to the Model A would therefore be a huge undertaking. Of the thirty-two thousand machine tools used in building the Model T, more than half were scrapped or rebuilt. The Model A would make use of deeper drawings (that is, sharper bends and deeper recesses in the sheet steel) than the Model T, thus requiring heavier and more sophisticated dies. These changes, wrote the *New York Times*, were "probably the biggest replacement of plant in the history of American industry." Years later Ford's tooling chief would say that the changeover "was just like starting out with a new machine shop."[8] Thus Ford would require thousands of new machine tools and even more dies, some almost experimental in their sophistication. But the company had badly misjudged the time and effort required for the changeover. Ford's tooling requirements on the Model A were only about one-quarter complete when Model T production stopped. The project was way behind schedule, and the company needed the services of virtually every tool-maker it could find.[9]

Walter Reuther was therefore the right man in the right place as he approached Highland Park's hiring door early in April 1927. But he almost missed his chance, for he encountered nothing but skepticism from the moment he stepped inside. The nineteen-year-old redhead, whose hairless face and pale complexion made him look even younger, seemed hardly qualified for the work of a die leader—an expert die maker who coordinated the labor of a squad of six or eight skilled crafts-men, usually a ten- to twenty-year veteran with some gray in his hair. The fresh-faced youth first had to spend hours talking his way past a 260-pound guard, then brashly convince the employment manager to call in the master mechanic to interview him. It took all morning before George Gardham, Ford's tall, white-haired man in charge of all skilled work, walked into the Employment Office and asked, "Where is the tool and die leader that I am to interview?" He was just as sur-prised and irritated as the others to find Reuther standing before him. "Look, this has been my problem all day," retorted Reuther. "Now you're here. Maybe you wouldn't have come if you had known I was waiting. But you're here. You've got the blueprints under your arm. It will only take a few minutes to find out how com-petent or incompetent I am. You've got nothing to lose."[10]

The Ford organization was a gigantic enterprise, full of competing cliques and barely hidden corruption. But it still recognized raw talent, unmediated by formal credentials or long experience in other firms, and the company did need die mak-ers. Gardham was both charmed and appalled by Reuther's talkative brashness. "Let's see what you know!" he challenged the cocky intruder, his tone reflecting the sentiments characteristic of an auto industry still on the far side of Depression-era job scarcity and postwar personnel management.

Reuther easily demonstrated that he could read a complicated blueprint and answer Gardham's technical questions. "You know much more about this than one would believe," admitted the Ford supervisor. "I don't deny I look like a farmer boy," retorted Reuther, "but I do believe that if you give me a job, I can prove I know a great deal more than you would think." To this Gardham replied with a "sporting proposition." Would Reuther be willing to work at Ford for two days without knowing his rate of pay? He would be watched closely, and at the end of the trial period his duties and his pay would be set. He should show up for work at 7:00 A.M. the next day.[11]

Reuther quickly accepted. Like all skilled workers, he carried his tools from job to job, so he immediately went back to Briggs to collect his toolbox. But the night-shift superintendent would not give him the special clearance needed to take any property, even his own tools, out of the plant. Reuther's boss at Briggs was a stubborn man to begin with; his intransigence, however, was a tribute not only to the quality of Reuther's work but to the industry's chronic shortage of skilled men. Reuther was frantic as the hours ticked away—at 5:00 A.M. he finally got his tools out. He rushed home for a bite to eat, then took a taxi to the Ford plant. There an exhausted Reuther spent the longest and hardest day he had ever worked, always under the watchful eyes of Ford supervisors. Another closely observed shift followed the next day, but Reuther had proved his métier: he would start tool and die work at Ford for $1.05 an hour.[12]

Reuther's five and a half years at "Fords"—so-called because its employees still thought of the company as the personal property of the founder—would prove one of the great character-molding and maturing experiences of his life. After about six months at Highland Park, Reuther was transferred to the toolroom of the B-Building in the new River Rouge complex, where assembly of the Model A was scheduled to begin in the fall of 1927. "The Rouge" was then an industrial marvel, the largest concentration of machinery and labor anywhere in the world. Since World War I, when he first manufactured Eagle Boats next to the Rouge River, Henry Ford had poured hundreds of millions of dollars into the construction of a gigantic complex that could take iron ore from Minnesota, coal from Ohio, and wood from Upper Michigan and, thirty-three hours later, turn these raw materials into an automobile that scooted off the assembly line under its own power. In the late 1920s more than seventy-five thousand labored at the Rouge. Consisting of more than twenty-three major buildings, including mills for steel and glass, two foundries, a huge powerhouse, a pressed-steel stamping plant, and assembly plants for motors and finished cars, the Rouge finally realized Henry Ford's dream of continuous, integrated manufacture. The tooling facilities were first-rate, and some were even air-conditioned, like those of the B-Building where Reuther worked. Wrote the Ford biographer Allan Nevins, "The Rouge was an industrial city, immense, concentrated, packed with power." Indeed, the great Mexican artist Diego Rivera captured some of the imaginative power, the physical complexity, and the sheer brutality of the enterprise in his famous series of murals painted in 1932 on the walls of the Detroit Art Institute.[13]

Reuther thrived at the Rouge; both his wages and responsibilities rose steadily. In 1929 he was classified as an "A-1 Diemaker Leader," at $1.40 an hour; still later he exercised the duties, if without the formal title, of a foreman in the B-Building tool and die room, where forty men worked under him. This experience put

Reuther at the very apex of the working class; he later bragged that he was among the twenty highest-paid mechanics in the Ford Motor Company. Reuther's lack of experience on the Model T might actually have been an advantage during his first years at Ford, a time when the Rouge production boss Charles Sorensen was determined to purge the organization of "all the Model-T Sons-of-bitches" who were too tightly wedded to the old production methods. But whatever the weight of this factor, Reuther was just the sort of energetic and reliable young worker who wins favor with his workmates and supervisors. Early in his career he successfully worked on the complex set of dies necessary to stamp out the soft, fragile brass, $^{15}/_{1000}$ of an inch thick, that made up the Model A head gasket; a bit later, probably in 1929 or 1930, Reuther helped construct the experimental wing section models that engineers used in the company's wind tunnel tests of the famous Ford trimotor airplane.[14]

As a die leader, Reuther had to bring foresight, planning, and initiative to even the routine work. Starting with blocks of steel and some blueprints, the die maker built a contoured steel form capable of stamping thousands of sheet metal parts. The metal was bent when a carefully constructed punch forced its shape into sheet metal pressed against a "female" image of the part, called the "die." The hardened steel impact surfaces of the punch and the die were each mounted on cast-iron "shoes," which slammed together to shape, cut, or press the metal into a useful part. Some iron shoes held twenty-five different kinds of steel, all precision-cut and measured. Front-office engineers designed the dies, but if die makers had merely followed the engineering blueprints, little more than scrap would have flowed out of the toolroom. Like all craft work, die making was an art as much as a science. Engineers could never precisely anticipate the complex reactions of metal under intense pressure; sometimes the die maker, or his leader, redesigned an entire die, especially the blanking dies used in complicated operations that not only bent but actually pulled the metal apart.[15]

As leader, Reuther was responsible for planning the sequence of steps necessary to build the die, assigning the work to those crew members most expert in each part, making templates and checking fixtures to precisely measure the finished work, and then seeing that any mistakes were promptly corrected. Throughout the process, some discussion might take place with engineers and foremen, but for the most part the die maker and the die leader were left unsupervised. If Reuther asked his supervisor for more men "to keep all the details working," these were promptly supplied. In truth, Reuther was a straw boss, but unlike the tough foremen, who held similar authority over the semiskilled production workers, he had cordial and cooperative relations with the die makers under him—an atmosphere that was the norm in most toolrooms.[16]

The work could be hazardous and dirty—especially the repair work—but tool and die makers had an enormous pride in their trade and its product. Many considered the die their own property and were reluctant to release it to production until it was finished to their satisfaction. These skilled workers were known for their orderly work habits, scrupulous neatness (lest a stray piece of metal ruin their work), cooperative work relations, and devotion to detail. Their work was not merely a job: it was a way of life that would have a lifelong effect on their personalities and politics.[17]

Reuther's purposeful intelligence and methodical personality were typical characteristics of a successful skilled craftsman, but he also had the capacity, evident since early in his youth, to win the attention of those in authority with a likable, self-reliant charm. Thus George Gardham became very friendly with the young redhead; he introduced Reuther to his wife and had him to dinner several times. At one point the older man explained to Reuther that he and his wife had never been able to have children of their own and that they would like Walter to come and live with them. Reuther was astonished, then deeply embarrassed, and he refused as delicately as he could, fearing that such an unusual arrangement would make life difficult and awkward at work.[18]

Yet Reuther was not entirely oblivious to the advantages of having well-connected friends in Ford supervision. Because of Henry Ford's reluctance to bureaucratize his organization, the Rouge, an awesome and smoothly functioning production machine to outside observers, was actually shot through with cliquish power struggles, ethnic conflict, and nepotism. Ford's infamous Service Department, run by the omnipresent Harry Bennett, represented one such nexus of power; the northern European, production-minded building superintendents and their general foremen represented another. The Freemasons' order, then at the height of its national influence, sustained a third system of authority at Ford, one that generally overlapped and reinforced the power of the building superintendents and general foremen. At Ford, as well as at scores of other factories, railroads, and offices, the Masons enrolled hundreds of thousands, drawn especially from the lower-middle-class world of male office workers and salesmen and from the ranks of skilled Protestant workmen. Anti-Catholic and anti-Semitic, the Masons took care of their own at Ford. Membership in the order was a virtual prerequisite for promotion, and sometimes was enough to keep one's job during layoff.[19]

Reuther probably knew all this when a friendly superintendent let him know, in early 1931, that membership in the Masonic order might save his job when Ford made its Depression-era layoffs. With a friend, the German-born Frank Braun, also a B-Building tool and die maker, Reuther swallowed his pride, paid the initiation fee of fifty dollars, studied the incomprehensible Masonic ritual, and earned his ring, which he discreetly flashed about the shop. This bit of youthful opportunism paid off handsomely in August 1931 when falling car sales, combined with the company's shift from Model A to V-8 production, gave Ford the opportunity to send tens of thousands of Rouge employees home on an "indefinite" vacation. But Reuther and Braun were among the skeleton staff Ford kept on to help work out the company's production problems.[20]

Thus the auto industry's boom-and-bust cycle hardly touched Reuther while he worked at Ford: he was among the most favorably placed of a stratum of skilled workers whose work culture was rewarding and full of larger opportunities. During the first half of the twentieth century, skilled metal workers, in both North America and Europe, were the aristocrats of labor, almost exclusively northern European white males whose strategic position in the production process won them the highest wages and the most privileged status in the blue-collar workforce. They were a self-confident and cosmopolitan lot, alternately more militant and more conservative than the thousands of relatively unskilled women and men, many but unlettered first-generation immigrants from peasant backgrounds, who filled the seemingly interchangeable work slots in the rest of the factory.

But the privileged position of these "aristocrats" did not necessarily make them conservative. Because of their self-confidence and their vital place in the production order, skilled craftsmen could be found both in the vanguard of those who posed a radical challenge to the existing industrial order and, almost simultaneously, among those workers who were most entrepreneurial and career-conscious in their outlook. When the relentless logic of Fordism challenged their privileges, skilled workers often took the lead in generalizing their grievances and giving them a socialist or syndicalist flavor. Skilled workers who were the masters of their own small workshops had little psychological difficulty making the leap to the idea that the working class itself might master the larger means of production. Among Reuther's Rouge workmates were Berlin veterans of the Sparticist uprising of 1919, refugees from the Tory suppression of the 1926 general strike in Britain, and Socialist militants who had lost their Bridgeport munitions industry jobs after World War I. Many of these same skilled workers, like Reuther himself, became leaders of the effort to unionize the auto industry after the Depression had once again turned their consciousness to the left.[21]

In the late 1920s, however, with jobs plentiful and their privileged standing still largely intact, skilled workers in the Detroit auto shops, certainly young workers like Reuther, could entertain dreams of steadily advancing their wages and shop authority or perhaps starting up small "alley shops" that would subcontract tooling work from the bigger companies. Logan Miller, who supervised Reuther's toolroom in the late 1920s and would later rise to become a Ford vice president, had been trained as a railroad machinist before hiring into the Highland Park toolroom in 1914. And John Findlater, a skilled die maker from Buffalo, became superintendent of the toolroom at Highland Park before transferring to the Rouge and taking over the steel division. He was joined there by his friend Alex Lumsden, an apprenticed blacksmith and toolroom worker at Highland Park who became head of the Rouge open hearth department in 1925. All three Ford managers had voted for Eugene Debs in 1912. GM president Charles Wilson, who had once worked at Ford, speculated later that, had Reuther arrived in Detroit ten years earlier, or even five, he might well have traveled high into Ford management.[22]

Reuther's path would probably have been through Ford's new aeronautical division. With some other young men, he had organized a flying club and bought a World War I Jenny, over which they labored on weekends. Encouraged by his workmates and supervisors, Reuther thought of becoming an aeronautical engineer, hardly an impractical dream in those formative years of aircraft manufacture.

In the late 1920s the Ford Tri-Motor had proved itself an advanced and highly competitive design. But Reuther's ambitions faded when the Jenny crashed, killing a clubmate, and when Ford abandoned trimotor production at the start of the Depression.[23]

Reuther's self-improving ambitions were nevertheless given a free rein when he decided to finish the high school education he had abandoned when he began his apprenticeship at Wheeling Corrugating. Reuther might well have first turned his eyes toward Ford because of the reputation of its famous trade school, located right inside the Rouge. But the school was closed to older adolescents like Walter, so he switched to the evening shift and enrolled as a tenth-grader at nearby Fordson High School, right after he transferred to the Rouge in the summer of 1927. Constructed just the year before with substantial funds donated by Henry Ford and his son Edsel, Fordson was housed in a magnificent, lavishly appointed building, a $3.5 million English Renaissance structure with towers, turrets, a beautifully tiled swimming pool, and a library modeled after that at the University of Michigan. Founded in the same spirit that Ford brought to his other Americanization efforts, the school was designed to inculcate in the offspring of the great immigrant tide then sweeping through Dearborn the cultural values of what Progressive-era educators thought of as Western civilization. The school did offer vocational courses, but the teaching staff sought to expose all students to the classical canon. An authentic seventeenth-century French tapestry hung in the lobby, while in the halls and library were situated half-sized statues of David, the Venus de Milo, Abraham Lincoln, and other icons of Protestant culture.[24]

Reuther would seem to have been a student who fulfilled Fordson's fondest ambitions. Most of his classmates were some five years younger than he, but Reuther did not see his high school experience in the crudely instrumental terms so common among working-class youth of later generations. After all, Reuther already had a vocation that most Fordson students would have envied. Instead, he savored the school experience and took seriously his courses in English, literature, and public speaking. Reuther's life was hectic: classes in the morning, followed by the 3:30 P.M. to midnight shift at the plant, then a full load of homework. He took lodgings near the high school in the rooming house of a young German immigrant couple, Emil Schmier, a Ford machinist, and his wife Ernestine, who provided for Walter a familiar and comfortable cultural setting.[25] In a 1929 school essay, "Time," he described his exhausting schedule:

The race is on. First a few hurried calisthenics; the dash to the bathroom, before someone else beats me there. Amid flying soap, water, and toothpaste I finish my toilet, rush downstairs, with the hope my landlady will have my eggs and toast ready to consume, I finish breakfast, dash back to my room, the clock says, "four minutes till your Geometry class starts." I grab my hat and books, and start down Horger Avenue on a run. . . .

I no more than get seated, than I hear Miss Barttlet say, "We will have to hurry this morning as I have a lot of work planned." Hurry! Hurry! Hurry! . . . For fifty minutes we juggle angles and triangles. The bell rings to end the second lap, and start activity hour. . . . I have German to conjugate, Algebra to study, material to read for debating. . . .

With the seventh lap over, my school worries are over for the day, so I rush to my locker, get my hat, and rush back to my rooming house, change clothes, and off to the restaurant. As I enter . . . the waitress, knowing I am in a hurry, gives me the quickest service possible. . . . Two minutes to catch my bus. . . . I hurry down Michigan Avenue. I shall miss the bus. No! I get a break! A feeling of envy comes over me as I sit there and notice the fleecy white clouds drift lazily in the sky. How I wish I could get away from this hustle and bustle, just to drift like a cloud. . . . Three minutes to go. I am off the bus before it comes to a dead stop—up those steel steps, polished by hurrying feet, over the bridge, down the other side.

Pushing, tugging, using all the football tactics I know of to get through the milling mob of Ford men, some coming in, others going out. A football player has an easy job. . . . I get in the clear, the goal post does not lie before me, but the time clock does. Thirty seconds to go, panting I hit the clock, the bell rings. No cheering crowds, just the roar of machines to acclaim my spectacular dash.[26]

During his years at Fordson High, Reuther made almost all his friends from among the other ambitious, hardworking young men who divided their time between Ford, high school classes, and extracurricular activities oriented toward self-improvement and athletics. Reuther organized a group of these older students into the Fordson Four-C Club (cooperation, confidence, comradeship, citizenship) and, as the spark plug of the group, took the uncontested presidency for the two years of its existence. The organization almost perfectly reflected the spirit of self-improvement and advancement that was so appealing to these young tradesmen in the late years of the confident, pre-Depression period known as the "New Era." The club's bylaws, almost certainly written by Walter Reuther, sought to "create a spirit of fellowship among the employed students" and "enable us . . . to come in contact with prominent men of the educational and business world." The club hosted talks, sold candy, and raised money by showing films in the high school auditorium. Fordson's principal and at least one bank vice president were made honorary members.[27]

Most Four-C members were young male immigrants—or at least recent migrants to Detroit—in their early twenties who wanted to move up and out of the working class. Joseph Ruzyski, a Polish-German toolmaker, and Harold Landgarf, a German-American apprentice toolmaker, both wanted to become engineers; Fred Brierley, born in Lancashire, looked forward to medical school; the Hungarian-born John Vitalari, an inspector at Ford, wanted a white-collar job; Harold Moore, another Englishman, "had a desire to associate with people with a higher standard than my own." Reuther's good friend Merlin Bishop, from Illinois farm stock, held a high-paying job as a crane operator at the Ford steel mill, but he also recognized that to get out of the shop, he would have to finish high school.[28] Reuther struggled to salute these classmates in verse:

Comradeship sincere and true
Is the seed from which we grew
Seasoned by work, nourished by joys
Banded together just we boys . . .
We are a team in the game of life
Seeking knowledge to eliminate strife
We toil in the shop not just for pay
But rather experience gained in a way . . .
The thing in life that counts the most
Isn't the man that gives the toast
But rather they who never shirk
Honest duty, honest work. . . .[29]

By 1929 Walter Reuther had transmuted his father's Socialist tutelage into little more than a humane but unfocused ambition. He remained a faithful son, of course, frequently returning to Wheeling to enjoy his mother's German cooking and the warmth of a tight-knit family. And until his twenty-first birthday he sent half his pay home; thereafter, and at his father's urging, he banked the rest and even invested in real estate, making payments on a $1,600 commercial lot in Dearborn and two other pieces of property in the nearby Hazelcrest subdivision.[30] On his own Four-C Club application, Reuther wrote, "I seek knowledge that I may serve mankind." He wanted to go to the University of Michigan and study law. It may not have been an idle thought: Frank Braun remembered Reuther as a man who loved to talk, on the job and off. At one point in 1929 Reuther urged Braun to sue Ford Motor Company when he sustained a leg injury, after which the red-haired die leader kept in close touch as Braun investigated the possibility of a lawsuit. "We called him the 'corporation lawyer,'" Braun recalled.[31] With their guileless ambition, it is no wonder that Reuther and Bishop were paraded before the Rotary and Kiwanis clubs of Detroit as sterling examples of young workmen who had completely internalized the values of an upwardly striving lower-middle class.

Reuther's high school compositions reveal a young man full of lofty but undirected idealism. He was a terrible poet, though he seemed to compose verse often. Reuther was better at prose, especially when he described his workaday world, but he preferred, or was assigned, themes that dealt with more abstract historical or political subjects. He began a work on Thomas Paine with the famous quotation, "The world is my country and to do good is my religion." In keeping with his time, Reuther admired Paine more for his religious rationalism than for the eighteenth-century writer's denunciations of illegitimate power. Indeed, Reuther either ignored much of what made Paine a radical or interpreted his radicalism as an exercise in reasoned moderation during turbulent times.

In other essays he often celebrated the powers of mass education and selfless intelligence, perhaps understandable in a youth who was making such an effort to win a high school diploma. He praised Thomas Edison and Luther Burbank, two of Henry Ford's favorites as well, as men who had "elevated civilization from the rut of superstition, fear and religion." Reuther thought Prohibition a failure, of course, but much to the chagrin of his teacher, he thought sufficient education would eventually eliminate the desire on the part of young people for alcoholic drinks. Indeed, all great questions could be settled by sufficient appeal to "truth, knowledge and reason."[32]

Such sentiments are not uncommon among adolescent schoolboys, but Reuther was hardly a raw youth in 1929 and 1930 when he wrote these compositions. He was a veteran worker, a man of some authority in the world's most technically advanced manufacturing complex. It is possible, of course, that Reuther was just giving his teachers what he thought they wanted, but guile of this sort was not Reuther's style. And in truth, his unfettered idealism was abundantly apparent outside of school. In the early 1930s, after he had gravitated toward Socialist circles, he sometimes lapsed into rhetoric characteristic of the Fordson Four-C Club; he often spoke, for example, of "the intellectual revolution" for which he struggled.[33] In later years his comrades would note Reuther's "Boy Scout" sincerity, his sometimes didactic rhetoric, and his devotion to an unfocused, universal humanitarianism. For a student, an intellectual, an engineer, or a politician in placid times, such sentiments might have seemed sophomoric and embarrassing, but for the leader of a mass movement that sought to create a new world of social justice and comradeship, these expansive, morally earnest sentiments would prove of immense value.

3

TOOLING AT GORKY

Soviet power plus American technique will build Socialism.
—*front-page motto*, Moscow Daily News, 1933

Walter Reuther began to think of himself as a Socialist once again after his brother Victor joined him in Detroit during the fall of 1930. "He got Walter all steamed up about the Socialist movement," remembered Merlin Bishop, Reuther's friend from Four-C Club days. "I think Walter had pretty well forgotten about it up to that point. He was a very frugal fellow and invested his money."[1]

As the youngest of the Reuther boys, Victor had come of age when the family finances were in better shape. Thus he was the only Reuther brother to finish high school straight through and the only one of the boys who did not commit himself to a trade in his adolescent years. Unlike Roy and Walter, he had no passion for sports in high school: "Reading and debating were my loves," Victor later recalled. His temperament was closest to that of his father, Valentine, who called him "the professor." Victor would spend his spare hours after classes in the school library; he had "Patrick Henry tendencies," said a schoolmate, and he incorporated into his schoolwork many of the radical, iconoclastic themes Valentine loved to preach. He served as president of two debating clubs during 1929–30, his senior year, and it was for his forensic skills that his teachers chose him to deliver one of the graduation valedictories. Typically for a Reuther, his talk was entitled "The Blessing of Citizenship," and it celebrated, in patriotic language, the struggles of colonists, pioneers, and abolitionists to advance a progressive and expansive set of American rights.[2]

In 1929, with financial help from Walter and Ted, Victor entered the University of West Virginia, where he spent just one year. Like Walter, Victor toyed with the idea of becoming a lawyer, but college life in Morgantown proved disillusioning. His grades were not spectacular, he disliked the compulsory reserve officers' training corps (ROTC) course, and he hated the social world of fraternities and sororities that dominated the campus. As the Depression grew deeper, the university remained a complacent island for the state's elite; meanwhile, Victor reconfirmed his sense of social outrage after a visit to a nearby mining camp full of squalor and ill health. Moreover, Victor felt uncomfortable being the only Reuther male still dependent on the family for support. In a letter to his father, he called himself a "parasite."[3]

With Walter's encouragement, Victor decided to move to Detroit and take classes with his older brother at Detroit City College (DCC) (now Wayne State University). He lived with Walter in a basement apartment near the college; there Victor cooked the meals and kept house by way of rent, since it seemed pointless to search for a job in these Depression years. Walter also paid his tuition at DCC. For a time in 1930 and 1931 the Reuther brothers shared their lodgings with a young Indian, Mukerji, who explained the nationalist movement to them. Merlin Bishop joined them when he finished Fordson in 1931, and Roy moved in during the summer of 1932 after he lost his job in Wheeling. By this time the Reuther brothers had rented a larger apartment on Merrick Street and South Boulevard with two ambitious toolmakers from Ford, Walter's workmate Frank Braun and Cecil Halbert, a friend from the Fordson Four-C Club.[4]

The Great Depression hit the Motor City with a force virtually unequaled in any other metropolitan area. Between 1929 and 1932 auto production dropped by two-thirds, and auto industry employment by more than one-half. By the winter of 1932 the Michigan jobless rate had reached 40 percent; 125,000 Detroit families, one in three, were without any financial support whatsoever. The shacks and hovels of the vagrants and evicted mushroomed along rail lines and highways and in vacant lots. Meanwhile, the city juggled its books to put even the small sum of $3.75 a week into the hands of those on relief, but as tax receipts plummeted, that effort courted municipal bankruptcy. By 1932 city employees were being paid in script and the Detroit banks tottered on the verge of collapse.[5]

Walter Reuther and his roommates were making good money, but they were hardly blind to this social catastrophe. Victor took the lead, exploring the city slum areas, Hoovervilles, and unemployment lines, as well as Socialist Party headquarters on Erskine Street, where he met Norman Thomas and heard lectures by Scott Nearing and other radicals. One weekend Victor and Walter spent a night at the Salvation Army flophouse; later a class discussion on crime and prostitution sent Bishop and the Reuther brothers off on a tour of Detroit's red-light district. Victor and Walter photographed Detroit's Hoovervilles and spoke with the unemployed and the hobos; then, in a joint class project, they photographically juxtaposed the social misery of Detroit with the Grosse Pointe mansions of the auto elite. All this politicized Walter Reuther's conception of the world, dissipating the private ambitions nurtured in his Fordson High days. He now kidded his roommate Cecil Halbert, "the capitalist," because he dressed well and still wanted to start his own tool and die shop. "The common road that we have both travelled for the past three years" has ended, Reuther wrote to Halbert with a touch of sadness. "The argumentative spirit sweep [sic] us into revolutionary combat," he explained. It was not a fight about "personalities" but "between ideas, concepts, ideals, aspirations and all things that go to make up one's philosophy of life." The important thing, Reuther lectured Halbert, "is not so much what your ideas are, as how sure you are of them. In other words the fellow on the fence is lost."[6]

Reuther began to put this new sense of commitment into action at Detroit City College, the Motor City's version of that more famous municipal institution, the City College of New York. DCC, which held most of its classes in a former high school building on Cass Avenue, enrolled about nine thousand, largely the second-generation offspring of Detroit's upwardly striving immigrant community. The Reuther brothers took as much economics and sociology as they could handle and got to know personally several of the more radical instructors. By 1932 the faculty and student body were polarized but shifting leftward. A conservative school board ran the place, but a straw poll found that Norman Thomas was second only to Herbert Hoover in faculty support, with Franklin Roosevelt a distant third. Student sentiment was just a bit more centrist, with 606 for Hoover, 419 for Roosevelt, 316 for Thomas, and 48 for the Communist ticket headed by William Z. Foster.[7]

Victor and Walter forged a solid, intimate, trusting friendship in these early Depression years. For more than five years, from the fall of 1930 until their return from the Soviet Union in October 1935, they spent few days apart. Walter was almost five years older than his brother, and he was the one who paid the bills, so he clearly took the upper hand in their relationship, certainly when it came to speaking or writing for a larger public. But Victor did not exactly subordinate himself to Walter: he often had the more critical political insights, and he was full of ideas and ambitions as well, even if he could only realize them with and through his brother.

So the Reuther brothers thrived at Detroit City College, taking many of the same classes and working on their assignments together. Remembered Merlin Bishop, "Their minds were like one. Walter would start a college paper and then say, 'Vic, you finish it up, I've got to go to work.'" According to Frank Braun, "Walt and Vic collaborated beautifully. Walt wrote solid prose, and Vic would finish it up with a Demosthenes gesture." Despite his evening work at Ford, Walter averaged a B-plus during the two and a half years he took classes at City College; Victor kept up a B average. "Walter and I shared the same childhood experience," wrote Victor in his memoirs, "and we were both fighting for the same social reforms. The cooperation was both practical and satisfying."[8]

With Bishop, Braun, and a few others, Victor and Walter organized the DCC

Social Problems Club, which was affiliated with the League for Industrial Democracy (LID), a youth group whose lineage went back to John Reed, Walter Lippmann, and the pre–World War I Intercollegiate Socialist Society. The league stated its objectives, somewhat vaguely, as "education for a new social order based on production for use not profit," but it was for all practical purposes a branch of the Socialist Party (SP), then in the midst of a long-awaited revival. Starting in 1928, when Norman Thomas, the attractive, Princeton-educated young minister first headed up the Socialist presidential ticket, the SP began to slowly regain membership. From eight thousand members at the end of the 1920s, the party grew to ten thousand in 1931, and to seventeen thousand in 1932. With a new generation of young people and college students pouring into its ranks, the SP became much more active, organizing unemployed workers' councils, supporting the Harlan County mine workers, and fighting militarism, racism, and social snobbery on campus. Ninety-six new party locals were organized during 1931, and another 114 were formed during the first five months of 1932.[9]

In Michigan the SP grew as well, although it could hardly hope to restore itself to the standing it had held at the end of the Great War. Then, the state party had enrolled six thousand members, published eleven newspapers, and elected mayors and other municipal officials in eight cities, including Flint and Kalamazoo. But the Michigan SP had just about disintegrated by 1920, when much of its industrial base left for the underground Communist movement, and when an important group of left-wing intellectuals split with the Debsian Socialists to found their own (non-Communist) Proletarian Party. By 1928 only a pitiful 129 dues payers were still counted on Socialist Party rolls. Rebuilding began with the Depression. In Detroit the party tripled in size, and by 1933, the year the Reuther brothers left for their foreign tour, the Motor City branches could, for the first time in a generation, host a Labor Day picnic for thousands of workers and their families.[10]

But this growth did not mean that the Debsian party of Valentine Reuther's youth had been reborn. Thousands of working-class families still considered themselves Socialist, but the politics of the older generation had either become so diluted as to be increasingly indistinguishable from New Deal reformism (with which it would soon merge) or retained a Marxist rigor only at the cost of an arid and spiritless scholasticism. Through the early 1930s the party was led by an "Old Guard," men like the Latvian-born party secretary Morris Hillquit, whose politics had been shaped years before, first during the fight against IWW syndicalism and then, even more decisively, in reaction to the Bolshevik Revolution and the Leninist consolidation of power that followed. The Old Guard spoke for the leadership of the New York garment trades unions, still the largest element within the Socialist Party, but they had no strategy for building the party or remaking its message. Their language was unmistakably European; an unfriendly contemporary described them as "complacent, over cautious" men who lacked "imagination, initiative, and energy."[11]

Norman Thomas had few programmatic disagreements with the Old Guard, but his approach to rebuilding the party was to make a giant wager on youth, on recruitment of intellectuals and middle-class professionals, and on a "Socialism in our time" that offered a concrete program of social reconstruction to those troubled by the misery and disorder of the Depression. Thomas proved a tribune of "industrial democracy," two words that artfully linked concrete Socialist programs and the grand sweep of the American political tradition. "Democracy," Thomas wrote, "means in Lincoln's phrase, government of the people, by the people, and for the people. . . . Industrial democracy is the application of that same idea to our economic life." Thomas himself was an ethicist, a pacifist, hardly a Marxist at all, but he was passionate and energetic. Many of his young, enthusiastic followers, who had formed themselves into a "Militant" faction, sought to depose the Old Guard and put some Marxist backbone into Thomas's reformism. The Militants were almost all recent college graduates, some young ministers out of Union, Vanderbilt, and Crosier theological seminaries, or Ivy Leaguers like Paul Porter, Mary Fox, and Joseph Lash, all of whom would speak before Reuther's Social Problems Club.[12] These young SP activists found that pacifist and antimilitarist themes mobilized students even more than a critique of American capitalism. Norman Thomas himself never succeeded in reconciling the bedrock pacifism engendered during his radicalization in World War I with the antifascist imperatives he followed after the Spanish Civil War. But Thomas and his partisans found in transatlantic antimilitarism—famously encapsulated when the upper-class Oxford Union resolved that "this House will in no circumstances fight for its King and Country"—an enormously effective organizing tool for campus radicals, who mobilized to eliminate ROTC at Chicago, Columbia, and Oberlin.[13]

The Reuther brothers announced their presence at Detroit City College with a spectacular fight on this issue. Within three weeks after Frank Braun and the Reuther brothers had organized the LID Social Problems Club in October 1931, these "fighting pacifists" plunged into a headline-grabbing controversy that would have lasting consequences for the left in Detroit. The Detroit Board of Education had just petitioned the U.S. War Department to establish an ROTC unit at the college; in response, the campus LID immediately organized a protest meeting, which attracted two hundred students. To be the featured speaker the Reuthers called on Socialist Walter Bergman, a young professor of education at Detroit Teachers College and organizer of a pacifist American Legion post. Bergman denounced "militarism" at City College as a violation of the Kellogg-Briand Pact, and he urged students to pass out petitions demanding the immediate "dissolution of ROTC." Conservatives were outraged by this "seditious and unpatriotic" lecture. One Detroit Board of Education member, the politically ambitious Burt Shurly, asserted his determination to fire Bergman at the next meeting of the board. This attack was part of a larger right-wing backlash against the Democratic mayor, Frank Murphy, whose liberal municipal administration permitted Communists and other radicals to hold demonstrations and rallies at city hall and

Grand Circus Park in the heart of downtown. The battle over Bergman's fate would be another test of strength between Mayor Murphy and his many adversaries. As Burt Shurly put it, "We had this thing licked once in Detroit, but now, under the patronage of Mayor Murphy, the propaganda is creeping back again, and it is time for another fight."[14]

In the days leading up to the Board of Education meeting on December 8, 1931, the controversy commanded front-page coverage in Detroit's papers and energized the long-quiescent forces of the city's labor-liberal community. Bergman was a respected figure, antimilitarism was a popular issue, and free speech was seen as a key to the revitalization of the labor movement. A packed Board of Education meeting, which the *Labor News* described as "the most splendid gathering of the leaders of liberal thought the city has ever seen," turned into a triumphant support rally for Bergman and the free speech rights of public school teachers. Walter Reuther's speech for this radical educator echoed some of the upwardly striving earnestness of his Fordson Four-C days: "It is we students of today who will be the members of the Boards of Education of tomorrow," he announced. "If you limit the right of expression of our professors how can you expect them to teach us how to take up the burdens of the future?" Pushed forward by its liberal members, the Detroit board repudiated Bergman's critics that very night.[15]

The board's endorsement of free speech marked a turning point in the ability of radicals to organize and agitate throughout the city. Teacher activism increased immediately, and Walter Bergman, who would become a friend and supporter of the Reuther brothers in the 1930s, campaigned as the Socialist Party's candidate for state superintendent of public instruction in the spring of 1933. The Detroit Federation of Teachers emerged from the "underground," giving Socialists and other radicals a larger organizational platform, which they used to offer material and moral support to the auto industry organizing drive just getting under way. For more than a decade Detroit high school auditoriums served as the routine venue for almost all the big automobile union meetings.[16]

This success made LID and the Reuther brothers notable elements on campus. Early in 1932 the Reuthers and the Social Problems Club used their influence to make citywide headlines again—in this case, over City College's agreement to abide by the Jim Crow policies of a nearby apartment house when students used its swimming pool during the morning hours. Organizing their first picket line, the Reuther brothers and the LID group generated publicity so unfavorable to the college that it had to cancel the pool contract. The Reuther brothers were now well known among radical students and interested professors; when a year later they left for the Soviet Union, the dean of men noted their departure with some relief.[17]

During the summer and fall of 1932 many of the Detroit City College LID activists threw themselves into support work for Norman Thomas's presidential campaign. Walter Reuther and Merlin Bishop campaigned on weekends in southern Michigan, while Victor Reuther and Loren Walters, a schoolteacher in his midtwenties, toured farther afield upstate. In rural areas and small towns they called on SP contacts from the party's Debsian era; on college campuses they set up "Thomas for President" clubs to build Socialist support.[18]

The campaign of 1932 was Norman Thomas's most successful presidential bid. At a time when Roosevelt and the Democrats had no program for countering the Depression, other than government budget austerity, Thomas's emphasis on a series of immediately implementable reforms to aid the jobless and restore production won him the support of a wide variety of prominent ministers, economists, writers, and leftward-moving journalists. The Socialist Party still retained the formal support of unions like the Pulp and Paper Workers, the International Ladies' Garment Workers, and the Amalgamated Clothing Workers, and it seemed to be winning a large following on campuses, where it outpolled Communist youth by a wide margin.

Of course, radical-sounding stump speakers still had trouble with the law in small-town America. Walter and Bishop traveled in a big Buick with a speaking platform hooked onto the back bumper and an eight-foot wooden sign, "Vote for Norman Thomas—Repeal Unemployment," anchored to the roof. They experienced a good deal of harassment from the police; in one town Reuther and Bishop got a permit after they told the city manager they were going to lecture on "applied Christianity." In Dearborn, Reuther cleverly chose to speak from a platform on his own lot; he kept the police at bay by whipping out the deed when they came to disrupt his rally. Reuther proved an enthusiastic soapboxer. The old Socialists hailed "Comrade Reuther" for his speeches ridiculing Hoover. "He could sit with a chicken farmer and talk economics for five or six hours," said Bishop. "He was very warm that way." Reuther traveled some three thousand miles on behalf of the Thomas ticket, Victor possibly a few miles more. The Socialists had expected to poll two, perhaps three million votes, but in November Thomas got 885,000 votes nationwide and 39,205 in Michigan. This figure amounted to about 2 percent, less than Debs received in 1912 but more than three times the 1928 count.[19]

Many older Socialists, including Thomas, were somewhat disappointed by these vote totals, but for the younger Militants the campaign had been an energizing experience. Certainly this was true for Walter Reuther, who by this time was far more politicized than he had been even a couple of years before. At Ford he had begun to talk politics with his workmates more frequently, and in 1931 he joined the Auto Workers Union (AWU), a radical group largely inside the Communist Party orbit. He also became close friends with John Rushton, a workmate and a bit of a mentor, the first of several older men who would influence Walter Reuther's thinking over the next two decades. Rushton, then in his late forties, was a tool and die maker with a quarter-century in the trade and sixteen years' experience at Ford. He was a Communist who had traveled to the Soviet Union in 1930; on his return, he and Reuther "often talked with enthusiasm about the success of young Soviet Russia."[20]

Rushton made his pro-Soviet, prounion views well known, so he was fired just after the Ford Hunger March of March 1932. This march, one of several Depression-era demonstrations of the unemployed sponsored by the Communists, ended in a dramatic clash at the very gates of the Rouge; four workers were killed, and the subsequent funeral march, which attracted upward of seventy thousand, became a rallying point for the Detroit left. Ford responded with a plantwide purge of hundreds of workers, firing virtually anyone they could identify as radical or sympathetic to the aims of the march. But Reuther was not fired. Though he had not participated in the original Hunger March, he did walk in the much larger funeral procession several days later. Perhaps his skill and his Masonic connections protected him, or perhaps he had just kept his increasingly radical political ideas discreetly hidden from those in authority.[21]

With his wife and two teenage daughters, Rushton soon left again for the Soviet Union, where he had arranged work at the newly constructed automobile plant at Nizhnii-Novgorod, five hundred miles east of Moscow. The Soviets were then in the midst of their First Five-Year Plan, a gigantic, convulsive effort to industrialize backward Russia and catch up with the West. Part of this plan involved the wholesale transfer of Western technology to the new industrial zones, of which Nizhnii-Novgorod was at the epicenter. The Soviets were particularly eager for Ford machines, technicians, and production processes, for Ford assembly-line methods symbolized all that was efficient and scientific in the realm of production. As the Soviets began to grapple with the enormous cultural and social difficulties involved in transforming a peasant society into one of disciplined industrial workers, they looked to the Detroit experience as a guide to the technical reconstruction of their society. "Fordizatsia" was a watchword for up-to-date technique even in those sections of the country where motor vehicles were rarely seen.

The Soviets had bought thousands of tractors and trucks from Ford in the 1920s. They sent technicians to Dearborn for training in 1926 and three years later signed a major contract with Ford for the purchase of all the tools, dies, jigs, and fixtures necessary for the manufacture of the Model A (which Ford would discontinue in 1931). A giant factory complex, modeled after the River Rouge plant, began to rise at Nizhnii-Novgorod, both soon renamed Gorky. By 1932 Amtorg, the Soviet trading company in the United States, began recruiting skilled workers, including Rushton, who got his job at that time building dies in the raw, half-finished complex at Gorky.[22]

Rushton and Reuther corresponded; the older man's letters confirmed the fact that skilled workers with a Ford pedigree were in exceedingly high demand in the Soviet Union. Reuther also had occasional conversations with the Soviet technicians then at work in the design rooms on the second floor of the B-Building, where many had had a fine, ironic vantage point from which to witness the bloody conclusion of the Hunger March and note the anti-Communist sweep that followed.[23]

Walter Reuther was intrigued. The Reuther brothers shared in the growing enthusiasm for the Soviet "experiment," then reaching its peak among the newly radicalized in left-liberal and Socialist Party circles in the United States. Few Socialists endorsed the one-party rule of the Communists, but aside from the Old

Guard, most were eager to give Soviet planning and social experimentation a chance to prove itself. To liberals as well as Socialists, "planning" had achieved a cultlike status in the early 1930s. In contrast to the aimless drift of the Hoover years, Soviet industrialization seemed purposeful and dynamic. An intercollegiate LID conference in late 1931, "Guiding the Revolution," assumed the imminent collapse of laissez-faire capitalism and pointed out, quite correctly, that competition had already begun among planning advocates from big business and those representing more democratically organized forces.[24] Six months later, in a resolution whose passage at the Socialist Party's Milwaukee convention signaled the rise of Militant influence, the SP declared that the success of the "Soviet experiment" in "the economic field will give an immense impetus to the acceptance of Socialism by the workers, while its failure will discredit an economy based on planned production and abolition of Capitalism." The American Socialists urged the release of political prisoners and the restoration of civil liberties in the Soviet Union but nevertheless endorsed the Soviet effort to "create the economic foundations of a Socialist society."[25]

On September 30, 1932, Walter Reuther spent his last day at the Ford Motor Company. According to his Ford employment record, he quit voluntarily, and it is possible that he actually did so in order to take his first full load of classes at Detroit City College. But Reuther always maintained that he was fired for his increasingly visible Socialist activity, which was reaching a peak during the Thomas campaign. According to Reuther, his building superintendent could give him no clear explanation for his discharge, and his employment record still listed him as a "first class worker" on his termination date.[26]

In any event, Walter came home smiling. "Guess what happened to me today? I feel like a liberated man." The brothers were now free to travel. They had been talking of taking a trip abroad that would offer them the chance to visit their relatives in Germany and tour a bit of Europe, then end with a toolmaking stint in the Soviet Union that would provide them with the funds to return home via Asia and the Pacific. With Rushton's recommendation, Walter had no trouble winning a place among those Amtorg recruited from Detroit; his expertise on a particularly tricky die for the Model A head gasket proved convincing to the Soviets. So vital were his talents, in fact, that he persuaded Amtorg to sponsor his brother Victor as well, who had no industrial experience.[27]

Before they left Detroit in January 1933, the brothers withdrew Walter's one thousand dollars in savings from the bank (just weeks before widespread bank failures culminated in the Michigan bank holiday that precipitated the New Deal's first crisis), bought heavy sheepskin coats, warm boots, and two sets of die makers' tools from a pawn shop. They dropped in at the office of Detroit's leading labor and civil liberties lawyer, Maurice Sugar, who had visited Gorky the summer before, and they said good-bye to Roy at the gates of the Briggs plant, where all three Reuther brothers had been activists in support of one of the first mass strikes of the Depression-era auto insurgency.[28]

Then they left for Wheeling. There Walter gave Victor a crash course in tool and die work at Wheeling High's machine shop. At a farewell party reported in the local paper, Walter announced, "We are going to study the economic and social conditions of the world, not the bright lights." More farewells followed in New York, where they spent a talk-filled night at the home of Norman Thomas. And with Victor's assistance, Walter wrote his first essay, an enthusiastic and optimistic report on the Briggs strike (it would fail after a long battle) for the LID's *Student Outlook*. On February 16 they sailed for Germany on the SS *Deutschland*.[29]

The Reuther brothers could hardly have chosen a more dramatic moment to visit their parents' homeland. They landed in Hamburg on February 24 in the midst of the Nazi revolution; they saw a working-class city on the brink of civil war. The entire town seemed to be in uniform, with the banners of the Nazi, Communist, and Social Democratic parties displayed on every block. They soon explored both sides of the political and social divide. A letter of introduction from one of their DCC German professors won them an invitation to a tense and awkward luncheon with an upper-class conservative in a plush neighborhood. They spent most of their time, however, with distant relatives who brought them into conversation with left-wing dockworkers who wanted the Social Democrats to call a general strike. When news of the Reichstag fire reached them, the Reuthers headed straight for Berlin, where on March 1 they saw the building's smoldering remains. The Nazis blamed the Communists for the conflagration and used the fire to mobilize mass support in Germany's last "free" election of March 4, after which they consolidated their political control. Victor and Walter were conducted through the ruins by a brown-shirted guide.

On the train to Berlin Walter and Victor had met a trade union organizer of the Social Democratic Party, and he put them in touch with Socialist university students. With these left-wingers they talked politics, attended clandestine political meetings, and shared quarters on the top floor of a warehouse. Just after the election they watched their roommates barricade the windows and doors against a storm trooper attack, which came at 3:00 A.M., when Nazi partisans raided their quarters in search of Socialist Militants. The Nazis just missed their prey—among them Emil Gross, the chairman of the Social Democratic Student Organization at the University of Berlin, who escaped down a rope ladder—but they did find the Reuther brothers, whose U.S. passports offered protection. The next day the storm troopers and police raided trade union and Social Democratic Party headquarters all over Germany.[30]

"Almost stunned by events," the Reuthers boarded the train out of Berlin. Passing through Dresden and Nuremberg, where they again saw the Nazis take full power, they made their way to Swabia and their Uncle Ernst's village of Ruit. This was the base to which they would return from tours of Germany and western Europe while they awaited, with increasing anxiety, their long-promised visas to the Soviet Union. Here the Reuther brothers found most of their relatives to be staunch Social Democrats, but they were nevertheless made painfully aware of the spread of Nazi culture and control. An Uncle Adolph, from their mother's village of Scharnhausen, a farmer and deputy mayor, loudly defended the new regime, and in one argument threatened Uncle Ernst: "When we march on Moscow I hope I shall have the privilege of shooting you down if you oppose me."[31]

The Nazification of German society was proceeding quickly, even in these remote villages. In nearby Neumagen the mayor and five members of his council had been beaten and imprisoned; at Nellingen, where the Reuther brothers also had relatives, and at Scharnhausen, the workers' singing societies were disbanded. The Nazis transformed German Memorial Day, March 23, into an occasion for fascist rallies. All houses had to display the Nazi flag, and at a bonfire in Scharnhausen that night Hitler Youth led the crowd in chanting "Heil Hitler." When a Nazi threw a Communist flag onto the fire, brownshirts beat and arrested a worker who shouted, "You stole that!" The Reuther brothers themselves almost suffered a similar fate a few months later when they failed to rise for the "Horst Wessel" song at the end of a German propaganda movie they saw with their relatives in Stuttgart.

As the weather improved, there were still no visas, so the Reuther brothers bought bicycles for a series of long tours. With "a positive euphoria," they pedaled through the Black Forest, down the Rhône Valley of France, and along the Riviera into Italy. In Rome they took in the usual tourist sites and mingled with the crowds assembled for a tenth anniversary celebration of Mussolini's fascist revolution. In Austria they admired the workers' housing and child care centers built by Vienna's Socialist government, but they noted the spread of Nazi flags throughout the countryside. When they toured European auto factories—Citroen near Paris, Morris on the outskirts of Oxford, Ford near Cologne—they reconfirmed for themselves the Socialist understanding that America stood in the industrial vanguard. Nothing equaled the Rouge in pay, pace, or efficiency.

They met many politically active people. In August they were in Paris for a sad, dispiriting conference of the Second International. The American delegation was sharply divided between the Old Guard and the younger university-oriented Militants, including Edward Levinson and Maynard Krueger, both of whom would become close friends of the Reuther brothers. Most of the Americans allied themselves with a group of radical European Socialists who favored a resolution written by Henryk Erlich and Victor Alter of the General Jewish Workers Bund of Poland. This initiative, with which the Reuther brothers were undoubtedly in sympathy, called for extraparliamentary joint action with the Communists in the fight against fascism. It went down to a crashing defeat, but the old Social Democrats who dominated the international Socialist movement had no better answer to the Nazi catastrophe.[32]

In England the Reuthers introduced themselves to Fenner Brockway, a leading spokesman for the Independent Labour Party, a member of Parliament, and an advocate of a British opening to the Soviets. He put them in contact with Labourleft comrades all over the British Isles, including the firebrand Jenny Lee, whom they met at a Brighton trade union meeting. A nasty fall while cycling on a country lane cut Walter up badly and slowed them down, but with the help of left-wing doctors and their characteristic perseverance, the Reuther brothers pushed on to complete their 12,000-kilometer tour.[33]

In Amsterdam they attended a Militant anti-Nazi rally and were reunited with Emil Gross, by then the editor of an anti-Nazi paper. Here they agreed to serve as couriers for the Socialist underground in Germany. They mailed their diaries back to Wheeling, memorized their messages, and set off for the Ruhr, where they were told to make contact with a "Fritz" by asking for a particular rare book in one of Dortmund's bookshops. Shunted from one shop to another, they finally reached their contact in the afternoon. They never met "Fritz" again, but Victor long remembered the intense bond of comradeship they instantly felt with this fellow anti-Nazi.[34]

By this time it was late fall and the Reuther brothers were getting desperate. Short of funds, they had their parents cash in one of their insurance policies and mail the proceeds to Berlin. There they made a last call on the Soviet consulate, which, after some further inquiries with London and Moscow, produced the long-sought visas. These were issued during the same week the United States formally recognized the Soviet Union, which may or may not have eased their visa problem.[35]

Their nine months of enforced tourism had two important consequences. First, it gave the Reuther brothers an exceptional view of Europe at the moment it entered one of its greatest crises. They had become cosmopolitan and adventurous young men, confident of their ability to grasp the politics of any situation and to communicate with a wide variety of people. Their political tourism certainly confirmed their antifascism, but it also pushed them toward the left margins of the Socialist movement, where cooperation with the Communists and appreciation of the strength of the Soviet Union were becoming increasingly attractive ideas. They would enter the Soviet Union convinced that Soviet power was an essential bulwark against the spread of fascism. Second, their nine-nation tour through central and western Europe would prove a kind of "cover" in later years when the nearly two years they spent in the Soviet Union came to seem like an embarrassing interlude. The Reuther brothers would then describe their sojourn in terms that made their visits to Britain, France, Germany, Austria, the Soviet Union, China, and Japan sound like a lengthy study tour devoid of the political commitments that had motivated their Soviet trip in the first place.

Walter and Victor left Berlin on November 15, 1933, and arrived in Moscow two days later. Here they confronted Soviet life for the first time: bitterly cold weather, a jammed railroad station, scores of street urchins, and a slow, peasant-filled train to Gorky. There a nasty surprise awaited them. Loaded down with luggage and conspicuous in their thin Western clothes, they had their pockets slit as they stood in a packed tram on their first trip to the *avtozavod*, or auto factory. It was the only word of Russian they knew. At Gorky they lived in the "American Village." Conditions were rough, but far better than those for native workers. There were a dozen plain, two-story apartment buildings, some communal rooms, a dining hall, and a store stocked for the foreigners alone. Insulation against the Russian winter consisted of mud, straw, and manure wedged within the walls. Their lodgings were new; in fact, construction difficulties had been largely responsible for the Soviet delay in issuing their visas, for they would have had no quarters had they come earlier. Even so, they were given a room so small that they had to hang their bicycles and footlockers from the ceiling to conserve space.

The Soviets were still completing the massive Gorky Auto Works when the Reuthers arrived. The complex's power plant was in operation, and the shells of most of the important buildings were standing, but otherwise it was a sprawling construction site strewn with machines, materials, and barracks, all set down in a sea of frozen mud. A wall of the building they were to work in was enclosed only by a tarp, through which boxcars delivered load after load of Western machinery. The wind came through too, which kept the Reuther brothers, as well as the rest of the toolroom workforce, bundled up. Tooling proved virtually impossible that first winter. To make any progress at all, they had to thaw out their fingers every so often in the nearby Heat-Treat Department, where die metals were hardened in high-temperature furnaces. Walter and Victor kept their sheepskin coats on beneath their shop aprons.[36]

Of the thirty-two thousand who labored at Gorky, the Reuther brothers were part of a contingent of about two hundred foreign workers, including about one hundred Americans. Perhaps thirty were from the Ford Motor Company. Such foreign specialists never composed more than 1 or 2 percent of a factory workforce anywhere in the Soviet Union, but their technical importance was considerable and their ideological significance even more so in these years of capitalist crisis and Stalinist industrialization. Many Western workers of the early 1930s were committed, at least initially, to building Soviet power, but the regime also insisted that during these years of hectic industrialization only those "foreign engineers, foremen and skilled workers" who could fill absolutely vital positions would win a post in the new factories.[37]

Perhaps as many as one hundred thousand American workers contacted Amtorg in 1931; in Europe, where both the depression and political crisis were stimulating widespread flight, applications reached upward of one million. By the time the Reuther brothers arrived, more than forty thousand foreign workers were filling key technical slots in the Soviet Union. About half were Germans (many of them refugees from the Nazi terror), and another 25 percent were Americans, of which a large Finnish contingent made up of veterans of labor radicalism in the Pacific Northwest was particularly notable. After 1934, in an era of growing insularity and xenophobia, the Soviets stopped recruiting skilled workers in the West, although politemigranty (political immigrants) still flowed eastward: several hundred young Austrian Schutzbunders arrived in May 1934 after their defeat at the hands of the reactionary Heimwehr in Vienna street fighting that winter, and in 1939 as many as five thousand Spaniards arrived after Franco's victory in the civil war.[38]

As valued foreign workers, Walter and Victor Reuther were privileged witnesses to a second revolution in the Soviet Union, one that may well have transformed the society far more profoundly than that of 1917. The collectivization of agriculture in 1930 and 1931 had destroyed the semiautonomous peasant villages, starved millions in the Ukraine and the North Caucasus, and reduced the standard of living for both rural and urban dwellers well below that of 1913. But the Communist war against the peasantry had given the Soviet state the political and economic tools to shift resources, in brutal and massive fashion, from consumption to investment, from agriculture to industry, from countryside to the new cities being built in the Urals, the Don River basin, and west of Moscow. By 1932 no fewer than nine million peasants had left the villages and entered the urban and industrial labor force; within little more than a decade one out of four peasants had become an urban industrial worker.[39]

In theory, Soviet industrialization was a well-planned, centrally organized effort that coordinated the deployment of raw materials, machinery, and workers in an efficient, fast-paced program of large-scale construction and production. By the time the Reuther brothers arrived, the First Five-Year Plan had laid the groundwork by dramatically expanding the industrial infrastructure, sometimes in massive new complexes: Magnitogorsk ("Russia's City of Steel"), Gorky ("The Auto City"), and the tractor plants at Kharkov and Stalingrad were notable examples. At Gorky a few Ford cars were already being assembled from imported parts when the Reuthers arrived; the Second Five-Year Plan called for manufacture of an all-Soviet Ford car, assembled at the rate of one hundred thousand a year. But Soviet industrialization had a chaotic and improvised quality that never failed to exasperate the foreign workers, who had arrived with such contrary expectations. The enormous difficulties inherent in the effort to acculturate and train the mass of peasant workers who streamed into Gorky and other new centers proved a huge obstacle to efficiency and order. Soviet workers in the early 1930s had an average of 3.2 years of schooling, and in new factories like Gorky the level was probably less.[40]

The overwhelming persistence of peasant poverty and culture struck the Reuther brothers with particular force: in the summer many workers walked to the factory barefoot to save on shoe leather; others knew nothing of indoor toilets; and one nomadic family, assigned to a new second-floor apartment, reportedly built a fire in the middle of the room to cook their dinner. Accident rates in the factory were high, scrap production enormous, and machine breakage not infrequent. Few workers could entirely shed the characteristic apathy of peasant life. Victor and Walter nicknamed one former street waif in the toolroom "Nitchevo," after his favorite expression, which he always accompanied with a shrug of the shoulders that meant, "What's the difference?" Moshe Lewin, the distinguished historian of Stalinist industrialization, has described such phenomena as part of a "ruralization" of Soviet urban life that took place in the early 1930s.[41]

But like many other foreign specialists, the Reuther brothers took enormous satisfaction in teaching ex-peasants the skills necessary to operate the imported machinery and begin turning out a finished product. "The entire factory was like one huge trade school," remembered Victor Reuther many years later.[42] Both Walter and Victor first gave instruction in German, which was then translated into Russian. Soon, however, they absorbed enough of the native language to communicate directly with their student workers. Walter Reuther was in charge of a brigade of peasant lads who had seen nothing more complicated than a wheelbarrow before they were enrolled in a technical training school operated by the factory. These were handpicked workers, and most were eager to learn. As early as January 1934 Victor wrote a friend in Detroit, "We are seeing the most backward nation in the world being rapidly transformed into the most modern and scientific with new concepts and new social ideals coming into force."[43] And by May 1934 the English-language *Moscow Daily News* quoted Walter: "The untrained workers of yesterday are taking rapid strides that soon will overtake auto workers anywhere in the world." This was bravado, of course, but skill levels and production did rise quickly. When the Reuther brothers arrived, a toolroom workforce of eight hundred built hardly one usable die a month; upon their departure twenty months later, the Soviet workers themselves were turning out five or six a month.[44]

The Reuther brothers were also enormously impressed with the communal elements of the life they now shared with other Soviet workers. At the American compound they surrendered their ration books to the general pool, thus providing the children of the community with a little more butter and meat than they otherwise would have had. Seeking to share the life of ordinary Russian workers, they ate their lunches in the factory cafeteria instead of the special restaurant for foreigners. The food was poor and they both lost weight, but Walter found "a wonderful spirit . . . among the workers. A foreman produces a guitar, strums a few chords. A greasy mechanic and a red-kerchiefed Komsomolka, forgetting work, swing into gay dancing. Everybody keeps rhythms, shouts and laughs. I enjoy every minute here."[45]

The Reuther brothers also had fun on the occasional weekend *subotnik*, or volunteer labor day, organized by a youth group or trade union for special projects such as cutting ice on the Oka River for summer storage or finishing a school or other construction project. In the summer, workers from Gorky and other factories often traveled to collective farms to help with the harvest. These were partly social events as well, with music, dancing, and extra food provided. During their first few months in the Soviet Union the Reuther brothers were enormously impressed at the high levels of participation in subotniks. Only later did they realize the subtle coercion involved in recruiting volunteers: those who failed to show up were soon noted and became subject to discrimination by Communist Party or factory officials.

The two brothers enjoyed a full social life. They were single, of course, and among the very youngest foreign workers at Gorky. In contrast to the experience of many older radicals who had brought their wives and children, the hardships of living in a raw and spartan land fell less harshly upon these adventurous young souls. Walter and Victor were pleased to note the substantial presence of women in jobs that were all-male in the United States, and on a vacation trip to central Asia they admired Soviet efforts to emancipate Muslim women there. Like many of the other single foreigners, they had Russian girlfriends. Such relationships were a real step upward for Russian women, who were thus able to share some of the privileges enjoyed by the skilled Westerners. Indeed, Victor discovered that his girlfriend traded on the black market—news that quickly ended the affair. But Walter developed a more serious relationship with "Lucy," the educated daughter of a former railroad official. For several months they lived together in the American Village.[46]

Within the factory itself, Walter and Victor found the Soviet effort to construct a new political culture of production, involving participatory structures unknown in the United States, quite extraordinary. It was thrilling to see red banners with slogans like "Workers of the World Unite" draped across the craneways, and they found the friendly "Hello, comrade" from the plant superintendent a refreshing change from the deference expected in Western factories. "We are watching daily socialism being taken down from the books on the shelves and put into actual application," Victor wrote to a friend in Detroit. "Who could not be inspired by such events?"[47]

When factory administrators announced a "socialist competition" to raise the "cultural level" of the workers, the Reuther brothers took the lead in the Tool and Die Department to come up with a project. Before 1935 such schemes had not yet degenerated into the brutal competition of the Stankhanovite movement but instead were somewhat more benign, involving suggestions for improving technique, group efficiency, and health and safety. For example, the Brake Drum Department at Gorky had shipped artificial palm trees from Moscow and scattered them about their section of the factory. Tool and die workers pondered a response, and the Reuther brothers hit upon a more practical idea: replacing the traditional wooden spoons in the workers' cafeteria with metal spoons stamped from the scrap left over from the fender dies. The project proved a great success, and the factory organized a festive ceremony when the spoons were distributed in the lunchroom. But such was their value in the impoverished region that all the spoons disappeared the next day, and a system that involved exchanging a factory worker's pass for the use of a spoon at each meal had to be devised to keep the utensils in the cafeteria.[48]

Most important to their favorable impression was the "genuine proletarian democracy," as they called it, in the structure of political participation that governed their department. This was the *Treugolnik*, or tripartite administration of Soviet industry, composed of factory management, union leaders, and the Communist Party. Meetings were frequent, and often a trade union official or worker would berate plant supervisors for supply difficulties or food problems. The actual authority of such shop meetings was highly problematic, but the Reuthers, delighted that they took place at all, saw such give-and-take as factory socialism itself. In what would become a celebrated and controversial document, the "Gorky letter" dated January 20, 1934, and addressed to Merlin Bishop's younger brother Melvin, Victor wrote that Walter and he were amazed to see workers voting and talking back to their department chiefs at shop meetings. "Imagine this at Fords or at Briggs. This is what the Outside World calls the Ruthless Dictatorship in Russia. I tell you, Mel, in all the countries we have thus far been in, we have never found such genuine proletarian democracy. It is unpolished and crude, rough and rude, but proletarian workers' democracy in every respect."[49]

Such were the Reuther brothers' impressions after but two months at Gorky. We know, however, that Stalinist industrialization was at that very moment reproducing most of the inequalities of capitalist social relations, but even more harshly, owing to the low wage level, the disorganized character of the new working class, and the fusion of political and economic power in the hands of the rapidly expanding state bureaucracy. Foreign workers, many of whom were former trade union militants, found to their surprise that virtually all production was conducted on a piece-rate or bonus system; production quotas were enforced not just by Taylorite wage schemes but by organized social pressure and selective administrative discipline. At Gorky, for example, the Reuther brothers found red flags placed on the machines of those workers who advanced production, and burlap ones on the machines of those who fell behind. *Udarniks*, or "shock workers" (most of those in the toolroom, including the Reuthers, qualified for this status) had privileges, like access to longer vacations and better housing that was unavailable to ordinary workers.

Meanwhile, the direct management of labor was becoming increasingly harsh. Although shop authority was formally in the hands of the Treugolnik, "one-man management" had increasingly become the prevailing practice in most shops. Unions had some responsibility for social services but little role in production; meanwhile, penalties for absenteeism and theft were draconian at Gorky and elsewhere. A 1932 law gave shop managers the authority to fire workers and deprive their families of housing if they were chronically late to work. As the 1930s advanced it became Stalinist policy to build new social hierarchies in the factories through the expansion of wage differentials and preferential access to food, housing, and education for those considered the most skilled or politically reliable workers.[50]

It is perhaps understandable that the Reuther brothers seemed unaware of these radical distortions in the socialist ideal: their perspective was limited and favorably focused by their privileged status. But like many other foreign workers, they were appalled at the chaos and inefficiency of the factory itself. At the Gorky Auto Works, a vastly overstaffed complex, coordination between the various production departments and between the foremen and their supervisors was poor—but only partly because of the newness of the factory and the vast influx of peasant workers. Equally important was the character of Stalinist-style production "planning" in the first two Five-Year Plans. Although expectations had moderated somewhat by 1932, Stalin and other high-level officials of the Communist Party still saw the plan as little more than a minimum set of production quotas that industrial managers would be expected to exceed. This expectation put a premium on improvisation, Bolshevik "storming" campaigns, heroic spurts of intense labor, shoddy output, and, ultimately, falsification of production figures. Some factory managers were therefore known to hijack raw materials and ignore tool maintenance in order to overfulfill their quota. Failure was blamed on sabotage and "wrecking," some of which did take place as a sort of protest against the brutalities of the industrialization drive. Reuther understood that such innovations were the opposite of what a successful industrial system needed, namely, systematic work, steady rhythms, and good coordination of effort among large cooperative communities.[51]

Walter Reuther sent a stream of letters to the English-language *Moscow Daily News* complaining that production problems in the toolroom were the result of "administrative," not technical or cultural, backwardness.[52] He attacked the Gorky piece-rate quota scheme: blueprints, castings, and steel arrived late, so that "the first half of the month sees insufficient work and the second half a mad rush to complete the program with quality being sacrificed." Reuther had no doubt that the principles of production he had learned at River Rouge had to be transplanted to the Soviet Union. In the U.S. plant, dies were completed on a staggered basis, generating "a constant flow of new work into the shop and a steady flow of finished dies out." And Reuther denounced Gorky's notoriously unsafe working conditions, also in Fordist terms: "The administration seems to be under the illusion that safety measures are entirely divorced from efficiency, something more or less superfluous." He was irritated that managers did not provide workers with rags with which to clean metal surfaces; after an expensive accident, he complained that safety holes were not drilled in the base of heavy dies and castings so that cranes and hooks could hoist them from place to place.[53]

Reuther's complaints created some unpleasant moments at Gorky, but his skilled status and American passport protected both brothers from reprisals. Walter often remarked to his brother that "the way to beat the bureaucrats was to get Moscow's ear, because they had respect for technicians." Indeed, after the appearance of his letter in the *Moscow Daily News*, safety holes were finally drilled in all heavy dies. For many foreign specialists, a critique of Soviet industrialization that began with suggestions for improving shop practice ended, after months of frustration and observation of the manifest inequalities of Soviet life, in disillusionment and opposition to Soviet communism itself. This reaction was particularly common after 1934, when many of the privileges enjoyed by foreign workers were withdrawn and the purge that began with the assassination of Sergey Kirov in December 1934 gathered its bloody momentum. At that time, most of the Austrian Schutzbunders and Finnish-Americans, as well as hundreds of left-wing workers from the United States, Germany, and Italy, desperately sought passage out of the Soviet Union. For those who retained their foreign passports, escape was relatively easy; for the vast majority of the remainder, arrest and deportation to the Gulag was the usual fate.[54]

The Reuther brothers never experienced such a painful disillusionment. Despite their sharp critique of industrial practice at Gorky, they had nothing but overwhelming praise for the larger social and economic arrangements that they found at the dawn of Soviet industrialization. Later this appraisal would become an extremely sensitive subject: the Reuther brothers, and especially Walter, would claim that, despite their initial enthusiasm, their shop-floor experience and close political observation had turned them into critics of the Soviet regime by the time they left. But there is little evidence that such an evolution took place. In letters signed by both brothers, they continued to identify with Soviet society, not just with its program of rapid industrialization, although that impressed them most forcefully, but also with its claim to socialist egalitarianism and workers' power. "Mel, you know Wal and I were always strong for the Soviet Union. You know we were always ready to defend it against the lies of reactionaries," wrote Victor two months after they arrived. "But let me tell you, now that we are here seeing all the great construction, watching a backward peasantry being transformed into an enlightened, democratic, cultured populace, now that we have already experienced the thrill, the satisfaction of participating in genuine proletarian democracy, we are more than just sympathetic toward *our* country, we are ready to fight for it and its ideas."[55]

Seven months later the enthusiasm of the Reuther brothers remained untarnished, despite a good deal more experience at Gorky, a bit more facility with the language, and a monthlong, 4,000-kilometer vacation tour down the Volga to Stalingrad and back through Ukraine to Moscow. It was a taxing and trying trip, admitted Victor, again the author of a letter to friends in the United States, but the construction projects, collective farms, and tractor factories they inspected filled them with a "strange pride." Here was a "new life in the making . . . we began to see life as it should be." At Stalingrad they saw new tractors being driven off the assembly lines and then "thrust into production," while the new Dnieper Dam, constructed with but primitive earth-moving equipment, demonstrated that "Bolshevism knows no barriers that cannot be surmounted." They traveled through Ukraine, just two years after an appalling terror-famine, but they found the collective farms they were allowed to visit endorsed by a prosperous peasantry. They were particularly impressed by the nurseries and the collective preparation of food. "All housewives in capitalist countries who are chained to the kitchen stove should see this, and I guarantee that the following day they would all join their local Communist Party branch." Among the Volga Germans, who had lived in South Russia for generations, they found a peasantry more prosperous than that of Scharnhausen, a living and pointed refutation of Hitler's anti-Bolshevik propaganda.[56]

In the spring of 1935, as the Reuthers prepared to leave Gorky, it became impossible to ignore the police-state character of the regime, even in the relatively protected environs of the American Village. As early as August 1934 an Italian worker whom the Reuthers knew as a gentle, sensitive person was arrested in a midnight raid. He was accused of being a Trotskyist. Five months later came the assassination of Kirov, the popular Leningrad Communist leader. He was shot by a party member named Nikolayev, whose trial, broadcast over the Gorky plant's public address system, became the basis for Stalin's accusation that a widespread Trotskyist plot threatened Soviet power. The secret police became more active, arrests were more frequent, and open political discussion ceased. Walter remembered seeing the wives and children of workers who had been taken away during the night, red-eyed and despondent at breakfast the next morning. "It was only on those rare occasions when we were alone with friends on a walk through the woods or perhaps in a rowboat in the middle of the Oka," Victor later wrote, "that we could talk to any Russian worker about his opinion of the Stalin regime and the political oppression that was hanging like a sword over his head."[57]

The Reuther brothers therefore had complicated feelings about what they had seen in the Soviet Union. They could hardly ignore the willful inefficiency of shop-floor production management, nor could they close their eyes to the purge that had begun to engulf even their foreign specialist comrades. But the Reuther brothers, and especially Walter, returned to the United States as committed and vocal defenders of the Soviet Union to an extent quite extraordinary among foreign workers who came back to the West in the mid-1930s. On June 20, 1935, just before they set off for the Far East, Walter and Victor still could write, in a letter to Maurice Sugar, of "the atmosphere of freedom and security, shop meetings with their proletarian industrial democracy; all these things make an inspiring contrast to what we know as Ford wage slaves in Detroit. What we have experienced here has reeducated us along new and more practical lines."[58]

It was one thing for sympathetic intellectuals like Scott Nearing, Lincoln Steffens, and Sidney and Beatrice Webb to celebrate the regime's accomplishments, for their knowledge of the Soviets, like that of many fellow-traveling visitors, was shaped by their political predispositions and hardly disturbed by their relatively brief and well-guided tours of the country. But the Reuther brothers had a far more gritty and intimate understanding of what Soviet life was like. It would seem difficult for them to have remained uncritical. The historian Andrea Graziosi found that the great majority of those foreign workers who succeeded in returning to the West offered their comrades there a somber picture of Soviet institutions, the effect of which was to substantially diminish the appeal of revolutionary politics in that era and to strengthen social democratic tendencies in the labor movement. In the United States, for example, the news from the Soviet Union may well have struck a heavy blow against Finnish-American radicalism, even before the Soviet invasion of Finland in 1939 finished it off.[59]

After their return to the United States, Walter and Victor Reuther would become publicly vocal critics of the Soviet regime, but Walter Reuther certainly did not adopt this stance during the first two and a half years he spent back on American soil. During his first few months back in the United States he offered several quite salutary lectures on his experiences abroad, some under the sponsor-ship of the Friends of the Soviet Union, others for Socialist Party and university groups. Reuther's notes have not survived, but those who heard him—among them, both Socialist Party comrades and FBI informants—described Reuther as still enthusiastic about the achievements of the Soviet regime and the character of the new society it was building.[60]

The Reuther brothers were not blind to the sinister elements inherent in Sta-linist industrialization. Rather, their favorable impression of the Soviet Union derived from their limited perspective, colored by the relative privileges they enjoyed as skilled workers holding U.S. passports, as well as from the value they put on the Soviet effort to plan directly economic growth and to politicize the structure of shop production, no matter how poorly these aims were realized in practice. The Five-Year Plans were transforming a peasant society into an indus-trial one, and in the process the Soviets seemed to be building a counterweight to the fascism that had so alarmed the Reuther brothers during their tour through western Europe.

Thus Walter and Victor were impressed with the Soviet government's effort to add a military component to the industrial scene. Gorky had marksmanship classes and a parachute training group, and the factory was earmarked from the beginning as a military standby facility, tooled and geared to produce tanks, gun carriages, and airplane parts. From the end of 1934 onward, technicians and engi-neers from the Red Army appeared almost daily in the toolroom to supervise the construction of dies and fixtures, which were then tested, oiled, and put on the shelf for emergency use. According to Victor, this integrated deployment of tool-making technology in the Soviet Union would provide some of the initial inspira-tion for Walter Reuther's celebrated effort, early in World War II, to force the auto-mobile industry to convert a portion of its tooling capacity to military aircraft production.[61]

The Reuther brothers returned to the United States via Asia and the Pacific. Early in the summer of 1935 they traveled south, through the Caucasus Moun-tains, across the Caspian Sea by steamer, and then on to Samarkand and Tashkent, visiting areas rarely seen by foreigners. Soviet officials insisted they return to Moscow to board the trans-Siberian train for the thirteen-day journey to Manchuria and North China. This leg of the journey proved typically adventure-some. They shared a railway compartment with Hayley Mills, Britain's top spy in the Far East, who pumped them for information on Gorky and the remote parts of the Soviet Union they had visited. They were unaware of his status, but the Japan-ese, who had just taken control of Manchuria, were suspicious enough to hold them all up at the border and then put a police agent on the Reuther brothers when they toured Japan a few weeks later.

In China they were appalled by the poverty and enormous inequalities of wealth, symbolized by the impoverished rickshaw drivers who continually implored them to take a ride. Boarding a riverboat in Nanking, they were horrified to see Sikh guards beat a crowd of destitute peasants back from the boat. Victor recalled: "As the peasants fought to get on board, grabbing the railings, they were savagely clubbed, and sank in the muddy waters beneath us. No one made any effort to save them from drowning, and when we protested, we were told that they would soon have died of starvation anyway!" The Reuthers left China for a brief and pleasant bicycle tour in Japan. There Walter was captivated by the Japanese aesthetic and its expression in domestic architecture. They arrived in Tokyo virtually broke, but the U.S. embassy helped them get jobs on an American liner to Los Angeles, where they arrived in mid-October. They had been away for two years and eight months. In their absence, much had changed—in Detroit, in Washington, and throughout the labor movement.[62]

4

RADICAL CADRE AND
NEW DEAL UNION

We really were not organizing the workers. We were just giving them a kind of
constructive leadership.

—*May Reuther*

ineteen thirty-six may well have been the most important year in Walter
Reuther's life, a turning point that divided a youth of hard work and
adventure from an adulthood of politically engaged leadership and national
prominence. He got married, won election to the United Automobile Workers
(UAW) executive board, ran a successful strike, and established a powerful union
base among the thousands of autoworkers on Detroit's West Side. A footloose
world traveler and Socialist lecturer only a year before, Reuther had become, to
use the title of C. Wright Mills's later book, one of the "new men of power"
spawned by the eruption of the working class onto the New Deal's political landscape.

When Walter Reuther returned to Detroit after his trip to the Soviet Union, he
was twenty-eight years old, no longer a youth, but part of that growing class of semiprofessional agitators and organizers engendered by the radicalization of the Great
Depression and the opportunities opening up in the labor movement and left-wing
politics. Immediately after landing in Los Angeles, Victor and Walter took the bus
to Wheeling for a family reunion, then returned to Detroit to catch up with old

friends in the Socialist Party and get a firsthand look at the labor movement in the Motor City.[1]

Much had changed, both in Detroit and all across America. By 1935 Detroit still remained a capital of the "open shop," but for more than two years trade unions of every sort had waxed and waned in the Motor City. Most strikes still ended in defeat and disarray and there were precious few employers who actually negotiated with their employees, but whatever its limitations, the New Deal had put trade unionism, even "industrial democracy," at the top of the political agenda. From the moment in June 1933 when Roosevelt signed the National Industrial Recovery Act (NIRA), with its famous section 7(a), which guaranteed workers the right to organize and bargain collectively, both liberals and radicals had come to see the revival of trade unionism as essential, not only to the protection of workers against autocratic employers, but also for a more equitable redistribution of national income and the increase in working-class purchasing power essential to a consumption-driven economy. This difficult and sometimes contradictory linkage between industrial democracy in the shop and mass purchasing power in the pay-check proved an enormously powerful idea that virtually defined the social agenda of the New Deal—and the politics of Walter Reuther—for more than a generation.[2]

If the idea of mass unionism was in the air, its reality was but fragmentary and episodic. Section 7(a) was little more than a hopeful sentiment that contained no administrative mechanism to ensure that the insurgencies that swept across industrial America were translated into stable and independent unions. Among the skilled metalworkers of Reuther's generation, unemployment, wage cuts, and skill dilution had subverted most entrepreneurial dreams and replaced them with a syndicalist militancy given shape and politics by the immigrant, Anglo-Irish radicals who came to the fore within this strategically placed sector of the auto workforce. They organized thousands of machinists and tool and die men into the innocuously named Mechanics Educational Society of America (MESA), whose violent strikes and verbal contempt for both managerial prerogatives and government authority still reflected the tradition of Labourite radicalism that had sustained the 1926 British general strike.

But for all its élan, MESA could hardly speak for the mass of unskilled workers whose consciousness was shaped by the parochial world of ethnic neighborhood, immigrant church, and grinding work. Although millions of eastern Europeans, African-Americans, and transplanted Appalachian whites now voted Democratic and looked to the New Deal state for a measure of economic security, the repressive insularity of the factory regime—gestapo-like at the Rouge, bureaucratically claustrophobic in most General Motors plants—muffled the New Deal's emancipatory message and made union-organizing work a sub-rosa activity. Auto unionists had their greatest success among the supplier plants and single-factory firms that lay on the margins of the oligopolistically structured industry. Energized by the New Deal's rhetorical endorsement of trade unionism, shop activists at White

Motor in Cleveland, at Studebaker in South Bend, and at Midland Steel and Kelsey-Hayes in Detroit built local unions whose character often stood halfway between a company-dominated employee representation plan and a genuinely independent union. The most spectacular battles took place in Toledo, where in 1934 an organizing effort at Electric Auto-Lite, an independent parts manufacturer, soon escalated into a citywide general strike. Success at Auto-Lite gave Toledo unionists the organizational momentum needed to shut down the city's Chevrolet transmission plant, forcing General Motors to halt production in factories employing thirty-two thousand workers. To resume work, GM made numerous concessions, but in a pattern that would be repeated again and again, the giant corporation transferred half of the plant's machinery to other locations, thus eliminating hundreds of jobs and undercutting the vitality of the new Chevy local.[3]

In Detroit the largest of these early unions took root at the great Dodge Main plant in Polish Hamtramck. There the Automotive Industrial Workers' Association (AIWA) arose out of the paternalism and self-confidence of Walter Chrysler, who sought to parry NIRA section 7(a) by establishing an elaborate works council scheme in October 1933. As the limited authority of the Dodge Main council became apparent, its leaders pushed for greater autonomy: wage bargaining with management, an independent shop steward system, and negotiations over the pace of production. They soon found a powerful ally in the charismatic "Radio Priest" Father Charles E. Coughlin, whose weekly broadcasts preached "social justice" for industrial workers, collaboration with employers, and, after 1934, an increasingly virulent brand of anti-Roosevelt, anti-Communist corporatism. By 1935 the AIWA was known as "Coughlin's union."[4]

The American Federation of Labor (AFL) did little to unite these weak and fragmented organizations. Given its political caution, its commitment to craft organization, and the barely concealed ethnocentricism of its northern European leadership, the AFL proved reluctant to put much energy behind any sort of trade unionism in the auto industry. William Collins, the Irish-American street railway unionist delegated to Detroit, once joked, "My wife can always tell from the smell of my clothes what breed of foreigners I have been hanging out with." When the federation finally chartered the independent United Automobile Workers union in August 1935, the AFL president, William Green, chose another business agent, the ever-cautious Francis Dillon, to preside over the sketchy organization. His timidity had much to recommend it, for neither the scattered "federal" locals chartered by the AFL nor the city's growing community of radicals had the staying power or the strategy to actually confront the big auto corporations. "We were all uninformed," recalled Dan Gallagher, an American-born production worker at Timkin Axle in Detroit. His coworkers and he were "naive, ignorant shop people who knew nothing about unions, organization, or anything else except that we knew our problem, each of us." By the time Reuther revisited Detroit early in the fall of 1935, virtually every strike in the industry signaled the destruction of the organization that had called it.[5]

To build an industrial union in the automobile industry would therefore require not just "militancy" but a cadre of organizers who could deploy the new language of industrial democracy to link shop-floor problems with union promise and New Deal politics in a persistent, systematic effort that seized a fleeting moment of social turmoil and legal advantage, the latter symbolized by Roosevelt's 1935 signature on the Wagner Act, perhaps the most radical piece of legislation in twentieth-century American history. Within little more than a year Reuther would prove himself one of the most resourceful of these radical cadre, but in the fall of 1935 he was still exploring America's new political terrain; indeed, he was shrewd enough to personally attend the two most significant conclaves of that season. In October 1935 he drove to Atlantic City with a carload of Detroit comrades to observe the tumultuous AFL convention, where John L. Lewis broke decisively with the stolid defenders of craft unionism to emerge as the great tribune of industrial organization in the auto, steel, rubber, and other basic industries of the day. Two months later both Victor and Walter attended the student congress in Columbus, Ohio, where Socialists and Communists merged their rival organizations to form the American Student Union (ASU), one of the key institutions that gave life to the new Popular Front, whose politics so dominated the American left in the last half of the 1930s.[6]

Victor and Walter Reuther were by now unusually cosmopolitan young men, seasoned speakers who could win an audience beyond that of Socialist youth on many a Midwest college campus. Walter gave talks in Ohio, Michigan, and Ontario, and just before Christmas both brothers lectured on their European trip at Brookwood Labor College in Katonah, New York, where Roy Reuther was teaching for the year.[7] Brookwood was an important resource for laborite radicals of Reuther's political generation. Founded during an era of enthusiasm for workers' education, in the years right after World War I, Brookwood would become a key institution of the labor left. Since 1933 the school, one hundred miles north of New York City, had been directed by the Socialist Tucker Smith, a former YMCA secretary and pacifist with extensive contacts among collegiate youth radicalized in the peace movement. Although Brookwood still enrolled some authentic proletarians on union-funded "scholarships," in the 1930s it was recruiting largely from the colleges, the radical community, and the Socialist Party itself. In the 1920s the school had never had any students from Detroit because the union movement there was so weak, but after Brookwood's shift toward service of a more self-consciously radical constituency, several young Detroiters spent time at the school, including Roy Reuther and Merlin Bishop, who had some of their expenses paid by a group of older SP supporters of greater means.[8]

The shift at Brookwood was important, because it actually made the school more relevant to the needs of the industrial union movement that was beginning to stir; it was among the politicized, ambitious semiproletarians of that movement that the new unions of the Congress of Industrial Organizations (CIO) would find so many essential cadre. These young radicals came to Brookwood for a summer or a season to sharpen their understanding of the new union movement and win the political credentials to become organizers or staffers after "graduation." Brookwood became an intellectually exciting institution in which urban Jewish radicals from New York and Philadelphia could make contact with the more "American" proletarians of Detroit, Newark, and Buffalo. Half-commune and half-classroom, Brookwood offered both its students and its faculty the kind of rich, personally gratifying experience that often marks off a generation.[9] Len De Caux, a Brookwood student and future CIO publicist, remembered the school as offering "ease, security, the fresh-air pleasures of the well-to-do. . . . Spiritually, Brookwood was a labor movement in microcosm—without bureaucrats or racketeers—with emphasis on youth, aspirations, ideals."[10]

Here all three Reuther brothers made contact with a cohort of future UAW "Reutherites." Victor Reuther made Brookwood a base during 1936 after Tucker Smith got him a job doing labor outreach work for the Quaker-funded Emergency Peace Campaign, and it was here that he met and married Sophia Goodlavich, a young Catholic working-class woman from Massachusetts. Frank Winn, a twenty-two-year-old Dallas newspaperman, spent much of 1935 at Brookwood; later he would become an editor and publicity man for the Reuther forces in the UAW. The National Student Association (NSA) leader George Edwards led a League for Industrial Democracy (LID) workshop at Brookwood in the summer of 1935; within a year he would be an organizer and political leader of several thousand autoworkers on Detroit's West Side. Journalists and intellectuals like Edward Levinson, Norman Thomas, Benjamin Stolberg, Robert Lynd, David Saposs, and Lewis Cory spoke frequently at Brookwood, and in their audiences were Socialist youths like Nat Weinberg and Brendan Sexton, the postwar directors of the UAW research and education departments.[11]

Roy Reuther was steeped in the Brookwood culture. Since 1933 he had been a student, teacher, and circuit lecturer with the school. Late in 1934, when he began teaching workers' education in Flint for the Federal Emergency Relief Administration (FERA), he simply re-created the Brookwood curriculum: labor history, public speaking, and "labor dramatics," which offered a "revolutionary" interpretation of labor's cause. His warmth, competence, and energy made him an instant hit among the beleaguered band of Flint unionists who dared to sign up for his courses. Though radical, FERA was a government program, so it legitimized union talk even inside some GM shops; within weeks of his arrival Roy Reuther had orchestrated their devastating testimony for a National Recovery Administration (NRA) committee investigating labor relations in heavy industry. General Motors soon forced his dismissal, but Roy Reuther had won the connections and confidence that gave him a leadership role among the activists who precipitated Flint's great sit-down strike of 1937.[12]

Walter Reuther was ready to replicate Roy's experience when he accepted Tucker Smith's offer to teach labor education at Katonah, then head up a Brookwood branch, partly funded by the CIO, in either Pittsburgh or Detroit. "I had not thought of going into workers' education," Reuther wrote to Smith late in January 1936, "but if you think I can contribute more to the movement and better utilize my experience . . . I am ready to come along." Reuther's hesitancy was uncharacteristic, but it reflected his simultaneous effort to find a useful niche in the nascent unions of the auto industry. His chance there came in February, when he won membership in the Ternstedt UAW local, which promptly elected him a delegate to the Wayne County Central Labor Council. Prospects now looked good for his participation in the upcoming UAW convention at South Bend, at which union radicals were expected to take control from the maladroit conservatives appointed by the AFL. Meanwhile, Reuther's SP comrades pressured him to stay in the auto industry organizing drive. Merlin Bishop berated Reuther for "running away" from trade union work, while his brothers Victor and Roy weighed in with a letter stressing the "necessity" of staying in Detroit. "Having just recently returned from a country where the opinion of one's comrades cannot be overlooked or minimized," Reuther wrote Tucker Smith in late February, "I feel the resentments of the Detroit comrades very keenly."[13]

And finally tipping the scales for a longer stay in Detroit was Reuther's courtship of May Wolf, a vivacious, five-foot-four physical education teacher active in the Detroit SP. May was a daughter of the immigrant working class. Her parents were Russian Jews, Frank Wolfman and Dora Rubin, who had immigrated to the United States in 1902 and 1903, when they were still teenagers. Married in 1904, Frank held a succession of working-class jobs in Pittsburgh and Cincinnati before the family moved in 1915 to Detroit, where he worked as a streetcar conductor, cigarmaker, and then, more permanently, as a freight handler on the Michigan Central Railroad. The family spoke Yiddish at home, were active in the Workmen's Circle, and voted Socialist when they could. Walter Reuther had briefly met both May and her father at Socialist meetings in the early 1930s. May had been born in Cincinnati in 1910, the second of three children and the only daughter. She was a precocious, hardworking child, a striking contrast to her older brother Earl, who remained something of a delinquent well into his twenties. She graduated from high school at fourteen, then took a two-year teacher training course at Detroit Teachers College, where she specialized in gym and health education, then the surest track to a public school job. But she was also something of a bohemian and a radical; she taught in one of Detroit's most racially integrated public schools, where she was indefatigable in her efforts to build a strong teachers' union.

Devoted to modern dance, May Wolf gravitated toward the avant-garde wing of the Socialist movement, where she participated in the "Rebel Arts" group and attended classes sponsored by Michigan's Proletarian Party, a Marxist sect with a somewhat more youthful and activist character than that of the SP. The Proletarian Party, which had emerged out of the chaotic fissure that split the Socialist movement in 1919, eschewed electoral action, in its place emphasizing the acculturation of the working class through party schools, public lectures, political demonstrations, and publications of all kinds. At home in such a milieu, this striking twenty-five-year-old redhead cut a glamorous figure in 1935. May Wolf was courted by, among others, V. F. Calverton, who edited the important Marxist literary journal *Modern Monthly* out of New York.[14]

Walter encountered May in the fall of 1935 when he reentered the Socialist world of Detroit. They attended dance concerts at the Detroit Institute of the Arts and participated in a three-day state conference of the Socialist Party in Flint early in 1936. Married on March 13, 1936, in a civil ceremony, the couple immediately drove to suburban Mount Clemens, where Walter gave an evening speech at a labor rally. Here was their life in a nutshell: a constant round of meetings, conferences, and caucuses, often exciting but sometimes merely tiring. May's teacher's salary of sixty dollars a week—then a bit more than what a skilled autoworker could earn—provided most of their income during the first nine months of their marriage, when Reuther was still largely an unpaid organizer. Until 1941 they lived near May's parents in a modest house on LaSalle Boulevard in a working-class district on the West Side of Detroit.[15]

Like any romance, their mutual attraction had its unique chemistry: in his love letters written from union meetings in distant cities, Walter saw himself as a "dope" in need of May's warmth and guidance. But their marriage also represented something of that fruitful connection nurtured at places like Brookwood and in the left-wing political parties between the cosmopolitan world of Jewish radicalism and the more solidly "American" proletarianism of the Protestant working class. Although Reuther was hardly a parochial youth in 1936, he certainly found May's fluency with the cultural avant-garde most refreshing. Likewise, May was herself a Socialist and union organizer, but Walter must have seemed like the real thing to her: a man with years of experience at Ford and in the Soviet Union, and a forceful orator ready to make his mark as a leader of the American working class.[16]

With May, Walter plunged into organizational work for the fledgling UAW, still little more than a tenuous group of organizing committees scattered about the city. At first this work took place almost entirely through Socialist Party contacts and connections. Backed by the wave of students and intellectuals who joined the party in the early Depression years, the Militant faction had won control of the party machinery in 1934, thereby precipitating the withdrawal of the pro–New Deal trade unionists who had long provided the financial and organizational backbone for the party.[17] "The legitimate autoworkers in the Socialist Party you could count on one hand," remembered Alan Strachan, an English immigrant active in the Detroit party. There were more than five hundred Socialists on the Michigan roll, but many were barely dues payers—doctors, social workers, older working-class veterans of the Debsian era—whose allegiance to the party of Norman Thomas was ethical and pacifist, often at odds with the new generation.[18] Thus in Flint the SP local refused to sponsor Walter Reuther for a talk on his experience in the Soviet Union because they thought him too much of a red. Instead, Roy

Reuther's friends in the Young People's Socialist League (YPSL) rented the hall, where Walter defended the Soviets to a packed house.[19]

In Detroit the really active SP element were the schoolteachers and young intellectuals. Indeed, when Walter rejoined the Detroit SP in 1936, the hardest workers in the branch Labor Committee—aside from Strachan—were Jewish schoolteachers: May Wolf, Walter Bergman, Robert Kanter (a Works Progress Administration instructor and future UAW organizer who had taken a job at Cadillac), and two Detroit Federation of Teachers activists, Jean Seidel and Celia Stern.[20] "It is not enough that workers are organizing. We socialists ask 'Organizing for What?'" proclaimed an SP Labor Committee leaflet drafted by May and Walter. "As Socialists we must be in the front ranks . . . helping to direct them along lines that will make the trade union movement a vital factor in the building of a new society."[21] Here was the Brookwood spirit, and these were the kind of young people with whom May and Walter felt most comfortable, but if Reuther were to actually stand in the front ranks of the new organizing drive, he would need help and comradeship of a far more substantial sort.

During the next two years the Communists proved indispensable to Reuther's rise. Although the SP had not been inactive, the Communist Party (CP) played a more central, more organic role in virtually every effort to organize a union of autoworkers. The CP was far more deeply rooted within the community of skilled craftsmen and second-generation immigrants who would be the shock troops for the nascent UAW. At the Rouge, for example, the Communists had maintained a virtual underground organization since the early 1920s, with important groups of activists in the toolroom and the motor building, where radicals of German, Polish, and Italian extraction found themselves once again organizing an antifascist underground.[22]

Victor and Walter therefore paid a visit to Maurice Sugar, the most prominent figure on the Detroit left, whose legal work and frequent intervention in municipal politics kept him in touch with almost every element in the progressive community. From the Soviet Union the Reuther brothers had written Sugar that they wished to reenter the labor movement, "to take up the work once more—this time with a more definite understanding of our goal and methods of attaining it." At the very least, this intention required a close working relationship with the Communists; at their first meeting with Sugar in the fall of 1935 he suggested that they see William Weinstone, the Communist Party district organizer, who had a thorough knowledge of the political terrain in the city's auto shops.[23]

It was in these months that Walter Reuther worked most closely with the Communists in Detroit; according to several well-placed observers, he may have actually paid the party monthly dues. William Weinstone claims that Sugar brought Reuther to a weekly district meeting and that shortly thereafter Weinstone asked him to join the party, which he did. Nat Ganley, later the Communist Party whip in the UAW, asserted that it was he who then accepted Reuther's dues. Indeed, Reuther did attend a twelfth anniversary commemoration of Lenin's death in January, at which the Communist leader Robert Minor spoke, and Reuther made a special note to listen to an Earl Browder radio broadcast in early February 1936. It was at this time that he started speaking on behalf of the Friends of the Soviet Union, and he made a point of seeing Anna Louise Strong when she appeared on the Detroit lecture circuit.[24]

The best evidence that Walter became very close to the Communist Party was that he obtained a union membership in Ternstedt Local 86, thanks to the good offices of the party unit chief in that GM plant. In the winter of 1936 Local 86 represented but a dozen or so activists who were struggling to spark the union idea among the twelve thousand largely Polish and Hungarian women who worked at the giant GM parts factory on Detroit's West Side. Of course, Reuther never actually worked at Ternstedt. As he remembered thirty years later, "Because we felt we ought to distribute our active young fellows where they would do the most good, we just made a tactical decision that I would be associated with Ternstedt. . . . I didn't care where I worked. It was really an unimportant detail where you were because all the locals put together weren't very much."[25] His affiliation was designed not so much to begin organizational work at the multiunit plant—Ternstedt would be the last big West Side factory organized by the UAW—as it was a device whereby Reuther could take part in the work of the UAW "progressives," the alliance of disenchanted AFL unionists and politicized organizers like himself who were determined to take control of the union at the South Bend convention two months later.[26]

What are we to make of Reuther's close connection to the Communist Party during the first half of 1936? After all, this was the era of the Popular Front, when the party sought the broadest possible alliances with other groups on the left, including the Socialists, and when the Communists assiduously courted energetic young radicals like Walter Reuther. The 1936 May Day celebrations exemplified this carefully constructed mood: in Detroit speakers from the Socialist, Proletarian, and Communist parties shared the platform at a packed meeting in the Deutsche Haus, while in New York 175,000 radicals of every persuasion marched through Union Square. Socialist Party activists were less enthusiastic than the Communists in their embrace of the Popular Front, but in the great CIO organizing drives, radicals of all stripes worked in relative harmony beneath the expansive banner raised by John L. Lewis. To his brothers at Brookwood, Reuther would soon declare that progressive victories in the UAW were "possible because of a complete united front between the SP and the CP."[27]

Still, Walter Reuther's close connection to the Communists, including a possible brief membership, has a meaning and a legacy that is of more than sectarian interest. To most of his conservative opponents, Reuther's sojourn in the Soviet Union and subsequent alliance with the Communists sustained the accusation that he was simply a red. To union activists this charge was something of an accolade in the mid-1930s, but a few years later, the suspicion among Reuther's left-wing rivals that he used the CP's influence to advance his fortunes in the UAW lay behind their frequent assertions that he was a political opportunist at the very birth of his union career. Nor did the issue fade even after his death more than thirty years later—less because of what an association with Communists said about Reuther the man than because of the legitimacy it seemed to give to the presence of ideological radicals in UAW ranks, both at the union's founding and for all the years thereafter.

Reuther quickly emerged as a key figure within UAW progressive ranks. He spoke publicly for the Ternstedt local at citywide auto meetings, attended a progressive caucus meeting in March, and won election as a delegate to the UAW's South Bend convention.[28] As Reuther humorously embellished the scene later in his career: "The constitution of our union said you had to have fifteen members to have a charter. We had only thirteen. We paid for two people by taking up a collection every month for two guys who hadn't joined yet. . . . I stood before this great mass meeting of organized workers—there were five others there beside myself—and thanked them for the great honor."[29] This convention proved to be a turning point in Reuther's life. Before then he was known as a young man with a colorful and politically engaged pedigree, a Ford worker who had been around the world, an organizer to be sure, but not so much of autoworkers as of an American left he hoped to rebuild. He was becoming well known in Detroit's progressive circles, but he was without a job, almost without a regular residence. The South Bend convention, which made him a Michigan executive board member, gave Reuther a definite project, a vocation upon which to lavish his considerable talents and within which to mobilize his growing network of friends and comrades.

The 1936 convention forged an alliance between the UAW and the new Committee for Industrial Organization (which would become the Congress of Industrial Organizations in 1938). Arriving in South Bend a few days before the convention opened, Reuther and other auto union progressives met with CIO emissaries like Powers Hapgood, Adolph Germer, and Rose Pesotta, who had little trouble steering the fledgling UAW toward the Lewis-led group. Almost immediately Homer Martin, a fiery speaker and Protestant minister who had spent a few years working in a Kansas City auto plant, replaced the AFL's Francis Dillon as union president. Martin was joined in the top leadership by the sage and well-respected Communist Wyndham Mortimer, out of the White truck plant in Cleveland, and George Addes, one of the leaders of the Toledo Chevrolet strike. From Detroit came Ed Hall and Walter Wells, who were elected top union officers not as a tribute to their organizational ability (they would soon disappear from the leadership) but because they were representatives of the still phantom army of Detroit autoworkers among whom the UAW had such a tiny foothold. As Murray Kempton put it, with only a little exaggeration, "In those days any Detroit delegate to an auto workers' convention was a candle in the night."[30]

Indeed, the South Bend convention hardly represented the vast body of unorganized autoworkers. Only about thirty thousand of the industry's half-million workers were then members of the UAW, and 70 percent of the new union's membership lived outside Michigan. The local unions with large delegations were not those of the Detroit area or Flint but hailed from Wisconsin, Indiana, and Ohio. For example, the Bendix and Studebaker locals in South Bend probably supplied more than half of all those who attended the convention, while Toledo, with some ten thousand organized workers, certainly had a membership greater than all the locals in Michigan combined.[31]

Some unionists more solidly grounded in their home communities greeted Reuther and other Michigan radicals with hostility because Detroit represented, in a sense, a vast rotten borough. The conflict was one of both politics and culture, a conflict that would resurface over and over again in the history of UAW factionalism during the next decade. UAW locals in cities like South Bend, Atlanta, and Kansas City were the pioneer organizations. They could be exceptionally militant, but their leadership was often parochial and insular. These shops were characterized by a homogeneous, largely Protestant workforce capable of reaching an accommodation with plant managers, who shared with them a similar set of social values. They were suspicious of the cosmopolitan radicals, Socialist or Communist, who seemed to be winning control of the union. In contrast, the cultures of Detroit, Cleveland, and Toledo were ones of ethnic heterogeneity, political radicalism, and industrywide consciousness. Flint, where GM clustered more than fifty thousand autoworkers, always represented something of a special case. The workforce was heavily Protestant, with many recent migrants from the middle South, but the massive corporate presence and the brutal working conditions forced the thin stratum of active cadre there to think of the union-building project in the broadest terms.[32]

This division in the union ranks explains the vituperative debate that erupted over a resolution that UAW locals "immediately expel from membership all known Communists." The progressive majority succeeded in shelving this divisive issue, but UAW radicals recognized the explosive character of these sentiments; thus, they backed the Missouri-born preacher Homer Martin over the Cleveland-based Communist Wyndham Mortimer as the new UAW president.[33] Unable to win on the convention floor, the conservatives aimed much of their fire at Reuther's accreditation, pointing out that he had never worked at Ternstedt. "Dewey Smith, chairman of the credentials committee and reactionary studge [sic] of Dillon put me on the spot as a red—direct from a 2 year stay in Moscow," Reuther wrote to May just after he arrived in South Bend. But Walter had the backing of friends on the credentials committee, including Robert Travis, a progressive stalwart from Toledo, and he was vouched for by both Wyndham Mortimer and Leo Krzycki, the Socialist Party national chairman and Amalgamated Clothing Workers of America vice president.[34]

Reuther was duly seated, but his troubles were hardly over: skeptical conservatives pounded away at his credentials almost every day; after he returned to Detroit, they again questioned his work record at Ternstedt. In combat Reuther felt almost elated. As he triumphantly described the scene in a letter to his brothers Victor and Roy, "Thanks to the reactionaries my name was before the convention every day, time after time they tried to have me kicked out of the convention and each time they were beaten and each time they made me more popular . . . until the unknown Reuther became a convention figure and altimately [*sic*] a member of the General Executive Board." Reuther showed a "surprising grasp of things for a novice," recalled Henry Kraus, the left-wing UAW publicist who worked closely with Mortimer in Cleveland. When a sensational and misleading headline in Hearst's *Chicago Herald-Examiner* asserted that the UAW had "quit" the AFL, Reuther picked a routine moment in the proceedings to rush the podium and denounce the publisher. Soon, he told his brothers, "I had the entire convention on its feet fighting mad." Still later, as part of the progressive strategy to get more radicals on the executive board, Reuther made an effective pitch for electing three vice presidents instead of one.[35]

The recognition and credibility Reuther had won made him the floor leader of the Michigan delegates and probably ensured his election as one of the four members Michigan had been assigned on the new UAW executive board. The UAW progressives had a tricky situation here, for they mistrusted the politics of several of the delegates from outside Detroit. Indeed, they were fairly certain that spies for GM were among the Flint group, and in one preconvention meeting a fight broke out in Reuther's hotel room.

The pace of the convention was devastating: Reuther subsisted on the occasional Hershey bar and hardly slept during one three-day stretch. "I am developing an acute case of caucusosis," he wrote to May. "They have me going in a whirlwind." But Reuther was in high spirits: "I learned a great deal about practicle [*sic*] politics and earned the title of John L. Lewis, Jr." he told his brothers. To May he reported, "Our machine worked to mechanical perfection."[36]

Though he was now a UAW executive board member representing Michigan autoworkers, Reuther made a fitful transition from political activist to full-time unionist. The union president Homer Martin did make Reuther chairman of the executive board's education committee, a post urged on the UAW by Tucker Smith, who promised several thousand dollars in Brookwood scholarships for the autoworkers. But Martin thought Reuther both a political liability and an unproven organizer, so Reuther won no salary or authority from the UAW.[37] He therefore had plenty of time for politics. He was a strong supporter of the Farmer Labor parties that had sprung up in several midwestern cities and states, a commitment that again put him in close collaboration with the Communists, who backed these reform parties as part of their general Popular Front program. However, Reuther's work for a Farmer Labor Party (FLP) immediately put him at serious odds with the bulk of his Socialist comrades. Old Guard SPers attacked the FLP idea because they considered it a Communist front; the younger group of left-wing Socialists, especially those influenced by the several hundred Trotskyists who had just entered party ranks, considered the Farmer Labor Party sheer reformism. So bitter was their opposition to Reuther's FLP collaboration with the

Communists that the Detroit Socialists made an effort (which was eventually dropped) to expel Reuther and Walter Bergman, another FLP supporter, from party ranks.[38]

His brothers Victor and Roy were also critical of this turn in Walter's politics. Both were more loyal to the SP; Roy had been a member of its Revolutionary Policy Committee, whose politics reflected the bitter anti-Stalinism of Jay Lovestone and his Communist Party opposition. In a long and passionate letter to his brothers, Walter defended his participation in Popular Front politics but still asserted his Socialist—nay, even his revolutionary—credentials. "To dismiss the many attempts to set up local Farm Labor Parties that are being made through the country as premature, as CP opportunism, or to take the sectarian Trotskyite view is not this dangerously stupid. By holding our nose, pointing our finger at these attemps [sic], and shouting it aint kosher we have not solved the problem, we have only tried to side step it." The Socialists had failed to build their own party even as labor awakened in the last few years, wrote Reuther, so "to build a Socialist Party we must first build the FLP, they are as much a part of one another as sowing and reaping." But from this point on, Reuther asserted a party-building strategy of classic Leninism. "By working within such a party, as a disciplined unit, with courage and clarity we can use the mass party as a resovour [sic] from which we can draw the most advanced workers into our revolutionary party. This revolutionary party within the mass party must carry on a relentless struggle against the reformist policy . . . constantly pointing out the impossibility of acchieving [sic] freedom, peace, and security without a complete change in our social system."[39]

All this seems a bit of a posture, perhaps designed to reassure his skeptical brothers. Whatever its meaning, Reuther still thought of himself as a Socialist in good standing. In late May he spent four days at the party convention in Cleveland that nominated Norman Thomas for another presidential campaign. Here he successfully defended himself against criticism from the Michigan Socialists, and he undoubtedly supported the majority of the party when it cut its ties with the New York Old Guard. Despite his views on the need for a farmer-labor third party, Reuther was caught up in the spirit of the convention. "When Thomas was nominated we sang and yelled, paraded and waved the red flag until I thought the house would come down," Walter wrote May. "The whole afternoon session bubbled with enthusiasm, determination and solidarity—a most fitting send off for an effective socialist campaign."[40]

Meanwhile, Reuther took the last industrial job of his lifetime in June, when he briefly worked for Coleman Tool, a small tool and die firm on the West Side. He needed the money, and he probably hoped to recruit into the UAW some of the skilled men there who belonged to the Mechanics Educational Association of America, with whom the UAW sought a merger. Reuther was fired when the boss found out he was a union officer; his account of this incident perfectly captures the transformation of craft pride into union consciousness. As Reuther remembered it:

At the end of 30 days I completed a perforating die. It had 200 perforated punches which had to pierce 12- or 15-thousandths thick brass. I put this die in the press for the tryouts and the chief inspector put a sheet of the *Free Press* under the die and brought the die down. It pierced all the punches clean without a burr. He said to me, "Man, that is one of the best jobs we have put out in this shop in some time."

I said, "Don't waste your praise on me. Tell it to the boss, because I'm going to demand a wage increase."

And the boss came over. He was called "Highball John" . . . because he rode the guys hard. I said to Highball John, "If that job is as good as the chief inspector says it is, I ought to get a ten-cents-an-hour raise." He said, "I will talk to the old man." He meant Frederick Coleman, who owned the shop.

The next morning at seven o'clock, Highball John came over and said, "We are giving you a ten-cents-an-hour increase." I said, "Thank you." At nine o'clock, I was discharged for being incompetent. [Reuther exaggerates here: it was at least a few days later] . . . I said to Highball John, "I'm going to finish the job of organizing this shop before you physically throw me out of the plant." And I did.[41]

Reuther spent the last part of August at the UAW summer school he had set up with Merlin Bishop, so it was early September before he really got down to the hard work of daily organizing on the West Side of Detroit. This area was a sprawling field of parts and assembly plants that flowed westward from Woodward Avenue toward Dearborn and the great River Rouge works. Here were big plants like Cadillac, Fleetwood, Ternstedt, and a collection of smaller independent parts plants like Coleman Tool, Timkin Axle, and Kelsey-Hayes. Altogether, the West Side, including the Rouge, employed more than one hundred thousand autoworkers in 1936.[42] To organize this immense region, the UAW chartered Local 174. Reuther borrowed $350 from Dave Miller, a Communist then working at Cadillac, and opened an office in a former bank building at Thirty-fifth Street and Michigan Avenue, a streetcar transfer point for many Ford workers. His new local had seventy-eight members on its books.[43]

Local 174 was an "amalgamated" local; amalgamation enabled the scattered activists on Detroit's West Side to pool their resources to take on one or two key shops. But organizational efficiency was not the only advantage. By taking leadership away from the weak organizing committees, amalgamation offered many union-minded workers their first "legitimate" opportunity to affiliate with the UAW and thus "frustrate the activities of stool-pigeons who have been instrumental in getting the pioneers of many of the locals fired." Once the UAW became established, most unionists thought the amalgamated locals would naturally fragment as each shop became strong enough to stand on its own.[44]

Reuther found the Communists to be essential to this organizing work. In particular he relied on the guidance of Bill McKie, a soft-spoken tinsmith from Scotland and Rouge Communist already legendary for his knowledge of the Ford works and for his stamina as an organizer. McKie guided Reuther to the plant gates, ethnic halls, and modest kitchens where Reuther's new West Side local made its first recruits. He was a methodical, hardworking organizer, a publicly acknowledged Communist who had visited thousands of workers in Dearborn and the West Side of Detroit in their homes and meeting halls. Between 1935 and 1941 he single-handedly signed into the UAW nearly two thousand workers. McKie was the first of a series of mentor figures who would provide Reuther with political and practical guidance during the early years of the UAW.

McKie and Reuther formed an effective team. From September through December Reuther met the Scotsman over coffee at dawn. Reuther would ask, "What meetings have we got lined up for us today, Bill?" and McKie would pull out his bulging notebook and leaf through the pages. Their final objective lay in Dearborn, but the path to Ford lay through organization of the lesser plants on the nearby West Side. McKie soon introduced Reuther to most of the shop activists who would later spark the sit-down strikes at Kelsey-Hayes, Cadillac, Fleetwood, and several of the smaller shops in the West Side's jurisdiction. Progress proved painfully slow; there was a "complete lack of co-operation with the workers inside the shop," reported one West Side organizer in October 1936.[45]

But the presidential elections transformed the social landscape of industrial America. Under pressure from the CIO's John L. Lewis, the UAW's South Bend convention had reluctantly voted down a labor party resolution, so in August the UAW formally endorsed Franklin Roosevelt. Reuther did not publicly dissent from the official UAW line, but he offered no support of the Democrats either. He and May and other SP comrades did their small part in boosting Norman Thomas in what turned out to be his most disappointing campaign since the late 1920s.[46] But as the days grew shorter that fall, it slowly dawned on activists like Reuther that the pro-Roosevelt excitement sweeping the working-class wards of the city might provide the key to the organizational breakthrough that had so long eluded them. This was an election in which Roosevelt seemed to draw a class line across American politics, a contest in which he denounced the "economic royalists" and "business and financial monopoly, speculation, reckless banking, class antagonism." "Never before in all our history have these forces been so united against one candidate as they stand today. They are unanimous in their hate for me—and I welcome their hatred."[47] The 1936 election mobilized the ethnic working class as no other, decisively confirming the power of the emergent Roosevelt coalition. Before the election, Adolph Germer had observed that the autoworkers were "still gripped with a feeling of fear," but he soon realized that "the election of Roosevelt will inject some stiffening in their backbone." The contest, Homer Martin told union loyalists, is a "mandate to organize," so the UAW displayed a Roosevelt remark, "If I were a factory worker, I would join a union," on every factory-gate leaflet distributed in the fall of 1936.[48]

Roosevelt's campaign tour of the Midwest was one continuous triumph. In the auto centers, workers often shut down their lines and crowded the windows to cheer him. In Flint, with a dues-paying UAW membership of but 136, over 100,000 people lined the streets. In Pontiac, where the UAW had no members at all, the *Detroit News* reported a "tremendous gathering." Half a million lined the streets from Hamtramck to Detroit, and more than 250,000 gathered at City Hall Square to hear Roosevelt lash the auto magnates.[49] The rush to the polls was of flood proportions in November, and FDR took every industrial city in Michigan. Wayne County's vote swelled by almost one-third over that of 1932, and the county gave the president an unprecedented 65 percent of its votes.[50] Roosevelt's victory depended heavily upon the mobilization of a new generation of working-class ethnics, who were seeking a sense of participation in the political, cosmopolitan world that stood outside—and in a certain sense was counterpoised to—the insular realm of the extended family and neighborhood parish. The election landslide was a result of the remarkable political awakening of the mass of new immigrants—the Poles, Slovaks, Croatians, Lithuanians, Ukrainians, and Italians—whose sense of citizenship, of participation and rights consciousness within the larger American polity, had been marginal so long as they remained trapped within the deferential world where workplace hierarchies mirrored the ethnic and social discrimination they faced in the general society. But the shock of the Depression and the rise of a sense of pluralist Americanism engendered by Roosevelt and the New Deal helped transform immigrant consciousness. The reelection of Franklin Roosevelt may not have been the cause of this immigrant upheaval, but it certainly helped to focus and express it in something very close to class terms.

Polish Detroiters had become the single most important bloc of voters in the Democratic Party: in some precincts FDR took more than 90 percent of their ballots. Naturally the UAW made a strong effort to tap this greater sense of political involvement and prounion activism among the forty thousand Detroit autoworkers of Polish extraction. In the summer of 1936 the union put Stanley Nowak, a second-generation Communist, on the UAW payroll. He organized an all-Polish autoworkers' local, began a series of Polish-language radio talks, and wrote a column in the left-wing Polish weekly *Glos Ludony*. In tune with the new mood, the Polish paper put a picture of Abraham Lincoln on its masthead and changed its self-description from "Only Polish Worker's Periodical in the U.S." to "Join the Struggle for a Just America" (in Polish, of course). Polish autoworkers themselves played a relatively muted role throughout the organizing era, but their hesitancy merely spurred the UAW's accommodation of this decisive constituency. The UAW's West Side meetings were usually held in one of the two Polish fraternal halls in that section of the city, and Nowak soon became a pivotal figure in the life of the Polish community, first as a strategist for thousands of Polish cigar workers, who organized their own union during the spring of 1937, and then as chief negotiator for the heavily Polish, twelve-thousand-worker Ternstedt trim and parts complex organized by Local 174 during that same dramatic season.[51]

Roosevelt's victory in November 1936 gave auto industry organizers the confidence that the time had come to crystallize the new mood in a bold and aggressive union-organizing effort. All across industrial America the election had seemed a referendum on the old order. In Pennsylvania, Michigan, and Ohio, pro–New Deal governors were elected or reelected. The elevation of Frank Murphy, Detroit's liberal, prolabor mayor in the early Depression years, to the Michigan governor's mansion seemed particularly propitious, for he could be relied upon to act with restraint, if not outright sympathy, when the autoworkers disrupted production in Flint, Detroit, or Pontiac. For a brief historical instant, businessmen seemed stunned, the police hesitant, the usual structures of deference and authority unsteady. A sea change in the social climate gave to a corps of dedicated activists the opportunity to build a new set of institutions that could capture the unfettered energies so briefly liberated during a plastic moment in history. The new mood was instantly apparent in the auto industry. In South Bend, one thousand Bendix workers began the industry's first recorded sit-down strike in mid-November. After an eight-day occupation, the UAW eliminated the company union and won exclusive bargaining rights. Two days after this settlement, skilled tradesmen led by the Scottish-born Communist John Anderson precipitated the first Detroit sit-down when nineteen hundred day-shift workers occupied Midland Steel, which supplied body frames to Ford and Chrysler. Although Midland was but a supplier plant, the strike there proved to be a turning point: it was spirited, solid, and a real victory. Thousands of autoworkers from throughout the city visited the Midland strike headquarters at Slovak Hall on the East Side. "The solidarity among the workers in favor of the union is definitely surprising," confessed *Ward's Reports*, an auto industry publication.[52]

Reuther knew that the time for a bold gambit was at hand, and it was toward Kelsey-Hayes Wheel Company that his West Side group turned most of its energies. The company was a good first target because the four thousand workers employed there already included a number of shop radicals, and unlike the River Rouge plant and the two West Side GM plants, Fleetwood and Ternstedt, it was neither too big to handle nor too dependent on management decisions made elsewhere. But Kelsey-Hayes was big enough, with two separate plants and six big departments, including a foundry, stamping unit, tool and die department, and assembly line. About 80 percent of its production went to Ford, which was dependent on it for about half of its wheels and brake drums. Thus a victory at Kelsey-Hayes would give the organizing drive a real push forward, perhaps a big step toward the conquest of the River Rouge complex itself.

Most important, Kelsey-Hayes workers had already had a good deal of experience with trade unionism. They had been among the first in Detroit to organize a federal labor union, which had maintained an episodic presence within the plant for almost three years. At its height, AFL Local 18677 represented more than 95 percent of the company's employees. Polish workers comprised probably 40 percent of the workforce; "hillbillies," Hungarians, and a sizable group of northern

European males in skilled jobs made up the rest. Mass meetings were held periodically at nearby Falcon Hall, home of a Polish fraternal order.[53]

Leadership at Kelsey-Hayes typified the shop-floor cadre who built the CIO. They were all inspectors or skilled men whose career progression into factory supervision or white-collar work had been frustrated during the Depression. They numbered just a dozen or so: no Poles or Hungarians, but at least one Jew, three or four Irish Catholics, and a couple of English immigrants. This male leadership cadre included a couple of Socialists (at least one of whom had migrated from England in the 1920s), a group of union partisans from the toolroom, and several foremen, of whom a good majority would become staunch unionists.[54]

Michael Manning and Frank Manfried were emblematic leaders of this early brand of Kelsey-Hayes unionism. Manning, an Irish Catholic in his forties, had worked in Detroit factories since 1920 but never abandoned his aspirations to join the lower ranks of management. He hired on at Kelsey in 1930 as an inspector and in 1935 was promoted to foreman. He was a generation older than the young Socialists in the Reuther group and remained untouched by the radical currents of the day. His experience, maturity, and negotiating skills made him president or chief bargaining representative of the Kelsey-Hayes AFL union, but unlike so many other UAW pioneers, he had worked well with Francis Dillon, with whom he shared ethnic and generational bonds. Manning served as chairman of the AFL's Detroit autoworkers' council, but he doubted the ability of autoworkers themselves to build an international union. "They are not experienced enough to conduct it and they have no money to run it," he told top AFL officials toward the end of 1935.[55] Manning therefore opposed the UAW revolt against Dillon, and as a consequence he was largely unaware of the Kelsey-Hayes strike preparations hatched by Reuther's younger group of CIO organizers in the fall.[56]

Frank Manfried, on the other hand, proved more adept at bridging the gap between the old union at Kelsey-Hayes and Reuther's organizing effort. He was a much younger, German-Jewish electrician from New York who had found work at Kelsey after Ford's notorious anti-Semitism excluded him from the Rouge. His skills had kept him employed in the early Depression years, but his wages had fallen more than 30 percent when he was demoted to production work at Kelsey-Hayes. Manfried was secretary-treasurer of Local 18677 and was either a Communist or fairly close to the party. Unlike Manning, Manfried did not inspire a natural confidence or respect, but he was willing to stick his neck out. He represented what was left of the Kelsey local at the South Bend convention and enthusiastically backed the CIO affiliation of the auto union. Manfried organized several meetings between Reuther and small groups of Kelsey workers, and he kept Reuther informed when job openings appeared at the plant.[57]

Kelsey-Hayes had long accommodated a form of trade unionism, and in the years after 1933 the company was quite willing to negotiate with Manning and Manfried, who spoke for AFL Local 18677. Like many other plant managers in the auto parts field, Kelsey-Hayes President George Kennedy wanted to accommodate the pressure emanating from Washington, from his workforce, and from the AFL, so he kept wages 10 percent above those in other auto parts firms, set up a seniority list, and settled minor grievances with the twenty-five-odd shop stewards—"the watchmen"—elected by Kelsey unionists. The company's policy was one of calculated paternalism. "I do not think there is a fairer man in the city to work for than George Kennedy," Michael Manning told federal investigators in 1935. Even Manfried thought Kennedy a "fair guy."[58]

But Kelsey management made sure that unionism remained a tentative institution. Because of its dependence on Ford for the overwhelming bulk of its sales, the company, like so many other auto parts plants, followed Henry Ford's lead on all industrial relations questions. As Kennedy told Manning on more than one occasion, Kelsey-Hayes would not be a "guinea pig" for automobile unionism. "Why don't you get some of the big fellows that we do business with to get some of these things and then we'll go along." And despite their good record on shop grievances, Kelsey managers repeatedly undermined the legitimacy of the AFL federal local by unilaterally announcing the work rule changes or wage adjustments they put into place. With other auto companies, Kelsey-Hayes defended the NRA-era "proportional representation" scheme that deprived its early unionists of exclusive jurisdiction. Kennedy therefore refused to hold an NRA labor board election in April 1935, claiming that it was the steadfast policy of the company "to deal with any individual employee or with any group of our employees . . . in relation to hours, wages, or other working conditions."[59] This combination of benevolent paternalism and steadfast antiunionism kept the local off balance. When the company blocked the 1935 certification vote, union membership, which had reached twenty-seven hundred that winter, collapsed for the final time. As Frank Manfried recalled several years later, "We did not have anybody that actually knew [what to do] and we . . . were just beginning, with the result that we were maneuvered."[60]

Reuther and the young band of activists he recruited for organizing work at Kelsey-Hayes provided the leadership and self-confidence the company's shop-floor unionists lacked. They would fill the gap that yawned at Kelsey-Hayes, as in so many other workplaces, between the tenuous shop organizations that had emerged in the early Roosevelt years and the national structures of power and purpose embodied in the new CIO and the far-flung network of political and legal allies with which the new union federation defended working-class interests. The industrial unions of the late Depression years were built from the ground up in a massive surge of rank-and-file participation, but the CIO unions were also built from the outside in, by well-connected and ideologically motivated organizers who saw their trade union work as part of a larger project of social reconstruction.

The group of young Socialists who gathered around Reuther on the West Side typified these semiprofessional agitators. A few were Jewish, and still more married Jewish women, but unlike so many Communist militants of this era, most of these young Socialists were native-born Protestants. Their participation in the early UAW was a compound of political adventure, personal ambition, and family-bred social commitment. Several, including the Reuther brothers, May Wolf, Merlin Bishop, George Edwards, and Robert Kanter, were the offspring of families whose Socialist roots went back to before World War I. None except Reuther and Bishop were really indigenous autoworkers, and these two had left the Detroit auto shops more than four years before. By any objective standard, they knew little of the West Side working class or of the particular factory culture at Kelsey-Hayes or the other plants they so rapidly organized in the months after December 1936. Their season of shop activism came and went quickly, and most ended up with union staff jobs of one sort or another. But these young radicals were nevertheless key leaders during that brief moment when managerial authority faltered and the social mold of the well-insulated factory regime broke open. They were able to emerge as genuinely popular tribunes whose practical political skills and rhetorical talents made powerful and coherent the aspirations and hopes of the many thousands for whom they spoke.

Because of the mid-decade auto boomlet, many West Side shops were hiring that fall; Kelsey-Hayes was building up its workforce by more than one thousand unskilled workers. Among the first to "industrialize" were Merlin Bishop and Robert Kanter, both of whom had worked closely with Roy Reuther in the FERA workers' education division. Kanter, a draftsman and pacifist whose entire family had spent World War I in a prison compound, got an industrial job at Cadillac in October 1936; two months later Bishop hired on at Kelsey-Hayes, just two days before the strike.[61] From Dallas came two additional recruits, Frank Winn, whom the Reuther brothers had gotten to know at Brookwood, and his good friend George Edwards, Jr., who landed a job on the enamel line in Department 49, the key unit at Kelsey-Hayes, where an unskilled workforce of 350 assembled Ford brake shoes.[62]

Aside from Walter Reuther himself, Edwards was by far the most remarkable of the young radicals who helped build the West Side local. Like the Reuther brothers, he was the offspring of a father well known in his community as a radical and iconoclast, an SP stalwart who waged a lonely battle on behalf of civil liberties and labor rights in the old Southwest. But the Edwards family was otherwise solidly bourgeois. Although the Depression prevented the younger Edwards from enrolling at Harvard, it did not keep him out of Southern Methodist University, to which all respectable members of the Dallas upper class sent their children. There Edwards had a grand time, even circulating the Oxford pledge to his fraternity brothers, most of whom signed the Socialist-sponsored manifesto.

After graduating in 1934, Edwards spent a year at Harvard, where he studied under radicals like F. O. Matthiessen, headed up the LID-dominated Liberal Club, and organized Harvard's high-profile antiwar strike. He soon shot to the leadership of the YPSL. He met the Reuther brothers in 1935 when he was working as college secretary for Norman Thomas, in whose service he had just been arrested when he spoke for the Southern Tenants Farmers Union in Fort Smith, Arkansas.[63] Edwards was boyish and handsome, but also a terrific speaker who exuded sincerity and intelligence. "He had a wonderful voice that traveled," remembered Alan Strachan, who called him "able, smart, attractive."[64] A gentile from the American heartland, Edwards was a natural choice for the presidency of the American Student Union when that organization was formed in 1935 out of the merger of the Student League for Industrial Democracy and the Communist-dominated National Student Union. But unlike such well-known ASU leaders as Joseph Lash and Molly Yard, Edwards resisted Communist efforts to move the student organization toward a collective security formula that would put it in support of Roosevelt's foreign policy.[65] Edwards therefore loosened his ties with the student organization in the summer of 1936, and that fall he headed for Detroit, perhaps with dreams of writing the great American novel he had planned since his Harvard days. Winn soon told him of Reuther's effort to take on Kelsey-Hayes and of that company's wide-open hiring.[66]

Victor Reuther was one of the last of these young Socialists to begin work at Kelsey. Once the Midland Steel strike made it clear that bold strike tactics paid off, Roy and Walter cabled Victor in Philadelphia, where he was still lecturing for the Emergency Peace Campaign: "Recent developments in auto make it necessary that you come at once to decide several very important issues that will effect [sic] our future work. Get in touch with us immediately and let us know when you can be here. Time is very important." Victor rushed back to Detroit and literally within hours of his arrival landed a job with Edwards in Department 49. There were now eleven unionists at work there, at least four of whom were Socialists: Bishop, Edwards, and Victor Reuther, plus George Young, a Detroit SP member who had worked at Kelsey for several years. With the union stalwarts from the old AFL local, Walter Reuther could probably count on about a dozen militants inside the plant, perhaps thirty-five unionists in all, out of a workforce that now approached five thousand.[67]

Although the Kelsey-Hayes strike would soon become one of the UAW's most famous early sit-down strikes, Reuther and his comrades were unprepared for a plant occupation. Instead, they hoped to precipitate a series of stoppages and disruptions that would prod the company into increasing pay, slowing down the production pace, and recognizing the renewed existence of a union in the plant. Reuther knew that there were enough activists inside the factory to disrupt operations, at least in Department 49. But the tenor of the rest of the workforce was suspect: the old local there had been moribund for more than a year, and since Reuther's closest associates were virtually unknown to the other Kelsey workers, they hardly expected to have the strength to pull off either a mass walkout or a lengthy sit-down.

Still, Reuther, Edwards, Bishop, and the others prepared carefully. Early in the week Reuther scheduled an appointment with Kelsey President George Kennedy for Friday, December 11. The conference set, Reuther and Manfried arranged for a woman in Department 49 to "faint," which would signal a coordinated shutdown of the line. Catching the company by surprise, the Brake Assembly Department went down just before the afternoon shift change on December 10. Immediately Merlin Bishop and George Edwards led a handful of Kelsey militants through the plant, pulling the switches that stopped the line and shouting that they were on strike. As a crowd gathered to see what was happening, Victor Reuther jumped on a crate to rally his hesitant, bewildered audience. When the personnel manager, Charles DeMong, demanded that everyone get back to work, Victor informed him that he had to speak with the union president, Walter Reuther, before he could get the strikers back on the job. DeMong immediately put in a phone call to Walter at the Local 174 office. Their conversation went something like this:

> "Is your name Reuther?"
> "Yes."
> "I want you to tell these men to get back to work."
> "Where are you?"
> "I'm inside the plant."
> "But I'm outside the plant and can't tell anybody to get back to work as long as I'm out here. Send a car over to pick me up and take me into the plant and I'll talk to the guys."

DeMong agreed. Victor was still holding forth on the crate when Walter arrived and smoothly picked up where his brother had left off. "What the hell is this? You're supposed to tell them to go back to work," protested the exasperated personnel man. "I can't tell them to do anything," replied Walter, "until I first get them organized."[68] Such would be the dilemma, and the fate, of industrial unionism at its moment of birth.

During the next two weeks Reuther and other unionists held talks, off and on, with DeMong and Kennedy. The company's negotiating posture was in part dictated by outside pressure. The Employers Association of Detroit (EAD), whose greatest strength was in midsized supplier firms like Kelsey, took a hard line against the union. EAD President Chester Culver, who sat in on all Kelsey negotiations, hoped to forestall a wave of sit-downs by denying the UAW even the appearance of a victory in the Kelsey strike. But counterpressure would soon come from the Ford organization, which wanted supplier plants like Kelsey to stay open even if doing so required making some concessions to the union. Ford thought itself entirely capable of taking care of its own labor problems; indeed, Henry Ford had long held the EAD in contempt and thought of his supplier firms as little more than dependent vassals.

Kelsey's George Kennedy wanted to avoid an intermittent series of slowdowns and stoppages, and to this end he was prepared to work with Local 174 in much the same fashion as he had with Manning's AFL group two years earlier. He would talk, offer another wage increase, but avoid any concessions that might amount to a de facto recognition of the union. Above all, Kelsey officials thought time was on their side. With the Christmas holidays fast approaching, they expected the Reuther group's agitation to grow tiresome to the large mass of workers who had time and again demonstrated such a tepid and transitory allegiance to the union.

In truth, Reuther's small band of militants had stuck their necks out. While Reuther and a newly elected strike committee met with Kennedy on the morning after the stoppage, production continued as usual in all the Kelsey shops. Reuther told Kennedy that the UAW wanted union recognition, a general wage increase, and overtime pay. The company quickly agreed to raise the minimum wage to seventy-five cents an hour, regardless of sex, but Kennedy reiterated his commitment to an open shop, rejected overtime pay, and announced that wage increases for the more skilled and longer-term employees would be made on the usual individual merit basis. Reuther's committee returned to Department 49 and called for a resumption of the strike, but the response was decidedly mixed. Bishop, Edwards, and other activists urged workers to stop work, but Kelsey management, fearful of a sit-in, ordered the plant shut and everyone out. At quitting time, about four hundred remained in the plant, but they voted to leave a few hours later after Walter Reuther and Richard Frankensteen, the citywide director of organization for the UAW, announced that Kennedy had again agreed to meet with a union committee at the start of the new week.[69]

Luckily for Reuther, the company blundered over the weekend. In an effort to revive Kelsey's employee association, management sent out thousands of telegrams announcing a mass meeting Sunday afternoon. Of course, Local 174 held its own meeting that morning, after which Reuther led five hundred Kelsey unionists over to the company-sponsored assembly at the nearby Dom Polski Hall. With the help of several husky men, Reuther and Frankensteen hustled the company spokesmen off the platform and took over the association's meeting. Perhaps two thousand workers were standing in and around the hall, so Reuther's forces pushed through a vote of confidence in the UAW and a resolution disbanding the company employee association. Hundreds of workers joined Local 174 that exciting afternoon.

But the union's coup merely stiffened resistance, for the EAD's Culver and Kelsey management now understood that they were dealing with a leadership considerably more resourceful than the company had ever faced before. On Monday morning Reuther's negotiating committee found Kelsey-Hayes intransigent. Kennedy announced that he would not disband the employee association and that the company would continue its open-shop policy; he therefore dismissed out of hand the union demand that UAW Local 174 be recognized as the sole employees' organization in the plant. Although few logistical preparations had been made, Reuther and his committee felt they had no choice but to call a sit-down strike. Again, Bishop, Edwards, and a few score union militants spent several difficult hours trying to convince workers in poorly organized departments to stop production. Toward Monday afternoon these experienced speakers had a virtual debate with DeMong, who told employees to vacate the plant or be fired. His threats proved effective: by quitting time only two hundred workers were still inside the factory.

Suddenly, Local 174, prepared for a series of short work stoppages, was forced to organize a prolonged sit-in. For the first two days food arrived erratically. Strikers obtained their evening meal Monday by asking workers on the afternoon shift to throw their lunches over the fence. On Tuesday, with the men getting restless, Merlin Bishop sent out a message: "Walter, *please*, send some food in for us. We had only bread and coffee today so far and it is now 2:00 P.M."[70] Reuther improvised under pressure. The union canvassed local merchants, opened a soup kitchen, and began supplying regular meals to the sit-in strikers. Local 174 published a daily strike bulletin, and Frank Winn offered reporters frequent briefings designed to counteract company propaganda. During most of the strike Victor assisted Walter outside the plant, often from the UAW's ubiquitous sound car. May spent virtually all her time at the West Side union office, as did Sophie Reuther, who translated union flyers into Polish. Constantly on the go, Walter hardly slept for the next week.[71]

Now that it had a real sit-down on its hands, Kelsey management maneuvered to wear down the strikers. The company promised individual workmen a wage increase and tried to lure others out of the plant by sending them telegrams that their wives or children were ill. Management was unable to ship finished parts out of the plant, but the company did succeed in slipping additional watchmen and foremen into the struck facilities. Led by Bishop and Edwards, an increasingly well organized group of sit-down strikers checked each company gambit. A climax of sorts came on Friday evening, December 18, when twelve strikebreakers were sent into the plant. Bishop organized a squad of strikers that trapped the intruders in the first aid station, while Walter mobilized outside help. Since several locals were just then holding their meetings, he had little trouble reinforcing Local 174's thin picket line with four thousand union sympathizers from all across town.

Bishop demanded that the "pug uglies" leave in fifteen minutes, and his ultimatum was echoed outside the plant by ominous chants of "fifteen minutes" and "throw the scabs out." Kelsey-Hayes wanted the police, who were on the scene in force, to protect its men, and Police Commissioner Heinrich Pickert, long known for his bitterly antilabor views, would certainly have ordered the police into action if he had not been restrained by Mayor Frank Couzens, who was loathe to look like a strikebreaker in the months immediately following the landslide electoral victories of Frank Murphy and Franklin Roosevelt. Still, the police might act on their own and clear the plant, in which case a riot seemed certain that frosty night. After Reuther promised the police that the crowd would let them pass through peaceably, management finally removed the strikebreakers. "Another victory had been won!" Merlin Bishop would later exult.[72]

With the strike lengthening into its second week, both sides found a settlement of increasing urgency. The sit-downers put up Christmas trees and organized songfests, but Reuther and his comrades feared morale would collapse if the strike actually continued until Christmas. Kelsey-Hayes, on the other hand, was coming under pressure from the Ford Motor Company. Harry Bennett told Kennedy that if the strike were not settled quickly, Kelsey would lose the Ford contract; other Ford officials threatened to send in a detachment of "servicemen" to seize the vital brake shoe dies and move them into the Rouge. The breakthrough came after Bennett's man John Gillespie, a tough character in charge of Ford's supply network, got in touch with Richard Frankensteen to find out what the union considered its minimum terms. The union could stick with its demand for an hourly rate of seventy-five cents for both men and women, Gillespie said, but had to drop the quest for union recognition—that was intolerable to Henry Ford. After much wrangling, Reuther, Frankensteen, Kennedy, and Culver, with Harry Bennett on the phone, worked out an agreement on December 23. It totaled seventy-one words in length. As arranged, Kennedy agreed to the minimum wage of seventy-five cents, which mainly applied to new hires, and he said that overtime pay and wage increases for all workers in higher brackets would "be adjusted." The company reiterated its "high wage" policy and asserted that there would "be no discrimination against any employee."[73]

Virtually dictated by the prince of Ford's open-shop empire, the settlement hardly represented an economic or organizational victory for the Kelsey unionists. The company had not recognized the union, and there would be no wage increase for most workers, none at all for the skilled workers who comprised the core of the union in the shop. Moreover, the company's concessions, such as they were, seemed reminiscent of the kind of dealings that had characterized its relationship with the old AFL federal local. For the large majority of those workers who had remained outside the factory, the agreement came as a relief and a victory. They would resume their jobs after Christmas, and an immediate 15 percent wage increase was promised for many women and new hires. But among the more dedicated group of sit-down strikers still holding the plant, news of the settlement came as a shock. George Edwards, who had won enormous respect from these workers, argued that the union's failure to win higher wages for the skilled men would breed resentment after they returned to work. Yes, retorted Reuther, and they will fight to raise their pay once they are back at work. He persuaded Edwards not to oppose the settlement, but Frankensteen and Reuther faced a tense and difficult group when they tried to sell the deal to the rest of the sit-downers. They angrily objected to the bargain, putting particular emphasis on the company's failure to recognize their union or even abolish the old company-dominated employee association. Chester "Moon" Mullins, whom Victor Reuther later described as a "hillbilly anarchist," led the rebellion. "We ain't gonna sign it," Mullins told Walter at the crucial meeting inside the plant. "Is there something in here you don't agree with?" asked Reuther. "I don't trust the sons of bitches," replied Mullins.[74]

Reuther faced a potential disaster if the militants still occupying the plant continued to reject the settlement. "Workers throughout Michigan were watching the strike," wrote Victor Reuther in his memoirs. "In a sense, the survival of the UAW depended on some sort of victory that December."[75] If the agreement were rejected, union ranks would be publicly split, and with the Christmas holidays imminent and a settlement already announced, there was little hope of resuming the strike. Acknowledging that management's offer was no victory, Reuther argued that a Kelsey-Hayes settlement was now essential, so that the UAW could free up all its resources for the impending battle with General Motors. That struggle won, the unsatisfactory state of affairs at Kelsey-Hayes could be rectified. If, however, the GM organizing campaign were aborted, the entire unionization effort might collapse. Not all the Kelsey militants accepted Reuther's logic, but his argument persuaded most of those still occupying the plant to accept the agreement and march out of the gate. There, in the December darkness, their spirits soared as thousands of chanting, torch-bearing unionists marched pass to acclaim their courage and stamina. To these autoworkers and to the wider public, the strike settlement was seen as a victory, even as Walter Reuther declared that "negotiations for pay adjustments in the higher brackets continue. This is merely an armed truce."[76]

If the Kelsey-Hayes strike was not the first victory of Walter Reuther's union career, it nevertheless demonstrated the resourcefulness and flexibility he would need in the difficult days ahead. Reuther proved not only that he could deal with management but that he could persuade a reluctant rank and file to accept a poor settlement—and by implication, his leadership—in the interests of a larger collective interest. His tactical retreat proved a wise strategy. At Kelsey-Hayes, union militants like Moon Mullins emerged as the long-term plant leadership, and in the next few months they made a small revolution in the Kelsey shops and foundries. Kelsey managers now remembered to call workers by their names, not their badge numbers, and a strong shop steward system soon began to function inside the plant. Fear evaporated, and the union routinely held shop meetings at lunch. Acutely aware of the forward march of the UAW all about him, George Kennedy agreed to recognize Local 174 as the sole representative of the workers shortly after the great Chrysler sit-down of March 1937 convinced most of the city's supplier firms that they too would have to deal with the UAW. The company eventually agreed to most of the demands Reuther had failed to win in December: premium pay for overtime, higher pay for the more skilled workers, a system of seniority to govern both layoffs and job promotions, and a 20 percent reduction in the speed of the assembly line.[77]

Kelsey workers were part of Reuther's Amalgamated Local 174, but they proved a maverick bunch. Like the old Industrial Workers of the World, the Mullins group refused to sign a regular contract with Kelsey management, relying instead on the minutes of the bargaining sessions between the plant manager and the stewards' committee to serve as the basis for the union's status there. Mullins and his associates enforced the union shop not with a checkoff but by seizing nonunion men and parading them about the plant in a wheelbarrow, then dumping them in the street. Such arrangements naturally put a premium on a forceful shop-floor presence, which in turn convinced Kelsey foremen that unionism for themselves and an alliance with the UAW was essential to their own well-being. Thus Kelsey-Hayes was the scene of frequent departmental work stoppages, and the union there acquired a well-deserved reputation as the stormy petrel of Local 174, with opponents of the Reuther caucus usually in control. After years of bitter debate, a dissi-dent Kelsey leadership finally pulled the unit out of the West Side amalgamated local in 1947.[78]

The same sense of self-confidence, even liberation, that so utterly transformed Kelsey-Hayes quickly flowed throughout Detroit in the weeks and months after the evacuation of the plant. Workers clearly perceived the strike settlement as a victory, and after the evacuation of Kelsey-Hayes the phone at the West Side local union headquarters was ringing every hour of the day and night. Within ten days Local 174's membership had jumped to three thousand; in another eight months it reached thirty thousand, organized in seventy-five shops and factories. "We really were not organizing the workers," remembered May Reuther, who took a leave from her teaching job to work full-time with Walter at the local's headquarters. "We were just giving them a kind of constructive leadership."[79]

But this was the key to the whole remarkable phenomenon that was the CIO at its most dynamic moment. Reuther and his band of young Socialists had no inti-mate knowledge of shop problems, and none of the long experience of those unionists who had actually negotiated with men like Kelsey's George Kennedy. In point of fact, they were hardly autoworkers at all, but their brashness and their con-nections with the larger world of politics and national unionism made them a lead-ership cadre to whom thousands of Poles and Hungarians could for a brief and decisive moment offer their allegiance and their hope for a better world.

THE WEST SIDE LOCAL

They picked me up about eight different times and threw me down on my back
on the concrete and while I was on the ground they kicked me in the face, head
and other parts of my body.

—*Walter Reuther, May 1937*

History sometimes turns on a narrow pivot. The deep structures of economic power and social consciousness usually constrain the opportunities and shape the choices men and women have to make. But there are also times
when circumstances conspire to greatly diminish our usual sense of social inertia
and institutional stasis, when tradition's chains begin to crack and old fears diminish, thereby making the world once again seem plastic and open, not just to an
ambitious few of will and vision but to a multitude of ordinary people who burst
forward onto the stage of history. In the auto centers of the American Midwest,
such a time came late in the winter of 1937. Our attention has been rightly
focused on Flint, Michigan, where UAW activists organized the great sit-down
strike that forced General Motors to bargain with a multiplant union of its workers. Victory in this contest, or at least the appearance of victory, opened the floodgates to a great mobilization of workers throughout midwestern industrial centers.
Beginning in February thousands who had once stood on the sidelines surged into
the CIO, boosting UAW membership to more than a quarter-million. Overnight,
the autoworkers' union became a powerful political and social force whose amazing success laid the basis for an even more bitter round of conflict, not only with
capital but within working-class ranks as well.

During the six weeks of the GM sit-down strike, Walter Reuther had his hands full consolidating Local 174 in Detroit. But he also understood the stakes at Flint. His whole career as a radical and a unionist would be shaped by the outcome of that struggle, just as the GM sit-down opened the door to the whole subsequent history of industrial unionism in the United States. Reuther therefore spent endless hours driving the Dixie Highway north in order to play his role in the Flint drama. A University of Michigan student journalist, the budding playwright Arthur Miller, found Reuther sleepless but excited when he encountered the unionist in the UAW headquarters in Flint early in the struggle. "He was a pale and reflective man with red hair and a simple, direct quality of respectful attention to me. . . . I realized that he did not think of himself as controlling this incredible event but at best guiding and shaping an emotion that had boiled up from below."[1]

As a tribune and strategist, Walter was often eclipsed by his brothers Victor and Roy, who roomed together in Flint. They played genuinely heroic roles in two legendary confrontations of the strike: the famous "Battle of the Running Bulls," when Victor manned the sound car during a violent repulse of a police attack on January 11; and the seizure and occupation of the vital Chevrolet Engine Plant No. 4 three weeks later, in which Roy Reuther had a large hand. Both incidents involved a physical confrontation between the strikers and the police; here and in several other conflicts the unionists were organized into paramilitary formations, "flying squadrons," of which the Women's Emergency Brigade was but the most famous.

These dramatic, military-style engagements tell us something important about the political and social character of the strike. First, the UAW victory was possible not so much because of the vast outpouring of union sentiment among autoworkers, but because General Motors was temporarily denied recourse to the police power of the state. The transformation of the 1936 election into something of a referendum on the industrial status quo led political figures like Michigan's Governor Frank Murphy to hesitate about using the militia to restore public order in the accustomed fashion. Such restraint could not be expected to last forever, however, and the window of opportunity would remain open for only a brief season. Its closure began early in April 1937 when the U.S. Senate erupted in an emotional denunciation of the sit-down strikes, and it was shut tight in June after the governors of Ohio and Pennsylvania called out National Guard troops to open the way for strikebreakers in the violent Little Steel strike that had begun in May.

But so long as political circumstances constrained state and federal officials, the contest in Flint and other industrial cities would be fought out in the factories and streets and neighborhoods, where union activists held the greatest leverage. Yet here GM's defensive posture was matched by the surprising weakness of the union forces, the second significant feature of the strike. Throughout its course, most workers in Flint—indeed, most General Motors employees across the nation—continued to report for work each morning. In Flint alone, thousands remained on the GM payroll. These workers were not necessarily procompany, or even neutral in the conflict. But they were bystanders whose union consciousness would crystallize only after the UAW had won the strike and stripped the company of its capacity to penalize their allegiance. Then tens of thousands would pour into the union. But until their fear had been banished, the burden of conducting the actual struggle with General Motors rested upon a relatively narrow base: a few hundred sit-downers in each plant, an energetic group of ideological radicals who ran the day-to-day affairs of the strike, and a few older unionists of national reputation posted to Flint during all or part of the conflict.[2]

The General Motors strike began on the morning of December 30 when shop activists shut down a Fisher Body plant to restore the jobs of three inspectors fired by the company. This stoppage caught most UAW leaders by surprise. They wanted to wait until January at the earliest, when Frank Murphy would take over the governor's office in Lansing. Reuther remembered that "we analyzed our strength in the different locals. We knew it would be suicide." But these were wondrous days of innovation and initiative. Several outlying GM factories were already on strike, notably those in Atlanta and Kansas City, so UAW activists in Flint moved quickly to spread the stoppage to the more important factory, Fisher No. 1, which supplied bodies to Chevrolet and Buick.[3]

In Detroit Walter Reuther and his comrades on the West Side, still exhausted and exhilarated from the Kelsey-Hayes fight, began a desperate effort to extend the Flint strike into GM's factories there. Reuther turned his attention first to Cadillac, which employed thirty-eight hundred assembling the corporation's top-of-the-line automobile. Here the political configuration of the shop activists resembled that at Kelsey-Hayes, with skilled workers, ex-coal miners, and a handful of Socialists and Communists in the lead. Pushed forward by Reuther and the Kelsey-Hayes flying squadron, these activists pulled a sit-down on January 8. About three hundred stayed in the plant overnight, but with police patrolling the nearby streets, the sit-down seemed anything but secure. Had it not been for the overwhelmingly prounion mood of the city, remembered one SP militant, the police "could have wiped us out."[4] The sit-down strike was even more tenuous at the smaller Fleetwood plant, which a handful of leftists shut down four days later. Piece rates were a big problem at Fleetwood, which supplied bodies to Cadillac, but most of the production workers were older Catholics who feared both the radicalism and the uncertain prospects of the CIO campaign. Just ninety workers participated in the sit-down on January 12, and when a vote was taken to determine the fate of the occupation, only a bare majority chose to remain in the factory. Francis Tribeau, a French-Canadian electrician who spoke for many of these skeptics, told UAW militants he had twenty-seven signed applications for union membership in his pocket. "If you win the strike they'll be members; if you lose, I'll tear them up."[5]

Tribeau's fence-straddling reflected a realistic assessment of the union's prospects. On January 4 the UAW executive board declared the strike national in scope: a corporationwide work stoppage that could end only when GM recognized the union as the sole representative of its workers. UAW activists rushed to Flint, and John L. Lewis sent in his best organizers as well. They found that General Motors was willing to talk to union leaders, but its top executives insisted that the locus of such negotiations remain at the plant level, where local managers hoped to end the work stoppages one by one. When John L. Lewis made it clear that the CIO would reject this gambit, General Motors and its allies in Flint mobilized directly against the strike, seeking an injunction on January 2, beefing up the city police force with GM security men, and setting up the Flint Alliance, an organization of foremen, loyal employees, and local businessmen, as a counterweight to the UAW.

Frustrated by their inability to get Governor Murphy to oust the sit-downers, local authorities struck on January 11: GM shut off the heat in Fisher No. 2, and the city manager sent in a large squad of police who fired off barrage after barrage of tear gas canisters. The strikers replied in kind, raining metal hinges down upon the police from the roof and soaking the law enforcement officers with high-pressure fire hoses. Roy and Walter were in the thick of the twilight battle, but Victor proved the real hero. For hours he manned the UAW sound car, from which he poured forth a constant stream of encouragement and tactical guidance described by one observer as "an inexhaustible furious flood pouring courage into the men." Twice the police assaulted the plant and the pickets surrounding it, and twice they were repulsed. Thirteen unionists were wounded by gunfire, but the day, thereafter known in labor folklore as the Battle of the Running Bulls, belonged to the UAW-CIO.[6]

The fight strengthened the morale and the mass support of the sit-down strikers and precipitated Governor Murphy's decision to send National Guard troops to Flint, not as strikebreakers but as a buffer between the contending forces, a move that, in practice, would weigh against the police and the hostile city government. Murphy also got negotiations started in his Lansing office between top officials of the company and the CIO. Soon a deal seemed at hand: the strikers would evacuate the plants, and GM would keep them closed while it negotiated an agreement with the UAW. Lewis and his lieutenants were highly suspicious—GM refused to put the agreement in writing—but the relative weakness of the union and the fear that time worked against the strikers compelled them to take a chance. In Detroit Walter Reuther had misgivings as well, but he too hoped that any agreement that even remotely appeared as a union victory could be parlayed, with enough energy and organization, into something of substance. He therefore met with Cadillac and Fleetwood strikers on January 15 and won their acceptance of the settlement. Under banners reading "We Have Just Begun to Fight!" 49 strikers from Fleetwood and 208 from Cadillac marched out of their factories the next day. But GM's understanding of the so-called Lansing Agreement was hardly the same as the CIO's, or else it was an outright double cross. Within hours the company sent thousands of employees telegrams telling them to report for work two days hence. And in Flint the UAW organizers Robert Travis and Wyndham Mortimer learned that GM intended to open negotiations not only with the auto union but with the right-wing Flint Alliance as well. UAW leaders immediately blocked the pullout, denounced the deal, and steeled themselves for a long strike.[7]

The Flint conflict had turned into a stalemate, even as John L. Lewis enlisted the aid of Labor Secretary Francis Perkins, then of President Roosevelt, in an increasingly desperate effort to persuade GM officials to come to terms. But GM again mounted new attacks upon the union. It secured another injunction against the sit-downers, while criminal charges were handed down against Roy and Victor, among others, for their part in the Battle of the Running Bulls. In Detroit Reuther's West Side local mobilized three thousand picketers to block GM's effort to reopen Cadillac on January 25, but in Flint, the Alliance put eight thousand procompany demonstrators in the street.[8] Although Roy and Victor had been sleeping with bodyguards, Walter and other UAW leaders in Detroit insisted that Victor, the most prominent activist in the Battle of the Running Bulls, get out of town. He left on January 24, joining his wife Sophie in Anderson, Indiana, another cockpit of GM-sponsored violence and police repression. Two days later, on January 27, GM called back to work about forty thousand idled workers, eleven thousand in Flint alone. Several UAW organizers were attacked, including Roy Reuther, who was dragged from the sound car when GM loyalists smashed its loudspeakers.[9]

The UAW was losing the strike. To again demonstrate the union's potency, strike activists realized that a bold counterattack was essential. A scheme to revive UAW fortunes by seizing Chevrolet Engine Plant No. 4, one of the most vital factories in the GM system, emerged in mid-January when Kermit Johnson, a Socialist in the Chevy plant, outlined the idea to an expanded SP caucus in the city. The key to the plan's success involved a carefully constructed ploy: a well-publicized attack would be made on Plant No. 9, a smaller factory several hundred yards away, drawing off GM security personnel and thus enabling UAW activists to take over Chevy No. 4, the real target. According to Johnson's young wife, the YPSL activist Genora Johnson (then emerging as the celebrated leader of the Women's Emergency Brigade), Roy Reuther thought the idea worth thinking about, but Walter exploded in derision, calling the plan "insane," a prescription for disaster and embarrassment. Indeed, it was a measure of Walter Reuther's stature, even in Flint, that his opposition stymied the proposal.[10] Johnson's gambit did have an adventuresome character, especially given the weakness of the sit-down forces, the need to retain the goodwill of the governor, and the possibility that any peaceful settlement would be better than the state militia being deployed against the strike. As at Kelsey-Hayes in December, Walter Reuther matched strategic vision with tactical caution. The UAW had to get its foot in the door with even the most minimal sort of settlement; then it would have the time and opportunity to build an effective organization throughout General Motors.

What happened next demonstrated the creative fashion in which the political initiative of radical groups like the SP and the organizational structure of the union were constructively interlinked. Because UAW President Homer Martin had proven himself such an inept spokesman, the Flint strike had no single chain of command; important decisions were made by the citywide strike committee, which held its nightly meetings in the Pengally Building, where Roy had once taught FERA classes. Young Socialists were particularly active here, so Genora Johnson wrote to Norman Thomas outlining her husband's plan; Thomas, who had no flair for strike tactics, turned the problem over to the SP's labor secretary, Frank Trager, who hurried to Flint on January 21. Trager was a full-time functionary, well respected by SP activists like Roy Reuther and George Edwards, and he thought the Johnson plan feasible. Roy now swung squarely behind the idea at an SP caucus; outvoted, Walter reportedly shouted, "I wash my hands of it," as he left the meeting.[11]

Roy Reuther then took the proposal to the rest of the strike committee, which discussed in greater detail the idea of a feint to draw guards away from Chevy No. 4. Significantly, none of the CIO officials advising the UAW were informed of this paramilitary exercise—which was just as well, since they might have wished to distance themselves from its failure, should it have come to that. So the counterattack was on. Beginning on the afternoon of February 1, a furious battle broke out in front of Plant No. 9, drawing off the GM guards and thus allowing a smaller force to occupy the main target, Chevy Engine Plant No. 4. Despite his misgivings, Walter threw all his energies into the battle. He recruited several carloads of West Side militants into the fight; once the plant was taken, Reuther and Edwards organized the construction of huge barricades at the gates. Then, in the predawn hours, Reuther and Powers Hapgood, one of Lewis's veteran CIO organizers, crawled under a set of boxcars to get through the National Guard blockade and negotiate the restoration of power and light for the three thousand men still inside. The takeover of Chevy No. 4 electrified strike supporters: when Walter Reuther again led a West Side caravan to Flint three days later, the turnout from Kelsey-Hayes was so great that the Detroit company lost a day's production.[12]

GM finally capitulated on February 11 when its president, William Knudsen, agreed to recognize the UAW as the workers' sole bargaining agent for not less than six months. Under this contract, a mere four pages in length, the UAW evacuated the plants while the company committed itself to negotiating, on a national basis, a more elaborate collective bargaining agreement covering the abolition of piecework, the establishment of a seniority system and a shop grievance handling structure, and the creation of "a minimum rate of pay commensurate with an American standard of living."[13] The contract language guaranteed a tough struggle ahead, but announcement of the GM agreement was taken as an enormous union victory. In Flint sit-downers marched out of Fisher Body No. 1 to the cheers of thousands of supporters and the strains of "Solidarity Forever." Huge crowds thronged the streets: it was a celebration that Roy Reuther would later "liken to some description of a country experiencing independence." Soon the tens of thousands of fence-sitters would pour into Flint's Amalgamated Local 156, lending enormous vitality and immense problems to the giant union.[14]

Across industrial America the GM settlement transformed the expectations of workers and managers alike. It was the making of the CIO. On March 1, 1937, U.S. Steel signed a contract with the Steel Workers Organizing Committee, and in April the Supreme Court finally endorsed the constitutionality of the Wagner Act. A fever of organization gripped working-class communities in a huge arc that spread from New England through New York, Pennsylvania, and the Midwest. From mid-February onward, a rolling wave of sit-down strikes seized dozens of factories in Detroit. In contrast to the Flint sit-downs, these plant occupations represented a real mass movement largely uncoordinated even by the local radicals on the scene. "Somebody would call the office," recalled Robert Kanter of Local 174, "and say, 'Look, we are sitting down. Send us over some food.'"[15]

In March came the epiphany. More than thirty-five thousand workers joined the Detroit sit-in movement. They occupied every Chrysler Corporation plant in the region, including the giant Dodge Main complex in Hamtramck. At least twenty-five auto parts plants were closed by sit-ins. Workers occupied four downtown hotels, along with a dozen industrial laundries, three department stores, and scores of restaurants, shoe stores, and clothing outlets. Five trucking and garage companies, nine lumberyards, ten meatpacking plants, and all the city's major cigar plants were shut by sit-ins.[16] When the police evicted female strikers from a cigar company and a few shoe stores along lower Woodward Avenue, the UAW called out working-class Detroit for a gigantic demonstration in front of city hall. Municipal authorities refused a permit, but the UAW, joined by the Wayne County AFL, nevertheless mobilized a half-day general strike that brought almost every factory, streetcar, and downtown enterprise to a halt. On behalf of the strike, the CIO self-consciously deployed the symbols of American patriotism. From the back of a flatbed truck Walter Reuther held aloft a ten-foot American flag, which the huge West Side delegation followed to Cadillac Square. There George Edwards led 150,000 in the national anthem, though he had to swallow much Socialist internationalism to remember the words. Leo Krzycki of the CIO was cheered loud and long when he called for a labor party, while Frank Martel of the Detroit AFL got an enthusiastic reception when he promised "a police commissioner who puts human rights above property rights" after labor won the next election.[17]

The peaceful rally opened the way for a last round of unionization among the city's small employers. On the West Side, Local 174 mushroomed in size. In addition to big auto supplier firms like Kelsey-Hayes, Timkin Axle (2,200 workers), and Michigan Malleable Iron (800 workers), Reuther's West Side local signed contracts with Revere Copper and Brass (900 workers), Universal Cooler (600 workers), Universal Products (350 workers), Federal Screw (350 workers), and Federal Motor Truck (450 workers). By the summer Local 174 held bargaining contracts with 48 firms covering close to 30,000 workers, making it one of the two largest amalgamated locals in the entire UAW.[18]

A fragile relationship sustained the organization of these middling shops and the huge companies they supplied. The auto parts firms were production satellites of the integrated producers, but labor relations were rarely uniform between the two sectors, especially when the shops producing automotive trim, wiring, locks, and fabric tended to generate bipolar workforces: a handful of northern European craftsmen/foremen presided over a heavily female, Slavic, and southern European production workforce. Given the competitive and decentralized character of the parts sector, it required an act of political will to unionize the small shops and bring their wages anywhere close to those of the core firms. This reality became painfully clear when a sit-in by scores of women workers at the Yale and Towne Lock Company ended in springtime disaster.

Because so much Yale and Towne production went to Chrysler, Reuther thought he had had an understanding with Richard Frankensteen that linked a Y&T settlement to that of the number-three automaker. But Frankensteen and most other top CIO officials, John L. Lewis chief among them, were desperate to end the Chrysler sit-down, whose prolongation, they thought, merely prepared the ground for a political backlash against the labor movement. Thus five hundred Yale and Towne strikers were left without a settlement when Chrysler resumed production in early April. Without pressure from its biggest customer, factory management held fast. Steeped in the paternalism and arrogance of old-line New England manufacturing, executives at Y&T's Stamford headquarters had no intention of recognizing a union in the company's Detroit outpost. The Connecticut firm therefore won an injunction against the sit-down; Gov. Frank Murphy, also feeling the heat from Michigan conservatives, allowed the injunction to stand. George Edwards organized the resistance from within the factory, but an attempt to reenact the Battle of the Running Bulls failed utterly when two hundred deputy sheriffs and police, firing tear gas and wielding riot sticks, stormed the West Side plant on April 15, arresting 120. On the streets outside, Victor and Walter marshaled hundreds of unionists from all over the city; in a running battle with the police scores of picketers were injured and many more arrested, including the Reuther brothers, who spent several hours in jail until George Addes and Wyndham Mortimer bailed them all out. The successful police assault proved but the opening gun in a militant counteroffensive against the CIO. Announcing that the issue at hand was not a labor dispute but a challenge as to whether "we have a government of law and order," the judge gave George Edwards and another young activist thirty days in jail. More disastrously still, Yale and Towne fired all its employees and simply shuttered the Detroit factory, an act Reuther condemned as "a piece of supreme treachery toward a group of underpaid, exploited women."[19]

Although this debacle was almost forgotten in the euphoria that engulfed labor activists during the marvelous spring of 1937, the collapse of unionism in this small feeder plant highlighted the importance of two unfinished tasks before the auto union: the organization of the Ford Motor Company, and the conquest of enough political power in the Motor City to neutralize the corrupt and hostile police force. Unionization of the Ford Motor Company was particularly vital to the defense of the new wage standards and working conditions negotiated in the factories organized by Reuther's West Side local. Even more than Chrysler, Ford established the economic and political environment in which scores of supplier firms operated. It spread antiunion propaganda from its citadel in nearby Dearborn and intimidated tens of thousands of West Side workers who took the Rouge trolley line out Michigan Avenue. The UAW put up billboards and banners proclaiming, "Fordism is Fascism! Unionism is Americanism!"

Among all the great work sites of American industry, the Rouge did have a fascist odor about it. Ford maintained the largest and most feared internal police force and spy organization in the auto industry. The infamous Service Department, whose two thousand employees were well salted with underworld types whom boss Harry Bennett had recruited from the Michigan prison system, replicated inside the Ford factories many features of the police states of central Europe. The servicemen were a law unto themselves, intimidating even foremen and lower-level supervisors. Among the eighty thousand employees at the Rouge, hundreds of stool pigeons earned extra pay as Service Department informers. Bennett gave this apparatus a political flavor by organizing the "Knights of Dearborn," an anti-Semitic, antiunion front group headed by the Ford serviceman Sam Taylor, a former prizefighter expelled from the Molders Union for embezzling strike funds. The pro-Nazi Silver Shirts had also recruited heavily inside the Rouge, especially among a recent wave of immigrant German technicians and skilled tradesmen. And, of course, the Ford Motor Company had the police and Dearborn city officials under almost complete control.

Ford's was a fascism far less of Prussian efficiency than of Italian intrigue. The entire factory was shot through with ethnic cliques, personal fiefs, and religious rivalries. Ford had hired so heavily before World War I that a remarkably large proportion of his production workers were still industrialized peasants trapped in an insular world of fear, family, and deference. In 1937 many Italian and Slavic workers still kept a picture of Henry Ford on their mantle. The Masons, the Black Legion, the Knights of Columbus, the Padrone-like job salesmen, the gambling kings, and the African-American ministers who brokered the occasional job for one of their parishioners—all these and a dozen other particularist hierarchies generated a whole universe of meaning counterpoised to the CIO's egalitarian program of social reconstruction.[20]

Despite these obstacles, Bill McKie and a few other left-wingers had signed up about four thousand Ford workers by May 1937. While prospects for a union breakthrough at the Rouge were problematic, it seemed just possible if the UAW could snap the pervasive fear that held so many workers in check; then the union could start an emancipatory wave of democratic, prounion sentiment rolling through the Rouge. Certainly Henry Ford himself understood the threat. "We'll never recognize the United Automobile Workers Union or any other union," he announced, following the Supreme Court's April 1937 decision declaring the Wagner Act constitutional. The company began its own distribution of antiunion propaganda, and Bennett's man John Gillespie, whom Reuther had last met at the Kelsey-Hayes negotiations, spent five thousand dollars on guns and tear gas and hired scores of new servicemen.[21]

In a *Daily Worker* interview that spring, Walter Reuther reported: "For the past eight months, while all on the surface was quiet, we have been holding these small group meetings throughout the plant with the aim of developing leaders in the shop who can carry through the campaign." Secret meetings were also held in the Local 174 hall.[22] But underground work alone could not make the union tangibly visible to the thousands of hesitant and fearful Ford workers. The great Rouge plant was both physically and psychologically insulated from union influence. Indeed, the Dearborn complex was surrounded not by the West Side's friendly ethnic neighborhoods but by a sprawling set of highways and parking lots under Ford control. The union's problem was an immense one: to reach tens of thousands of Ford workers with union propaganda that would make the UAW seem as legitimate and powerful as the regime Henry Ford had constructed in his Dearborn fortress. To contest this space, to break the isolation, to demonstrate union potency, something dramatic would be necessary. Thus in April Victor and Walter actually rented a small plane from which they broadcast prounion slogans over the Rouge. Richard Frankensteen, Reuther's intraunion rival then in overall charge of the Ford drive, wanted the UAW to sponsor classical music broadcasts on the radio to compete with Ford's popular "Sunday Concert Hour."[23]

But nothing could substitute for the physical presence of the union itself. Reuther therefore scheduled a massive leaflet distribution for May 26. In preparation, Frank Manfried paid the Dearborn city clerk five dollars for a license, the UAW opened two nearby headquarters, and May Reuther typed out a flyer, "Unionism, not Fordism," consisting largely of quotations from the Wagner Act. Reuther knew that extraordinary steps would have to be taken if a distribution of leaflets were to take place without opposition from the Ford Motor Company and its thuggish Service Department. Reuther, Kanter, and McKie visited the principal site of the distribution—the overpass at Gate 4—on two occasions to plan the operation. Ford had constructed the overpass that linked a streetcar stop to the gate, but the company had also leased it to the Detroit Street Railway Commission. It was a public thoroughfare, as was Miller Road, which ran for hundreds of yards along the east side of the Rouge.

To forestall Ford assaults on the leafleteers, Reuther invited a wide range of observers: clergymen, reporters, photographers, and staffers from Sen. Robert LaFollette's Civil Liberties Subcommittee, which had helped the CIO expose company spies on the eve of the big sit-down strikes. Responsibility for the mass distribution went to Local 174's women's auxiliary. Reuther addressed one hundred of these women on the morning of May 26 and gave them armbands, leafleting assignments, and maps designating public and private property. While the women leafleteers stood along Miller Road, Reuther, Frankensteen, Kanter, and J. J. Kennedy, the UAW's East Side regional director, planned to climb to the top of the Miller Road overpass, where they could observe the operation and have their photograph taken with the Ford Motor Company name clearly visible behind them. Reuther dressed for the occasion: he wore a suit with vest and watch chain.[24]

The situation was tense, but Reuther was still in a confident mood when he drove out to the Rouge just before 2:00 P.M. At the urging of newspaper photographers on early deadline, he immediately climbed to the top of the Miller Road overpass with Kanter, Frankensteen, and Kennedy. They were smiling for the cameramen when about forty men surrounded them. Reuther heard a shout, "This is private property, get the hell out of here!" and then the pummeling began. The attack was led by Sam Taylor and Wilfred Comment, a Ford supervisor. Frankensteen and Reuther were the main targets, although the 200-pound Frankensteen got the worst of it because his resistance was so spirited.

Reuther described his ordeal a few days later:

> I didn't fight back. I merely tried to guard my face. . . . They picked me up about eight different times and threw me down on my back on the concrete and while I was on the ground they kicked me in the face, head and other parts of my body, and after they kicked me awhile, one fellow would yell, "All right, let him go now." Then they would raise me up, hold my arms behind me and begin to hit me some more. They picked my feet up and my shoulders and slammed me down on the concrete and while I was on the ground, they kicked me again in the face, head and other parts of my body. This process went on about eight times. Finally, they got me next to Dick who was lying on the bridge and with both of us together they kicked us again and then they picked me up and threw me down the first flight of steps. . . .
>
> After they kicked me down all the stairs, they then started to hit me again at the bottom of the stairs and slugging me, driving me before them, but never letting me get away. The more we tried to leave the worst it was for us. They simply wanted to slug us out, not let us out. They drove me to the outside of the fence. . . . And all the time I had the permit to distribute the leaflets in my pocket, but no one would look at that.[25]

Raymond Sanford, a Chicago minister, had accompanied Reuther and Frankensteen to the top of the overpass. Of Reuther he later testified: "He had his fists crossed over his forearms and . . . a look of terror written upon his face, with his face blanched white around his upper lip and nose and mouth, with the exception of a trickle of blood coming from his nose." During a pause in the beatings, Reuther grabbed the handrail and began to move toward the steps, but "a very husky individual from the rear wrenched him loose and endeavored to hurl him down the first flight of steps, which I should say, were about nine or ten in number."[26]

Frankensteen had no less trouble than Reuther. As he later told an NLRB inquiry: "Kicking was quite the practice. They at one point put their heel into my stomach and twisted on it, and at another point they held my legs apart and kicked me in the groin. And then a man whom I have since learned was Taylor would say, 'That's enough—let him up.' They would stand me on my feet and Mr. Taylor would then proceed to knock me over again."[27]

Reuther and Frankensteen, both bloodied and dazed, found each other after escaping the Service Department thugs and flagged down an auto driven by the *Detroit Times* photographer Arnold Freeman. With Kanter in the car as well, they were driven to the office of one of the UAW's left-wing doctors, Eugene Shafarman, who found no broken bones but plenty of bruises and cuts. In photos that would soon appear all across the country, Frankensteen is bleeding from the mouth and nose, his shirt is torn, and he has no coat. And Walter Reuther's head is swollen so badly on both sides as to almost close his eyes. That night May, Victor, and Sophie kept watch, periodically waking him to make sure he did not slip into a coma.[28]

Meanwhile, along Miller Road, the elimination of the union leaders hardly ended the assault. As the women tried to get off the streetcars, servicemen blocked the exits, shoving, punching, and kicking them. Katherine Gelles, head of the Local 174 auxiliary, traded punches with a Ford goon, and the Ternstedt Communist Tony Marinovich suffered a permanently disabling skull fracture. Bill McKie, aged fifty-six, was roughed up at the entrance to Gate 5. Some leafleteers were beaten up blocks from the factory. In all, scores of women and men were injured.[29]

Ford officials had enough sense to know that pictures of the assault would be devastating to the company; thus, most of the photographers were rudely threatened and their film destroyed. This treatment made the press even more determined to get the story. The *Detroit News* photographer James Fitzgerald had captured the initial assault on the top of the overpass, and in a series of Pulitzer Prize–winning photographs, first in the Detroit newspapers and then in the Luce publications, the crisp and telling images of "the Battle of the Overpass" were circulated throughout the world. They are among the classic photographs in the tradition of Depression-era social realist photography. In the first frame, three of the UAW organizers smile as the thugs walk toward them; perhaps they felt secure as they stood on the overpass surrounded by newsmen and photographers. Only Walter Reuther, well-groomed and well-dressed, looks back with concern. Then comes the brutal assault; the servicemen use Frankensteen's coat to pin back his arms. The image is one of labor-capital conflict in its most violent and direct form. And finally, the denouement: Reuther and Frankensteen look directly into the camera, blood-spattered and swollen, but dignified and determined. Reuther, in an uncharacteristic but moving gesture, has his arm around Frankensteen.[30]

The publicity proved disastrous to Ford. Although some newspapers, like the *Detroit Free Press*, declared that the UAW was "looking for trouble" at the Rouge, most publications denounced Ford's attack. *Time's* coverage was particularly graphic, and in response Henry Ford withdrew all its advertising from *Time*, *Life*, and *Fortune* for the next seventy weeks. The unique reputation of his company, which had still been at least a notch above that of his competitors, now sank far lower. As the union stated, "Today the world has seen the true character of the Ford Motor Co. We don't intend that it shall forget it." At Reuther's instigation, the UAW soon distributed two hundred thousand copies of *The Flivver King* (1937), Upton Sinclair's devastating account of Henry Ford's ethical devolution. After the Battle of the Overpass, the Ford Motor Company lost the moral edge that its long history of paternalism and civic activism had once sustained. The company's ability to control its workers would henceforth rely even more on simple terror.

Not that the Ford Motor Company would soon be unionized. In a crackdown quite similar to the one that had followed the bloody Hunger March of 1932, Ford successfully attacked the foothold the UAW had won at the Rouge and outlying plants. In all, Ford fired some four thousand actual or suspected unionists during the next four years. In St. Louis, Kansas City, Long Beach, and Richmond, California, Ford used the annual layoff of 1937 and the sharp recession that followed to smash the relatively solid UAW locals in these regional assembly plants. Led by its attorney, Maurice Sugar, the UAW would use the NLRB and the courts to compile a huge and utterly convincing case against Ford Motor Company. The union would eventually charter a new Ford local, Number 600, and vowed time and again to "Organize Ford!" But for four long years the world-famous American company would remain an open-shop fortress, an economic threat to the wage standards and working conditions the union sought to establish, and a constant reproach to the legitimacy of the UAW itself.[31]

The Battle of the Overpass put Walter Reuther among the front rank of the UAW's publicly visible leaders. Until May 26 a dozen auto unionists were better known than the young president of Local 174. *Time* focused its coverage of the overpass incident on Richard Frankensteen, calling Reuther "his lieutenant"; and because of the paramilitary leadership they displayed at Flint, his brothers Roy and Victor had also received more coverage in the Detroit papers. But now Walter Reuther became far more widely known.[32] Even before his cuts had healed, Flint unionists recruited Reuther to speak at a huge rally in their city demanding that municipal authorities finally drop felony charges against Victor Reuther, whose effective command of the UAW sound car on the night of January 11 had so infuriated city law enforcement officers.

With Flint autoworkers now at the height of their unpredictable power, the city caved in, after which UAW organizers transformed the protest into a celebration of the union's remarkable power. Among the principal speakers were Victor, Roy, and Walter Reuther, the embodiment of youthful militancy on a beautiful afternoon in June. Recalling the now famous Battle of the Overpass, Walter announced, "We'll make Dearborn a part of the United States just as we made Flint a part of the United States." As dusk approached, the entire assembly of forty thousand, directed by two thousand shop stewards, formed a line of march for a torchlight parade that filed through the heart of Flint, all units marching under their own factory banners, with spectators often eight and ten deep along the sidewalks. It must have been a moment to savor.[33]

Maurice Sugar made Reuther the leadoff witness in the NLRB's well-reported Ford hearings, which opened on July 7. Reuther told his story of the beating again, and although it was not their purpose, other witnesses made it clear that the Rouge leaflet distribution had been largely a Local 174 operation. In the first of what would become a long series of similar efforts by Walter Reuther's opponents in management and politics, the Ford attorney Louis J. Columbo attempted to discredit Reuther by baiting him over his trip to the Soviet Union. But Reuther, looking relaxed and confident on the witness stand, was imperturbable and resorted to what had become his standard line of explanation: "We went there to study, as I said before, the social conditions of Russia, as we did in other countries."[34]

While the NLRB hearings were exposing Ford brutality, Sugar and Reuther scheduled another mass distribution of union literature at the Rouge. This time there would be a thousand people to hand out a special edition of the UAW newspaper, and they would be accompanied by the Wayne County district attorney, state police, and special representatives of the governor. The distribution would send the message that the UAW had not been frightened off by the company's musclemen, and it would put a clear Reuther imprint on the Ford organizing drive, an important advantage in the UAW's increasingly factional internal politics. Reuther had just flown into Detroit from a Milwaukee meeting of the UAW executive board when he received an irate phone call from rival Richard Frankensteen demanding that he return to the meeting, on pain of suspension from the board. "Go to hell," Reuther shouted into the phone, but Wyndham Mortimer soon persuaded him to take the next plane back to defuse the conflict. Although Reuther missed the actual leaflet distribution, the operation went off without a hitch, even as the incident made clear the West Side leader's controversial new prominence. When reporters learned that the UAW executive board had forced Reuther's absence from Dearborn, the antiunion *Detroit Times* took advantage of the UAW's internal dispute to throw a banner headline across its front page: "Reuther Quits Ford Drive."[35]

Walter Reuther's stature was confirmed again when the UAW selected him and Frankensteen as the two CIO leaders who would run on a labor slate in the city council elections of November 1937. The autoworkers slotted Maurice Sugar, who had built a broad labor-liberal-black constituency in his previous runs for municipal office, as a third candidate, and they expected the Detroit Federation of Labor (DFL) to select two more, including its president, Frank Martel. Under his leadership, the Detroit AFL had been quite supportive of the industrial union insurgency: Martel had denounced police attacks on union picket lines as much as any CIO partisan, and he seemed to look forward to a joint campaign.[36]

But the effort to construct a broad labor slate immediately collapsed. By the summer of 1937 the organizing war between the AFL and the CIO had reached a fever pitch; UAW locals in Flint and Detroit were signing up any workers who sought admittance, not a few of whom were in jurisdictions claimed by powerful AFL craft unions. From Washington, AFL officials hurled broadsides against the CIO's poaching, and despite its more progressive character, the Detroit AFL felt aggrieved as well. Spurred on by the building trades, Martel ended his cooperation with the CIO in late July, so the UAW had to go it alone in the fall campaign. It filled out the labor slate with two more local union presidents, the Hudson local's Tracy Doll, also a member of the International executive board, and Chrysler's R. J. Thomas, an ally of Homer Martin and vice president of the UAW.[37]

The labor slate's exclusively UAW character gave conservatives an open shot. The *Detroit Free Press* called its candidates "the Five Conspirators" and characterized Reuther in particular as "one of the extreme left wing political radicals and as such one of the chief advocates of the sit-down strikes."[38] Indeed, the labor campaign was shaped by the same coalition of political unionists that had led the work stoppages. The labor candidates' central theme was the elimination of police violence against sit-down strikers and the dismissal of the city's reactionary and corrupt police chief, Heinrich Pickert. Reuther, who had pounded away at this theme since the Yale and Towne strike in April, declared that labor would make "its best picket captain" the new city police commissioner; the labor slate itself demanded the "removal from office of the present military-minded, dictatorial commissioner of police," who has "shown a greater concern in crushing strikes than in battling increased crime and protecting the lives and sanctity of our womenfolk."[39]

Detroit's 1937 labor campaign was part of a wave of state and local labor tickets that took to the hustings in the wake of the 1937 industrial union upsurge. In Akron, Toledo, Flint, Canton, Aliquippa, and Woonsocket, unionists ran for municipal office against long-entrenched, corporate-dominated city administrations. While their efforts clearly stood to the left of the New Deal, they were not hostile to the Democrats and Franklin Roosevelt. In New York, Sidney Hillman, David Dubinsky, and George Meany had founded the American Labor Party in 1936 with the explicit intention of shifting the still-important Socialist constituency there into the Roosevelt column, but in the industrial cities of the Midwest the labor campaigns often had a somewhat more independent character.[40] This was the case in Detroit, where a large section of the state Democratic Party attacked the labor slate and where the Socialist Alan Strachan managed the campaign entirely outside the usual political channels. Programmatically, the labor slate pushed the outer limits of New Deal reformism, calling for public ownership and operation of the utilities that supplied gas and electricity to the city; for development of a city-owned milk-distributing plant; and for a city-owned radio station and low-cost public housing. Even mayoral candidate Patrick O'Brien, an independent liberal not formally part of the union slate, struck a radical note, calling on "labor to seize the reigns of government."[41]

The CIO expected to do well, and it mobilized thousands of its cadre to get out its message and its vote. Many of the unemployed Yale and Towne women were hired to work in the campaign's central office, where they laboriously translated union rolls into precinct voter lists. In October Reuther's West Side local mobilized more than one thousand shop stewards for a thorough canvass of the city's wards west of Woodward. Local 174's weekly newspaper, the *West Side Conveyor*, bragged that, "in number of election workers, in amount of money raised, in energy and talent of its committees, in enthusiasm and cooperation of its membership, West Side led the parade."[42]

In the October primary the slate did even better than it had expected. The turnout of 328,000 was the highest in the city's history, even larger than the record-breaking turnout for the presidential election eleven months before. All the labor slate nominees made it to the runoff: Sugar and Frankensteen, who had well-established roots in the city, came in seventh and ninth; Doll, Reuther, and Thomas placed slightly lower. Their success had national repercussions. From Washington, the *Detroit News* correspondent reported that "an amazing amount of national publicity has been given the Detroit battle, far exceeding in interest any local issue in years." Naturally this news gave a shot in the arm to Labor's Non-Partisan League, the CIO political organization that John L. Lewis had put together for the 1936 election. "We consider the Detroit elections to be an indication of what can be done in every industrial city in America when labor is properly organized for political action," asserted a spokesman for Lewis. Sugar and Frankensteen were given an excellent chance of winning seats in November. According to the *New York Times*, they were "sure winners," and in the closing days of the campaign Gov. Frank Murphy endorsed them.[43]

Reuther and other UAW politicos understood well the intimate connection between CIO electoral muscle and the evolution of an advantageous relationship with the auto corporations. As the *West Side Conveyor* editorialized just before the November election: "A Big Vote Will Scare GM." The labor slate's victory in the October primary had already softened up GM foremen and plant managers, reported the *Conveyor*. "That's why, regardless of how the election turns out, we want a whopping big vote next Tuesday. Those hundred thousand primary votes looked like a hundred thousand pickets to the bosses. They looked like a hundred thousand sit-downers. Let's make it two hundred thousand next Tuesday!"[44]

The prospect of a labor victory evoked near-hysteria, and not only from the Detroit establishment. On October 29 the *Detroit Free Press* warned: "CIO success will be a blow to the reputation and standing of Detroit throughout the world. . . . This city belongs to the people who live and work in it, and not to Mr. Lewis. Let us keep it that way." Denouncing the "tyranny of labor government," Father Coughlin pounded home much the same anti-CIO message to the thousands of Detroiters who still tuned into his Sunday afternoon broadcasts.[45] Even more damaging was opposition from the Detroit Federation of Labor, which enlisted in the AFL's militant war against the CIO after its leaders attended the AFL convention in October 1937. Not only did the DFL endorse its own slate of council candidates, but after a bitter internal fight it also threw its weight behind the

Republican mayoral candidate, Richard Reading, an inveterate red-baiter. The endorsement may not have won the conservatives many labor votes, but it did legitimate right-wing assertions that the labor slate represented a narrow, alien wing of the union movement. The *Free Press* asked whether voters would allow Detroit "to become a part of a tail to the kite of John L. Lewis' personal ambition?"[46]

Reuther made a valiant effort to counter this assault. In a radio speech just before the election, he returned to the Debsian cadences of his youth to turn the anti-CIO accusations on their head. The real "outside interests" were "the Wall Street financial groups, that already control our public utilities, our banks, our milk supply, and other vital items of civil life." During the big strikes of early 1937, "who came to Detroit to negotiate for General Motors and Chrysler? Not local people. Certainly not! But lawyers like Donaldson Brown, John Thomas Smith, and the Chrysler lawyer, Kelly, who represented the DuPont and Morgan interests." The issues were sharply drawn, concluded Reuther: "Can we, you and I, as citizens of Detroit, afford to turn over our city government even for one more term to these outside forces that have already milked it for so long? Your vote on November 2nd can mean only one of two things—a vote for outside interests and Wall St. financiers or a vote for the citizens of Detroit."[47]

When he appealed to an exclusively working-class constituency, Reuther deployed the gritty language of proletarian solidarity to repulse the red-baiting campaign against him. Writing in the Ternstedt-unit newspaper of Local 174, Reuther saw the "red scare" as but another effort by the "bosses" to divide and conquer. "They pay stools to go whispering around that so-and-so—usually a militant union leader—is a red. They think that will turn the other workers against him. What the bosses really mean, however, is not that the leader is a red. They mean they don't like him because he is a loyal, dependable union man. . . . So let's all be careful that we don't play the bosses' game by falling for their red scare. Let's stand by our union and our fellow unionists."[48] Such were Reuther's sentiments at the height of his collaboration with the Communists, at the apogee of the New Deal–Popular Front–CIO alliance. These were words the UAW left would never let him forget.

Rhetorical polarization of this sort generated an equally pronounced political division in the voting booth. On November 2, the labor slate won about twice as many votes as any previous left-wing insurgency in the city, but the CIO effort was nevertheless soundly defeated. O'Brien trailed Reading in the mayor's race by 100,000 votes, and the UAW candidates failed to finish among the top nine who made it to the city council. With 145,342 votes, Sugar came in tenth; Reuther, at fourteenth with 126,323, was bunched between Doll and Thomas.[49] So why did the labor slate fail? Why, at the very moment when the union movement commanded such precious resources, in energy, organization, and spirit, did it fall short in one of the most overwhelmingly working-class cities in the United States?

The answer is found in both the specific circumstances of the Detroit election and the more general dilemma faced by the industrial union movement even at the very height of its power. First, large sections of the industrial working class remained untouched by, even actively hostile to, the CIO. Ford Motor Company was still unorganized, which meant that tens of thousands of potential voters lived and worked in the shadow of this old regime. Despite all of Local 174's efforts, the labor slate won no wards on the West Side, where Ford's sway was most pronounced; it did considerably better in the working-class neighborhoods east of Woodward Avenue where CIO influence had penetrated more deeply. Detroit blacks, about 15 percent of the city population, also remained largely outside the ambit of the industrial union movement and lent only tepid support to the labor slate. The National Association for the Advancement of Colored People, the Urban League, and the black church were led by members of the black community who were skeptical of the CIO and still oriented toward Ford and other paternalistic white elites. Thus, when a UAW local held a segregated dance, the most important black newspaper in the city pounced with a streamer headline, "Jim Crowism in the UAW."[50]

More important, the defeat of the labor slate was also part of the larger stalemate in American politics that set in almost immediately after the Roosevelt landslide of 1936 and the great CIO breakthrough a few months later. The class tensions made manifest by the mobilization of a specifically working-class constituency evoked a specter of social chaos that generated divisions within the working class, defections from liberal ranks, and a right-wing countermobilization that soon put both the new unions and the New Deal on the defensive. Campaign manager Alan Strachan thought the middle class "obsessed with the fear of anarchy," while Ben Fischer, whom the Socialist Party had sent into Michigan to help coordinate their work in the auto industry, concluded that "the middle class went overwhelmingly to the reactionaries."[51] Ford's brutal victory at the Battle of the Overpass and the CIO's failure to establish itself as an independent political force determined that the conflict between the new industrial unions and their corporate adversaries would have to be fought on a terrain that was far narrower and more difficult than the one that had seemed to open up in 1936–37. The stalemate of the New Deal, followed almost immediately by the devastating recession of 1938, put the CIO in a desperate battle to maintain its presence in the mills and factories it had so triumphantly entered less than a year before.

In these difficult circumstances, the UAW survived because its most committed cadre had built a series of remarkable institutions that would sustain them in the coming storm. Among these was the West Side local, UAW Local 174, over which Walter Reuther presided with enormous skill and energy. Because of its large size and amalgamated character, Local 174 was essentially autonomous within the UAW. With an income of more than twenty-five thousand dollars a month, the local had its own paid staff, sound truck, newspaper, and recreation program—indeed, its own political line on virtually all policy questions, foreign, domestic, and intraunion. The local was the very first in the UAW to buy its own headquarters, an Odd Fellows Hall on West Mayberry Grand, with bowling alleys, billiard tables, and a big kitchen. Here the offices, meeting halls, and corridors were filled with a constant buzz of activity. In one thirteen-day stretch in the summer of 1937, the local scheduled more than fifty-one separate shop meetings. Unknown workers often appeared, their hands gripping a stack of signed membership cards.[52]

The localwide council, consisting of proportional delegations from each plant, met on Saturday mornings in the union's 150-seat auditorium, on the walls of which were spread social realist murals of labor's rise and triumph, including a larger-than-life rendering of the Battle of the Overpass. "In the beginning . . . joint council meetings of 174 were wonderful," remembered Irene Young Marinovich, a Ternstedt worker and council delegate close to the Communist grouping in the local. "They would last three or four hours; people would get up and they'd fight, they'd discuss anything. You discussed the conditions in the plant, what you oughta do. Everybody talked." After the collapse of Brookwood Labor College — because so many of its students and instructors were furiously building the CIO — Local 174 acquired its extensive library and hosted many speakers from its faculty, including the economist Joel Seidman, the sociologist Robert Lynd, as well as Tucker Smith and Norman Thomas.[53]

Walter Reuther proved himself a resourceful and effective trade unionist during his two and a half years as Local 174 president. He helped negotiate scores of agreements, spoke hundreds of times each year, and organized dances, picnics, demonstrations, and picket lines. His pay was $57.70 a week, plus travel expenses paid by the International, a little less than what most tool and die makers earned.[54] Like other young industrial union leaders in the 1930s, he almost always wore a suit and tie when he spoke to a large audience or negotiated with an employer. Autoworkers expected the dress and demeanor of their spokesmen to reflect the dignity and respect they were so often denied at work and for which they so self-consciously fought. Reuther's speaking voice was not quite the equal of other UAW orators, like Richard Frankensteen, George Edwards, and Homer Martin; on the radio it sounded just a bit too high, sometimes even whiny. But Reuther was well organized and programmatic. His notes for speaking or writing usually took the form of a list: problems to solve, people to involve, action to be taken. Even at his most extemporaneous, he made a careful analysis of the problem at hand, followed by a multipoint program to resolve it. "Now let's be realistic about the whole matter," was one of his favorite phrases.[55]

Although his amalgamated local was a highly politicized institution, representing workers in an amazing variety of work sites, Reuther's handling of its day-to-day affairs faced almost no criticism. Thus Stewart Strachan, who allied himself with Homer Martin in the UAW's bitter factional combat of 1937–38, nevertheless thought that Reuther "ran a very good local, a model local." And Adolph Germer, who considered Reuther a bit too much of a radical, wrote John L. Lewis in October 1937, "There is no denying that Walter Reuther is very popular with the rank and file." Should Homer Martin seek his ouster, warned this top CIO aide, "he is just going to stir up a hornets' nest." Not unexpectedly, Reuther partisans were convinced that the twenty-nine-year-old militant had a good shot at the presidency of the UAW when and if the Missouri preacher faltered.[56]

Reuther surrounded himself with talented men and women, a well-balanced group that reflected the politics of the leading left-wing activists on the West Side. The local usually had five paid organizers: three were Socialists, two were allied closely with the Communist Party. The organizers were kept busy negotiating contracts, adjusting grievances, and "servicing" the membership. Although much of the work was routine, it was vital to the morale of the West Side organization. Organizers handled between ten and fifteen shops each, including a large plant that was the primary focus of their work. Thus George Edwards negotiated for Kelsey-Hayes during his first eighteen months in the local, Robert Kanter serviced Timkin and Cadillac, and Stanley Nowak took on the extraordinarily difficult task of organizing Ternstedt and rationalizing its wage structure. Bill McKie always saw his primary responsibility as the organization of Ford, whose clandestine local met in the Local 174 hall. Victor Reuther—"the voice"—was a popular speaker but, as a Local 174 organizer, not adept at collective bargaining.[57]

Edwards and Nowak were the key men. Polar opposites in politics and personality, they were equally vital to the organizational health of Local 174. Reuther disliked Stanley Nowak but found him indispensable. Edwards remembered Nowak as a "little power pigeon and a miserable guy, very theoretical in his adherence to the [Communist] line." For almost two years Reuther depended on the Polish-speaking organizer to make Local 174's presence felt inside the West Side's largest factory, GM's Ternstedt auto parts complex, where second-generation eastern European women represented more than half of the twelve thousand who labored there. Nowak proved himself a brilliant, popular organizer among Polish workers, an aptitude he eventually parlayed into a decade-long career as a Democratic state senator from the West Side district. Indeed, he symbolized the UAW's capacity to compete with other Polish institutions, including even the church, for the loyalty of working-class Polonia. As a senator, Nowak often officiated at the weddings and funerals of the sizable group of Polish anticlericals hostile to the priesthood and its ceremonial role. Reuther appreciated Nowak's unique appeal, but he could hardly ignore the influence Nowak had come to exercise at the West Side's largest factory. "Stanley has too much power," Reuther once remarked. "He holds Ternstedt in the palm of his hand."[58]

Reuther's collaboration with George Edwards was far warmer. At age twenty-three, Edwards was Reuther's key political operative, a comrade to entrust with the most difficult tasks. He was boyish, charming, and a quick-witted, engaging speaker. Despite the SMU and Harvard degrees in his pedigree, Edwards had a genuine rapport with the autoworkers. "The crew in my department has in it some of the most natural, unaffected, warm hearted and courageous people whom I have ever known," he wrote in early 1937. "If the whole of the working class resembles the workers at Kelsey-Hayes—then it is certainly worth spending a life time fighting for."[59] Rank-and-file autoworkers thought of him not as an interloper but as an emissary from another class whose very presence among them validated and sustained their struggle. Despite his heavy involvement with the UAW, Edwards remained an SP stalwart; thus, he scolded Reuther for his collaboration with the Communist grouping in the auto union, and he complained of the political "dirty work" Walter often foisted upon him. But Edwards remained a comrade and friend, and Reuther shamelessly exploited his energy and intellect. Indeed, the president of Local 174 was hardly a gracious boss. Throughout his union career Reuther rarely gave public recognition to his dedicated comrades and collaborators. It was not simply that Reuther was insecure or personally ambitious but, more fundamentally, that he counted his own leadership a corporate enterprise in which the advancement of his person merged so cleanly with the fate of the union that the rituals of collective leadership and the requirements of friendship seemed frivolous indeed.[60]

Two other full-time staffers were also important to Reuther's extraordinarily effective leadership of Local 174, and they helped him project his influence well beyond the West Side of Detroit. In July 1937 he hired Carl Haessler to edit the *West Side Conveyor*. Haessler was a sophisticated and experienced newspaperman, an editor at the left-wing Federated Press, and the architect of the excellent newspaper coverage the UAW had won during the GM strike. He was a full generation older than Reuther, a Rhodes scholar, and a Socialist for most of his adult life who moved into the Communist orbit in the mid-1930s. With Haessler on the payroll, Reuther became the only local union president who had the services of a professional publicity man to issue press releases, polish his radio talks, and meet with newspaper reporters and magazine writers. Reuther listed himself as "president and editor" on the masthead, but it was Haessler who made the *West Side Conveyor* the finest local union paper in the UAW, a weekly that offered detailed coverage of union politics and lively reports from all the major shops in Local 174's jurisdiction. The *Conveyor* was the recognized voice of those unionists who opposed Homer Martin's increasingly maladroit leadership in the union. Thus it circulated far beyond the West Side of Detroit; its subscription list included virtually every actual or potential member in the unionwide opposition grouping.[61]

Finally, there was May Reuther. In early 1937 she quit her teaching job to work full-time as her husband's secretary in the West Side office, at a salary of twenty dollars a week, a substantial pay cut. Still using her maiden name and discreetly keeping her identity as Reuther's spouse generally unknown, she functioned as far more than a mere typist who put her boss's prose into workmanlike English. At the West Side local and the UAW General Motors Department, which Walter took over in 1939, May made numerous day-to-day decisions for her husband. She participated in the SP caucus until it disintegrated in the fall of 1938, and she was president of the Detroit local of the United Office and Professional Workers, which represented the clerical staffs in the many union offices opening up all over town. To the annoyance of her female friends, May usually joined the circle of male politicos when Walter's comrades talked shop after dinner.[62]

May put in ten- and twelve-hour days at the office, and Walter often had a meeting in the evening. They bickered under the strain, but Walter's frequent out-of-
town trips brought affirmations of his love flooding back to her in letters. Between
descriptions of the political infighting that consumed the union's executive board,
Walter offered May kisses and hugs: "Even though we do fight a lot the world is
an empty place without you," he wrote from Cleveland in March 1937. "It ain't
right my being here and you being in Detroit. . . . I would like nothing better than
to . . . pull back the cover and crawl in bed and hold you tight. Would you love
it."[63] Guilt over spending so little time together, even in Detroit, was a recurring
theme. "I act like a perfect fool sometimes. I neglect you," wrote Walter from the
UAW's Milwaukee convention in August 1937. "I give the movement all of my
time only to find that by neglecting you I destroy a relationship without which I
can never hope to accomplish anything."[64]

Ten months later Walter made the same complaint: "Mayichka, I think you're
wonderful and I can't wait until I get back and we can go away together. That has
been our main trouble. We have never had time together. . . . We can be such
swell kids together if we can stop being machines. I can't wait to get started—can
you?"[65] But the union's growing factionalism only made the pace more hectic during the summer and fall of 1938, and in November, May wrote Walter, again in
Washington for an executive board meeting, "There is a good deal that I would
like to say that's awfully nice, but I can't say the nice things without prefacing it
with others that aren't so nice and that I feel we ought to talk about rather than
write. . . . For a long time we have been settling all of our difficulties by going to
bed which creates a situation where grievances accumulate and which finally pre-
cipitates an explosion. (Like a GM strike). Such is the situation at the present
time." Walter proposed a solution: "When I am away from the mechanical-like
existence we live, I begin to see why we are on edge all the time. Please let's try to
work out a schedule and stick to it. . . . We must do something so that we won't
keep going like two machines."[66] But Walter's schedule continued to frustrate
them both, a situation that was resolved, or at least displaced, only by the birth of
their daughter Linda early in 1942, after which May stopped her work for the
union, withdrew from her high level of political engagement, and focused much
of her emotional energy on Linda and her sister Lisa, who arrived in 1947.

Both friends and foes knew that Walter Reuther would soon move beyond the
presidency of Local 174, but he was determined to keep the big amalgamated
organization firmly in his camp. In Local 174's first real election, held in March
1938, Reuther again put trade unionists on his slate who leaned toward the Communists: Frank Manfried of Kelsey, who had worked closely with Bill McKie, was
reelected treasurer; and Irene Young from Ternstedt, a protégé of Nowak, became
the new recording secretary. Few questioned Reuther's hold on the presidency, but
the vice-presidential slot occasioned much dispute. George Edwards desperately
wanted the post, which would put him in line for Local 174's presidency when
Reuther moved on and up. But the Communists vigorously objected to Socialists

dominating the two top jobs in the local; moreover, Reuther himself found his comradeship with Edwards overlaid by something close to a sibling rivalry. He therefore pushed Edwards out, into the UAW department that organized the unemployed, and chose for the vice presidency a more conventional figure, Michael Manning, who could appeal to the more conservative element in the West Side shops. Manning, it will be recalled, was the middle-aged Irish Catholic foreman who had skipped the organizing drive at Kelsey-Hayes because of his allegiance to the AFL. Although a bumbling and maladroit speaker, he was a "stabilizing force," as Victor Reuther remembered him, whose presence in the leadership would help deflect antiradical sentiment and consolidate the local.[67]

In the local elections Reuther's left-wing coalition swept the field by more than four to one, but the most potent threat to his power came from another quarter: the growth of a self-confident independence, leading to a demand for unit autonomy, among Local 174's shop leadership. For example, Francis Tribeau, who had remained on the sidelines during the Fleetwood sit-down, quickly reemerged as a leader there, especially among the older workers of northern European background who nearly dominated this quality production shop. As shop chairman, Tribeau, a onetime follower of Father Coughlin, aligned himself with UAW President Homer Martin and his increasingly antiradical, anti-Communist outlook.[68] Tribeau was Reuther's unsuccessful opponent in the Local 174 elections, but his efforts to win Fleetwood its own separate charter won backing from a far broader group of unionists. Homer Martin had already begun to break up the amalgamated organization that encompassed all the GM factories in Flint; naturally he also targeted Local 174, where even many radicals wanted separate charters for their own factories. An important group of Kelsey-Hayes sit-down strike veterans, for example, agitated long and hard for an autonomous local; at Fleetwood and Cadillac leftists would also push for their own charter. Within the GM system most locals consisted of a single factory or a closely related set of production facilities, so once plant bargaining relationships were established on anything like a routine basis, the Local 174 situation seemed anomalous indeed. As a group of Cadillac secessionists put it, "We want democracy. We are large enough and strong enough to run our own affairs. At present nearly 60 other plants with entirely different problems are telling us what to do. . . . We want to vote on our own questions and elect our own officers."[69]

Reuther, who obviously had more power within the UAW as the head of a big local, fought these centrifugal tendencies. As the *Conveyor* bragged in July 1937, the ninety-five delegates the local would send to the UAW convention in Milwaukee gave it the biggest representation there of any local. And aside from the UAW itself, Local 174 had more paid organizers on its staff than any other unit in the UAW. These advantages were organizational weapons of considerable value in the UAW's growing factional warfare. The amalgamated setup also ensured the Reuther forces' effective control within Local 174. The local's joint council overrepresented the numerical strength of the unionists from the smaller automotive parts plants (about one-quarter of the membership), who were far more dependent upon the tutelage of the local's politically astute organizers than were the workers at factories like Kelsey-Hayes or Cadillac, who had their own set of experienced officeholders.[70]

But beyond these elements of realpolitik, Local 174's amalgamated structure expressed the very real sense of class solidarity felt by the more activist elements within the UAW. In its early years the West Side local was as much a community organization as a collective bargaining institution. Workers frequently switched jobs among the many small metal fabrication shops, which were themselves embedded in the neighborhoods of closely spaced wood-frame houses that characterized Detroit's working-class districts. Local 174 backed West Side rent strikes and organized a union auxiliary for those employed in New Deal work relief programs. Reuther therefore saw the mixed character of Local 174 as an embodiment of his vision of the union movement, in which collective bargaining and political mobilization were organically and fruitfully linked.[71]

In particular, the amalgamated character of Local 174 helped energize and integrate women workers into the labor movement and the civic culture. Reuther would never have put it in these terms; in fact, neither he nor any of the other leaders of Local 174, male or female, played up the fact that Local 174 was one of the most heavily female locals in the UAW (at least 40 percent). More likely, the men who ran Local 174 considered the high proportion of women in the auto parts industry a source of weakness, for the conventional wisdom among unionists of both sexes held that women were both more difficult to organize than men and less reliable as unionists. Certainly employers and the police thought so, for their counterattacks, both physical and ideological, invariably targeted the low-wage, heavily female shops and factories. Reuther therefore discouraged Stanley Nowak from tackling Ternstedt, with its thousands of women workers, until after several more heavily male factories had been organized.[72]

Whatever their privately held views, none of the radicals in Local 174's leadership put much effort into an attack upon the gender hierarchies that governed the factory work regime of that era. Sexually segregated seniority lists remained the norm, and the employment rights of married women were barely tolerated. Walter Reuther did not put equal pay for equal work on the union's bargaining agenda. Until 1940 and the wartime labor shortage, he thought such a bargaining strategy would merely encourage companies to substitute women workers for men. Not unexpectedly, women workers were underrepresented in the union's official life. Among the Local 174 female activists, few were married or had children. Single women predominated, inspired in their union work either by a newfound political commitment or by a history of unionism in their families. Although Edwards, Nowak, and Victor Reuther encouraged women to take a greater role in the local's affairs, female delegates comprised but 13 percent of Local 174's joint council membership. For a time Local 174 had an active women's auxiliary, but it was composed largely of the nonworking wives and daughters of union members.[73]

Despite these limitations, Reuther's determination to preserve the unity of Local 174 put the union firmly on the side of greater gender equality in the workplace. The breakup of Local 174 would leave the heavily female production units in the auto parts sector vulnerable to the competitive, low-wage pressures characteristic of supplier firms. Local 174 organizers therefore sought to increase wages in these shops to the GM level and to install simple grievance and seniority systems. Eventually the UAW would organize special departments and councils that took on these same tasks for each segment of the industry—foundries, wheels, nut and screw shops, and so forth—but in the late 1930s the effort to link the fortunes of this subordinate and less well organized section of the industry to the big centers of union strength reflected even more directly the sense of shared expectation that linked workers in West Side shops both large and small. Women workers often defended their interests through slowdowns and other job actions, but in an era when so much class conflict was decided in the street, they needed the muscle that Local 174 could supply when the union confronted police, scabs, and strike-breakers. As the *West Side Conveyor* boasted, "An amalgamated local doesn't have all its eggs in one basket. When democratically run like the West Side, it can't be beat for solidarity and union power."[74]

The violent Federal Screw strike of April 1938 proved an extraordinary example of the elementary combativeness of the community-based local and of Walter Reuther's capacity for both tactical militancy and strategic vision in these creative and exciting years of his life. By late in the winter of 1938 the Roosevelt recession that had begun five months before was having a devastating effect on the UAW and other new unions. U.S. industrial production seemed in a free fall, with steel, auto, and rubber all down over 50 percent from their 1937 highs. Many employers threatened to cut wages by 10 or 20 percent, especially those in industries, like auto parts manufacturing, where sizable wage inequalities existed between union and nonunion plants.

On the West Side, production and employment plummeted. Ternstedt cut its workforce by 50 percent and worked the remainder a total of five days during the entire month of February 1938. Smaller firms cut their workforces by even more. Most unionized employers demanded that the UAW accept a wage cut if it hoped to renew the contracts the union signed the year before. History, after all, seemed to be on the employers' side. They had cut wages during the recession of 1921 and again when the bottom fell out of the auto market after 1931. Employers may well have been encouraged by UAW President Homer Martin's assertion in January 1938 that the union had no intention of penalizing unionized supplier firms in the Detroit area by insisting on wage rates higher than those of their small-town competitors.[75]

Reuther took the lead in resisting these wage cuts. "This is no time for concessions," announced Local 174 early in the year. Reuther and his comrades in the local leadership believed that layoffs and short workweeks had already dampened union enthusiasm among the production workers so recently recruited to its ranks.

"We have faced 20 managements on the West Side in the last two months and 18 of them wanted wage cuts." Therefore, any accommodation to even the most financially shaky of these employers would open the gates to a tidal wave of demands by all employers, generate even more disillusionment with the union, and cause a permanent loss of members.[76]

Local 174 was therefore prepared to fight. One of the shops demanding a wage cut was Federal Screw, a parts supplier for Ford and GM. It had already reduced its workforce from 350 to 150 when its management demanded that the local agree to a 20 percent pay cut. There was some evidence that the company was acting in close coordination with police officials, other supplier firms, and the Ford Motor Company. As a management attorney told Stanley Nowak, the plant organizer: "Things have changed in the City of Detroit. Labor is going to be put in its place, and any strikes, sit-downs or otherwise, will no longer be tolerated."[77]

The social structure of the plant workforce replicated in microcosm the ethno-technical terrain upon which the entire CIO did battle. A majority of the production workers in the plant were women, many of them residents of the surrounding Polish neighborhood whose crowded streets fronted directly upon the small factory. But a group of better-paid male job setters, several of German and Irish parentage, bitterly opposed the union, and they offered the company the core group of employees needed to operate the factory and supervise the new workers management hoped to recruit from the mass ranks of the unemployed. Stanley Nowak reported that the shop was still 75 percent organized, that "morale is good," and that the company was making a profit. With the rest of the plant bargaining committee, he recommended a rejection of the company's wage cut and preparation for a strike.[78]

Despite the wariness of their relationship, Reuther was ready to back Nowak and throw such resources as Local 174 commanded into a fight at Federal Screw. Reuther knew that the UAW could still mobilize tens of thousands of workers and supporters; in early February Local 174 had again contributed a sizable contingent to a big Cadillac Square rally demanding rent reductions and more relief funds during the recession. The local therefore established a strike headquarters near the company, alerted physicians friendly to the union cause, and made plans for a picket line that would include workers laid off from shops all over the West Side. As Reuther put it in Carl Haessler's press release issued at the height of the battle, the Federal Screw strike "is a test case for the entire wage structure of the auto industry. If the employers succeed here they will chop wages everywhere else. For this reason not only West Side Local but union men and women everywhere are fighting it. They are fighting on behalf of law and order against the employers' defiance of the Wagner Act."[79]

The strike began on a Monday, March 28, when the company unilaterally imposed a wage cut of ten cents an hour. That day and the next, hundreds of police successfully shepherded thirty or so workers through UAW picket lines. The UAW wired the governor, demanding a reduction in the massive police presence, but there were soon scuffles between the police, the picketers, and local residents who shouted insults at the scabs from their porches and sidewalks. "The battle field for all West Siders is in front of the Federal Screw plant," announced the *West Side Conveyer* on Tuesday. "Every West Sider in fighting trim will be there. This is not a conscription, but an enthusiastic volunteering in the mass."[80]

The battle came as the shift changed on Wednesday afternoon. By this time between three thousand and five thousand picketers, marching resolutely behind a huge American flag, had filled the streets around the plant. Victor Reuther resumed his command post in the Local 174 sound car. Virtually every activist in the Detroit labor movement was present. Confronting them were six hundred Detroit police, including a large squad of mounted patrolmen. As the horsemen came charging through their ranks, the pickets swung back, sometimes in a calculated effort to break the kneecaps of the riders. A Cadillac steward described the scene: "The cops began to swing their clubs and charge the crowd with their horses. Bricks began to fly. Three cops pile onto one man. He goes down. They hit him over the head. . . . A club sails through the air and knocks a cop off his horse. The cop tries to rise. He falls again with blood streaming from his head. The air is full of bricks, rocks, bottles, police sticks swinging, horses hoofs."[81] In all, forty pickets were hospitalized, but so were twenty-five scabs. Thirteen policemen were injured. Timkin's shop steward, Daniel Gallagher, reported that the floor of the West Side union hall was "so bloody you slipped down on it taking the people in there."[82]

The social ecology of the Federal Screw strike was characteristic of many industrial conflicts of the pre–World War II era. The strike had strong neighborhood support. Although the shock troops of the battle—the pickets who actually fought the police—were not workers at the Federal Screw plant, the closely packed Polish neighborhood offered them a friendly environment upon which to fall back. In at least one celebrated instance, a neighborhood woman poured boiling water on the police riders as they trotted up the narrow streets. Many of the women in the community around the plant were cigar workers who had been through their own bitter strikes the year before. They saw the police as an alien force and identified with the CIO. This was Stanley Nowak's turf, a fact that Reuther, Edwards, and other Socialists in Local 174 implicitly recognized, for they gave his faction of the local de facto control of the day-to-day strike tactics.[83]

But neighborhood resistance would never have been enough to confront the hundreds of police, whose aim was to protect company operations. The UAW also called out its paramilitary arm: the specially organized flying squadrons from Kelsey-Hayes, Dodge, and other well-organized shops. The squadrons were composed of youthful militants, ready to hop in their cars and drive anywhere in southeastern Michigan for a fight, either against the union's corporate antagonists or, with equal frequency, to protect the meetings and strengthen the picket lines of the union faction to which they offered their loyalty. They wore a sort of uniform: an overseas cap and a leather jacket with an armband. Kelsey-Hayes had the best flying squadron on the West Side, and its members were positively cocky after the

Federal Screw battle: "The trouble with a lot of unions is lack of good fighters. For those so troubled, Kelsey can spare a few. . . . The Kelsey boys are always there when they're needed." They armed themselves with "picket signs" that easily converted into two-by-two clubs. As a Kelsey militant put it: "Police and unionists argue hotly about when is a banner a shillalee? A shillalee is a club that dangles downward from the hand while a banner is a stick held upright. Our pickets always carry banners."[84]

The level of violence was high, but in such late-Depression strikes, police and pickets battled it out on almost equal terms. Unionists assembled rocks, steel hinges, and other objects to throw at the cops, and the police organized tear-gas attacks and mounted charges. While many bones were broken, there were few arrests and no indictments for incitement to riot or criminal conspiracy, common practice in the next large-scale wave of civil unrest in the 1960s. Detroit's police force, a corrupt and politically fractionalized institution—it was marbled with elements of the Black Legion and the Ku Klux Klan—had great difficulty in making credible its claim to uphold law and order, even among non-working-class elements of the population.[85] It was the union that claimed to speak for the lawful community; with huge American flags and rhetoric defending an "American standard" of living, strike leaders tried to define the conflict not as a contest over the maintenance of civic order but as a confrontation with those who sought to disrupt the new system of economic justice the UAW had begun to impose on the industrial landscape. Reuther denounced "the savagery of Mayor Reading's police," and at a packed city council meeting held just after the battle, unionists demanded that the city call off the police: "When old ladies stand at their windows with boiling water to pour on vicious officers, it's time for the council to act," asserted Reuther. "The union is opposed to violence and wants to settle this by peaceful negotiations, but you can't let Pickert have his men run wild at strikebreakers without meeting some resistance."[86]

The violence of the battle on March 30, 1938, and the relative sympathy the union was winning throughout Detroit, forced Federal Screw management to capitulate. The company agreed to call off the police, close the plant, and negotiate a new contract with Local 174. The contract was signed on April 9: wages were kept at the old level, seniority and overtime schedules were improved, and the unit won sole collective bargaining rights.[87] Reuther, Nowak, and Haessler had piloted the West Side local to a remarkable victory, but the violent consequences of the Federal Screw strike were not quite over.

The UAW victory at Federal Screw was almost as much a defeat for the Ford Motor Company as it had been for its screw supplier. Ford did not oppose the high wage standard that Local 174 had taken the lead in defending. But John Gillespie, the shadowy figure in charge of keeping the supplier plants in line for the Ford organization, did fear the thoroughgoing unionization of the many parts plants: it was bound to drive up unit costs and set an example for the tens of thousands of Ford workers who lived on the West Side. The Ford Service Department had kept track of Reuther's activities since the Battle of the Overpass, and in the weeks leading up to the Federal Screw strike its operatives had actually rented an apartment from which they could more closely observe Walter and May, then living in a second-floor flat at 13233 LaSalle Boulevard. Among those watching the Reuthers was Willard "Bud" Holt, a onetime personal bodyguard to John Gillespie and, until late March, a full-time employee of the Service Department. On the evening of April 9, the very day Local 174 signed a new contract with Federal Screw, Holt and another tough character, Eddie Percelli, a former rumrunner, pulled out their guns and knocked on the Reuthers' door.

But instead of a lone couple, the gunmen were surprised to find a small party in progress. It was Sophie Reuther's birthday, but Walter had come down with a bad cold, so the party had been moved to the LaSalle Boulevard apartment. The guest list reveals that the Reuther circle of friends still comprised mostly Socialists active in the auto union. Aside from May, Sophie, the three brothers, and George Edwards, those present included Al King and Frank Marquart of the Detroit SP and two Socialists recently sent into Michigan from out of town: Ben Fisher, who would coordinate the party's auto industry work, and Tucker Smith, the head of the Socialist Party in Michigan and former director of Brookwood.

The unexpectedly large group may well have saved Reuther from "taking a ride" or at least prevented another severe beating. Victor Reuther remembered the next few moments as melodramatic, played like a scene from a gangster movie of the era. With revolvers drawn and snap-brimmed hats pulled low over their eyes, the hoods pushed their way forward. "Okay, Red, you're coming with us!" yelled Holt, the bigger of the two. Then bold talk from Roy, Victor, and Edwards: "You're not getting him out of here. You may shoot some of us, but you will not get out yourselves."[88]

Holt beat Reuther with a floor lamp, then a blackjack. As at the overpass, Walter Reuther had the self-control not to resist. Instead, he backed into a corner to ward off the blows. At one point Holt shouted to Percelli, "Kill the son of a bitch!" Reacting instinctively, the men nearest Percelli took the slightest step forward. The Ford thugs hesitated; from the kitchen, Sophie threw a pickle bottle, which landed with an ominous thud that put a feeling of emptiness in their stomachs. Meanwhile, Al King had managed to slip out the kitchen window and jump onto the street, shouting for help. At this, the gangsters abruptly withdrew, plunging the room into long minutes of hysterical laughter.[89]

In the aftermath of this attack, Walter and Victor bought revolvers, practiced shooting with their wives at an out-of-town firing range, and for a brief time had union bodyguards assigned to their homes. In exchange for cash from Local 174, an informer soon supplied Reuther with the names of his assailants, who were easily identified in a police lineup. But the trial in September proved a farce. The prosecution offered no motive for the crime, and the well-paid lawyer who defended the gunmen claimed that Reuther had arranged with Holt to stage a sham battle that might help advance the West Side union leader's fortunes in the

UAW. Much testimony was given as to whether or not Reuther and George Edwards had met Holt before the night of the attack; although Reuther denied any acquaintance with Holt, it seems probable that he had been in the same room with him during one of the UAW's several negotiating sessions with Gillespie. Ford lawyers again took pains to point out Reuther's radical background, as well as that of the other Socialists present in the apartment. Holt and Percelli were acquitted, although it seems certain they were gun thugs working for Harry Bennett.[90]

Long before the bizarre story ran its course, Reuther had begun putting together a comprehensive program by which the UAW could capitalize upon the energy mobilized during the Federal Screw strike to take "wage, hours, and working conditions out of the sphere of industrial competition." In a twelve-page report to the UAW executive board, Reuther offered a strategic analysis of the auto parts industry, the character of interfirm competition, and the organizing strategy the UAW had to adopt to avoid a crisis. The task at hand was therefore clear: hundreds of nonunion "competitive" plants had to be organized and their wages raised to the Detroit standard. Local 174 could not accomplish this job alone; thus, Reuther argued for a national "Competitive Shops Department" to begin the work.

Here was the kernel of the first of the series of "Reuther Plans" that would follow: a carefully conceived program that dissected the contradictory character of contemporary capitalism and then offered a practical union program to reorganize and rationalize, if not the whole system, then at least a significant and well-defined slice of it. And like so many of Reuther's plans over the next two decades, this initiative had a decidedly political bite: "There has been much talk of the necessity for stabilizing the union," Reuther chided Martin and his antiradical allies, "often without recognizing that stabilization is impossible without completing the job of organizing the unorganized plants." A purely defensive posture undermined "the union spirit," argued Reuther, but "we can conduct successful strikes now and conclude successful new agreements with wage increases. . . . It is being done."[91]

But a reconstruction of the UAW would not be so easy. In Local 174 Reuther had proven himself an exceptional unionist whose hard work and carefully modulated leadership made the West Side organization one of the most solid in the UAW, even though the local had to contend with more than its share of unemployment, political factionalism, and management hostility. But a well-led local hardly represented the limits of Walter Reuther's political vision or personal ambition. He would soon demonstrate the expansive character of both as he grappled with the near-collapse of the UAW in the months that followed its stunning emergence as a national institution.

6

GENERAL MOTORS AND GENERAL MAYHEM

The whole trouble in the UAW is that it is too democratic. Thus, it can't be controlled by its leaders. They are out in front and the mob, led by the belligerent minority of radicals, are always at their heels.

—*Stephen DuBrul, GM chief economist, January 1938*

In November 1937, 282 union delegates from General Motors plants across the country met for two days in the Arabian Room of the Tuller Hotel just off Grand Circus Park. The meeting was not a festive one: the chandeliers and plush velvet of the glitzy ballroom seemed to mock the spirit of the hard-driving UAW activists. Long gone was the euphoric mood of February and March 1937. In its place, the unionists felt only anger, confusion, and a sense of betrayal. General Motors had the whip hand again, and a bitterly divided union seemed unable to respond. Less than ten months after the UAW's famous victory, plant managers had begun to fire union activists and lay off thousands of workers. "The fighting spirit in the union is down low," admitted Walter Reuther, expressing a sentiment that no one bothered to contest. "The important task that we face is to reestablish ourselves with General Motors on the same sort of relationship we had back there during the strike period. We have to make them realize that we still have some fight in the old Union."[1]

It would not be an easy task, and things would get a lot worse before the UAW turned itself around. The union still boasted 350,000 members, but it stood at the edge of an organizational abyss. During the next eighteen months the UAW would split into two warring factions, lose many of its collective bargaining contracts, and relinquish the loyalty of tens of thousands of its members. This debacle had several sources: ideological combat, ethnocultural conflict, personal ambition, and the sharp economic falloff known as the Roosevelt recession. But at the root of most of the UAW's troubles was General Motors—"the corporation"—whose contest with the new union over the shape and meaning of the new industrial democracy would have consequences as far-reaching and politically significant as the Flint sit-down strike.

In 1938 *Fortune* magazine called General Motors "the world's most influential industrial unit in forming the life patterns of the machine age." With 110 manufacturing and assembly plants scattered through 14 states and 18 foreign countries, with 250,000 employees and 400,000 stockholders, General Motors was "the perfect exemplar of how and why American business is Big. Every way you can measure it, the business of General Motors is not big but colossal." The company built two million cars each year, twice as many as Ford and Chrysler combined. And GM did more than build automobiles: it was the largest producer of locomotives and buses in the country, a major home appliance manufacturer, a partner in two California aircraft firms, and a giant finance company. GM turned a profit during every year of the Great Depression, and despite the sit-down strikes of early 1937, the corporation would build more cars and make more money in that turbulent year than in any since 1928.[2]

But General Motors was more than simply big. Under the leadership of the austere Alfred Sloan, General Motors saw itself as a model of bureaucratic rationality. Ownership at General Motors was highly concentrated, far more than in most heavy industry firms (Ford being the most proximate and visible exception). The DuPonts owned about one-quarter of all GM stock; Sloan and the other top managers held 10 percent more. GM executives were therefore rich, but equally important, because they feared neither their shareholders nor their competitors, top managers were given the freedom to plan the corporation's investment strategy, capital requirements, and production targets almost a decade ahead. Roaring past the archaic Ford organization in the late 1920s, Sloan and the DuPonts looked beyond the business cycle, including the Great Depression, to project a set of price and production guideposts (a 20 percent return on investment, a 40 percent market share) that transcended the market itself. GM executives were rhetorical partisans of competitive capitalism, of course, and in the mid-1930s several contributed handsomely to the reactionary Liberty League, a DuPont political front. CIO political objectives, reported Sloan to his stockholders, meant "the economic and political slavery of the worker, and an important step toward an economic and political dictatorship."[3] Yet General Motors was a remarkably successful planning bureaucracy in which market fluctuations were displaced almost entirely onto the production workforce. Thus, when the 1938 recession cut auto sales in half, GM kept its price schedule intact and its dividend substantial. But the firm immediately slashed production and employment, so that by April 1938 plants like Ternstedt were down to 20 percent of their summer payroll.[4]

GM's key innovation was the "standard volume" concept, first developed in the early 1920s by Donaldson Brown, a DuPont in-law and GM vice president. Brown generated a set of accounting devices that measured unit costs not in terms of the corporation's episodically shifting sales but according to a standard volume of production spread over the entire business cycle. This accounting method gave top management the tools to measure the relative efficiency of its autonomous divisions and their individual production units, an assessment that was essential to Alfred Sloan's celebrated deployment of a functionally decentralized management system at General Motors. Each division manager submitted monthly reports to the General Office, and that data, forwarded in a standardized format, helped determine the rate of return on investment for the division and any needed corrective action. Peter Drucker would soon declare Sloan's system "not a mere technique of management but an outline of a social order."[5]

Corporation publicists claimed, "We exploit tools, not men." In fact, GM did pay the high wages characteristic of the automobile industry, and the corporation did pour huge sums into the purchase and deployment of new production technologies. Yet because automobile manufacturing was one of the nation's more labor-intensive industries, right up there with textiles and lumber, efficient production required close and continuous supervision of the work process. GM managers therefore understood that their own career prospects required the reduction of unit labor costs to the lowest possible level, regardless of whether output levels were high or low. It was said of GM President William Knudsen, the Ford production chief Sloan had recruited in the 1920s, that he knew how to shout "Hurry up!" in fifteen languages.[6]

Alfred Sloan's labor relations system proved Janus-faced. Individual plant managers were expected to exploit any and all advantages inherent in their local labor market, but when faced with a specific set of union demands, they immediately deferred to GM headquarters in Detroit, especially after 1938, when Sloan established a new Industrial Relations Department to regulate local negotiations and systematize long-term personnel planning. Here the sheer size of the corporation offered enormous advantages. Unlike Ford and Chrysler, which had concentrated more than half of their manufacturing resources in one large facility (the Rouge and Dodge Main in Hamtramck), GM retained the flexibility to decentralize its production facilities in order to make them less vulnerable to union pressure tactics. As a result of the strikes the company faced in the mid-1930s, first at Toledo and then at Flint, it became GM policy to ensure that the company had at least three sources of supply for every component it needed. As Chairman Alfred Sloan put it just after the 1935 Toledo Chevrolet strike caught GM "napping," the corporation would "place itself in a position so that interruption of production at one plant manufacturing vital parts will not affect the continued operation of other plants."[7] For every GM production facility in which the UAW had a strong foothold, the corporation built, expanded, or retooled another factory making identical parts. Thus GM transferred much of Toledo's capacity to build transmissions to factories in Saginaw, Michigan, and Muncie, Indiana; built a new plant to assemble Buicks, Oldsmobiles, and Pontiacs in South Gate, California, near union-free Los Angeles; duplicated Fisher Body stamping capacity in Cleveland with a new facility in Grand Rapids; added foundries in Tonawanda, New York, and Pontiac, Michigan, to the Chevrolet gear and axle capacity in Detroit; and built a new Ternstedt parts factory in New Jersey, thus cutting into the strategic importance of the large complex that Local 174 would organize on the West Side of Detroit. Even the Roosevelt recession did not slow the pace: GM opened five new plants in 1938 alone.[8]

The sit-down strikes came as a shock. As Alfred Sloan put it in his autobiography, written some twenty years later, "Our rights to determine production schedules, to set work standards, and to discipline workers were all suddenly called into question."[9] A social revolution was at work in dozens of GM factories, an insurrection whose spirit and tactics almost overwhelmed GM's multilayered defenses. Thousands of workers signed union cards after the February 11 agreement; the UAW organizer Robert Travis reported from Flint: "Everybody wants to talk. Leaders are popping up everywhere. One of the healthiest situations I have ever seen." Sometimes highly political, more often merely popular, the new union activists collected the dues, attended the union meetings, and linked, on a daily, intimate basis, the world of the shop with the life of the union and the realm of a larger politics. "GM was not supposed to recognize stewards," remembered Ted La Duke, who worked at Chevrolet No. 9 in Flint, "but they did and they bargained with them." With solid backing from their workmates, stewards took shop grievances directly to the foreman and frequently resolved them on the spot. "With the coming of the union, the foreman finds the whole world turned upside down," declared a union guide for the new shop stewards. "His small-time dictatorship has been overthrown, and he must be adjusted to a democratic system of shop government."[10]

In Flint the union had become a genuine mass movement, enrolling more than forty thousand workers in a single local union—No. 156—that represented not only five GM factories but also dozens of smaller enterprises, including the employees of dime stores, hotels, restaurants, and the city bus system. The UAW had suddenly replaced GM as the hegemonic institution within the working class. There were meetings every night, a huge union sports program, and the political mobilization of thousands of workers throughout Genesee County.[11] Workers and supervisors fought constantly throughout the spring and summer of 1937, the former to consolidate and expand their shop-floor power, the latter to defend management authority and retake lost terrain. GM locals denounced the company for "chiseling," for "provocations," for "undermining the union." Activists campaigned to force recalcitrant workers and dues "freeloaders" into joining up and paying up. When faced with opposition of a determined sort, "accidents" were arranged or brief stoppages instigated. Every element of the shop-floor work regime seemed up for grabs: wages, of course, but also the pace of production, the power of the shop stewards, the meaning of seniority, even the deference due company foremen outside the factory gates. GM naturally claimed that the UAW broke the contract with a series of slowdowns and wildcat strikes, of which the company counted 170 between February and June 1937.[12]

GM must have been particularly alarmed that work stoppages and confrontations had become commonplace at the factories that had remained placid during the sit-down strikes of January and February. This was the case at the big Ternstedt complex on the West Side of Detroit, where thousands of Polish, Hungarian, and Appalachian women joined the UAW in March and April. Because plant management remained contemptuous and hostile, and the union infrastructure too fragile for a strike, Stanley Nowak got Reuther's blessing for a factorywide slowdown in which employees cranked down their output over several days. With 80 percent of all workers participating, Ternstedt shop stewards soon exercised effective command of their departments; indeed, this industrial action proved the psychologically decisive event that demonstrated the union's authority to workers and supervisors alike. Serious negotiations began on April 12, leading to union recognition and the abolition of piecework. When the difficult transition to hourly rates generated an impasse two months later, the Ternstedt unionists were strong enough to put up a massive picket line and close the factory for eight days.[13]

Radicals like Reuther and Nowak posed a serious challenge, but GM regained its bearings with remarkable speed. As long as the UAW seemed to hold together as a working institution, the company would bargain with it; however, GM officials were convinced that they could deal with the UAW only if they regained substantial control of the shop-floor work environment. Plant managers therefore made it clear that they were willing to "take a strike" when faced with demands from shop stewards and committeemen that seemed to threaten what the company considered its vital interests in controlling the pace of production and the maintenance of shop discipline. The precise delineation of GM's hard line would take a few years to work out, but the corporation had the production resources to make its policy stick. The contrast with Chrysler is instructive. Managers there were as tough-minded and ideologically hostile to trade unionism as those at GM. However, the smaller firm's essential manufacturing capacity was concentrated at Dodge Main, so foremen and superintendents found themselves whipsawed by departmental shutdowns whose ripple effects could cripple the entire firm's production. Thus shop stewards at Dodge Main and other Chrysler factories came to exercise far more authority than those in any GM facility. Chrysler executives hated this system of "dual power," but for the time being they were stuck with it.[14]

To avoid Chrysler's fate, GM executives relied upon the loyalty of more than ten thousand first-line supervisors. They were the "noncommissioned officers" upon whom the corporation depended for the maintenance of "discipline" on the shop floor. Their loyalty to the Sloan organization might not seem surprising, given the corporation's repeated assertions that foremen were part of "the management team," but under the pervasive social and organizational pressure generated by the CIO's newly empowered workers, low-level supervisors often defected to the union, either by actually joining the new UAW locals or, even more frequently, by reaching their own private accommodation with local union officials and shop representatives.

GM was acutely sensitive to such disloyalty. In 1934 it took the unusual step of putting these supervisors on salary, thereafter ensuring that foremen earned at least 25 percent more than their best-paid subordinates. The General Motors Institute, which the corporation established as a sort of technical college and personnel department, enrolled more than five thousand foremen in its classes, where they were indoctrinated into GM's "tough but fair" version of the new "human relations" ideology propagated by psychologists like Elton Mayo, fresh from his pioneering industrial relations experiments at Western Electric's Hawthorne works near Chicago.[15] To sustain the authority and allegiance of their foremen, GM officials were determined to shield them from the intimate, hourly shop-floor contact with union activists that almost inevitably spelled demoralization in such turbulent times. The corporation therefore refused, even in its contract talks of March and April 1937, to recognize the legitimacy of UAW shop stewards, insisting instead that management would process grievances only through the far less threatening "committeeman" system. The difference was decisive: where shop stewards were given de facto recognition, as at Chrysler, a foreman confronted a working steward who might represent the same twenty or thirty workers the foreman supervised. But under the GM system, union representation was limited to about one committeeman for each four hundred hourly rated employees. Moreover, workers were first required to discuss their problem with the foreman before bringing it to the attention of the committeeman, whose hours as a union functionary were limited to twenty per week. Reuther found the committeeman setup a "distinct advance" over preunion conditions, but no substitute for the steward system, "which is imperative in the plants if true collective bargaining is to be attained."[16]

From GM's point of view, this system worked. The corporation succeeded in retaining the loyalty of its foremen, certainly to a far greater degree than did top management at Chrysler, Ford, Packard, Kelsey-Hayes, and Hudson, where foremen sought to organize their own trade unions in the late 1930s and early 1940s. As one Ternstedt supervisor put it, with consummate belligerency: "I'm a foreman, and I doubt if there's a man in the shop what would put out a hand to save me from drowning. I have stuck with the company through two strikes. People still call me a SCAB . . . but I would still have the company for my friend than you guys."[17] Moreover, the corporation came to understand that the interests of the UAW's top leaders and of its constituent units were not always identical. Before the sit-down strikes, General Motors had sought to avoid negotiating with "outside" unionists, whom it saw as a well-connected group of interlopers motivated by either left-wing ideology or the most cynical kind of business unionism. But once GM had signed with the union, it sought to turn UAW officials into allies in its effort to maintain control of the production process. After all, the agreement that ended the sit-downs implied that, in return for union recognition, the UAW leaders who signed the contract would get the men back to work. Thus GM executives insisted that the national officers of the UAW work to end slowdowns, wildcat strikes, and other disruptions of what the company defined as an orderly production regime. "The whole trouble in the UAW is that it is too democratic," asserted Stephen DuBrul, the corporation's chief economist, in a moment of frustration. "Thus, it can't be controlled by its leaders. They are out in front and the mob, led by the belligerent minority of radicals, are always at their heels."[18]

A well-orchestrated backlash against the CIO strengthened the company's hand early in the spring of 1937. The sit-down strikes that winter had come during the very season when President Roosevelt had placed his ill-fated Supreme Court–packing plan before the U.S. Senate. To many, and not only the Republican old guard, both actions seemed to be assaults on the social order and property rights. Such fears and resentments exploded on the floor of the Senate on April 1 when both Democrats and Republicans denounced the CIO and its sit-down tactic. The very next day General Motors issued its own blast at the continuing series of UAW work stoppages, ominously declaring that "agreements not lived up to are no agreements."[19]

There followed an uneasy truce as the actual number of strikes and sit-downs declined, both nationally and in the auto industry. But the political assault against the CIO resumed two months later as tensions over the violent Little Steel strike generated the kind of polarization that mobilized all those uneasy with this new social force. In quick secession, three events put the UAW on the defensive in Michigan. On June 7 a strike in an auto plant near Lansing escalated into a city-wide "Labor Holiday" after the local sheriff arrested union leaders in a 2:00 A.M. raid. Thousands of workers swarmed downtown, blocking traffic and occupying municipal buildings. Two days later UAW-organized workers went on strike at Consumers Power Company, which cut off electricity for a few hours to nearly half a million people in the Saginaw Valley. And shortly thereafter, a strike in a steel mill at Monroe, fifty miles south of Detroit, turned violent when management reopened the plant. UAW flying squadrons from Pontiac, Dodge, and the West Side rushed to the scene, generating a series of well-publicized clashes with local vigilantes.

The events of early June sent a wave of anxiety surging through the political and financial elite of mid-America, and the conflicts stimulated the formation of law and order leagues in several cities to support local police departments. "When the state's capital is taken over, power lines are shut off and streets are barricaded," a Michigan business journal declared, "there is an approach to anarchy which honest citizens cannot stomach." Nor were such sentiments confined to employer circles. Reporters who revisited Flint in the late spring of 1937 were far more skeptical of the union viewpoint than they had been during the winter sit-down. Indeed, influential newspapermen like William Lawrence of *U.S. News* and Louis Stark of the *New York Times* began to highlight GM claims that the recurrent wildcat strikes were evidence of endemic irresponsibility and radicalism in the union leadership.[20]

Such accusations stung, so that union leaders of virtually every political persuasion sought to accommodate GM's demand for greater stability at the point of production. At the top, CIO President John L. Lewis feared that even if the UAW did not self-destruct, the example set by the feisty union would damage his efforts to extend organization into steel, meatpacking, textiles, and aircraft. Thus Lewis had insisted that tens of thousands of Chrysler strikers evacuate their plants for a contract no better than that at General Motors, and in a Detroit speech of April 7 he both saluted UAW militancy and warned unionists that "your union has given its pledge that during the life of this agreement there will be no stoppages of any kind. . . . That means sit-down, stand up, walk out or stay in."[21] Adolph Germer, Lewis's man in Detroit, kept the pressure on during the next few months. "Frankly, it is a hell-of-a-mess," he wrote his boss. "Every CIO rep is looked upon as a walking strike and this epidemic is going to make it difficult to organize other industries, particularly in the south."[22]

Union radicals endorsed Lewis's efforts to regularize UAW bargaining. Vice President Wyndham Mortimer, the UAW's leading Communist, negotiated an agreement with General Motors just a month after the end of the Flint strike that left unrecognized the dense system of shop stewards that had arisen in most GM shops. When problems arose, Mortimer cautioned, "sit-down strikes should be resorted to only when absolutely necessary."[23] Reuther agreed. He still believed a vigorous shop steward system was essential to the growth of in-plant "workers' councils," which would constitute a giant step toward the vision of "industrial democracy" that had been such a staple of SP propaganda since his father's time. But Reuther and his Socialist comrades supported the Lewis policy because so much seemed at stake; thus, Reuther was among those who persuaded a conference of GM workers to accept Mortimer's disappointing contract with GM. Reuther thought it was important simply to get the union in the door at GM; with tens of thousands of workers pouring into the UAW, the formal language of any agreement seemed far less important than a signed contract that legitimized a union presence in the shops.[24] Moreover, neither Socialists nor Communists in the union leadership wanted to instigate a fight that might antagonize John L. Lewis or give their new union a reputation for irresponsibility and politically damaging radicalism. As Reuther put it in the summer of 1937, after the issue of wildcat strikes at GM had embroiled the union leadership in bitter controversy: "We want a disciplined organization. We believe that in a union, as in an army, discipline is of first rate importance. There can be no question of that whatsoever."[25]

The contest with General Motors was bound to generate tensions within the UAW, regardless of who held the union presidency, but the occupation of the top spot by Homer Martin ensured that the political infighting would take place in the most self-destructive fashion. As the sit-down strikes began to ebb in the spring of 1937, a "right-wing" UAW faction crystallized under Martin's mercurial leadership. Motivated by both a visceral anti-Communism and a search for some kind of accommodation with General Motors, his "Progressive Caucus" soon dominated the UAW executive board and waged war upon union radicals. In response, Reuther, Mortimer, and other leftists pulled together their own "Unity Caucus," which defended the cadre who had built the UAW and opposed GM's effort to push back union power on the shop floor. Both of these union factions were highly unstable, mirroring the UAW's larger failure to win from either employers or workers the recognition and loyalty it so desperately sought. By 1939, when top CIO leaders rescued the auto union from its own fratricide, Walter Reuther had broken with his old comrades and replaced Homer Martin as the most prominent of the UAW anti-Communists.

Like so many activists in the Depression-era industrial unions, Homer Martin's place in the lower-middle class vanished during the great slump. Martin spent the 1920s in rural Missouri, preaching in small Baptist churches, teaching high school, and attending college, where he was a national "hop, skip, and jump" champion. After seminary study in Kansas City, Martin assumed the pastorate of a nearby Baptist church in 1931, but his increasingly radical sermons, which combined populist attacks on big business with a revival of social gospel themes, antagonized some of his parishioners, who forced him out of the pulpit. He immediately took a job in the Kansas City Chevrolet plant, helped form a federal labor union there, and became its president. He lost his job in 1934, but his self-confidence and oratorical talents soon made him part of the UAW's early leadership circle.[26]

A well-dressed man of medium height, with blue eyes and perfect teeth, Martin cut an impressive figure at the pulpit or podium. His speeches were full of biblical imagery, moral exhortation, and instructive humor. "No other man could pierce the hearts of Southern-born workers as he could," wrote B. J. Widick, then an organizer of rubber workers in Akron. "He made men feel that in organizing a union they were going forth to battle for righteousness and the word of God."[27] But Martin was an utter failure at all the tasks essential to the everyday work of a trade union. To both his friends and enemies, Martin was impulsive and vindictive: he failed to keep appointments, disappeared in the midst of important meetings, and used his fists when words failed to persuade. During the last, crucial days of the GM strike, John L. Lewis sent him on a speaking tour just to get him out of Flint. Among rank-and-file autoworkers who were the beneficiaries of his far-flung and frequent speeches, Martin's popularity soared, but in Detroit and Flint he quickly lost influence to the sophisticated politicos who were building lusty union locals from the ground up. "He was a lamb among some very tough wolves," remarked Stewart Strachan, one of Martin's few politically adept supporters in Local 174. Soon Martin came to see the radicals as opponents, even as conspirators, with whom he could not avoid a showdown.[28]

Martin's combativeness reflected much personal instability, but he also took skillful advantage of the sociocultural fissures that the emergence of the industrial union movement had opened within America's class structure. On one side — often Martin's side — stood the Protestant lower middle class and the old labor aristocracy of northern European descent. These men and women had a substantial stake in the old order, be it the comfortable politics of a small midwestern town or the chance to climb a few steps higher within the workplace hierarchy. Through the Masons, the Knights of Columbus, the evangelical churches, through kinship and friendship, they had forged a hundred and one social and cultural links with those more solidly bourgeois. In the early 1930s, when the whole social structure seemed on the verge of collapse, these plebeian elites had swung into the ambit of corporatist radicals like Huey Long, Upton Sinclair, and Father Coughlin. Desperate and insecure, thousands also flocked to the banner of the new unions and the CIO, which they saw as the vehicle that would sustain their status and dignity in turbulent times.

But the industrial unions also mobilized, organized, and gave voice to that huge strata who had stood just below, or just outside, the social structures the factory elite saw as their own. The CIO made shop-floor citizens of eastern European Catholics, African-Americans, French-Canadians, and migratory Appalachians whose relationship to the old German- and Irish-American elite had been one of deference and subordination. Moreover, the CIO, with its leaven of radical Jews and anticlerical Catholics, its rationalizing, modernizing, and cosmopolitan outlook, threatened the lifetime of social capital and ethnic privilege built up by those whose outlooks were more parochial and insular. No wonder that the late 1930s saw a recrudescence of right-wing agitation and red-baiting wherever the new unions disrupted the old order. Thus the terroristic Black Legion flourished in Pontiac and Flint and the KKK at Packard and at assembly plants in Indiana, Missouri, and Texas. Company-sponsored vigilante groups were at work in California agribusiness and in the industrial towns of upstate New York and New England. It is hardly surprising, therefore, that Homer Martin had come to share and shape the more general transformation of Protestant, evangelical radicalism into an equally adamant, anti-Communist, sometimes anti-Semitic impulse that characterized so much of American cultural politics in the late 1930s.[29]

Had the UAW been less spectacularly successful, the influence of the union radicals, in the shops and on the executive board, would certainly have remained paramount, but the overnight influx of three hundred thousand new workers, and the patronage jobs their dues supported, gave Martin and his allies a chance to deploy their politics on a far broader scale. This opportunity was taken explicitly in June 1937 when Richard Frankensteen and Russell Merrill organized UAW antiradicals into the Progressive Caucus. Under Father Coughlin's tutelage, Frankensteen had presided over the transformation of the Dodge Main company union into UAW Local 3, but he was alarmed at how rapidly shop radicalism seemed to get out of control once the Chrysler sit-down had come to an end. Likewise, Russell Merrill, a founder of the Studebaker local, thought the UAW of the sit-down strikes a "red outfit," quite alien to the world of South Bend, Indiana. There UAW Local 5 had established an orderly bargaining relationship with Studebaker, a former wagon maker that smoothly accommodated a tradition of managerial paternalism to the language and structures of the new industrial unionism.[30]

With this kind of backing, Martin moved against the radicals: Roy Reuther, Henry Kraus, and Robert Travis were taken off the International payroll; Victor Reuther was transferred out of Detroit; Frank Winn and Merlin Bishop were demoted and then fired. Martin would have gotten rid of Walter Reuther too if he had not been an elected board member. The UAW president thought Reuther a cocky, sharp-tongued radical; when Walter complained at one 1937 meeting about Martin's high-handed ways, the heated exchange quickly turned into a fight. "He rushed at me like a mad bull," remembered Reuther a few months later. "I ducked and picked him up and threw him over my shoulder. He was kicking his feet and pounding on my back." Once Martin had been pulled away, Reuther quipped, "I'm very new at this and don't know much about parliamentary procedure, but isn't it customary for the chairman to use the gavel instead of his fist?"[31]

Martin could war against Reuther and his comrades, but if he were to consolidate his control of the union, he needed a cohort of ideologically motivated functionaries who could deploy the language of industrial unionism to advance his fortunes. Like so many of the new unions, the UAW had yet to generate its own set of trade union intellectuals who could link the micropolitics of the shop-floor struggle with the programmatic thrust of the top officialdom. Martin soon found such help in New York City, among the men and women of the Communist Party Opposition (CPO), Jay Lovestone's political sect. By 1937 Lovestone was a man of near-legendary guile. He had been ousted as secretary of the American Communist Party in 1929, charged by Stalin himself with "right-wing" deviationism during the Comintern's shift into its ultraradical Third Period phase. Almost immediately he formed his own political group, whose raison d'être was, of course, warfare against what he once called the American "lackeys of the gangster Stalin clique." In the New York needle trades Lovestone worked cooperatively with the Old Guard Socialists, including David Dubinsky of the International Ladies' Garment Workers Union (ILGWU), who played a key role in recruiting the dozen or so Lovestoneite staffers who came to work for Martin in 1937.[32]

With Homer Martin and John L. Lewis, the Lovestoneites favored a policy of accommodation with General Motors. Because of their hostility to the Popular Front and the Roosevelt New Deal, Lovestone and his followers had little faith in the possibility that the state could play a role in either reviving the economy or defending the unions, an outlook seemingly confirmed by the mass layoffs that swept the newly organized industries during the Roosevelt recession of late 1937. This belief generated a self-limiting assessment of what could be accomplished, either through a mobilization of the rank and file or in negotiations with the auto companies—above all, with General Motors. The Lovestoneites championed

Lewis's effort to conciliate the giant corporation and impose a measure of discipline on shop-floor militants.[33]

In response to the Martin-Lovestone offensive, most of the UAW radicals organized the oppositional Unity Caucus early in the summer of 1937. Reuther thought "90% of unauthorized strikes were provoked by the company," not undisciplined UAW radicals. The Lovestoneites were therefore "playing a treacherous game," thought Reuther, while Homer Martin was more often simply inept and inconsistent. Reuther wanted John L. Lewis to take a larger hand in the UAW's affairs. "I went down the line on Martin in the presence of Lewis on the question of incompetency and irresponsibility," he wrote from Washington late in April 1937. "Martin came back at me with the red scare and so the session ended as usual. . . . We shall pound away some more tomorrow."[34]

In this fight Walter Reuther again worked closely with the UAW Communists. His most important comrade was Wyndham Mortimer, a steadfast organizer and union strategist who was part of the same generation as John L. Lewis, a fact that may account for the CIO chief's confidence in him despite his clear membership in the Communist camp. Reuther looked to Mortimer as something of a mentor, and the two shared an occasional intimacy during their long car trips to distant cities, as when Reuther told "Mort" that he missed May "terribly," to which the older man laughingly replied, "Wait until you are 50, then you won't mind."[35] On the UAW left, Mortimer commanded enormous respect, but Reuther thought him "extremely modest," someone who "does not talk enough." His close relationship with Mortimer opened the way for Reuther to become Unity's chief spokesman, a role for which he had both Communist approval and the appropriate flair.[36]

Reuther and his comrades worked to stop Martin from making good on his promises to clean out the "reds." Indeed, Martin's intentions provided the name for the caucus, for the union radicals proposed that when the UAW met for its first big convention in Milwaukee, the delegates reelect, in the spirit of "unity," all the UAW's top officers, whatever their politics. "Unity means cutting out all political maneuvering and conniving," explained Reuther at one of his own caucus meetings. "There is but one test of leadership—that is, merit, experience and competency." This comment on leadership would become a familiar theme, but it was not mere rhetoric, for Unity partisans were convinced that if they could reach an accommodation with Martin, their talent and energy would prove decisive, especially if they could then eliminate the influence of the Lovestoneites. Twice Reuther and a Unity delegation traveled to Progressive Caucus meetings, and twice they were rebuffed. "We do not want a dogfight," reported Reuther in an exasperated moment. "We do not want name calling. . . . Red baiting is a crime. . . . We want a sincere and honest discussion of our problems and a meeting together." But Martin's partisans were not interested; they looked forward to a showdown in which they would sweep their opponents from union office. "It would be healthy to have a fight in the Union," one CPO activist told Reuther.[37]

The stage was thus set for a tumultuous convention in Milwaukee late in August

1937. The West Side local chartered several railroad passenger cars to speed some ninety-five voting delegates on their way to Wisconsin. There they met more than one thousand other wide-eyed unionists, some staying in a hotel for the first time in their lives. "Most of the delegates were 'rank and file' members," reported the *New York Times* labor reporter Louis Stark with a certain alarm. "They were excited, argued heatedly, and waves of emotion ran through the meeting mounting to turbulence."[38] Hundreds of delegates, not to mention the tens of thousands of workers who had elected them, were bringing into the UAW the political passions and social prejudices of a working class largely untutored in union politics. This was Homer Martin's natural constituency. As Henry Kraus, Mortimer's journalist friend, noted when he first stepped into the packed lobby of the convention hotel, "They were all unknown to us and we felt that this was no longer 'our UAW' but a mass of strangers."[39]

Martin seemed poised for a thoroughgoing purge of his opponents when the Unity forces were rescued by the dramatic appearance of John L. Lewis, who took the podium on August 25. The hall erupted in a guileless celebration of the man who had so magnificently backed the sit-downers at Flint eight months before, the man whose spellbinding voice and substantial presence symbolized CIO power and self-confidence. To Reuther and other UAW activists, Lewis stood above the factional squabble, not because he did not take sides—he did—but because his authority so transcended that of virtually any combination of his foes and friends. Near the height of his power and prestige, Lewis offered autoworkers a vision of themselves in "one great union ... marching with the other militant mass of American workmen under the farflung banners of the CIO." His advice could hardly be ignored.[40]

Lewis wanted the UAW to achieve stability as quickly as possible; indeed, he favored a strong, even autocratic union executive, and he was willing to give General Motors just about whatever it wanted in order to win a renewal of the old contract. To this end, Lewis had sent W. Jett Lauck, his most trusted economic adviser, to Detroit to guide the UAW in its recurrent negotiations with GM. But Lewis could also see that the UAW was too evenly divided for the kind of factional purge Martin had in mind; the press was having a field day reporting the disarray into which the convention had fallen, and the auto corporations were certainly taking note as well. So it was with enormous relief that Reuther and his partisans listened to the CIO president denounce "political rivalry" and then, in effect, call for the reelection of Reuther, Mortimer, and other radicals to the union's executive board. The formation of the UAW was one of labor's "most outstanding accomplishments," intoned John L. Lewis, ". . . and I think that the officers . . . who led you throughout that enterprise and to that objective of success are deserving of your commendation." Martin could not resist the CIO chieftain, not yet anyway, so the Unity Caucus retained its influence in the UAW's high councils, though the Progressive Caucus did get the Chrysler unionists, Richard Frankensteen and R. J. Thomas, as two additional vice presidents. The new executive board would have sixteen from the Progressive group and eight from Unity.[41]

To maintain the fragile equilibrium, Reuther demanded of himself and his comrades a characteristic self-discipline. The Progressive Caucus had challenged the credentials of eight Unity delegates from Flint, who swung enough votes to put Roy Reuther on the new executive board. Martin's people kept their fate off the agenda until the very last hours of the convention. When the Unity floor leader George Edwards finally made his case for the legitimacy of these delegates, Martin ruled the subsequent, chaotic voice vote a Progressive Caucus victory. Martin then denied Reuther the floor, after which Unity delegates leaped to their feet and onto the tables, chanting, "We want Reuther! We want Reuther!" The factional compromise forged by John L. Lewis seemed ready to collapse in a brawl.[42]

But the radicals kept their heads. First, Wyndham Mortimer and then George Addes pleaded with their supporters to act as "sane, sensible people," in the interests of "harmony and unity." Then the thirty-year-old West Side leader mounted the platform and addressed the assemblage in what was practically the first quiet moment since the session had opened. Reuther had intended to argue the Unity position on the credentials dispute, and he still maintained that the Progressive Caucus had made the Flint delegates an issue in order to steal an additional executive board vote. But the fate of the union hung in the balance. "It was just an invitation to disaster," he recalled years later. "I got up there and I looked around and said to myself, 'My God, if I make the speech I came up here to make, the blood is going to be running in the streets.'" Urged Reuther, "The only thing to do is to accept this under protest. Let's accept it and settle down and go back to build this union."[43]

Martin smashed the Milwaukee truce within a month. Throughout the summer General Motors had demanded, as a prerequisite to renegotiation of its first contract, a clear statement from the union granting the corporation unilateral authority to discipline those participating in slowdowns or wildcat strikes. On September 16 Martin shocked Unity leaders by conceding the point. He wrote to GM's William Knudsen that "the corporation will be allowed to discharge, or otherwise discipline, union members known to be or found guilty of instigating unauthorized strikes." The UAW president also committed the union itself to taking "effective disciplinary action" against those GM targeted as wildcat strike agitators. Martin backed up this coup with a new purge of UAW organizers and staff. This time the victims included Victor Reuther, Robert Kanter, and Stanley Nowak. Richard Frankensteen pushed Walter Reuther out of the Ford organizing drive, and Martin sought editorial control of all the UAW's local newspapers, including the *West Side Conveyor*.[44]

Local 174 proved the center of resistance to Martin's new offensive. Conflict began in a sensational fashion on September 30, when a West Side delegation of unionists seeking an audience with the UAW president were turned away at his office door by Homer Martin himself, who greeted them with a pistol pointed straight at the stomach of Daniel Gallagher, chairman of Timkin's shop committee. The UAW president's claim that "hoodlums" had attacked him made the front pages of the Detroit papers. But Local 174's side of the story soon proved more credible. Carl Haessler put out a long rebuttal that was mailed to every local in the UAW, and Walter Reuther, who now concluded that the Unity group had to defend itself in a far more determined fashion, described the protest as "a spontaneous reaction of the men in the shops against the policy of the international in the recent discharge of organizers." Reuther put those Martin had fired on the Local 174 payroll and, with George Edwards, spearheaded the effort to hold a conference of all GM workers to make it clear that the rank and file was opposed to the contract Martin seemed on the verge of negotiating with General Motors.[45]

A delegated conference finally assembled after the municipal elections, when almost three hundred anxious autoworkers from more than forty GM plants took their seats at the Tuller Hotel on November 14 and 15. In the spring of 1937 West Side Socialists had been satisfied with a "foot in the door" approach to union recognition and shop steward development, but Reuther now saw that, for the sake of both union politics and UAW-GM relations, the union had to reassert its power in the GM shops. A well-developed shop steward system was essential if the UAW were to "accept responsibility for its members" and establish its "authority in the shop." As Reuther's *West Side Conveyor* put it: "So-called wildcat strikes arose because the company chiseled on the agreement. . . . A steward system with teeth in it will compel the company, and not only the union, to live up to its word."[46]

Naturally Reuther and the Local 174 Socialists also demanded repudiation of the wildcat strike letter endorsed by Homer Martin. "This clause is bad under any circumstances. . . . It leaves the active union members completely at the mercy of the corporation. . . . Democracy demands that final acceptance of the completed agreement be put up to those who have to work under it."[47] Most GM workers agreed. They wanted to codify on the shop-floor level the legal norms and procedural safeguards found in civil society; Martin's capitulation to GM seemed to legitimize a new era of shop-floor autocracy without any improvement in wages, seniority, or hours of work. The contract Martin would sign was "a crime to the working class of General Motors," announced a delegate from Chevy Gear and Axle, a big Detroit local that had earlier lined up with Martin's Progressive Caucus. Another delegate captured the outrage of workers who saw their newly won shop-floor rights at stake: "I want to ask this body of men and women here whether we, as organized people, will give the right to the company to accuse and judge, convict and sentence one of our members for an unauthorized strike. . . . Before the national [UAW] or the local, or the operators can pass sentence on any one of our members, we should be allowed as members of the organized union to give our evidence."[48]

Given such clear opposition, Martin and his Progressive stalwarts simply repudiated the contract they had spent so many months negotiating with GM, in particular their assurance that GM had the unilateral right to fire those who slowed or stopped production. Indeed, Martin told some delegates, "you are not going to have a lot of trouble getting authorization for strikes."[49] But this apparent change of heart was mere bluster. In its place Reuther wanted a plan of action that would back up the UAW in a new round of negotiations with GM. And quite characteristically, Reuther had a program neatly worked out. To "let General Motors know that we are building up a fighting spirit," Reuther proposed a massive publicity campaign against the giant corporation: a weekly bulletin, demonstrations, and another conference in thirty days, "ready to take action if need be." The time was ripe for such calibrated militancy: "If the plants in Flint, Pontiac, Saginaw—way out in California—up in Tarrytown, New York—if every one of those plants went down with a bang and the workers had a meeting and we could use those two hours to collect back dues and get the weak sisters in line, let me tell you when that old switch went up again at the second hour, that Union would be a stronger Union than it was when the switch was pulled." To "put the heat on General Motors," asserted Reuther, ". . . you have to have power under control, disciplined power." Reuther's vision swept the conclave, after which hundreds of enthusiastic unionists linked arms and bodies to snake-dance out of the hotel and into the cold of Grand Circus Park.[50]

Reuther and his Unity partisans had a chance to test this new resolve almost immediately, when twenty-five hundred night-shift workers at Fisher Body in Pontiac occupied their factory. The union cadre at Pontiac had backed Martin during the summer, but since then shop conflicts—over speedups, dues payments, the authority of foremen and shop stewards—had become endemic. And Pontiac workers were infuriated that management had transferred much of their work to GM's new, nonunion facility in Linden, New Jersey, laid off 1,350 workers, and put the rest on a four-day workweek. "General Motors has cast aside all pretense of keeping any contract," editorialized the Pontiac Auto Worker.[51]

The sit-down ended within a few hours after local management agreed to negotiate layoff procedures and resolve other grievances, but GM President William Knudsen and other top corporate officials were not about to preside over a new era of labor insurgency. GM therefore dismissed four leading activists in the factory the next day, insisting that Martin's September letter gave the corporation the undisputed authority to discipline those who instigated unauthorized strikes. Pontiac unionists denounced the reprisals as "lawless company aggression" and accused the corporation of provoking wildcats by its insistence on a "terrific speedup and wholesale sabotaging of the union agreement." On November 17 about five hundred workers again occupied the Fisher Body plant, welded shut the gates, and moved in blankets and food. Their militancy was confirmed the next night by a packed, five-hour meeting of workers from all GM plants in Pontiac. Wild applause greeted those who denounced Homer Martin; more important, the sit-down strike won the endorsement of at least two thousand Pontiac unionists.[52]

The strike at Pontiac Fisher Body marked a high point in rank-and-file militancy during the formative years of the UAW. It demonstrated that layoffs, even the specter of mass unemployment, had hardly crippled the will to fight; indeed, such layoffs were but more tinder, more evidence of the crisis of legitimacy that undermined managerial authority and politicized all shop conflicts. Despite the caution of its own top leadership, CIO trade unionism had thus put powerful weapons, both ideological and collective, into the hands of workers at the point of production. As the debate and discourse at the Tuller Hotel had so passionately demonstrated, workers saw their new contract, their new grievance procedure, and their budding shop organization as a charter of rights and entitlements whose violation demanded a massive, immediate response. Given this impulse, the Pontiac strike simultaneously demonstrated the extent to which the left might yet capture the social terrain normally occupied by the right. Pontiac was a thoroughly Protestant town, a Martin stronghold, and a center of Black Legion strength and goon squad violence, which had not been absent in the early stages of the sit-down. But in this bitter conflict with the corporation, UAW militants had succeeded in mobilizing a substantial layer of the working-class community and bringing to prominence new leaders who were more congruent with the cosmopolitan radicals of Detroit in their secularism and politics. Within days Pontiac seemed on the verge of turning into another Flint.[53]

For five days the UAW executive board sat in almost continuous session. All union officers denounced GM management, but Martin and his faction proved ineffectual in their plea that Pontiac workers resume work. Only Reuther and Mortimer argued for an outright authorization of the strike, followed immediately by an orderly evacuation of the factory. Then, as part of the campaign Reuther had outlined at the Tuller Hotel, the UAW would press for the reinstatement of the local leaders GM had fired. Unity leaders warned that if GM successfully victimized these shop leaders, the corporation would inaugurate an assault upon everything the union had won in the last year.[54]

Whether it won or lost, UAW authorization of the Pontiac wildcat strike would have represented a huge gamble, a lunge toward union power and a syndicalist-flavored industrial democracy at the nation's most powerful corporation. Even at this late hour, a factory social order of the sort that had given UAW stewards dual power at Kelsey-Hayes, Midland Steel, and Dodge Main now seemed within grasp, if only there were spirits bold enough to seize it. But General Motors would have none of this. Accommodations might well be made in the routine give-and-take of shop grievance handling, but when it came to the formal powers of foremen and plant managers, when it became a question of management's prerogative to run its factory, determine production schedules, and discipline the insubordinate, GM was ready to abandon its tenuous truce with the UAW. Thus William Knudsen warned on November 18 of the grave consequences attendant upon the union's failure to immediately end the sit-down: "Irresponsibility on the part of the locals, unauthorized strikes and the defiance of union officers will eventually make agreements valueless and collective bargaining impossible in practice."[55]

John L. Lewis could not have phrased the alternatives with more precision. When told that General Motors workers had thrown out the September 16 wildcat strike letter, Lewis remarked with a studied contempt, "Will someone let them in out of the rain?"[56] Understanding that the recession was shifting the balance of class forces against the new unions, Lewis wanted to shield the CIO behind solid contracts, no matter how unfavorable. In no uncertain terms, he let Martin and the UAW executive board know that the Pontiac wildcat strike had to end. Erstwhile allies like Gov. Frank Murphy—who was fearful that strike-generated headlines were stripping away votes in the next year's election—sought to shore up support on the right by threatening to send in the militia to clear the plant of sit-downers. How the political terrain had shifted, and all in one year, 1937![57]

Reuther was again in the national spotlight, but now as a disruptive radical in league with the Communists. Beginning on Monday, November 22, Louis Stark, the influential labor reporter for the *New York Times*, published a series of UAW articles that closely followed the Martin-Lovestone line, whose anti-Communist credibility had risen, in New York if not Detroit, with every dark dispatch from Stalin's purge trials in Moscow. Stark identified opposition to the Martin administration almost entirely with Socialist and Communist elements in the union, and he asserted that "militant Socialists," including the Reuther brothers and the leadership of the West Side local, "adhere to the CP line." He concurred with Martin's charge that these "union opponents wish to foment unauthorized strikes in order to cast discredit on the chief leaders."[58]

Stark's reportage sent shock waves through left-wing circles in Detroit and New York. In the Motor City the Reuther brothers were amazed and indignant. Frank Winn wrote Stark that his attitude was "thoroughly incomprehensible. . . . The Reuther brothers do not follow the line of the Communist Party. They follow the line of the Unity caucus which they help to determine."[59] But the articles had their most dramatic impact upon the Communists. To Earl Browder and other top CP strategists, Stark's report on the Pontiac wildcat strike represented another example of how Communist cadres in the industrial hinterland threatened to sabotage the tentative trust the party had won from CIO and Democratic Party leaders on the national scene. Browder therefore personally ordered the party's auto faction to end the sit-down immediately and get Pontiac's Fisher Body plant back into operation. His dictate had the desired effect: Mortimer tempered his support for an authorized strike, and the handful of Communists in Pontiac abruptly repudiated their own leadership of the sit-down. Reuther still thought Martin's failure of nerve at Pontiac a monumental blunder, but he nevertheless voted for an executive board resolution condemning the strike in the interest of leadership unity.[60]

The Pontiac disaster inaugurated nearly eighteen months of confusion and retreat for the UAW. On the industrial front the UAW virtually abandoned its fight against GM. At Pontiac defeat was total: the four strike leaders stayed fired, the UAW put the local under a trusteeship, and union loyalty collapsed as thousands abandoned the trade union idea. Then the Roosevelt recession hit the auto industry with hurricane force. Within weeks, all thought of a coordinated campaign of industrial action and union publicity evaporated as UAW strength withered away. U.S. car production dropped by almost half between November 1937 and January 1938. One-quarter of all GM workers were laid off; even more stopped paying their dues to the UAW. On Reuther's West Side, Ternstedt membership dropped from

5,896 to 1,751 in these two months; at Cadillac the number of dues payers shrank from 2,665 to 1,209. Payrolls were slashed even more severely among the supplier plants organized by Local 174; more than half of all these workers were on short time. When no relief appeared in the spring, all organizers were cut from the Local 174 payroll.[61]

Under such conditions, even Reuther agreed that the union had no choice but to sign the unauthorized strike letter demanded by GM. The signing took place on January 17, after which Martin and a handful of his aides proceeded to negotiate and then, in March 1938, to sign a new contract with the company, "the best we can get out of the Corporation at the present time."[62] Reuther, Mortimer, and other Unity leaders labeled it a "wretched surrender to the corporation," the responsibility for which "lies not in the depression or other outside factors but in the ruinous factional policy of President Martin himself." Indeed, the agreement materially weakened the union's presence at the point of production. The new contract reduced the number of committeemen, cut from four hours to two the hours each could spend on grievance adjustment, forbade union shop stewards from collecting dues on company property, and gave Martin the right to exclude other union officers from meeting with GM factory management.[63]

It proved a huge defeat. With the Depression as their ally, GM plant managers exploited every advantage the new contract had given them. "Abuses have poured into our office," admitted William Dowell, whom Martin had plucked out of Kansas City to direct GM affairs; plant managers "would place a very narrow and technical interpretation on some clauses, thereby making them unworkable."[64] Dues revenue dropped even more sharply than the recession might have warranted, while foremen and other workers loyal to the company were put on regular production jobs. The contract proved extraordinarily unpopular, but the recession proved so devastating that strikes and job actions nearly ceased in the auto industry. "We could easily take care of the employers who want to take advantage of the fight in the UAW if times were normal," mused Reuther late in the spring of 1938. "We could pull sit-downs galore. Now that the factories are empty there isn't anything we can do."[65]

Like a revolutionary army in retreat, the collapse of the GM "front" reduced the UAW to its most ideologically committed core, thus ensuring that political factionalism would exceed even the expansive limits seen in the latter half of 1937. Real issues were at stake, but during the next several months the warfare took on a life of its own whose intensity stood in inverse proportion to the union's impotency at GM and the other corporations. With the rest of the Unity group, Reuther wanted to contain Martin and eliminate Lovestone's influence. The Communists sought to accomplish the same end by making a deal with Richard Frankensteen, the ambitious vice president to whom Martin had already turned over much of the day-to-day running of the union. Reuther never liked this gambit: Frankensteen and he were simply intense personal rivals who both sought the UAW presidency. Reuther scorned the former Dayton University football player as an opportunist, which he was, unashamedly: a fundamentally apolitical figure, Frankensteen had the bearing and ease of a popular, urban politician.[66]

All this put Reuther into difficulty and contradiction, even among his own Socialist Party comrades. By 1938 Detroit Socialists had formed themselves into two sometimes antagonistic branches. The older group comprised lawyers, social workers, and physicians who stood four-square for Socialist Party principles: independent political action, anti-imperialism, and faith in the moral and political authority of Norman Thomas. Meeting as Branch 1, these regulars applauded Homer Martin's staunch anti-Communism, as well as the support he offered the SP's own "Keep America out of War" campaign.[67] The UAW Socialists, organized into Branch 2, were torn between the all-encompassing tug of union work and their party's comradeship. They saw the Branch 1 regulars as "an impotent group of well intentioned people"; some Branch 1 comrades, on the other hand, denounced the young UAW activists for "using the Socialist Party as a training ground to promote their union careers."[68]

Walter Reuther came in for plenty of criticism, both from the older generation of party regulars and from his Branch 2 comrades in Detroit. By 1938 Reuther's West Side local was by far the Socialist Party's most important point of contact with the new industrial unions. Indeed, within liberal circles "the fabulous Reuther brothers" and their UAW comrades virtually defined Socialist trade union practice—thus the close attention, intense resentment, and continuous pressure that poured down upon them from the SP regulars.[69] "The Reuthers, Edwards, Kanter and these fellows are pragmatic as hell," complained Ben Fischer, an SP organizer from New York who served as a liaison between the SP auto faction and the national party. "They will not climb out on a limb: be certain of that."[70]

Indeed, Reuther's closest comrades were the first to label him an "opportunist," an accusation that would plague Reuther throughout his rise to power in the UAW and beyond. It was not simply that Reuther was ambitious, for most Socialists applauded his growing stature in the UAW; nor was he merely criticized for forming and shifting his alliances during the course of the faction fight. Rather, there was a more subtle sense that even among his confidants in the Local 174 SP faction Reuther was not entirely reliable or predictable. In 1938 almost every meeting of the auto group centered around one question: how could the activists persuade or cajole or threaten Walter Reuther into being a "good Socialist"?[71] Their chief complaint was that Reuther had linked himself too closely to the Communists within the Unity Caucus. "When Walt wants to, he can present a very thorough analysis of the CP," reported Ben Fischer.[72] Yet Reuther remained too dependent on or too fearful of Communist strength inside Unity and among Local 174 activists to put his politics fully into play. Thus Tucker Smith, who now headed up SP work in Michigan, thought Walter Reuther "not an SP fan—but a trade union politician with socialist sympathies. I don't believe he will ever be a socialist except when we have votes to impress him. He is not a CP stooge."[73]

This assessment touched upon another closely related sore point in Reuther's relationship to the Socialist Party. His failure to "build the party" in the UAW was a source of constant complaint; indeed, even on the West Side the Communists had outpaced the SP in their recruitment efforts. Although some Socialists still hoped that the growth of the CIO would generate a parallel explosion in recruitment to the SP, the size of the two organizations was inversely related. Thousands of potential recruits who might have once found an outlet for their humane and radical politics in the Socialist Party now found the new unions and the New Deal a more robust substitute.[74] As a result, when Reuther advocated a clearly "socialist" political line, his comrades and he feared that rank-and-file support would be tepid, or worse, that the growing Communist element in the local would take factional advantage of SP difficulties. This apprehension constrained his leadership and devalued the potency of his own politics.[75]

Finally, many SP regulars pounded away at Reuther to reach an accommodation with Homer Martin. Norman Thomas thought the UAW president "ready to do business with socialists in so far as temperamentally he is capable of doing business with anybody." In practice, such an accommodation spelled the destruction of the Unity Caucus, for as Thomas told the SP auto group in March 1938, "On two great questions of importance—the popular front in America and our war stand—we are completely opposed to the Communists. How is it possible then for you people to work with them in the Unity caucus without a sharper differentiation than has yet occurred?"[76] Some of Reuther's closest comrades—George Edwards and Roy Reuther among them—agreed that the working alliance with the Communists had to end, but Reuther remained loyal to the Unity Caucus and the fight against Homer Martin. Indeed, Reuther won the tentative endorsement of the Unity group as its candidate for president of the Michigan CIO council; when Communist functionaries objected to his candidacy, however, on the grounds that he was too "factional" a figure, Reuther quickly withdrew in favor of the CIO's Adolph Germer, whom the Progressive Caucus could hardly oppose. As a consolation prize, Unity unanimously agreed to nominate his brother Victor for CIO council secretary-treasurer, a lobbying job in the state capital.[77]

The stage was thus set for what Walter Reuther would always remember as the great Communist "double cross" at the state CIO convention late in April 1938. The factional politics of the episode were more nuanced than Reuther would later choose to recall, but for him this realignment within the Unity Caucus marked a decisive moment at which he crossed a psychological divide that forever put him at odds with his erstwhile comrades within the Communist orbit.

By the spring of 1938 UAW Communists were ready for a rapprochement with Richard Frankensteen, who finally recognized that Homer Martin could not last as union president. Though many UAW Communists distrusted him, the party's key Michigan operatives, State Secretary William Weinstone and Bill Gebert, head of the party's auto faction, insisted upon Frankensteen's recruitment into the Unity Caucus. They argued that an alliance with the popular leader was essential to split the Progressive Caucus, eliminate Martin, and keep the Reuther brothers in their place.[78] Although such an arrangement had been rumored for months, Reuther was genuinely surprised on the third day of the state CIO convention in Lansing when Frankensteen asked for a ten-minute caucus to work out "a deal which could unify the meeting." Walter soon discovered Frankensteen in a huddle with Gebert, Weinstone, and leading UAW Communists, who had decided to abandon Victor Reuther and throw their support to Richard Leonard, a popular DeSoto unionist who had theretofore backed Martin's Progressives.

Walter Reuther felt a deep, personal sense of betrayal. He had taken much heat from his closest friends among the UAW Socialists to remain a leader of the Unity Caucus, but now Reuther's Communist allies had violated his trust and spurned his ambitions. "What are you bastards doing?" Reuther exploded. "Don't you realize you are going to destroy the Unity Caucus, which is the only thing that can save this union?"

"We know what we're doing," Weinstone replied coldly.

"If you carry through this double-cross, then count me on the other side, not only in this fight, but from here on out!"[79]

Victor Reuther lost his CIO council post by a wide margin, and Walter forever after turned a cold, impersonal shoulder to the union pioneers who still remained within the Communist orbit. But the immediate political impact of the Lansing double cross was actually muted, for Reuther's outburst against the Communists had been over a question of factional tactics, not grand ideology. As long as Homer Martin's presidency continued, Reuther felt he had little choice but to maintain some kind of alliance with all those who opposed the disastrously maladroit leader. Top CP leaders also realized that it was a mistake to dissolve the link between the Reuther brothers and the party. "Our greatest problem today," Earl Browder asserted in reference to the Lansing maneuvers, "is breaking down all suspicions in the minds of people who have no other obstacles to collaboration with us except their suspicions. People suspect us of merely biding our time until we can make a coup and stab them in the back."[80]

So Reuther's alignment with the Communists and the Unity Caucus was not yet ready for the dust heap of history—as became clear in early June when, because of Frankensteen's defection, Martin lost his working majority on the UAW executive board. Although the union's officers were meeting in Washington, where John L. Lewis was attempting to mediate the internal UAW conflict, Martin provocatively suspended five of his opponents—among them, Wyndham Mortimer, Richard Frankensteen, Secretary-treasurer George Addes, and Vice President Ed Hall. Martin said he had acted to combat the Communist Party, whose "guilty hand" had created the "confusion and division that for months has brought reproach upon our union."[81]

However much he distrusted Frankensteen and the Communists, Reuther instinctively recoiled from Martin's coup. Just hours before, he had written May that "some of the hot heads in Martin's group want to expel several Ex. officers. This is impossible and I don't think they dare try it as this would destroy any possibility of peace."[82] Reuther was therefore incensed by Martin's suspensions the next day, and in a gesture of protest and solidarity he led a walkout of the six remaining Unity board members, courting his own suspension in the process. The suspensions were "the biggest mistake they had ever made," Reuther immediately announced. "It was equivalent to a declaration of war ... [that] would tend to destroy the union." Agreeing with his "erstwhile comrades in the Unity Caucus," he was convinced that "peace with Martin and his Lovestoneite brains trust was out of the question. The suspensions would have to be fought, the UAW reconstituted."[83]

When he got back to Detroit, Reuther was surprised to find that his realignment with Mortimer and the Unity group had generated a burst of criticism among his closest Socialist comrades. At a brutal meeting of the SP auto faction, Reuther found himself almost completely isolated, under withering attack not only from George Edwards and Ben Fischer but from Victor and May as well. Edwards thought Reuther's continuing alignment with Mortimer and the Communists disastrous, both to the integrity of Socialist Party auto work and to the revival of the UAW. "Walt began to weaken," reported Ben Fischer. "Then he said he did not know who was behind him, who would back him." Edwards insisted that Reuther could maintain the confidence of the SP's auto cadre only if he organized a "peace camp" that clearly defined itself as counterposed to the principal UAW antagonists.[84]

This would be Reuther's program for the balance of the faction fight. In a hectic round of speeches and meetings Reuther sought to differentiate himself from the officers expelled by Martin and to build a middle-of-the-road caucus in the UAW. Reuther declared the suspensions "absurd and illegal," but he also asserted: "I want to make it clear that I believe the war in the UAW must be stopped immediately. No amount of name-calling between international officers will stop wage cuts or organize competitive plants or solve the problems of workers."[85] He argued with the suspended board members against a per capita dues strike by the big locals they controlled, and he warned that any call for a separate convention would lead to dual unionism and the breakup of the UAW. Reuther told friends that the suspended board members were "acting like nuts. They want to carry the fight on indefinitely regardless of the harm to the union. They are a bunch of irresponsible bastards. The crowd on the other side are just as bad." Concluded Ben Fischer, "We at last find Walter Reuther solidly lined up with us and willing to fight the CP openly."[86]

But Reuther could not break his ties with his old allies quite so easily. In 1938, in Detroit, the Communist Party had not yet been demonized, and it was still high noon for the New Deal's dalliance with the left. Reuther and most of the active SP autoworkers saw identification with "anti-Communism" as a distinct liability, even as Norman Thomas and the rest of the Socialist Party moved toward a more systematic set of anti-Stalinist politics. When the *Socialist Call* praised Reuther and his new caucus as the "force that can rescue the union from the strangling grips of the Communist Party," George Edwards led the SP's Detroit auto group in publicly repudiating the article.[87] Reuther's politics were further constrained by the approach of the 1938 election season. The key test would be Frank Murphy's reelection campaign. Despite his rolling shift to the right, the governor's identification with the new unions made him a popular figure in UAW ranks. But it was not Murphy's popularity alone that made Reuther reluctant to stray far from the CP-Frankensteen alignment and endorse an SP gubernatorial candidate that fall. More to the point, Reuther was trapped by the Communist Party's determination to make endorsement of New Deal Democrats a central feature of the party's political profile; the Local 174 president feared that the substantial Communist element in the local would "plan a vicious campaign to put him and the party on the spot" if he did not also endorse the Michigan governor. By late summer of 1938 Stanley Nowak's ability to mobilize hundreds of West Side activists in his grass-roots Democratic primary campaign for the Michigan Senate had demonstrated the potency of such a Popular Front strategy.

Reuther's dilemma made his membership in the Socialist Party virtually untenable. Some comrades toyed with the idea that he should remain in the party but back Frank Murphy, since the SP was not "obliged when running a candidate to insist on suicide for key people in the labor movement." But most Socialists, in Detroit and nationwide, thought such a strategy a clear betrayal of vital party principles. "If we make it kosher for Party members who happen to be big shots to fight the Party, then we have no party," asserted a Socialist from Branch 1. Walter Reuther came to share this viewpoint, for he thought that any arrangement whereby he stayed in the party and still supported Murphy "would be embarrassing and impossible for both."[88]

Walter Reuther's decision to actually resign from the SP came after several long talks with Roy in early August. Roy, the party stalwart among the Reuthers, urged his brother to resign so that the comrades in auto could put aside the divisive Murphy question. With this albatross thrown overboard, Reuther could actually work in greater harmony with the other Socialist autoworkers, for they would no longer feel compelled to square their own politics with that of the SP's most prominent trade union leader. And for his part, Reuther would no longer fear that an open break with the Communists opened him up to a devastating attack on the Murphy question. Reuther's resignation would therefore be "friendly," for his day-to-day relationship with the SP comrades in auto would remain virtually unchanged.[89]

It is doubtful that Reuther felt a profound sense of liberation upon his resignation from the Socialist Party; he neither issued a public statement nor offered any ideological justification. To Reuther, American Socialism was not the God that failed. But he did demonstrate a new sense of political decisiveness after his departure. Reuther publicly endorsed Murphy and other Michigan Democrats; more important, he finally broke all his ties with the Communist group in Local 174.[90] After the November elections, Reuther easily marshaled the votes to eliminate Stanley Nowak and Bill McKie as West Side organizers, and in the spring of 1939 he crossed off his slate the rest of the CP-oriented pioneers in Local 174:

Recording Secretary Irene Young Marinovich, Financial Secretary Frank Man-fried, and several others from the Ternstedt group Nowak had built. In the larger UAW Reuther also increased his distance from the Unity Caucus and recruited to his middle-of-the-road group unionists who would form the core of a newly pow-erful Reuther caucus.[91]

Meanwhile, the faction fight within the UAW had reached an ugly climax. The "trials" of the suspended officers, to determine if their suspensions should stand, lasted from July 26 to August 6, 1938. Reuther described a night session in which "Martin became hysterically belligerent, two of his board members went to the door of the board room to summon the strongarm squads and the defendants and their attorney were fiercely threatened with violence. Eight board members pack guns."[92] The main event was the verbal slugfest between Maurice Sugar and Lawrence Davidow, the Old Guard Socialist who "prosecuted" the case for Martin and the UAW board majority. Sugar had come into possession of scores of highly revealing letters written between Jay Lovestone, Homer Martin, and other Progres-sive Caucus stalwarts. By publicizing the damaging correspondence, Sugar scored the most points, but the free-for-all turned the trials, which ended in the expulsion of the principal Unity leaders, into a public relations disaster for the union.[93]

Walter Reuther wanted John L. Lewis to reinstate the suspended officers and take over UAW affairs. He had no special confidence in John L. Lewis; like most Socialists, he thought Lewis an autocrat, much too willing to accommodate both General Motors and Homer Martin. But Reuther saw CIO intervention in the UAW's affairs as far superior to the proposal advanced by Frankensteen, Addes, and the Communists: a dues strike followed by a special convention. Reuther and Sugar clashed bitterly over the issue at a Toledo meeting of opposition forces in mid-August. Reuther thought the CP-backed gambit would merely generate a dual union, almost certainly dominated by the Communists, a perfect foil for both the companies and the Martin group still in control of the executive board.[94]

Thus Reuther competed with his erstwhile comrades for the favor of the CIO chief. They made repeated trips to the UMW headquarters in Washington, and on one crucial occasion in August Reuther battled it out with Sugar and Franken-steen before an informal CIO court composed of Lewis, Sidney Hillman, John Brophy, and the industrial union federation counsel, Lee Pressman.[95] Exasper-ated, Lewis finally decided to put the CIO in direct charge of the auto union, and when the plan was announced in late August, Reuther may well have played a cru-cial role in getting Martin to swallow it. The UAW president's only realistic hope of avoiding Lewis's dictate would come from David Dubinsky, the staunchly anti-Communist leader of the ILGWU whose links with Jay Lovestone were increas-ingly cordial and whose ties to John L. Lewis and the CIO were correspondingly frayed. Thus Martin and several of his UAW allies rushed to New York to plead for Dubinsky's political and financial support. But Reuther got wind of their plan, and through Norman Thomas he also had an entrée to the ILGWU chief. Dashing to New York on September 1, Reuther convinced Dubinsky that if Martin fought

Lewis, the conflict would wreck the auto union. Not wanting "to support a loser," Dubinsky told Martin that he would be "foolish" to fight the CIO.[96]

Lewis assigned his two most important CIO collaborators, Philip Murray and Sidney Hillman, to preside over the rehabilitation of the UAW. They spent weeks in Detroit. Mortimer, Frankensteen, and Addes were returned to their posts, regular dues payments were restored, and several Lovestoneite staffers were sent back to New York. Meanwhile, auto production bottomed out and thousands of workers were recalled to their jobs. In the *West Side Conveyor* Reuther sounded a note of relief and determination: "On the picket line and in the negotiating room, West Side has come through a bitter layoff season with flying colors. We stuck together and we won. . . . The UAW now gets back on its real job and will be going places. Employers, take notice."[97]

Politically, Reuther could live with a tightly leashed Homer Martin, at least until the next scheduled UAW convention in August 1939. But Martin was unwilling to go quietly into the night. Thus he tried to break up Local 174 by issuing a separate charter to Reuther's opponents at Fleetwood; and on the East Coast, his chief lieutenant, Frank Tucci, blocked organization of a New Jersey Ternstedt factory because of the fear that radicals would control the local union. Martin resisted the tutelage of Murray and Hillman and remained as mercurial as ever. Wrote Walter to May in the midst of an exasperating executive board meeting that November, "He is America's number one screwball."[98]

Reuther also noted something far more ominous in Martin's behavior that fall. After the CIO's 1938 convention Reuther was made a member of a new UAW-CIO Ford organizing committee, but despite his every effort, he could not get Martin to sit down with the committee; nor could he get Martin to sign off on the organizing propaganda they had prepared. It soon became apparent that Martin had been secretly negotiating a deal with Harry Bennett designed to shift the UAW out of the CIO and "unionize" one hundred thousand Ford employees in locals entirely controlled by the UAW president himself.[99] When news of these dealings became public in January 1939, the crisis in the UAW came to its final climax. Martin's opponents denounced the UAW president; he in turn attacked John L. Lewis, resigned his post as a CIO vice president, and suspended fifteen of twenty-four executive board members, including Reuther. Representing the CIO, Hillman and Murray finally repudiated the UAW president and gave the suspended officers their "complete support and recognition." Amid fistfights, threats, and strong-arm parliamentarianism, both sides mobilized their supporters for special conventions: Martin's to be held in Detroit, the CIO loyalists' in Cleveland, where their faction had always enjoyed complete organizational supremacy. Ominously, General Motors and Chrysler announced a suspension of collective bargaining in plants with two rival organizations.[100]

Philip Murray and Sidney Hillman were well aware of these difficulties as the UAW-CIO's convention drew near. Equally dangerous, the departure of the Martin forces shifted the center of political gravity far to the left; UAW delegates would certainly have chosen the steadfast, popular George Addes, perhaps even Wyndham Mortimer or Walter Reuther, had they been left to their own wishes. Addes was the clear favorite, although Reuther and his middle-of-the-road group controlled some of the biggest locals: West Side, Briggs, Chrysler-Jefferson Avenue, and Willys-Overland in Toledo. They would have given the UAW secretary-treasurer a bruising run for his money. But such a contest was not to be. Hillman and Murray were fearful that if a radical like Addes or Reuther were president, UAW turmoil would continue. Addes and Reuther were both resourceful leaders with well-organized support within the union. Under such leadership, CIO influence would be limited, internal factionalism would persist, and the Martin hard-liners would have their fears of Communist or Socialist domination of the CIO confirmed. Equally important, the UAW would make itself vulnerable to the red-baiting chorus that now featured not only the usual enemies of the union movement but also the aggressive House Un-American Activities Committee (HUAC) and a reawakened American Federation of Labor.

To avoid all these difficulties, Hillman and Murray chose as the new UAW president R. J. Thomas, a former electric welder from the Chrysler Kercheval plant who had played but a limited role in the UAW's early organizational campaigns. Briefly influenced by Father Charles Coughlin, he was elected a UAW vice president with Martin's blessing and remained a supporter of the UAW president until late in the fall of 1938. Thomas proved everything the CIO could want: personable and easygoing, a pragmatic trade unionist, a man with no ideologically committed following within the UAW. "Murray felt Thomas was his boy," George Addes recalled. "He could lead Thomas around by the nose." Murray anointed Thomas at the steel union's headquarters in Pittsburgh late in January 1939. There Thomas was told he would be acting president of the UAW and provided with a check in his name to finance the UAW convention two months later.

When the convention assembled in March, Murray and Hillman pressured key UAW leaders to back their choice for the top spot. And they were assisted by several of the Communist Party's key functionaries, including Gebert and Roy Hudson, the party's national trade union secretary. Unlike Wyndham Mortimer and Robert Travis, militants who resented R. J. Thomas's absence from the UAW's early union-building struggles, the Communists most attuned to the logic of the Popular Front were convinced that only a demonstration of their complete alignment with John L. Lewis could sustain the CIO, the laborite New Deal, and the party's newfound legitimacy in labor-liberal circles. All such discussion took place during a fevered round of closed convention meetings and late-night hotel room conclaves. Rank-and-file delegates still chanted, "Addes is our leader, we shall not be moved," but the UAW secretary-treasurer bowed to Hillman, Murray, and the Communists. "George Addes made a supreme sacrifice at that convention," observed the CIO's Lee Pressman. "If he had lifted a finger, he could have been elected president of the Auto Workers Union."[101]

Reuther made no play for the presidency at the grueling eleven-day convention in Cleveland, but his influence in UAW affairs took a quantum leap upward. With Martin gone, Reuther began to coalesce under his wing all those elements of the union hostile to the old Communist-tainted Unity group: the Martin crossovers, an emerging group of Catholic-influenced unionists, and the shop-floor militants who remembered Reuther's defense of wildcat strikers and his consistent opposition to Martin's GM contract. More immediately important, Sidney Hillman tilted decisively toward Reuther's version of a reconstructed UAW. Indeed, Hillman is said to have told R. J. Thomas not to become too comfortable in his new office, "because Walter Reuther will be the next president. I don't know how long he will sit still but he's bound to go after it."[102]

Hillman favored Reuther as a reliable counterweight to Addes, Mortimer, and the Communists. In January the CIO vice president selected the labor journalist and longtime Socialist Edward Levinson as the new UAW publicity director, a job entirely factional in its purpose and duties. Levinson would command the propaganda war against Homer Martin, keep an eye on UAW internal politics for Hillman, and become a mentor and intimate of Walter Reuther. Levinson had been a reporter for the *New York Post* and the *Socialist Call*, and in 1935 he wrote the exposé *I Break Strikes!*, which helped persuade the Senate's LaFollette Committee to investigate industrial spying. He was a brilliant propagandist and a shrewd tactician. The Communists were understandably "inflamed and enraged" by his selection.[103]

Hillman and Murray also constrained the power of the Communist-oriented left wing of the union by demanding the elimination of the UAW's five vice presidencies. This tactic removed from high office three of Reuther's most resourceful opponents, Wyndham Mortimer, Ed Hall, and Richard Frankensteen. They had hoped to retain posts on the UAW executive board on an at-large basis or through a realignment of board regions, but Reuther apparently stanched the scheme at a late-night session in Hillman's hotel room, the real power center of the convention. Frankensteen retained his board seat as one of the four Detroit-area regional directors, but Ed Hall faded into oblivion, and Wyndham Mortimer, the most highly respected of all the UAW Communists, could no longer play a role in shaping the union's fortunes at the top levels.[104]

Finally R. J. Thomas appointed Walter Reuther director of the UAW General Motors Department at the Cleveland convention. He was the unanimous choice of the new GM Committee, composed of local union officials from the corporation, and even at age thirty-two, he seemed a far more energetic and experienced candidate than any of his rivals.[105] Reuther's new post was the largest, most challenging job in the American labor movement, and he was starting from scratch.

POWER UNDER CONTROL

GM PRESIDENT CHARLES E. WILSON: Walter, you are an awful pusher, there
    is no compromise in you.
WALTER REUTHER: I am a very practical young man and I happen to have a
    job seven days a week to handle the headaches and bellyaches of your
    employees.

— *transcript, National Defense Mediation Board, May 1941*

When Walter Reuther assumed control of the UAW General Motors
Department in May 1939, he found that only 6 percent of all GM
workers were paying dues to the UAW. In Flint there were but five hundred workers in good standing, out of a potential membership of forty-two thousand. He
thought the membership "demoralized and disillusioned," with "organization . . .
practically non-existent" in many corporation plants.[1] Indeed, Homer Martin's
supporters had their greatest strength in GM: dual shop committees were present
in eleven plants with more than fifty thousand workers, and in twelve smaller
plants in the South and East Martin's men dominated the union representation
structure. GM officials claimed that they did not know who represented the workers, forcing the UAW's new president, R. J. Thomas, to concede that UAW contracts had become no more than "scraps of paper."[2]

Taking charge with characteristic energy, Reuther immediately called into operation the hierarchy of GM councils and subcouncils that had been mandated by
unionists determined to institutionalize rank-and-file input at the UAW-CIO's
Cleveland convention. Such structures, representing workers in each major corporation or industry sector, were more than expressions of democratic goodwill;

they enabled Reuther and the other union officers to get a tangible sense of the shifting moods and specific grievances of the autoworkers they sought to rewin for the CIO. In return, the constant round of meetings gave to Reuther's leadership a legitimacy far greater than that of mere appointment as GM director by the UAW executive board. By the middle of May 1939 Reuther found "new hope, new life and a genuinely new and vigorous spirit" among these council activists.[3] He categorically reconfirmed as his own the radical bargaining agenda of these steadfast union loyalists. The UAW was committed to sole recognition from the company, a guaranteed annual wage based on a thirty-hour workweek, complete recognition of the shop steward system, and joint control of production standards. Above all, even the most syndicalist of the council activists wanted to rebuild an organization whose totality represented more than a collection of militant locals. They wanted a system of multiplant *collective* bargaining that would have real meaning on the shop floor. Reuther promised national negotiations on a new GM contract "at the earliest possible date, depending upon our organizational position and the new production schedule."[4]

But how could such an ambitious agenda be won? "We must demonstrate that we are a disciplined, responsible organization," answered Reuther, "that we not only have power, but that we have *power under control*." Thus wildcat strikes were out. The chaos of the Martin years, the admonitions of the CIO high command, the real sense of organizational responsibility that came with the job of GM director, all forced Reuther to adopt as his own the hectoring language of John L. Lewis and Homer Martin. "There can be no grounds or justification for an individual or a group of individuals taking things into their own hands and causing a stoppage," Reuther told hundreds of GM local leaders in early June. "The International Union and the National GM Department is unalterably opposed to, and will not tolerate any unauthorized strikes or stoppages of work. . . . We who claim the right to strike must assume the responsibility of striking when it is right to strike."[5] Such a policy was easy to enunciate in 1939; its test would come later.

Reuther appointed none of his intimates from the West Side Socialist group to his GM Department staff. Instead, many of Reuther's key people were former Martin partisans who switched to the CIO at the height of the faction fight. He chose them not for their politics but because they would be most efficacious in the fight for Martin's old constituency. George Merrelli was typical: a skilled maintenance man from Chevy Gear and Axle, he had battled the Communists for control of Local 235 all through the faction fight. When Homer Martin shouted out to a packed meeting of that local in early 1939, "All good union men, follow me!" Merrelli's credibility with the conservative faction turned the tide. Leaping to the mike, he shouted, "Don't go out, fellows—stay here, stay with the CIO!"[6] Southern-born John Livingston was another GM staffer of this sort. As founder and president of Fisher Body Local 25 in St. Louis, Livingston had demonstrated his political finesse by keeping his big local largely neutral and therefore solidly organized all during the Martin era. Livingston hardly knew Reuther when he joined the

GM staff in April 1939, but his excellent contacts with border-state unionists made him just the man to battle Martin in his own southwestern stronghold.[7] Likewise, Reuther also recruited Art Johnstone of Pontiac, a Michigan-born Socialist and union militant, but an anti-Communist who had leaned toward Martin in the faction fight. All of these men would be identified with the more parochial and socially conservative wing of the intraunion caucus built by Walter Reuther in the 1940s. Their rise through the hierarchy reflected not only Reuther's politics but the pressure upon all of the CIO's original cadre to broaden and deradicalize the union leadership so as to reflect the heterogeneous character of the factory population to which they were unavoidably linked.[8]

Eddie Levinson's appointment as UAW publicity director represented a very different changing of the guard. The son of a Russian-Jewish tailor, Levinson was only six years older than Walter Reuther, but he soon became an indispensable mentor, putting at Reuther's disposal all of the newspaper savvy, personal connections, and political sophistication he had amassed during twenty years of Socialist Party politics and labor journalism in New York City. Levinson proved a brilliant propagandist, a more adept and politically attuned version of Carl Haessler, who was now aligned with Reuther's factional opponents in the UAW. Clayton Fountain, a Reuther partisan in 1939, remembered Eddie "at a desk in his shirt sleeves, a cigarette drooping from his mouth and the lights shining on his nearly bald head. . . . His energy was boundless, his spirit unflagging, his sense of news and timing and strategy keen as a knife."[9]

Living just across the street from each other on Appoline Street, in a working-class neighborhood where May and Walter had bought a modest home, Reuther became as intimate with and dependent upon Eddie Levinson as he could with any man. Levinson quickly learned all the details of the UAW factional scene and made his influence felt when Reuther's closest political comrades gathered for late-night strategy sessions. Levinson was but the first of a series of labor intellectuals who found in Reuther's ambitious energy a vehicle through which their oft-deferred social vision might finally be fulfilled. "Watching the fellow work is an experience," remarked Levinson shortly after his move to Detroit. "Barring accidents, I predict he'll be at the top of the labor movement in ten or fifteen years."[10] For his part, Reuther appreciated Levinson's "gay and pixy sense of humor," his capacity to see "the world through both ends of a telescope. He saw it large and small, the emerging historical era was as plain to him as the smallest idiocies." One of the very few individuals to whose intellect and judgment Reuther deferred, Eddie Levinson, a battle-scared veteran of New York's hothouse left-wing political culture, would play a major role in Reuther's rapid evolution from antiwar militant to anti-Communist interventionist and laborite social planner.[11]

But first the UAW had to force General Motors to again recognize the CIO union as the sole representative of its many workers. In 1939 GM was having a good year: car and truck production was up by one-third, and market penetration stood at more than 43 percent.[12] Even more important, two years after Flint, GM economic strength seemed fully matched by its ability to project its own techno-political vision of the American future. When the 1939 New York World's Fair opened in April, GM's Futurama exhibit, which offered visitors an elaborately crafted world of express highways, green suburbs, and well-planned cities, proved the hit of Flushing Meadows. In May fair-goers voted GM's 44,000-square-foot exhibition the most popular by far; when fifteen thousand lined up on July 4, the crush was so great that the World's Fair police stopped newcomers from joining the line.[13]

General Motors was the employer of the UAW's largest single bloc of potential members and the key to the union's revival. But despite much brave talk, Reuther and his comrades knew that they could not attempt a full-scale shutdown of the corporation's sixty-odd production facilities. The UAW had never closed the majority of GM's factories—not even in 1936–37—and prospects for such a general strike looked even less promising in the summer of 1939. A national GM council meeting in early June confirmed Reuther's belief that Martin's strength was quite limited in the shops of the giant automaker, but he also learned that thousands of workers had suspended their confidence in CIO-style trade unionism as well. After the long recession, the UAW-CIO held the allegiance of a core group of activists in virtually every factory, but this union loyalty had yet to be mobilized, and in several key factories, especially Fisher Body No. 1 and Buick, both in Flint, Martin's group had its own articulate spokesmen. When these anti-CIO men pulled a strike on June 11, Martin sent in additional pickets, who scuffled with CIO partisans and disrupted production for several hours. Reuther hurried to Flint, ordered UAW-CIO loyalists across the picket lines, and broke his strike, but Martin had done enough damage to reconfirm GM's determination to avoid formal recognition of either faction.[14]

The crisis demanded that Reuther find a way to win management recognition of the UAW-CIO as sole representative of all GM workers. The corporation stalled and, in a complete policy reversal, petitioned the government for an NLRB ruling on the UAW's jurisdiction followed by an election to determine the loyalty of its employees. But Reuther rejected the idea of a labor board vote as far too risky; Martin might well pick up enough votes to divide Flint and take several of the border-state assembly plants. Instead, Reuther chose "direct action" to reassert UAW power and turned to the one group of autoworkers who had both the union commitment and strategic leverage to dent GM's armor: the skilled tradesmen furiously at work building the tools and dies for the 1940 models that would roll off the assembly lines at the end of the summer. "If William Knudsen insists that only the courts can decide who shall speak for GM workers," Reuther warned, "we will be compelled to tell him to see if the courts can make his tools and dies."[15]

Since the onset of the Depression, the skilled workers had been the most union-conscious of all autoworkers, and they were almost universally loyal to the CIO. Although he had been out of the country at the time, Reuther certainly knew the significance of the militant job action organized by the Mechanics Educational

Society of America in 1933, which had briefly shut down Detroit-area tool and die shops in one of the earliest multiplant strikes in the auto industry. Now Reuther and other leaders of the skilled trades would reinvent the pre-UAW strike tactics as the union again turned to these union pioneers for salvation in a moment of deep peril. Skilled tradesmen were willing to battle for an industrial union in 1939 because they saw the CIO as essential to the integrity of their craft. Thus the skilled trades contract supplement that Reuther set out to negotiate with GM sought to tighten apprenticeship requirements, restore the relative wage advantage these workers had once held over the semiskilled production hands, and stamp a union label on all tools and dies used by GM, regardless of their origin. These provisions would stanch the flow of low-wage, nonunion work from the smaller "alley" shops that were threatening to undercut the standards the UAW had won in the big "captive" toolrooms of the major automakers.[16]

Reuther had been discussing the idea of a tool and die strike with skilled trades leaders since early May. Indeed, the idea of such a limited work stoppage was not Reuther's alone. Bill Stevenson, the new chairman of the national GM bargaining committee and a MESA strike leader in 1933, remembered "long talks with Walter" about such a stoppage. Few in Reuther's inner circle doubted that most skilled tradesmen would strike, but if the stoppage either proved incomplete or simply dragged on too long, Reuther's daring gambit would signal a major defeat, not only for the UAW but for his newly minted leadership. "The Commies were just waiting for me to fall on my face," gloated Reuther. It was thus highly reassuring to know that the shock troops for the strike would come from Local 157, the West Side tool and die local with a heavy complement of old Socialists in its leadership and two of GM's most important shops in its jurisdiction.[17]

Reuther cleared the tool and die strike plan with Sidney Hillman and Philip Murray in Washington, then won UAW executive board approval on July 2, 1939. After overwhelming strike votes in all the principal GM toolrooms, the stoppage began on July 5 when Reuther called out the eight hundred skilled workers at the Fisher No. 21 shop on the West Side of Detroit. The next day tool and die craftsmen walked out of four more GM facilities in Detroit, including Fisher No. 23, the largest tool and die shop in the world. On July 7, three more Detroit plants — Fisher No. 47, Fleetwood, and Ternstedt — followed suit. And on July 10, GM shops in Cleveland and Saginaw, the first outside of metropolitan Detroit, were shut down. The gradual escalation, "not unlike amputating one finger at a time to cripple a hand," wrote *Time* magazine, demonstrated UAW solidarity, kept the strike on the front pages, and gave unionists and the public a definite sense of movement.[18]

By the middle of July less than seven thousand unionists were on strike, but the stoppage had captured national attention as thousands of production workers were laid off and GM's fall production schedule fell apart. "The UAW-CIO fights with discipline, with intelligence, and with strategy," Reuther asserted shortly after the first craftsmen had walked out, and thus it was as the leader of this "strategy strike" that Reuther again came to the fore as a unionist of unusual flare and talent. Wrote the *Cleveland Plain Dealer's* Spencer Fullerton, "The strategy . . . is mostly the product of the imagination of canny Walter Reuther, who is rapidly being recognized as one of the more able labor leaders now operating."[19]

The 1939 tool and die strike generated one of the CIO's last community-based mobilizations of the prewar era. With the loyalty of the production workers an unknown quantity, Reuther feared strikebreaking initiatives instigated by GM, the AFL, or both. The union therefore remobilized its women's auxiliaries to nurture support for the strike in working-class districts, and Reuther called out the flying squadrons to add backbone to the picket lines in Pontiac and Cleveland, where pitched battles of the old-fashioned sort forestalled management-sponsored back-to-work movements.[20] Reuther's leadership of the strike had a distinctly radical edge to it: on July 27 he surrounded GM headquarters with a picket line twelve thousand strong, then scheduled a radio speech on July 30 in which he intended to denounce GM's DuPont connection and advertise the enormous salaries of Alfred Sloan and William Knudsen. Station WJR censored those passages, but Reuther and Levinson turned the incident to the union's advantage. As a UAW leaflet put it, the "industrial barons not only want to dominate their own plants, like kings of old, but, they want to rule God's free air."[21]

Because of UAW instability and Reuther's own reputation for radicalism, when GM decided to open negotiations with the union in mid-July the CIO vice president Philip Murray would play a leading role in the settlement talks, with Reuther handling the technical details. GM President William Knudsen, a hard-driving production boss, took an instant dislike to Reuther, whom he soon denounced as a would-be "commissar."[22] But Knudsen and the rest of the GM production hierarchy recognized the logic of the UAW demand for exclusive recognition. Union factionalism and instability had caused some 435 strikes since 1937; the time had come, said Knudsen, "to settle the whole issue now and forever."[23] Within a few days GM offered to recognize the UAW-CIO as the exclusive bargaining agent for those plants, forty-one in all, where only the CIO had shop committees.

Because of GM's resistance to a companywide standardization of skilled trades wages, the strike dragged on into early August, with much haggling over job classifications and wage rates in GM's many tooling facilities. "Young man, I wish you were selling used cars for us," barked Knudsen after a particularly exhausting session. "*Used cars!*" squawked Reuther. "Yes," replied GM's president, "*used cars.* Anybody can sell new cars."[24]

Fortunately, Reuther's bargaining clout increased when the Michigan Unemployment Compensation Commission ruled that laid-off production workers not themselves on strike could collect weekly payments. Faced with the UAW's ability to sustain an even longer strike, GM agreed on August 4 to a somewhat higher wage structure for the skilled trades, enough for Reuther to claim victory. In truth, the wage adjustments were paltry and the UAW failed to make GM use only union-label dies. But in a situation not dissimilar from that at Kelsey-Hayes thirty-two months before, Reuther knew that a symbolic victory, properly exploited, was just as efficacious as a real one. To the country, and to most workers, the UAW had decisively reestablished itself at GM, signing the first companywide wage agreement with the giant automaker since the spring of 1937. "Six months ago," trumpeted Edward Levinson in the union paper, "we were torn by the treachery of men whom we had trusted. Since then we have set our house in order and reached out with the strength of lions to tame one of the toughest and richest industrial corporations in the country."[25]

UAW strength in the GM empire was confirmed after the union petitioned the National Labor Relations Board to conduct a companywide, 55-plant election, which was finally held in April 1940. Livingston and Reuther spent hundreds of hours at union meetings in Flint, sometimes not returning to Detroit until five in the morning, just in time to prepare for a 9:00 A.M. grievance-handling session at the General Motors building.[26] Reuther also made periodic swings through the East to shore up UAW strength in New Jersey, Connecticut, and New York. In October he spent a grueling week in Oakland to forestall a strike at GM's East Bay assembly plant: "I have been meeting day and night," he wrote May after getting back to his hotel. "I am so exhausted I am unable to hold my head up. . . . All local leadership completely opposed to my position. . . . I spoke for 2 hours and won them over." May, who described herself as "the most capable secretary a GM Director ever had," juggled the correspondence and telephone calls in his absence with a keen sense of the factional implications.[27] By the spring of 1940 Reuther was energetically mobilizing UAW resources for the NLRB campaign, which was climaxed by the appearance of Lewis, Murray, and Hillman at huge rallies in Detroit and Flint.[28]

With over 134,000 votes cast, it was the largest election ever conducted by the NLRB. The UAW-CIO took 68 percent of the vote, wiping out the AFL in all but five outlying plants. The election returns faithfully reflected the ethnopolitical demography that had structured UAW factionalism since the union's founding. The CIO won a smashing 84 percent of the total vote in Detroit and Cleveland, with their large Catholic, Slavic, and Anglo-Gaelic populations, but only 64 percent in Protestant, Appalachian Flint and Pontiac, where several big factories were captured by uncomfortably narrow majorities. Reuther lost GM's border-state assembly plants in Anderson, Indiana (45 percent), Kansas City (30 percent), and Norwood, Ohio (23 percent), but these units would soon reunite with the UAW after CIO opponents realized the futility of a go-it-alone bargaining effort.[29]

Reuther and the UAW had won the right to bargain for the two hundred thousand hourly workers who labored in America's most important company. Now what would they build with this newly confirmed power? The NLRB election resolved none of the problems that had brought the union to its knees: General Motors remained a steadfast and powerful adversary. "We have got the toughest problem of any group of organized workers in America," asserted Reuther. "We are dealing with a two billion dollar corporation that has all of its authority vested in a small group of directors in Wall Street who are not connected with production problems."[30] GM sales and profits were up as the Roosevelt recession finally came to a close, but the war scare generated by the Nazi blitzkrieg in western Europe clearly chilled the already doubtful prospects for a corporationwide strike to raise wages or institutionalize the shop steward system, the two big questions pushed by the union. In what would soon become a bargaining season ritual, UAW locals rejected GM's first offer, which at least made the dispute visible in Washington despite all the war news. Hillman and Murray scurried to Detroit, and the U.S. Conciliation Service sent in its top mediator.[31]

The peaceful resolution of these negotiations was ensured by a change at the top of GM's hierarchy. In May 1940 President Roosevelt appointed William Knudsen a member of the new National Defense Advisory Commission, the government's key war mobilization agency. Knudsen's replacement at GM was the fifty-two-year-old Charles E. Wilson, who would take an unusually close interest in the corporation's industrial relations. Like Reuther, Wilson had been a unionist in his youth, and he always claimed to have voted for Eugene V. Debs in 1912. He also shared Reuther's great faith in technical competence; he had sharpened his own skills at Carnegie Tech and at Westinghouse, where he began his career in pre–World War I electrical design. But Wilson was a generation older than Reuther; he had entered industry at a moment of unparalleled opportunity for energetic engineer-mechanics. Wilson therefore quickly shed his youthful politics and, after shifting to GM in 1919, rose to the presidency of Delco-Remy, the electrical parts subsidiary headquartered in Dayton. There Wilson assimilated many of the ideas of progressive personnel management practiced at the nearby National Cash Register Company, a welfare capitalist pioneer of the 1920s.[32] Returning to GM's Detroit headquarters in 1929, Wilson served on the General Motors negotiating team during the Flint sit-down strike and then presided over many of the difficult poststrike negotiations with the union. Knudsen was happy to turn over this vexing responsibility. "C. E., you handle this union business," Knudsen reportedly told Wilson during one of his fits of exasperation with the UAW. "You have more patience than I do and you like to talk more."[33]

Wilson got on well with Alfred Sloan and Donaldson Brown, architects of the GM managerial system, but he was not a DuPont man, and his elevation to the presidency opened a sliver of light between the reactionaries of New York and Wilmington and the merely hard-boiled production men of Detroit. Unlike most of the DuPont hierarchy, who presided over a paternalistically structured, nonunion enterprise, Wilson immersed himself in the details of the collective bargaining contract, a process that inevitably generated an element of collaboration with union officials. During one set of arduous prewar negotiations, Wilson snapped, "Walter, you are an awful pusher, there is no compromise in you." To which Reuther replied, "I am a very practical young man and I happen to have a job seven days a week to handle the headaches and bellyaches of your employees. . . . Why shouldn't I try to eliminate them in the future if I can by being practical at the moment?"[34] Soon Wilson came to respect Walter Reuther's drive and energy, once calling his adversary "the ablest man in American industry." But more important, the GM president understood something of the dynamics of modern industrial unionism. As he put it to the management theorist Peter Drucker: "A union is a political organization and needs adversary relations and victorious battles. And a company is an economic organization and needs productivity and discipline. At GM we get both."[35]

The 1940 UAW-GM contract, finally signed on June 24, therefore represented the first settled accommodation between the corporation and the UAW. It was a detailed blueprint, several times longer than the 1937 contract. Indeed, it even looked more substantial: bound as a gray booklet, this contract and its many successors served as the template that would structure the attitudes and actions— indeed, the whole worldview—of hundreds of thousands of men and women. At GM, foremen were told, "Be tough but fair, and don't deviate from the little gray book."[36] GM recognized the UAW as the "sole and exclusive" bargaining agent for almost all of its hourly workers, and the union won the right to solicit membership and collect dues on company property. Reuther negotiated a "CIO dividend," a week's vacation pay for most GM workers. More important, he won for the UAW a $5 million wage equalization fund and access to a "complete breakdown" of GM's entire hourly wage structure. Plant committees could now adjust and rectify inequitable wage differentials within and between plants for individuals doing the same work. Although the total monetary benefits were small—an average of one and a half cents per hour overall—the UAW had forced GM to concede that the principle of companywide wage standardization superseded local labor market conditions in establishing individual wages on specific jobs.[37] In turn, GM had "subcontracted" many of its most difficult wage rationalization problems to Reuther and his colleagues, who now presided over the politically sensitive task of defining the precise meaning of equal pay for equal work in more than three score of the corporation's factories.

Regardless of its motivations, GM's shift toward a uniform, nationwide wage pattern represented one of the industrial union movement's most significant steps toward the New Deal era's transformation of the American class structure. Factories within the same firm, and companies within the same industry, would cease to compete for lower wages, and within those factories and occupations wage differentials would decline, compressing and restructuring the blue-collar social structure. Reuther championed this program as "in keeping with the whole philosophy of the CIO on Industrial Unionism."[38] For more than two decades he used the frequent renegotiation of the GM contract to push forward the wages of the lowest-paid production workers: janitors, loaders, assemblers, checkers, and foundrymen. By 1960 relative wage differentials within GM's production workforce had declined by 60 percent, a pattern replicated throughout unionized industry. Given the ethnic, gender, and racial character of so many auto factory jobs, the slow but steady equalization of working-class incomes provided the economic bedrock upon which the industrial unions championed midcentury cultural pluralism and racial equality. In the GM contract, as elsewhere, gender discrimination remained overt, but the actual wage differentials between the work of men and women, even at their carefully segregated jobs, declined over time.[39]

But if the UAW could make slow and steady economic progress with GM, Reuther faced a stone wall when he sought anything approaching a real transformation of power relations between workers and managers within GM factories themselves, where the frontier of control remained as contested and contentious as ever. As auto production picked up in 1939 and 1940, all the old shop issues had come to the fore again: speedup, favoritism, job assignments and promotions, disciplinary suspensions, and firings. Remembered Art Johnstone of the GM Department, "We were constantly bedeviled, aggravated and embarrassed by the fact that we had many cases in which the equities were clearly all on our side, but the corporation would not settle." Reuther himself complained to Hillman that hundreds of grievances and disputes had been "hanging fire" for as long as three years. New shop-floor explosions, followed by a punishing GM retaliation, awaited but the right moment and the opportune spark.[40] To resolve such workplace conflicts, the industrial union movement had a clear and unambiguous solution: scores, even hundreds, of wide-awake shop stewards in each factory, mill, and office. The UAW called these worker-spokesman-organizers "a weapon of democracy" powerful and numerous enough to overthrow the foreman's "small-time dictatorship" and establish a "democratic system of shop government." In a brilliantly educative 1940 pamphlet, "How to Win for the Union," the new UAW Education Department defined the shop steward as "at once a diplomat negotiating with a foreign power and a general preparing his troops for possible conflict." Shop stewards were told, "Your relationship with the foreman should be that of equals seeking a solution to a common problem." Thus grievances were best settled on the spot: "A little more pressure on your foreman or superintendent may win a satisfactory settlement which higher officers of the company would not be willing to give."[41]

Reuther endorsed this vision of shop democracy. Indeed, he argued for a kind of shop "mutuality" in which foremen as well as workers would find themselves subject to a new system of industrial justice. Above all, Reuther asserted the need for a dense system of shop stewards: one for each foreman. Then "no time is wasted bringing a committeeman from some other department and getting him informed on the background."[42] Reuther understood that the multistep grievance procedure first codified in 1937 was but a poor substitute for direct negotiations at the point of production. "We must establish a shop steward system so that grievances can be settled at the machine and on the assembly line and not referred to the General Motors Building in Detroit."[43] Chrysler remained the model. In the fall of 1939 the UAW fought management there to a standstill during a bitter, monthlong stoppage—the so-called speedup strike—that defined with some precision union power at the point of production. The UAW won de facto recognition

of hundreds of "blue button" stewards who retained the authority to write up grievances, collect dues, negotiate directly with their departmental foremen, and exercise a measure of control over production standards. Indeed, UAW shop-floor
strength proved so great that most Chrysler foremen decided to "join" rather than
"fight" the union tide. Several hundred sought their own CIO union during the
1939 strike; Philip Murray turned them aside, but two years later they again
spurned top management when they flocked to the independent Foreman's Association of America.[44]

Such shop-floor turmoil redoubled GM's determination to maintain control of
production standards and sustain the authority of its foremen. Sloan saw the union
effort to demoralize the foremen as an assault on "basic management prerogatives." GM President Wilson later defined the very existence of a shop steward system as constituting "a form of joint management which in our plants would lead
to much friction and inefficiency."[45] To stanch such a prospect, GM insisted upon
inclusion in the 1940 contract of a definitive assertion that management's "right to
hire; promote; discharge or discipline for cause; and to maintain discipline and
efficiency of employees, is the sole responsibility of the corporation. . . . In addition, the products to be manufactured, the location of plants, the schedules of production, the methods, processes and means of manufacturing are solely and exclusively the responsibility of the corporation."[46] This declaration, a virtual preamble
to all subsequent UAW-GM contracts, was further buttressed by "paragraph 78,"
which maintained that "production standards" were subject to the "full authority"
of local management.[47] Such language remained the fortress from which General
Motors would defend its power and that of its foremen at the point of production.
It was not a contract clause so much as an ideological manifesto reflecting a worldview that saw in the natural rhythms of the factory an inherently hierarchical and
authoritarian social order. If the UAW ever tried to alter the wording of these paragraphs, a GM official later remarked, the struggle would have to be waged by nothing less than "revolutionary means."[48]

GM's defense of what the corporation considered proper shop management
also mandated a thorough recentralization of its industrial relations apparatus.
The decentralized system that so famously characterized production, sales, and
finance at GM had always looked rather monolithic when seen from the bottom
up. Chevrolet, which operated thirty-two assembly and manufacturing plants and
built more than 60 percent of GM's North American automobiles in 1940, was a
giant enterprise in its own right with a clear profit-and-loss responsibility. This
huge GM division was an utterly centralized institution, and the Chevy boss Marvin Coyle—Peter Drucker called him "a flint-hearted bookkeeper . . . ham-fisted
and hard, with small, mean eyes"—kept his plant managers on a tight leash. But
even autocrats like Coyle bowed to a higher authority when it came to virtually
any level of corporate contact with the UAW. By 1940 GM industrial relations
were a top-management function, administered by a strong central staff working
out of the GM building in Detroit.[49]

Such centralization blocked UAW efforts to play one plant off against another. Reuther had wanted a contract that offered unionized "weak plants" a minimum sort of protection but allowed enough local flexibility so that in factories with more union-conscious workers "you can get more if you can work it out locally." But in the GM system, factory superintendents and managers were left with little authority to cut the sort of informal and opportunistic deals that were commonplace throughout the rest of unionized industry. Staffers from the corporation's new office of industrial relations carefully monitored the flow of grievances to avoid any erosion of management's shop authority. Reuther called this "collective bargaining by remote control," and he complained that "we have fought more on this one point than any other. . . . We have raised hell with the Chevrolet central office."[50]

But all to no avail. Virtually alone among the prewar titans of unionized heavy industry, General Motors had the immense resources and systematic will power— Sloan called it "management by policy"—to undercut shop steward power and keep union influence well contained. GM therefore insisted in the 1940 contract that where shop stewards did exist, their only function would be to collect dues, not represent the men or process grievances. Foremen and supervisors would negotiate only with those individuals the corporation recognized as shop committeemen. The 1940 contract increased their numbers (to about one for every 250 workers) and gave them more job security, a somewhat greater freedom of movement about the plant, and additional time to process grievances. But the committeemen were scattered too widely throughout the factory to offer GM foremen any effective social or psychological competition. No matter how militant the union committeeman, he was almost always an "outsider" in a shop-floor contest of will.[51] John Anderson, a committeeman at Fleetwood, described how the new system functioned just before the war. "I could only take up a grievance when the foreman told me where it was and who wanted to see me. Then I would have to sign out of my department and when I got to the department where the grievance was I had to notify the supervisor there and sign in. After dealing with the problem I would then sign out and on returning to my job I would have to notify my foreman and sign back in again. Our movements were completely controlled."[52]

Intransigence of this sort made life exceedingly difficult for Reuther. Unlike other top union strategists, such as those at Chrysler, Studebaker, and Allis-Chalmers, where steward-led shop-floor confrontations won for the union a kind of veto power over management decisions within the shop, Reuther quickly came to see that such aggressive tactics would fail at GM, especially after the turn to the right in American domestic politics made "militancy" a doubtful prospect. GM had the redundant productive capacity, the market share, and the programmatic will to "take a strike" and make it stick.[53] Thus Reuther pounded home the dangers of undisciplined shop-floor militancy. "Members have been given notice," he declared in the immediate aftermath of the tool and die strike, "that when they get out of line in the future, there will be no wildcat departmental strikes to back them up."[54] In effect, Reuther was repudiating the factory-centered militancy he had advocated two years before. "You cannot strike General Motors plants on individual grievances," Reuther told one meeting of autoworkers. "One plant going down will affect the 60 other plants." Instead, the UAW needed solidarity and unity, not another Tuller Hotel "snake dance and everything."[55]

But if Reuther was not to suffer Martin's fate, he needed a strategy other than that of simple capitulation to the giant corporation's monolithic defense of its authoritarian work regime. He continued to argue in favor of the steward system, of course, but UAW rhetoric on the issue became increasingly formalistic in the years after 1940. Reuther would soon see such a system as inherently destabilizing, especially when steward power became identified with the shop militancy and political opposition that thwarted his larger collective bargaining agenda. He therefore sought to counter the enormous power of GM management with the countervailing authority of the one institution that seemed anything like GM's equal: the New Deal state. He moved to dilute management authority by calling to the union's rescue quasi-governmental institutions that could intervene both at the level of the shop and in the realm of corporate finance, investment, and pricing. The GM director was not the only unionist to seek union influence over corporate governance through an expansion of the New Deal regulatory apparatus, but Reuther had a singular capacity for packaging a state-sponsored solution to the UAW's internal problems with a larger political agenda that offered Americans a laborite interpretation of what constituted the national interest.

But before exploring Reuther's effort to plan the political economy on a left-corporatist basis (see chapter 8), we turn first to the application of this strategy at the microsocial level, where Reuther began a pioneering effort to codify or "constitutionalize" management authority at the point of production. With the establishment of a shop steward system beyond his reach, Reuther still hoped to limit management's shop-floor power through a system that might yet temper the authority of GM foremen and shop superintendents or, as he later put it, "substitute civil procedure for war in this industry."[56] The key feature of the 1940 UAW-GM contract was therefore the establishment of grievance arbitration under a permanent "umpire," an industrial supreme court that would rule on those disputes unresolved in the first three steps of the grievance procedure.

The idea of an industrial jurisprudence lies close to the heart of the New Deal system of industrial relations. Although grievance arbitration is not mentioned in the Wagner Act, mechanisms for peacefully resolving the "labor question," for constitutionalizing and ameliorating shop conflict, were a product of more than half a century of agitation, experimentation, and legal reform. They were predicated upon the triumph of a pluralist ideology that saw the establishment of strong unions and stable industrial relations as the key to a Keynesian reflation of the economy and the extension of political democracy to the realm of shop and office. Although well tested in the needle trades, less than 10 percent of all union contracts contained an arbitration clause, and in heavy industry managers instinctively resisted any institution that seemed to further undercut their prerogatives.

The UAW-GM contract therefore represented a nodal point in the elaboration of this New Deal vision, a breakthrough for the conflict-displacing mechanisms and pluralist ideology that had been pioneered in the industrially marginal world of cloak-making, hosiery, and women's clothing.[57]

If Walter Reuther was the father of this imperfect transition, Sidney Hillman, his sometime mentor, proved the anxious and imperious godfather. Hillman was a member of that generation of immigrant Jewish labor leaders whose political education had begun in the revolutionary movement against the czar and then continued in the clothing shops of Chicago and New York in the equally ideological struggle against the low wages and instability of the needle trades. He had risen to the leadership of the Amalgamated Clothing Workers of America (ACWA) in the great upheavals that mobilized Jewish and Italian immigrant workers in pre–World War I America, but thereafter Hillman combined his waning Socialist faith with a degree of technocratic planning and Progressive-era commitment to the amelioration of social conflict. Working closely with Progressives like Felix Frankfurter and Newton Baker and with maverick employers like Edward Filene and Joseph Schafner, Hillman sought to turn the rebellious and unpredictable clothing workers into the sturdy citizens of a well-regulated "industrial democracy."[58]

In the men's clothing industry, and then in the full-fashioned hosiery shops of Philadelphia, union leaders like Hillman and Emil Rieve, head of the United Hosiery Workers, reached an accommodation with the managers of highly competitive, labor-intensive industries heretofore characterized by ethnopolitical militancy, periodic mass strikes, and acute economic instability. By the end of the 1920s therefore, a species of industrial democracy had been built in both industries; its key features were employer recognition of union strength and permanency, a union commitment to industrial self-discipline, including a program of wage rationalization, and the establishment of a quasi-judicial umpire system that would resolve any outstanding disputes between the parties.[59] Harvard's Sumner Slichter, the dean of American labor economists, foresaw an emerging "industrial jurisprudence"; likewise, William Leiserson, an architect of early New Deal labor policy, thought collective bargaining but the latest step forward in the great liberal tradition that had begun with the Magna Carta, the Long Parliament, and the U.S. Constitution.[60] Indeed, unions like the Amalgamated Clothing Workers, the Hosiery Workers, and the ILGWU had interpenetrated industry decision-making at virtually every level. Union officials in these labor-intensive industries jointly set piece rates, influenced the appointment of foremen, bailed out bankrupt firms, and negotiated the introduction of new technology. Hillman's ACWA even helped managers of the largest clothing firms plan and market their new product lines.[61]

Hillman, Reuther, and Levinson therefore saw the needle trades system of grievance arbitration and labor-management collaboration as a potential solution to the danger and instability that faced the UAW. Reuther's first effort to adapt that model came in the auto parts field, whose organization and stabilization had bedeviled Local 174 since the disastrous Yale and Towne strike of 1937. This industry sector had almost the same economic structure as that of the needle trades. It was a labor-intensive, highly competitive industry plagued by runaway shops, piece-rate wages, and near sweatshop working conditions. A heavily female workforce employed in relatively small, widely scattered shops had proven difficult to organize, thus keeping Local 174's organizers on a perpetual treadmill. "If this type of competition is permitted to continue," argued Reuther, "the workers in higher paid shops will have organized themselves out of a job." In the aftermath of the bloody 1938 Federal Screw strike, Reuther sought to ameliorate some of these problems, first by pushing for a vigorous organizing drive coordinated by the new Competitive Shops Department, later by seeking an accommodation with parts industry management that would parallel the cooperation built in hosiery and men's clothing. In the parts field, as in clothing, the unionized, high-wage firms had an immediate and pressing interest in any scheme that would regularize wages and conditions among their nonunion competitors.[62]

With Hillman's collaboration, Reuther began exploratory negotiations with top executives of the Automotive Parts Association after the conclusion of the tool and die strike. The association president, Ternstedt's C. O. Skinner, had several meetings with Hillman and spent time in Philadelphia observing the work of George Taylor, the highly respected University of Pennsylvania economist who served as "impartial umpire" in the full-fashioned hosiery industry. For a few months in the fall of 1939 a deal seemed in the offing: as in the needle trades, the UAW would agree to the continuation of a piecework pay standard, and leaders of the auto parts industry would offer Reuther a blanket agreement covering most of the principal firms. Sidney Hillman promised to "guarantee" union adherence to the letter and spirit of the agreement.[63]

But the needle trades model of industrial democracy simply would not fit the Detroit-centered auto parts industry. As of the late 1930s, the UAW had not succeeded in organizing as high a proportion of the workers in its industry as had ACWA or the Hosiery Workers. Firms in the auto parts industry remained bitterly divided, and many managers still saw resistance to the UAW as "protecting the constitution from the Reds."[64] Moreover, even unionized firms insisted that piece rates were essential to maintain labor discipline and compensate for the industry's wide variations in productivity. Yet the UAW had made elimination of piecework part of its very raison d'être: Local 174 counted the difficult shift to day work wages at Ternstedt and the smaller West Side shops among its proudest achievements. And Reuther himself feared that union collaboration with management in setting production and piece-rate standards "would probably cause a lot of friction" at the shop level because the actual timing and piece-rate pay determinations would be made by engineers a step removed from the social and political pressures generated by the production line.[65]

So the Hillman-Reuther effort at parts industry rationalization came to nought. But Reuther learned two things from these exploratory steps. First, he began to think more seriously about the larger structure of each industry in which the UAW bargained and about how the union might apply economic and political pressure to generate a more stable and socially efficient industrial order. Thus emerged the central idea for the next decade's series of high-profile "Reuther Plans," which offered a program of social planning and union influence that won Reuther the enthusiastic endorsement of politically influential New Dealers and the grudging respect of even the CIO's most conservative opponents. Second, and more immediately useful, he became quite familiar with the idea of industrial arbitration. At the most immediate and crudely political level, Reuther wanted an umpire system at GM to protect the union leadership from the consequences of undisciplined shop-floor activism. Citing the experience of the clothing workers in Chicago, Reuther convinced a corps of sometimes wary GM local officers that the new institution would protect them from the corporate reprisal and inner union factionalism that were so often the product of unconstrained departmental militancy. "Out of the frying pan and into the Umpire," was the catchphrase soon coined by GM unionists to describe the new system's conflict-displacing properties.[66]

The political difficulties inherent in the situation became clear even as the UAW and General Motors wrangled over the choice of their first arbitrator. Less than three months after signing the 1940 agreement, the presence of AFL loyalists at Fisher Body No. 1 in Flint touched off a fight, a CIO effort to eject the die-hard Martinites and a GM lockout of the entire shift. The company fired seventeen of the most active unionists in the plant, to which Local 581 responded with a solidly effective strike that put thirteen thousand on the street. In an additional display of solidarity, union leaders at nearby Buick initiated a sympathy strike that closed that factory.[67] Reuther and R. J. Thomas rushed to Flint and got everyone back to work on September 20. To Reuther, the Flint wildcat, no matter how justified, represented a threat to the larger and more stable relationship the GM Department sought to build with the corporation. Like Martin, Reuther had become a prisoner of the corporation's demand for continuous production, and like Martin, he was coming under attack from the militants in the shop. William Genske, a Fisher Body union leader, later recalled, "On each occasion Reuther came down and told the people that they had to live up to the contract. He would just not permit any wildcat strikes. . . . He was determined to sell the company the idea that the UAW was a responsible union. The membership did not always see eye to eye with that because it ruled out a lot of the activities they thought would eliminate some of the problems they were confronted with."[68]

Reuther's stock plummeted. To get the Fisher workers reinstated, he spent the better part of two months in a series of fruitless negotiations with GM managers. Wilson wanted to teach the Flint unionists a lesson; thus, he refused UAW requests for a special arbitrator in the case. Reuther's failure in Flint opened the door to attack from the militants in that auto city—Reuther labeled them "Trotskyites"—as well as to more factional intrigue among the UAW's top officers. Secretary-Treasurer George Addes, emerging as Reuther's most powerful rival, eventually negotiated a compromise settlement that got the men returned to work.[69] But Reuther's difficulties were not over yet. GM's trench warfare tactics generated a companywide chorus of complaints once the implications of the 1940 contract became clear. Because they resented top management's takeover of industrial relations, plant managers in the Fisher Body and Chevrolet divisions simply ignored many clear-cut provisions of the contract. Grievances were then bucked upward to the arbitrator. Unionists soon bombarded Reuther and the UAW executive board with demands for a conference that would put restoration of the shop steward system and joint control of production standards at the top of the agenda. These demands were championed by Reuther's increasingly well organized factional opponents, who made Philip Murray, R. J. Thomas, and the GM director himself fear a Tuller Hotel–style revolt, which might once again destroy the UAW's credibility with the corporation.[70]

But Reuther was not Homer Martin. When 120 angry GM delegates assembled at the Fort Shelby Hotel in early February 1941, they found that Reuther had come thoroughly prepared. Unlike Martin, Reuther faced the crisis GM had precipitated with a clear message that combined a far-reaching vision of union militancy with a program of tactical caution. Reuther admitted that the 1940 contract was far from perfect, and that GM's "remote control" bargaining generated a huge grievance backlog that frequently brought tensions to the boiling point. The UAW would therefore fight for the shop steward system, for the thirty-hour week, for a big wage increase, even for union participation in company governance. But wildcat strikes and stoppages were out. "I want to be brutally frank with you on this point. I want to say . . . that unless you have a recognition and observance of these provisions [of the contract] then instead of having democracy, you have 'mobocracy.' When you fight for the right to have a democratic organization, you also take on the responsibility to function within that organization in a democratic manner . . . because otherwise you destroy the very thing you are trying to defend."[71]

In the meantime, argued Reuther, the grievance arbitration system had begun to work: the arbitrator "is going to do a real constructive job and help us solve some of our most difficult problems." Reuther himself pushed appeal cases where shop tensions were most severe. Following a long debate in which Reuther's opponents denounced the umpire setup as a "dictatorship," GM delegates voted by almost two to one to keep the grievance arbitration scheme.[72] Reuther's leadership had been sustained, but without great enthusiasm. Indeed, the GM director would find that he never enjoyed an unchallenged administration of his massive department, especially in Flint, the very heart of the corporation's empire. There anti-Reuther rhetoric was the common coin of shop politics, so Flint's regional directors were often his factional opponents.[73]

Such were the difficulties of union leadership in the untamed UAW. But the umpire system was not simply a mechanism designed to displace shop-floor conflict; many unionists came to see that the system of industrial jurisprudence contained a certain autonomous dynamic that might well be turned to the advantage of the union. "Management has no divine rights," Reuther would declare after World War II. "Management has only functions, which it performs well or poorly. The only prerogatives which management has lost turned out to be usurpations of power and privilege to which no group of men have exclusive right in a democratic nation."[74] Reuther clearly hoped that the UAW could use a combination of well-organized pressure, grievance bargaining, and umpire decisions to build a system of democratic, rule-bound governance on the shop floor. "The contract is your constitution, and the settlement of grievances under it are the decisions of an industrial supreme court," declared the UAW in its steward's handbook of 1940. "*A complete record of such decisions is sometimes more important than the contract itself* [italics in the original]."[75]

Indeed, the effort to structure the shop-floor struggle into a system of quasi-legal rights and obligations had a powerful, and initially quite advantageous, impact on the way many unionists conducted their conflicts with foremen and plant managers. The early UAW-GM umpires were contractual activists, far more influential than the series of legal technicians who would follow them. The first umpire was Harry Millis, an early student of John R. Commons and a University of Chicago economist with long experience as an arbitrator in the men's clothing industry. Millis had participated in shaping New Deal labor law since the experimental days of 1933, and like most of Commons's students, he saw in the new unions and the new labor law the keys to an evolutionary transformation of industrial society. But he proved acceptable to GM management because he had clearly demonstrated that the limits of this evolution were governed by management's interest in an orderly production process. Roosevelt appointed Millis NLRB chair late in 1940, before he could impose his ideas about good labor relations, but he was replaced by the like-minded George Taylor, who spent a crucial year in Detroit until the president again snatched away the UAW-GM umpire, this time to become vice chairman of the new National War Labor Board.[76]

Millis and Taylor shared a belief that industry itself would find in the constitutionalization of the work regime a road to social peace and high productivity. Taylor was so committed to this task at GM that he often tilted his decisions toward the company to ensure management's continued participation in the arbitration scheme. Reuther was more than annoyed, but he also understood Taylor's larger purpose.[77] The GM arbitrators were paid twenty thousand dollars a year, more than a Supreme Court justice. Indeed, they were full-time jurists who ran a kind of "court" in which the top officials of the GM industrial relations staff battled it out with written briefs and oral arguments against equally well prepared unionists. Of the tens of thousands of grievances that made their way upward through the grievance procedure, between one hundred and two hundred reached the arbitration stage and a definitive "umpire decision." These decisions were then rushed into print and distributed up and down each of the two huge organizations out of which the dispute had emerged: twelve thousand to the GM foremen, superintendents, and plant managers who staffed the corporation's seventy-odd production facilities, more than double that number to every UAW local union committeeman, officer, and activist.[78]

Reuther thought their "decisions have reflected a very enlightened point of view." Both umpires held informal discussions with the parties before writing their decisions, and both Millis and Taylor transgressed their formal role by suggesting modifications in the contract that tended to clarify and strengthen the web of rules the union sought to impose on the relationship between workers and foremen.[79] Early in 1941 George Taylor played a decisive role in changing management practice on two key questions. For years GM back-pay policy had been easily summarized: "Wages are not paid for work not performed." Under this policy, GM faced no monetary penalty for inequitable discharges or suspensions; however, in a sweeping opinion rendered in early 1941, Taylor reversed GM's back-pay policy, prompting Reuther to comment, "I think their blood pressure is going to go up considerably when they read it Monday morning."[80] And Taylor also demonstrated the unworkability of GM's harsh disciplinary code, which mandated outright discharge for a wide variety of offenses. By ruling "not guilty" in a series of 1941 cases that might well have merited a penalty less than discharge, Taylor virtually forced GM to concede to the arbitrator considerable discretion in assigning industrial penalties.[81]

The seniority question was undoubtedly the most important shop-floor issue "litigated" through the grievance arbitration system. Seniority was a key facet in the moral economy of American automobile workers. Both as an antidote to arbitrary personnel decisions and as a kind of vested property right in a job, seniority was a key index to union status and to the validation of worker rights on the job. Thus the definition and interpretation of seniority rights had taken up fully 35 percent of the text in the UAW-GM agreement of March 1937.[82] GM conceded that seniority would cover the layoff and recall of workers, but the corporation was determined to limit the extent to which seniority governed the promotions and transfers of workers already on the job. GM managers feared a loss of the "flexibility" needed to run the shop, and in the 1940 contract GM insisted that "in transferring or promoting employees, seniority will be secondary to other qualifications but will be given reasonable consideration."[83] Reuther found such corporate argumentation little more than a cover for supervisors' efforts to reward procompany workers with the best job assignments. In the absence of a strong shop steward system, argued Reuther, an "explicit" set of rules constraining the foreman's discretionary authority was essential to the defense of employee rights.[84]

This need became clear in 1941 after union committeemen took the language of the UAW-GM seniority clause and used it to protest every time a foreman promoted any worker out of the line of strict seniority. By pressing thousands of grievances and presenting scores of fourth-step arbitration cases, the GM Department succeeded in reshaping actual practice on this key issue. In an important series of decisions, Umpire George Taylor first subordinated the phrase "seniority will be secondary" to the idea that "reasonable consideration" had to be given to seniority in all promotions and transfers. Then Taylor invented an entirely new seniority test: the company had to prove that an individual was "head and shoulders" above all others before he or she could be promoted or transferred out of line of seniority. The "head and shoulders" doctrine effectively shifted the burden of proof from the union to the company, made seniority the norm in most promotions to new job classifications, and established a new auto industry work rule that was destined to last for decades.[85]

Despite the drift of such early arbitration rulings, General Motors found the new system enormously advantageous. Charles Wilson recognized that the maintenance of industrial order demanded a measure of employee consent, a legitimization of the disciplinary function. He therefore accommodated the Hillman-Reuther demand for grievance arbitration despite grumbling by Knudsen, Sloan, and the top officials most closely associated with the DuPont interests. "This umpire in our kind of situation is an industrial experiment," asserted the new GM president. It would prove a success if it helped engender "a new kind of thing in social relations, and that is an industrial crime," whose punishment would be seen as just not only by plant supervision but by union officials and fellow workers alike.[86] On this fundamental level the system worked as GM management had hoped. More than half of all cases that came before GM arbitrators in the 1940s involved disciplinary charges by supervisors against workers. Such penalties were often modified by the umpires, but the legitimacy of a system in which management could act and the union could bring grievances was reaffirmed time and again. When charged with an industrial crime, management invoked its penalty right away, then litigated the issue through the grievance procedure. Workers were guilty until proven innocent.[87]

Likewise, the grievance arbitration system greatly strengthened the prohibitions against wildcat strikes. Umpires at GM and the other big automotive companies held union committeemen and local leaders to a standard of conduct higher than that of rank-and-file workers during stoppages. In his very first decision, Taylor referred to "the duty" of committeemen "to take proper steps for meeting the Union obligations" when a wildcat strike occurred. Committeemen who remained at work but did nothing to halt wildcat strikes exhibited "negative leadership" and were therefore subject to management discipline even greater than that accorded the strikers. When union leaders complained that a commitment to elementary solidarity demanded that they align themselves with rank-and-file workers during extracontractual stoppages, a 1944 umpire decision at Ford denounced such a view as "a romantic expression of a perverse and debasing view of the committeeman's obligations."[88] Of course, GM was not willing to rely merely upon the general ideological power of the grievance arbitration system to reinforce its control of the shop-floor work regime. The corporation had its own very precise conception of how industrial arbitration should function. The largest corporation in the world had no need for the kind of economic tutelage and freewheeling intervention so often meted out by the industrial relations "fixers" who had pioneered in the economically chaotic clothing trade. GM therefore insisted that the umpire's job was merely to "call the balls and strikes," not to "add to, subtract from, or modify" the collective bargaining agreement. Moreover, issues that the company saw as central to the maintenance of discipline and economic efficiency would simply not be subject to umpire review. These issues included disputes over the speed of operations and wage payments fixed in the collective bargaining agreement. The adjustment of piece rates and the determination of work norms had been central to the umpire's duties in clothing, but at GM disputes over these issues could be resolved only by strike action authorized by the union.[89]

Within a decade grievance arbitration became nearly universal within unionized industry. The National War Labor Board insisted that every contract contain an arbitration setup; still later, the federal courts virtually mandated an arbitration clause in all postwar contracts.[90] But the very pervasiveness of the institution belied its efficacy as a mechanism for establishing industrial justice on the shop floor. For all their influence, Millis and Taylor were transitional figures at GM. After Taylor's departure in early 1942, umpires at the corporation were men of far less experience and prestige who presided over the system's transformation into one of rigid legalism and lengthy deliberations. Shop disputes reduced to writing took between two and three months to work their way up the grievance ladder. GM executives thought their resolution tended to keep the management-union relationship "on the beam" and made "contract-stretching" by the union more difficult. At Ford and Allis-Chalmers, umpires played a more wide-ranging role, but there too the general drift was toward a strict construction of the contract.[91]

The UAW responded with its own turn toward a highly structured legalism. Reuther delegated day-to-day control of the GM Department's arbitration setup to Thomas Johnstone, who saw the umpire system as "the keystone of the collective bargaining arch in GM."[92] Not unexpectedly, Johnstone soon became the system's disciplinarian and used his staff as a "fire department" that suppressed local job actions and enforced contracts. Johnstone's hand was strengthened in 1944 when the UAW set up its own board of review to screen all General Motors grievances before they went to the umpire. The board eliminated hundreds of grievances whose adverse resolution might set a bad precedent, but the new administrative apparatus proved to be a highly effective political filter that generated even greater distance between American automobile workers and the world of industrial justice they sought to win.[93] The result was a kind of "dehydration" of the dispute resolution machinery: union committeemen were often transformed into contract policemen charged with keeping the lid on difficult situations. At Chrysler shop stewards exercised considerable authority well into the postwar era, but even there the influence of the GM system could be felt by the early 1950s. "Time and time again management does things that I know it has a right to do under the contract," reported a union official at the number-three automaker, "but the men don't know it. If I explain to them that the company has the right under four or five rulings made previously they get sore at me." As a consequence, politically savvy commit-

teemen "become demagogues. They tend to fake on all this stuff. They write grievances when they know they shouldn't, the art of buck passing is developed to the
nth degree."[94]

The great expectations with which Reuther and Hillman introduced the system
of industrial jurisprudence at GM were therefore stillborn. A web of rules regu-
larized and limited management power, but the constitutionalization of the shop
regime fell far short of even Reuther's limited hopes. The underlying problem lay
in the very nature of an orderly system of industrial jurisprudence, for the orderliness so imposed shifted the balance of class power into management's hands. Like
the law of gravity, the collective power of workers is evident only when the everyday structures collapse. Only in the midst of "disorder"—sit-down strikes and
demonstrations and even the self-destructive wildcat stoppages—do workers have
the leverage to focus capital's attention on the concessions necessary to restore a
sense of predictability to the labor of their human assets. But as Reuther well
understood, disorder of the sort that might have given the union an opportunity to
win real power in GM shops was also so disruptive that it would certainly bring
into question the institutional existence of the UAW itself. If Reuther was to escape
this conundrum—and his ambition and intellect gave him no real choice but to
try—he would have to look outside the increasingly claustrophobic world
promised by a purely private, firm-centered collective bargaining relationship with
GM. In short, he would have to look to the realm of national politics and to the
amazing transformation of the American state, then in the midst of its most explosive season of growth in this century.

500 PLANES A DAY

The plane, from certain points of view, is only an automobile with wings.
—*Walter Reuther,* "*500 Planes a Day—A Program for the Utilization of the
Automobile Industry for Mass Production of Defense Planes*,"
December 1940

L ittle more than a week before Walter Reuther and Charles E. Wilson
signed the 1940 General Motors contract, Nazi troops marched into
Paris. The world was at war, and it would remain so, hot or cold, for the remainder of Walter Reuther's life. In the UAW virtually all activity—from the summer education camp agenda to the negotiating strategy at one of the big automakers—took on a political coloration that linked the internal life of the union to the great world historical conflicts that racked the middle decades of the twentieth century. Strikes, wage demands, organizing drives, political endorsements, and the scramble for office were measured by a yardstick that stretched all the way from the body shops of Flint and the toolrooms of Detroit to the White House, the Kremlin, and the battlefronts of Europe and the Far East.

Walter Reuther had an acute understanding of this new world. Indeed, the word *Reutherism* first surfaced in the early 1940s, an addition, albeit of a minor sort, to the great "isms" of the era: Communism, Fascism, Socialism, and Americanism. Like any highly charged ideology, Reutherism had no fixed meaning, but in its most dynamic phase, Reutherism articulated a union strategy informed by the recognition that in an era of wartime mobilization and postwar tension the state would serve as a battleground between the working class and its adversaries.

Reuther saw that the use of the strike weapon would become immensely more difficult, and that the government's direct role in shaping production, wages, and investment would necessarily expand.[1]

To the non-Communist left, Reuther became a sensationally attractive figure in the 1940s because of his overall strategic approach: an assault on management's traditional power in the name of social and economic efficiency, an appeal for public support in the larger liberal interest, and an effort to shift power relations within the political economy, usually by means of a tripartite governmental entity empowered to plan for whole sections of the economy. Still merely a subordinate officer of the UAW, Reuther nevertheless encapsulated a vital strand of social democratic thought. An imaginative planner, he would link union power with government authority in what we might label today a "corporatist" framework designed to reorganize American capitalism within a more stable and humane framework. Yet because his program would limit the freedom and authority of individual corporate enterprises, it was bitterly resisted by most spokesmen for American business.

Reuther's political economy proved particularly attractive because he wedded his reformist planning initiatives to the profound realignment then taking place in the political culture and program of the American left. Until the end of the 1930s the agenda of all progressive Americans—from New Deal technocrats on the right to Trotskyist intellectuals on the left—had been resolutely focused upon the transformation of American capitalism, its metamorphosis into a political economy in some fashion responsive to the popular forces unleashed by the Depression and the rise of the labor-left in that decade. Such dreams did not die, but by the decade's end the reform of capitalism had to share emotional commitment with a bitter opposition to another ideology that also claimed to speak the language of progressive reform and outright anticapitalism. Communist faith in the Soviet Union, now exposed as a cynical and imperialist state, made renewal of the old Popular Front, even during World War II, a temporary expedient at most. As American Communists accommodated themselves to the domestic political imperatives mandated by the Nazi-Soviet pact of August 1939, liberals, radicals, and Socialists who had once collaborated with the CP fled from its embrace. Whatever their good works, the Communists had put themselves beyond the pale, where they had to be exorcised from the body politic.[2]

For Reuther and other politically engaged activists, the break with the Communists was not merely a question of foreign policy but a profoundly ideological and moral issue as well. This was the moment in American history when the word *totalitarian* entered the popular vocabulary, when Communism and Nazism were insolubly linked as "isms" diametrically counterpoised to the pluralism of American democracy. It was 1939, not 1946 or 1947, that marked the inauguration of the ideological cold war between those who still saw the Communist movement as an integral part of the American progressive tradition and those whose hostility to the Communists was fundamental and intransigent. On the anti-Communist left, it became a matter of principle to exclude Communists outright from the leadership of liberal, labor, and professional organizations.[3]

Meanwhile, a wave of prowar, pro-British sentiment swept through the non-Communist left as Nazi tanks blasted their way through western Europe. Interventionist sentiment was linked to a defense of "civilization" against what the columnist Dorothy Thompson called "a tidal wave of red-brown counter-revolution." Among Socialists a "silent split" stripped the party of almost all its young activists, including those in Reuther's UAW circle: his brothers Roy and Victor, as well as Leonard Woodcock, Frank Winn, and George Edwards.[4] As late as October 1939 Reuther still identified with the Socialist tradition of radical antimilitarism. But he too came to favor U.S. aid to Britain to defend "not the Chamberlains, not the paid imperialists, but the British working class who are struggling today to protect their homes, their institutions and their rights." This was the outlook of the new Union for Democratic Action (UDA), whose most prominent personality, the theologian and ex-Socialist Reinhold Niebuhr, sought to regroup all those interventionists who were both prolabor and pro–New Deal. Parent to the postwar Americans for Democratic Action, the UDA provided a haven for former radicals in transit toward militant anti-Communism, Democratic Party liberalism, and an activist foreign policy in the early cold war years. Reuther was clearly the UDA's kind of trade unionist; thus he was soon collaborating with the cosmopolitan liberals of New York and the interventionist New Dealers of Washington, whose early ranks included the journalist I. F. Stone, the *Washington Post* publisher Frank Graham, the UDA's founder, James Loeb, and the defense mobilization lawyer Joseph Rauh.[5]

Intellectuals and political activists were not the only people who began to see the world in a different light after 1939. The outbreak of war in Europe had its greatest impact on that slice of immigrant America that the left had once thought of as its own. The movement of the Red Army into Finland, Poland, and the Baltic states shifted the political terrain sharply to the right, crystallizing an anti-Communist, antiradical sentiment among millions of eastern European workers whose fraternal lodges and social halls had once given comfort and succor to the unions and the left. Operation Barbarossa would do little to reverse this shift. Indeed, the ease with which the Nazi invaders found collaborators in Croatia, Romania, Hungary, Slovakia, Poland, Lithuania, Moldavia, and Ukraine was echoed in the United States by the emergence within these communities of a virulently anti-Communist sentiment directed with unsurpassed bitterness toward those landsmen who still championed Popular Front and pro-Soviet illusions. Thus did the Finns of the upper Midwest shift decisively toward a conservative isolationism after the Soviets breached the Mannerheim Line in the winter of 1940. And among Polish-Americans right-wing leaders won new support after the Nazi-Soviet partition of the homeland, the Soviet failure to recognize the pro-Western government in London, and the discovery that the KGB had slaughtered virtually the entire Polish officer corps at Katyn Woods. As early as 1942 Chicago's largest Polish newspaper argued for a postwar military offensive against the "red liberators" of the homeland.[6]

Reuther capitalized upon this new constellation of forces almost immediately. At the St. Louis convention of the UAW late in August 1940, the Reuther forces easily pushed through a resolution condemning "the brutal dictatorships, and wars of aggression of the totalitarian governments of Germany, Italy, Russia and Japan," after which delegates further isolated the Communists by barring from union office any member of an organization declared "illegal" by the U.S. government. When George Addes warned against a political "purge," hundreds of delegates cheered the Reutherite ex-Socialist Harvey Kitzman when he reminded CP stalwarts that there were "boats leaving every day for Russia."[7]

Reuther also rolled over Communist efforts to forestall a UAW endorsement of President Roosevelt for a third term. The Communists were aligned with CIO President John L. Lewis, whose growing estrangement from FDR was fueled by his fear that U.S. participation in a new world war would merely recapitulate the "war hysteria" and reactionary social tensions generated by the last war.[8] Lewis was still a towering figure whom Reuther feared to attack directly. He therefore denied that the delegates had to choose between Lewis and Roosevelt, and he ridiculed the hypocrisy of his opponents who were now attacking Roosevelt for insufficient liberalism. Waving a copy of the 1939 convention proceedings, Reuther denounced "the beautiful resolutions that [the Communist whip] Brother Nat Ganley introduced, praising Roosevelt, because those were the days of collective security and the People's Front. That is no more; there has been a deal between Stalin and Hitler, and therefore People's Front and collective security have been put in the ash can once and for all." Reuther concluded, "Let Lewis lead the CIO and let Roosevelt lead the nation." The auditorium resounded with cheers of approval, catcalls, and whistles for those who had tried to delay the vote. Only the thirty Communist delegates held their ground.[9]

Reuther came out of the union's 1940 convention the equal of any other leader within the UAW, and a national spokesman for the prodefense, pro-Roosevelt "right wing" within the American labor movement. His stature was confirmed late in October when John L. Lewis threw the CIO into turmoil with his election-week endorsement of Roosevelt's Republican opponent, Wendell Willkie. Speaking of Roosevelt, Lewis asked a nationwide radio audience: "Are we to yield to the appetite for power and the vaunting ambitions of a man who plays with the lives of human beings for a pastime?" Promising to resign the CIO presidency if FDR were reelected, Lewis called upon his union followers to "sustain me now, or repudiate me." The CIO leader soon got his answer. The UAW immediately called a conference of more than 700 local union officers—a meeting the size of a small convention—who quickly confirmed the union's endorsement of President Roosevelt and invited him to Detroit, promising a turnout of 250,000 workers in Cadillac Square. In response, FDR invited Thomas, Frankensteen, and Reuther to lunch at Hunter College in New York. Most in the UAW leadership still coupled their endorsement of FDR with continuing support for Lewis as CIO chief, but the Reuther group was willing to take Lewis's resignation threat at face value. A

Kelsey-Hayes stewards meeting urged R. J. Thomas to "use every means at his command to speed removal of John L. Lewis from office."[10]

Walter Reuther minced no words when he delivered the UAW's thirteen-city radio reply to Lewis. In a hard-driving speech that bore the unmistakable mark of Eddie Levinson's craftsmanship, Reuther denounced the "mad dictators loose in the world" and defended Roosevelt's program of rearmament and aid to Great Britain. But the bulk of his talk was devoted to what for Reuther was a remarkably uncritical defense of the Rooseveltian New Deal and a refutation of Lewis's charge that the president was moving the nation toward "dictatorship." "No President in the history of our nation has struck such hammer blows for social justice. In this process he has stepped on the toes and rapped the knuckles of the coupon clippers and speculators. . . . It is from this source that there originated the mythical charge, the scarecrow of 'dictatorship,' and the 'lust for power.'" Indeed, argued Reuther, Wall Street had "lost some rights—the right to cheat the consumer and the little man—the right to brow beat labor. I see nothing to fear in that." After a contemptuously brief denunciation of Willkie as a "synthetic liberal," Reuther returned for a last stiletto thrust at his onetime chieftain. "The personal spite or the hatred of one man will not switch labor's vote from Mr. Roosevelt. . . . The issue is wholly and simply, Roosevelt or reaction! American labor will take Roosevelt!"[11]

Of course, "Roosevelt or reaction" was a profound misreading of American politics as the United States mobilized itself for a war of global proportions. The real fight lay within the long and hidden corridors of power, where bureaucrats, executives, and military officers were shaping America's new war economy. Just before he beat Willkie, Franklin Roosevelt is said to have told Thomas G. Corcoran, the New Deal "fixer" and presidential confidant, "Tommy, cut out this New Deal stuff. It's tough to win a war."[12] Such was the conventional wisdom, of which Roosevelt was both victim and architect, after the Nazi blitz put defense mobilization at the center of U.S. politics. Within weeks Roosevelt called for a tripling of the military budget, massive aid to Great Britain, and a peacetime draft. Most dramatically, he called for the production of fifty thousand military aircraft a year, a figure that far surpassed the number of warplanes then in existence on the entire globe. A new warfare state was in the making, symbolized by a giant office complex, the twenty-nine-acre Pentagon, which now began to rise from the mudflats on the south bank of the Potomac River. Unlike the wooden "temporaries" that had been built to house an expanded military establishment in 1917, there was nothing flimsy about the five-sided concrete structure. It was built to last.

Roosevelt reasoned that in any rearmament effort, business and financial interests that had once been bitterly hostile to the New Deal would have to be accommodated. In May he established the National Defense Advisory Commission (NDAC), the first of a series of mobilization agencies that Roosevelt hoped would bring order to the burgeoning military-industrial apparatus. In these wartime agencies the highest posts were invariably staffed by dollar-a-year businessmen

and career military officers whose worldviews and operating methods were antithetical to the New Deal ethos. Roosevelt did make Sidney Hillman a member of
the NDAC—in recognition of labor's strategic power and Hillman's personal loyalty—but most authority went to industrialists like Edward R. Stettinius of U.S.
Steel and the Burlington Northern's Ralph Budd. William Knudsen held the
most important post on the new commission. His appointment as head of production planning was a tribute to the enormous productive power of Detroit and
reflected the key role General Motors and the automobile industry would be
expected to play in the mobilization effort. Alone, General Motors controlled 10
percent of the nation's entire manufacturing capacity! In July 1940 Roosevelt
reorganized his cabinet to reflect the nation's new geography of power and policy. To top positions at the War and Navy Departments Roosevelt appointed the
Republicans Henry Stimson, secretary of state under Hoover, and Frank Knox,
Alf Landon's running mate in 1936. Both were leaders of the internationalist,
interventionist wing of the GOP; from the familiar law offices and investment
banking firms of New York and Boston, Stimson and Knox brought to Washington a corps of civilian managers who would dominate war and postwar politico-
military strategy for more than a generation. Among them were John Lord
O'Brien, Robert Lovett, John J. McCloy, Robert Patterson, James Forrestal, and
the Dulles brothers, Allen and John Foster.[13]

Although Roosevelt had ceded the administrative high ground to his erstwhile
opponents, the mobilization process did not go smoothly. The armed services
believed that awarding prime contracts to the nation's largest corporations on very
lucrative terms guaranteed speed and reliability. Naturally, the dollar-a-year men
in the planning bureaucracies applauded the effort to franchise out the production
details: the U.S. Treasury's fiscal stimulus would be turned on full blast, but the
money pouring out of Washington would reinvigorate the traditional structures of
corporate power and privilege. Thus, of more than eleven billion dollars in prime
contracts awarded by the services during the seven months from June to December 1940, 60 percent went to twenty firms and 86 percent to the top one hundred
corporations. However, these core corporations were both unprepared and, in
some respects, unwilling to tackle the mobilization program, no matter how great
the purely economic incentives. Politically, this was the era when the isolationist
America First Committee had its greatest impact, and precisely in those midwestern manufacturing sectors upon which defense production would rely. If the war
were to end quickly or in a negotiated peace, then defense mobilization would
have been merely a rational for higher taxes and a larger federal presence. Such
were the private thoughts of many, and they were given voice by the public pro-
nouncements of men like Charles Lindbergh, Joseph Kennedy, and Robert Taft.
Henry Ford actually rejected a multimillion-dollar contract for the manufacture of
Rolls-Royce aircraft engines after learning that they would be sent directly to
England: he flatly refused to build weapons for export to the Allies.[14]

The industrialists who staffed the new mobilization agencies were not America

Firsters, but they did share with their comrades on the right a fear that the war would generate the kind of overcapacity that had so plagued both agriculture and heavy industry in the Depression decade. This fear was particularly strong at U.S. Steel and Alcoa Aluminum (the latter an outright monopoly), both of which opposed building new mills to expand production, even with huge government subsidies. In the automobile industry few worried about postwar overcapacity, but manufacturers did fear that defense orders and raw material shortages might crimp the industry's ability to fill the burgeoning demand for new cars.[15] "We must remember that war orders are a boom business, and that there is a definite end to it," asserted Harvey Campbell of the Detroit Board of Commerce in May 1940. ". . . I don't believe that manufacturers are anxious for war business. They would rather see a steady line of production and employment." The automakers therefore took defense orders but chose to build new facilities and add new production lines rather than convert existing factories and machine tools to military production. A year after the Nazi invasion of the low countries, the bulk of the defense work assigned to the auto industry still consisted of engineering studies and new plant construction. Not unexpectedly, 1940 and 1941 turned out to be banner car production years, the best since 1929.[16]

To New Dealers and liberal interventionists, Detroit's unwillingness to contribute more to the war effort seemed to confirm the Tory indifference and "business as usual" mentality of its leading figures, including the defense commissioner William Knudsen. Nazi bombs were pounding British airfields in the late summer of 1940, yet Knudsen shielded the auto firms, enabling them to order new machine tools for their 1941 models and assign millions of hours of skilled-work time to make the tools and dies that went with them. GM itself devoted less than 3.5 percent of its output to defense work that year, and only about 10 percent in the first half of 1941. Wrote I. F. Stone, the Nation's Washington correspondent: "If war means a boom business in cars, the automobile industry is prepared to swallow its pacifism. But if war means curtailment of civilian business in the interest of defense, the automobile industry isn't so sure. Detroit suddenly feels far, far removed from the sea."[17]

Walter Reuther agreed; indeed, he and Levinson had been key sources for Stone ever since the Nazi-Soviet pact had put him in their political camp. Reuther and his comrades could see that the industry's mobilization failure created a political opportunity for labor-liberals by demonstrating both the technical and organizational bankruptcy of their managerial adversaries and the necessity for a measure of laborite influence and corporatist control in the governance of America's largest industry. The airframe makers of America were batch producers: production runs of only a few score units were made, then the designs were altered, the bugs ironed out, and limited production resumed. On the eve of war capital investment per employee in this relatively new industry was less than one-third that of the typical Chevrolet assembly plant. Technological change was therefore rapid, but unit costs were high, skilled labor was essential, and output was low. In Germany and

Great Britain well-embedded craft traditions within the workforce enabled manufacturers to convert a wide variety of metal fabrication factories to airframe production. But in the United States the mass-production ethos meant that the expansion of aircraft production would require huge numbers of machine tools and millions of hours to fabricate the dies, jigs, and fixtures required by the Fordist regime and its unskilled workforce.[18]

If, as seemed likely, new aircraft factories were built in southern California, Texas, Georgia, and Kansas, then the defense program and the UAW would face enormous difficulties. Despite around-the-clock construction and high-priority machine tool orders, delay and inefficiency were inevitable in bringing a new production facility on line. Driving to work in the summer of 1940, Reuther watched the rapid progress of the construction crews at Packard's new aircraft engine factory, yet even with all the frenetic activity, no Packard-built Merlin engines would fly until 1942 or later. Machine tools were a key bottleneck, as was the recruitment and training of an unseasoned workforce. Reuther may well have remembered the waste, confusion, and delay that he found so frustrating while on his sojourn as a Gorky toolmaker during the Soviet Union's era of forced draft industrialization. "New plants cannot be built and put into operation in less than eighteen months," forecast Reuther in the fall of 1940, although even this estimate turned out to be several months short of the World War II average. ". . . Britain's battle, for all her people's bravery, may be lost, and our own country left to face a totalitarian Europe alone."[19]

Reuther was not the only one to see Detroit as the potential aircraft capital of the nation. Late in May 1940 *Wards Automotive Reports* announced that a "painstaking survey of the present situation indicates that the widespread worry over tooling for volume output of airplane engines may be somewhat overdone; that our ability to produce motorized equipment is available almost in a twinkling." *Wards* estimated that in ninety days "a small army of craftsmen can be transferred to aviation, tank, truck and ordnance tooling." From Washington the *New York Times* reported that "mass production experts" were saying that the aviation industry's machine tool bottleneck could be "broken quickly by calling on the automobile factories to turn out aviation engines." Indeed, General Motors had already begun making parts for the Allison aviation engine in Detroit, much of it with retooled Cadillac machinery.[20]

The problem was that no single firm wanted to convert its facilities to military production if doing so were to lead to premature loss of its share of the booming civilian market. Walter Reuther therefore proposed a "short-cut" that would solve the structural dilemma by aggregating the auto industry's unused capacity into one huge plane production unit. Detroit operated at 80–90 percent of its maximum capacity for only a few months each year. Tool and die work for the automakers was notoriously cyclical: half the skilled workers averaged six months or less employment per year. Most factories operated on a single shift, and in 1940 there were still many plants, including those of Cadillac, Studebaker, Chrysler,

Willys-Overland, and Nash, operating at well below one-third capacity. To each firm individually, such idleness represented a rational use of its resources, but given the needs of the national defense program, Detroit's haphazard deployment of its vast productive machine was a social and economic debacle. Reuther's plan would continue civilian auto production but postpone tooling for the 1942 models by six months, thereby making available the labor time of as many as fifteen thousand skilled mechanics to build the tools, dies, jigs, and fixtures for the production of an all-metal fighter on a mass-production basis. At Gorky the Reuther brothers had been part of a similar tooling program in which skilled workers prepared for future use military dies for tanks and heavy artillery. In the United States military tooling would be needed immediately, but there were plenty of idle body plants, like those of Hupmobile, Murray, Detroit Fisher, and Ford Highland Park, in which to mass-produce wings and fuselages. Meanwhile, engine manufacture and assembly would take place at a central facility to which many of the industry's redundant machine tools would be consigned.[21]

In May 1940 Sidney Hillman had appointed Reuther to an NDAC manpower training committee, so Reuther naturally broached this plan with his sometime mentor. After they conferred in August, Hillman spoke with Knudsen, who was directly responsible for coordinating defense production. Not unexpectedly, Knudsen told Hillman, "We can't get the automobile industry to move that fast," but his brush-off was hardly the last word in what would turn out to be a yearlong campaign for the "Reuther Plan." Hillman was already in the midst of a protracted and frustrating conflict with the dollar-a-year men, who were ignoring efforts by the dwindling band of administration New Dealers to inject an element of social planning and laborite participation into the organization of the emerging war economy. Hillman therefore urged Reuther to forge ahead; he did so by assigning Victor and Ben Blackwood, his skilled trades staffer in the GM Department, to make a careful survey of idle production capacity in the industry. By November Reuther's team had assembled enough data to hold an unofficial production council at Cass Technical High, where skilled tradesmen from more than a dozen factories endorsed the feasibility of the Reuther Plan.[22]

Here was a vital element in the excitement the Reuther Plan would soon evoke: counterplanning from the shop floor up. Organized and coordinated through the union, veteran machinists and tool and die men had a better overall understanding of industry technics than did any individual corporate manager. They were a practical example of Thorstein Veblen's "soviet of engineers," whose road to power crossed the new economic terrain carved out by wartime production politics. Power seemed to be lying not in the streets but on the underutilized and ill-coordinated shop floors of a score or more Detroit production facilities. Could Reuther pick it up? Certainly he had a Bolshevik flare for sloganeering. Reuther gave his auto industry conversion plan a sensational name, "500 Planes a Day"—a commitment to actually build, and build quickly, the waves of warplanes that Roosevelt had promised for the defense of Great Britain. Polished with the aid of Edward Levinson and I. F. Stone, who "coined a few phrases" as Reuther dictated the plan late one October night, the introductory prose perfectly captured the sense of destiny and technocratic vision that American industrial supremacy still inspired in this season of fascist triumph. "England's battles, it used to be said, were won on the playing fields of Eton. This plan is put forward in the belief that America's can be won on the assembly lines of Detroit." Like Roosevelt in the presidential campaign, Reuther did not assert the need for the use of U.S. forces abroad, but he did believe that "in an age of mechanized warfare, victory has become a production problem. . . . Time, every moment of it precious, its tragic periods ticked off by bombs falling upon London and the Midlands, will not permit us to wait until new mass production factories for aircraft and aircraft engines finally swing into action late in 1942. . . . This plan is labor's answer to a crisis."[23]

It was a crisis indeed, and not only for the U.S. aircraft program. The crossroad at which the industrial union movement stood in the fall of 1940 was a political crisis that arose directly out of the militarization of the economy and the internal transformation of the New Deal. The long-sought revitalization of heavy industry had finally arrived, but unless labor-liberals could again grasp the levers of administrative power, the reconfiguration of the political economy would be guided by hands hostile to labor's great decade of struggle. Sidney Hillman seemed to be well situated to make labor's weight felt on the administrative apparatus: at the NDAC he stood as the bureaucratic equal of industrialists like Knudsen and Stettinius. But Hillman's power was a rapidly ebbing commodity that was largely dependent upon Roosevelt's assessment of the CIO's potentially disruptive impact on the defense program. By the fall of 1940 it was clear that for all his prominence Hillman could not prevent the military from signing procurement contracts with labor law violators, nor could he ensure that the distribution of the new billions flowed to small business, to regions of chronic unemployment, or through channels that gave the planning wing of the New Deal real clout. He came to represent less the needs of labor within the decision-making chambers of the capital than the viewpoint of an aggressive and self-aggrandizing state within the councils of the labor movement. As his biographer Steve Fraser put it: "Hillman's actual power to determine the contours of public policy declined in inverse proportion to his official position and prestige."[24]

Thus the Reuther Plan filled the vacuum created by Lewis's abdication and Hillman's impotence. Reuther's proposal mandated the establishment of a tripartite aviation production board that would have the power to ignore corporate boundaries, markets, and profits as it presided over the conscription of machine tools, working space, and manpower where and when needed. In structure the board harked back to the corporatist experiments of the NRA era; in power it would mimic Great Britain's Ministry of Supply, which Winston Churchill's coalition government had put in place to ensure a level of industrywide production coordination that neither the American military nor its prime contractors would tolerate. The Reuther Plan would thereby resolve union problems that collective bargaining had thus far proven incapable of resolving. First among these was regularity of employment—the long-sought annual wage would be virtually guaranteed through the tripartite pooling of idle production capacity. Second, the plan gave labor a voice in industry's government-financed investment decisions, an enormous breakthrough for a war economy in which aircraft accounted for 30 percent of all military expenditures and the Treasury financed three-quarters of all new plant and equipment.

And finally, the Reuther Plan promised to strengthen the UAW in the shop. Aircraft was a notoriously antiunion, low-wage industry. But if engine and airframe production were reconcentrated in the unionized Midwest, the UAW could avoid the time-consuming and problematic effort to organize hundreds of thousands of new aircraft workers, especially difficult in the emerging industry center, southern California, the "white spot of the open shop." Because of his relative strength within General Motors and among the skilled tradesmen of Detroit, Reuther would enhance his factional power, while diminishing that of rivals like Richard Frankensteen, the new director of the UAW aircraft drive whose West Coast organization was largely under Communist leadership.[25]

Reuther and his plan burst upon Washington immediately before Christmas 1940 when Philip Murray, the new CIO president, and R. J. Thomas forwarded the proposal to President Roosevelt. Thomas was a most reluctant emissary: "You're not going to make a horse's ass out of me." Union men should "stick to their knitting," he is reported to have told Reuther when asked to back the program.[26] But Murray found Reuther's idea more than useful: it represented the most concrete application of his own all-encompassing program for a series of "industry councils," inspired as much by the social reformist encyclicals of Pope Leo XI as by the NRA planning experiments of the early New Deal years. Unlike John L. Lewis, whose mistrust of the New Deal intensified after he stepped down from the CIO presidency, Murray saw the state apparatus as a terrain of struggle that the war had made suddenly favorable once again. And like Reuther, Murray wanted industry governance put in the hands of tripartite committees that would allocate raw materials, channel manpower, and set wages and prices into the postwar years. In the following months CIO unions developed specific plans for steel, aluminum, farm equipment, and nonferrous metals, but it was Reuther's scheme, with its daring promise of five hundred planes a day within six months, that generated the greatest enthusiasm and evoked the most pointed debate.[27] Roosevelt publicly announced his interest in the idea, the New Dealers were enthusiastic, and the dollar-a-year businessmen grudgingly respectful. Reuther explained his "500 planes a day" production plan to a nationwide radio audience on December 27, then had a Sunday morning breakfast meeting at the Cosmos Club with a cohort of embattled New Dealers, including Jerome Frank, chairman of the Securities and Exchange Commission, Leon Henderson of the NDAC, the Treasury Department's Harry Dexter White, John Carmody of the WPA, and the FDR confidant Tom Corcoran. All found Reuther charming and forceful and his ideas persuasive, encapsulating that combination of technical self-confidence, social reform, and wartime urgency that captured the spirit of the defense-era New Deal. White arranged for Reuther to meet that afternoon with Secretary of the Treasury Henry Morgenthau, who quipped, "There is only one thing wrong with the program. It comes from the 'wrong' source."[28]

Joseph Rauh, a self-described "war hawk" in the fall of 1940, remembered Reuther's bravura performance at the Washington Press Club early in the New Year. "This young man took Washington and all of its cynical reporters by storm that day." To Rauh and his circle of interventionist New Dealers—"Everybody I knew was so much for the war we could taste it"—Reuther's plan to accelerate aircraft production was "the greatest thing he ever did . . . because it combined his gigantic knowledge of the social forces in America, his mastery of the technical forces and his idealism."[29] I. F. Stone proved an equally enthusiastic proponent in the pages of the *Nation* and Marshall Field's ardently liberal newspaper *PM*. "Our full potential capacity can be mobilized only by enlisting in the effort the widest participation of American enterprise, engineering ability, and labor. Defense must be democratic if it is to be efficient; only a democratic defense can be a total defense in a total war. This is what the monopolists do not understand, dare not understand, for though a democratic defense would protect our country it would undermine their power."[30]

But embattled New Dealers were not alone in finding Reuther's proposal attractive. *Time* magazine, whose founder was about to announce the dawning of the "American Century," commended Reuther's plan as "on a braver, broader scale than Mr. Knudsen's proposal." Likewise, Walter Lippmann, no friend of New Deal economic planning, nevertheless devoted two columns to Reuther's scheme, the author of which was "playing an active and responsible part in the battle of production." The *Washington Post* called the plan "a remarkable example of the way in which our people are waiting to be led and organized in making aid to Britain a reality." Finally, Blair Moody, the influential Washington correspondent for the *Detroit News*, reported that Reuther's plan was "being seriously regarded as perhaps the most constructive production proposal ever to come from the ranks of organized labor."[31] Reuther's ideas even won a measure of respectful curiosity from the Wall Street Republicans Roosevelt had so recently put in charge of the defense apparatus. Though fundamentally hostile to labor's aims, they were also impatient with the parochialism that seemed to characterize so many in manufacturing management. Thus Undersecretary of War Robert Patterson had already begun to force a sometimes reluctant aircraft industry to curb its civilian output and replace it with military production. Within weeks he would agitate for a similar switch among the major auto corporations.[32]

Patterson's efforts were spurred on by his special assistant, Robert Lovett, a Stimson recruit from Brown Brothers Harriman; in his globalist vision of postwar U.S. power, dominance in commercial and military aviation was essential. Like Reuther, Lovett saw auto industry parochialism, machine tool bottlenecks, and

Knudsen's timidity as obstacles to a vast increase in military aircraft production. Intrigued by Reuther's ideas, he told Patterson that it would be better "to have one plant completely equipped" than to have "several plants all lacking a certain proportion of tools so that none of them are in operation." He asked Knudsen to turn over aircraft engine blueprints to Reuther, and he put a military aircraft at the UAW leader's disposal for a January tour of defense plants.[33] Accompanied by Army Air Force officers, Reuther inspected the Pratt & Whitney engine factory in Hartford and the Glen L. Martin plant in Baltimore. At both facilities, reported the military, management attitudes toward the unionist quickly changed from "hostility to tolerance" because "he was earnestly trying to help the cause of National Defense."[34]

Despite such high-level interest, the Reuther Plan proved anathema to auto executives, the aircraft manufacturers, and their allies in the military. "Everyone admits that Reuther is smart," argued GM President Charles Wilson, "but this is none of his business. . . . If Reuther wants to become part of management, GM will be happy to hire him. But so long as he remains Vice-President of the Union, he has no right to talk as if he were Vice-President of a company."[35] Reuther and Hillman met with Knudsen and his staff on March 1, 1941, but the discussions proved frustrating. "They wanted to come into the shop as a union committee and try to design fixtures for the present machinery," Knudsen remarked later in the month. "We had to stall on that one and say that it couldn't be handled."[36]

Given the production pressures emanating from the War Department, Detroit could not denounce the plan on such purely ideological grounds. Knudsen and other auto industry experts therefore attacked Reuther's plan as technically inadequate: Detroit's machine tools were too imprecise for aircraft production; pooling arrangements were difficult and cumbersome; the U.S. government wanted to emphasize production of bombers, not fighters. There were indeed technical difficulties with Reuther's conversion plan: fighter planes had at least ten times as many parts as did a Fisher-built auto body, and they required frequent design changes, dictated by the performance of their enemy counterparts. Apart from engine production, aircraft was less a manufacturing industry than a contracting business, like construction and shipbuilding; the Reuther vision of row upon row of fighters moving down the assembly line proved but a seductive mirage.[37]

Nevertheless, Reuther's vision, linking technical innovation and patriotic purpose, had enormous power. The counterattack was therefore also certain to question Reuther's Americanism, even as his ideas were subject to tests of their productive practicality. Thus it was no surprise that the Reuther Plan came under almost immediate assault from America's fast-growing security apparatus. To the FBI and army intelligence, Reuther was still considered a Communist in late 1940. A report from G-2, the army's domestic intelligence branch, argued that the Reuther Plan was but a ploy to transfer "a large percentage of our plane production" from the nonunion aviation industry to the UAW-organized auto plants, "in which the CP has a strong voice."[38] FBI Director J. Edgar Hoover naturally concurred. Indeed, Victor and Walter Reuther had been given prominent places on the FBI's new "custodial detention" list of dangerous individuals slated for arrest should the president declare a national emergency.[39]

When Reuther's name popped up in the headlines shortly after Christmas, Hoover quickly sent a long summary of Reuther's substantial file to those the director thought would be most interested. Among these were FDR's secretary Edwin Watson, William Knudsen, and the Dixiecrat demagogue, Eugene E. Cox of Georgia. The centerpiece of the FBI file was a copy of the enthusiastically pro-Soviet letter that Walter and Victor Reuther had written from Gorky to Melvin Bishop and his wife Gladys on January 20, 1934, the so-called Gorky letter. Hoover flatly accused Reuther of being a Communist, and from this time on, whenever Reuther sought a security clearance for service on a government committee or was considered for a Washington job, the FBI director circulated the Gorky letter, along with much other evidence of Reuther's radical activities in the late 1930s.[40] Eugene Cox told the House of Representatives that Reuther was "as violent a red as ever turned on the American public by Russian Communism," and he inserted into the *Congressional Record* Hoover's copy of the 1,500-word letter.[41]

The letter was written just after the Reuther brothers had arrived in Gorky and was the first of several they sent from the Soviet Union to their SP comrades and Brookwood friends in the United States. Most were written by Victor but usually signed "Vic and Wal." The January 1934 letter was full of enthusiasm for the Soviet industrialization drive: "We are actually helping to build a society that will forever end the exploitation of man by man," wrote the twenty-two-year-old Victor. "Let no one say that the workers in the USSR are not on the road to security, enlightenment and happiness." In 1934 such sentiments were unexceptional among Socialist Party youth; in July of that year most of the letter was printed in the YPSL *Challenge*, including its entire last sentence, "Carry on the fight."[42]

The letter proved controversial from the start. Roy Reuther, who was then part of a Lovestoneite grouping within the SP, thought his brothers had apparently "gone completely Stalinist." Because the letter had appeared in print and, indeed, was ammunition for both sides in the Militant–Old Guard faction fight, it is not surprising that it soon found its way into antiunion hands. The Liberty League propagandist Joseph Kamp quoted from the letter in his March 1937 booklet, "Join the CIO . . . and Help Build a Soviet America," as did Michigan's Republican congressman, Clare Hoffman, in an anti-CIO declamation of June 1, 1937. It was at this point, probably as a result of Kamp's pamphlet, that many reprints of the letter began to carry the last line "Carry on the Fight for a Soviet America." This was the version that appeared in all subsequent FBI reports and most anti-Reuther publications.[43]

The Gorky letter was clearly an embarrassment, and no more so than in the spring of 1941 when Reuther's advocacy of more aircraft production, his high-profile negotiation of a new GM contract, and his bitter feud with the UAW Communists kept the energetic union leader constantly in the headlines. In May, Michigan Republicans again used the letter to denounce Reuther as a Communist, even as his Communist rivals charged him with promoting "war and speedup."[44] The months before Pearl Harbor constituted a dress rehearsal for the later cold war: it was a time for political orthodoxy, with scant recognition that a person's views might have evolved over the previous decade. Reuther made his public capitulation during an interview with Blair Moody of the *Detroit News*, when he foisted onto his brother Victor the sole responsibility for the tone and content of the letter Congressman Cox had put in the *Congressional Record* four months earlier. Denying that he had ever endorsed the letter, Walter asserted that Victor had written it "in the flush of enthusiasm at seeing all those stupid Russian peasants, who had never had anything, working in a fine factory."[45]

Victor was furious, as was Roy, and in a confrontation with Walter the youngest brother insisted that he would not be used as his sibling's ideological dumping ground. Walter immediately retreated—he hated such moments of unresolved tension within the family—insisting that Moody had misquoted him. To his brothers Walter apologized profusely, but he then proceeded to further muddy the public waters by claiming that the letter Cox read into the *Congressional Record* was a complete forgery, "concocted by foes of the UAW-CIO during the 1937 strikes."[46] This lie fooled no one on either the left or right; indeed, it gave credibility to the charges of opportunism and hypocrisy that had become the predictable accusations hurled at Reuther in the new round of factionalism that convulsed the UAW in the summer of 1941.

As if this were not enough, Reuther also faced the charge of dodging the draft just as he was becoming known as a prominent spokesman for labor cooperation with the defense effort. At the age of thirty-three, and in excellent physical condition, Reuther registered for the military draft early in 1941 claiming two dependents, his wife May, then his UAW-paid secretary, and his seventeen-year-old sister Christine, who had recently joined the Reuther household in Detroit. Reuther did not request a deferment on the basis of the dependency of his wife and sister, but UAW President R. J. Thomas did request an occupational deferment for the GM director because of his key job in the union. Reuther's draft board was not persuaded, and on April 30, 1941, it gave him a class 1-A rating, with a tentative induction date of May 21.[47]

Reuther's draft status became national news shortly thereafter because Thomas and CIO President Philip Murray announced that they would appeal the decision of the local board on the grounds that Reuther "has direct supervision for the union on labor regulations covering seventy-eight plants and 173,000 workers. A great many of these employees are engaged in defense production."[48] Reuther undoubtedly sought to keep out of the army, but Murray's intervention was more than a personal favor: the CIO wanted the government to defer high-level trade union officials on the same grounds as their corporate counterparts. Selective Service was unwilling to make Reuther such a concession on occupational grounds, but he did win a lower-ranking dependency deferment after it became clear that May would be forced off the UAW payroll if he were drafted. Within just a few weeks May did quit work, became pregnant, and in February 1942 gave birth to the couple's first child, Linda, whose arrival ensured that Reuther's draft deferment would remain intact throughout the war.[49]

Reuther's troubles with the draft were hardly unusual: hundreds of thousands of young men sought to manipulate their deferment status in the hopes of postponing or avoiding induction into the armed services. But the symbolic politics of such efforts were treacherous indeed for those in the popular arena; the fast-rising warfare state was transforming family arrangements and personal inclinations into ideological constructions of the most public sort. Thus Reuther's deferred draft status—on the basis of his wife's dependency—subjected him again to bitter recrimination, especially from the Communists, whom he had repeatedly denounced for seeking to undermine the defense effort. A typical blast came at the UAW's 1941 convention in August; John Anderson of Local 155 tried to deflect a Reutherite attack by announcing that "the 'Royal Family' that sponsored this resolution has in its ranks a man that would sooner face cameras than bullets. . . . He hid behind the skirts of his wife, and every man in this hall knows that."[50]

These controversies added to the Reuther Plan's sensational quality, but it was the war economy itself that undermined the social democratic corporatism inherent in his CIO-sponsored scheme. Indeed, Pearl Harbor brought the Reuther Plan not its most promising opportunity for implementation but its bureaucratic demise. All at once, the government banned civilian auto production and swamped Detroit with production contracts. The difficulties of partial conversion, which would have disrupted competitive relationships in the civilian market, were postponed for the duration of the war. All this became clear in early January 1942 when Reuther used a two-day meeting of the auto industry division of the Office of Production Management (OPM) to make one last effort to salvage the most rudimentary elements of his production plan. By this time, a month after Pearl Harbor, the military had five billion dollars' worth of orders for the Detroit manufacturers to take over immediately, yet the chaos of the industry's overnight conversion had generated a wildly checkered production pattern. More than 225,000 autoworkers were temporarily unemployed, including vital tool and die workers whose every hour of idleness represented lost employment and production for scores of others. In a scrappy exchange with Charles Wilson, whom he now met more frequently in government offices than across the negotiating table, Reuther pointed to the eight hundred highly skilled tool and die men underemployed at GM's Ternstedt auto parts complex, even as Ford desperately scrambled for workers to build the twelve thousand dies needed to equip its new Willow Run bomber plant.[51]

To avoid such inefficiency, Reuther wanted Detroit-area pooling of all tool and die facilities. Victor Reuther had already negotiated the seniority guidelines that facilitated the transfer of workers from civilian to military production. Now Walter argued for a parallel transfer of production contracts under the coordination of a "central agency to route the tooling jobs to see that the right job gets to the right shop in terms of machinery and tools and manpower." Reuther demanded that "every tooling hour in industry regardless of where it is . . . be utilized at all times."[52] Knudsen and Wilson no longer had any doubt that most Detroit machine tools could be converted to war production, but they saw in even this stripped-down version of the Reuther Plan an insidious challenge to managerial capitalism. Reuther wanted to "regiment industry," charged Knudsen; Wilson thought government-sponsored pooling of tools and facilities was tantamount to "complete socialization of industry." It "would be just about as much help as the boys in the rank and file of the Army and Navy if they were to tell the General Staff how to get this thing done."[53]

American capitalists were not adverse to planning, but only if they were the ones to determine its essential character. Although Reuther's machine tool–pooling idea expired within the OPM bureaucracy, where labor had just the slightest leverage, the auto industry began to share, subcontract, and convert its tools, manpower, and factory space in a fashion not even Reuther had fully imagined a few months before. Detroit converted its production capacity to build all sorts of aviation engine parts, subassemblies, and equipment: by June 1942 the industry was using 66 percent of its machine tools on military goods, and late in the war the president of Chrysler boasted that his company had converted 89 percent of its automotive capacity to war work.[54] The Reuther brothers took such statistics as vindication of their 1940 plan, but the success of management-led conversion clearly undermined the most potent rationales for labor participation in the industry's collective management. Even Reuther admitted to Wilson and Edsel Ford, "We have no argument on what we are trying to achieve. We are discussing the question of how we get at it."[55]

Unlike the early New Deal, when labor's political and economic participation was essential to restore political legitimacy to the system and generate a higher level of consumption, the military Keynesianism of the 1940s ameliorated the still-unresolved economic dilemmas and social conflicts that had given rise to corporatist thinking and the New Deal. With virtually unlimited funds, military procurement officers found it most convenient to contract out a program with a large corporation such as Ford or Chrysler and then let the corporate management handle the subcontracting in the normal business fashion. The system generated delay and waste, but even when the production crisis of 1940 and 1941 prompted greater centralization, direction of the warfare state remained bureaucratically divided, ad hoc, and essentially responsive to the traditionally volunteerist values of American business. Sidney Hillman and the ever-shrinking band of New Deal systemitizers steadily lost whatever influence they had possessed during the defense-era production crisis. The scale of funding and the resources available rapidly subsumed the disorder and inefficiency, which in any event heavy industry preferred to the coercions of a corporatist state whose operations were beyond their immediate control.[56]

Reuther's plan was dead, but the unionist had won new prominence as one of the nation's most exciting advocates of technosocial planning. As a trade union leader, Reuther now stood just below Philip Murray, Sidney Hillman, and John L. Lewis. Twice he spoke to nationwide radio audiences in the month after Pearl Harbor. *Time* and *Business Week* devoted respectful columns to his politics and program, while the *New York Times Magazine* opened its pages to his views on labor's rightful place in the war effort. *Fortune* called Reuther the "Plan Man." Even General Motors conceded the potency, if not the correctness, of Reuther's spokesmanship. On March 31, 1942, the corporation invited scores of journalists to witness a debate on auto industry conversion between management and union teams headed up by Charles Wilson and Walter Reuther. The debate, often highly technical, became a six-hour endurance contest, with Reuther addressing "Mr. Wilson" and the General Motors president speaking to "Walter." When a reporter asked Wilson why he was willing to publicly debate the Reuther Plan when he had cold-shouldered it for fifteen months, the GM executive paid his adversary a grudging tribute. "The Reuther plan is dead. It never had any merit but . . . if a corpse is not properly buried with due ceremony its ghost may haunt the living."[57]

But Reuther himself was more alive than ever. He was now in Washington for a few days almost every month. Most of his contacts were New Dealers, like Interior Secretary Harold Ickes, his deputy Abe Fortas, and the liberal economists Robert Nathan, Leon Keyserling, and John Kenneth Galbraith. He got on well with Texas Congressman Lyndon Johnson—still in his New Deal phase—upon whose spare couch Reuther slept during several visits. Reuther had also won the personal confidence of the powerful undersecretary of war, Robert Patterson, who was in charge of overall procurement for the army. To Patterson and his aides, Reuther was smart, knowledgeable, and full of energy. Despite the eclipse of the Reuther Plan, his faith in the power and logic of American Fordism remained undiminished. Reuther found enormous satisfaction, even joy, in the clever deployment of Detroit's most efficient mass-production technique in industries, like aircraft and ordnance, that were still dependent upon small-batch manufacturing methods. Thus Reuther convinced the Army Air Force that the "shaved" gears manufactured for automobile engines in Detroit were just as accurate as the far more labor-intensive gears "ground" by Pratt & Whitney machinists in Hartford. And he convinced army officers at the Imperial Arsenal in Philadelphia that the hand labor necessary to turn out 75-millimeter tank barrels could be cut by more than 90 percent if the military turned to the "broaching" machinery standard in Detroit metal shops.[58]

Reuther's passion for the transcorporate pooling of machine tools and skilled labor finally had some impact as well when the army insisted, as Reuther had first proposed, that Chrysler, Ford, and GM adopt a single engine, built in the converted Lincoln factory, for the M-4 tank each manufacturer was rushing into production.[59] Reuther took the idea a step further in 1944 when, during a season of labor shortages and unpredictable production requirements, he urged the Pentagon and the War Manpower Commission to establish a series of "technical commando units" composed of tool and die makers, designers, draftsmen, and engineers, who could quickly shift their attention from factory to factory when bottlenecks appeared.[60]

Reutherite Fordism extended to housing construction as well as machine tools. In the fall of 1941 Reuther took the lead in the UAW's advocacy of a federally subsidized "Defense City" designed to shelter fifty-five thousand at Willow Run, the site forty miles west of Detroit where the giant Ford bomber plant was under construction. In this project Reuther had the assistance, and inspiration, of a remarkable architect and friend, Oskar Stonorov, who helped crystallize Reuther's sense of the modernist aesthetic. Born in Frankfurt and educated in France, Switzerland, and Italy, Stonorov had assimilated the radically modernist spirit of the Bauhaus school by the time he immigrated to the United States in the early 1930s. Stonorov, a pioneering architect of New Deal housing, attacked privately constructed, single-family homes as "fortresses of individualism." This viewpoint informed his design for Defense City, whose schools, shops, gardens, and pedestrian byways were integrated into a harmonious and permanent "new town."[61]

Reuther was captivated by the vision, and his enthusiasm for every detail of the vast project soon infected New Deal mobilization planners. Hillman put his housing man on the project, while Leon Keyserling, then commissioner of the federal government's Public Housing Authority, began to work out the funding.[62] But the bomber city idea collapsed before the same forces that had eviscerated Reuther's production planning proposals. The Ford Motor Company had purposefully sited the Willow Run plant in rural, Republican Washtenaw County, where Ford hoped to keep the local government and tax code in friendly hands. Detroit real estate interests were equally opposed to a publicly subsidized model city, so Ford refused to sell its property near the plant as long as the federal government endorsed the UAW's housing idea. Ford also blackmailed the UAW by linking renewal of its collective bargaining contract to the union's abandonment of the ambitious Reuther housing plan. UAW Secretary-Treasurer George Addes, now emerging as Reuther's chief rival, accepted Ford's offer in October 1942 when he announced that the union favored the diversion of "critical materials" from housing to the production of war implements. Within days the government withdrew support for the bomber city plan, after which Ford agreed to sell its land for dormitory-style war housing.[63]

Reuther lost this battle, but his interest in the redemptive power of modern architecture and the promise of the planned community never flagged. To Reuther, Stonorov proved a powerful and visionary figure, one of his few friends outside the union movement, to whom he would turn for the design of the UAW's most important postwar projects. It was fortunate that Reuther relied upon Stonorov's aesthetic sensibility, for he himself often favored a crudely Fordist solution to the nation's postwar housing problems. He was an enthusiastic supporter of Buckminster Fuller's ugly "Dymaxion Dwelling Machine" when he toured the inventor's Wichita shops in 1944, a visit that prompted yet another Reuther Plan, this time for the postwar production, at Willow Run and elsewhere, of mass-produced, modular housing units for veterans.[64]

Reuther's public presence, his energy, and his ideas won him the attention of the White House itself. "Here's my young red-headed engineer," FDR beamed in one Oval Office meeting. But it was Eleanor Roosevelt who took a genuinely personal interest in Walter Reuther, just as she had cultivated Joseph Lash and Aubery Williams, two other young radicals of similar energy and idealism. "Mrs. Roosevelt and I became really very, very close and warm friends," Reuther remembered several years later. He called the First Lady "my secret weapon," because "every time I had an idea, good or otherwise, I always talked to her." She clashed with Knudsen on Reuther's behalf, invited him to Hyde Park, and put him in touch with other liberals who distrusted the dollar-a-year men occupying so many key Washington posts. She was attracted to his boyish enthusiasm, his flair for publicity, and the power he commanded within the union movement. They would remain friends for the remainder of her life.[65]

Reuther's high profile made him an obvious candidate for a top post at the War Production Board (WPB), organized right after Pearl Harbor. In April 1942 Franklin Roosevelt personally recommended that Philip Murray and William Green agree to Reuther's appointment as head of the new Labor Production Division in the WPB. The CIO endorsed the idea, but AFL leaders vetoed the appointment. To them, Reuther was still a radical collectivist.[66] Reuther nevertheless craved the opportunity to demonstrate labor's administrative creativity. The entire shape of the postwar economic landscape was on the drawing board, and Reuther was constantly in the capital, frequently appearing before the wartime boards and commissions that now calibrated the incomes and employment prospects of millions of workers. As he told a CIO convention late in 1942, the executives running the mobilization agencies feared that "we might make a real contribution, that we might show the world that if you can harness the democratic, creative forces that lie dormant inside of labor . . . that might have a lasting effect upon the economic pattern of America in the postwar period."[67]

From Hillman's sad experience, Reuther knew that the authority he sought had to be concentrated to be effective, yet the War Production Board established by FDR in January 1942 resembled a feudal empire: the corporate-staffed industry divisions held the real power, at the expense of the remaining New Dealers, like Robert Nathan and Leon Henderson, who sought a more centralized and coordinated national production plan. Wrote Roy Reuther, then serving as a WPB staffer, "The Brass Hats here and [in] industry just have not and seem determined not to take labor into camp and deal honestly with them." Labor's interests, observed another WPB staffer of liberal inclinations, remained "undigested lumps in the stomachs of the management people."[68]

Reuther was twice offered high-level posts at the War Production Board, but in each case the appointment was a tribute to his personal energy and expertise more than to his role as a spokesman for American labor. When in October 1942 the former Wall Street banker Ferdinand Eberstadt picked him to be his "partner" in charge of cracking open the most sensitive labor and commodity bottlenecks, Reuther asked whether the post represented a higher level of recognition for the trade unions at the WPB. Replied Eberstadt, "No, I want you; I don't want the labor movement."[69] Reuther could not take the job on these terms, so months of negotiations between the White House, other WPB officials, and the two labor federations followed. By the spring of 1943 Reuther was slated to fill a new post, as one of the WPB's two labor vice chairmen. He was more than intrigued. Finally he would be able to demonstrate the social efficiency of a well-planned production effort while protecting the interests of his constituency, the autoworkers, in the battles that consumed the highest levels of the production bureaucracy.[70]

Such were Reuther's fleeting hopes. But could they be realized in wartime Washington? The effort would be "suicide," wrote Roy to his older brother in April 1943. The WPB's industry divisions had been functioning for more than a year with virtually no labor input, the New Deal's cohort of civilian planners and economists were on the way out, and the issues of most vital concern to rank-and-file workers—wages, prices, housing, the military draft—were under the control of other boards and commissions. "I certainly feel you would be making a most serious error if you came to Washington now," argued Roy. "No strong, intelligent individual can be a substitute here in Washington for a well organized and united labor group such as the English Labor Party has." Equally important, Reuther would be savaged by his UAW opponents if he took responsibility for the war production setup or for the wage freeze, housing shortage, and bureaucratic squabbles that made Washington so frustrating to war workers. Admonished Roy, "if you come to D.C. and are here for six months or a year—you will have to start out at the bottom in the UAW again."[71] If such were the stakes, then Reuther really had no choice, for he knew that no prize could be as exciting and important as the leadership of America's most powerful trade union.

9

FAUSTIAN BARGAIN

In the North American situation it was obvious that the Communist Party was making political capital of workers' legitimate demands for wage adjustments in order to sabotage defense production and to discredit the administration in Washington.

—*Walter Reuther, June 1941*

By the middle of 1941 the Great Depression was over. America's steel mills were running at full capacity, as were the shipyards, locomotive shops, machine tool firms, and other capital equipment companies that had staggered through the great slump. The auto companies were having their best year since 1929, boosting the payrolls of Detroit's many satellite industries: rubber, glass, electrical equipment, sheet steel, and ball bearings. Unemployment declined by almost a percentage point each month; soon millions of Americans would begin a great migration from the low-paid world of domestic service, cotton mill drudgery, and hardscrabble farming to the great centers of war production. Force-fed by an endless stream of government dollars, the sprawling industrial infrastructure that would characterize the postwar era was under construction. Pittsburgh, Baltimore, Buffalo, Long Beach, Seattle, and Detroit attracted hundreds of thousands of new factory workers, but the real industrial explosion came in once sleepy towns like Ypsilanti (Michigan), Tacoma (Washington), Wichita (Kansas), Marietta (Georgia), Richmond (California), and Melrose Park (Illinois), where the government sited huge production facilities. Factories were gigantic, not only because of the great requirements of the war but because of the Fordist technology of the era: men, women, and machines were massed together in amazing density.

In the new aircraft industry one hundred thousand would soon work at Douglas in Long Beach and El Segundo, fifty thousand at Curtiss Wright in New Jersey, and forty thousand at Ford's famous Willow Run bomber plant. Excluding farm labor, 43 percent of all employed Americans were now blue-collar workers, a proportion that would never again be surpassed.[1] Fifteen million Americans—one-third of the prewar workforce—used the new demand for their labor to move into new jobs. At least four million crossed state lines: half these migrants poured out of the rural South, many to the two fastest-growing war production centers, California and Michigan.[2]

Despite inflation and wage controls, real earnings jumped, generating the most progressive redistribution of income in the twentieth century. Promotions, reclassifications, and overtime came easily during the wartime labor shortage. Thus weekly earnings in manufacturing leaped 65 percent after December 1941; taking into account both inflation and the higher payroll taxes imposed upon the working class in 1943, real wages still managed to grow by 27 percent. "For a skilled factory hand, Detroit was the biggest boom town of all," reported *Time* in 1942. Tool and die makers lured from one high-paying job shop to another could take home two and three times their prewar pay. New "girls" at Briggs Body got eighty-five cents an hour, double what they made as waitresses. When the Detroit branch of Saks Fifth Avenue invited GM clerical workers to an evening fashion show, thousands of factory women from all over town packed the store.[3] By 1945 the family income of the bottom two-fifths of the population had increased by over 60 percent, more than double that of the rest of the population. Housing, transportation, and food distribution deteriorated in the crowded war production centers, but health care and educational opportunities increased dramatically: the military alone "socialized" medical services for a substantial portion of the male population (sixteen million) who passed through its ranks. War workers ate better and worried less; thus, infant mortality declined by more than one-third between 1939 and 1945, while life expectancy surged ahead by three years for the white population, by five for African-Americans.[4]

Such dramatic material changes were accompanied by a transformation in social expectations. The New Deal was ending, but its legacy retained the power to validate a range of plebeian entitlements, even as the language of patriotism and production became an ideological terrain contested by workers, managers, government officials, and union leaders. Full employment, high pay, and the ideological recognition offered war workers in the production effort generated an enormous sense of self-confidence and self-respect. Despite the tilt to the right in Washington, the economic leverage now in the hands of millions of workers inaugurated a new era of union growth. The CIO was on the march once again, and in the vanguard stood the autoworkers. After doubling membership in 1941, UAW officers rechristened their union the United Automobile, Aircraft, and Agricultural Implement Workers of America, indicative of an ambition to make the union the largest independent organization of workers in the world, a status finally won when UAW rolls topped one million a year after Pearl Harbor.

If Reuther wanted the unions to make their presence felt in Washington's corridors of power, America's new warfare state expected from the trade union movement industrial discipline and political orthodoxy. From Roosevelt on down, the military, the dollar-a-year production bosses, and the new generation of government arbitrators, mediators, and commissioners constructed an elaborate apparatus of industrial control that demanded the collaboration of Reuther and his generation of trade union militants. In 1941 Reuther thought the bargain well worth it: labor-liberal influence in Washington might yet shift the balance of power between labor and management in Pittsburgh, Detroit, Los Angeles, and Dallas, ensuring the growth and security of the trade unions and their democratic participation in factory, mill, and office. The opponents of this corporatist accord were all Reuther's bitter enemies: John L. Lewis, the Communists of the Nazi-Soviet pact, and "brass hat" industrialists like Max Babb of Allis-Chalmers, Ernest Weir of National Steel, and Henry Ford, men whose isolationism seemed but another front in their hostility to the New Deal, the new unions, and the new pluralist Americanism that was the official ideology of the mobilization effort.

The most bitter and decisive round in the politics of this accord would be fought during the spring and summer of 1941. There were three UAW fronts upon which Walter Reuther deployed his forces and chose his allies: first, a set of disruptive, politically charged industrial conflicts at some of the nation's most important defense firms; second, the construction in Washington of a new political-administrative framework for wartime industrial relations; and finally, the eruption within the UAW body politic of a long-running, full-scale debate over the relationship between industrial militancy, trade union program, and mobilization politics. Conflicts on all of these fronts were grist for a political mill that tested the politics and temper of all the leading figures in America's most dynamic trade union. Sheer ambition did much to motivate Reuther, his antagonists, and their respective spear carriers. But the UAW convention debates of this era also embodied the range of ideological choices facing the New Deal and the new unions at a moment of enormous tension and transformation. The chronic factional battles that began in 1941 were fueled by the protracted difficulties inherent in the effort to accommodate an increasingly self-confident generation of workers to the political and economic imperatives of America's new warfare state.[5]

Defense strikes were the burning issue in the spring of 1941. In May Secretaries Henry Stimson and Frank Knox wrote FDR that "strikes and deliberate slowdowns . . . have so far been more harmful in their total effect than actual physical sabotage."[6] Some of the men and women responsible for inaugurating the stoppages were Communists, but their chief crime was less a conspiracy to cripple military production than a failure to recognize that in America's new warfare state the unions were expected to subordinate their interests to the production imperatives and nationalist rhetoric of a mobilized polity. Walter Reuther understood the new reality and used it as a bludgeon with which to pummel his now-vulnerable enemies within the UAW. But he had to walk a fine line: it was one thing to denounce Communists for their strike tactics, and another to allow opposition to work stoppages to overwhelm the union movement. Indeed, the defense emergency had already breathed new life into a right-wing assault upon labor law and the New Deal welfare state. Explaining the fall of France, editorial writers at the *Saturday Evening Post* denounced the wage and hour laws enacted during Léon Blum's Popular Front government for the internal weakness that led to the rapid collapse of French resistance. In Congress, conservative forces under the leadership of Rep. Howard Smith of Virginia steadily pressed for new legislation curtailing the right to picket, providing for a thirty-day "cooling-off" period after a strike vote, and implementing compulsory arbitration procedures in labor-management disputes. In Texas, California, and Wisconsin, state legislatures enacted laws that made organizing more difficult.[7]

The Allis-Chalmers strike of March and April 1941 proved to be a case in point. Producing a wide variety of the most complex engines, generators, tractors, and construction equipment, the Allis-Chalmers workforce was bitterly divided between a heavily German and Catholic minority faction that sought to sustain an AFL craft organization and a majority of equally skilled workers who gave their allegiance to UAW Local 248 and Harold Christoffel, a tall, lanky militant now working closely with the Communists. UAW unionists confronted a truly reactionary management whose efforts to subvert Local 248 generated both chronic industrial combat on the shop floor and an unusually tough, ideological local, which boasted a paramilitary flying squadron that Christoffel freely deployed against his opponents, within the working class or without. The strike halted production of naval turbines and generators, so the federal government rushed into the fray: first Sidney Hillman, who failed to work out a compromise on union security, and then William Knudsen and Navy Secretary Frank Knox, who more sternly demanded that the plant reopen at once. Three days of bloodshed, riot, and police violence followed as Local 248 strikers battled company loyalists and Milwaukee police.[8] The Allis-Chalmers debacle put the issue of "Communist" defense strikes squarely, and hysterically, on the national agenda. In response, Hillman convinced Roosevelt to set up a tripartite mediation board to resolve such politically embarrassing work stoppages. Reluctantly, CIO leaders accepted the new National Defense Mediation Board (NDMB), but many feared that state mediation would soon lead to compulsory arbitration and a ban on strikes. A unanimous UAW executive board rushed to remind readers of the *United Auto Worker* that the right to strike was still the "Keystone of Liberty."[9]

Indeed, the UAW demonstrated the liberatory potential of direct action on one last, magnificent occasion: thousands of workers finally shut down the great River Rouge works on April 1. For years Reuther had coveted control of the Ford organizing effort, but in the winter of 1941 the national CIO itself mounted the well-funded and carefully orchestrated campaign that overcame the ethnic particularism, political rivalries, and Service Department intimidation that had made the Ford Motor Company such a standing rebuke to UAW-style unionism. The strike itself was "unauthorized," but neither Reuther nor his rivals hesitated to seize the opportunity and sanction the huge stoppage. At UAW headquarters across town,

Anna Stocker and Valentine Reuther just before their marriage in 1903. From his red-haired mother Walter Reuther took his sense of order and duty; from his father a love of talk and ideas. Valentine tutored his children in Socialist principles, but his career as a trade unionist ended when West Virginia went dry. *Archives of Labor and Urban Affairs, Wayne State University.*

By 1910 Walter Reuther already seemed to have a firm grip on life, but his older brother Theodore looks characteristically apprehensive. *Archives of Labor and Urban Affairs, Wayne State University.*

Walter *(foreground)* and Victor *(right, standing)* with Italian, Finnish, Polish, and Soviet toolmakers in the Gorky auto plant, 1934. "It is unpolished and crude, rough and rude, but proletarian workers' democracy in every respect." *Archives of Labor and Urban Affairs, Wayne State University.*

Walter and May shortly after their marriage. They met as Socialists and built Local 174 together. *Archives of Labor and Urban Affairs, Wayne State University.*

Union officials lead Cadillac sit-downers out of their Detroit plant on January 17, 1937. The evacuation was a mistake. *left to right:* Julius Hochman of the Amalgamated Clothing Workers, Richard Frankensteen, Leo Krzycki (also of the Amalgamated), Homer Martin, and Reuther. *Archives of Labor and Urban Affairs, Wayne State University.*

Roy, Victor, and Walter after visiting Milwaukee Mayor Daniel Hoan, also a Socialist, in August 1937. *Archives of Labor and Urban Affairs, Wayne State University*

Reuther worked closely with Communists like Wyndham Mortimer to build the UAW and fight Homer Martin's maladroit leadership. Here Mortimer holds the pen with which he signed the first General Motors contract. *Archives of Labor and Urban Affairs, Wayne State University.*

Reuther became nationally famous at the "Battle of the Overpass." During a leaflet distribution on May 26, 1937, men from the Ford Service Department attacked UAW organizers Robert Kanter, Reuther, Richard Frankensteen, and J. J. Kennedy. Frankensteen, a former football player, fought back and took the roughest beating. Within months the scene had become labor lore. Artist Walter Speck included the incident in a mural on the wall of Local 174's auditorium. *Archives of Labor and Urban Affairs, Wayne State University.*

Police attack pickets at the Federal Screw strike, March 1938. With clubs in hand the West Siders are ready. *Archives of Labor and Urban Affairs, Wayne State University.*

Reuther explains the union's stategy during the 1939 tool and die strike. To his left are his brother Victor and William Stevenson, a skilled trades leader from the West Side of Detroit. *Archives of Labor and Urban Affairs, Wayne State University.*

Philip Murray, John L. Lewis, and Sidney Hillman pose for one last time at a CIO convention in November 1940. Jacob Potofsky of the Amalgamated Clothing Workers stands to Murray's left, Emil Reive of the Textile Workers to his right. *The George Meany Memorial Archives.*

Rivals. *left to right:* R. J. Thomas, George Addes, Walter Reuther, and Richard Frankensteen late in World War II. Their ambitions kept the UAW in turmoil. *Archives of Labor and Urban Affairs, Wayne State University.*

During the General Motors strike of 1945–46, Reuther insisted that the company could raise wages without increasing car prices. To prove it he wanted GM to open its books to a government panel. *Archives of Labor and Urban Affairs, Wayne State University.*

During the bitter UAW faction fight of 1947, Reuther's opponents published *The Bosses' Boy*, which put Reuther in league with racists, fascists, and big business. He never forgave them.

Victors. *left to right:* Richrad Gosser, Emil Mazey, Walter Reuther, and John W. Livingston after their sweep at the 1947 UAW convention. In power, Reuther eclipsed them all. *Archives of Labor and Urban Affairs, Wayne State University.*

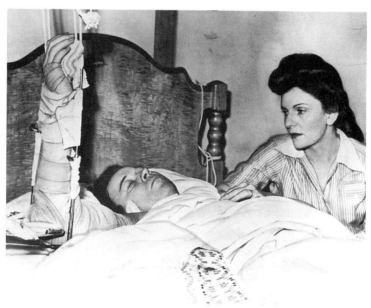

May watches Reuther after one of Santo Perrone's gunmen almost killed him in April 1948. His recovery was remarkable. *Archives of Labor and Urban Affairs, Wayne State University.*

General Motors Board Chairman Alfred Sloan, Research Director Charles F. Kettering, and President Charles E. Wilson in 1951. Reuther thought Sloan, who refounded GM in the 1920s, both arrogant and remote, but he considered Wilson a tough, fair negotiating partner. *Provided by General Motors Media Archives. Copyright © 1978 General Motors Corp., used with permission.*

Ford Vice President John Bugas and Reuther sign the 1955 contract. *Time* put Reuther's portrait on the cover when the UAW won supplemental unemployment benefits, but thousands of Ford workers wildcatted anyway. To Reuther's right, UAW Ford Director Kenneth Bannon; to his upper right, Carl Stellato, president of Local 600. *Archives of Labor and Urban Affairs, Wayne State University.*

Within weeks after breaking bread with George Meany at the AFL-CIO's first convention in December 1955, Reuther would trade insults with him on foreign policy issues. *The George Meany Memorial Archines.*

"If you want the Labor Bosses to control the American scene, vote the straight Reuther ticket." 1958 campaign flyer, Beverly Hills Republican Club. *Archives of Labor and Urban Affairs, Wayne State University.*

KNOW YOUR OPPONENTS
Here's the Labor Slate.   Study it carefully.

For Governor, Walter Reuther   For Lieut.-Governor, Walter Reuther

For State Senator, Walter Reuther   For Atty.-General, Walter Reuther

For Treasurer, Walter Reuther   For Secretary of State, Walter Reuther

Joseph Rauh and Roy Wilkins. Rauh saw Reuther as his client and friend, not his employer. The distinction would become important at the 1964 Democratic National Convention. *Photo by Yoichi R. Okamoto, LBJ Library Collection.*

union officers could hardly believe the reports pouring out of Dearborn. Ford was shut down! Reuther and others organizers immediately drove to Gate 4 next to the infamous overpass. Ford servicemen stopped the car, checked with the Ford hierarchy, and brusquely informed the unionists, "They will not meet with you—get off our property."[10] Soon thousands of Ford workers flowed out of the Rouge to an all-night meeting on the grounds of Local 600's new union hall in Dearborn. For leaders and new recruits alike, it was an inspiring and cathartic experience, the last time unionists celebrated such massive defiance with a genuinely unqualified sense of solidarity. Quickly and effectively, the UAW transformed the enormous energy of the Ford workers into the structure of an expertly run strike, with soup kitchens, a hospital, flying squadrons, and picket lines. To block Ford's multiple gates, the union completely surrounded the plant with an automobile barricade.[11]

Despite the magnificent show of strength, UAW leaders still feared that the turmoil and delay that had crippled the Allis-Chalmers strike might sour the potential victory at Ford. Harry Bennett denounced the strike as "Communistic" and sent out emissaries, including Homer Martin, to address "back-to-work" rallies in the black community. On April 2 and 3 violent melees broke out on Miller Road between hundreds of African-American strikebreakers, who remained within the Rouge, and the picketers, most of whom were white. The strikers returned to work on April 10 after Ford agreed to negotiate with the UAW and abide by the results of an NLRB election. The UAW eventually won its best contract at Ford: a union shop agreement covering employees throughout the nation. But the negotiating process had been exceedingly ticklish: until the last moment UAW negotiators feared that Ford lawyers might still use public alarm with union militancy and Communist influence to deprive the union of the fruits of its victory.

Ford's capitulation hugely complicated UAW politics and strike strategy. The breakthrough at the Rouge touched off a revolution on the shop floor. In a recapitulation of the most tumultuous months of 1937, production standards were cut back, petty shop rules suspended, and unpopular foremen forced out of their departments. Ford's primitive management structure had none of the depth or resilience of GM's, so wildcat strikes and shop-floor conflict continued well into the war. Almost overnight more than ten thousand African-American workers embraced industrial unionism, infused it with a rights-conscious militancy, and raised up a phalanx of articulate, aggressive leaders. The new Local 600, now touted as the largest in the world, tilted toward the left; for more than a decade it would remain a cockpit of factionalism and a prize earnestly sought by Walter Reuther and his union rivals.[12]

Such were the pressures that confronted the GM director as the UAW sought to renew its contract with General Motors late in April 1941. Reuther wanted the same ten cents an hour just won by the Steel Workers, and he wanted to further entrench the UAW in GM shops by winning the union shop (compulsory union membership). However, Reuther sought to avoid a real showdown with the automaker. GM's Wilson claimed that a work stoppage would halt military production. Reuther insisted that 95 percent of all GM facilities were still dedicated to civilian output, but he nevertheless conceded the ideological point: UAW members on defense work would not strike. Reuther's caution did not go down well with many GM locals, especially those in Flint, which favored strike action to again challenge GM on the shop steward issue. "Reuther does *not* control GM," asserted Joe Brown, an unusually acute observer. "Flint, [the] most powerful GM center, is overwhelmingly against him and Hillmanism."[13] The big Buick and Fisher Body No. 1 locals even demanded Reuther's dismissal as head of the GM Department because of his failure to make the fight against speedup a higher priority. Such sentiment contributed to Reuther's fear that a strike might win the UAW a reputation for careless militancy, thereby jeopardizing both his influence in Washington and the outcome of the NLRB election at Ford.[14]

Reuther was taken off the hook on April 26 when Secretary of Labor Francis Perkins certified the GM dispute to the new National Defense Mediation Board, thereby postponing the work stoppage, scheduled for just two days later. Reuther immediately dispatched telegrams calling off the imminent strike, but in an emergency session of the UAW executive board the next day he came under fierce attack for endorsing such government intervention. Led by George Addes, Reuther's factional opponents feared that the GM director had set a dangerous precedent. "Are we to assume," asked Addes, "that when entering negotiations with the corporation in the event our case is certified to the mediation board, our union will follow a 'no-strike' policy?" Addes probably reflected the views of a majority of the board when he called Reuther's capitulation "hasty"; he asserted, "We must follow an aggressive policy and not one of appeasement."[15]

Reuther's difficulties at General Motors demonstrated the extent to which the power to shape the wartime balance between capital and labor was shifting to Washington. A new labor relations apparatus sprawled out of the bureaucracies housed in the Federal Triangle, setting the wages of one hundred thousand steelworkers in the morning, the duties of a dozen bomber plant shop stewards that afternoon. Reuther would spent much time and energy arguing before these new tribunals. The National Defense Mediation Board and its successor, the National War Labor Board (WLB), were the most ideological and intrusive institutions of the warfare state. Unlike the defense production agencies, which were little more than governmentally sanctioned defense industry cartels, these tripartite labor boards were dominated by a cohort of academically inclined lawyers and economists who saw management accommodation to the trade union movement as essential to social stability and efficient production. These men were not the young "New Dealers" who had so vexed the corporate boardrooms, but an older generation whose political outlook had been shaped in the late Progressive Era, when reformers had seen the resolution of the "labor problem" as part of a general amelioration of the contending claims of both labor and capital.

NDMB Chairman William H. Davis proved an energetic and highly visible proponent of this sociopolitical outlook. A leading New York patent attorney, Davis had helped write NRA codes in the early years of the New Deal and then had won a national reputation as a resourceful "fixer" at the New York State Mediation

Board, which he chaired in the late 1930s. He was joined on the WLB in early 1942 by George Taylor, the umpire under the UAW-GM agreement. Not only did Taylor propagate grievance arbitration throughout unionized heavy industry, but he was also largely responsible for the elaboration of the War Labor Board's early wage program, which, in the famous Little Steel cases of 1942, put a ceiling on overall wage claims but established guidelines that tended toward a leveling-up of incomes across the entire working class. Other public members included Frank P. Graham, the liberal president of the University of North Carolina who handled many difficult race relations issues, and Wayne Morse, the brilliant Oregon Law School dean who had won the confidence of both the radical San Francisco unionist Harry Bridges and the shipowners as a longshoring industry arbitrator in 1939 and 1940. Their vision was one of "industrial pluralism": the factory social order would be sustained by the establishment of legal and administrative procedures that structured and channeled conflicts between labor and capital. The Wagner Act was their greatest triumph, and routine collective bargaining and the grievance arbitration scheme their model of "industrial democracy." Thus the NDMB hailed the progress in UAW-GM bargaining relations, from the "relatively chaotic condition which existed four years ago . . . to that stable and peaceable relationship which emerges when parties have been accustomed to deal with one another on the basis of equality . . . mutual confidence and respect."[16]

Reuther found these government boards an irresistible forum to which he would return again and again during the next half-decade. There, Reuther and Wilson seemed finally on equal terms, pleading their cases like rival lawyers from two big-city firms. Indeed, the preparation of the union's annual labor board brief became one of the GM director's most time-consuming tasks, and he soon had several staff members assigned full-time to the government panel. The work distanced Reuther from ordinary workers and feisty local union officers, whose interests he now felt to be but one pressure among many within this half-constructed corporatist order. Given the "practical machinery" to resolve shop conflicts, Reuther saw labor-management relations as finally "coming out of the jungle" during the war. Such a broad approach, Reuther admitted, often involved taking an "unpopular position" with the rank and file, thus opening officials to charges that "your leadership is selling you down the river." The union needed a higher degree of institutional security—the union shop—as management recognition that it had become an accepted partner in factory governance.[17]

Clearly there were advantages to such a corporatist bargain. Both the NDMB and the WLB socialized much of the trade union movement's prewar agenda, thus making seniority and grievance systems, vacation pay and night-shift supplements, sick leave, and paid mealtimes standard "entitlements" for an enlarged section of the working class. The socialization of the union agenda was especially important for those represented by unions of less strength than that of the UAW or other big industrial unions. Likewise, government wage policy tended toward an equalization of wages within and between industries and among men and women and blacks and whites. Thus the NDMB easily acquiesced in the UAW demand for a wage hike of ten cents an hour at GM; that increase set the pattern for the entire industry and further compressed the wage hierarchy for one million autoworkers.

But was Reuther making a Faustian bargain? Even in the spring of 1941, nearly a year before the labor movement offered the government its formal no-strike pledge, the unions had become ensnared in a process that would cede much freedom and legitimacy to the warfare state. Already the mediation board's staff saw "continuous operation of the General Motors plants [as] imperative in this time of national peril." Those who would shut them down were therefore a "selfish interest" that stood athwart production for national defense.[18] With their situation framed in these terms, who would speak for the workers at Ford and Flint and a hundred other mills, mines, and factories whose quest for industrial democracy remained unrealized? Their vision and their voices were now increasingly muted, their solidarity seen as but an unpatriotic and pointless assault upon the national purpose.

The tensions inherent in Reuther's bargain soon exploded, in southern California, where the UAW was organizing aircraft workers in a high-stakes competition with the AFL's machinist union. By mid-1941 over one hundred thousand youthful workers were employed in Los Angeles–area aircraft factories alone.[19] The industry's Aeronautical Chamber of Commerce enforced a fifty-cent-an-hour rate for semiskilled labor, little more than that paid in the southern textile industry. Meanwhile, the skilled core of the workforce were either company loyalists, who still remembered the camaraderie of the experimental, cottage industry days, or AFL craftsmen hostile to the UAW brand of social unionism. CIO Communists were largely in charge of the actual organizing campaign in southern California, then the second-largest center of Communist Party strength in the United States. Both Lew Michener, the UAW's California director, and Wyndham Mortimer, Reuther's erstwhile mentor who now played a key role in the California aircraft drive, were party members.[20] The showdown came at North American Aviation, where Mortimer had poured UAW resources into organizing the fast-growing workforce at the big Inglewood plant, one of the nation's two main producers of fighter aircraft. When negotiations deadlocked in May, Frankensteen flew to California and won an overwhelming strike vote designed to both prod management and speed certification of the dispute to the NDMB.

By this point prounion sentiment had reached a fever pitch, but the new mediation board, now swamped with such cases, was slow to make arrangements for a hearing. When on the night of June 4 a departmental wildcat turned into a mass turnout, Mortimer and Michener decided to authorize and organize the stoppage, in much the same way top UAW leaders had capitalized upon the unplanned Ford strike two months before. Most of the CIO apparatus in southern California came to the aid of the strike, which was the largest in the state since the San Francisco general strike of 1934. In Washington the news from Inglewood generated near-hysteria. Only a week before, on May 27, the president had issued the "Declaration of Unlimited National Emergency," rhetorically linking defense plant strikes with fifth-column activity. Secretary of War Henry Stimson, who was "morally certain" that defense strikes were "instigated by Communist and other subversive elements," pushed the president to seize the North American Aviation plant.[21] But before the army could act, Hillman and NDMB Chairman Davis persuaded the military to see whether UAW leaders could end the strike themselves. Davis understood, as the military did not, the crucial importance of making sure that the army did not take over the plant until the aircraft director, Richard Frankensteen, had had time either to settle the dispute himself or to declare the stoppage unauthorized.

Frankensteen again flew to California and demanded that Mortimer and the North American Aviation unionists end their walkout. When they refused, he took over the local, suspended its negotiating committee, and fired the organizers, including Mortimer. In a nationwide radio speech he declared the strike a wildcat, denouncing the "infamous agitation and vicious underhanded maneuvering of the Communist Party." But such rhetoric failed to end the walkout, for when Frankensteen then spoke to thousands of workers in a bean field near the plant, they shouted him down, rejecting his plea for a return to work. This sealed their fate. With the explicit approval of Sidney Hillman and the certain knowledge of top CIO leaders, Roosevelt sent in twenty-five hundred troops on June 9. The army broke up the picket lines, detained hundreds of activists, and ordered North American Aviation management to fire all leaders of the rebellious local. Repression? Certainly, but of the sort appropriate to the corporatist regime of laborite co-optation under construction in Washington. In Inglewood the army encouraged the CIO to build a new UAW local at North American Aviation; prodded by Sidney Hillman, who had his own agents on the scene, the National Defense Mediation Board instructed corporate management to meet virtually all the union's wage demands. Slowly Frankensteen's men rewon the confidence of North American Aviation's workers, making it possible for the *United Auto Worker* to greet news of the wage award with the headline "Responsible Unionism Wins at Inglewood."[22]

Consumed with the Ford organizing drive and the GM negotiations, Reuther had played no direct role in the Allis-Chalmers stalemate or the North American Aviation debacle. But he was certainly prepared to capitalize upon their notoriety and the wave of anti-Communist sentiment that had swept over UAW ranks. Thus Reuther and Frankensteen sealed a factional alliance late in April when they announced that they would propose an outright ban on Communists, Nazis, and Fascists holding elective or appointive office in the union. By discrediting the Communists, the pair planned to drive out Addes as secretary-treasurer and elect each other to vice presidencies. Frankensteen, who had moved from Father Coughlin to Homer Martin to the Communists and back, had all the qualities and bearing of a successful legislative horse trader, accounting perhaps for the remarkable equanimity with which even Reuther greeted his rank political opportunism. After the North American fiasco, Reuther took to the airwaves to support Frankensteen, calling his handling of the situation "fearless." Reuther would not defend the government's use of troops to break a strike—here he joined other unionists in their growing estrangement from "Hillmanism"—but he nevertheless directed most of his firepower at Communist "un-American union wrecking tactics." The party, charged Reuther, was "making political capital of workers' legitimate demands . . . in order to sabotage defense production and to discredit the administration in Washington."[23]

The Nazi invasion of the Soviet Union on June 22 and the subsequent Communist Party endorsement of an all-out defense effort did nothing to moderate Reuther's factional steamroller or his rhetorical fireworks. Indeed, the abrupt shift in the Communist line simply deepened the contempt in which the Reutherites held the "comrades." They made much sport of—and long remembered—the contradictory resolutions submitted to the Wayne County CIO council by the Communist leaders of Plymouth Local 51. The first urged the CIO to call a national conference to "take America out of the war and keep it out of the war." But the second, submitted immediately after the German invasion, called for all-out aid to the Soviets. Amid much laughter, both resolutions came up for a vote at the same meeting. One doubts whether Reuther cracked a smile, for a few days later, at a CIO conference in Washington, he encountered the "glad hand" of the leader of the United Transport Workers, Mike Quill, long one of the Communist Party's closest allies in the CIO. "Such complete hypocrisy turns one's stomach," he wrote to May. "What a hell of a spot they will be in if Joe folds up and patches things up with Adolph."[24]

George Addes was not a Communist, but Frankensteen and Reuther were correct to see him as the embodiment of Communist influence in the very highest union councils. Addes, the dark-haired child of Lebanese Christians, would not defend the party in open debate, yet he turned to the Communists for the same kind of ideological guidance and organizational support that the Socialist network had once offered Walter Reuther. In turn, party loyalists saw Addes as the one popular leader who would be sure to stand against the Reuther juggernaut. UAW Communists, who now numbered as many as five hundred shop activists, therefore made Addes's reelection a key task in the union, for his survival measured their actual influence in UAW politics far more than the ideological denunciations that so often swept through union conclaves. Addes had been caught unaware by the energy with which Reuther played the anti-Communist card in 1940; he spent 1941 shoring up his own caucus, lining up with the Flint militants who rejected Reuther's brand of industrial jurisprudence. As secretary-treasurer, Addes had the resources to build a unionwide political machine, but Victor Reuther also conceded that he was "a tireless worker and the kind of guy who had real appeal for factory workers." In April 1941 Addes demonstrated new clout when he lobbied a majority of the UAW executive board to replace Edward Levinson with Carl Haessler as editor of the *United Auto Worker*.[25]

And then there was Walter Reuther. He was the most polarizing figure in the

UAW, the most ideological of the top union leaders, a man who instinctively clothed his ambitions in the programmatic language of the labor-left. Reuther lived and breathed the union: he was constantly on the road, rarely took a vacation, and had few friends outside his political circle. Novels and small talk bored him. To relax he took a long vigorous walk, sometimes followed by a cold shower. At night his mind kept ticking away, and if he awoke with an idea, he jotted down a few notes on a pad and pencil he kept handy on a night table before he went back to sleep. When *Who's Who in Labor* asked him to list his outside interests, he wrote "wood & metal craft work; development of economic & production plans."[26] Reuther possessed little of Frankensteen's warmth or Addes's organizational strength, but he had linked his persona so closely with his politics that he nevertheless generated a remarkable commitment among thousands of unionists. The *CIO News* editor Len De Caux, who was close to both John L. Lewis and Philip Murray, remembered Reuther as "signally lack[ing] the charisma of a Lewis, a Debs, or other crowd-stirrers. Nothing could make him appear so lustily broad-gauged as Lewis, so seemingly loving-kind as Murray, so subtly—almost spiritually—appealing as Hillman." Nevertheless, "Reuther was a leader, not just an officeholder. . . . Others might relax and say, 'A-a-aw, what the hell!' Not Walter Reuther, he didn't drink, smoke or dillydally in any way to distract him from giving his all to his purpose." Bert Cochran, then a Trotskyist active in the auto union, remembered Reuther as unlike "other auto union officials who avidly sought power; it was as if he were biologically structured for the quest."[27]

Reuther did have a private life, a conventional one for his time and class. After his draft deferment had been finalized in mid-1941, Reuther and May bought a $7,750 white brick-and-frame, six-room bungalow at 20101 Appoline Street in a Northwest Detroit neighborhood of largely white, working-class homeowners. He put a workshop in the basement; there Reuther found the mastery and precision that proved so elusive in the wider world. Soon the house was filled with kitchen cupboards and maple furniture of a modernist line.[28] After their daughter Linda was born early in 1942, May entered fully into a world of maternal domesticity. She was pregnant again in 1944, but the child, a "blue baby," died at birth. A second daughter, Lisa, arrived safely in 1947. May kept abreast of union politics, but after the factional attacks on the "royal family," she never again took on even temporary duties with the UAW, an arrangement that some observers—possibly including Eleanor Roosevelt—thought one of frustration and self-denial. Walter was on the road more than ever, in part because the UAW executive board now had both the funds and the inclination to hold its bimonthly meetings in the distant production centers of the South and West.[29] Reuther would have much preferred Detroit meetings: his letters to May are full of plans and schemes for taking the earliest possible train or plane back to the Motor City. Reuther was appalled early in 1942 when, at Richard Frankensteen's insistence, the executive board held a ten-day session at the ritzy Ambassador Hotel in Los Angeles. "The sham tinsel that shouts at you here is so much like him," Reuther wrote to "Mayichka

Darling." New Orleans got the same response; he thought the French Quarter "certainly is overplayed." Still, Reuther was at least aware of his own dour reputation. While in the Crescent City, Reuther was pleased to read the same comic strips that appeared in the *Detroit News*, prompting a query to May, "Don't you think that this is a definite sign that I might possibly be human?"[30]

For the next six years the partisans of Walter Reuther fought a nearly continuous battle for office and influence within almost every UAW region and local union. Their contest with the Addes-Communist group generated much of the energy and creativity that made each UAW convention in these years a political event of national importance. Reuther's caucus was commonly labeled "right-wing," but this was not an adjective he would endorse for either his followers or himself. Instead, Reuther saw his UAW faction as the embodiment of militant, independent trade unionism, whose adherents extended across almost the entire political spectrum. To many of his partisans, especially those on the anti-Communist left, Reuther's fierce ambition signified not personal opportunism but an almost Leninist appreciation of the vanguard role played by the leadership of the nation's most dynamic trade union.

Though Reuther was in frequent touch with Washington defense planners and New York liberals, his own brain trust still consisted almost exclusively of the close-knit group of former Socialists who had been his comrades for almost a decade. Robert Kanter, Frank Winn, and Eddie Levinson frequently joined Victor and his wife Sophie, Roy, and May and Walter for a half-social, half-political round of meetings and meals at the Reuther household or at Levinson's nearby home. They were joined by Leonard Woodcock, a young prowar Socialist who served as Reuther's political secretary, and Brendan Sexton of Brookwood and the SP's Workers Defense League, who now battled it out with the Communists in the Ford bomber local at Willow Run. During the war there were always two or three former Socialists on the UAW executive board, and a dozen or more served as local union officers. At the 1940 UAW convention Woodcock counted seventeen delegates who were still Socialist Party members, not far from the number of Communists (twenty-five) in attendance.[31]

The Reuther caucus had at least two well-defined wings. On the syndicalist left, Emil Mazey and his "young turks" at Briggs Local 212 emphasized a shop militancy well beyond that advocated by the ex-Socialists who gravitated to Reuther's inner circle. Mazey was six years Reuther's junior but just as battered in the auto struggle. The son of Hungarian immigrants, Mazey sharpened his politics in the classes offered by the Proletarian Party, as well as in the streets of Detroit, where he acquired a well-deserved reputation as a pugnacious picket captain. He thought of Reuther as something of an interloper and of himself as the more authentic proletarian. "The guy had guts—he had more Goddamn guts!" admitted Mazey's brother Ernest, then a militant in the rival Socialist Workers Party.[32] Mazey never learned a trade but got a job at Briggs, the notoriously authoritarian employer of low-wage immigrant labor. Briggs had been a concentration point for Communists in the early 1930s, but the mass firings that accompanied the failure of a violent, Communist-led strike in 1933 created a leadership vacuum that Mazey and a handful of non-Communist militants would fill later in the decade. Mazey gave the political machine he built in Local 212 a multilayered resilience and ideological influence that sustained the union's reputation for combativeness long after several of its key officers, including Mazey, were drafted into the military. This pattern was replicated in other venues where the fortuitous presence of a few pro-Reuther radicals gave a unique left-wing coloration to several of the big unions that mushroomed out of the defense boom, including Brewster Local 365 in Long Island City, where dozens of New York leftists were employed, and Local 6 in Melrose Park, where a handful of student Socialists shared in the leadership of sixteen thousand workers who built Pratt & Whitney engines for Buick.[33]

Socialists and syndicalists were hardly enough to sustain the growing power of the Reuther caucus in the UAW. Reuther was a man of the left, but he nevertheless forged a solid alliance with an organization whose ideology was decidedly hostile to the secular, radical traditions that Reuther shared even with his Communist foes. This new ally was the Association of Catholic Trade Unionists (ACTU), whose emergence late in the 1930s represented a heroic effort by a wing of American Catholicism to simultaneously accommodate and reshape the new industrial unions. In the 1920s and 1930s a new language of "social Catholicism" had emerged in the United States, derived from the writings of Thomas Aquinas and revived in the modern era by two papal encyclicals, Leo XII's 1891 *Rerum Novarum* and Pius XI's 1931 *Quadragesimo Anno*. In response to the industrial revolution and the emergence of working-class radicalism, both encyclicals rejected the individualism, exploitation, and class conflict that lay at the heart of laissez-faire economics. In their place, church teaching called for "social justice" that emphasized both a "family wage" and the social responsibilities of capital. The encyclicals defended private property and denounced socialism, so many Catholics still saw in the CIO not only an institution that was open to atheistic collectivism but one that competed within the Catholic working class for the faith, hope, and institutional allegiance that the parish priest had long monopolized. In Detroit Father Charles Coughlin was but the most shrill and reactionary of those within the hierarchy who considered the UAW little more than a Communist front; during the 1939 Chrysler strike his Sunday broadcasts vigorously defended the corporation and called for a back-to-work movement among the heavily Catholic workforce.[34]

But to many Catholics, both lay and clerical, simple repudiation of the new industrial unions was neither ethically wise nor strategically appropriate. A wing of American Catholicism, ranging all the way from Monsignor John A. Ryan ("the right Reverend New Dealer") in the center to Dorothy Day and the Catholic Worker movement on the ascetic left, saw in the new industrial unions a fulfillment of much that was close to the heart of Catholic social doctrine. Many younger Catholics, almost all laymen of Irish extraction, were also swept up in the

CIO organizing drives and sought to bring a specifically Catholic impress to the movement. In 1937 they formed the Association of Catholic Trade Unionists, whose chapters soon spread from New York to Chicago, Detroit, Pittsburgh, and other Midwest cities. The ACTU became a presence on the Detroit labor scene early in 1939 when a new Detroit archbishop, Edward Mooney, signaling a leftward shift in the church's approach to the UAW, sponsored the first Detroit meeting of Ryan's prolabor "Catholic Conference on Industrial Problems." Led by a thirty-five-year-old priest, Raymond Clancy, the archdiocese set up ACTU chapters and Catholic labor schools throughout southeastern Michigan. Clancy proved a firm ally of the CIO: he defended the UAW during the 1939 Chrysler strike, repudiated Coughlin on the radio, propagandized for the union among conservative Polish priests, and worked with the Ford organizing drive in 1940 and 1941.[35]

The Michigan ACTU soon became a force in UAW politics and, after New York City, the second-largest chapter in the nation. Its newspaper, the *Wage Earner*, covered factional politics from an anti-Communist, anticapitalist, corporatist perspective and was the only publication to penetrate UAW shops as well as the *Daily Worker*. In Detroit as elsewhere, the ACTU saw its chief task as organizing the apathetic Catholic rank and file in order to counter Communist influence within the industrial unions.[36] The stakes could not be higher, argued the ACTU executive secretary, Richard Deverall, who was also the UAW education director in 1940 and 1941. "It is not Moscow gold, but Communist sweat that is building the Communist Party in America." Catholics must emulate CP dedication and stop "raving verbally about Communism" if they were to mobilize America's twenty million Catholic workers. The ACTU trained cadre and built caucuses at Dodge, Buick, Pontiac, and Plymouth; the Catholic opposition threatened the Communist-line leadership at these plants all during the war. Most important, the ACTU was active at Ford, both before and after the UAW organized the giant automaker. Paul St. Marie, an ACTU founder, defeated a Communist for the local presidency in 1942. At the Rouge, Reuther found the core of his support among ACTU Catholics of German, Irish, and Polish extraction. The UAW executive board members Jack Kerrigan and Alex McGowan were publicly identified with ACTU.[37]

ACTU denounced socialism, secularism, and class conflict, but its strategic goals clearly paralleled those of the Reuther group. "We were forced, intellectually and conscientiously, to agree with most of his basic policy," explained the *Wage Earner*'s editor, Paul Weber. Catholics and Reutherite socialists were equally anti-Communist, and both groups favored arbitration and government tribunals as mechanisms for defusing class conflict, although liberal Catholics tended to see such institutions as a definitive solution to industrial strife, while the Reutherites saw them as but another venue for labor-management struggle. Likewise, both the Reutherites and the ACTU favored government planning and a corporatist governance of the emerging war economy along the lines CIO President Philip Murray advocated in his plan for "industrial councils." The ACTU even wanted unionists to serve on corporate boards.[38] And although many of the Irish Catholics in the leadership of the ACTU were pacifist, or simply anti-British, both Reuther and the Catholic group favored aid to opponents of the Axis well before the German invasion of the Soviet Union. Thus ACTU members participated in Reuther caucus meetings, campaigned for joint candidate slates in local union elections, and applauded Reuther's frequent denunciations of the Communists. They called Walter and Victor Reuther "sound leaders, whose socialism, we think[,] will be mitigated by events."[39]

Reuther's opponents saw this alliance as unprincipled at the very least. The secular-minded Reutherites had linked their fortunes to an organization whose central ideology was counterpoised to all for which the left had stood for more than a century. Indeed, only months earlier Reuther had helped raise money for loyalist Spain, fund-raising that the hierarchy of the American Catholic Church denounced in the most hostile language. Even many anti-Communists raised their eyebrows. Joe Brown, the Detroit journalist who had long applauded Reuther's brand of effective and militant leadership, labeled him a "stinker" who "worked in cahoots with the unspeakable American Catholic Trade Union bloc." Predicted Brown, "After the Reuther crowd and the ACTU eliminate the CP's, the ACTU will turn on the Reuther crowd and ease them out."[40]

But in the UAW, the ACTU never became the tail that wagged the Reutherite dog. The autoworkers were a predominantly Protestant group, so that in Detroit, unlike Pittsburgh, New York, and other centers of ACTU activity, Reuther could hardly rely too heavily upon their specifically Catholic strain of anti-Communism. More important perhaps, ACTU influence depended not only on its vocal anti-Communism but on its prounionism as well. The very legitimacy of a Catholic caucus in the UAW, as well as other unions, was predicated upon the New Deal–era emancipation of the Catholic working class, itself one of the chief fruits of the industrial union upsurge. But this social emancipation was one of secularization too, which limited the extent to which Catholic anti-Communism alone could structure the politics of these workers. Indeed, enthusiasm for the ACTU among Catholics in the auto industry would wane when the organization came to identify itself almost entirely with anti-Communist factionalism in the union.[41]

Reuther would test the power of this caucus coalition at the union's 1941 convention in Buffalo, where all the social tensions and political crosscurrents of the new war economy exploded in a rhetorical slugfest of the first order. The tumultuous UAW conventions of the 1940s were some of the most remarkable social phenomona of that era, at once among the most impressive and profane institutions through which the twentieth-century working class could make its political consciousness visible. Usually held during the auto industry's late summer shutdown, these convocations, attended by upwards of three thousand officers, delegates, staffers, and a big contingent from the national press, lasted ten days and more. To many workers whose experience in a hotel or a strange city was minimal, the conclaves were an all-expense-paid holiday not unknown for heavy drinking, late-night poker games, water balloon fights, and the occasional tryst. At Buffalo fifteen hundred delegates sat at long tables that completely filled Memorial Auditorium, otherwise used for hockey games. Wearing overseas caps proudly embroidered with their local union name, the delegates listened to speeches, demanded the microphone, threw paper airplanes, and paraded about in demonstrations behind bands sent by the Dodge and Ford locals. These delegates were hardly representative of American workers in general, or even of those who labored in the unionized auto and aircraft factories. They were part of the small minority in every local that paid attention to union politics and scrambled for the part-time offices and minor privileges that eased their work lives and sustained their egos. Many unionists saw politics in the UAW as a simple scramble for such posts. Compared with the rest of the industry workforce, they were more likely to be male, white, and skilled. By the early 1940s there were probably one thousand union jobs to which they could aspire: four or five hundred full-time local union officers and an equal number of staff jobs, either at the national office in Detroit or, more likely, with one of the nineteen regional directors.

The UAW executive board stood at the apex of this patronage democracy. The union's 1939 Cleveland convention had strengthened the board at the expense of the union's president; thus, the nineteen regional directors elected by delegate caucus constituted the real locus of power in the UAW. In 1941 the board faithfully reflected the character of the original cadre who had built the UAW: Thus there were no Italian-, Polish-, or African-Americans on this relatively well-educated, all-male body (average age thirty-six). A large region, such as 1A on the East Side of Detroit, might have jobs for thirty International representatives. Reuther's GM Department offered employment to twenty, while at its peak Frankensteen's Aircraft Department put sixty staffers on the payroll. Executive board members were intensely jealous of their turf and status. When Paul Miley, an Addes partisan from Cleveland, once asked for technical assistance from Reuther's GM Department, R. J. Thomas blurted out, "What the hell is going on with Miley, asking Reuther to come into his region?"[42]

But the annual UAW conventions were not just about the quest for position and power; they were genuinely democratic forums for developing the ideas and ideology with which the union movement could best express itself. "They all clamor for recognition," observed a Buffalo journalist. "They argue with the chairman on points of parliamentary law and sometimes prove their point. . . . They work nights and Sundays at the convention because their fellow workers back home want a run for the money they vote to send delegates down." Dozens of participants were full-time political activists, delegates who saw their vocation as one of agitation and organization. Their voices shaped the debate, yet during eleven grueling days at the Buffalo convention more than 250 other delegates took the floor. All were convinced that what they did and said was important, that what transpired in these big-city auditoriums might well shape the fate of both labor and the nation.[43]

The Reuther forces swept into Buffalo in a confident mood, buoyed by the backlash against the botched defense strikes and ready to capitalize on the anti-Communist current that ran so deep among the politically alert delegates who settled in for the long convention. Edward Levinson prepared a comprehensive program for the union, including a complete brief detailing the Reuther case against George Addes.[44] At the convention itself, the Reutherites commanded the high ground: Victor chaired the constitutional committee, and the ACTU's Tom Doherty held sway on the credentials committee, which would decide the fate of the hotly disputed Allis-Chalmers delegation. Meanwhile, Reuther's alliance with Frankensteen seemed stronger than ever: with their wives the two had taken a leisurely vacation drive to Buffalo. Both convention arithmetic and the fervor of the times gave the Reutherites the conviction that this was the moment to make their lunge for supremacy.[45]

Doherty struck first with a credentials committee report that rejected the big delegation from Allis-Chalmers Local 248. Their transgression had been technical—the delegates had been nominated and elected at the same meeting—but the charge was political to the core: "Hitler and Stalin believe that treaties are scraps of paper," thundered Doherty. "They believe constitutions are only made to be broken, and the majority of this committee believe that the ruling officers of Local 248 believe the same thing." This accusation opened up a free-for-all. Addes, noting his own Catholicism, denounced the ACTU as an "outside organization creating factionalism within the auto union." Richard Leonard, a DeSoto unionist whom Reuther had tapped to run for Addes's job, attacked Local 248 for continuing its strike in the face of the Knox-Knudsen demand to reopen the plant. Walter Reuther denounced Christoffel and his flying squadron "goon squad" that effectively disenfranchised opponents of his "political machine." The issue before the delegates, he said, "is a simple question of whether or not . . . the highest tribunal of our organization is going to put the stamp of approval on the worst kind of strong-arm political racketeering in this union." When nearly 60 percent of the delegates voted to exclude Local 248's representatives, the Reuther faction had clearly won the first skirmish.[46]

But not the battle. Reuther's alliance with Frankensteen had begun to unravel almost as soon as the two arrived in Buffalo. Vain as he was, Frankensteen could plainly see that in a UAW dominated by the dynamic Reuther forces he was destined to play second fiddle. Leaders of the national CIO were also uneasy with Reuther's rise to power. Philip Murray, ever-sensitive to his prerogatives, did not want the leading union in the CIO under the control of an empire-builder. Thus Allan Haywood, Murray's man at the convention, advised Frankensteen that the CIO was opposed to any attempt to remove Addes from the UAW's leadership. Haywood would persuade Addes and his supporters to back Frankensteen so that he could win a vice presidency without Reuther's help.[47]

As a result of this intrigue, Frankensteen broke with Reuther over how to deal with the aftermath of the North American Aviation debacle. He concluded a deal with the Addes forces that condemned the North American Aviation strike and sacrificed Wyndham Mortimer but merely excluded from the UAW leadership Regional Director Lew Michener, a Communist "influential" on the West Coast. Michener himself made the factional meaning of their rapprochement explicit: "If Walter Reuther, Sidney Hillman or any one else who subscribes to the principles of the OPM . . . think for a moment that Richard Frankensteen and I are going to engage in a death struggle . . . while Walter Reuther sits back there gleefully as a spectator and laughs and smirks at what he apparently considers his high-handed maneuvering, I want to state here and now he is going to be mistaken."[48] Michener was right: a more punitive proposal supported by the Reutherites could not command a delegate majority. Philip Murray soon put Michener on the CIO payroll; the next year California unionists reelected him to the UAW executive board.[49]

It became clear that the tide had turned when the messy Allis-Chalmers case again roiled the delegates. Twice the UAW sent committees to Milwaukee to hold new delegate elections, and each time Christoffel clung to power. On the sixth day of the convention he defended himself in a magnificent oration that celebrated the raw combativeness of those who remained steadfast in the great battles waged by Local 248. When Christoffel's men finally marched into the convention hall on the ninth day of the proceedings, they were met with a thunderous reception.[50] The Reuther faction had overreached itself. Their constitutional amendment barring Communists, Nazis, and Fascists from office generated an extraordinarily bitter debate that made the radical pasts, contemporary politics, and possible ambitions of the Reuther brothers themselves the central question. The Addes faction distributed copies of the Gorky letter to any delegate who cared to read its pro-Soviet text, and they recited passages from Walter Reuther's factional career in which he condemned red-baiting as "the boss's ploy." Reuther's opponents insisted that if political tests were to be applied to unionists, then Socialists, whose party still sought "to convert the capitalist war crisis into a victory for Socialism," should also be barred from UAW office. After all, insisted James Lindahl, a Communist leader of Packard Local 190, "the real question is whether or not the Socialist Party in the person and voice of Walter Reuther and Victory Reuther and the rest of the Reuther family is going to have a privileged minority position in this union."[51]

Such fireworks aside, Reuther's amendment barring Fascists and Communists from union office passed easily. By this time American political culture had become so rigid that even within the Communist orbit only those radicals whose politics were formed in the syndicalist era of World War I—men like Wyndham Mortimer, Bill McKie, and John Anderson, the skilled trades leader from the East Side of Detroit—were willing to actually defend the party and admit their own membership. The more typical response, from George Addes and from most Communists themselves, was to denounce red-baiting and political "bickering" within the union. They were unwilling to defend, on even civil libertarian grounds, the legitimacy of a Communist presence within the body politic.

But Reuther's ideological victory had only the most limited organizational consequences. The UAW executive board remained almost as divided as before the convention. Indeed, Reuther was just barely reelected to a Michigan board seat, a vote that may well have reflected the growing strength of the new Ford locals, where he would struggle to build a following.[52] Meanwhile, Richard Leonard won only 43 percent of the vote in his effort to unseat George Addes. Scores of delegates from big locals like Dodge, Chrysler, Toledo, River Rouge, and West Side Tool and Die voted first for Reuther's ban on Communists and then cast ballots for George Addes, the union leader most closely associated with the continuation of a Communist presence in the UAW.[53]

From this switch Reuther came to understand two things. First, the anti-Communist litany that swept through working-class assemblies was not the same thing as an actual repudiation of the veteran unionists whose leadership was linked to the still sizable Communist cohort within the UAW. To most, anti-Communism was essential to their sense of Americanism, but the actual content of that patriotism remained pluralistic, progressive, and prounion on the eve of the Second World War. And second, Reuther now knew that he had become the most dynamic and the most polarizing figure in the UAW. His identification with the warfare state and its agents within the union movement troubled many of the most active unionists, including those who otherwise endorsed Reuther's programs for the UAW. They feared his seizure of the union's commanding heights and made a conscious decision to divide power at the top. It would require a radical transformation of the political landscape to break this stalemate.

10

PATRIOTISM AND POLITICS IN WORLD WAR II

Regardless of what reactionary legislation is passed . . . this war . . . still remains a just, progressive war against Fascism.

—*Nat Ganley (UAW Communist), 1943*

This is a war against . . . all brands of fascists, foreign and domestic.

—*Victor Reuther, 1943*

Early in 1942 a new ballad, "UAW-CIO," offered thousands of autoworkers a rousing salute to their patriotism and their production effort. Baldwin "Butch" Hawes of the Almanac Singers composed the urban folk song, and with Woody Guthrie on banjo and Pete Seeger on guitar, the piece perfectly captured a left-progressive vision of unionized workers in the antifascist struggle.

I was there when the Union came to town,
I was there when old Henry Ford went down:
I was standing at Gate Four
When I heard the people roar:
"Ain't nobody keeps us Autoworkers down!"

It's that UAW-CIO
Makes the Army roll and go—Turning out the jeeps and tanks and airplanes
  every day

It's that UAW-CIO
Makes the Army roll and go—Puts wheels on the USA

There'll be a union-label in Berlin
When the union boys in uniform march in:
And rolling in the ranks
There'll be UAW tanks—
Roll Hitler out and roll the Union in![1]

Detroit workers, a federal observer noted in 1942, "are completely identified with the American army and look forward with at least as great interest to their technological triumph over the enemy as to triumphs of generalship and strategy." Understanding this impulse, Reuther used his contacts with Undersecretary of War Robert Patterson to organize 270 local union officials for a weekend junket to Camp Atterbury, Indiana, early the next year. There Reuther and his men donned army uniforms, took part in basic training exercises, and were allowed to operate the tanks, jeeps, machine guns, and artillery the factories were turning out.[2]

Working-class identification with the war effort did not translate into a simple endorsement of an elite-managed control of defense work; unionists who had long battled away on shop-floor grievances now used the military production effort to legitimize an even broader critique of their employers. The auto industry's reluctance to plan the conversion of its facilities from civilian to military production generated numerous bottlenecks, much temporary unemployment, and considerable friction within Michigan factories. Unionists therefore denounced GM plant managers for failing to secure an adequate supply of steel, for hoarding skilled labor, and for incompetence in converting to war production. "We have been doing everything in our power to put the heat on the Management to fight for more material," wrote a Buick committeeman to Reuther in July 1942. And from the company's Diesel Engine Division came a similar complaint: "The union has fought hard and long to make Management realize what a tremendous amount of idle machinery they have in the plant and how important it has been to the 'ALL OUT' war effort that this machinery be manned and operated 7 days a week." A UAW survey found that many war workers saw their bosses as incompetent. A grinder denounced "'90 day wonders.' They toil not, neither do they spin." From a rigger in a bomber plant came the admonition, "Crack down on inefficient foremen. . . . Make big shots *show* their ability or replace them immediately."[3]

Hierarchy and inequality rankled during the war because an economy subject to far-reaching political controls lends an element of conscious purpose to every economic exchange. As the historian Mark Leff has pointed out, the term "relative deprivation" was coined during World War II, for modern war is necessarily based upon an ideology of common aspirations and responsibilities. As John Kenneth Galbraith, then an Office of Price Administration (OPA) official, would observe, "No feature of World War II . . . has been more striking than the scrutiny which each of the several economic groups brings to bear upon what the others are getting."[4]

Walter Reuther's campaign for a "Victory through Equality of Sacrifice" sought to parlay such egalitarian sentiment into a wartime economic program for the union movement, but the gambit's rapid collapse demonstrated even more clearly the polity's deeply embedded inequalities of power and privilege. Immediately after Pearl Harbor the trade union movement, including the UAW, had offered the president its "unconditional no-strike pledge." In return, the new National War Labor Board won the power to arbitrate contract disputes, set wage levels, and impose upon unionized employers a form of union security known as "maintenance of membership," which automatically enrolled all workers in a certified union unless they chose otherwise within fifteen days of starting employment. Reuther endorsed this bargain, but he quickly came to see that establishment of the WLB had done little to reduce the UAW's need for a mobilized and combative posture. This need became clear after President Roosevelt demanded seven-day-a-week operation for all defense plants. A steel shortage and the conversion muddle made such a mandate rhetorical, but General Motors and the War Production Board nevertheless insisted that the union immediately forgo the "premium pay" bonus from their contracts. These provisions, mandating time-and-a-half pay for work on Saturday and double time on Sunday, had been negotiated to discourage weekend operations and spread existing work, but managers now claimed that such pay penalties thwarted the production effort. In February 1942 GM President Charles Wilson even took his case directly to a meeting of UAW leaders from ninety corporation plants, but the auto executive's assertion that premium pay now represented "business as usual for the union" persuaded few, especially after Reuther let loose with a statistical barrage indicting the multimillion-dollar salaries and bonuses of GM's top executives: "Maybe these things ought to be brought up when Mr. Wilson talks of sacrifices and business as usual."[5]

But union opposition proved politically dangerous. Pearl Harbor did little to stanch right-wing assaults upon either the New Deal ethos or the trade union movement. Congressional conservatives led by Virginia's Howard Smith and Georgia's Carl Vinson gained substantial support for legislation that would suspend for the duration of the war not only premium pay but other federal labor standards as well, including ordinary time-and-a-half pay for any work beyond forty hours a week. The Roosevelt administration wanted to keep union problems out of the hands of Congress, where the ascendancy of the Republican-Dixiecrat alliance promised to disrupt the process of corporatist accommodation that constituted the essential work of the wartime labor relations apparatus. Thus Roosevelt told Philip Murray in March 1942 that the CIO must itself voluntarily relinquish premium pay in order to have "a salutary effect upon the public state of mind." More bluntly, Donald Nelson of the WPB warned the industrial unions that if they did not agree within thirty days to give up such pay, the government would press for a law to compel surrender.[6]

CIO unionists capitulated on March 24. Demonstrating the Janus-faced quality of wartime production rhetoric, Philip Murray justified the retreat "in the light of the same single touchstone which has guided all [the CIO's] policies—the necessity for maximum war production."[7] Given the CIO lead, Reuther and the rest of the UAW executive board had little choice but to reverse policy as well, but they knew that the symbolically important concession would not go down easily. With some 250,000 autoworkers still unemployed during the long conversion process, industry's demand for such a concession seemed entirely premature, if not simply arrogant.

George Addes collaborated with Reuther to package the premium pay concession as part of the "Victory through Equality of Sacrifice" program offered to local union leaders at a war emergency conference held in April. Their cooperation reflected the brief factional truce that had temporarily settled over the post–Pearl Harbor UAW. In return for labor's no-strike pledge, premium pay concessions, swing-shift scheduling, and an all-out production effort, the Reuther-Addes program called for sacrifice by industry and management as well. The UAW asked the government to step up its rationing program, maintain tight price controls, guarantee a living wage for dependents of those in the armed services, and institute a rigid ceiling on profits and executive salaries—the latter at twenty-five thousand dollars, about eight times the annual wage of a fifty-hour-a-week war worker. Working through Eleanor Roosevelt, Reuther arranged for the president to send a message to the UAW conference, announcing that much of the "Equality of Sacrifice" program had his blessing. But there was grumbling in the ranks, even from such otherwise conservative Reutherites as Local 174 President Michael Manning, who feared that the end of premium pay was but the first in a series of backward steps. Reuther admitted that the new program was an exercise in appeasement: "I say the surest way to see that a tidal wave is launched in Washington that will engulf all of us is to refuse to recognize the double time issue as something we cannot fight on at this time, but we can fight on the 40 hour week." As usual, Frankensteen put the matter much more bluntly. He challenged the delegates: "Are you going to tell the President to go to hell?"[8]

As an ideological counterthrust aimed squarely at the business culture, the "equality of sacrifice" idea won Reuther new fame within the progressive community's embattled ranks. Liberals like Eleanor Roosevelt and William O. Douglas applauded, but when the details were actually worked out, Reuther's gambit proved an embarrassing debacle for the UAW leadership. Roosevelt did make the UAW's $25,000 salary limit part of his 1942 anti-inflation program: it "clarified the whole situation as far as labor was concerned in the Detroit area," explained one Treasury Department official. But hard-nosed congressional conservatives, who regarded such regulations as but another New Deal assault upon the authority of traditional elites, soon gutted the salary limit, eroded the administration price control program, and opened loopholes in the rationing schedules.[9]

UAW leaders also misjudged the impact of the union's premium pay concession on the temper of rank-and-file workers. Reuther advertised "Equality of Sacrifice" as "the kind of program you can rally around and make the fight for in the shops," but the union's abandonment of premium pay hardly proved an incentive to wartime organizing efforts. The main threat came less from employers, most of whom now acquiesced in unionization, than from a revitalized AFL, which sought to take advantage of the UAW's newfound social patriotism. Union leaders were shocked in July 1942 when the International Association of Machinists (IAM) handily won an NLRB election at the huge Buffalo plant of the Curtiss-Wright Aircraft Company, a top-priority organizing target in Frankensteen's aircraft drive. Because so many AFL unions like the IAM had never entertained the CIO's policy-shaping ambitions, they naturally took a more parochial view of the extent to which labor should subordinate its interests to the total war effort. Thus many of the IAM's powerful, virtually autonomous lodges simply refused to relinquish premium pay even after the government requested that they do so. At Buffalo the IAM attacked the UAW: "Can the CIO's masterminds tell you why they know what's good for the worker better than he knows himself? . . . The CIO sacrifices workers' pay, workers' overtime as the CIO's contribution to the war effort. Big of them, huh?" To this, the Machinists counterpoised pure and simple trade unionism. "While the AFL has been loyal to the country, it has also been loyal to its members. *It has not felt called upon to make sacrifices of workers' pay or of labor's gains.*"[10]

Reuther had been backed into a corner. Desperate, he joined the rest of the UAW high command in appealing to FDR for an executive order that would force all labor to yield the double-time standard for holiday and Sunday work. When Roosevelt hesitated, Victor Reuther's War Policy Committee proposed that the union rescind its premium pay sacrifice in thirty days unless the government took action to force uncooperative AFL unions to relinquish the extra pay provision in their contracts as well. With much grumbling, delegates to the UAW's 1942 convention in Chicago endorsed this half-threat, and on August 28, Reuther, Frankensteen, and Thomas met with Roosevelt and reached tentative agreement that the president would accommodate the UAW with an executive order banning all premium pay for the duration of the war. Thus was the "equality of sacrifice" idea reduced from a grand vision to an exercise in administrative theft.[11]

The 1942 convention in Chicago must have left a sour taste in Reuther's mouth. He supported Addes for reelection as union secretary-treasurer: "There is one fight that we have got and that job is against Hitler, so as I say, let's vote Brother Addes in unanimously." Addes returned the favor with an endorsement of Reuther, "an able leader, an energetic leader," to one of the two newly created vice presidencies.[12] Richard Frankensteen got the other. But just below the level of this cynical office-trading, a majority of the seventeen hundred delegates demonstrated a pronounced reluctance to follow the lead of their unusually united leadership. Dwight Macdonald described the delegates as "eager, alert, suspicious." They complained that grievance procedures were ignored by management, that the Little

Steel formula was unfair, and that price and profit controls were rigged in favor of the rich. Spurred on by Emil Mazey's delegation from Briggs and by a growing, vocal Trotskyist contingent in the UAW, unionists sharply cut the salary increase proposed for UAW officers, defeated an increase in union dues, and forced the executive board to call its next convention in 1943 rather than 1944.[13]

To Reuther the "equality of sacrifice" idea had become an albatross. Despite his fervent denunciations of the "war millionaires," the idea had linked Reuther to all the frustrations and impotence that rank-and-file unionists had begun to experience.[14] "I am for doing everything we possibly can in this nation to win the war and to lick Fascism once and for all," announced Richard Gosser, the Reutherite president of the big amalgamated local in Toledo, "but by God, I am not in favor of letting our employer kick the hell out of us all around the place behind the American flag." Indeed, Reuther found that the most disaffected at the convention were unionists who would normally have been solid Reuther caucus partisans. The vote to raise officer salaries was a kind of referendum on the UAW leadership. It narrowly passed, but core Reuther locals, including his usually faithful West Side home, voted heavily against it.[15]

And Reuther's troubles were just beginning. By mid-1942 it was clear that wartime collective bargaining had turned into little more than a holding action. When Reuther sat down with GM executives in March 1942, *Business Week* accurately gauged the automaker's newly aggressive mood: "The company sees the war, its role as the government's biggest supplier and a rising tide of public resentment that is anti-union as an opportunity not only for rebuffing the UAW's current ambitions—but for actually cutting down on the union's power."[16] GM called on the UAW to reduce by half the number of union grievance committeemen, open the way for larger pay differentials, and allow the company to make unilateral changes in shop-floor work rules. Company negotiators embarrassed Reuther by demanding that UAW locals stop "accusations of 'speed up' on management's efforts to increase production of war materials." And breaking with prewar precedent, GM asked that the negotiations be open to the press; Reuther vetoed this idea, fearing the company would try to "exploit the anti-labor hysteria."[17] At the behest of the War Production Board, GM and the UAW did set up scores of plant-level, labor-management production committees, but the corporation made sure that these fledgling institutions were consigned to the most routine activities. Within a year Reuther would denounce them as "window dressing for fake propaganda campaigns."[18]

Reuther spent the summer of 1942 arguing the union case before a War Labor Board panel in steamy Washington. He wanted to continue the CIO's great work: raising wages and reducing inequalities across the whole auto industry, but he now found "more confusion and less stability today than a year ago."[19] Ironically, Reuther's greatest success came among the new surge of women war workers whose profile had long remained barely visible through his political periscope. As late as October 1941 Reuther had seen the new influx of women workers as a low-wage threat to the wage standards enjoyed by higher-paid men. In a period of still-considerable unemployment, most UAW leaders sought not the application of the "equal pay for equal work" principle but the exclusion of women from "male" jobs. Thus Kelsey-Hayes unionists conducted a successful, authorized strike demanding "the removal of all girl employees from machine work," after which the 1941 UAW convention adopted a resolution opposing "any attempt to train women to take the place of men on skilled jobs until such time as the unemployed men have been put back to work."[20]

But such a strategy quickly became untenable. Women were pouring into the defense plants, accompanied by a barrage of government propaganda that hailed women's war work as essential to the production effort. By October 1942 nearly seventy thousand women were employed in the auto industry, 12 percent of the workforce, more than double the proportion of the year before. Within a year their numbers would double again. As chairman of the union's War Policy Committee, Victor Reuther took charge of working out the UAW's policy reversal. If the new surge of low-wage women workers was not to dilute the wage standards enjoyed by a predominantly male workforce, the UAW would have to deprive management of its incentive to substitute women for men. As the Ternstedt Communist Irene Young put it, "We do not want you to discriminate against the men and take their jobs away from them by permitting women to scab for lower pay."[21] The UAW therefore demanded "equal pay for equal work," a principle for the first time endorsed by the War Labor Board in its landmark General Motors case of September 26, 1942. Directing GM and the unions to include in their contracts a clause stating that "wage rates for women shall be the same as for men where they do work of comparable quantity and quality in comparable operations," the WLB rejected GM's claim that the necessity of employing male helpers to assist women on certain operations warranted lower pay for women.[22]

Reuther hailed the decision as a "milestone in the fight for the rights of women workers," but the assertion of the "equal pay for equal work" principle hardly resolved the issue, as became clear at GM plants in Bay City, Michigan, and at Buick in Flint and Melrose Park. Reuther's GM Department contended that new wartime jobs, like aircraft inspection, were comparable to those once held exclusively by men. Women aircraft inspectors should therefore receive the "male" rate. When GM balked, the issue went back to the WLB, where arbitrator William Simkin substituted the terms "light" and "heavy" for the controversial "female" and "male" job labels, establishing a ten-cent wage differential between the two categories. Art Johnstone, who handled the case for Reuther, challenged the WLB's distinction, but the UAW could not free itself of a gendered vision of work in the automobile industry. Thus Johnstone and Reuther found themselves arguing that women employed in "male" jobs should receive the "male" rate and those employed in "female" jobs should receive the "female" rate.[23]

The corporatist effort to micromanage the industrial relations order generated its own form of trench warfare at the War Labor Board, where more than eight hundred cases from Reuther's GM Department eventually found their way. The WLB offered GM workers a four-cent-an-hour wage increase in September 1942, in line with the Little Steel formula promulgated two months earlier, but Reuther thought this increase was less than half what was necessary to compensate for the inflationary surge that had just swept through the industrial Midwest. A year later Reuther was again irked by the board's effort to establish a set of regional "wage brackets" to which auto wages might be adjusted. This system—the "bracket racket," Reuther called it—perpetuated the geographical wage variations to whose abolition he was so committed.[24]

Reuther found the rationalization of wages particularly troublesome among the fifty thousand skilled tradesmen of the Detroit region. These politically potent maintenance and tool and die workers were raking in the money, but the frenetic conversion program had generated a whole new set of "relative deprivations." Tool and die makers in the big "captive" shops jealously watched the pay of their "job shop" comrades skyrocket upward, while maintenance workers demanded that their pay match that of the AFL craftsmen who installed much of the new machinery in the converted auto factories. The WLB raised "captive" tool and die rates a dime an hour in October 1942, but the board failed to equalize wages between AFL and CIO craftsmen. The WLB directive met with a howl of opposition and leaders of the Detroit Tool and Die Council demanded that Reuther resign as head of the UAW skilled trades department. Reuther promised to fight harder for his men, but he could do little to stop the transmutation in the consciousness of Detroit-area skilled workers. In the 1930s they had stood in the vanguard of the industrial union movement; now and for the next generation, they were putting their self-confident militancy at the service of an invidious craftism. After top officials of the UAW Maintenance Council became members of the Mechanics Educational Society of America, which had spurned the no-strike pledge, the latter struck scores of Detroit factories in a stoppage that put ten thousand skilled tradesmen on the street.[25] MESA's organizing activities soon petered out, but the audacity of its gambit demonstrated how plastic were union loyalties under wartime wage constraints.

The revolt of the skilled tradesmen proved but a prologue to the larger distemper that now began to sweep through Michigan factories and foundries. The alienation of the foreman from the ranks of factory supervision proved another key element in the reemergence of a syndicalist movement during the war. The dramatic expansion of the wartime labor pool forced managers to recruit thousands of ordinary workers into the supervisory ranks. At GM 42 percent of its nineteen thousand foremen in 1943 had been on the job for less than a year. Recruited from a unionized workforce, the new foremen complained of long hours and low salaries. Veteran foremen from the Ford Rouge plant, who had sparked the formation of the Foremen's Association of America (FAA), were appalled at the chaos they saw engulfing the factory hierarchy. While management fumbled the conversion program from above, they encountered a revolution from below: "The bosses were just people to look down on after the union came in," remembered one supervisor. "We were just dirt after that." The FAA had signed up thirty-three thousand foremen by mid-1944, about 80 percent in Detroit-area auto and aircraft plants.[26] These foremen also lost caste because the technics of wartime production put new power in the hands of shop stewards, committeemen, and production gangs. The conversion of the auto industry to critical aircraft, gun, and tank assembly increased the degree to which war work required small-batch, task-oriented production that enabled war workers to set informal production quotas and work norms on a group basis. The difficulty of costing out such "government work" accounted in part for management's wartime campaign to abandon daywork (straight hourly wages) and restore incentive pay.[27]

The labor shortage, the conversion of the factories to high-cost military production, the decline in the loyalty and power of the foremen, and the new expectations generated by top-level demands for an equality of sacrifice, all taken together created the conditions for chronic industrial warfare. Capital still held much of the ideological high ground, but management's disciplinary tools were growing dull. Workers were scornful of supervisors' attempts to set production standards, assign work, and discipline employees. A production manager at Packard Motors reported that "the stewards at the plant objected every time we went in. A number of times they told the time-study man to get out, so he got out." Wildcat strikes mounted steadily, involving one in four autoworkers in 1943, one in two in 1944. By then almost 83 percent of lost man-hours involved disputes over discipline, compared with 4 percent in 1940.[28] The work stoppages reflected the heterogeneous and disorganized consciousness of the swollen wartime workforce. As the draft took its toll of veteran unionists, the UAW cadre became a thin stratum somewhat older and somewhat more skilled than the mass of new recruits, who had not experienced the deeply transforming process of actually building the unions of which they were now a part. As a frustrated officer of the UAW's 42,000-member Willow Run local put it, "The majority are paying $1 a month for the privilege of work. They have no understanding at all of the union and are probably a little mystified as to how they ever got into it."[29]

Illegitimate in terms of the patriotic, production-oriented ideology advanced by management, state, and union, these job actions therefore lacked the overall leadership that had given prewar strikes of this sort a more consistently progressive character. Strike violence was not uncommon, and some supervisors were assaulted or even stabbed. As a consequence, such shop-floor syndicalism easily coincided with a determination by some workers to retain elements of an older work regime, which had been structured by race, skill, and gender. Certainly this was the level of consciousness of many in Detroit's white male workforce who feared that factory managers would use the influx of black workers to erode work standards and dilute job security. The frequent wildcat strikes to protest the upgrading of blacks during the first half of the war climaxed in June 1943 when twenty thousand Packard workers staged a weeklong "hate" strike, which was followed within a fortnight by the explosive Detroit race riot itself.[30]

By early 1943 Walter Reuther could see that his close identification with the administration of the war effort held considerable danger. As his brother Victor remarked in February, "It is common knowledge that enthusiasm for the Union has bogged down considerably in a great many circles because we have not continued to win economic gains for our members."[31] As if to prove the point, a union-wide referendum turned down another leadership-sponsored dues increase, and a series of local union elections in the winter deposed numerous incumbents, including those at Packard, Chrysler, and Briggs, where Emil Mazey took back the local presidency on a militant "preserve the union" ticket. Michael Manning resigned from office in Local 174, "fed up with rank-and-file bitching."[32]

Such turbulence put Reuther on guard against further government efforts to transform work standards and labor relations. The War Production Board's campaign to revive incentive pay in war plants presented Reuther and his union with a particularly complex problem. Inspired by ever-influential GM executives, the WPB argued for a vast extension of group piecework plans, under which the pay of all employees would rise in partial proportion to the increase in production, regardless of the wage ceilings imposed by the War Labor Board. This provision made the scheme particularly attractive in the aircraft industry, where productivity was rising rapidly but the Little Steel formula had kept wages far below those in nearby shipyards or in the converted auto factories of Detroit. In California tens of thousands of teenagers and rural migrants poured in and out of the plants. "We no longer have the approach we once had of telling these workers that if they join up with us, we have a very tangible something to put into their hands," complained UAW Aircraft Director Richard Frankensteen, "that we will get them five, ten or fifteen cents an hour and their retroactive pay."[33]

Frankensteen naturally jumped at the WPB incentive pay plan, and in early March the UAW executive board opened the door a crack by giving union locals the opportunity to negotiate such schemes if they could avoid erosion of labor standards and wage rates. Reuther was skeptical from the start. Piecework was already well entrenched within the industry, especially among the supplier firms, including those organized by Reuther's old West Side local. He knew that incentive pay violated an ideological commitment to the solidarity of labor, and that such pay schemes, which generated huge differentials within the wage structure, sustained a factory's technocultural hierarchy. Welders, machinists, operators of complicated batch-production tools, all those who occupied strategically advantageous posts in the production order or who enjoyed a high level of individual control of their work pace, found they could manipulate the system to their advantage, unlike other, less well-situated workers.[34]

Two political developments soon made the incentive pay question a white-hot issue in the UAW. Within a month the Roosevelt administration promulgated a tough "hold the line" executive order that tightened WLB wage guidelines and blocked trade union efforts to liberalize the Little Steel formula. UMW President John L. Lewis and many AFL leaders vigorously denounced the new edict as a unilateral breach of the government's implicit deal with the union movement, but the

CIO responded with much more equivocation. Philip Murray, who saw the industrial union federation's political fate as inextricably linked with that of the administration, announced that "today we must accept the basic principle of stabilization of wages," thus reaffirming the CIO's staunch defense of its no-strike pledge and opening the door to implementation of the WPB incentive pay plan.[35] Second, American Communists, inside the CIO and out, enthusiastically championed the incentive pay idea. Their persistent theme was the need for the unity of all "progressive win-the-war forces." They defended the no-strike pledge with passion and urged the labor movement to agree to all concessions demanded by the government, not so much as a necessary tactical retreat, which was often the perspective of leaders such as Philip Murray and Richard Frankensteen, but as a progressive step in itself, one that mirrored on the home front the Big Three unity that Churchill, Roosevelt, and Stalin would forge at the Teheran Conference in mid-1943. In a widely distributed pamphlet, "Production for Victory," the Communist leader Earl Browder forecast that all wartime wages would soon be tied to increased productivity. "If we still have any prejudices that make it impossible to talk to anyone who works for Bedaux [a management consultant and time-study company] let us get rid of them. The Bedaux production experts, in alliance with the labor movement will help smash Nazism everywhere in the world."[36]

Such rhetoric did not play well in Flint, Detroit, Toledo, and other prewar centers of UAW militancy. In the core firms of the auto industry, where Fordist production principles had been most decisively deployed, incentive pay schemes had been discredited and replaced during the union-building agitation of the mid-1930s. "Piecework" thus became incorporated into the union liturgy and was denounced because of the arbitrary fashion in which management had imposed it, the often incomprehensible pay calculations time-study required, and the corrosive impact such pay schemes had on workshop solidarity. Reuther quickly championed such sentiment, turning distaste for the WPB gambit into a larger critique of the state labor-relations apparatus. Since labor did not have a large enough "voice in the authority of industry," corporate "chiseling on engineering changes" was inevitable, Reuther told a CIO executive board meeting in May. But even where the adoption of incentive pay schemes might well raise wages, as in the aircraft industry, the scheme would wreck the UAW effort to win industrywide wage standards. Frankensteen and Addes argued on behalf of "local autonomy," but Reuther insisted that "if this union does not . . . begin to think in terms of wages with the whole industry, we are going to go into a postwar situation where the shop having the lowest wages is going to have the job and the shop having the highest standards is going to be on the street. We have got to take labor out of competition!"[37] Finally, Reuther denounced the WPB-Frankensteen proposals as an obstacle to an upward revision of the Little Steel formula. "We must shake off the attitude of defeatism and weakness which is holding us back," he told a conference of two hundred GM union delegates. Those who supported the WLB scheme saw "the so-called incentive plans as the only way to get wage raises. If labor even indicates that it is considering piece work, such an attitude will be used to make the labor and wage freeze stick."[38]

Reuther's campaign against incentive pay soon became intertwined with the great wave of industrial militancy that swept the heartland that spring. In a frontal attack upon the Little Steel formula, the War Labor Board, and the entire corporatist apparatus, John L. Lewis put half a million miners on strike in May and June of 1943, marching them in and out of the mines in a daring, tension-filled game of maneuver with his multiple adversaries. Their example proved potent: "Many workers in the plant say to me John Lewis has the right program," admitted UAW President R. J. Thomas. Soon a major wave of stoppages swept through Detroit, Akron, and the East Coast shipyards, a movement that the commissioner of labor statistics labeled a "fundamental swell of industrial unrest." These were not shop walkouts of a balkanized few but well-organized, citywide strikes designed to pressure management and the War Labor Board to raise wages and enforce contracts. In Detroit, where a companywide action put twenty-seven thousand Chrysler workers on the street, "it was just like old times," reported one Dodge Main worker. "The stewards walked through the plant and announced the meeting, and in five minutes the plant was dead."[39]

With this industrial turmoil, Communists, both in New York and Detroit, thought they saw an opportunity to discredit and diminish Reuther's influence in the labor movement. The GM director opposed the mine strikes and the Chrysler wildcat, but he had clearly positioned himself as the UAW leader most opposed to the government's economic mobilization program. Earl Browder toured Detroit and other midwestern cities with a message of denunciation, linking Reuther with a Socialist/Trotskyist "strike wave conspiracy" and calling the auto leader "less bold but more hypocritical than Lewis." Browder's attack was carried into the UAW, where Chrysler Department Director Leo Lamotte, the executive board member most closely allied with auto union Communists, denounced the wildcat and blamed "Reutherism" for the citywide strike. Said LaMotte of Reuther, "His weak and irresponsible position gave encouragement and comfort to those who wanted to avoid their responsibilities against strikes in this war period."[40]

No doubt, Reuther's critique of the War Labor Board did give ideological cover to the strikers, but the Chrysler walkout was largely organized by regulation trade unionists normally allied with Richard Frankensteen. A mass meeting of Chrysler workers called for LaMotte's replacement, after which Reuther demanded and won an executive board censure of the Chrysler Department director. The board divided along strictly factional lines, with R. J Thomas providing the essential swing vote for Reuther.[41] "As of today," wrote the labor reporter for the *Detroit News* in June 1943, "Reuther is the fair-haired boy of the rank and file." At regional UAW conferences in New York and Detroit, delegates applauded Reuther's attacks on the Communists, on incentive pay, and on the government wage freeze.[42] The issue would again come under debate at the UAW's Buffalo convention in October 1943, but by then the Reutherites deployed it merely as a bludgeon with which to batter the Communists and their allies in the union. Carousing along Buffalo's streets, Reuther partisans sang an immortal bit of campaign doggerel:

> *Who are the boys who take their orders*
> *Straight from the office of Joe Sta-leen?*
> *No one else but the gruesome twosome,*
> *George F. Addes and Frankensteen*

> *Who are the boys that fight for piecework,*
> *To make the worker a machine?*
> *No one else but the gruesome twosome,*
> *George F. Addes and Frankensteen . . .*

> *The Auto Workers have their sideshow*
> *One is fat and one is lean.*
> *Who are they but the gruesome twosome,*
> *George F. Addes and Frankensteen.*[43]

During the war years, conceded the UAW Communist leader Nat Ganley, Reuther's "most effective slogan was 'Down with Earl Browder's piecework in the UAW.' "[44]

In preparing for the 1943 convention, Reuther must have calculated that his caucus was finally on the verge of a stunning breakthrough. From a champion of corporatist collaboration between labor and the state, the incentive pay fight had transformed Reuther into a sharp wartime critic riding a wave of shop-floor radicalism. The Reuther group was determined to eliminate Addes and Frankensteen from the leadership and decisively repudiate the Communists. R. J. Thomas would remain little more than a titular president, but Reuther would set an aggressive, independent agenda for the UAW. To this end, Edward Levinson prepared an elaborate preconvention brief that pounded home Communist-line "double-dealing," not only on the incentive pay issue but on virtually every union question since the days of the Nazi-Soviet pact.[45]

It was a devastating critique, but not a knockout blow. Reuther would have to wait four additional years to become supreme within the UAW; indeed, by the summer of 1944 Reuther's fortunes had actually declined to such an extent that he nearly lost his union vice presidency. Two obstacles confronted him, both central problems in the midcentury reformulation of labor-liberal thought and praxis. The first, involving Reuther's awkward perception of the relationship between racial liberalism and class politics, generated a chronic alienation from the most dynamic elements of the newly unionized African-American working class. Meanwhile, the second dilemma embodied a recapitulation of all the insoluble tensions that arose out of the still-unresolved "labor question," which was now exploding out of its shop-floor crucible and into the politically sensitive realm of union governance, management strategy, and warfare state politics.

The modern civil rights movement arose out of the proletarianization and unionization of black America. More than two million African-Americans migrated to northern and western industrial areas during the 1940s, while another million moved from farm to city within the South. In Detroit the proportion of black autoworkers more than doubled during the war, to 10 percent. There, as elsewhere, a key moment in the transformation of African-American consciousness came in 1941 when the UAW finally broke the back of Ford paternalism; overnight, black workers became among the most steadfast of UAW members. For all its limitations, the union offered African-American workers a sense of rights-conscious entitlement and a new focus for their collective empowerment. Soon a whole cohort of talented, politically sophisticated black officers and staffers emerged out of the UAW to offer the African-American community a new source of leadership. A dozen or more were appointed as highly visible UAW staff representatives; still more, upwards of two hundred, won election as delegates to the union's annual conventions, where they represented almost 10 percent of the total voting roll. The Rouge foundry sent more than a score to every UAW convention, provided at least half of all black staffers hired by the UAW, and customarily supplied the giant Ford local with at least one of its top officers.

With almost one hundred thousand black workers organized in the Detroit area, African-American unionists from the Rouge and other UAW plants poured into the Detroit NAACP chapter (making it the nation's largest), demanded the promotion of black workers in metropolitan war plants, and mobilized thousands to defend black occupancy of the Sojourner Truth Homes, a federally funded project that became a violent center of conflict between white neighborhood groups and the housing-starved black community. Black workers at the Rouge, Packard, Hudson, and Briggs plants organized scores of on-the-job protests and short stoppages; indeed, there may well have been as many walkouts led by black workers as there were racially inspired "hate" strikes.[46] The great Detroit race riot of June 1943 continued this pattern. Beginning as a racial turf fight among picnickers at overcrowded Belle Isle Park, the riot had many elements that harkened back to the antiblack pogroms of the World War I era, including widespread black victimization from white mobs roaming the streets. But the conflict was clearly a transitional event in the shift toward the kind of "riots" that characterized urban racial uprisings in the 1960s. Three-quarters of the twenty-five blacks killed were shot down by law officers. There was little conflict in Detroit's factories, but neither was there much production, for absenteeism ran high among both blacks and whites who feared violent assault on their way to or from work.[47]

Black activists encountered enormous resistance in their struggle, not only from Detroit's old elite but from large sections of the white working class and the union leaders they elected. Beginning in late 1941 a spectacular wave of racist strikes shut down scores of factories as blacks broke out of their traditional job ghettos and

moved into formerly all-white departments. The "hate" strikes were a manifestation of the wartime recomposition of an ethnically heterogeneous, episodically
employed proletariat into the self-confident, white working class of the postwar
era. The New Deal, the industrial union movement, and the still-segregated military provided the institutional and ideological basis for a culturally pluralist Americanization movement that subordinated ethnic identity within a transcendent
sense of "whiteness." Fraternal organizations of the foreign-born, which had once
reaffirmed the cultural and political heritage of many second-generation Americans, lost thousands of members in the 1940s, and American Catholics—Polish
and Italian as well as Irish—abandoned much of what remained of their defensive ghetto mentality. In many factories and mills they came to see their committeemen and union seniority systems as protectors of a new sort of property
right to the job, which they defended with almost as much steadfastness as they
did their racially segregated neighborhoods. Add to this the continuing influx of
southern migrants, and Detroit became fertile soil for the racialist propaganda of
the KKK, of Gerald L. K. Smith, and of a score of lesser-known preacher-evange-
lists. Smith, who had just moved his church headquarters from Louisiana to the
Motor City, took more than one-third of the votes in the 1942 Republican senatorial primary.[48]

But like the civil rights movement of the early 1960s, white resistance failed to
slow the political and social momentum won by the African-American militants.
The movement had achieved the kind of ideological legitimacy that made "fair
employment"—though not integration—an integral part of the labor-liberal
agenda. During the hate strikes top UAW officers often sought the protection of a
WLB back-to-work order to deflect white rank-and-file anger, but few of them
made an outright capitulation to the racism that bubbled up from below. At the
1942 CIO convention Reuther exhorted delegates to "take up the fight against
racial discrimination, [and] not as a secondary consideration . . . this fight . . . must
be put on the top of the list with union security and other major union demands."
In 1943 he told an NAACP rally in Detroit that "the UAW-CIO would tell any
worker that refused to work with a colored worker that he could leave the plant
because he did not belong there." Indeed, in the aftermath of the Detroit race riot,
the UAW stood out as the only predominantly white institution to defend the black
community and denounce police brutality. Reuther himself had watched in hor-
ror as police stood aside when a white mob attacked some of the African-American students to whom he had just finished speaking at a high school graduation.[49]

Reuther spoke out against racial discrimination as much as any leading figure in
the UAW; nevertheless, the overwhelming majority of UAW blacks backed the
union caucus led by George Addes and Richard Frankensteen. Observers saw
Reuther's following as progressive at the top, but far more likely to be the milieu
of racist elements at the bottom. In 1941 the black Trotskyist E. R. McKinney
observed that "virtually all the most blatant and hidebound reactionaries flocked
to the Reuther banner," a judgment endorsed four years later by George Crockett,

the first director of the UAW Fair Employment Practices Department. Reuther was an impressive unionist with an "innate sense of theoretical justice in all inter-racial matters," admitted Crockett, who was then close to the Communist Party. "Nevertheless, the perpetual question that constantly bobs up when Negroes in the UAW talk about union politics is 'Why is it the great majority of the prejudiced elements in the UAW are Reuther's most vociferous supporters?' "[50]

A look at industry demographics is a good way to start answering this question. The workforce at General Motors was practically lily-white. Unlike Ford, Chrysler, Briggs, and Packard, GM completely excluded blacks from all body plants and consigned them to the foundries. The corporation payroll stood at but 2.5 percent African-American at the start of World War II, and with its factories typically sited in heavily Appalachian cities such as Flint, Saginaw, Lansing, Anderson, Norwood, and Toledo, its black employment during the war rose more slowly than that of Detroit-based firms like Packard, Plymouth, Hudson, Chrysler, Ford, and Briggs. Thus Reuther felt little pressure to put blacks on his staff, nor in the course of his daily work did he become as intimately acquainted with the prob-lems facing black workers as did many of his rivals. This estrangement seems to have reflected the situation at Kelsey-Hayes, where segregated seniority lines kept several hundred African-Americans stuck in the foundry. When blacks at Kelsey-Hayes lodged a protest with the UAW early in 1941, they took their problems to George Addes, not Reuther.[51] Indeed, the Addes-Communist group had much greater credibility with black workers. Again the Rouge proved pivotal, for it was a key center of Communist Party strength within the UAW. Skilled Bohemian, Ger-man, and Anglo-Irish workers had proved the party mainstays during the preunion years, but after 1941 the Communists recruited far more successfully among blacks. At its peak in the mid-1940s the party enrolled 450 Rouge workers, almost half from the foundry. Communist influence among black workers rested on the party's identification with civil rights issues; indeed, many blacks saw the party's foundry "club" as little more than a militant race organization. By the late 1940s more than 40 percent of all Communist Party recruits in Michigan were African-American.[52]

The relative success enjoyed by the Communist Party among blacks was matched by a nearly symbiotic counterorganization from the Reutherites. The ACTU proved especially important because it fought the Communists in precisely those locals and among precisely those second-generation immigrants who had populated the party's own most fruitful social terrain. At the Rouge, ACTU activists like Joe McCusker, John Blaich, and Paul St. Marie were almost all skilled Irish or German tool and die makers who formed an episodic alliance with Reutherite radicals. In the elaborate electoral campaigns of the 1940s "Communism" and the fight against Ford's effort to establish higher production standards were often the ostensible issues, but in Dearborn, a notoriously Jim Crow city, racial tensions always remained a barely hidden subtext. Nor was anti-Semitism far beneath the surface, especially in a staunchly Communist-line union like Plymouth Local 51, where Jews filled most of the top staff jobs and where the ACTU organized the long-frustrated opposition.[53]

Factionalism aside, the legacy of Reuther's Debsian youth provides a final insight into his approach to racial politics in the 1940s. The American Socialist tradition put the difficulties confronting black workers firmly within a class framework, perhaps too firmly. From Eugene Debs to Norman Thomas, American Socialists had seen the "Negro question" as but a function of a larger class inequity. Reuther therefore thought "racial tensions and hostility toward minorities . . . a product of irrational emotions and impulses . . . bred and grown strong in an economic environment of scarcity." Labor's goal is "fundamental reconstruction," he wrote in the Urban League's *Opportunity*. "Only in such a new society can the Negro hope to end his tragic search for justice." His "particular economic plight is for the most part an intensification of the general predicament of all workers."[54]

Such was Reuther's evocation of the Debsian vision in the 1940s. Racial and class antagonism were insolubly wed; little progress could be made in resolving one without the other. Unlike the Communists, who had already forged a multigenerational relationship with many of the most activist elements of the black community, Reuther and other old Socialists were slow to understand the extent to which a radical shift in race relations had become as much a precondition to the transformation of society as it would be a product of their revolution. Thus the Reutherites often saw a special focus on the particular disabilities under which black Americans labored as tangential at best, even divisive and demagogic within a union context. Reuther explained his own policy as an "appeal to Negroes, not as racial nationalists, but as unionists and fellow Americans." In polemical debate, the Reutherites were wont to describe blacks in or allied to the Communist Party as "stooges" manipulated by clever party operatives. Privately, and sometimes in public, Reuther questioned whether any blacks were "qualified" to fill high UAW posts.[55]

The issue boiled over at the 1943 UAW convention in Buffalo—held there again because of persistent segregation in St. Louis hotels—when a newly constituted black caucus proposed that the union create a "Minorities Department" headed by an African-American who would also be an executive board member. The proposal had strong backing from the Addes-Frankensteen caucus, as well as from all the African-Americans active in the union, including the few black staffers allied with the Reuther group. But the Reutherites were convinced that the proposal was but a factional ploy, a gambit on the part of the Addes-Frankensteen forces to win another anti-Reuther vote on the executive board.[56] They called it "Jim Crow in reverse." In response the Reuther caucus proposed the creation of a "Fair Practices Department," whose appointed director would hold no executive board vote. The objective differences between the two proposals were minor but charged with racial symbolism. "For years George F. Addes has made himself appear to a large segment of our Negro brothers as being the savior of the Negro race," Reuther seethed at a preconvention caucus. "Well, I'm going to explode that erroneous belief." Addes and his partisans were "intellectually dishonest" because their hands were hardly clean when it came to collaboration with UAW racists. Later, during convention debate, Victor Reuther offered a classic attack on what would eventually enter the political lexicon as "affirmative action." "We must not establish the practice of giving special privileges to special groups, because that is a Jim Crow privilege, and will . . . kick in the teeth the very people it is trying to help. If there is a special post for Negroes, then in all justice there should be a post at large for the Catholics, the women, the Jews, the Poles and the rest."[57]

On both sides racial progressives dominated the public discourse, but hidden just below simmered a vast cauldron of prejudice, resentment, and belief in the racial hierarchy of Jim Crow America. Thus both proposals were defeated, after which two white delegates, one from Local 174, let loose with outright denunciations of "social equality" between the races. The debate seared a racial divide into the UAW body politic. From this point on at least 90 percent of all African-Americans active in the union aligned themselves with Reuther's opponents; the four or five hundred votes they commanded at the 1943 convention almost certainly provided the margin of victory for George Addes and Richard Frankensteen when Richard Leonard again challenged them, with the Reuther group's backing. In 1944 the union finally created the Fair Employment Practices Department; not unexpectedly, Director George Crockett became a key figure in the Addes-Frankensteen caucus, rallying black unionists against Reuther's takeover of the UAW.[58]

Reuther played his cards with somewhat more finesse when he confronted the second great question that roiled the UAW's wartime waters: the no-strike pledge. As strikes, stoppages, and shop-floor controversy escalated, a new political left had begun to emerge within the UAW; it was essentially syndicalist in its shop orientation, but tinctured with a highly ideological critique of the war effort. Indeed, at its heart the no-strike pledge was an ideological formulation, a pledge of allegiance to the idea, if not the reality, of cross-class unity and common endeavor. As a factor in war production, strike activity had virtually no impact; at one point Reuther calculated that the working time lost from all of the stoppages in GM's one hundred war plants during 1943 and 1944 added up to far less than that generated during the July 4 holiday the company reinstituted in 1944. But the political meaning of the pledge—and of its possible recision—had to be carefully calculated. In June 1943 the UMW mine strikes had given congressional reactionaries their chance to slap the labor movement with the Smith-Connally Act, an awkward piece of anti-strike legislation that the Republican-Dixiecrat alliance passed over Roosevelt's veto. Unionists feared more of the same if the stoppages were not tamed. Philip Murray put his great prestige behind the "solemn commitment" embodied in the no-strike pledge, warning of the "well entrenched interests . . . hellbent upon your destruction" should the union movement abandon its compact with the government.[59] Likewise, R. J. Thomas pleaded for an end to wildcat strikes because "public opinion has become inflamed. . . . Our union cannot survive if the nation and our soldiers believe that we are obstructing the war effort." Reuther would not dissent from this judgment. By the middle of the war he saw maintenance of the no-strike pledge largely as a question of political tactics: it represented a position that the labor movement could hardly abandon "without literally crucifying itself and the ideals for which it struggles."[60]

The issue looked quite different from down below. Given the chronic tensions with management and the episodic eruption of shop-floor conflict, many veteran unionists came to see strict adherence to the no-strike pledge as a danger in and of itself. As one local union official put it, "Workers begin to ask each other, 'What good is our union? What are we paying dues for, anyway? Why do our leaders let us down like this?'" Thus many local union officials sought to defend what they saw as traditional union practices, not by championing the "quickie" walkouts and departmental strikes but by channeling the unrest they represented into a more unified and powerful movement. Especially when key union activists were fired, the local leadership sometimes "adopted" a departmental stoppage and authorized a plantwide closure. They did so to aggregate parochial grievances, reintegrate their locals unions, and "close the gap between the rank and file and their elected leadership." Certainly this was the motivation of Lawrence Wilkey, a Cleveland local president who told a UAW executive board committee investigating a four-day strike at Ohio Crankshaft: "The only time I have ever had respect from the membership is when I finally had guts enough to stand up and face the people we had directing things in Region 2A and tell them I didn't give a damn what they done, I was sticking with my membership."[61]

By mid-1943 the movement against the no-strike pledge had become a considerable force within the UAW. At its core were veteran militants like John Anderson of Fleetwood, Emil Mazey of Briggs, Paul Silver of Detroit Steel Products, and John McGill of Buick, syndicalist-minded unionists who had never been reconciled to the no-strike pledge or to the corporatist bargain the CIO had sought to negotiate with Roosevelt and the War Labor Board. They were joined by elements of the ACTU, especially those in the Chrysler locals, who found that their hopes for a patriotic corporatism were daily undermined by the opportunism and intransigence of a management cohort that made no secret of its distaste for CIO-style trade unionism. Much to the chagrin of high CIO leaders, the Mazey-Silver-ACTU grouping demonstrated its potency at Michigan's state CIO convention late in June 1943. There the wartime mavericks captured virtually all the top posts and pushed through resolutions calling for repeal of the no-strike pledge, support for the UMW, and advocacy of a third party modeled after that of the Canadian Commonwealth Federation, which had made a spectacular debut in Ontario's industrial ridings.[62]

The veteran militants of southeastern Michigan were reinforced by a cohort of industrialized students and intellectuals, many politicized in Socialist or Trotskyist circles at the City College of New York, the University of Chicago, or the University of Michigan. Unlike the Communists, who eagerly sent their best cadre into the military, the non-Communist left saw the war with much greater political ambiguity; many young radicals were happy to accept draft deferments in the new war plants, where they moved with remarkable ease into the leadership of several of the UAW's giant "war baby" locals. There the workforce was new, the social structure plastic, and the opportunities for even a minimally organized political grouping virtually limitless. Among the most important, and radically led, of these wartime locals were Brewster Aeronautical on Long Island (Local 365), Ford's B-24 factory in Ypsilanti (Local 50), the Pratt & Whitney Aircraft Building at the Rouge (Local 600), Bell Aircraft in Buffalo (Local 501), and Buick in Melrose Park outside Chicago (Local 6). At Melrose Park, where sixteen thousand men and women built aircraft engines for B-29 bombers, the sociology graduate student Jack Conway made the shift from Hyde Park intellectual to chairman of the plantwide bargaining committee in less than a year. Conway and his comrades were staunch opponents both of the no-strike pledge and of the considerable influence of the Communists within the UAW locals of Wisconsin and Illinois. Soon Local 6 was a center of opposition to both.[63]

Walter Reuther maintained a respectful relationship with these wartime radicals. Many had been in his factional camp before Pearl Harbor, and almost all would return to his caucus right after the war. "Ideologically, emotionally, I identified with the Reuther forces in the UAW from the very beginning," remembered Conway, who would become Walter Reuther's key assistant in the early postwar era.[64] Reuther also blamed management and the War Labor Board for many of the "provocations" that led to wartime strikes, and like others on the anti-Communist left, he came to see the government's appeal to wartime patriotism as a cynical exercise in the manipulation of an increasingly stale set of slogans. After 1943 Reuther approached mobilization politics almost exclusively in terms of its capacity to prepare labor for the inevitable battles that would erupt as soon as the war was over, conflicts to which he looked forward with considerably more relish than did most of his erstwhile comrades in the CIO high command. Victor Reuther, Walter's ambassador to this wartime insurgency, argued that "the difficulty of supporting the war effort in co-operation with domestic social forces whom labor knows to be violently opposed to the democratic objectives of the war is by far the most serious problem labor faces today."[65]

But Walter Reuther would go just so far in accommodating the political turbulence stirring within the ranks of his million-strong union. As a UAW vice president and a frequent visitor to the Washington corridors of power, Reuther was not about to cut himself off from the main body of legitimate wartime politics. He therefore "straddled" the issues, offering autoworkers a carefully nuanced critique of the government's wartime policies and the CIO counterstrategy. He defended Lewis's wage demands but not his strikes; and Reuther supported Roosevelt for a fourth term, but he fought the effort by Addes and the Communists to endorse the president in 1943 before FDR had laid out his postwar plans. Reuther condemned the Little Steel formula and attacked the War Labor Board and the corporations for precipitating many unauthorized strikes, but he cooperated with the UAW executive board to discipline wildcat strike leaders.[66]

Reuther's free ride ended late in the summer of 1944 when he found himself politically wounded in his effort to traverse the minefield that constituted UAW enforcement of the no-strike pledge. Until 1944 GM had been the most strike-free of all the major auto companies—a status that had nothing to do with Reuther's effectiveness as a negotiator but rather reflected the corporation's ability to keep its foremen loyal, union committeemen on the defensive, and retribution for strike action swift. Reuther described GM's labor relations policy as "tough," but "at least they have a policy and you know about where they are going."[67]

Late in July 1944 seven thousand workers at Chevrolet Gear and Axle walked out to defend the jobs of five workers fired by management for not meeting stepped-up production schedules. The local officers were largely Addes partisans, but neither Reuther nor his factional opponents could persuade them to return to work. GM fired seven top local leaders as fomenters of the strike, after which the UAW executive board suspended them from office and installed Melvin Bishop, the East Side regional director and Reuther's onetime housemate, now in the Addes camp, as administrator of the local. Work resumed after Reuther assured an angry meeting of two thousand Chevy workers that the War Labor Board had ordered all workers rehired. But General Motors still demanded its pound of flesh, which it took a day later when it fired for the second time the seven Local 235 leaders. GM's unexpectedly harsh discipline—Reuther called it "subterfuge and trickery"—precipitated an even larger work stoppage that sent Reuther and Bishop scrambling to an emergency meeting of the War Labor Board in Washington. There Reuther tried to turn the tables on GM, announcing that the "corporation is using every pretext to weaken and undermine the UAW-CIO in the hope of destroying its power in the post-war period."[68]

But no matter how accurate his counterpunch, Reuther was politically exposed and personally embarrassed. He had aligned himself with the tough no-strike policy of his factional opponents, been doubled-crossed by GM, and then was publicly admonished by the UAW's former umpire, George Taylor, who now served on the War Labor Board: "We had your word there would not be any [work stoppages]. . . . Walter, we cannot afford this kind of thing and you know it. The unions cannot afford it either."[69] With all these pressures bearing down on him, Reuther must have seen that a CIO-line defense of the no-strike pledge would prove a political and personal disaster. It was time for a certain creative opportunism. Thus, when the UAW assembled for its annual convention in Grand Rapids in September 1944, three resolutions on the no-strike pledge confronted the twenty-four hundred delegates: a majority position, backed by most of the leadership and the Communists, reaffirming the pledge for the duration of the war; a separate Reuther caucus resolution proposing that after the defeat of Germany strikes might be selectively authorized in factories converted to civilian production; and a "superminority" plank sponsored by the UAW radicals, who were now organized into their own Rank-and-File Caucus, that simply revoked the pledge immediately, subject to later ratification by a unionwide referendum.[70]

In a typically disorganized and bitter two-day debate, Reuther's equivocal effort utterly collapsed. His minority proposal rested on two remarkably untenable propositions. First, the false distinction it maintained between civilian and military production had been disparaged by virtually all unionists, including Reuther himself, in an era of consumer rationing and manpower controls.[71] Equally important, Reuther assumed that as Allied troops completed their rush across France, a German defeat might well come before Christmas, making it possible for the War Production Board to order a big cut in military production to "clear the deck" for a massive reconversion to civilian output. But Reuther's calculations proved naive, and not only because the fortunes of war delayed V-E Day until May 1945. At the War Production Board a small business–oriented faction led by Donald Nelson had favored the rapid reconversion to civilian production of as much excess plant capacity as possible. But their efforts were blocked by the dominant alliance between the giant corporations and the military, which feared that even the most tentative steps toward civilian reconversion would threaten the oligopolistic structure of the durable goods manufacturers and open the gates to chaos in the labor market. By August, when Roosevelt exiled Nelson to China as a special emissary to Chiang Kai-shek, the small-business faction had lost the initiative at the WPB, thereby dooming the civilian reconversion program even before Reuther staked his claim to it.[72]

The convention hooted down Reuther's plan in a voice vote. Meanwhile, the real debate took place between those who favored and those who opposed outright revocation of the no-strike pledge. Roosevelt and the CIO mobilized their big guns to defend the pledge: Murray, Hillman, Secretary of Interior Harold Ickes, and the Catholic New Dealer Bishop Francis J. Haas, all put in a word for labor's pledge. Just back from the war front in France, R. J. Thomas once more justified the pledge by an appeal to the patriotism of the union delegates, whereas Philip Murray, in an extraordinary plea to UAW delegates, laid special emphasis upon the need to retain the strike prohibition in order to ensure Roosevelt's reelection.[73] But unreflective calls to support the commander-in-chief had worn thin by late 1944. "When the flags were waved in 1942 . . . we sang 'America,' we sang 'The Star Spangled Banner,'" argued the Rank-and-File Caucus leader Paul Silver, "and we thought we were voting in favor of the song 'America' and 'The Star Spangled Banner,' [but] we wound up with a No Strike Pledge."[74] When some UAW officers made ready to bring wounded war veterans to the microphones in support of the pledge, leaders of the Rank-and-File Caucus threatened to bring their own recently hospitalized servicemen to the convention floor. Both sides agreed to forgo the macabre confrontation.[75]

When the votes were counted, the superminority resolution revoking the pledge took 37 percent, but backers of the pledge also failed to win a majority, so the UAW found itself with no formal position on the crucial issue. In the ensuing confusion,

Victor Reuther and the leaders of the Rank-and-File Caucus worked out an interim compromise: the strike pledge would be reaffirmed, but only until a unionwide referendum resolved the issue.[76] Meanwhile, Reuther's factional prospects had reached their wartime nadir as Richard Leonard, the Reuther bloc's candidate for UAW secretary-treasurer in 1941 and 1943, bolted to form a third faction with R. J. Thomas, who finally sought more than merely titular leadership of America's largest trade union. In the ensuing three-way race for first vice president, Frankensteen beat Reuther by more than nine hundred votes. Now the Addes-Frankensteen faction smelled blood. If they swung all of their support to Leonard in the balloting for the second vice presidency, they might actually eliminate Reuther from the top leadership. "For the first time Walter was totally isolated," recalled Conway, who thought the convention was Reuther's "low point in his political career."[77]

Reuther was in trouble, but he did not panic. "Walter during this period took upon himself the task of speaking personally to every delegate upon whom he could lay a hand," observed Elizabeth Hawes, who shared the factional outlook of the union's Communist-led Education Department, for which she worked. "For hours on end, The Redhead would come grimly downstairs, take his stand near the UAW bookstore display, and harangue little groups of delegates. . . . Certainly the indefatigable energy of the man paid off."[78] Moreover, in 1944 as in previous years, top CIO emissaries, including Allan Haywood and Sidney Hillman, sought to maintain a balance of power in the federation's largest affiliate. They also feared that Reuther, whose reliability on the no-strike pledge seemed suspect, might well emerge as a powerful spokesman for the radicals if he were forced into opposition. Even the Communist group at the convention may have been persuaded to back off: before the second vote, Pat Touhey, the top party organizer in Michigan, told Leonard, "We hate this little redhead sonofabitch but we hate Hitler worse."[79]

Thus Reuther recaptured the second vice presidency, but his close call at the 1944 convention put him at odds with what passed for CIO orthodoxy during the last year of the war. Reuther formally backed an affirmative vote in the UAW referendum to uphold the no-strike pledge, but he put little energy into the task and refused to serve with the other top officers on a Communist-sponsored "Committee to Uphold the No-Strike Pledge." Early in 1945 auto unionists ended up voting two to one in support of the no-strike pledge, but their ballots did little to thwart the stoppages that local union officers organized during the very same months. Reuther therefore proposed that the CIO withdraw from the War Labor Board, at least until the government agency adopted a more liberal policy on wages and fringe benefits. He demonstrated the practical meaning of such sentiments in March 1945 when he insisted that the UAW executive board not impose the usual disciplinary measures on the leadership of the Dodge and Briggs locals then on strike. His faction carried the day on this issue, and as a result the work stoppages continued unabated, forcing the WLB to consider the grievances of these locals even while picket lines ringed each plant. In June 1945 Reuther told a conference of four hundred local union leaders that the no-strike pledge had to go: "Our union has to begin to speak the kind of language the people in Washington will understand."[80]

After V-E day in May the institutional and ideological structures that had sustained the truce began to come apart. Each day brought headlines about a new layoff, a new strike, or a union call to throw off the authority of the War Labor Board. Strikes of maintenance men, rubber workers, and foremen made picket lines a common sight. In nearby Ontario general strike sentiment swept the industrial districts after Canadian militia attacked UAW picket lines at a Ford factory in Windsor. Running for mayor of Detroit, Richard Frankensteen surged to the top of the primary list in early August, perhaps an American echo of the Labour Party landslide in Great Britain just the month before. As many as three hundred thousand Michigan war workers lost their jobs in the weeks ahead, but the massive layoffs did nothing to temper the wave of unauthorized strikes. On the UAW executive board Reuther called for a new referendum on the no-strike pledge: to his surprise, he won the votes of Melvin Bishop, Richard Reisinger, George Burt, and Carl Swanson, once hostile regional directors from Detroit, Cleveland, Ontario, and Flint, where even President R. J. Thomas declared the factories full of "chaotic labor unrest."[81]

A wildcat strike of forty-five hundred Kelsey-Hayes workers exemplified the new militancy. Nine years before Reuther and a small band of Socialist youth had struggled to sustain the strike action of a committed few, but in 1945 Kelsey-Hayes workers were bursting with the self-confidence that a half-decade of full employment and effective union representation had engendered. Kelsey unionists had never signed a contract with management, but union committeemen were powerful figures in the shop, exercising a kind of veto over the decisions made by the foremen, the most obnoxious of whom were sometimes thrown out of the plant. By dramatically raising the wages of its many women operatives, the Kelsey unit of Local 174 had won near-universal respect within the shop, and it had begun to move African-Americans out of the foundry and into cleaner jobs in the semi-skilled production departments.[82]

In company president George Kennedy the Kelsey unionists faced an old foe. In 1936 he had not feared unionization so long as UAW wage demands did not make Kelsey a high-cost supplier to the Big Three automakers; nine years later wage rates were largely out of his hands, but Kennedy worried that if Kelsey-Hayes did not discipline its aggressive committeemen, unpredictable unit-labor costs would put the firm at a disadvantage in the postwar scramble for Big Three contracts. He was determined to rewin the "right to manage." Kennedy therefore cracked down hard, firing thirteen union activists after a wildcat strike in April. The WLB reinstated nine that summer, but the government board supported the company's dismissal of four key committeemen, including the popular militant Chester "Moon" Mullins. After V-J Day, Kelsey unionists agreed that the time had come to ignore WLB arbitration machinery and to "revert back to prewar methods" to teach management a lesson. "We haven't lost a steward or commit-teeman all through the war and we don't intend to start losing them now," declared Mullins. On August 23 they closed the factory. It would not reopen for nearly eight weeks.[83]

In the great labor battles of 1945 and 1946, the Kelsey strike was a minor affair, yet the capacity for self-organization demonstrated there reflected a far larger empowerment. In the entire social history of twentieth-century class relations, the months immediately following the end of World War II may well stand as the moment of greatest potency for working-class America. The élan so noticeable in many sections of the labor movement rested upon a remarkable degree of union consciousness, in some cases amounting to working-class loyalty. "Picket lines, no matter how small, are rarely crossed," admitted GM's Harry Anderson early in 1945.[84] The war, with its legacy of full employment, patriotic entitlement, and democratic expectation, had offered millions of workers an emancipatory vision, one as yet unfocused and ill defined but of greater depth and substance than that of 1919 or 1937, when repression, slump, unemployment, and ethnosocial con-flict had broken the spirit of these earlier mobilizations.

Because of the wartime growth of the unions—from nine to fifteen million—it became the norm, not the exception, for industrial workers to find themselves members of an institution that used all the tools of modern propaganda and effi-cient organization to explain the world to them as one in which their political and economic interests were counterpoised to the greed of those who owned and oper-ated the nation's factories. And to the alarm of all who saw "labor" as but another word for the unskilled and the poorly educated, the unions had begun to enroll elements of the once stolidly loyal lower-middle class—foremen, draftsmen, news-paper reporters, insurance agents, airline pilots, and automobile salesmen, men and women whose drift toward labor's orbit shattered the unitary facade of "man-agement" and opened the door to a much larger definition of what constituted a self-conscious working-class identity. Thus did Elizabeth Hawes observe that upper-class Detroiters "had that cold, hard look in their eyes that people get when they talk of an enemy whose strength they do not underestimate, and whom they therefore loathe and fear."[85]

To what end would UAW leaders seek to mobilize this power, now unleashed by the union's formal abandonment of the no-strike pledge after the fall of Japan? When the executive board met in Flint on September 10, all of its officers, but especially those of the Addes faction, faced a quandary. Outside, one hundred angry unionists picketed their hotel, demanding strike sanction for walkouts at Kelsey and a dozen other factories. Among the top officers, Thomas and Leonard toyed with the idea of authorizing the Kelsey stoppage. The strike was solid, the pressure from below intense, and they might well outflank Reuther, whose shift away from a defense of the no-strike pledge had proven so popular in the last few months. Yet they also feared that a rash of bitter strikes would utterly deplete the treasury, fragment the union, and wreck the program, largely identified with Philip

Murray's CIO leadership, to win from the Truman administration and the major corporations a strike-free postwar compact that would raise wages across the industrial landscape. "Labor will be asked what it is doing and what it intends to do about these strikes," complained a beleaguered R. J. Thomas. "Discipline and order within the ranks of labor must be regained[,] otherwise[,] if the present unruly condition is permitted to increase the Union will be destroyed."[86]

In this crisis, Reuther knew precisely what he wanted. However popular it was, Reuther thought the Kelsey strike a disaster. The bitter stoppage threatened the UAW's ability to organize a well-defined postwar offensive against the major corporations. Indeed, by the time the UAW executive board met in Flint, Ford had laid off thirty thousand additional workers in Detroit, blaming the Kelsey shutdown for holding up needed parts. The union had come to a "crossroads," asserted Reuther, for unless the UAW began to look upon the possibility of a postwar strike as a "well thought-out program properly timed, then the union will be dissipating its power and when the time arrives for a real show-down with a big corporation, the effect will be null."[87]

On the morning of September 13, 1945, the UAW executive board finally gave the defiant Kelsey strike leaders a definitive no to their demand for strike sanction, then suspended them from office and ordered all workers back to work. None would return for almost a month, even in the face of a company injunction, mass arrests, and UAW advertisements urging that the strike end. But whatever its drama, the Kelsey strike remained a sideshow, for that afternoon Reuther announced to the executive board that the UAW must target General Motors for a corporationwide strike that would establish the wage standard for all heavy industry. He also used the Flint executive board meeting to make another announcement, though only the most trusted members of his caucus were present to discuss its contents. Reuther had decided to make the move so many had expected for so long. He would challenge R. J. Thomas for the presidency of America's largest union at the UAW convention in March 1946. But first, the United Automobile Workers had to take on General Motors.[88]

11

ON STRIKE AT
GENERAL MOTORS

The fight of the General Motors workers is a fight to save truly-free enterprise
from death at the hands of its self-appointed champions.

— *Walter Reuther, January 1946*

hree days after the UAW executive board voted to squash the Kelsey-Hayes wildcat, the *New York Times Magazine* published a major essay under Reuther's byline. "Our Fear of Abundance" neatly summarized his postwar economic program in a set of lively propositions strikingly different from the laborite worldview embodied in his struggles against General Motors in the 1930s or in the "500 Planes a Day" plan of 1940. Reuther's themes were both Veblenite and Keynesian, combining a sanguine faith in the perfection of Fordist production technology with a piercing critique of capitalism's apparent failure to make the transition from the warfare state's command economy to the consumer-driven market of the postwar era.

"We suffer," Reuther wrote in the *Times*, "from what Thorstein Veblen called the 'inordinate productivity' of the machine. We have mastered technology and possess a complex, high-octane B-29 production machine. But our productive genius has always been stalemated by our failure at the distributive end. We have found it impossible to sustain a mass purchasing power capable of providing a stable market for the products of a twentieth century technology." Or, as Reuther would put it in a speech just a month later, "The war has proven that production is not our problem; our problem is consumption."[1]

This dichotomy, between the machine and its product, between production and consumption, represents a theme of paramount import to the ideology of labor-liberalism in the 1940s. Of course, such counterpositions had always been present in the language of the labor movement and the left. Indeed, the UAW theme song, "Solidarity," condemned the "untold millions" that the capitalists "never toiled to earn." But what was new after the war, for Reuther and for American labor, was the way in which the unproblematic celebration of industry's productive capacity displaced so much conflict from the realm of the work site to that of the pay packet and the shopping mart. With Reuther in the vanguard, the labor movement began to substitute the language of technical Keynesianism—"purchasing power," "aggregate demand," "wage-price stability"—for much of the prewar lexicon of power, justice, and industrial democracy.

The reconstruction of the political economy during World War II proved central to this sea change. By 1945 America's large business corporations had gone a long way toward relegitimizing their role as autonomous and efficient generators of the nation's wealth. The top one hundred corporations had substantially increased their contribution to the gross national product, which by 1946 was double the 1940 figure. Chevrolet's wartime advertising slogan, "Volume Production for Victory," may have been ungainly, but it nevertheless offered magazine readers an accurate celebration of the production, by General Motors Corporation, of more than 12 percent of all war material made of metal. As the historian Alan Brinkley has pointed out, the wartime economic experience had discredited the Depression-era idea that the U.S. economy had become "stagnant" or "mature" and replaced such pessimism with a vision of limitless postwar growth. For liberals, structural changes in the distribution of economic power, such as those envisioned by the CIO's various schemes for tripartite governance of industry, now seemed less important, since the essential structures of corporate enterprise had proven their enormous productive capacity during the war. Economic growth was still not automatic, of course. It required the careful application of the lessons taught by Lord Keynes, but the possibility of a postwar "economy of abundance"—the term was first used in a 1943 National Resources Planning Board report—now lay within the nation's grasp.[2]

A powerful union movement played a particularly vital role: now labor's traditional demand for higher income meshed easily with the emerging Keynesian view that aggregate demand must be sustained and income redistributed to avoid a new slump. With the collapse of military spending, the nation faced an annual loss of $35 billion in annual wages. Reuther therefore saw labor's demand for a postwar wage boost as a struggle to maintain purchasing power, a "holding action" designed to forestall a disastrous deflation and to prepare the ground for an advance toward a $200 billion economy.[3]

Of course, Reuther's brand of Keynesianism demanded a good deal more attention to the micromanagement of the production system than that espoused by many of his erstwhile allies. For example, the UAW was particularly concerned with the postwar fate of the giant airframe industry, especially when the military announced plans to abandon such giant facilities as Brewster Aircraft on Long Island and the famous Willow Run factory near Ypsilanti. When the navy shut down Brewster in May 1944, the plight of war workers first captured national attention. Local 365's radical leadership organized a plant occupation, Frankensteen demanded new military work for the factory, and Reuther used his good relations with Undersecretary of War Robert Patterson and Eleanor Roosevelt to plead for a reemployment scheme.

But all to no avail. When Willow Run was closed a year later, the CIO News offered a graphic commentary: "They gave the workers Army-Navy E's and told them to go home because the government and Mr. Ford didn't want the plant any more. Nobody wants Willow Run, the $95 million factory that produced almost 9,000 Liberator bombers. Nobody wants the 51,950 pieces of machinery. . . . And nobody wants the more than 20,000 human beings who go with the plant."[4] Working with Local 50's Brendan Sexton, a Socialist out of Brookwood and the Workers Defense League, Reuther used the manifest inefficiencies and social dislocations accompanying the abandonment of these giant war plants to advocate a postwar program to bring their production capacity under the control of a tripartite "Peace Production Board." Reuther wanted Willow Run converted to the production of railroad cars or prefabricated housing under the aegis of a government agency styled after the Tennessee Valley Authority (TVA). But such schemes had little resonance outside liberal-labor circles. The big corporations and the Truman administration saw physical reconversion of war production facilities as largely a process of rapid privatization and regulatory dismantlement, so Reuther's proposal that the government itself reconvert its war plants never entered the policy debate.[5]

With the structural reorganization of American capitalism clearly blocked at the end of World War II, Reuther could hardly avoid tackling what had become the central issue in the political economy: the postwar relationship between wages and prices in the manufacturing sector. Labor's practical case for a substantial wage increase rested upon both the government's failure to restrain inflation and the sharp cutback in overtime pay that began after V-E Day. The Bureau of Labor Statistics found that living costs had gone up by 30 percent since January 1941; union economists argued that 45 percent was a more accurate measure. The CIO therefore insisted upon a quick upward revision of the Little Steel formula: an across-the-board 20 percent wage increase to sustain working-class living standards and put billions of dollars of purchasing power into the hands of workers during the uncertain transition from war to peace. As Reuther put it in a voluminous economic brief filed with the WLB on June 30, 1945, "Wages can be increased without increasing prices. Increased production must be supported by increased consumption, and increased consumption will be possible only through increased wages."[6]

Reuther's turn toward an explicitly Keynesian formulation reflected not only the general drift of labor-liberalism in the mid-1940s but the detailed tutelage offered the UAW leader by a new confidant, Donald Montgomery, who ran the union's consumer office in Washington. Like Eddie Levinson, who had died of a stroke in August 1945, Montgomery served Reuther as both a public relations flack and a genuine policy mentor. While Levinson had an unsurpassed feel for labor politics, Montgomery's expertise extended to the broader world of macroeconomic policy-making and liberal politics. Eleven years Reuther's elder, Montgomery was representative of the cohort of still-vital Progressives who flocked to the New Deal agencies in the early 1930s. Educated at the Universities of Pennsylvania and Wisconsin, Montgomery administered antitrust and unfair competition laws for the state of Wisconsin, then worked at the Federal Trade Commission, the Securities and Exchange Commission, and the Department of Agriculture. He was a friend of Ben Cohen and other young New Dealers sent to Washington by Felix Frankfurter.

During his seven years at Agriculture, Montgomery proved a vigorous and combative spokesman for the "consumer movement" of the late 1930s, a coalition of liberal activists and government regulators who saw organized and educated consumers as an essential counterweight to oligopolistically organized processing industries and predatory retail chains. Montgomery battled the farm bloc for taking advantage of the food shortage during the war, but his was an isolated voice within a department whose vestigial reformism had all but vanished with the departure of Henry Wallace and the coming of war. In December 1942 Montgomery resigned from his post when the department refused to go ahead with a program of grade-labeling he had championed. Upon Victor's recommendation, Walter hired Montgomery as his staff lobbyist in the UAW's new Washington office.[7]

Montgomery quickly established himself as one of Reuther's closest and most influential advisers, and he soon became the CIO point man on the inflation front. For three years he proved a friendly adversary to Chester Bowles, the wealthy but liberal advertising executive who had taken over the Office of Price Administration (OPA) in early 1943 and made it labor's sometime ally within the mobilization apparatus. Montgomery insisted that under wartime conditions industry reaped enormous productivity gains through high-capacity production; therefore, most corporations could easily absorb a wage increase without a corresponding price rise. He urged the OPA to deconstruct the corporate balance sheet so that the public would understand what relationship the price of individual products bore to wage and material costs. Working as both a defender of the OPA's overall mission and a critic of its price-setting calculations, Montgomery refined and popularized many of the concepts—and catchphrases—that Reuther would later deploy in his GM strike program: "wage increases without price increases," "open the books," and "purchasing power for prosperity."[8]

Reuther signed the UAW onto Montgomery's analysis in a June 30, 1945, memorandum, "How to Raise Wages without Increasing Prices," submitted to William H. Davis, who as director of economic stabilization was responsible for both the

OPA and the WLB. The UAW argued that workers needed an immediate 30 percent increase in their hourly pay, both to sustain aggregate demand and to compensate for the income they lost when the postwar workweek shrank from forty-eight hours to forty. To drive home their argument, Montgomery and Reuther revisited the stagnationist critique of the late 1930s, even quoting the gloomiest of the Keynesian economists, Alvin Hansen, to the effect that wartime savings had been greatly exaggerated and a postwar consumer goods boom was hardly a sure thing. Indeed, Montgomery and Reuther shared the view, widespread among economic forecasters of even moderate views, that the nation stood on the brink of a postwar depression unless the government took immediate action.

Montgomery and Reuther argued that a macroeconomic remedy was at hand, if only America had the will to push it through. They were not interested in a new round of government spending, the Keynesian prescription favored by liberals half a generation later. Instead, left-Keynesians of the immediate postwar era saw the progressive redistribution of income as the key lever by which unions and the government could sustain aggregate demand. As Montgomery put it in his June 30 memorandum: "Discovery of our full productive potential in civilian production will depend to a large extent upon the creation of conditions that stimulate discovery. Wages that press forward ahead of prices are one such condition, persuading management to discover new highs in productive efficiency." Stagnation was the alternative to such a program, warned the Montgomery-Reuther brief:

> Going into the postwar period with a wide gap between prices and wages, industry will not need to find markets for the products of full employment. It can produce at half or three-quarters of capacity and break even. . . . It does not intend to adopt a new pattern just because we have passed through a war which has demonstrated—to its embarrassment—the tremendous, but strenuous, profit potential of capacity operations. . . . A government stabilization policy that fails to challenge this industry objective, promotes it.[9]

But how could the labor movement win such a government stabilization policy? Two choices confronted labor-liberals, one identified with the consensus-building leadership of Philip Murray, the other with the more confrontational militancy Walter Reuther would come to embody. Philip Murray was a man beloved by all those with whom he worked closely. The Scottish burr of his gentle voice soothed and reassured his auditors even when it hailed labor's power and denounced corporate greed. But even as he presided over America's most dynamic labor federation, Murray was a man beset by public fears and private doubts, not all of them irrational by any means. He feared God, he feared John L. Lewis, and he feared for his "manhood" when even mildly dissident voices challenged his leadership. Above all, Murray feared chaos and conflict, either within the CIO or between the unions and their corporate adversaries. Like so many trade unionists of his generation, Murray had been seared by the mass unemployment and the antilabor, antiradical mobilizations that followed the 1919 strike wave. Thus Philip Murray told the 1944 CIO convention, "only chaos and destruction of our industrial life will result if employers look to the war's end as an opportunity for a union-breaking, wage-cutting, open-shop drive, and if labor unions have to resort to widespread strikes to defend their very existence and the living standards of their members."[10]

To forestall such a prospect, Murray's reconversion strategy forecast a government-backed accommodation with industry, one that ensured continuation of the no-strike pledge, price controls, and a new wage pattern that finally revised the Little Steel formula by at least 20 percent. In March 1945 the CIO had been the principal motivator behind the "Labor-Management Charter" cosigned by William Green of the AFL and Eric Johnston, president of the U.S. Chamber of Commerce. Hailing both the virtues of unfettered free enterprise and the rights of labor, the charter symbolized the CIO's hope for cooperation with the liberal wing of American capitalism in stabilizing postwar industrial relations along roughly the lines established during the war. "It's Industrial Peace for the Postwar Period," headlined the CIO News. In return for management support for the unamended Wagner Act and a high-wage, high-employment postwar strategy, the unions pledged to defend "a system of private competitive capitalism," including "the inherent right and responsibility of management to direct the operations of an enterprise."[11]

By the fall of 1945 the CIO and its friends in the government had begun to assemble the materials out of which such a corporatist accord might be fashioned. Immediately after the fall of Japan, President Truman announced that the government would no longer stand in the way of voluntarily negotiated wage increases so long as management held the price line. Many New Dealers, like Commerce Secretary Henry Wallace and William Davis, now head of the Office of Economic Stabilization, endorsed the kind of laborite Keynesianism that Montgomery, Murray, and Reuther were advocating. Thus Davis, who had spent the war holding the line on the Little Steel formula, suggested that American living standards would have to rise by 40–50 percent over the next five years to avoid a postwar slump, and Robert Nathan of the Office of War Mobilization and Reconversion projected a 24 percent increase as essential to maintain aggregate demand over the next year. OPA Chairman Chester Bowles worked out a tentative deal with Murray, Green, and Johnston to hold the price line, raise hourly wages 10 percent, and avoid a postwar strike wave. This accord collapsed soon after V-J Day, but Murray nevertheless urged CIO unions to avoid "provocations" and await a White House labor-management conference in November, at which he hoped to nail down a strike-free wage increase for much of the trade union movement.[12]

Philip Murray's vision had much to recommend it. The New Deal had thoroughly politicized all relations between the union movement, the business community, and the state. For more than a decade issues of vital concern to labor had been negotiated through a set of tripartite political structures in Washington. From the National Recovery Administration of 1933 to the Wage Stabilization Board established just after V-J Day, the successive appearance of these agencies seemed to signal that in the future as in the past the fortunes of organized labor would be determined as much by the process of politicized bargaining in Washington as by the give-and-take of contract collective bargaining.

Had American labor reached such a postwar accord with the government and the large corporations, the United States would have taken a giant step toward the sort of social democratic corporatism that came to characterize countries like Austria, Sweden, and Germany in the 1950s and 1960s. Under such conditions, key elements of an overall wage pattern are established when, under a sympathetic government eye, representatives of an entire union federation periodically negotiate with officials of a nation's most important business associations. Although union officials had not been uncritical of the War Labor Board and the Office of Price Administration, liberal and labor spokesmen saw the maintenance of corporatist institutions such as these as the kernel of a postwar "incomes" policy. In Western Europe a similar corporatist model promoted a more egalitarian wage structure, a remarkably low level of industrial conflict, and a business community that saw little economic advantage to the avoidance of trade unionism.[13]

Unfortunately, the CIO president's program never had a chance. First, not all trade unionists shared such a vision. The AFL had never been as committed as the CIO to the tripartite bargaining arrangements of the war era; AFL unions now demanded a return to unrestricted collective bargaining. Their approach stemmed in part from the AFL's tradition of Gompersarian voluntarism, but it also reflected the contrasting organizational bases of the two labor federations. The CIO industrial unions were overwhelmingly concentrated in the manufacturing sector of the economy where they faced oligopolistically organized employers who were themselves capable of imposing a new wage pattern. But only 35 percent of AFL membership lay in this heavy industrial sector; construction, transportation, and service trades were the AFL's most important centers of strength. These decentralized, and now booming, sectors of the economy were less subject to the pattern-setting guidelines established by core firms like General Motors and U.S. Steel.[14]

Although he was an industrial unionist, John L. Lewis spoke most forthrightly for the AFL viewpoint. Repeated clashes between the UMW and the Roosevelt administration during the war had soured the mine leader on the kind of state-sponsored industrial planning arrangements he had once advocated as the CIO's first president. Lewis was now determined to exercise his union's power unfettered by a new set of federal regulations. "What Murray and the CIO are asking for," declared Lewis at the November labor-management conference, "is a corporate state, wherein the activities of the people are regulated and constrained by a dictatorial government. We are opposed to a corporate state."[15]

Second, Truman and his principal policymakers equivocated. Representing a border state, Truman stood geographically as well as politically between the liberalism of the late New Deal and the conservative opposition that had arisen against it. In the perceptive analysis of Samuel Lubell, Truman was a man of "persistent irresolution," whose political hallmark was the "faculty for turning two bold steps into a halfway measure."[16] From August through November, presidential speeches and policy directives were almost as progressive as any labor-liberal might wish. Immediately after V-J Day, Truman told the War Labor Board to lift the cap on wages, and in late October, on the eve of the labor-management conference, he endorsed essential elements of a left-Keynesian program that would allow industry to offer the unions a substantial increase in wages without raising prices.

But Truman failed to put administrative backbone into the implementation of these wage-price policies. The wartime agencies that regulated production, wages, and prices lost power and prestige in a swirl of rapid personnel and policy changes. As the old New Dealers drifted away, Truman replaced them with a domestic policy staff of a decidedly parochial and conservative cast. Key posts were staffed by men like Lewis B. Schwellenbach, the new secretary of labor, who opposed continuing most price controls; John C. Collet, a Missouri crony of Truman's, who replaced, ineffectually, William H. Davis at the Office of Economic Stabilization; and John Snyder, a Missouri banker at the Office of War Mobilization and Reconversion whose affinity for the business point of view was neatly matched by his "ideological fear" of Walter Reuther. Although liberals still retained important posts in the battle over price controls, the OPA chief Chester Bowles, for one, was "beginning to look like a man who got into government by parachute, and is trying to defend a small clearing against the enemy," commented journalist Samuel Grafton.[17]

Moreover, Truman had none of the patrician equanimity with which FDR faced the leaders of the labor movement. The new president certainly recognized that in order to govern the unions and their liberal allies had to be accommodated—this was the lesson that the White House aide Clark Clifford would drill home in his famous strategy memorandum on the 1948 campaign—but despite the pride Truman took in his humble origins, he found emotionally jarring and somehow illegitimate the power and resources commanded by trade union leaders. Thus Clark Clifford remembered a bitter 1946 showdown with the UMW's John L. Lewis as "the moment when Truman finally and irrevocably stepped out from the shadow of FDR to become President in his own right."[18]

Truman's inadequacies aside, the CIO had profoundly misjudged the tenor of the postwar business community. The progressive industrialists with whom the industrial union federation hoped to achieve an accord—men like Paul Hoffman of Studebaker and Henry Kaiser, whose West Coast fortune had been built through New Deal construction and shipbuilding contracts—were in fact a relatively uninfluential minority. Key business spokesmen were the practical conservatives who presided over the core manufacturing firms in the steel, chemical, electrical, auto, rubber, and transport industries. Led by men such as John A. Stephens of U.S. Steel, Ira Mosher of the National Association of Manufacturers, Walter Carpenter of DuPont, and Wilson of General Motors, these industrialists had emerged from the war with enormous sophistication and self-confidence. Unlike their counterparts in continental Europe, or even in the British Isles, who had been tarred with the brush of collaboration or appeasement, American business leaders found the wartime experience one of both commercial success and political advantage. They felt little need for the kind of state-sponsored labor-management collaboration that helped legitimize a mixed capitalist economy in Germany, France, and Italy in the immediate postwar era.

Executives of corporations at the core of American industry sought the restoration of the managerial prerogatives that wartime conditions had eroded in the areas of product pricing, market allocation, and shop-floor work environment. They were intensely suspicious of the kind of New Deal social engineering favored by labor, and only with some reluctance did they accommodate themselves to the modest degree of economic stimulation that would later go by the name "commercial Keynesianism." Looking forward to a postwar boom, they wanted to be free of government or union interference in determining the wage-price relationship in each industry. General Motors had its own top-level postwar planning group, which saw an imminent threat to "private capitalism and free enterprise. . . . The system we know, and under which we have operated, is one that must be preserved in principle as affording the best future promise for society."[19]

Thus did DuPont's Jasper Crane, summing up the general views of the GM-DuPont hierarchy, denounce Eric Johnston and his Labor-Management Charter as "irresponsible" and a step toward "state socialism." As for progressives like Hoffman and Kaiser, they were "unsound business men."[20] As a consequence, the long-awaited labor-management conference that President Truman convened on November 4, 1945, was doomed to failure. No accord proved possible on either the prerogatives of management or the scope of legitimate union demands, and on the crucial issue of a general wage policy the CIO got nowhere. Philip Murray offered industry a de facto policy of labor peace in return for a pattern wage increase, which Truman had endorsed in a speech of October 30, but the opposition was so great that the issue never secured a place on the formal conference agenda.[21]

Walter Reuther had a more realistic, and therefore a more confrontational, understanding of the obstacles facing the industrial unions in the immediate postwar era. Like Murray, Reuther wanted the government to preside over the establishment of a new postwar wage pattern—still possible without a strike—but he understood that only a direct assault on a key corporate adversary would blunt industry resistance and prod the government into putting some backbone into the OPA's postwar price guidelines. In a thinly veiled attack on Murray's strategy, Victor Reuther spoke for his brother: "It is time to debunk the notion that labor can meet in parlays with government and management and by some miracle, fashion a compromise that will keep all parties happy and contented." Reuther's GM strike program would therefore harness the restless energy of the autoworkers, restore legitimacy to top union leaders, and advance his own fortunes in the internal scramble for office. The key GM strike demand—for a 30 percent wage boost without an increase in the price of cars—was but a militant restatement of the CIO's postwar wage policy. Yet the demand excited union ranks because it was made directly and backed by union strike power, rather than offered to a government agency for tripartite negotiation and compromise.[22]

Reuther made his GM wage program public on August 16. A month later, at the Flint executive board meeting, he won the rest of the executive board to a "one at a time" strike strategy directed at General Motors. Reuther would have the UAW "blockade" GM production while encouraging other auto companies to build cars, take profits, and steal market share. Under the provisions of the wartime Smith-Connally Act, still in effect, the NLRB set a strike vote for October 24. In the meantime, Reuther insisted upon "effective self-discipline," from the shop floor up. "Local union officers and members must clearly understand that there shall be no strike action in any plant until the instructions are received form the International Union."[23]

When Charles Wilson finally rejected the UAW's wage demands on October 3, he agreed with Reuther that the dispute with the UAW was "no ordinary collective bargaining quarrel. . . . It is a national problem." Of course, Wilson saw the conflict in terms diametrically opposite to those of his thirty-eight-year-old adversary. Reflecting a corporate culture that complacently asserted the identity of interest between company, polity, and society, Wilson announced that "if strikes are called and our plants are closed, the strikes will be against the interest of all the people of our country as much as they will be against General Motors." Indeed, by the time formal negotiations began on October 19, GM executives had probably concluded that a strike could not be avoided. Thus GM offered a 5–8 percent wage increase, coupled with a provocative proposal that the union join the corporation in calling for a revision of the Wage and Hours Act to increase the standard workweek from forty to forty-five hours. Wilson told a press conference that in the auto industry as in steel, OPA price limits were the real stumbling block to settlement. "It is either going to be solved, or our plants are all going to be shut down completely." Reuther therefore charged that "General Motors wants a strike. It is baiting labor, it is baiting the Government; it is planning to use its vast economic power to coerce Congress."[24]

He was right, for GM executives sought to hold the line against any linkage between wages and a price structure subject to government review. General Motors had long been a pioneer in market forecasting, production planning, and cost containment. Since the 1920s the corporation had sought a 20 percent annual return on invested capital. While its sales and profits had more than doubled during the war, the corporation had accommodated itself to a broad system of government controls and settled for a rate of return somewhat less, in part because Sloan and the DuPonts feared a return of public outrage over the "war profiteering" that had plagued the munitions maker in earlier years. But with the end of World War II, GM executives were determined to return these planning functions to the corporation itself so that the entire automobile industry would again assume its "virile leadership" within the American economy.[25]

Top executives privately acknowledged that Reuther's pay and price program had much validity. William "Buck" Harrington, a DuPont vice president, circulated a letter to other GM board members admitting that "the possible advance in technique" during the war "would justify General Motors to take a reasonable business risk with respect to increases in wages notwithstanding the freezing of selling prices." In contrast to the situation in steel, where technological change had been limited, "General Motors . . . is not in a position in my judgement, to go to OPA as did [U.S. Steel Chairman Benjamin] Fairless in the Steel case and say 'No wage increase until OPA relaxes its position with respect to selling prices.' . . . Frankly, I would not advocate General Motors taking the same position as Fairless took."[26]

But this stance was precisely what GM Chairman Alfred Sloan insisted upon. "I am greatly exercised—perhaps unduly so—by the philosophy of 'capacity to pay,'" wrote Sloan to DuPont President Walter S. Carpenter. "General Motors has taken the position that it will not bargain for wages with an operating statement in its hands. . . . Personally, I dislike to see the U.S. Steel Corporation indicating that they will go up in wages if the Government will let them go up in prices. . . . I think the relationship is very dangerous. . . . In the final analysis, it gets down to production plus a fixed fee." GM's vast Public Relations Department soon turned such private sentiments into a public fusillade. The company sent its response to the UAW's proposal to every congressman, senator, and governor. Its advertisement, "Danger on the Production Front," appeared in scores of metropolitan dailies. And in late December another widely placed advertisement warned: "America is at the crossroads! It must preserve the freedom of each unit of American business to determine its own destiny. . . . The idea of ability to pay, whatever its validity may be, is not applicable to an individual business within an industry as a basis for raising its wages beyond the going rate." George Romney of the Automobile Manufacturers' Association exaggerated but slightly when he personalized the darkest fears of American capital: "Walter Reuther is the most dangerous man in Detroit because no one is more skillful in bringing about the revolution without seeming to disturb the existing forms of society."[27]

Given such guidance from on high, it is not surprising that the UAW-GM negotiations soon came to an impasse after they began on October 19. Since both sides saw their fight as fundamentally political, the talks were little more than a public relations battle. Naturally Reuther wanted the negotiations open to the press. When GM balked, citing Reuther's demand for secrecy during the 1942 bargaining round, the UAW brought in its own stenographer; the livelier exchanges were therefore reprinted in the newsweeklies and the daily press. In addition to Don Montgomery, Reuther beefed up his negotiating team with three other liberal activists (all of whom would eventually join the UAW staff): Paul Sifton, a prewar Socialist who helped found the Union for Democratic Action; Abe Zwerling, a lawyer from Ann Arbor who had worked on WLB cases for Reuther's GM Department; and Joe Rauh, who had just returned from the Pacific theater.[28] Sifton and Montgomery crafted the UAW's economic brief, "Purchasing Power for Prosperity," as a highly readable pamphlet that the union mailed to thousands of government officials, businessmen, and journalists. "Mass purchasing power is our new frontier," asserted the union brief. "The whole style of the postwar economy is being set now. The action of business on wages is determining whether we intend to maintain permanent prosperity on a broad base. . . . In 1946, when the reconversion boom will be past its peak . . . we shall then be hell-bent for depression, and the moderate remedies which can be applied now will be insufficient then."[29]

General Motors sent only its labor-relations men to the negotiations; they had no authority to discuss corporate profits or price policy, and their attitude was one of studied contempt for Reuther's economic analysis and his larger social ambitions. GM's Harry Anderson cleaned his fingernails during the UAW's opening presentation. Harry Coen, who had played hardball with the union since his days as a plant superintendent in Flint, read a magazine.[30] When "negotiations" did take place, they soon turned into a cat fight:

WALTER REUTHER: But don't you think it is constructive for us to try to relate our wage question to prices?

HARRY COEN: Nobody else is doing that but you. You are the fellow that wants to get the publicity out of this whole thing. You want to enhance your own personal political position. That is what the whole show is about.

REUTHER: I see. This is just a political thing?

COEN: That is right. If it wasn't for that, you wouldn't be on the radio and you wouldn't be putting out these statements.

And later:

REUTHER: Unless we get a more realistic distribution of America's wealth, we won't get enough to keep this machine going.

COEN: There it is again. You can't talk about this thing without exposing your socialistic desires.

REUTHER: If fighting for a more equal and equitable distribution of the wealth of this country is socialistic, I stand guilty of being a Socialist.

COEN: I think you are convicted.[31]

A strike was inevitable, but its timing proved a crucial and contentious issue for Reuther, his UAW rivals, and the CIO. About half the GM workforce was still on layoff, but in the NLRB election of October 24, eighty-four thousand participating workers nevertheless voted six to one for a strike. Led by Philip Murray, most CIO officials still hoped that some agreement with industry could be negotiated at the labor-management conference President Truman had called in early November;

in a speech of October 30, the president had seemed to once again back union claims that a substantial wage advance might be negotiated without a major shift in OPA price guidelines. Moreover, even if such an accord proved out of reach — Murray himself thought the failure of collective bargaining a product of "a national sit-down strike" by employers determined to "secure substantial price hikes for the manufacture of almost every civilian commodity"—many unionists still wanted to postpone an industry showdown until January 1946. Until then, industry balance sheets would suffer little damage because the Treasury guaranteed corporations a refund from their wartime excess profits tax for any losses suffered during the reconversion period. In effect, the U.S. government would reimburse General Motors for virtually all strike-related losses it might bear during 1945. Moreover, the steel industry, not autos, had established big labor's wage pattern during World War II; it was the price of this commodity, now being furiously debated by the OPA and industry, that would inevitably determine the cost of all other durable goods. At a CIO executive board meeting in early November, Van Bittner of the United Steel Workers (USW) warned Reuther against "jumping out into the forefront," because a UAW failure would derail Philip Murray's entire reconversion wage strategy.[32]

But Reuther simply ignored CIO policy and maneuvered for the most favorable terrain upon which to call an early stoppage. He applauded Truman's speech of October 30, called upon the OPA to make public GM pricing data for its 1946 model cars, and invited GM President Charles Wilson to personally participate in the negotiations. When GM finally presented its formal answer to the UAW demand for a 30 percent wage increase—thirteen and a half cents, with no guarantee on prices—Reuther excoriated the offer as a "conspiracy against the public," a "bribe offer because we will not be a party to sand-bagging the American customer." The UAW also filed an unfair labor practices complaint against GM, charging, among other things, that GM had refused to discuss "ability to pay." By the time Reuther convened a conference of two hundred GM delegates in Detroit on November 19, a strike was but hours away. As a rhetorical gesture designed to shore up support on the public relations front, Reuther proposed that a three-person arbitration board examine GM's books and make a binding decision on just one question: the corporation's ability to raise wages 30 percent without a price increase. He called for an answer in twenty-four hours; when GM hardly took notice of this gambit, Reuther called on some 175,000 workers to strike eighty GM plants and warehouses in more than fifty cities. Voting Reuther's strike resolution through with a roar, the exhilarated GM delegates burst into a booming rendition of "Solidarity Forever!" When slapped on the back by a well-wisher, Reuther replied, "Just like old times, isn't it?"[33]

Begun on November 21, the GM strike would last for 113 days, by far the longest major stoppage of the great 1945–46 strike wave. Reuther had been high-handed in his preparations for the strike, barely consulting the rest of the executive board except to ratify his strategy. But even Reuther's factional opponents recognized the popularity and decisive character of the stoppage. Addes, Thomas, Leonard, and Frankensteen downplayed their differences with the GM director, and each helped by mobilizing his own partisans in support of the big strike. They endorsed Reuther's assessment that if the stoppage had not begun in late November, the union would have been faced with "a wave of unauthorized strikes [and] walkouts . . . in the industry throughout the country." George Addes recalled, "We reached a point where we had to do something. . . . We weren't prepared to accept a decision from the CIO."[34]

Reuther had "jumped the gun" on Murray and the CIO because the GM strike was a fundamentally political phenomenon. Upon its success, or at least its vigorous prosecution, rested Reuther's prospects for election to the UAW presidency. But it was also a political strike in the sense that its outcome was hardly dependent upon GM's profit-and-loss statement during the 1945–46 automotive season; the stakes, as GM propaganda never ceased to remind the public, were far higher than that. The success of the strike lay in its shock value, its capacity to mobilize a broadly strategic constituency in behalf of Reuther's political economy. Indeed, by early December a note of socialist millenialism had crept back into Reuther's rhetoric. Before a union audience in Buffalo he weighed the price of failure: "a short and steep toboggan ride" to mass unemployment. "If we fail, if depression comes again, another generation will go out to die."[35]

The strike proved massively popular and utterly solid, winning enthusiastic support up and down the union hierarchy. The UAW had never before been able to shut down all of General Motors, so for even veterans of the 1930s the postwar stoppage was exhilarating and cathartic. After years of wartime constraint, even unionists hostile to Reuther recognized the enthusiasm his strike had unleashed. The Cleveland Communist Leo Fenster thought the strike had been called prematurely, but he recalled, "Emotionally, they really wanted to strike. . . . The participation of the membership was fantastic." By its second week the prolabor *Federated Press* reported "strong spirited turnouts" on the Detroit-area picket lines. "The auto workers were fed up with the status-quo," recalled B. J. Widick. Picketing dwindled by midwinter, but autoworker support for the strike never flagged. Reported Edwin Lahey of the *Detroit Free Press*, "The workers have sweated out Thanksgiving, Christmas, New Years and now are tramping into spring. Their war savings are about depleted. . . . Yet there is no recorded instance of revolt or threatened revolt against the union leadership in all the far flung locals." Indeed, in Flint, where every strike against GM had been accompanied by bitter internal union conflict, and where Reuther had been virtually persona non grata during the last half of the war, the GM strike put Reuther and his erstwhile opponents on the same side of the barricades. "Reuther was a big hero," conceded the Addes partisan Jack Palmer in an oral history fifteen years later. "Everybody was a Reutherite in 1946."[36]

In Detroit a citywide strike committee, dominated by radicals but equally divided between Reuther friends and foes, met daily to coordinate picketing, strike benefits, and local publicity. The UAW had no strike fund, but workers got along without much hardship. The union raised six hundred thousand dollars from within its own ranks; as a matter of course, all the top officers, including Reuther, donated their salaries to the strike fund. Meanwhile, almost all GM workers had at least a few hundred dollars' worth of war bonds that could be turned into cash. "They can't scare us with the boggy that the kiddies will have a cheerless Christmas," reported a grinder at Chevy Gear and Axle. "We are ready to sit this out till next Labor Day." After more than three months on strike, only 7 percent of all GM strikers had applied for family assistance in the city of Detroit.[37]

The UAW's strike slogan, "We fight today for a better tomorrow," rested upon not only the logic of Reuther's economic program but upon the social weight and cultural prestige of a working class whose experience had been so central to the triumphant war effort. The strike, asserted Reuther, was "the fight of every veteran coming home in search of a job and a tangible stake in the future of the country he saved from international fascism."[38] Unlike 1919, when elements of the army's officer corps had organized the American Legion to spearhead an attack upon popular radicalism, World War II veterans remained virtually immune to antilabor political mobilization.

To millions of working-class youth the war experience had ratified the new sense of citizenship born in the late 1930s. After V-J Day, U.S. troops in the Far East organized a "bring the boys home" movement that demanded rapid demobilization of American occupation troops in North China, the Philippines, and Indonesia. In Manila, the storm center of the movement, Sergeant Emil Mazey played a key role as one of the savvy organizers of a highly successful protest campaign. The symbiotic resonance between this insurgency and that in the Midwest auto centers was hardly lost on the top brass. Thus, when four thousand U.S. troops in Manila marched on an army headquarters depot in December 1945, the commander ordered them back to their barracks with the wisecrack, "You men forget you're not working for General Motors. You're still in the Army." Back home, GM strikers who had served in the military wore their uniforms as a symbol of their entitlement and their patriotism; when the UAW declared January 12 "Veterans' Day," a huge uniformed picket line ringed the corporation's giant office complex in Detroit, while smaller lines paraded outside outlying factories.[39]

This strike, and the series of even larger CIO and AFL walkouts that followed in the winter, may well have marked the very apogee of union strength during the twentieth century. More than three million workers participated in the strike wave that extended from November to June, second only to 1919 as a year in which such a large proportion of U.S. workers withheld their labor. Although neither Reuther nor his corporate adversaries could know it, the strike movement of 1945 and 1946 was the last in the great cycle of industrial conflicts that began with the railroad strikes of the 1870s and then each decade reminded the nation of the seemingly insoluble conflict that brought labor and capital into violent confrontation. Certainly this was the last great strike in which unionized workers could claim, with even marginal credibility, that their struggle embodied the immediate hopes and popular aspirations of all Americans.

Yet even as Reuther sought to frame the strike as a struggle between GM and "the rest of us," his very rhetoric belied a new defensiveness born of the realization that union labor was seen and had come to see itself as an entity distinct, perhaps even at odds, with "consumers," with the "community," and with society itself. "Labor is not fighting for a larger slice of the national pie," Reuther argued in the *New Republic*. "Labor is fighting for a larger pie." Reuther insisted that "we are not going to operate as a narrow, economic pressure group," because the UAW now fought "to make progress with the community and not at the expense of the community." But Reuther's use of this very counterposition made it clear that even the most adventuresome champions of labor's cause knew that their movement had lost an organic identification with society's middling strata.[40] The sectorial structure of collective bargaining and the constipation that overcame the union movement's quest for industrial democracy had already begun to sever the links between the struggles of organized labor and the aspirations, both psychic and material, of the still larger mass of pink-, white-, and blue-collar Americans.

The General Motors strike generated little of the violence and sidewalk conflict that had given such drama to the UAW mobilizations of the late 1930s. In the auto centers of Detroit, Flint, Toledo, and Cleveland, the strike proved peaceful because General Motors made no attempt to operate its facilities. Here was a concrete manifestation of the legitimacy won by the industrial unions over the previous decade, an institutional recognition shared by the corporations, the local bourgeoisie, and virtually all elements of the blue-collar working class. In Flint the UAW regional office presided over the strike of forty-two thousand GM workers from its headquarters on the twelfth floor of a downtown bank. Reporting from the factory city, Edwin Lahey found that businessmen and professionals there faced the strike with "the resignation of people who have been snowed in, not the fierce antagonism of property's myrmidons beating back the proletarian horde."[41]

Most significantly, the fault lines that had long divided autoworkers according to race, ethnicity, skill, and politics were now deeply buried within a larger commitment to the union and its cause. These divisions had not disappeared, of course: Richard Frankensteen's unexpected defeat in November's mayoral election had demonstrated the capacity of those forces backing Mayor Edward Jefferies to use racist and anti-Semitic innuendo and outright slander to pry Polish and Italian voters from the CIO, even in solidly working-class neighborhoods.[42] And within the realm of union politics the furious conflict that was soon to erupt over the Communist issue reflected many of the ethnopolitical tensions that had long divided workers in heavy industry. But such fissures no longer threatened the existence of the UAW itself, even in those factional giants, like Ford Local 600 or Allis-Chalmers Local 248, where rival unionists fought for leadership with the intensity of a civil war.

In the auto centers the confrontations that did take place represented a union effort to extend the strike and challenge GM authority over those the corporation considered management. Almost immediately after the strike began, many locals remobilized their flying squadrons and put out energetic picket lines to block the foremen and white-collar employees who were still reporting for work. The city-wide strike committee favored such initiatives, but Reuther and others on the UAW executive board feared that confrontations of this sort might generate a backlash against the strike, especially after General Motors won a court injunction barring such tactics. Of the Big Three automakers, GM had been the most determined and successful in keeping its salaried staff union-free. The UAW's top officers therefore ordered local unions to let the white-collar workers in, and the local pickets reluctantly acquiesced.

A more serious conflict between union militants and UAW officers came early in December when General Motors asserted its willingness to open several of its supplier plants in order to keep other auto and truck firms in stock. To the extent that the success of the UAW's one-at-a-time strike strategy seemed to depend upon continuous production at GM's competitors, the union released a letter in R. J. Thomas's name welcoming the company's "generous" offer. When the *Detroit Free Press* reported that dozens of plants might well be reopened, a storm of opposition erupted among union militants. Reuther had probably approved the letter as well, but once he saw the psychological damage generated by the deal, he quickly denounced the idea. Thomas backtracked as well, but he took the political hit, appearing to be an ineffectual leader. Regardless of the internal union squabble, the incident demonstrated the clear limitations of Reuther's "blockade GM" strategy, given GM's enormous weight within the industry and the shortages of steel and finished parts that hobbled the other automakers.[43]

Reuther knew that solidarity and militancy on the picket line were insufficient to win the strike: if his radical program were to stand a chance, he had to make his case with both the larger public and the Truman administration. The UAW did not have the financial resources to counter the full-page advertisements GM placed in hundreds of daily newspapers, but Frank Winn in Detroit and Paul Sifton in Washington made sure that the newspapers and the radio were flooded with a stream of releases and reports. Sifton remembered that fall and winter as one long press conference in which "Reuther is on his toes, weaving, feinting for an opening, keeping the air as full of gloves as possible, seeking to wear his opponents down. Arm-weary from blocking, leg-weary from shifting to keep up with him, General Motors President C. E. Wilson . . . will eventually expose a mighty jaw for the second necessary to land a straight short punch."[44]

Early in December Reuther invited about fifty high-profile figures likely to sympathize with the union to assemble in Detroit as the "National Citizens Committee on the GM-UAW Dispute." The financier Bernard Baruch turned him down, as did the Macy executive Beardsley Ruml, both players in the debate over postwar planning. But a dozen influential people, including such reliable New Dealers as the former OPA chief Leon Henderson, the laborite Catholic bishop Francis Haas, Walter White of the NAACP, Murray Lincoln of the Ohio Farm Bureau, and the University of Chicago sociologist Ernest Burgess, signed a report lauding the UAW's determination to lift "collective bargaining to a new high level by insisting that the advancement of Labor's interest shall not be made at the expense of the public." Soon thereafter, the even more prominent "National Committee to Aid the Families of GM Strikers," headquartered in the NAACP's New York offices, put such luminaries as Eleanor Roosevelt, Henry Morgenthau, Wayne Morse, Reinhold Niebuhr, Harold Ickes, and Harold Stassen on its letterhead.[45]

In the battle of the press releases, Reuther won little backing from the metropolitan newspapers, which considered the more innovative elements of his negotiating posture irrelevant, if not actually dangerous. For example, the *Detroit Free Press*, the less conservative of the two Motor City papers, called Reuther's 30 percent wage demand an "inflammatory ultimatum," and his call for GM to open its books "a mere subterfuge."[46] But support did come from an unexpected quarter: the Luce publications, then at the height of their influence, offered Reuther and the strike surprisingly favorable coverage. The powerful publisher of *Time*, *Life*, and *Fortune* was a Republican, and by 1945 an increasingly partisan one, but Henry Luce was also something of a corporatist who favored "a new democratic capitalism" that could accommodate both Keynesian economics and the strong trade unions necessary to sustain the new capitalist order.[47]

Time therefore put Reuther on the cover of its December 3, 1945, issue, and both *Life* and *Fortune* gave him large and notably favorable spreads just after the strike began. Calling Reuther a "smart young strategist," *Life* characterized the unionist as a man "who can rise above the bear-pit level of wage-and-hour battling to attack the great problems of the national economy." And *Fortune*'s John Chamberlain told his business audience:

> More than any other one man in labor he symbolizes the stresses and strains within the capitalist system. Indeed, no aspect of his complex character is more marked than his almost impish delight in worrying the archetypes of capitalist leadership—Detroit's auto manufactures. . . . He believes that labor's political and economic power must be brought to bear for one great purpose: to gain for labor—and thus, he believes, for the consumer—a true partnership in the U.S. productive machine. To this mission, thirty-eight-year-old Reuther brings an energy and native intelligence unmatched by any other union leader.[48]

Such sentiments were certainly shared by Henry Luce himself, whose postwar internationalism had given him an appreciation of both Reuther's anti-Communism and his social democratic politics. By February Luce had lent his name to the National Committee to Aid the Families of GM Strikers. He served as a co-chair, along with Eleanor Roosevelt and Harold Ickes.[49]

The UAW won a mixed victory in the propaganda war. In early December polls found that 60 percent of the country felt that the autoworkers deserved a raise, and that 44 percent of Americans sided with the strikers, as against 35 percent with General Motors. By a two-to-one margin a January poll found that Americans wanted labor to have more to say than big business about what laws were passed in the next year or two; indeed, the citizenry thought management could raise wages without increasing prices, and a small plurality even endorsed Reuther's "open the books" demand. However, the General Motors work stoppage itself was unpopular: one poll found that 42 percent blamed the UAW for the strike, as against 19 percent who thought GM at fault. (Twenty-six percent blamed both sides.) And here was a warning of future trouble: if long strikes failed to generate the social and economic payoff trade unionists claimed for them, then the public might well listen more attentively to those in politics and management who sought to cripple labor's capacity to conduct such inconvenient work stoppages.[50]

On December 3, President Truman intervened in the strike, but in characteristically maladroit fashion. Without consulting Murray or Reuther, he called on Congress for legislation creating fact-finding boards in strikes of national importance. The boards would not be arbitration panels, but while they met unions would have to observe a thirty-day cooling-off period. Here was a hint of the Taft-Hartley Act eighteen months in the future. In the meantime, Truman appointed presidential fact-finding boards in both the steel and GM disputes, and he called on the UAW to return to work while deliberations proceeded.

Truman's gambit was clearly unacceptable to either Reuther or the rest of the CIO. Philip Murray was particularly vexed, claiming with considerable justification that the president sought "continuous appeasement of American industry" and had taken "the first step for ever more savage legislative repression." Stung by the GM parts plant fiasco, UAW leaders joined in the attack on Truman. Thomas asked why the president had not appointed a fact-finding board one hundred days before; Reuther asserted that Truman had "bum advisers" and claimed that the new president had made a "clean break with the labor policies" of Franklin Roosevelt. "The way out is for GM to negotiate a satisfactory agreement," Reuther told the press.[51]

However, General Motors was not about to accommodate the UAW. The corporation took seriously the vanguard role it played in organizing American capitalism in the crisis. Reflecting a slight liberalization of OPA guidelines, General Motors had sweetened its wage offer to thirteen and a half cents, but the corporation also terminated its contract with the UAW on December 10, thereby casting out all nineteen contract clauses inserted by the War Labor Board, contract modifications that, as GM now made clear, it had accepted only under duress. The corporation was determined to extract its employment relations from the state tutelage with which it had been burdened since Roosevelt, Perkins, and Murphy had intervened to settle the 1937 sit-down strikes. Two clauses in particular were important: maintenance of union membership, and paragraph 63, the clause that covered the acquisition of seniority and its application to promotions and transfers.

The first clause was ideologically symbolic of the wartime legitimacy the Roo-seveltian state had conferred upon the union movement; the second represented one of corporate management's weakest links in the chain of contractual elements that defined and defended the hierarchial organization of GM's factory empire.[52]

Having thrown down this gauntlet, GM's Alfred Sloan, Charles Wilson, and Donaldson Brown convened a December 19 meeting in the Waldorf-Astoria with the top executives of U.S. Steel, Bethlehem, General Electric, Westinghouse, and other companies facing CIO wage demands. With Truman's fact-finding board scheduled to start work the next day, Wilson wanted to make sure that other exec-utives, especially those in steel, proved as resolute as the automakers. "We don't believe in this industry-wide bargaining or forcing the whole industry of the coun-try into a group that would take [the same] position," asserted Wilson.[53] The big auto company was determined to resist the authority of this postwar board, whose very existence seemed to promise an indefinite continuation of the corporatist pol-icy-making from which GM managers sought to extricate themselves. Indeed, the fact-finding board's chairman was Lloyd Garrison, a pillar of the old War Labor Board, and the two other members of the board were cut from the same cloth: Mil-ton Eisenhower, president of Kansas State University, and Walter Stacy of the North Carolina Supreme Court. All saw a corporation's profitability, both current and future, as highly relevant to its wage standards.[54]

GM's determination to resist Reuther's program was made manifest in its choice of chief counsel at the board hearings: Walter Gordon Merritt, a lawyer of the old school who still remembered the 1906 Danbury hatters case, in which he had won a sweeping injunction that crippled labor's capacity to undertake strikes and boy-cotts. Reuther called Merritt the "cave-man of American labor relations." At the fact-finding board's first meeting, on December 20, Merritt announced that GM would withdraw from the proceedings if ability to pay was considered relevant to the deliberations—exactly the approach Truman adopted, as Garrison learned in a message delivered to the board at 2:30 that same afternoon.[55]

At Garrison's urging, the parties returned to Detroit to negotiate, fruitlessly, through the Christmas break. When the board reconvened in Washington on December 28, Merritt and the rest of the big GM delegation filed into the room but remained standing, winter overcoats in hand. Would the fact-finding board still look into GM's profitability? inquired Walter Gordon Merritt. When Garrison answered yes, the GM men simply decamped en masse, though not without another denunciation of Reutherite economics and the Rooseveltian state. Gen-eral Motors did not plead "inability to pay" as a reason for rejecting the board's jurisdiction. Instead, asserted Merritt, the issue was one of "ideology and national policy . . . a broad [union] attack on American industry and free enterprise." Given the high stakes inherent in the union's program and the board's prerogatives, only Congress had the right to "write a new charter for industry and the nation." GM recognition of the fact-finding board would therefore legitimize "the revolutionary and uncompromising character of the union's proposals." Asserted Alfred P. Sloan in a more private moment, "It took fourteen years to rid this country of prohibition. It is going to take a good while to rid the country of the New Deal, but sooner or later the ax falls and we get a change."[56]

"We're going back to Detroit to hold the line," responded a gloomy Reuther. "That's what you do in a strike, hold the line." Still, with GM's phalanx of lawyers and economists absent, Reuther and Montgomery had a clear field to make yet another highly publicized advertisement for their wage program. The board found a consideration of GM profitability hardly precedent-setting; after all, GM itself had submitted detailed evidence bearing on the firm's cost structure during the war when it sought to counter UAW pay claims. Reuther quickly regained his poise, and the presentation of the union case in the news-hungry capital may well have marked the apogee of Reuther's fortunes in the strike.[57] The *New Republic* celebrated his appearance before the fact-finders as if he were a Lochinvar from the West:

> Your first impression is of youth. He has brownish-red hair, almost pitch-black eyes. His voice is high and loud, he is speaking easily and excitedly. . . . His eyes are narrow, like a plainsman's. He is self-confident, young and sure of himself. . . . This is a new kind of strike, a new kind of leader. Reuther is emphasizing again and again the concept that workers have got to have high pay to buy the goods they produce. . . . What he implies is that this isn't a strike; it's a crusade.[58]

When the fact-finding board issued its report on January 10, Garrison and the other members asserted that its recommended wage increase—17.5 percent, or nineteen and a half cents an hour—hardly necessitated an increase in the price of the products built by the giant corporation. Indeed, the board's entire 12,000-word report reflected the economic logic, if not all of the quantative assumptions, upon which Montgomery and Reuther had made their 30 percent wage claim. "Certainly, as GM's new plants come into operation, it may exceed in 1947 its 1941 production by as much as 50 per cent," asserted the board's report. "This desirable development will greatly increase the company's profits and will give it the pleasant task of determining how such profits shall be distributed to stockholders, to reserves, and to consumers generally in the form of higher quality and of lower priced products."[59]

Reuther hailed the board's recommendation as a "complete endorsement of the union's position and . . . an historic step in the fight to establish full production." He expressed delight that no wage increases would be paid in the "wooden nickels of inflation." And Reuther agreed to settle on the board's terms if the General Motors Corporation approved the pay raise by January 21. Of course, Reuther was extremely disappointed with the board's monetary award: it was little more than half of what the union had demanded in August. When Milton Eisenhower told him what the recommended amount was likely to be, he "protested that his men would have to work for years to recover the losses incurred in the strike." In fact, the GM fact-finding board's unexpectedly low wage award may well have reflected the political economy of the labor negotiations in the steel industry far more than it did in auto. Productivity growth had simply not been as great in basic steel as in auto, so by early January Philip Murray had worked out a preliminary deal with U.S. Steel's Benjamin Fairless for about a twenty-cent-an-hour wage increase; thus, the CIO president feared that if the GM board gave the UAW more, the USW would find themselves under overwhelming pressure to strike for a like amount.[60]

GM was unsettled by the board's recommendations as well. President Charles Wilson immediately rejected the fact-finding report, in particular the "unsound principle that a specific company should be forced to pay higher than competitive wages because of its financial ability." Privately, GM executives worried over the Truman administration's apparent decision "to play into Reuther's hands on this very fundamental issue." Indeed, the very modesty of the panel's wage award would now swing the government and the public against GM. "Reuther has gained a moral victory," admitted Donaldson Brown, who sought to ensure that the corporation continued to uphold its managerial autonomy. The actual size of the wage award was of secondary importance, but the GM board of directors had to tough it out "for the sake of the principle we have stood for."[61]

GM's task would soon prove far less arduous, for the whole structure of the negotiations in the 1945–46 bargaining round were about to shift decisively against the Reutherite wage program. Indeed, the publication of the auto panel report represented Reuther's last best hope of winning an auto settlement on anything like his original program. From this point on, it would be all downhill as the GM negotiations entered nearly two months of stalemate and the bargaining spotlight shifted to other industry conflicts—above all, steel, where Philip Murray sought an accord quite different from the one sponsored by Reuther and his team.

At midcentury, steel remained America's most basic industry, the huge template that ponderously impressed its economic patterns upon the price, wage, and production levels of the rest of heavy industry. The industry's giant corporations had poured almost one hundred million tons of steel during each year of the war, but the technology and organization of its great mills and the mindset of its top executives still reflected the world of Charles Schwab, Elbert Gary, and Myron Taylor, instinctive oligopolists who mistrusted innovation and feared overcapacity. The U.S. Steel president Benjamin Fairless was cut from the same cloth: unlike executives of the GM-DuPont combine, Fairless and the other steelmen had reconciled themselves to a corporatist adjudication of the basic wage-price relationship in their industry. With its fixed market shares and feeble productivity growth, the industry bargained as a self-protective bloc with both the government and the union. For almost thirty years after the promulgation of the Little Steel formula in 1942, the industry's price level would therefore be set in the White House, though not without crisis and contention.[62]

Philip Murray was neither unfamiliar with nor unsympathetic to the steel industry's outlook. He had put the CIO on the line behind the GM strike, but he feared that a really staunch effort to shift the fundamental wage structure in the auto industry would generate a long and debilitating strike that might crack the CIO and open the way to factional chaos within the industrial union federation. Indeed, in early December Murray had summoned UAW leaders to Pittsburgh, where he warned Reuther to avoid boxing himself into a corner with his demand that GM agree to a price freeze on its postwar automobile line. For his part, Murray and his union aides wanted a substantial wage increase, but as long as it was at least equal that of other unions he was content to let big steel play a "poker game" over tonnage prices with the OPA and the White House.[63]

In a White House bargaining session on January 12, Fairless indicated that he would seek steel industry support for an eighteen-cent-an-hour wage increase, but President Truman vacillated between holding to the tough price line advocated by Chester Bowles and going along with the far more elastic price ceiling urged by Secretary of the Treasury John Snyder. At Truman's request, Philip Murray postponed the USW's strike, even as 200,000 electrical workers stopped work on January 15 and 260,000 in the meatpacking industry struck a day later. But when it became clear that Fairless did not speak for the Little Steel price hawks, Murray cried "double cross." President Truman put his prestige on the line by proposing a compromise agreement of eighteen and a half cents. Murray and his top aides quickly endorsed the presidential gambit, but when the steel industry still held a wage settlement hostage to its demand for price relief, the USW had little choice but to pull 750,000 of its members out of their mines and mills. American big business, charged Murray, was engaged in an "evil conspiracy . . . to exact unconditional surrender of the American people and the United States Government."[64]

For a moment it seemed as if the valiant General Motors strikers had been joined by a massive wave of reinforcements. In January alone the number of idle workdays reached almost twenty million, and in the following month strikes cut production even more, to levels not seen since the red autumn of 1919. More than two million Americans were on strike during the winter of 1945–46. Like the General Motors strike, the massive stoppages involved only minimal levels of rank-and-file mobilization and relatively little picket-line violence, yet like the proverbial 800-pound gorilla, they necessarily commanded the attention of the nation.[65]

The drama was real, but Reuther no longer stood at center stage. Closure of America's great steel industry had rendered Reuther's assault on GM largely superfluous. Equally important, the USW's endorsement of Truman's eighteen-and-a-half-cent wage offer had established a new set of bargaining goals and guidelines. And once Truman rejected Chester Bowles's suggestion that the government seize the steel mills, the administration had little recourse but to accommodate the industry demand for a virtual destruction of the OPA price ceilings. Certainly Philip Murray had little more than a rhetorical objection to such a settlement. Thus, on February 15, the steel industry and its union signed a contract for eighteen and a half cents an hour, and three days later the OPA authorized a price increase of slightly over five dollars a ton, more than double the relief Bowles had thought justified. Truman asserted that the increase was only a "bulge" in the price line, but it was the end of the line for labor-liberal efforts to sustain postwar price controls. "From this point on," concluded the OPA's own history, "a really firm price policy was in fact no longer possible, either administratively or politically."[66]

By this time the 1946 wage pattern had been carved in rock. As early as January 26, Ford and Chrysler reached wage agreements with the UAW at the eighteen- or eighteen-and-a-half-cent-an-hour level, and Radio Corporation of America, the one major electrical company not struck by the United Electrical Workers (UE), agreed to give its workers an eighteen-cent raise. Two weeks later the UE, which bargained for thirty thousand General Motors appliance and electrical workers, also settled with the corporation for eighteen and a half cents an hour. Many UE leaders were close to the Communists, so Reuther partisans immediately denounced their agreement as a "betrayal." Said Reuther, "Maybe there are others in the union movement who will sell their workers down the river, but I won't." UE leaders had failed to coordinate their negotiating strategy with Reuther, and they had bargained secretly with General Motors, but their February 9 agreement merely followed the eighteen-and-a-half-cent precedent agreed to by Philip Murray, as well as the pattern already set by the UAW leaders Richard Leonard and Norman Matthews in their negotiations with Ford and Chrysler. All three came in for much grumbling from the Reuther circle, especially Phil Murray, whose disdain for the upstart redhead was more than matched by the younger man's frustration.[67]

After the settlements in the steel and electrical products industries and at the other big carmakers, Reuther and the GM strikers stood alone and exposed. The economic parameters of the strike had been fixed; the only issue remaining was the extent to which GM, Reuther, or his factional opponents would reap a final advantage in the endgame. Reuther was clearly unnerved. When the federal mediator James Dewey urged Reuther to accept GM's "final" eighteen-and-a-half-cent-an-hour offer, the UAW vice president exploded: "I won't be made a damn fool of forever. The President's offer of 19½ cents was a compromise of our demand. I will be God damned if I will compromise a compromise. We are not going to take less than this, and this is all horse shit about going back to work."[68]

Reuther scrambled for some lever with which to pry an extra penny out of the giant auto corporation, if only to justify, even symbolically, the length and cost of the strike. At a GM conference in early March he demanded that Truman put his "moral" leadership behind the strikers, and the UAW again called on GM to submit the remaining issues in the dispute to arbitration. City councils in Detroit and other strike-bound cities called on the federal government to intervene, but Truman refused to take any steps to implement the conclusions reached by his fact-finding board. Indeed, the president had grown irritated with the strike and its leadership, publicly complaining of those labor leaders "who are running for headlines to settle things in the newspapers." To a Missouri friend Truman wrote, "Industry and labor have begun to lean on the government for decisions which they themselves ought to make. If we are going to have free enterprise and free collective bargaining, the sooner we get to it the better." GM would not budge, of course, for its negotiators saw that the single penny that stood between the company's final offer and the union's wage claim represented a most emphatic repudiation of Reuther's ideological assault on the corporation's determination to pay no more than the "going rate" for its labor.[69]

The wage stalemate brought to the fore the set of chronically unresolved shop control issues barely contained by the wartime truce. GM still insisted upon its own extensive set of contract revisions, including an end to maintenance of membership, severe penalties for wildcat strikers, a reduction in the hours committeemen could handle grievances, and a more extensive assertion of management prerogatives. Reuther's team had allowed such issues to fester, but now his UAW publicists shifted gears, claiming that the corporation's abrogation of its contract with the UAW had "tipped their hand to every striker. . . . This strike is not over another nickel or two on pay day, but over decent shop conditions every day, and over the very survival and growth of our organization." Such propaganda was not without a kernel of truth, for within the GM hierarchy there was certainly some debate as to how radically the corporation might seek to revise those sections of the contract imposed by the War Labor Board. Merritt's prominence at the fact-finding board hearings had been an ominous sign, as had the participation of several GM executives—including the company's chief economist, Stephen DuBrul—in founding the "Society of Sentinels," a Detroit-based organization that called for the immediate repeal of most New Deal legislation, including the Wagner Act.[70]

A corporate hard line on these issues would certainly have generated a real crisis, but in mid-February President Charles Wilson reemerged to take a direct hand in the negotiations. Wilson was then in the midst of a determined effort to enhance the operational autonomy of "Detroit" at the expense of the DuPont interests centered in the East. GM's tough defense of its macroeconomic prerogatives had been orchestrated from New York, but, according to Donaldson Brown, once this issue had been settled, "Sloan threw up the sponge completely and left matters wholly in C. E.'s hands." Wilson was ready to build cars again. He knew that during the war GM shop discipline had been better than at Ford or Chrysler, so he was willing to reinstate most of the WLB clauses the company had repudiated in December; in return, Reuther agreed to substitute a dues-checkoff program for the maintenance-of-membership clause that GM executives—east and west—still found anathema.[71]

Union and management continued to lock horns, however, over paragraph 63, the section of the UAW-GM contract covering promotions and transfers. The dispute was a classic example of a contract "technicality" that was mystifying to the press and the public yet commanded tremendous passion and conflict among the managers and the managed within industry itself. In nearly one hundred factories all across the nation, General Motors had defeated the UAW effort to counterbalance the authority of the foreman with that of the departmental shop steward.

The union therefore relied upon an increasingly elaborate set of work rules to define for its members the precise limits of both their shop-floor freedom and their industrial subordination. The language of the UAW-GM contract marked this union frontier of control, defined and redefined through a kind of linguistic trench warfare in which the addition of a single word or the revision of a simple phrase measured the contractual territory won or lost in an entire bargaining campaign.

Paragraph 63, formulated in 1941 after a long argument before a National Defense Mediation Board panel, stated that within a single department or job classification, "the transferring of employees is the sole responsibility of Management," but in the case of permanent promotions to new, usually higher-paid jobs, "when ability, merit and capacity are equal, employees with the longest seniority will be given preference." Unionists, who felt that long service gave them a proprietary stake in their jobs, wanted seniority to apply in both instances, while GM managers saw the seniority principle, especially if applied to a foreman's routine transfers, a dangerous subversion of management authority.[72] GM wanted language in the contract that clearly affirmed management's right to reassign work within a department regardless of a worker's seniority. Reuther saw this demand as a cynical ploy: "They want to turn the clock back to the days of foreman-favoritism and the Red Apple Club," he announced in a February strike bulletin.[73]

But was paragraph 63 of sufficient importance to further prolong the GM stoppage? As the strike dragged into its fourth month, only this issue and the elusive penny wage differential divided UAW and GM negotiators. The GM negotiating committee, composed of local union officials, insisted that the transfer and promotion issue remain a top priority. These secondary union leaders had been quite willing to let Reuther and his team determine strategy on the national wage package, but they knew that once their plants got back into production their leadership would be judged not by the pay increase, such as it was, but by the numerous disputes that were sure to arise over the pace of work and the distribution of jobs as their constituents returned to the factory.[74]

Reuther faced a different set of pressures. The UAW could not remain on strike indefinitely, and with his run for the union presidency now a virtual certainty, his leadership of the strike would no longer remain immune to attack by his factional opponents. "Why isn't the GM strike being settled?" asked R. J. Thomas on March 10, the day after Reuther partisans made public his presidential bid. "At the moment I am talking here [to a meeting of the UAW Ford council], members of the GM staff are at a caucus of my own local union trying to get my job." Moreover, paragraph 63 was a burning issue to only a fraction of the union membership, and even to them the actual impact of any contractual changes might well remain obscure for several months. Reuther therefore had every incentive to finesse the issue; he did so by formulating a new and still-ambiguous paragraph, finalized at 2:25 A.M. on March 13, just hours before the negotiators announced a settlement. GM agreed to give "preference" to those workers who applied for transfers to new positions or vacancies in a department, but the actual meaning of "preference" and the extent to which it applied to changes in all job assignments would be left to arbitration. Thus Reuther claimed a "tremendous" victory on the issue, but the union would still lose most of its grievances under the new transfer clause when it appealed them to the umpire.[75]

Reuther's extra penny remained equally problematic. He claimed that the final settlement was worth nineteen and a half cents an hour on the basis of an agreement that gave local managers authority to adjust intraplant wage rates. But unlike 1940, GM set aside no specific sum of money to deal with the problem, so the total wage increase proved impossible to calculate. Because the union had originally proposed a one-cent-an-hour fund to deal with intraplant inequalities, it was clear that something less was actually negotiated, a fact that Reuther supporters eventually acknowledged.

So the great strike was finally over, ending with far more relief than exultation. At a March 15 GM conference that voted to approve the settlement, Reuther claimed a moral and political victory but charged that the conduct of the steel strike "weakened our position," that the UE settlement was "Treason and Double-Cross," and that many in the labor movement were divided on the price question. Four days later the UAW advised GM that since a majority of locals had approved the national agreement, the contract was ratified. However, in a pattern that would emerge again and again after Reuther and his adversaries signed a national agreement, thousands of workers remained on strike over local contract issues, the most important of which was the difficult switch from piecework to day rate. Two of the locals remained on strike for another six weeks.[76]

The strike offensive of 1946 ended in a pyrrhic victory. Automakers won three OPA price increases in the three months following the conclusion of the GM strike; meanwhile, Congress shaped a revision of the price control regulations so weak that Truman vetoed it on June 29. Prices exploded: within two weeks the cost of twenty-eight basic commodities had risen by 25 percent. A new set of price controls were cobbled together at the end of July, but the inflationary genie could not be stuffed back into the bottle. Between March and November 1946 the cost-of-living index surged more than 14 percent, wiping out most of the wage increases won in the winter. All the big trade unions felt compelled to return to the bargaining table for a second round of wage negotiations early in 1947. Labor's many enemies soon complained of a vicious "wage price spiral" that was robbing the public and crippling commerce.[77]

The failure of Reuther's General Motors strike program marked an end to the New Deal's capacity for a direct and progressive reconstitution of the nation's political economy. More than a decade before, proponents of the Wagner Act had sought to bolster working-class purchasing power by creating a legal-administrative framework under which an organized working class bargained with capital to recalibrate the polity's distribution of income and power. By 1945 the success of this initiative could be measured by a dramatic decline in income inequality—to the lowest level in the twentieth century—and through a trade union movement powerful enough to put the overall distribution of profits, wages, and prices at the very heart of reconversion politics. Reuther's GM strike program proposed the further institutionalization of the New Deal's commitment to working-class purchasing power—through a reconfiguration of the wartime set of corporatist arrangements, thus recognizing the union movement's new leverage upon management's traditional prerogatives. American workers were easily mobilized to this end, but Roosevelt's heirs proved too feckless and trade union leadership too divided to overcome capital's intransigence. U.S. capitalism would now enter its postwar golden age, but under conditions that fragmented union power and eroded the capacity of farsighted laborites like Walter Reuther to champion a broad coalition of industrial workers and middle-class consumers.[78]

12

 "UAW AMERICANISM FOR US"

"Against Outside Interference"

—*Reuther campaign slogan, 1946*

It's not a question of right or left in this union. It's whether you are for or against Reuther.

—*R. J. Thomas, 1946*

Walter Reuther was elected president of the United Automobile Workers on March 27, 1946, in Atlantic City, New Jersey, at the union's tenth convention. After a roll call that took more than four suspenseful hours, the margin was paper-thin: just 124.388 votes out of a total ballot of some 8,765 delegate votes.[1] Reuther would spend the next twenty months of his life in a brutally fought campaign to transform this narrow victory into an anti-Communist mandate, but in early 1946 his margin accurately reflected both the balance of forces within the auto union and the fragile equilibrium that structured the politics of the CIO, the labor movement, and the liberal community. Across almost the entire spectrum of liberal and laborite opinion, the fear of a postwar depression at home remained far stronger than fear of Communist aggression abroad. Both Reuther and his adversaries wanted the U.S. government to reach an accommodation with the Soviets in Central Europe and to push France, Britain, and Holland to decolonize their empires. They expected American liberalism to help unionize the

South, end discrimination in hiring and education, inaugurate a system of national health insurance, and fund the construction of millions of working-class houses and apartments.

Within the broad outlines of the American left, Communists and anti-Communists were not yet at each other's throats. Inside the industrial union federation, Philip Murray was determined to maintain institutional unity by enforcing a political truce between left and right. The CIO's newly vibrant political action committee (PAC) linked Democratic Party stalwarts of the North and West with both labor-party advocates in Reuther's circle and Communist Party proponents of a postwar Popular Front. Just as their European comrades still participated in the coalition governments that ruled France, Italy, and Czechoslovakia, so too did U.S. Communists expect to play a continuing role in the politics of American liberalism.[2] On foreign policy issues both wings of the UAW leadership were sharply critical of President Truman. Indeed, the growing tension with the Soviet Union seemed to unite rather than divide Popular Front radicals and anti-Communist liberals. At the 1946 UAW convention, a foreign policy resolution, drafted by Victor Reuther, denounced Winston Churchill's "Iron Curtain" speech delivered just three weeks before at Westminster College in Missouri, especially the former prime minister's call for "an American-British military alliance against Soviet Russia." Communist delegates still criticized the Reuther text, but only because it attacked the Soviet Union—as well as the United States and Great Britain—for its "old imperialist, war inciting methods of power politics."[3]

Reuther's campaign for the UAW presidency was short because his unionwide networks were well in place. In early March, 17 Detroit-area union presidents— all longtime Reuther partisans—announced their organization of a committee to "draft" the redheaded leader. Imagination, leadership, and militancy were the themes Reuther and his supporters pounded home in the days leading up to the Atlantic City vote. In a frenetic round of speeches and caucus meetings, Reuther revisited his opposition's support of incentive pay, categorical no-strike pledge, and alliance with the Communists. He called the poker-playing R. J. Thomas a "desperate man . . . doing his best to hang onto a swivel chair."[4] In contrast, Reuther had been the leader of the union's most impressive mobilization since Flint. Any critique of his leadership now had the flavor of Monday morning quarterbacking. Thus, when Thomas finally gave vent to the privately held views of many CIO unionists—that Reuther had picked GM as the target "on his own hook" and then called the strike six weeks too early and ended it four weeks too late—the accusation held little bite.[5] Edwin Lahey of the *Detroit Free Press* summed up the conventional assessment: Reuther's attractiveness lay "in his remarkable technical competence, the brilliance of his public relations, his genius for making simple presentations of complex economic issues, and above all his increasing diligence in the art of building political fences."[6]

Philip Murray was hardly pleased with Walter Reuther's effort to upset the UAW's precarious equilibrium. Thin-skinned and quick to take offense, Murray resented Reuther's implicit critique of his leadership and feared the emergence of a brash young rival. Reuther's contempt for Murray was likewise an open secret, but because of Murray's huge popularity within the UAW, Reuther swallowed most of his pride. Thus, when Murray arrived on the Atlantic City boardwalk, Reuther shoehorned his way into the official welcoming committee and grabbed Murray's arm as they marched up to the convention podium. But the conversation was not friendly. Richard Leonard remembered Walter's indignant protest, "Well, damn it, Phil, I'm going to run!"[7]

Some Reuther partisans were convinced that their leader held at least a thousand-vote margin over Thomas when the convention convened. After Murray's speech, however, the Reuther advantage may well have shrunk considerably. Murray practically endorsed Thomas, "that great big guy for whom I have a distinct fondness." And the CIO president went out of his way to denounce as "a diabolical, detestable lie" the Reutherite supposition that Murray and the Steel Workers had been a party to the GM fact-finding board's disappointing wage recommendation in January.[8] Nevertheless, with a majority of only 50.7 percent, Reuther's victory had many sponsors. Winning more support in Flint than he had two years before in his vice-presidential run helped him take two-thirds of the votes of all GM delegates. He also benefited from the abrupt shrinkage of the UAW Aircraft Department, as well as the retirement from union politics of its former director, Richard Frankensteen, who would soon run for Congress. And Reuther did relatively well on the East Side of Detroit, the union's largest region, where opposition to the no-strike pledge had been most widespread and CIO orthodoxy most resented. Virtually all the activists in the wartime Rank-and-File Caucus supported Reuther in 1946, and the Trotskyists—followers of both Max Schactman and James P. Cannon—argued that Reuther's leadership of the General Motors strike gave him the radical credentials to lead the nation's vanguard union.[9]

UAW delegates had given Reuther the presidency, but they were not about to give him the union. Indeed, the next four days in Atlantic City were a disaster for the Reutherites. As soon as he was elected president, Reuther offered Addes and his forces an olive branch: pledging his loyalty to Murray and the CIO, Reuther proposed a kind of coalition in which the Addes-led caucus would repudiate its Communist allies and accept his leadership, in return for a substantial, if still subordinate, role in running the union. Such an arrangement seemed logical: the CIO favored it, Richard Leonard and R. J. Thomas had long rejected Communist support, and George Addes was a realist who had offered Reuther unflinching solidarity during the long General Motors strike.[10]

But the UAW Communists were not about to see themselves marginalized quite so easily. They thought the historical tide might still be running with the party, whose presence at the Atlantic City convention proved substantial: ninety-seven member delegates and a full complement of national leaders. So when Reuther squeaked through to the presidency, party activists redoubled their efforts to minimize the damage; to this end, party leaders found in R. J. Thomas an unlikely but effective ally.[11] In the United States, top union leaders rejected by their own membership are expected to retire to some harmless sinecure, which the CIO's Allan Haywood dutifully offered Thomas as soon as the votes were counted. But beneath his good-natured exterior, R. J. Thomas had a chest full of resentment and a backbone of newly hardened steel. Thus, when the Communists threw all their resources into a genuinely popular campaign to convince Thomas to run for one of the two UAW vice presidencies, R. J. proved easily persuadable. He quickly forgot his years as an anti-Communist, aligned himself with the Addes camp, and turned into one of Reuther's most bitter opponents.[12]

Reuther was caught off guard, and R. J. Thomas sailed to an easy victory over the Reutherite candidate Melvin Bishop, the director of Detroit's East Side region. Reuther also came up short in the contests that decided the composition of the rest of the UAW executive board. George Addes ran unopposed, and Richard Leonard squeaked by John Livingston, the conservative Reutherite, for the second vice presidency. The Addes-Thomas-Leonard coalition also won nine regional director elections, including two bitter contests in Reuther's West Side home base. The Reutherites took eight positions—among them, Bishop's vacant East Side seat, which now went to Emil Mazey, who learned of his election while he was still stationed in the Pacific. On the UAW executive board, where dues-paying membership determined the voting strength of each regional director, the Reuther group held but 324 votes, nearly 190 less than their opponents.[13] With much contempt, Reuther declared his opponents a "mechanical majority," unprincipled and inconsistent, but the Addes-Thomas-Leonard grouping proved creative as well as aggressive. At the new executive board's very first meeting in April, they surprised Reuther with a fully worked out economic program that repudiated much of the political economy—including his "ability to pay" theory—for which Reuther had fought during the GM strike. A reporter found Reuther hurriedly "scanning a copy of the Addes platform. He seemed stunned."[14]

When it came to the union staff, Reuther's strategy was to take control of those positions that gave his faction the widest ideological influence throughout the union. After the GM strike and the postwar layoffs, the UAW was broke, so Reuther flew to New York right after the convention to borrow $250,000 from Sidney Hillman's Amalgamated Clothing Workers. With the payroll secure, Reuther began to trade jobs and offices with his opponents. He kept the directorship of the GM Department but let R. J. Thomas have the Competitive Shops Department (organizing), with its patronage-rich staff, and Reuther kept Maurice Sugar on as UAW counsel. In return, the Reuther caucus took control of the Publicity, Education, and Fair Practices Departments. The newspaper went to Frank Winn, a socialist friend of Eddie Levinson, and Victor Reuther took over at Education, where he soon transformed this most political of all UAW departments into a factional weapon of the first order. He fired all the Addes loyalists and appointed Brendon Sexton of Local 50 and Lewis Carliner, a Don Montgomery protégé, to his staff. Together they turned the union's Port Huron summer school into a

Reutherite "training base" and reached out to the locals with a series of special education programs for thousands of union activists. In January 1947 the Education Department put on a huge educational conference in Cleveland where the featured speakers—Chester Bowles, Eleanor Roosevelt, and the NAACP's Walter White—offered more than one thousand delegates heavy exposure to an American liberalism decidedly hostile to the ethos of the old Popular Front.[15]

Reuther appointed himself codirector of the highly sensitive Fair Employment Practices Department. Here Reuther replaced George Crockett, a stalwart of the Addes camp, with William Oliver, an African-American of far less stature and experience. Reuther was well aware of his limited support among black autoworkers; he therefore made himself a highly visible UAW spokesman on civil rights issues—testifying before Congress, prodding local unions to establish their own fair employment practices committees, and pushing forward the UAW campaign to end discrimination within the leagues of the American Bowling Congress. The practical consequences of all this activity were limited—for example, Reuther failed to win an antidiscrimination clause in the 1947 GM contract—but the new UAW president successfully forestalled any attempts to use the racial issue against him. Indeed, the clearest indication that Reuther enjoyed the CIO's endorsement for a second presidential term came in September 1947 when Philip Murray presented him with an antidiscrimination award at a big Detroit banquet.[16]

From outside Detroit Reuther recruited an additional cohort of socialist intellectuals to the factional battle. For his administrative assistants he pulled in Leonard Woodcock from Muskegon and then lured Jack Conway, the Local 6 militant, away from law school at the University of Chicago. Through Conway, Reuther recruited Bill Dodds, another Melrose Park radical who was studying with Robert Lynd at Columbia when he got the call. Dodds was promptly sent to Indiana, where he helped swing the big Delco Remy local to the Reutherites. The new UAW president also shoehorned Nat Weinberg, an old Brookwood alumnus, into the union's Research Department. An Addes partisan controlled the department, so Weinberg had few duties. For his typing, he had to prowl through union headquarters, looking for secretaries friendly to Reuther.[17]

Walter Reuther was a superb administrator and an ingenious negotiator, but the collective bargaining regime in heavy industry had become so entrenched that neither side in the UAW faction fight could reasonably argue that upon its victory depended the survival of the union. Thus the fate of Reuther and his opponents would turn upon an issue external to the immediate economic mission of the union: namely, the meaning of a Communist presence in American life and politics. And yet the polemical debate on the issue proved hardly extraneous at all, for the UAW was a bedrock institution of American liberalism, and the Communist issue a metaphor that framed the limits of debate on every issue, from civil liberties and civil rights to bargaining strategy and political economy.

Reuther's anti-Communism had a variegated coloration that matched that of his audience and his enemies. To the union ranks and the larger public, Reuther conflated an anti-Communist appeal with a rejection of "outside" political influence. "I am going to get rid of people whose party loyalty is above union loyalty," Reuther told a press conference immediately after his election. He would mobilize 90 percent of the membership around the top leadership, "thereby isolating the 10 percent which has outside loyalties." The dichotomy was an instructive one, for it posited a clear distinction between the practice of American trade unionism and the ideological politics of the Communists, as well as the views of other laborite intellectuals in the ACTU and the Trotskyist movement. Though Reuther's entire claim to UAW leadership rested upon his own politicalization of the trade union function, the *Wage Earner* found Reuther "red faced and obviously angry" when he found Communist leaflets distributed at a union meeting. "What in the hell are these things doing here? Did the Ford workers in your plants send you here to discuss ways and means of improving your wages and working conditions, or did you come here to have the Communist Party line thrust down your throats?"[18]

Such fulminations were not simple hypocrisy. Despite the party's limited resources and the invective that now poured down upon American Communists from so many directions, Reuther saw these radicals as a rival of the most potent sort. He shared the fear common to a whole cohort of intellectuals on the anti-Stalinist left—that when postwar capitalism entered its long-expected slump, the Communists might well emerge, as they had in France and Italy, as a majoritarian current within the organized working class. The regulation unionists and reformers would prove useless then, for at its heart American liberalism was soft, perhaps even corrupt. Too many progressives—and here Henry Wallace served as the object lesson—had no understanding of the counterfeit radicalism propounded by the Stalinists. "The Communists have a complete political valet service," asserted Reuther in one of his most effective polemical thrusts, but their "customers" soon discover "that they have become boxed in, thoroughly dependent, and pliable instruments of the party linemen."[19] To the Reutherites, therefore, the very instability of American capitalism demanded the most vigorous brand of anti-Communism if America's working-class institutions were to remain independent and democratic.[20]

However, Reuther could not purge this opposition. He failed repeatedly to win executive board endorsement of his effort to enforce the UAW constitutional provision that banned from all elective and appointive positions anyone who was "a member of or subservient to any political organization . . . which owes its allegiance to any government other than the United States or Canada." His opposition certainly knew that their Communist allies were a growing liability; indeed, Leonard and Addes formally excluded the party from their caucus after Reutherite charges of Communist domination had helped defeat their center-left slate at the Michigan CIO convention in June 1946. Nevertheless, Addes, Thomas, and Leonard were not willing simply to abandon their Communist-oriented staffers. Usually they heeded the warning of Maurice Sugar, the UAW general counsel and left-wing caucus leader, who predicted that Reuther "is out to eliminate the generals by destroying their colonels and majors and captains."[21] The issue remained in abeyance until the GOP victory in the off-year elections, the onset of the cold war, and the passage of the Taft-Hartley Act transformed the Communist question into a far broader and even more explosive intraunion conflict.

In the meantime, the Truman administration's failure to back the unions and sustain a firm accord regulating wages and prices throughout the nation had left ticking economic and social time bombs that would soon explode upon a nervous body politic. Despite their widely noted orderliness, the legacy of the great strikes of 1946 was hardly one of labor peace. The big industrial unions won an eighteen-and-a-half-cent wage increase, but there was no national pattern; nor were there any corporatist institutions, either public or private, that might have compelled adherence to a social compact based on the settlements in steel and automobiles. The big CIO unions had set a target to which millions of less powerfully organized workers now aspired, but hundreds of firms simply refused to settle at this level. Standing just outside the oligopolistic core of the national economy, a phalanx of midsize businesses were determined to rewin the entrepreneurial freedom and labor market power denied them by nearly a generation of New Deal reforms and war-era regulations. Where unionism had established only a tenuous foothold—in scores of smaller cities and factory towns and along the whole white-collar–service worker industrial frontier—family capitalists and old-line managers still fought the unions with the fervor of those who were defending a whole social order. In the UAW-organized auto parts field, dozens of companies held out for a cheaper contract or a weaker grievance procedure. The union spent half a million dollars in an unsuccessful campaign to organize Thompson products in Cleveland. Likewise in textiles, trucking, retail trade, municipal transit, and agricultural implement manufacture, the 1946 round of wage increases were hardly uniform. The average raise throughout the manufacturing field was little more than eleven cents an hour, and in nonmanufacturing industries, it was only three and a half cents.[22]

The net result was a season of sporadic industrial warfare, punctuated by picket-line violence, consumer-goods shortages, and headline-grabbing confrontations that agitated the local bourgeoisie and mobilized the political right. American workers were hardly quiescent in 1946; as Peter Drucker noted, "It is the worker rather than the union leader who has been clamoring to strike and to stay on strike."[23] In late May came one of John L. Lewis's periodic coal strikes, as well as an administration standoff with the Railroad Brotherhoods, who threatened to shut down the nation's entire rail network to win the eighteen-and-a-half-cent pattern. President Truman, whose common touch now reflected the common prejudice, sparked an uprising of the labor-baiting conservatives when he denounced the Brotherhood officials A. J. Whitney and Alvanley Johnson in a vitriolic speech before a joint session of Congress. The legislature quickly passed the Case bill, which embodied virtually the entire labor law agenda advocated by the alliance of Republicans and southern Democrats who had so long chafed under the New

Deal order. Truman caught his breath and vetoed the measure, but the counteroffensive against union labor merely shifted its focus to more local battlegrounds. During that summer and fall police efforts to break picket lines touched off scores of violent incidents, including a set of citywide general strikes that stretched from Oakland, California, to Stamford, Connecticut. After Reuther became president, the UAW felt compelled to authorize at least eighty strikes during this season of turmoil, including three exceptionally long and bitter stoppages at Allis-Chalmers, Mack Truck, and J. I. Case.[24]

Industrial friction of this sort turned the political mood ugly, but the legacy of the CIO's abortive wage offensive had yet one more disastrous consequence. In theory, the Office of Price Administration still had a mandate after the steel settlement, but the price hikes authorized by Truman gravely undermined its political clout and social authority. The OPA was the last of the New Deal's great agencies of social regulation and economic nationalism. Its staff was large, its regulations intrusive, and under Chester Bowles, its leadership self-consciously liberal. Quite naturally it came under ferocious attack, drawing special venom from the jobbers, cattlemen, and cotton barons of the West and South, who now moved in for the kill. In June Congress renewed the OPA for a year, but in such a bastardized version that Bowles resigned and Truman vetoed the bill. Rents and food prices exploded during July and August, thereby wiping out all of labor's 1946 wage gain. When controls were restored on meat in the early fall, a producers' strike cleared the grocery stores, literally blackmailing Truman into lifting all price restrictions just before the 1946 elections.[25]

Reuther found this situation utterly frustrating. In May and June the UAW mobilized what forces lay at its command to defend Chester Bowles and the embattled OPA, but once prices shot up in midsummer all the wage gains won a few months earlier evaporated. Reuther could justifiably assert that his GM strike program had been vindicated, but doing so did nothing to assuage millions of urban food shoppers. For a moment he hoped the enormous reservoir of popular resentment might be tapped by the labor-left. Thus Reuther advocated meat boycotts, grocery store picket lines, and even rent strikes, as a counterweight to the "packers, profiteers and middlemen." The UAW encouraged such consumer activism with a big rally in Cadillac Square, where Reuther again proved himself a master phrase-maker. "I was in Minnesota last week, talking to some farmers, and for the first time I realized that you can make more money milking a farmer than you can milking a cow." To revive an alliance with working farmers, Reuther called on labor to take control of "the backside of the paycheck."[26]

The food boycotts soon faded, but they nevertheless lent a powerful impulse to a UAW-sponsored consumer cooperative movement, for which Victor Reuther and Don Montgomery propagandized in all the midwestern auto centers. This initiative, which evoked the communitarian spirit last seen in the back-to-the-land movement of the early Depression era, held some contemporary resonance: within a year dozens of union-sponsored co-ops had distributed thousands of dollars' worth of food in Detroit, Flint, Lansing, and Pontiac. The Reutherites sought to broaden the union's cultural reach and build in the United States a social democratic network in which the cooperatives would be the backbone for the sort of nonprofit retail distribution system that operated so successfully in Sweden and Denmark.[27] On the other hand, the Communists disdained such self-help efforts, which they correctly saw as an ineffectual and depoliticized response to the inflationary crisis. In the end, the debate proved moot, for the co-ops had all collapsed by 1952. In the metropolitan Midwest, the new supermarkets proved too competitive, the suburban sprawl too extensive, and the mobilization of working-class women too difficult to sustain such a project.[28]

The surge in food prices might have been less frustrating had the auto industry been operating at full throttle, but persistent shortages in steel and copper and episodic strikes in the auto parts field were limiting automobile production to 60 percent of prewar capacity. Many members of the car-starved public wrote directly to Reuther: some implored the UAW leader for help in coaxing a car out of their neighborhood dealer; others asserted that "all this is planned in Moscow. . . . The Communist OPA gang held everything down in order to help the CIO break the laboring man."[29] Reuther invited the auto companies to meet with the union to "jointly explore . . . the problems which are impeding production." Reuther hoped the big automakers would pressure the government to restore some commodity controls and price ceilings, thus tempering the industry's competitive scramble for specialty steel. Not unexpectedly, the Big Three turned him down, once again seeing a Reutherite effort to erode managerial production prerogatives. However, the independent auto firms—Studebaker, Kaiser-Fraser, and Willys-Overland—were eager to cooperate with the UAW, for they suspected, with much justification, that the Big Three's market power had deprived them of their fair share of the available steel, copper and glass. But Reuther and the independents could do little—they urged the government to begin a scrap metal drive—so auto production and employment limped into the autumn.[30]

By the end of the summer of 1946 the inflationary surge had driven real wages back to levels not seen since 1942, but most CIO unions approached the idea of a second round of wage negotiations with great caution. Reuther shared Philip Murray's timidity, which served to protect the UAW leader from a factional mauling at the hands of his intraunion opponents. Although some Chrysler unionists were anxious to confront their employer—the workers there had hardly missed a paycheck since 1939—Reuther promised Murray that the UAW would not go off "half-cocked." In this unsettled political season, the demand for a new round of wage increases seemed counterproductive, and mobilization for a strike out of the question.[31]

Indeed, the entire polity had turned increasingly hostile to labor-liberal prospects. The incapacity of either the Truman administration or the labor movement to make an effective fight against the inflationary surge discredited the Rooseveltian state and demobilized millions of working-class voters. Many now paid attention to the 1946 Republican campaign slogan, "Had Enough," which conflated labor unrest, the OPA failure, and Communist power abroad. GOP prospects were immeasurably improved in mid-September when Truman dismissed from his cabinet Henry Wallace, the titular leader of labor-liberal America, following his public criticism of the administration's hard line toward the Soviets. Thereafter, the GOP had a field day. Young ex-servicemen, like Richard Nixon in California and Joseph McCarthy in Wisconsin, unhesitatingly identified the CIO and its political action committee as near-synonyms for Communist. In the South an orgy of red-baiting and race-baiting stopped the CIO's postwar organizing campaign, Operation Dixie, dead in its tracks and snuffed out the political career of many a regional liberal.

In November Democrats lost control of Congress for the first time since 1930. More than half of all the liberal Democrats were wiped out, including the majority of those endorsed by the CIO-PAC. In one of the lowest turnouts in the twentieth century, apathy and discontent robbed the Democrats of more than ten million voters who had cast their ballots for FDR two years before. The most dramatic reversals took place in precisely those districts—stretching from Connecticut to Illinois—where the Democratic Party relied most heavily upon a labor-urban constituency. Reuther's postmortem—that the returns were "not a GOP win but a revolt against the Democratic Party and congressional indecision"—held much validity but not much comfort. The new, Republican-dominated 78th Congress cut back social security, passed the Taft-Hartley Act, and generated much of the legislative-investigative regime we have come to know as "McCarthyism."[32]

The election debacle precipitated a sharp turn against the Communists within virtually all labor and liberal organizations. Given the paralysis within its leadership, the CIO could do little to stem what Reuther admitted was a "period of growing reaction" in which "the Truman administration continues to yield to pressure." Appeasement on the Communist issue therefore seemed the only way to temper the conservative assault. Certainly this was Philip Murray's perspective when he told an executive board meeting just after the elections that the CIO was building for itself "targets, targets that can be easily hit" by labor's adversaries.[33] To stem this tide, Murray appointed Reuther to a six-man committee—composed equally of CIO presidents from the right and left—to exorcise the Communist element yet retain unity within the industrial federation. Reuther proved a bulldog during a weekend of tough negotiations, out of which came a resolution asserting that CIO delegates "resent and reject efforts of the Communist Party . . . to interfere in the affairs of the CIO." With no dissent from the left, Murray rushed this dictate through the CIO's 1946 convention, for the Communists now clung to Murray's leadership like a storm-tossed sailor to his raft.[34]

Reuther again took the offensive against the Communists within the auto union, leveling his big guns as the protracted and violent strike at Allis-Chalmers reached a climax. By November the Allis-Chalmers strike was six months old, but the bitter conflict between the company's self-righteous executives and its militant workforce had been running for more than a generation. Allis-Chalmers managers wanted to eliminate shop steward power in their factory; UAW Local 248, led by a cohort of battle-hardened Communists, was determined to pick up the gauntlet in a postwar showdown. The strike had attracted little attention outside Milwaukee until late September 1946, when management began to play the Communist card. Using research and personnel files supplied by the company, the *Milwaukee Sentinel* published scores of daily articles detailing the left-wing history of the Local 248 leaders. When negotiations collapsed in October, the company initiated a back-to-work movement, which gained many adherents among the large minority of the Allis-Chalmers workforce who had long battled the union's left-wing leadership.

The strike could hardly have been more fractionalized. Reuther hated Harold Christoffel and distrusted Robert Buse, then serving as president of Local 248. Reuther also had poor relations with Joseph Mattson, the UAW regional director for Illinois and Wisconsin who was proving a staunch ally of the Addes-Thomas-Leonard group in the UAW hierarchy. Reuther's hostility was shared by several of the "right-wing" locals in Milwaukee, whose leadership denounced Local 248 Communists, took a hands-off attitude toward the strike, and devoted all their political energy to the reduction of left-wing influence within the Wisconsin CIO. For most of 1946 Reuther handled the situation without much factional controversy. He voted to back the strike with UAW money and manpower, personally ordered his Milwaukee supporters to reinforce the Local 248 picket lines, and put R. J. Thomas in overall charge to get negotiations started with Allis-Chalmers.[35]

However, Reuther soon became convinced that the strike could be won only if the Communist leaders of the Allis-Chalmers union were deposed, an assessment shared by George Addes, who also favored a UAW takeover of the local. Many Local 248 officers and shop leaders had signed Communist Party nomination petitions, some of which actually circulated on the picket line. "Why," asked Reuther after Allis-Chalmers had advertised this connection, "did they place this gigantic club in the hands of their management with which to beat our union to the ground?"[36] Indeed, the strike—violent, protracted, and headline fodder for the resurgent right—was in desperate shape; when the Wisconsin Labor Relations Board scheduled a certification election for January 26, 1947, the fate of the UAW local at Allis-Chalmers lay in a most precarious balance.

But the elimination of the Local 248 leaders was not a simple matter. Despite all their difficulties, Christoffel and Buse had the support of Vice-President Thomas and Regional Director Mattson and the strike-tested loyalty of at least half the factory workforce. Thus Reuther had to step gingerly in mid-January when he received an unexpected phone call from Ensworth Reisner, a Methodist minister in Milwaukee—prolabor but anti-Communist—who had been in contact with Allis-Chalmers officials. The company president Walter Gise and his key labor-relations strategist, Harold Story, were willing to resume negotiations, but only if top CIO officials took a direct hand in the talks. Allis-Chalmers would not even meet with Local 248 leaders; in fact, Gise and Story insisted upon a UAW ouster of the left-wing leaders if a modest wage increase and a new contract were to take effect. Reuther therefore kept Thomas and the other UAW officers well posted when he and John Brophy, Philip Murray's designated representative, met with the management group in Chicago and Milwaukee. Reuther believed that even the appearance of bargaining progress improved UAW chances of winning the representation election, if only because the anti-Communist element at Allis-Chalmers now had reason to stick with the union.[37]

Buse and other Local 248 veterans correctly saw a Reutherite strike settlement as a huge defeat for their brand of shop militancy and left-wing politics. With a victory in the election seemingly assured—Thomas estimated the odds at four to one—Local 248 sought to wrest the initiative from Reuther with an announcement on January 23 that negotiations with the company were terminated "until after Local 248 [had] won the election" on January 26. Meanwhile, R. J. Thomas released a long letter indicting Reuther for what the Milwaukee left saw as the UAW president's "backdoor" negotiations with the company. Reuther had "swallowed" a corporate "divide-and-conquer scheme," charged the former UAW president.[38]

But this factional assault had no legs, for the workers at Allis-Chalmers failed to give Local 248 the mandate Thomas and Buse expected. The UAW won but a bare plurality in the representation election, an outcome that the company immediately challenged. Reuther's hope for a settlement evaporated as the company and its many allies in government and the press moved in for the kill. In February the House Un-American Activities Committee (HUAC) made a flying visit to Milwaukee, where Local 248 leaders were denounced by their anti-Communist opponents. Shortly thereafter, Thomas, Buse, and Christoffel were dragged before the House Education and Labor Committee in Washington. They were met with bipartisan contempt: two freshmen congressmen, Richard Nixon of California and John F. Kennedy of Massachusetts, were among the most hostile and persistent interrogators.[39]

Meanwhile, Reuther felt slandered. The accusations of R. J. Thomas, "published in the reactionary press," he now denounced as "false, malicious and irresponsible." From this point on Reuther and Thomas communicated only through long, accusatory memoranda.[40] More important, the Allis-Chalmers debacle—the strike finally collapsed in March 1947—proved one of those searing episodes, like the North American Aviation strike of June 1941 or the incentive pay fight in 1943, that confirmed for a generation of Reutherites an anti-Communist liturgy of enormous power and conviction. "Our failure at Allis-Chalmers was the result of the open interference on the part of the Communist Party in the affairs of the local union involved," asserted Reuther in a summary of his first presidential term. Ignoring both the determination of the management and the steadfastness of several thousand strikers, Reuther declared the membership betrayed, because "there were people in leadership positions in that local who put loyalties outside of their union, outside of the rank and file, and outside of this country. . . . That is why we lost."[41]

If this was the kind of rhetoric that came out of the union movement itself, it is not surprising that labor's legislative adversaries now conflated Reutherite efforts to eliminate Communist influence within the CIO with their own reactionary overhaul of the Wagner Act designed to strengthen employer prerogatives. Late in February 1947 Reuther himself spent three and a half hours in the Capitol sparring with Senators Robert Taft and Joseph Ball. Evoking little sympathy from these Republicans, Reuther complained that most of the postwar era's difficult strikes were a product of employer intransigence and government labor policy. He defended the J. I. Case strikers, then in their fourteenth month on the picket line, as "freemen . . . fighting for elementary economic security and social justice," but he avoided a similar justification for the long Allis-Chalmers stoppage.[42]

"We are living in a period in which there are going to be witch-hunts, hysteria and red-baiting by the most vicious group of congressmen that have gathered under the dome of the Capitol," Reuther reported to a UAW executive board meeting three weeks later. "What is happening in Local 248 is just a small . . . dress rehearsal." This was the season when the administration put together its loyalty-security apparatus, when the president dramatically announced the Truman Doctrine to repel Communist subversion in Greece and Turkey, and when HUAC began its highly publicized investigation of Hollywood. If Reuther's opponents defended the union's Communist element under such circumstances, they were demonstrating a willful determination to put the interests of an outside political group above the union's very survival. It was therefore "nothing short of criminal negligence for a union not to recognize these basic facts and attempt to get its house in order," asserted Reuther. "We should be putting on armored plates."[43]

Toward this end, Reuther offered the Addes-Leonard group a truce. He was willing to parcel out the union's offices and staff jobs on an equitable basis, but if the two caucuses were to cooperate, Reuther insisted upon a definitive price: a "policy of completely isolating members of the Communist Party . . . from leadership in the International and local unions."[44] The first to go had to be Irving Richter, one of the left wing's most effective political intellectuals. Reuther hated him. Like Don Montgomery, Richter knew Congress, the liberal advocacy groups, and the executive branch bureaucracy, but since 1943 he had worked this network on behalf of a Popular Front liberalism that gave legitimacy and influence to the programs advanced by Reuther's opponents. Reuther first tried to get rid of Richter in June 1946, but he could not muster the votes to drop him from the payroll. When Reuther tried again, in March 1947, he was ready with a prosecutor's brief: Richter's "loyalties [were] outside of the Union," he had lost the confidence of many of the congressmen the UAW sought to influence, and, most sensationally, he had put on his staff the Communist wife of Carl Marzani, whom the State Department had just fired as a potential spy. "Richter is conscientiously a part of that effort to use the American trade union movement as a sort of collaborating agency to carry out a program that meets the needs of the Communist Party, the Soviet Union," charged Reuther.[45] But even this full-bore attack was insufficient to breach the walls behind which Reuther's opponents were entrenched. The Addes-Leonard faction had the votes to save Richter's job once again, but their victory proved costly. Reuther was convinced that intraunion compromise was out of the question: from this point on he would accept nothing less than the elimination of his rivals from all posts in the UAW hierarchy.[46]

The debate over the Taft-Hartley Act in the spring of 1947 and its final passage over President Truman's veto on June 23 proved the decisive event that both ensured Reuther's victory within the UAW and determined much of the political meaning of his triumph. Reuther opposed the law, of course. Urging a presidential veto, the UAW leader declared that the measure would "set off a whole new era of industrial strife and friction," since its provisions gave "encouragement and new weapons to anti-labor employers."[47] But the law was not designed to destroy the union movement; rather, it would codify and crystallize all the legal and administrative procedures that had tended to constrain, contain, and discipline the unions since the defense strikes just before World War II. The requirement that union leaders sign anti-Communist affidavits, the prohibition against secondary boycotts, the enactment of section 14b allowing states to prohibit the union shop, the ban on foreman unionism, all these provisions strengthened state regulation, encouraged contractual parochialism, and penalized any serious attempt to project a classwide political-economic strategy.[48]

These were the political and social constraints that C. Wright Mills labeled "the main drift," what a generation of industrial relations experts would define as "free collective bargaining," what Walter Reuther himself would eventually, and perhaps somewhat reluctantly, endorse as the only practical road forward for American labor.[49] Thus, in a radio debate of May 1946, when he was still basking in the glow generated by his bold GM strike program, Reuther told his listeners that rhetoric about a "government-controlled economy" was a big-business scare tactic. The real question, he said, was "how much government control and for whose benefit." But in the wake of the massive Republican victory of November 1946, Reuther made a rhetorical about-face, now urging "free labor" and "free management" to join in solving their problems, or a "superstate will arise to do it for us." Still later, after the Taft-Hartley restrictions were in place, Reuther put the issue even more bluntly: "I'd rather bargain with General Motors than with the government. . . . General Motors has no army."[50]

The logic of such an approach devalued interunion solidarity and channeled labor's energy into a collective bargaining straitjacket that restricted the social visions and political strategies once advocated by the laborite left. Taft-Hartley lent credence to Reuther's factional slogan, "Against Outside Interference," because the new labor relations infrastructure held no place for the Communist Party or any other political tendency that advocated a program "outside" the new boundaries approved by the cold war state. Thus would Catholic-inspired visions of an "industrial council" corporatism wither as rapidly, if more silently, than the syndicalist militancy advocated by Trotskyist organizers or the third-party linkages urged by the Communists.

Although Truman hardly dissented from the political logic embodied within the Taft-Hartley Act—he would make use of its powers as vigorously as any postwar president—his initial veto of the measure played into Reuther's hands as well, for it made possible the eventual rapprochement between the Truman administration and those liberals who remained hostile to the Communists. This remarriage took more than a year, but Truman's lurch to the left—he also put forward a bold "Fair Deal" program of social reform—effectively blunted the appeal of a postwar Popular Front, ensuring that within the CIO left-wing unionists allied with the Communist Party would remain a minor current and the 1948 Wallace candidacy a marginal affair.

Two episodes in the spring of 1947 demonstrate how Taft-Hartley came to depoliticize and restrict Reuther's understanding of the collective bargaining function. In April the CIO mounted the first of a series of huge protests against congressional enactment of the law. Spurred on by many secondary union leaders, Reuther joined his factional opponents in an executive board vote to mobilize the entire Detroit-area labor movement for a massive demonstration in Cadillac Square on April 24, 1947. The UAW would be calling a political strike: Reuther sent telegrams to all locals ordering them to quit work at 2:00 P.M. and assemble downtown. Such demonstration strikes had been annual affairs in the late 1930s, and as recently as July 1946 autoworkers had shut down many factories when the CIO rallied against the decontrol of meat prices. Emil Mazey hoped that American unions were beginning to deploy "the kind of political power which is most effective in Europe."[51]

But Reuther lost his nerve. He was in final negotiations with GM for a second-round wage increase; more important, GM executives told UAW officials that such a work stoppage would be a violation of paragraph 117 of the UAW-GM contract, which prohibited strikes and stoppages. The company promised to penalize any workers who walked out even a few minutes early. When the UAW executive board considered the matter on April 22, Reuther refused to assent to the counter-strategy urged by George Addes (and endorsed even by Emil Mazey): the UAW must immediately tell GM that if any unionists were disciplined, the union would itself retaliate in a massive and concerted fashion. Asserted Reuther, "No board member no matter how righteous he may feel about the cause, has the right to shut down a General Motors Plant as a counter measure of the company's discipline."[52]

By 1947 Reuther had become a prisoner of the General Motors contract. He had held too many bargaining sessions, filed too many grievance appeals, and butted heads with C. E. Wilson and Harry Anderson too many times to risk the destruction of the social order with which both sides had made their decade-long accommodation. While Reuther never rescinded the strike call, he now considered it a "mistake," and he stood aloof as his assistant in the GM Department, Art Johnstone, warned General Motors militants against violating the contract. The demonstration itself proved a huge success. More than 250,000 from throughout the metropolitan region shut down their workplaces to converge on Cadillac Square at midafternoon. Ford, Chrysler, Briggs, Packard, and Hudson were all shut down. Police lined up shoulder to shoulder to keep storefront windows from being broken by the surging crowd. Virtually every leader of the UAW spoke, including Victor Reuther, but Walter was conspicuous by his absence.[53]

GM soon took its pound of flesh. The Fleetwood local president John Anderson described the scene at the appointed hour: "As 2:00 P.M. approached I was surrounded by five members of supervision. . . . As I was about to leave, all five of them . . . pointed their fingers at me, and [personnel director] Heikes said: 'Anderson, we are ordering you to remain on your job.' I brushed them aside with a wave of my hand, walked to the switch which stopped the conveyor, and pulled it." When Anderson and his workmates arrived at the square they were elated at the turnout, but alarmed when several Reutherite locals, representing a majority of GM's production workforce in the Detroit area, marched in their troops two hours late. Along with fourteen other key union officials, Anderson was fired when he returned to work the next morning, and GM gave more than four hundred others lengthy layoffs.[54]

These penalties sent a wave of fear and resistance through the union. The grievance procedure was useless because the umpire was sure to side with the corporation on so clear a violation of the contract. Amid a new round of mutual recriminations, Addes, Leonard, and Reuther scrambled to win back the jobs and limit the layoffs. GM managers were more than willing to ameliorate the penalties, because they extracted from the UAW a declaration that the mass work stoppage was indeed a violation of the contract. On May 8 Reuther offered the corporation a pledge that the UAW would never again call such a clearly political strike. "During the year that followed our labor relations were dramatically changed for the better," remembered GM Chairman Alfred Sloan, who considered the hard line GM took toward the Cadillac Square rally one of the corporation's most important initiatives.[55]

Reuther also proved equivocal a month later when the specter of Taft-Hartley touched off a bitter industrial dispute at the Ford Motor Company. The issue was nothing less than the character and extent of working-class solidarity in the postwar era. Corporate framers of the Taft-Hartley Act, especially those in heavy industry, were particularly anxious to ghettoize the unions into an isolated and fragmented blue-collar sector of American society. To this end, the new law sought the destruction of the remarkable impulse toward foreman unionism and intraclass solidarity that had swept through factories and mills during the late years of the war. Taft-Hartley's section 2(3) redefined the term *employee* so as to specifically exclude from NLRB purview all first-line supervisors. In response, the new Foreman's Association of America had little choice but to strike if it were to defend its existence. The FAA had been founded at the Rouge, and there held its greatest strength. When Ford management refused to renew its contract on May 21, this independent union put almost four thousand supervisory employees on the picket line. UAW members refused to take on foremen's work, but each day sixty thousand passed through the FAA picket lines to their own jobs.[56]

Not all industrial unionists favored foremen, but as a onetime supervisor at Ford, Reuther understood the high stakes at risk. Should the FAA fail—and by mid-June Ford management remained intransigent—the resentful supervisors would become "willing tools in the hands of the Ford company to break our own union." Moreover, Reuther cringed at the thought of so many autoworkers ignoring the FAA picket lines—the very symbol of class solidarity. With passage of the Taft-Hartley Act imminent, the UAW had to teach "respect for authorized picket lines regardless of what union they are." If necessary, Reuther favored a merger with the FAA and a UAW strike at the Rouge itself.[57]

But the Ford Motor Company was Richard Leonard's turf, and he thought he had bigger fish to fry. Leonard's department was in the midst of an exceedingly complex set of negotiations with the company, out of which he hoped to win both a pension plan and a clause immunizing the UAW from company lawsuits arising out of Taft-Hartley. Since Leonard was hostile to any industrial action that might complicate the negotiations with Ford, Reuther voted with the rest of the executive board merely to authorize UAW mediation in the dispute. When Ford management spurned the offer, the foremen were doomed; in such fashion did the union movement's sociological frontier cease its forward march.[58]

Until the summer of 1947 neither Reuther nor his factional opponents really knew the mood of the rank and file, but the impact of the Taft-Hartley Act on the union's activist core became apparent during the course of a unionwide referendum on a proposed merger between the UAW and the 43,000-member Farm Equipment Workers (FE). The merger plan was itself a product of the desperate condition into which the trade union left had fallen in less than a year. Fearing attack after Taft-Hartley became law, the Communist-led Farm Equipment Workers sought protection within the million-strong UAW, yet the merger agreement sought to preserve the political character of an "autonomous" FE division within the larger union, thus adding some 430 left-wing votes to the strength of the Addes-Thomas caucus at the UAW's 1947 convention.

Reuther was taken completely by surprise on June 13 when his opponents broached the secretly negotiated merger scheme during the last hours of an executive board meeting in Chicago. Reuther, who was about to catch a plane for a White House meeting on Taft-Hartley, denounced the plan as a "blitz attack . . . dangerous and unconstitutional," but his opponents had a solid majority locked up. Naturally the Reutherites saw the merger, to be ratified in a hastily organized referendum, as an utterly cynical piece of factional opportunism. They were right, but from a purely trade union perspective the merger had much to recommend it. To end their sometimes destructive rivalry, the CIO had long urged that the FE merge with the much larger UAW. Reuther had endorsed this CIO proposal, which would have certainly strengthened the UAW in its long and frustrating strike against the farm equipment maker J. I. Case. To halt the merger, Reuther therefore shifted the character of the debate, transforming the referendum from a technical question of union structure into a vote against the politics of his opponents.[59]

Reuther's partisans threw themselves into the struggle, rushing to locals across the country to debate both Thomas and Addes at noisy meetings. Ostensibly, both sides debated the constitutional and strategic merits of the issue, Reuther emphasizing that an autonomous FE division undermined the industrial union idea; soon the skilled trades and the Ford workers would follow their precedent. But such arguments, remembered Jack Conway, "were really unimportant." The key issue was always of a blunter sort: "The Communists are trying to take over the UAW; what are you going to do about it?" By this time Taft-Hartley had so thoroughly saturated union politics with the Communist question that Reuther and his comrades could eschew the cruder sort of red-baiting; all that was needed was the occasional reminder to the autoworkers that FE officers and their UAW allies had favored the government's incentive pay schemes during World War II. The novelist Clancy Sigal, who helped the Addes-Thomas group negotiate the merger, remembered their initiative as "the wrong move. Wrong and fatal. It gave [Reuther] just the issue he needed to push him over the top."[60]

Because each local voted as a unit, the merger fight gave the Reutherites the chance to organize a faction throughout every important union in the UAW. As usual, the meetings were lightly attended that summer, but this merely accentuated the political character of the struggle, since those participating in the debate were UAW cadre who would soon run for delegate to the next UAW convention. Conway, who chaired the Reuther caucus at the 1947 convention, recalled that the referendum "gave us a forum and we beat their ears off. And, in the process, converted a lot of the leadership to our point of view." The merger lost heavily in Detroit and in several regions headed by Addes-Thomas regional directors: Canada, Indiana, Chicago-Wisconsin, and Flint. "We give Reuther credit," admitted an FE leader. "His workers covered the country from coast to coast and down to the Gulf." When the votes were tabulated in August, the merger had failed by more than two to one. The Wage Earner now thought Reuther "unbeatable" in November.[61]

But one more hurdle remained before Reuther could sweep his forces to power in the UAW. Though the Taft-Hartley Act became law on June 23, many laborites hated the new law's requirement that trade union leaders sign affidavits certifying that they were not members of the Communist Party. Management officials were not required to sign, so even conservative trade unionists found the requirement a humiliating insult. John L. Lewis abruptly pulled the UMW out of the AFL when the federation went along with the law, and Philip Murray, who led the CIO defiance campaign, called the affidavit requirement "a diabolical piece of work, extremely discriminatory in nature, and revolting to a citizen who believes in decency and in justice and in freedom."[62]

In the UAW the "diabolical" character of the clause soon became evident, even as the union's 1947 Labor Day parade filled Woodward Avenue with tens of thousands of marchers and scores of floats advertising the union movement's loathing of Taft-Hartley. By not signing the anti-Communist affidavits, the UAW blocked itself from participation in NLRB certification elections. This had little impact on the well-organized core of the union, but it wreaked havoc on the UAW's coastal frontiers, where AFL unions had the resources to raid UAW jurisdictions. At the aircraft maker Glenn Martin in Baltimore, NLRB officials had already halted a ballot count in which the UAW sought to repel a raid by the International Association of Machinists. "We cannot hold our people much longer," reported the president of the aircraft local. "The people in the plant are not old militant union people. . . . They are young yet, and have read the papers, and they want to know the answers to certain questions that they have a right to ask."[63]

Reuther called Taft-Hartley "a vicious piece of Fascist legislation," but he still wanted UAW officers to sign the anti-Communist affidavits. "I agree completely with the principle the CIO stands on," he told a September executive board meeting, but "we have no alternative as a practical matter except to comply." The furious debate that followed turned on a fundamental assessment of working-class consciousness in the postwar era. An old radical like Percy Llewellyn, who had survived the red scare after World War I, argued for a return to "militant action" and an abandonment of any reliance on the state's labor relations apparatus. But Emil Mazey, whose credentials as a shop militant were no less distinguished, made a counterclaim: "We have already organized the advanced section of the working class in America. The workers that are still unorganized are the more backward element. . . . These workers will not, in a majority of cases, strike to win union recognition." Taft-Hartley made it harder to organize, admitted Reuther. "It was written for that purpose . . . but it does not make it impossible to get people to join a union." The militant rhetoric of his opponents was therefore essentially "defeatist." Unless the UAW continued to organize, it would be incapable of winning the political support necessary to stem the right-wing tide.[64]

The campaign for convention delegates that fall ratified the membership's overwhelmingly pro-Reuther sentiment and crystallized the meaning of that shift in loyalties. It was a wildly democratic contest in which both Reuther and his opponents distributed thousands of dollars' worth of literature and deployed virtually every International representative and staff intellectual at their command. In a secretly prepared "Report to the Membership" sent to all UAW dues payers, the Reuther camp attacked Addes for shoddy bookkeeping, Thomas for incompetence, and Leonard for his factionally motivated conduct of the Ford pension drive. Reuther defined his cause as one capable of ending the union's divisive factionalism and eliminating the influence of the Communist Party, whose "members in America and in our union are governed by the foreign policy needs of the

Soviet Union." Individual unionists might hold an unorthodox "personal political philosophy," but the UAW had the duty to "oppose with uncompromising determination the efforts of the Communist Party or any other outside group or individual to interfere in the affairs of our union."[65]

Reuther denied that such attacks amounted to red-baiting; indeed, he threw the accusation back, denouncing the Communists and their allies for "branding as a fascist and red-baiter everyone who has the courage to oppose or criticize the Communist Party line." As the frenzy and exhaustion of the campaign reached its November climax, Reuther and his circle saw the contest as starkly Manichaean; George Addes and other executive board opponents were reduced to little more than transparent ciphers. "We in the UAW took the Communists on without illusions," wrote Reuther in a *Collier's* magazine feature, "How to Beat the Communists," published just two months after the UAW convention. "We understood that the alternative to a finish fight was Communist control of our union." Such hyperbole had no objective basis, as even many Reutherites would later acknowledge, but his real target was much closer to home: it was what Reuther called "the united-front psychology . . . in which many non-Communist progressives made common cause with the Stalinists in the misguided belief that contemporary Communism operates from ethical and moral perceptions of a certain validity." Here was the Niebuhrian line over which postwar labor-liberals dared not step.[66]

Reuther's opponents could hardly lay a hand on him. In a widely distributed pamphlet, "The Bosses' Boy," they denounced him as a red-baiter and a tool of labor's corporate adversaries, but both arrows missed their mark. The red-baiting charge held little sting, but not because American autoworkers were militant anti-Communists in 1947. Rather, they were all fervent unionists. After the GOP victory in 1946 and the passage of Taft-Hartley six months later, autoworkers had come to see the interests of the UAW as counterpoised to those of any "politics," inside the union or out. Thus it was Reuther's pledge to end factionalism and deflect "outside interference" that seemed to so many workers both sensible and self-protective. Publicists for the Addes group were also mistaken when they sought to use against Reuther the respectful spreads that he received in the business press and in many of the mass-circulation publications. His opponents thought such "lavish praise" in the "monopoly press" a condemnation in its own right. But whatever the interests of the *Saturday Evening Post* in anti-Communism or the Luce publications in industrial relations stability, Reuther's credentials as a union progressive and corporate critic were still freshly minted. Most UAW members probably saw in this coverage a validation of their union's power and a further proof that Reutherite leadership was the UAW's best protection from corporate and congressional attack.[67]

As the whole debate got down to the shop level, savvy unionists had little difficulty in fusing a crude sort of ideological politics with the "pork chop" calculation pervasive in local elections. Victor Scott of Continental Motors summed up the popular sensibility as well as any activist. As a convention delegate, Scott had voted for R. J. Thomas in 1946, but now he thought the "commies were trying to control the UAW." With Leonard Woodcock set to become his regional director, Scott switched his allegiance to the Reuther group because they were not "using the union as a stepping-stone for themselves or some other philosophy."[68] In 1947 the Reutherites had taken over Chrysler Local 7, which R. J. Thomas had long considered his "home." Visiting the union hall after the end of the faction fight, the journalist Samuel Lubell found the slogan "UAW Americanism for Us" propped on the office desks. "In 1940 the flavor of the local was one of street barricades and sit-down strikes," reported Lubell. "Eight years later it was almost like a lodge hall."[69] Except for California and Cleveland, the Reuther forces took every region in the UAW. In Detroit they polled big majorities in almost all locals, even in units like Plymouth, East Side Tool and Die, and the Motor Building at the Rouge, all of which had been under Communist leadership. In late October Philip Murray, who feared the Reutherite sweep might propel some left-wingers out of the union, called Reuther and his top lieutenants to Pittsburgh to plead for the careers of Addes and Leonard. But Reuther told the CIO leader it was too late for "peace in our time."[70] His machine was running smoothly now. "We put a powerhouse together," remembered his campaign manager Jack Conway. "We just knew what we were doing every minute of the day. . . . We had a reading on the whole convention, every delegate, every union, every issue."[71]

When the UAW again met in Atlantic City, the drama of the last boardwalk conclave was entirely missing. Convention delegates easily backed Reuther's decision to sign the Taft-Hartley Act's anti-Communist affidavits and then moved on to give the Reutherites virtually total control of the union. In the most significant contest, Mazey ended Addes's twelve years as UAW secretary-treasurer by a nearly two-to-one vote. Then Richard Gosser of Toledo and John Livingston of St. Louis took over the two vice-presidential spots from Thomas and Leonard. The Addes group reelected only four regional directors, two of whom, George Burt of Canada and Cyril O'Halloran of California, promptly transformed themselves into compliant Reutherites. The left-wing delegates, reported Newsweek, "sat glum and silent" during the time-consuming ballots, "while Reuther's anti-Communist steamroller clanked over them."[72]

The new UAW executive board closely mirrored the Reuther caucus coalition. There were five staunch Reutherites, four with SP backgrounds: Reuther, Mazey, Woodcock, and Martin Gerber from New Jersey, plus Edward Cote, a loyalist from Local 174. They were precisely balanced by five Catholics, of whom three, Joe McCusker of Local 600, Raymond Berndt of South Bend, and Mike Lacey from the East Side, had been active in the ACTU. No Poles or blacks served on the board, but conservative unionists from the South were probably overrepresented: they included Livingston, Pat Greathouse of downstate Illinois, and Tom Starling of Atlanta.[73]

The Addes group simply disintegrated when Reuther recruited, replaced, or defeated its key leaders. Addes left the union to run a bar, Thomas took a staff job with the CIO, and Leonard, who briefly tried to rebuild a political base in his old DeSoto local, also ended up on the CIO payroll. Upwards of eighty union staffers who found themselves on the losing side were out of a job. Two activist liberals, Abe Zwerling in Detroit and Joe Rauh in Washington, took over the legal work and the political counseling, once performed by Maurice Sugar and his left-wing law firm; likewise, Nat Weinberg replaced James Wishart at the Research Department, and Reuther finally rid the Washington office of Irving Richter, who went on to help manage Henry Wallace's Progressive Party campaign. His replacement, Paul Sifton, proved Richter's mirror image during 1948, writing anti-Wallace pamphlets for the Americans for Democratic Action.[74]

All observers immediately recognized that the Reuther victory decisively shifted the balance of power within the entire labor-liberal community. The ADA hailed his sweep in the UAW an a vindication of its brand of anti-Communist liberalism. Within the CIO, anti-Communists from Philip Murray on down recognized that they could now move with far greater determination to isolate and then expel its Communist affiliates. In far-off Los Angeles, the CP leader Dorothy Healey remembered that until Reuther's sweep the party was still considered "a legitimate force in the union movement. We still enjoyed our 'citizenship.' Reuther's election, though, was the turning point." Indeed, Reuther was determined to smash all of the institutions that had constituted the decade-old Popular Front in America. In particular he saw the Wallace campaign, in which the Communists came to form the organizational backbone, as but another, and perhaps even larger, battleground in the same factional conflict that had brought him to victory in the UAW.[75]

Reuther's attack was therefore uncompromising and, within the liberal-labor camp, decisive. Though Reuther had warmly praised Henry Wallace as late as 1946, he now thought the former vice president "a lost soul," as he told a National Press Club audience in December 1947. The next month, when the CIO executive council met to debate the Wallace candidacy, Reuther pulled out all the stops, rhetorical and otherwise, to browbeat leaders of the left-wing unions that hoped to make an autonomous endorsement of the third party. Wallace was not "God's anointed apostle to carry on the Roosevelt tradition," declared Reuther. Instead, Wallace's Progressive Party movement was designed to block the Marshall Plan, divide the CIO, and generate the kind of political "chaos" out of which the Communists could rebuild their power. Reuther had seen it all before, during the "closing days of the Reichstag [when the Communists] voted with the Nazis against the trade union bloc and the democratic bloc. . . . That is the tragic philosophy which the Wallace thing is helping advance in America." To his face Reuther called Harry Bridges, the West Coast longshore unionist, a "prostitute." To the Wallace unionists he drew a line in the sand: all CIO affiliates had a "moral obligation" to repudiate the Progressive Party, in keeping with the executive council's vote against him of thirty-three to eleven. The postwar Popular Front was dead, and the third-party Wallace campaign crippled at its birth.[76]

In their moment of victory at the 1947 UAW convention, Reuther partisans had been giddy but Reuther himself betrayed no swagger from the podium. He dressed fastidiously, rarely loosening his collar or rolling up his sleeves in public. At forty, Reuther was still barrel-chested, with the well-preserved look of an athlete. The journalist James Wechsler thought him "always ebullient and fresh, as if he had just stepped out of a shower."[77] Irritated that most newspapers and magazines described his sweep as a victory for the "right wing," Reuther used his last speech to the 1947 UAW convention to repudiate those "editorial writers" and to "serve notice" on the corporations that under his uncontested leadership the UAW would be a far more formidable opponent than its divided predecessor. "Teamwork in the leadership" now matched the union's "solidarity in the ranks." Returning to the Socialist cadences of the early 1930s, Reuther offered UAW delegates a militant, comprehensive vision of their union as "the vanguard in America," "the architects of the future," whose task was nothing less than "the total job of fighting to save and make democracy work in the world." As if to ratify these ambitions, Reuther then introduced his father, Val Reuther, "an old soap boxer, an old rabble-rouser . . . an old fighter in the ranks of labor," who offered a stirring speech that recalled the Debsian movement of his own youth. When UAW delegates then gave Val an honorary UAW membership, they simultaneously made his second eldest son the contemporary unionist who most clearly represented that meeting of organized power and social vision so vital to the creative future of America's working-class movement.[78]

13

THE TREATY OF DETROIT

Pressures growing out of employee dissatisfaction, unrest, union politics . . . all
were interfering with our production processes. From our standpoint, a better
method of wage determination had to be found.

    —*Harry W. Anderson*, Behind the GM Wage Program, *1950*

The plain truth is that factory work is degrading.

    —*Harvey Swados, "The Myth of the Happy Worker," 1957*

On April 20, 1948, the UAW executive board meeting at the Book-Cadillac
Hotel ran well into the evening. There was much to discuss: strike
prospects at Chrysler, the complicated GM negotiations, Truman's chances in the
fall. After it was over, several officers headed for the bar, but as usual Reuther drove
straight home, only stopping briefly at the UAW headquarters to pick up a few
papers. He reached his house in Northwest Detroit at 9:40 P.M. Reuther ate a dish
of warmed-over stew at the breakfast bar, then went to the refrigerator to get a bowl
of peaches. As he turned to reply to a casual remark by May, a blast of Double O
buckshot from a twelve-gauge shotgun smashed through the kitchen window. Four
pellets ripped into Reuther's right arm, and a fifth plowed through his chest. He
fell to the floor, his arm a bloody confusion of bone and muscle. Most of the buckshot perforated a kitchen cupboard. Had Reuther not turned at the last moment,
the full force of the blast would have blown out his chest.

    Reuther remained conscious; indeed, he crawled onto the back porch to try to
glimpse his assailant. "Those dirty bastards!" he cried out to the neighbors who

soon poured into the house. "They have to shoot a fellow in the back. They won't come out in the open and fight." At the hospital he was given three pints of whole blood and one of plasma while undergoing two and a half hours of surgery. Reuther would survive, but his recovery was complicated and prolonged. He was in traction for weeks and in a cast for almost a year; as a result of the transfusions, he contracted both hepatitis and malaria. The seemingly irreparable damage to the nerves controlling the use of his right hand proved most disturbing. In November, after Duke University specialists had probed for five hours in a desperate effort to piece together tiny shreds of the radical nerve, Reuther began making twice-daily hospital visits for whirlpool bath treatments.[1]

Reuther's tenacity and capacity for hard work paid off. About eighteen months after the surgery, he was in the bath when he realized he could move his right thumb a sixteenth of an inch. He let out a yell of triumph. Now he exercised the withered arm by squeezing a hard rubber ball for several hours at a time. Soon he returned to woodworking with a vengeance: when the family moved to a remote and well-guarded cottage in woodsy Rochester, thirty-five miles north of Detroit, Reuther himself rebuilt and expanded their new home. Still struggling to get full use of his right hand, he would saw and hammer until his eyes filled with tears, then dunk the stiffened hand in a bucket of hot water. "I got a good house and a good hand—all for the same money," he later quipped.[2]

The attempt on Reuther's life was not an isolated incident. Thirteen months after that first assault on Walter, Victor Reuther nearly lost his life when another shotgun blast—from a gun of identical make—caught him at home reading the evening paper. Victor was hit in the face, throat, and right shoulder; at Henry Ford Hospital a surgeon removed his right eye. Both assassination attempts were accompanied by enormous publicity, a UAW reward eventually totaling more than two hundred thousand dollars, and what seemed at the time like a vigorous police manhunt. But Reuther's enemies were still not scared off. On December 20, 1949, a UAW watchman found a bomb containing thirty-nine sticks of dynamite just outside a back entrance to the union headquarters. The fuses had sputtered out because of a heavy rain, but according to one anonymous tip, "It was planted when the big guy was in the office."[3]

Who tried to kill the Reuther brothers, and why? No assailant was ever brought to justice, but the trail clearly led to an industrial underworld whose private arrangements and clan loyalties were threatened by the consolidation of Reuther's power in the UAW and the larger centralization of industrial relations that he championed. At midcentury the line between shop militancy, union organization, and personal aggrandizement was not always clear. The classic site of industrial criminality arose in those competitive yet highly unionized workplaces where working-class entrepreneurs leveraged the new power at their command to advance their own fortunes and those of their ethnic associates. By the late 1940s a dramatic leap in both union power and leadership corruption had made the cash payoff, the sweetheart contract, and the gangland beating a part of the "industrial relations system" that governed the construction industry, short-haul trucking, East Coast longshoring, and the bakery and restaurant trades.[4]

The same configuration of power and profit was often present in the auto shops, especially among the independent supplier firms and within the quasi-feudal Ford organization. During the war the spread of trade unionism and the recruitment of a huge, unskilled workforce gave plenty of room for a whole stratum of ambitious shop politicians to manipulate the entrepreneurial opportunities available to local union officials, shop committeemen, ration stamp distributors, numbers runners, and canteen operators. No UAW faction was untouched: Richard Gosser, Reuther's man in Toledo, tolerated the gambling rings at Willys-Overland, as did the Rouge Communists, who never interfered with the well-organized numbers racket that pulled in thousands of dollars each week from the foundry and the Motor Building.[5]

Reuther's assailants were paid by "the Shark," Santos Perrone, an illiterate but powerful Sicilian gangster who had a shadowy alliance with Reuther's erstwhile comrade Melvin Bishop. Perrone's base of operations was the Michigan Stove Works on the East Side of Detroit, where his family cleverly leveraged for their own gain the working-class insurgency that swept through Detroit. Until the 1930s Santos and his brother Gaspar had been core makers in the foundry, but organizing efforts at the stove works soon put a premium upon their thuggish talents. Twice they smashed unionization attempts; in return, the owners, one of whom soon became deputy police commissioner, gave Perrone the lucrative contract to haul away all the scrap metal from the works. Perrone also controlled the foundry, over which he presided like a traditional southern Italian padrone.

In the 1940s the Perrone gang moved into the larger world of industrial politics. In 1941 they supplied some of the thugs who helped Jimmy Hoffa and his Detroit Teamsters local smash a CIO effort to organize Ford's car haul business, and at the end of the war Perrone put his strong-arm men at the service of the Briggs Corporation and Regional Director Bishop when they confronted the union militants allied with Emil Mazey. In return for a big scrap metal contract at Briggs—worth upwards of one hundred thousand dollars a year—Perrone gangsters beat up six Local 212 leaders in 1945 and 1946, to the notable disinterest of the Detroit police, who still saw industrial violence of this sort as little more significant than a barroom brawl. The Perrone family was also active in black market operations during the war, in the numbers racket at Ford, and in ferrying illegal immigrants from Canada.[6]

Reuther's consolidation of power in the UAW threatened Perrone's expanding empire. In the staff purges of late 1947 and early 1948, Melvin Bishop and other Perrone contacts were dismissed from the union, and Emil Mazey supervised an investigation of the Briggs beatings. Reuther began to extend his influence and built a faction within many of the key locals on the East Side of Detroit, and the UAW again took steps to unionize the Michigan Stove Works.[7] Early in April 1948 John Bugas, the former FBI chief in Detroit who had taken over industrial relations at Ford, called Reuther to inquire whether the UAW president would have any objection to the dismissal of the key gambling operatives at the Rouge. Reuther, who had earlier told a congressional committee, "We did not organize our union to give the people the right to shoot crap in the toilets," gave Bugas the go-ahead. These firings may well have been the last straw for Perrone.[8]

The three assassination attempts—utterly audacious in view of the publicity they generated—were undoubtedly sustained by Perrone's knowledge that at least some strategically located police officers were complicitous either in the crimes or in a more general effort to thwart the subsequent investigations. For example, just before Victor's shooting, a Detective Sergeant Albert DeLamielleure, who was in charge of the Reuther case, insisted that Walter's younger brother get rid of his family's small guard dog, whose evening barks were said to have disturbed the neighbors. DeLamielleure, later known to have had friendly dealings with Santos Perrone, eventually resigned from the police force and went to work for Jimmy Hoffa's Detroit Teamsters local.[9] In 1948 and 1949 Michigan police interviewed more than five hundred suspects, but their general attitude toward the attempted assassinations was often one of contempt and disdain, a view ratified at the very highest levels by the notable failure of the FBI to enter the investigation. J. Edgar Hoover's position was clear: "Edgar says no" was the bureau response to calls for action from both the CIO and President Truman's own attorney general. "He says he's not going to send the FBI in every time some nigger woman gets raped."[10]

Perrone family fortunes finally declined in 1951 when the Senate's Crime Investigating Committee, under the chairmanship of Estes Kefauver, held a week of sensational hearings in Detroit. The Michigan Stove Works went bankrupt, and Perrone lost his scrap metal contract with Briggs. In 1953 one of the Perrone gunmen confessed to the Reuther shootings in return for $5,000 from the UAW, but he then slipped away from his police guards and fled to Canada. No one was ever convicted of either the Briggs beatings or the Reuther assassination attempts. Indeed, Perrone's son-in-law, Carl Renda, who had won the original Briggs scrap metal contract, successfully sued the UAW for "malicious prosecution" in 1958.[11]

Despite this unsettled legacy, Reuther did everything in his power to see that the shootings failed to alter the industrial history he knew it was his destiny to shape. From his hospital bed Reuther dictated a defiant statement for the press: "The momentum and power of our new kind of labor movement cannot be stopped and thrown back by slugs from a shotgun. The social and economic democracy for which we struggle . . . cannot be clouded or killed by assaults on one man." If Walter had any private doubts, he kept them deeply buried. He soon distanced himself from the long and frustrating investigation, whose supervision he left in Jack Conway's trusted hands. To his mother Anna, who had characteristically urged his return to the tool and die trade, Reuther confessed, "No, I'm all tied up in this thing, all involved. I must do it."[12]

Within the UAW, the assassination attempt immensely strengthened Reuther's leadership, adding a personal, moral dimension to the political supremacy he had demonstrated just months before. Since no perpetrator had been found, all of Reuther's opponents remained suspect. One of his critics, Carl Haessler, thought that until the mid-1950s "it was impossible to say anything against the Reuthers— no matter how true—that would find general credence." Reuther traveled in an armored Packard and kept two bodyguards close at hand; meanwhile, the UAW put up the fences, lights, and guard posts that transformed his homes, first in Detroit and then in exurban Rochester, into fortresses. Top UAW officials held more than fifty gun permits. Though Reuther himself never used the shootings as a bloody shirt with which to denounce his intraunion critics, he remained convinced that Sicilian gangsters alone could not have been responsible for a crime of such political magnitude. When finally interviewed by the FBI in early 1950, Reuther speculated that individuals from the old Addes-Communist alliance must have had a hand in the coup attempt.[13]

Once he had recovered from his wounds, Reuther's absorbing work and constant travel pushed the trauma to the margins of his consciousness, but his family paid a heavy price. Linda and Lisa resented the ever-present guards, the confining routine, and the frequent absence of their father. As they grew older, the assassination attempt remained a kind of dark secret whose emotional consequences were rarely acknowledged; Walter and May always spoke of it as "the accident." May kept up a brave front, vainly seeking an "illusion of normalcy" as she retreated even further into a sometimes lonely domestic world. "May Reuther was expert at sublimating her feelings," commented her daughter Lisa. "She had years of practice." Linda, who was six at the time of the assassination attempt, came to see her father as cold, remote, and Teutonic, a man whose failure to confront the family's extraordinary situation generated tension and estrangement. Her poor performance in Detroit elementary schools helped prompt the family's move to Rochester in 1953. Later her enrollment at the Putney School in Vermont served as a kind of liberation from the family.[14]

To Walter Reuther, the aftermath of the assassination attempt exacerbated the sharp compartmentalization of his life. Reuther retained the intense personal and political loyalty of those who had helped him battle to the top in the UAW, and he sometimes invited friends and colleagues like Brendan Sexton, Abe Zwerling, and Oskar Stonorov out to Rochester, often to help with the expansion of the cottage. But the easy give-and-take was harder to sustain now, for Reuther's social isolation increased his propensity to see even longtime associates as little more than instruments of his political ambition. "He never asks me about my family," one friend complained. "Walter," said a wry admirer, "is a dedicated fanatic." In their largely sympathetic portrait of 1949 the Trotskyist intellectuals Irving Howe and B. J. Widick described Reuther as an "unfinished personality" whose public personality reflected "a disturbing distance—a distance between himself and his followers; between the ultimate ideas tucked away in the back of his head and his immediate action . . . between his long-range passions and his day-to-day compromises."[15]

Whatever his inner conflicts, Reuther himself knew that the assassination attempt could not shift the flow of history. In 1948 the United States stood on the cusp of a great political settlement, a class accord that ended nearly two decades of industrial turmoil during which neither labor, capital, nor the state were quite certain of the rules of the game or the intensity of the contest. From this point on Reuther was forced to play his part in the construction of the postwar regime, which both constrained labor-management conflict within a world of "free" collective bargaining and offered a section of the working class—largely white, male, and unionized—economic security and social benefits that would double their real incomes within a generation. Reuther spent the rest of his life exploring the limits of this postwar settlement, a generation-spanning order of which he proved both enthusiastic champion and knowing victim.[16]

Of course, none of these consequences were apparent in early 1948. The rhetoric of American unionism still called for "security," but few economists were willing to stake their reputations on the continuation of the postwar boom, and no laborite could assert that the Truman administration had a realistic plan to ensure the medical care and retirement security of working-class Americans. On the wage front, real incomes had stagnated since 1945. All of the money won during the big postwar strikes had been wiped out by the inflation that engulfed the nation over the next ten months. The "imbalance" between wages and prices remained an ominous specter, warned the CIO in a widely discussed assessment of late 1946 prepared by Robert Nathan, the young Keynesian who had earlier defended national planning at the War Production Board. "Unless there is an immediate increase in wages or a sharp drop in prices, we are flirting with collapse," read the Nathan Report, in language remarkably reminiscent of Reuther's GM strike program issued the year before.[17]

But the unions were too weak, the administration too timid, and the corporate opposition too strong to do anything with such ideas in 1946 and 1947. Consumed with the faction fight and fearful that another big companywide strike might further excite antiunion agitation, both Reuther and his opponents had dodged the wage issue. Reuther was therefore chagrined in April 1947 when for the second year in a row the Communist-oriented leaders of the United Electrical Workers set the wage pattern for a big slice of heavy industry. By accepting a fifteen-cent-an-hour wage offer from General Motors—about 30 percent less than that considered minimal in the Nathan Report—the UE forced Reuther to take the same medicine when he signed the UAW-GM contract later in the month.

By 1948, therefore, Reuther needed to demonstrate that his newly minted slogan, "Teamwork in the Leadership, Solidarity in the Ranks," would finally pay off for the mass of ordinary autoworkers. But despite his bold rhetoric, UAW prospects for a breakthrough on the wage front were hardly promising. Although inflation still eroded weekly pay packets, the prospects for a renewal of price controls—still the cornerstone of the Reuther-Montgomery program to defend working-class living standards—appeared nil with the Republicans in control of both houses of Congress and labor-liberal disaffection with President Truman virtually unanimous. Meanwhile, all of the big corporations had taken a hard line as the unions geared up for a third round of postwar wage bargaining. Big steel set the tone by rejecting USW requests for any wage advance over 1947. General Electric followed suit in its industry, and Ford demanded an actual wage cut. Meatpacking workers launched an industrywide strike, but it collapsed after nine weeks.[18]

Reuther sought a total of thirty cents an hour from General Motors, but unlike 1945, he encountered active opposition to his bargaining strategy from within the UAW. In Flint the presidents of five big GM locals had organized a caucus to wrest the initiative from Reuther in the 1948 bargaining round. Their most immediate "radical" demand was for a "sliding scale of wages" linked to the cost of living. The idea had been popularized on the labor-left by Leon Trotsky, who argued for the concept as part of his 1938 "transitional program" (to socialism). During the war the idea of an annual cost-of-living adjustment (COLA) gained wider currency on the non-Communist left as an alternative to the more statist program of wage and price controls advocated by CIO leaders and Democratic Party liberals.[19]

Reuther was firmly opposed to the idea. Like most laborites from Samuel Gompers and Eugene Debs onward, he rejected any linkage of wages to the cost of living. With the general wage declines of 1921, 1930–32, and 1938 still a living memory, virtually all union leaders instinctively rejected the premise upon which a postwar COLA formula might be based: the emergence of a new era of inflationary prosperity and relative social peace. Trade union officials in both the AFL and CIO thought such a wage formula foreclosed the possibility of a large increase in the real standard of living, and they continued to fear that it would become a downhill escalator when the inevitable postwar depression finally arrived. Publicly debating the issue with his Flint opposition, Reuther had little trouble retaining control of the GM wage negotiations, but the price of the controversy was high. Sixteen locals, including Buick in Flint and the key tool and die shop, Fisher No. 23 in Detroit, voted against strike action in April and May 1948.[20]

General Motors was a close observer of UAW politics that spring. Charles Wilson had greeted Walter Reuther's consolidation of power in the union with a certain satisfaction. Reuther's larger social vision was clearly anathema to him, but nearly ten years of bargaining experience had convinced GM officials that here was a man with whom they could do business. Wilson thought a long-range accommodation with the UAW was now possible, to contain unionism within what he considered its "proper sphere." Otherwise, declared the GM president, the "border area of collective bargaining will be a constant battleground between unions and management." To lower the rhetorical temperature, Wilson reshuffled his industrial relations team, replacing shop-educated production bosses like Harry Coen, who had denounced Reuther as a socialist in the big strike of 1945–46, with the more adroit Harry Anderson and Louis Seaton, men with backgrounds in law and marketing.[21] Stability and control of the production regime remained of paramount importance to General Motors, but now the corporation was ready to pay a premium for such predictability, if only to ensure the success of its $3.5 billion expansion program designed to boost postwar production capacity by more than 50 percent over prewar levels. New factories were being built in California, New York, Texas, and Ohio, and GM's blue-collar payroll had grown by one-quarter, to nearly 280,000.

The corporation had staved off the UAW effort to link company pricing policy to its wage demands, but Charles Wilson recognized, perhaps as early as 1942, that the Reutherite effort to advance real wages in an inflationary environment had to be resolved. Many businessmen thought the solution to the wage-price spiral lay in the reduction of monetary inflation to an absolute minimum; their preferred strategy required a sharp cut in government spending, tough negotiations with the unions, and a spot of unemployment. Given the scope of GM's postwar expansion program, Wilson recognized the political and social impracticality of such a course in 1948. Despite Taft-Hartley, big unions like the UAW still had the capacity to disrupt management's production schedule. The auto union had authorized 409 strikes and organized more than two hundred thousand new members in the two years following Reuther's consolidation of power late in 1947. Often couched as part of a broader offensive against corporate power, these continuing work stoppages, as well as the union's annual set of wage negotiations, embittered shop-floor labor relations and hampered corporate planning. Given GM's sensational return on investment—28 percent during the first quarter of 1948—and the public's insatiable demand for cars, Wilson and his new team of industrial relations professionals were determined to reach a settlement with the UAW that stabilized production for as long as possible. To Peter Drucker, Wilson put all this in the language of Whig democracy: GM's corporate founders had built a most efficient and centralized institution, but "to develop citizenship and community is the task of the next generation. We are, so to speak, going to be the Jeffersonians to Mr. Sloan's Federalists."[22]

Further, Charles Wilson knew that the inflationary pressures generated by cold war military spending promised to be a permanent feature of the economic scene. In the spring of 1948 Marshall Plan spending had swept through Congress with only marginal opposition from the right wing of the Republican Party; likewise, the Czechoslovakian coup in February had seemingly ensured passage of both a new draft law and the Truman administration's $3.3 billion military procurement package.[23] Reuther rejected military Keynesianism, but labor did not have the power to influence the defense budget: "That is out of our reach," he told an executive board meeting in the fall of 1948. Instead, the union would have to adapt to the consequences of the militarized boom, "through collective bargaining."[24]

And finally, the assassination attempt on Reuther's life may well have convinced Wilson and his colleagues that the maintenance of UAW stability required a bold initiative from the corporation. GM therefore broke corporate ranks and offered the union what Reuther would ruefully call a "blue plate special." Wilson proposed a two-year contract that increased wages by a rather nice eleven cents an hour. But of far greater import than the size of the wage boost was what Wilson called a "new approach to the living cost problem." First, GM would make quarterly cost-of-living adjustments keyed to changes in the consumer price index of the Bureau of Labor Statistics (BLS); second, the corporation committed itself to a 2 percent annual improvement factor (AIF) wage increase each year, designed to reflect, if only partially, the still-larger annual rise in GM productivity. Against the inclinations of some DuPont-oriented executives, who wanted cost-of-living increases measured on a regional basis, Wilson's offer confirmed the success of Reuther's decade-long effort to establish corporationwide wage standards. General Motors, with 45 percent of the domestic market and no foreign rivals, could easily "administer" any price increases made necessary by the new labor contract.[25]

Just out of the hospital, Reuther discussed the GM offer at bedside meetings with key union aides. Then on May 25 Vice President Jack Livingston and Assistant GM Director Art Johnstone signed the two-year contract for the UAW. Reuther praised the agreement for breaking the "big business conspiracy" that had held up the long-deferred third round of postwar wage hikes. But he still rejected the larger political implications of the COLA/AIF principle. In a press release that undoubtedly reflected Reuther's views, the union described the 1948 pact as but a "holding operation" that would protect the income of GM workers in the "context of today's economic and political reaction." GM's wage formula was acceptable "only because most of those in control of government and industry show no signs of acting in the public interest. They are enforcing a system of private planning for private profit at public expense." The UAW still fought for price controls and an overall shift in the sociopolitical balance of power. "General Motors workers cannot be bribed with the wooden nickels of inflation into withdrawing from the fight against the greedy industrialists and subservient politicians who caused and condoned the price rises which are now undermining the living standards of millions of families."[26]

This was a brave and radical critique of GM's strategy, one final protest against the corporate effort to contain, constrain, and privatize industrial unionism's economic agenda. But against his spirited rhetoric and egalitarian social vision stood the lure of GM's money, the power of the corporation, and the remarkable productivity of the auto industry's postwar factories. In the UAW the ideological turning point, at least among the union leaders, came in February 1949 when the BLS index dropped and GM cut its wages by three cents an hour. There was much grumbling in the ranks, so for the first time Reuther had to mobilize his executive board to defend the 1948 contract as a progressive initiative—"a tremendous victory"—that preserved the real wages of hundreds of thousands of autoworkers. General Motors was also pleased with the results of the 1948 contract: inflation had proven modest, the level of work stoppages was lower than ever, and its annual productivity gain was well above 2 percent. The UAW "did a remarkable job of administering the contract," admitted Harry Anderson. ". . . The experience through the period from 1948 to 1950 was very, very good."[27]

Thus neither the UAW nor General Motors had much difficulty in reaching a new agreement in May 1950. Indeed, once Reuther's inner circle had made the decision to accept GM's requirement for a contract that ran a full five years, the UAW president was hardly needed at the bargaining table. GM made monetary improvements in the cost-of-living formula and the annual improvement factor, agreed to a pension of $125 a month, and paid half the cost of a new health insurance plan. Observers of American industrial relations greeted the contract with something close to incredulity. *Fortune* famously hailed the settlement as the "Treaty of Detroit." *Business Week* called it "industrial statesmanship of a very high order," and the *Washington Post* declared it "a great event in industrial history." By guaranteeing autoworkers a 20 percent increase in their standard of living over the next half-decade, the UAW-GM contract represented the greatest economic gain won by any of the big unions since before the war. Negotiated quickly and in complete secrecy, this industrial concord neatly sidestepped the protracted wrangling that had shut down steel mills and coal mines and forced workers at Ford, International Harvester, and Chrysler out on long and bitter strikes during the previous year.[28] The *New York Times* compared the GM contract with Ford's promulgation of the five-dollar-a-day wage thirty-seven years before; and just as Henry Ford's industrial innovations had made him something more than a successful business-man, so too, speculated the *Times*, would Reuther's next surprise put him on the road to the White House.[29]

Reuther himself called the contract—in which GM finally conceded the union shop—"the most significant development in labor relations since the mass production industries were organized." This time Reuther failed to denounce GM's effort to buy off the UAW at the expense of the consuming public; instead, he pointed to the "maturing relationship" between the union and the company and rationalized the union's five-year commitment to the COLA principle by claiming that GM had been compelled to "abandon the practice of capturing in the market place through higher prices what it yields at the bargaining table in higher wages." From this point onward Reuther and his comrades at the top of the UAW championed the COLA/AIF clauses as among the union's proudest achievements.[30]

Quickly spreading to much of unionized heavy industry, the Treaty of Detroit proved a milestone from which there was no turning back. It signaled the end of the era in which Reuther—as the boldest spirit in the leadership of the industrial union movement—could hope for a serious transformation in the governing structures of American industry. Writing for *Fortune*, Daniel Bell, once himself a comrade of Reuther's in the Socialist Party, summed up the meaning of the contract: "GM may have paid a billion for peace but it got a bargain. General Motors has regained control over one of the crucial management functions . . . long range scheduling of production, model changes, and tool and plant investment." It was the first contract "that unmistakably accepts the existing distribution of income between wages and profits as 'normal' if not as 'fair.'. . . It is the first major union contract that explicitly accepts objective economic facts—cost of living and productivity—as determining wages, thus throwing overboard all theories of wages as determined by political power and of profits as 'surplus value.'"[31]

The Korean War, which broke out in late June 1950, confirmed the solidity as well as the definitive limits of the Treaty of Detroit within the U.S. political economy. At the level of mobilization politics and corporatist bargaining, Reuther found that the UAW and the rest of the labor movement had even less voice than in World War II. With production requirements limited and the labor movement a known quantity, the Truman administration was uninterested in either a no-strike pledge or a general system of tripartite governance. Instead, the president let a virtually autonomous Federal Reserve Board use its credit controls to suppress consumer demand and fight inflationary pressures. Regulations X and W raised down-payment requirements and shortened loan schedules to slash the capacity of working-class Americans to buy cars and houses. Reuther thought this "meat-axe" approach discriminated in favor of high-income families, generated auto industry unemployment, and made no provision for the orderly shift of factories and jobs from civilian to military production. Reuther lobbied hard during the fall and winter of 1950–51, but all his efforts, and those of the AFL-CIO's United Labor Policy Committee, merely demonstrated labor's marginality in the administration of what many Truman aides were now calling a permanent war economy.[32]

But the UAW contracts were another story. Late on the afternoon of December 12, 1950, Don Montgomery phoned Reuther with the alarming news that Truman's new economic stabilizer, Alan Valentine, had prepared a draft order freezing auto wages. Reuther immediately flew to Washington with Richard Gosser, the UAW vice president whose reputation as Toledo's powerful labor boss was then at its height. The next day Reuther told Valentine and his superior, Stuart Symington of Emerson Electric, then chairman of the National Security Resources Board, that any government tampering with the UAW's escalator and annual improvement clauses would almost certainly generate "unrest and instability." Reuther's prediction was an unmistakable threat taken seriously by government officials, industry leaders, and the autoworkers back in the shop. Within days Valentine rewrote his order to exempt, for at least three months, COLA and AIF wage increases from any controls. Of course, Reuther's swift victory had a silent partner: the big auto corporations, which also saw the UAW's five-year contracts as a cornerstone of social and economic stability. This partnership was confirmed in May 1951 when the Wage Stabilization Board considered yet another ceiling on wage escalation. The National Association of Manufacturers spoke for many employers in labor-intensive industry who wanted the government to crack down, but GM's Harry Anderson offered a down-the-line defense of his corporation's labor contract. "Spoken like a true *yipsel* [YPSL, Young People's Socialist League], Harry," muttered a CIO observer in the hearing room.[33]

Given his assumptions about the stability of the automobile industry and its centrality to the American economy, Reuther saw the Treaty of Detroit not as a straitjacket but as a solid foundation upon which to build. At the top of Reuther's bargaining agenda stood the erection of what proved to be a private welfare state for UAW members. The stalemate that had descended over U.S. domestic politics had stymied labor-liberal efforts to win for working-class Americans adequate public funding of a range of social benefits: health care, pensions, unemployment insurance, vacations. Like almost all other unionists, Reuther had long found company provision of such welfare programs distasteful—their coverage was incomplete, the financing was indeterminate, and they smacked of old-fashioned paternalism. He favored a public, federal system for financing social provision. During the war both the CIO and AFL had worked for the passage of the Wagner-Murray-Dingell bill, which would have liberalized and federalized the American social welfare system in a fashion similar to that envisioned by the British government's pathbreaking Beveridge Report of 1942, the blueprint for the Labour government's postwar welfare state.[34]

But the lurch to the right after the war again sidelined labor-liberal efforts to increase the social wage. The Congress elected in 1946 failed to raise social security benefit levels and blocked Truman administration efforts to pass a national health insurance scheme. For a typical worker whose nominal wage had doubled in the decade after 1939, social security benefits dropped by half, to only 11 percent of working income. In 1949 the United States devoted about 4.4 percent of its GNP to social security, a proportion less than half that of even the austere economies of war-torn Western Europe.[35]

The political impasse drove American trade unionists toward negotiation of their own firm-centered welfare state. Company-financed fringe benefits had been put on the union bargaining agenda during World War II, initially when such schemes were given important tax advantages (1942), and then more forcefully when the War Labor Board exempted the cost of "fringe" benefits from the government's wage ceiling in a politically adroit maneuver designed to derail union efforts to break the Little Steel formula (1943).[36] During the war, industrial unionists proved notably unenthusiastic about exploiting such opportunities, but immediately after the 1946 elections the CIO announced that it was not going to wait "for perhaps another ten years until the Social Security laws are amended adequately." Reuther and other unionists of an explicitly social democratic outlook tried to give the new strategy a corporatist twist, theorizing that if collective bargaining saddled employers with large pension and health insurance costs, management itself would join "shoulder to shoulder" with labor-liberal forces to demand higher federal payments to relieve them of this burden.[37] Big business still rejected health care and pension bargaining as yet another union invasion of its prerogatives, but a protracted struggle waged by the United Mine Workers over these issues in 1946 and 1947 broke the dike, and the Supreme Court's 1949 decision in the Inland Steel case made management failure to bargain over such fringe benefits an unfair labor practice. By the end of 1949 more than half of all strikes were over health and welfare issues in labor contracts.[38]

Reuther saw pensions as the key bargaining issue of 1949. The UAW focused its firepower on Ford, where an aging workforce and a new management seemed to provide the best circumstances for winning the auto industry's first big pension contract. The negotiations were technically complex and fraught with political difficulty, but the September 1949 agreement established a collective bargaining tactic that Reuther would return to time and again. The power and political volatility of the big Rouge workforce always kept both Reuther and the Ford labor relations executives on their toes. Thus, when the UAW sought an innovation in its contract, Reuther usually turned to the second-largest automaker. Ford was still a family-held firm, but "young Henry" was thought to be something of a maverick: since taking over the company in 1945, he had set out to dismantle the autocratic system that flourished under his grandfather, replacing it with a spirit of "human engineering." Ford was also big enough to set the bargaining precedents that the rest of the industry had to follow and that General Motors might well sweeten in the next round of negotiations. Reuther called this connected bargaining "getting a foot in the door." Thus the 1949 Ford contract offered autoworkers with thirty years' service pensions of $100 a month, but the UAW persuaded GM to increase the payment to $125 when the two parties signed their famous "treaty" eight months later.[39]

The UAW was not the only trade union to win pension benefits at this time, but Reuther proved by far the most forceful and effective propagandist for the new "fringe benefit." Toward auto executives who already enjoyed handsome retirement packages, he opened the floodgates of class resentment. Privately, Reuther thought Charles Wilson "a very decent, genuine human being," but the UAW leader offered his corporate adversary no quarter in public debate. Reuther advertised GM's guarantee that Wilson would enjoy a pension of twenty-five thousand dollars a year in retirement, although his annual salary and bonus payments already came to more than half a million dollars. Exclaimed Reuther, "If you make $258 an hour, they give it to you. If you make $1.65 an hour, they say: 'You don't need it, you're not entitled to it, and we are not going to give it to you.'" Reuther popularized the telling phrase, "too old to work and too young to die," to dramatize the plight of many retired workers. Reuther proved equally passionate on the need for company-funded medical care, but because of its relatively low cost in 1950 and the union's decision to accept an insurance-based system, the issue raised little controversy until costs ballooned in the late 1960s.[40]

Unlike John L. Lewis, and later Jimmy Hoffa, Reuther did not demand union control of the pension funds, but he insisted that corporations fund their pension obligations according to the most actuarially stringent standards. When in the winter of 1950 Chrysler executives balked at this UAW requirement, Reuther insisted upon a strike despite much evidence that few autoworkers understood the concept of an "actuarially sound" pension plan. The work stoppage proved exceedingly bitter. When finally concluded after 104 days, Reuther refused to pose for the ritual handshake with Chrysler executives. Nor did he win the fully funded pension scheme he had demanded. But he had made his point: the UAW could inflict great damage upon any automaker that refused to follow the pattern established at Ford. In this case, Chrysler walked away from one billion dollars in sales and lost forever its chance to supplant Ford as the number-two automaker. Chrysler thereafter followed the auto industry pattern.[41]

Reuther was equally passionate about the UAW's next major campaign, to win a guaranteed annual wage (GAW) in the 1955 collective bargaining round. Advocates of the idea—which had been central to the industrial union agenda since the 1930s—proposed winning the GAW either through a reduction of the workweek to thirty hours or, as Reuther would advocate time and again, through tripartite governance of the industry. By the 1950s Reuther knew that the UAW was not about to win a direct hand in auto industry management, but he and Nat Weinberg, his key aide in the campaign to win a guaranteed annual wage, thought that the union might well negotiate a plan that both guaranteed laid-off workers an income stream and confronted employers with a set of financial penalties severe enough to force them to reschedule production and regularize employment on an annual basis.[42]

Reuther saw the GAW campaign, which lasted for the next four years, as economic policy-making on the grand scale. Weinberg had more than two decades of New Deal–Fair Deal investigation of the problem to build upon, and he set up a committee of sympathetic economists to advise the union and justify its program. Such elaborate preparations proved good "psychological warfare to convince employers that we really mean business on the guaranteed employment question." As in all his bargaining rhetoric, Reuther framed the union's push as part of an effort to transform the entire political economy. By committing themselves to the payment of an annual wage, American managers would come to "to see the virtues of broader planning, in their plants and in the national economy." Soon they would demand that government itself "shoulder its proper share of the cost of unemployment and its proper share of the responsibility for preventing it." Reuther reclaimed the language of his Debsian youth to denounce industry's "productive process" as one in which "Man, instead of being the end, becomes the mere means—a tool of production. . . . He is a cost to be eliminated the moment there is no need for his services." The union's annual wage was therefore "a demand for a proper scale of moral values which puts people above property, men above machines," thus eliminating "the immoral double standard under which the worker, of all those who draw their incomes from industry, has the least protection against economic adversity." Given such stakes, it is hardly surprising that in 1955 Reuther had convinced himself that millions of workers at home and abroad were asking one question: "Are the autoworkers going to break through on the annual wage?"[43]

By this point, collective bargaining in the auto industry had assumed a ritualistic form. In the months leading up to the start of negotiations, Reuther and other top union officials would hold scores of meetings and conduct dozens of conferences to sell their bargaining program to local union activists, measure their enthusiasm, and note the grievances that flowed upward from the shops. When negotiations actually began, Reuther would always speak first. Flanked by upwards of twenty union officials and staff experts, he would deliver a long and passionate presentation of the union's demands intended to win public approval, rally the troops, and convince his corporate adversaries that the union leadership had the will to strike. Company officials often bet among themselves as to how long Reuther would talk, but they made little effort to upstage the UAW president. When John Bugas rejected the UAW's annual wage proposal by asserting, "This is something that we will never, never do," Reuther replied with a certain twinkle, "Never say never, John."[44]

In the days just before the contract termination, Reuther would return to the bargaining table. Now the crucial decisions had to be made about what issues would be discarded, where trade-offs could be made, and whether the UAW would actually strike. These bargaining sessions often ran eighteen to twenty hours a day. If Reuther showed reporters his toothbrush, they took it as a signal that the bargaining was in a crucial phase. Reuther sometimes took a nap, but more often he kept himself alert with soft drinks, chewing gum, and constant talk. Since Reuther's birthday was usually spent in negotiations, somebody was sure to present him with a cake. In 1955 GM's Louis Seaton gave him a modest one; moments later reporters came in with a second, bigger birthday cake. "Like the GM offer," Reuther joked, "Mr. Seaton's cake was inadequate." Thereafter, the journalistic language of pattern bargaining was always that of a sweet shop: "Do you expect to get any frosting on the cake at GM, Walter? Do you expect to get à la mode at Ford?"[45]

In the GAW negotiations Ford was determined to set a definitive limit to its financial liability under any plan that mandated company payments to laid-off autoworkers. When Bugas offered the UAW a complicated proposal to make employees interest-free loans on the security of the stock they had accumulated in a payroll deduction scheme, Reuther exploded: "John, please don't insult our integrity . . . when you know and I know that this is the General Motors Corporation proposal, which we rejected two weeks ago—and you haven't changed a word of it." With no hint of a bluff, Reuther concluded, "You have just bought yourself a God-damned strike." Bugas countered with the claim that a Ford survey of its employees found that almost 90 percent favored the stock ownership plan to the UAW annual wage scheme. In turn, Reuther offered to put the issue to a referendum vote.[46]

Such was the gamesmanship of big-time collective bargaining in its heyday. In the end Ford agreed to a highly modified version of the UAW's annual wage idea. The company would put five cents an hour for each worker into a trust fund that could be drawn on to provide payments of twenty-five dollars a week for laid-off workers (up to half a year). With unemployment compensation added in, a worker might well take home up to 65 percent of his or her regular pay. The 1955 version of the GAW was therefore rather like the Holy Roman Empire—neither guaranteed, annual, nor a wage. It was best described by its new name: supplemental unemployment benefits (SUB). Of course, Reuther knew that the 1955 Ford contract was just the start: over the next twelve years, four contract renegotiations were required to finally bring SUB payments up to 95 percent of take-home pay for fifty-two weeks of idleness.[47]

The conclusion of the GAW negotiations brought Reuther his second appearance on the cover of *Time* magazine and an additional round of applause from the establishment press. Virtually all commentators took Reuther's bargaining rhetoric at face value: the *Christian Science Monitor* called the settlement "one more piece of evidence that the world in which we are living is evolving rapidly away from the calculations of Karl Marx." Even the *Daily Worker* called the GAW contract a "breakthrough," a sentiment confirmed on the right by the National Association of Manufacturers, whose president warned industry that capitulation to labor's demand for a guaranteed annual wage would lead straight to "a socialistic state and controlled economy."[48]

Reuther himself was increasingly convinced that his brand of collective bargaining offered working-class Americans all the hope and progress his generation had once invested in the socialist movement. Publicly, Reuther lost few opportunities to distance himself from a Marxist worldview and celebrate what he called "the genius of the American economy." He admired the social democracy of northern Europe but thought the productivity of American capitalism so great and the structure of American society in such flux as to make class politics counterproductive in the United States. Thus in 1958, when the British journalist Henry Brandon needled Reuther for his ideological confusion, the UAW leader shot back: "The American labor movement is as radical on basic things as the European labor movement, but we don't dress our things up with socialist slogans. . . . We are pragmatic; if a thing will work, we are for doing it—if it's radical or conservative—we're for doing it."[49] Like any trade unionist, Reuther had to duck and weave and make his compromises, but his vision of how he wanted collective bargaining to reshape American society was still an optimistic, Whiggish, evolutionary, and deterministic schema, echoing the socialist values of his youth. "Collective bargaining is an eternal struggle," Reuther once affirmed. "Fifty years from now . . . the standard of living will be fantastic. . . . They will look back at this period and think we were a bunch of cave dwellers." Observed a wry admirer, "Reuther is the only man I know who can reminisce about the future."[50]

By 1955 Reuther thought collective bargaining with the Big Three automakers might well generate in the United States the kind of classwide settlement that was characteristic of industry-labor relationships in northern Europe. The UAW, repeated Reuther time and again, was not interested "in just another nickel in the envelope." The innovations and monetary gains won at Ford and General Motors were bound to spread to the rest of the auto firms and parts suppliers and then to UAW-organized plants in the agricultural implement and aircraft fields. Economists called this "pattern bargaining," and virtually all observers thought it essential to a mature, responsible system of labor relations in the United States. Through friendly competition between the UAW, the Teamsters, the Steel Workers, and the Machinists, powerful unions in both the CIO and AFL made certain such contract improvements were widely diffused throughout heavy industry. To avoid unionization, firms like Weirton Steel and Thompson Products (a big auto parts firm), as well as virtually all manufacturing employers of white-collar labor, made their wage and benefit packages track those of the blue-collar unions. By the early 1960s the COLA principle had been incorporated into about half of all union contracts, and one-third of the entire workforce held some form of pension coverage.[51]

Reuther was equally convinced that the "special leverage that we have at the bargaining table" could be used to pry open the doors long closed to government expansion of the welfare state. The key to this strategy was the transformation of the big corporations from opponents into supporters of government social spending. As Reuther put it in 1951, "When you begin to put some pressure on their pocketbook nerve, they jump through hoops." Beginning with its 1949 push for pensions, the UAW structured its fringe benefit demands inversely to the level of government support. At first the strategy seemed to pay off. After the pension breakthrough in 1949, Congress increased social security payments by an average of 77 percent; then in 1955 the UAW's annual wage formula prompted legislatures in several industrial states to boost unemployment compensation.[52] "Our fight in this field of social security has not been for our members alone," boasted Reuther. "We have fought for all the people."[53]

During the 1950s it became a commonplace to assert that because of higher pay, greater job security, and better fringe benefits, American unionism had, in the words of a 1951 issue of *Fortune*, "made the worker to an amazing degree a middle-class member of a middle-class society." A generation of social commentators assumed that the consumerist embourgeoisement of the American working class—reflected, to take just one telling example, by the surge of advertisements for cars, kitchen appliances, and suburban homes that now appeared in the pages of many autotown papers—had accommodated this postwar generation to the alienating labor that still characterized factory life. The decline of overt strike violence and the routine character of much collective bargaining seemed to eclipse the old struggles at the point of production. As Reuther himself so often asserted, a larger economic pie was more easily divided than a small one. An "economy of abundance" ameliorated all social conflicts and generated a richer and more rewarding life for all.[54]

The extent to which American autoworkers readily traded alienating work for good pay proved a major fallacy of midcentury social science and popular journalism, but there is no doubt that UAW members enthusiastically endorsed their union as a prime vehicle for winning a higher standard of living. In the 1948 referenda mandated by the Taft-Hartley Act to determine the fate of their union shop contracts, autoworker turnout was both exceptionally heavy and almost unanimous in support of the UAW. More than 98 percent of all Ford workers voted to back the union, a result that management officials had to admit was "astounding."[55] The five-year contract of 1950 also won near-unanimous endorsement. At the Fisher Body local in Cleveland, Leo Fenster remembered that the left-wing executive board opposed ratification. "The membership listened politely, and then by a vote of ten to one agreed to accept the new contract. . . . In the minds of the members the union was firmly established; if its effectiveness were threatened they would resist. . . . But beyond this there was the realism of a new kind of life to live. . . . Now there were homes and autos and appliances to pay for; children to educate. The question of a five year contract was comparatively theoretical."[56]

Between 1947 and 1960 average wages in the automobile industry nearly doubled to almost six thousand dollars a year. This was not quite enough for an urban family of four to achieve a "moderate" standard of living, as defined by the Bureau of Labor Statistics (a five-room house, maintenance of a four-year-old Chevy, no savings), but it represented real progress for the generation of autoworkers who had come of age when Depression memories were still fresh. In Detroit, Flint, and Toledo the proportion of owner-occupied homes reached levels among the highest in the nation. However, their good pay was not matched by employment security: after 1948 big layoffs and plant closings were a regular feature of automobile employment. During the recession of 1957–58 it took almost seventeen years' seniority to retain a production job in Detroit. In that downturn, 70 percent of laid-off autoworkers reported that they had reduced the amount of money they spent on clothing, and 60 percent spent less on groceries.[57]

This combination—high pay and employment insecurity—generated widespread support for Reuther's bargaining goals. In 1961 a Louis Harris survey found that autoworkers strongly backed union efforts to secure better retirement and unemployment benefits and greater protections against layoffs and short workweeks. Although a remarkably high proportion of UAW members were unclear as to the actual composition of their fringe benefit package, autoworkers solidly backed the International as a wage-setting and welfare-enhancing institution. This support further consolidated Reuther's enormous prestige within autoworker ranks. Confidential interviews with delegates to the 1959 convention found that 87 percent regarded Walter Reuther as the outstanding labor leader in the United States. One local union president, long identified with the Flint opposition, flatly asserted, "Walter Reuther is qualified not only to be president of the UAW but of the United States of America."[58]

But whatever its economic benefits, the Treaty of Detroit did not transform American autoworkers into one-dimensional consumers, oblivious to the conditions of their work life. Indeed, the accord set the stage for a generation of trench warfare in the auto shops; casualties remained heavy, and the union defense unrelenting. There is little doubt that the big auto corporations interpreted their détente with the UAW as an occasion to mount a workplace offensive to rewin from their employees the control over production standards, work schedules, and job assignments that most corporate officials felt they had lost during the union drives of the late 1930s and the era of government-subsidized war production that followed. When during the GM negotiations of 1948 the UAW made yet another stab at winning some modification to section 63(b), the much-debated contract clause that restricted the application of the seniority principle in departmental transfers, company negotiators soon handed their union counterparts a fifty-five-page brief defending management prerogatives on this single issue. "I've been given the polite No, the long No, and the short No, but this is the first monumental No," quipped Art Johnstone, then standing in for Reuther as head of the General Motors Department. Under the 1948 agreement, boasted Harry Anderson, GM had "conceded no ground whatsoever on fundamental principle matters which would have the tendency of watering down management's responsibility to manage the business."[59]

GM's brand of midcentury Fordism proved as much an ideological construct as a business strategy. Because General Motors had so clearly established the industry norm for labor discipline and productivity, the management of every other auto firm felt it essential to conform to the new standard regardless of market niche or shop tradition. To make the transition, GM executives were often pirated outright and GM production technique and personnel policies closely emulated. Ford began its industrial relations shakeup in the late 1940s; Chrysler, Packard, Studebaker, and International Harvester followed suit in the mid-1950s. By 1958 a so-called new look in American industrial relations had put managers on the offensive throughout unionized heavy industry. Not all efforts were successful, but the shifting balance of power kept shop tensions high and the union political pot on the boil.[60]

Reuther was not insensitive to the corporate strategy. Within months of signing the 1948 accord he charged GM with a "concerted drive" to "speed-up" autoworkers. Instead of relying upon new technology or more efficient organization of production, the UAW asserted, GM managers sought "to recapture the productivity increase provided by the present agreement from additional demands upon the workers' energy alone." To demonstrate union resolve, Reuther dismissed Saul Wallen, the UAW-GM grievance umpire, because his rulings had penalized shop committeemen for "talking back" to foremen; the UAW president also beefed up the union's Engineering Department, where Robert Kanter, his old SP comrade, taught autoworkers time-study techniques with which to counter company foremen and engineers. Most important, Reuther and his union officers authorized scores of strikes, many over production standard issues. In 1949 Reuther bragged to his executive board that Detroit was still the strike capital of America. He was determined that the union would continue the "historic struggle in resisting speed-up with every weapon. . . . We will mobilize our Union to fight against speed-up wherever it raises its ugly head, whether it be in the small plant or Ford Motor Company or General Motors or Chrysler."[61]

Yet Reuther's capacity to lead this fight was subverted by both the ideology and the structure of the collective bargaining relationship he had built with the principal automakers. The concept of an "annual improvement factor" had made it clear that a "cooperative attitude" by the union and workers was a necessary ingredient in increased productivity. Reuther himself took pride in the UAW's rejection of "featherbedding." When asked whether he favored a ban on the introduction of new machines, he replied, "Nothing could be more wicked or foolish. You can't stop technological progress and it would be silly to try it if you could." In tribute, a railroad executive bedeviled by a century of encrusted work rules hailed "the management clause in the Ford contract [as] a production man's dream."[62]

Productivity became an issue again in the early 1950s, when a brief recession at the end of the Korean War gave automakers the opportunity to merge, close, or relocate scores of Detroit-area factories. Hudson, Motor Products, Packard, and Murray Body closed their doors, Chrysler took over Briggs, and Ford slashed the big Rouge payroll by twenty thousand. Ford won worldwide attention when it moved engine block production to an "automated" factory in Brook Park, Ohio, just outside of Cleveland. There a series of automatic machine tools, loaders, and transfer lines cut manpower by 90 percent on the traditionally labor-intensive operation. To liberal intellectuals and practical labor leaders, automation raised ominous possibilities. Typical were the authoritative views of MIT's Norbert Weiner, who had pioneered in the field of programmable machine tools. Initiating a correspondence in 1949, he wrote Reuther to warn that, "in the hands of the present industrial set-up, the unemployment produced by such plants can only be disastrous."[63]

Rouge Local 600, clearly Ford's chief target in the corporate decentralization drive, responded with a campaign for a sharp reduction in the workweek: thirty hours' work for forty hours' pay, a demand once endorsed by unionists of almost every political coloration. But as a solution to automation and job loss, Reuther rejected "30 for 40" in the early 1950s. Given the tenor of the times, the Reutherites denounced the Rouge proposal as a Communist-inspired effort to subvert America's cold war production effort. They would soon abandon such demagoguery, but Reuther proved far too much of a technocrat to temper his faith in the efficiency of the Fordist production regime. With some success, the UAW negotiated areawide transfer rights for workers displaced by plant closures and made certain that new job classifications generated by new technology did not erode the general wage structure. But the union's overall approach reflected a technological determinism that saw productivity growth as an autonomous process divorced from the character of class relations. Thus the union argued that the timing of a union push for a decrease in work hours depended upon "the forward march of science and technology [which] since the beginning of the industrial revolution has enabled men in our industrial society to create greater economic wealth."[64]

This argument was a repudiation of American labor's traditional view: that high wages and shorter hours themselves encourage capitalists to invent and buy new machinery. A shorter workweek became part of Reuther's long-range agenda, but in the meantime, he retained the faith that a combination of Keynesian demand stimulation and government economic planning were tools sufficient to handle unemployment, if only policy makers made use of them. Americans in general and autoworkers in particular were still in very real need of more of the world's basic material goods. Reuther's macroeconomic focus on such technological change is evident in what may well have been his most celebrated exchange with any representative of automotive management. When Reuther toured the new Brook Park engine plant in 1952, a Ford executive taunted him with the remark, "You know, Walter, not one of these machines pays union dues." To which Reuther shot back, "And not one of them buys new Ford cars, either."[65]

The automation hysteria of the mid-1950s soon passed. Automation—or rather, the capital-intensive and inflexible "Detroit automation" pioneered at Ford—spread throughout the industry, but it engendered no robot factories. Automobile industry employment grew by about 15 percent in the two decades that followed the Treaty of Detroit, even as factory productivity more than doubled. But technological change on the factory floor is not just about employment. It is about power, politics, and social choice. Some of the most bitterly fought battles of the postwar era were fought on this terrain: on the docks, where containerization transformed longshore work; in the press room, where the reign of the linotype finally gave way to cold type composition; and in the machine shop, where engineers and machinists battled for control of the programming function on the first generation of automated tools.[66] Similar conflicts took place in every UAW-organized factory. The annual model change kept work assignments, personnel schedules, and production technology in constant flux. As one Ford local discovered, "We had some 350 production standard disputes . . . but we found that in a number of cases after the disputes were settled, management would change the method, operation, and in some cases the work assignment of the employees. As a result of these changes other standard disputes developed, and we found ourselves going back thru [sic] the same occurrences."[67]

During the five-year contract, wildcat strike activity increased at all of the Big Three automakers, after which it retreated to a level only slightly less than that of the 1940s. General Motors retained its reputation for shop discipline, but the company's hard line merely shifted conflict to the formal grievance procedure: GM's volume of grievance filings rose more than fivefold in the decade that began with the Treaty of Detroit. In 1958 more than eleven thousand unresolved grievances were hanging fire at the expiration of the contract. When the UAW surveyed its membership in the 1960s, workers approved of strikes called over workloads and local issues to a greater degree than those called over the national contract, but they were also more likely to think the handling of such strikes "only fair" or "poor." When asked whether they thought their committeeman was a "stand up guy who protects the workers," only 16 percent answered in the affirmative in 1967, down from a less-than-impressive 26 percent six years earlier.[68]

These shop conflicts were often a jungle of conflicting claims, not only between union and management but between workers themselves: between skilled workers and the "upgraders" who sought admission to their craft, between high- and low-seniority workers, and between those who favored more overtime and those who wanted less work. Though the UAW negotiated remarkably egalitarian pay scales, the quality of the jobs under the Fordist regime remained radically uneven. In his classic study of a Lansing Oldsmobile plant right after the war, *Automobile Workers and the American Dream*, Ely Chinoy found that workers themselves understood the factory as a highly stratified set of jobs ranging from the assembly line at the bottom to skilled nonproduction work at the top. Like all work, it was not so much the physical labor itself that was objectionable but the condition of unfreedom in which it was performed.[69]

Because the union could do so little to transform the quality of these occupations—the emasculation of the shop steward system and the defeat of foreman unionism had already eliminated two essential tools—autoworkers and their local union officials did their utmost to build classification and seniority walls around the work considered most pleasant and dignified. Walter Reuther offered little leadership in this rearguard battle, but the incremental proliferation of a highly complex set of defensive work rules and restrictive job definitions would eventually come to play its part in the subversion of the very productivity gain upon which the UAW president had staked so much.[70]

Throughout its postwar history the UAW remained one of the few big unions whose contracts authorized local strikes over health and safety and production standard issues; this right was the union's main counter to the extensive list of management prerogatives contained in every contract. But the Treaty of Detroit made manifest the inherent tension between the exercise of this right and those elements of the effort bargain that the union leadership could most easily quantify and monetize—generally, wage and fringe benefit improvements in the national contract. In summing up the impact of the 1950 UAW-GM contract, the respected labor economist Frederick Harbison put it all too bluntly: "This kind of collective bargaining calls for intelligent trading rather than table-pounding, for diplomacy rather than belligerency, and for internal union discipline rather than grass roots rank and file activity."[71]

Reuther had to make this system work, but it was not easy. His difficulties first became apparent even at its moment of creation, during Ford Local 600's famous speedup strike of May 1949. When the Ford Motor Company finally swung into mass production of its first complete postwar model, Ford managers adopted a new policy: foremen increased the line speed above the daily standard to make up for the minutes lost when routine breakdowns halted the conveyor. Shop conflicts quickly escalated; in April 1949 workers in the B-Building (final assembly) voted to strike over this production standard dispute. With the union's pension drive topping his agenda, Reuther clearly saw the dispute as a distraction, "a detour, when every effort . . . ought to be keeping our main drive down the broad highway in terms of our 1949 economic demands."[72]

But Reuther could hardly ignore the conflict: Local 600 remained a cockpit of political factionalism and a powerful center of opposition politics. Reuther partisans dominated the B-Building, but the Communists at the Rouge skillfully championed the speedup issue to rebuild their strength. Reuther therefore assigned Emil Mazey and Ken Bannon to head up a "fact-finding delegation" that toured the B-Building in early May to resolve the dispute. But instead of settling the issue, the presence of top UAW officers touched off a wildcat strike. Ford then fired some fourteen committeemen whom they held responsible for the walkout, transforming the dispute into a Rouge-wide confrontation. The UAW executive board authorized a work stoppage, and in the first complete shutdown since 1941, some sixty-two thousand workers struck the Rouge for twenty-four days in May. "Reuther was right out in front leading the parade," observed the *Detroit Free Press*. "In fact, he gave the appearance of a man running hard to keep ahead of the mob."[73]

Because Reuther hardly wanted a premature showdown with Ford, the strike itself proved a weapon as useful to management as to the union. John Bugas and other Ford executives complained bitterly that wildcat strikes and other forms of disruptive shop-floor activity threatened to undermine good-faith bargaining at the national level. In turn, Reuther told Ford executives that his writ extended only so far: "Have you ever thought that to get control the leadership must fight to get the machinery necessary for control?" He was therefore amenable when Bugas agreed to take the issue to a special arbitration panel headed by Harry Shulman, the UAW-Ford umpire whose reputation was that of a consummate industrial relations "fixer." This agreement ended the strike, took Reuther off the hook, and returned the collective bargaining agenda to the key pension issue.[74] When the Shulman panel promulgated its decision several weeks later, the award proved both anticlimactic and ineffectual, for as the UAW and Ford both knew, no arbitration decision could resolve so complex and subtle an issue. The daily variation in auto body mix and options kept the fight against speedup one of Sisyphean struggle.[75]

The problem of production standards remained an issue that Reuther could neither ignore nor solve. At every UAW convention the leadership put forward a lengthy resolution declaring, among other things, that "the fight against speed up must be spearheaded at the plant level." But as Reuther regularly reminded his membership, to bargain successfully with the most powerful corporations in the world "requires central direction in terms of timing and strategy and tactics, and if we dilute this central direction that is built around authorization of strikes . . . you dissipate the power of the union at the bargaining table." Thus, after the 1949 speedup strike fiasco, Reuther and his executive board made certain that such local conflicts never again stood in the way of the national contract negotiations.[76] In this contest Reuther clearly had the upper hand, for the very language and structure of postwar industrial relations worked on his behalf. Shop-floor syndicalism was rooted in the concrete social and technical structures of the workplace, but it was doomed to militant parochialism without a leadership strata and a larger ideology with which it might transcend its localistic focus. The wage and welfare struggles for which Reuther won such public acclaim clearly resonated in postwar America, but the very language in which so many shop issues were now discussed—"production standards," "paragraph 63(b)," "plant versus departmental seniority rights"—belied an ideological attenuation that made them invisible to the larger public. Reuther himself understood something of the dilemma when he told a 1955 Ford Council meeting that local problems "close to the Ford workers' daily needs" might well "get lost in the shuffle." Two months later the Ford settlement left hundreds of shop issues unresolved, after which more than one hundred thousand workers shut down scores of factories in the hours immediately after Reuther and Bugas posed for the photographers at the signing ceremony. The *Detroit Free Press* labeled these strikes the "Revolt of the Victors."[77]

Reuther usually proved a consummate manager of such discontent. As early as 1951 he realized that the five-year contract had been a mistake. The COLA formula failed to fully compensate autoworkers for the inflationary burst that accompanied the outbreak of hostilities in Korea; equally important, local union officials hated the long duration of the contract because so many grievances and disputes accumulated. Reuther therefore turned on the pressure. First he fired Art Johnstone, the nominal director of the GM Department. Johnstone, in the words of one disgruntled staffer, operated a "fire department . . . using the staff . . . to prevent strike action and block locals from obtaining authorization for a legitimate strike."[78] Next Reuther pledged to negotiate no more five-year contracts. Indeed, he demanded that the employers reopen the master contract in 1953 on the grounds that such agreements were "living documents" that had to reflect unforeseen economic conditions. When GM and Ford balked, Reuther authorized a set of crippling production standard strikes at key foundry and transmission plants. "We didn't turn them off," remembered Jack Conway. "Normally . . . you'd get in and work like hell to settle the local issues. But . . . we just sat back." GM buckled first, after which the industry gave Reuther almost everything he wanted.[79]

"Reuther's like a guided missile," predicted the veteran *Free Press* reporter Edwin Lahey in 1957. "He'll go on and on being a dominant voice in the labor movement, just out of sheer brilliance." Why do employers hate Walter Reuther so much? a reporter asked Joe Rauh, the UAW's Washington counsel. "Because he is so effective," came the instant reply, an answer grudgingly accepted by most of Reuther's Detroit adversaries. Briefing its business readers on how to handle the UAW president, the *Nation's Business* had to admit that "he is hard to attack because . . . [he] is a devoted family man and shows no desire for personal wealth. His desire is for power, and this to some is worse than immorality. . . . He is inflexible in his thinking, and like most planners believes there is no compromise with the righteousness of his own cause."[80]

But such endorsements came just as Reutherism had moved past its apogee. By the end of the 1950s the great era of auto industry collective bargaining was at an end, and Reuther's capacity to shape the future, even in the limited universe defined by the Fordist bargaining regime, had given way to an increasingly routine give-and-take. The clarity and power of Reuther's strategic vision faded as he scrambled to respond to forces, both within the union and outside it, over which he had little control. He was becoming a prisoner of the institution he had done so much to construct.

Reuther's handling of the 1958 bargaining round proved a case in point. The recession of 1957–58 was like a fire bell in the night, warning of the industrial conflagration that would shortly gut the manufacturing core of the urban Midwest. The recession was the most severe since 1938, and it marked an end to the brief era of labor-management good feeling that had accompanied the boom years of the Korean War. Industry faced its first serious wave of foreign competition as steel imports exceeded exports for the first time in the twentieth century and smaller, cheaper foreign cars like the Volkswagen made their debut on the American market. Auto production plunged: by early 1958 there were three hundred thousand unemployed autoworkers and nearly nine hundred thousand unsold cars sitting in factory lots. Suddenly, management efforts to restrain unit labor costs took on a new urgency, and a Republican Party–business coalition launched a propaganda offensive that denounced as a vicious "wage-price spiral" the moderate inflation and industrywide wage standards men like Wilson and Reuther had built into the Treaty of Detroit. The marginal producers and nonunion firms were in an uproar, and they provided much of the energy that put right-to-work referenda on the ballot in California, Ohio, and other industrial states. For the first time since the immediate postwar years, "big labor" supplanted the Communist menace as a prime target of the American right.[81]

Ill at ease in this chilly climate, Reuther switched bargaining goals again and again. He abandoned a convention pledge to bargain for some version of the shorter workweek in favor of a union proposal that the auto companies reduce prices by one hundred dollars a car, in return for which the UAW would forgo a year's productivity bonus. Not unexpectedly, Reuther's effort to revive even a scaled-down version of his 1945 GM program met with a uniformly hostile response from automotive management; moreover, as the recession deepened it became clear that a uniform price reduction would have driven out of business high-cost producers like Chrysler and Studebaker. So Reuther and his top officers again changed union demands, this time focusing on an elaborate profit-sharing scheme that targeted only the money-making companies. "We tailor our economic demands to fit the economic realities," Reuther told the union convention that approved the switch in early 1958.[82]

Auto executives were certain that the same realities—both economic and political—were entirely on their side. Taking their cue from the hard-line tactics pioneered by General Electric's Lemuel Boulware, they insisted upon a simple extension of the contract: no profit sharing, no social pioneering, no "icing on the cake." In particular, Chrysler turned its own disastrous performance into a weapon by demanding UAW cooperation in its battle to discipline local shop stewards and bring production standards up to GM levels. If the UAW wanted to maintain pattern bargaining on economic and fringe benefit issues, Reuther would have to support Chrysler's tardy effort to recast its industrial relations along the most advanced principles of midcentury Fordism. When the contracts expired without agreement in May 1958, Reuther, knowing he was in a tight spot, told more than half a million UAW members to stay on the job. "Ignore everything the companies do and bide your time." Reuther told workers at the Big Three, "To strike now would be insane."[83]

Reuther's gamble again demonstrated the mixed character of the bargain his union had struck with automotive management. The companies did nothing to undermine the overall legitimacy of the union, autoworkers voluntarily paid more than 90 percent of their dues, and committeemen continued to process their grievances. Reuther thought working without a contract "good for the union's soul." In the fall he eked out another pattern settlement that preserved all the key features of the Treaty of Detroit. Except at a few smaller firms, profit sharing disappeared from Reuther's bargaining agenda.[84]

But the 1958 contract was not simply a draw: Reuther had been drawn into a subtle game of "concession" bargaining. Managers at Ford and GM used the no-contract period to tighten shop discipline another notch, and in the fall there were scores of inconclusive strikes. However, the real battle came at Chrysler, which used the summer of 1958 to land the decisive blows in its assault upon the last citadels of shop steward power. Reuther, who personally took charge of these negotiations, feared that unless the UAW helped Chrysler management, the company might well go the way of Hudson, Packard, and Kaiser-Frazer. When the UAW's big Detroit locals demanded strike authorization, Reuther and his executive board stalled. The intraunion stalemate gave Chrysler the chance to grind down the opposition, set new production standards, and suppress the wildcat strike tradition.[85]

Looking back from our vantage point at the end of the twentieth century, we can see that Reuther's faith in collective bargaining, even in its heyday, had proven a grave miscalculation. The American automobile industry's postwar boom lasted but a single generation. The extraordinary profits generated by the Big Three's unchallenged dominance of the world's greatest market for new cars fueled Reuther's social imagination, but even in the 1950s the beneficiaries of the Treaty of Detroit were neither as numerous nor as well rewarded as many had expected.

For all its apparent solidity, pattern bargaining in the United States had a remarkably anemic life. It never spread much beyond the oligopolistically structured core industries, and even there it required a strong union that could take labor costs out of competition to make the pattern stick. Where unions were weak, as in electrical products and textiles, or where competition was fierce, as in automotive parts and food processing, wage and benefit guidelines established in Detroit, Pittsburgh, or Chicago were reproduced only imperfectly. Reuther himself had announced as early as 1950 that the GM settlement of that year might have to be "trimmed" in firms without the big automaker's financial clout. Thus even in the unionized auto parts industry only about one-quarter of all companies, employing 40 percent of the workforce, followed the Big Three pattern during the 1950s. When inflation became a chronic problem after 1965, wage inequality within the blue-collar manufacturing sector increased dramatically.[86]

Nor did the corporatized welfare state encompass more than a highly segmented fraction of the American working class. White male workers in stable firms were its chief beneficiaries. Women, whose work careers were often episodic, were far less likely to build up the continuous work time necessary for a pension or a long vacation. Likewise, African-American men found that the firm-centered benefit system worked against them, because their disproportionate employment in marginal firms often deprived them of full access to the social wage negotiated at the core of the economy. For every black who retired with a full pension from Ford there were a dozen or more who lost their jobs and their benefits during the wave of plant closures and bankruptcies that swept through the metropolitan North during each postwar recession.[87]

Reuther's expectation that the UAW's version of collective bargaining had shifted corporate behavior, perhaps even neutralized capital's opposition to an expansion of the welfare state, proved equally misplaced. For example, the guaranteed annual wage that the UAW negotiated with the Big Three represented a well-defined commitment of corporate cash, not the kind of unlimited financial liability that Weinberg and Reuther had once hoped might prompt a management shift in production policy. This version of the annual wage did nothing to regularize production schedules and payrolls but functioned as a sort of company-financed insurance policy into which the UAW later dipped for additional contract benefits like severance pay, Christmas bonuses, and short-workweek supplements.[88]

And contrary to Reuther's expectations, heavy-industry employers did not respond to the proliferation of such fringe benefits by seeking government assumption of the costs. Given their well-insulated market and GM's leak-proof price umbrella, most larger firms proved quite willing to fold pension, health insurance, and SUB costs into their product prices. Moreover, managers recognized that company-specific benefits built employee loyalty, and at some level they understood that a low social wage was advantageous to their class interest, even if their own firm had to bear additional costs as a consequence. Ironically, it was the UAW's own commitment to an expansion of the welfare state that began to flag. Reuther and other top officials never relinquished their support for national health insurance or a higher level of unemployment benefits, but the capacity of the union to mobilize its members on behalf of these initiatives ebbed away as round after round of collective bargaining enhanced the attractiveness of the UAW's own private welfare state.[89]

At the end of the 1950s the magic had been drained from the collective bargaining idea. Reuther had just turned fifty, he had been negotiating with the auto companies for twenty years, and he understood that there were limits to social pioneering at the bargaining table. In the next decade Reuther made certain that autoworker pay and benefits were among the best enjoyed by any in organized labor, but the triannual bargaining ritual had become a burdensome necessity shouldered with competence by a team of trusted lieutenants. If Reuther were to again make the UAW a vanguard in America, he would have to refashion it within a wider world of politics and party.

14

AN AMERICAN
SOCIAL DEMOCRACY

The UAW, for the true believers in its midst, has the character of a full-scale religion.

—Murray Kempton, April 1951

What puzzles Europeans most about the American trade union movement is that it has not tried to create its own political party to advance labor's own interest. . . . How do you explain that?

—Henry Brandon of the Sunday Times, *interviewing Walter Reuther,*
July 1958

Shortly after he was elected president of the Congress of Industrial Organizations late in 1952, Walter Reuther received a telegram from UAW Local 6 in Chicago. It read: "You have been in office thirty minutes. The wage freeze is still on, the war in Korea has not been concluded. Get on the ball."[1]

In politics, as in collective bargaining, Americans had great expectations of Walter Reuther. At midcentury his adversaries often denounced him as an ambitious politician. The accusation was entirely accurate, but it did not sting. Reuther saw the UAW as an independent and powerful force in American society, and he made no apology for his efforts to magnify, unify, and deploy that power in the most efficacious fashion. He wanted influence in Washington, Lansing, and a score of city halls. Much speculation had him on the road to the White House; Reuther never trod that path, but his goals were hardly less sweeping. He understood, as so many did not, that for labor's voice to carry real weight he had to reshape the consciousness of millions of industrial workers, making them disciplined trade unionists, militant social democrats, and racial egalitarians. Here was ambition indeed, and on a scale that generated both hatred and admiration, within the labor movement and without. As Daniel Bell put it in 1953, "The source of his strength is that combination of ideology and self in which the idea is personified in the man and the man artlessly assumes that the idea he incarnates must triumph. It is the messianic urge of the man with a 'calling.' "[2]

But Reuther's political and social ambitions would be frustrated in the 1950s, and not only by his adversaries. His tragedy was that of a man imprisoned within institutions, alliances, and ideological constructs that were largely of his own making. Reuther was trapped, first by the poisoned legacy of an obsessive anti-Communism, then by an alliance with an unreformed Democratic Party, and finally by the transformation and demobilization of the UAW itself. Reuther struggled episodically to extract himself from these snares, but like a man in quicksand, his unsuccessful efforts were more likely to increase the suffocating pressures.

Whatever his difficulties, Walter Reuther's politics mattered in the years after World War II. Detroit stood at the geographical and political heart of the labor-liberal coalition: until 1968 every Democratic candidate for president launched his campaign with a Labor Day rally in Cadillac Square. Here Reuther seemed to be the commanding general of a well-organized industrial army. The UAW was the biggest union in the nation: with no less than 1.3 million members, Reuther offered political guidance to union families that composed almost 5 percent of the American electorate. In more than a score of midwestern political districts, his union had decisive clout. UAW monetary contributions to its favored candidates were modest, but during a campaign season the union would put nearly one thousand staffers on virtually full-time political work. Reuther's speeches were themselves political events; at Berkeley a 1948 talk dryly entitled "The Economics of Collective Bargaining" attracted eighty-five hundred to the university field house. At meetings of the Americans for Democratic Action (ADA), of which Reuther had been a founding officer, all labor officials were accorded a respectful hearing but, reported one awed observer, when Reuther took the floor, "an actual hush settles over the room."[3]

Of American workers Walter Reuther often told his supporters, "First we organize them, that's the easy part; then we must unionize them, that's the hard part." His remark was utterly characteristic of the social contract symbolized by the Treaty of Detroit. Management put up few obstacles to the growth of unionism in the industrial sectors where it already existed. Thus the UAW boomed along with the carmakers, winning almost three-quarters of all its NLRB contests in the first decade of Reuther's presidency. But Reuther and his generation had serious doubts as to the consciousness of these new workers, especially in the early 1950s when a new wave of rural migrants were recruited into the factories. Most were unaware of the union's early struggles; many thought their high wages and fringe benefits were "the philanthropic contributions of enlightened management and not hard-won gains wrested from stubborn bosses." Emil Mazey put it still more bluntly: rank-and-file autoworkers could hardly tell the difference between "unionism and rheumatism."[4]

Reuther was determined that they would know the difference, if only because "the single stroke of a pen in Lansing or Washington can wipe out all the progress gained around the collective bargaining table." He sought to build within the UAW body politic a kind of social democratic culture that would replicate in the American Midwest the political and social solidarities that so often magnified and sustained the influence of trade unionism in Austria, Germany, and Scandinavia. His task would not be easy. In the United States union-organized cooperatives, hospitals, recreation programs, and educational camps had rarely flourished outside of insular ethnopolitical subcultures; moreover, Reuther faced competition not only from the church, the lodge hall, and the growing culture of suburban insularity but from the corporations, which were determined to discredit the New Deal ethos and neutralize union influence upon their employees.[5]

Regardless of the growing stability of their collective bargaining agreements, few executives concluded that a postwar consensus existed between the ideological claims of labor and capital. The idea of an American "end of ideology" in the 1950s was the product of tired radicals, not newly self-confident corporate managers. General Motors, for example, made a sharp distinction between industrial relations, in which it bargained with the UAW, and "employee relations," managed by a separate department that competed with the unions for the loyalty of those same employees. Thus, in 1947, GM did not let Charles Wilson's growing accommodation with the UAW forestall the corporation's invitation to all employees to participate in a "My Job and Why I Like It" contest. Reuther complained that it should be called "What I Like or What I Don't Like about My Job," but nearly 60 percent of those eligible competed on the corporation's terms for more than $150,000 in new cars and kitchen appliances.[6]

More important than such one-shot public relations exercises were the more pervasive postwar programs—political, educational, and recreational—that so many corporations directed toward employees and their families. While some, like the Advertising Council's "Freedom Train," were rather crude propaganda exercises on behalf of anti-Communist patriotism and storybook capitalism, the more successful campaigns sought to displace union influence through a more subtle identification between company interests and those of family, community, and nation. In particular many executives saw the nonworking housewife as the militant union's weak link. "You would be surprised," contended the Timkin Roller Bearing executive R. L. Frederick, "at the pressure that a woman can place upon her husband if he is considering going out on strike for half a cent an hour. . . . Mrs. employee will often make it clear that she doesn't care for that."[7]

To counter such propaganda, the UAW wanted to maintain an active presence throughout what we would today call civil society. A keystone of this union influence would be the "lighted union hall," which, as Roy Reuther put it at the dedication of Flint's big grocery co-op, would serve as a "symbol of unity and solidarity, not only of labor but of the whole community ... extending democracy beyond the factory walls, into the neighborhoods." Walter Reuther also put money and personnel into an extensive sports program—"to make democracy come alive on the ball diamond"—and in his more ambitious moments foresaw a series of UAW hospitals and insurance schemes designed to engender a "union view of the world" among both workers and their families.[8]

Reviving some of the old Brookwood spirit, the UAW maintained the largest and most highly politicized education program of any major U.S. trade union. The biannual education conferences organized by Victor Reuther brought two thousand of the union's most committed cadre together for long weekends of debate and discussion. The pedagogically innovative UAW summer school at Port Huron enrolled even more—families included—for two weeks of classes in a racially integrated, informal atmosphere. The experience was complemented through the year by the monthly magazine *Ammunition*, which was mailed to the twenty thousand shop stewards, committeemen, and local officials who composed the indispensable backbone of the organization.[9] *Ammunition* was a sophisticated and radical magazine that pushed the left edge of midcentury political orthodoxy. Here were didactic reports on UAW conventions, strikes, and speeches, favorable reviews of books by C. Wright Mills, Sidney Lens, and Ray Ginger, and spirited attacks upon corporate management. After almost half a century, a short essay by the editor Brendan Sexton, "Deep Therapy on the Assembly Line," remains a devastating critique of the entire school of personnel management spawned by Elton Mayo and other social psychologists of the 1940s.[10]

To complement *Ammunition* and the UAW summer schools, Reuther wanted to publish a CIO daily paper, or at least a weekly version of the *United Auto Worker*. Such publications would have cost too much, but the UAW did win a large and timely audience with a series of daily radio programs during the 1950s. The key figure was the extraordinary Guy Nunn, a Rhodes scholar of working-class background and former OSS operative whom Reuther hired after he was fired by a commercial radio station for the evenhanded reportage he offered GM strikers in 1946. With its sharp and stinging news commentary, Nunn's twice-daily radio shows—"Eye Opener" and "Shift Break," timed to catch factory workers on their commute—generated more shop-floor political talk than any other union function during the 1950s. Broadcasting on forty stations, Nunn remained the most listened-to radio personality in Detroit; indeed, to the discomfort of some union officials, Guy Nunn *was* the UAW to most listeners.[11]

Reuther himself spent a huge proportion of his time on the stump. It was his natural method of discourse. When he was first elected union president, Reuther had Frank Winn or Guy Nunn write out his speeches, but he could never stick to the text. Thereafter, Reuther always spoke from notes, usually jotted down in a plane or hotel room from material assembled by Weinberg, Montgomery, Winn, or Conway. When in good form—which was more often than not—Reuther offered his audiences an evangelist's tour of American life in which the confusion, injustice, and hypocrisy of the day stood counterpoised and condemned by the order, harmony, and logic of the new world he spread before them. "For a time it seemed we were listening to one of the Hebrew prophets," observed Bishop Bromley Oxnam of a 1950 Reuther speech to the Federal Council of Churches. "Reuther was a superb entertainer," wrote Stanley Levey in the *Reporter*. "He asked questions and gave answers. He swept up his audience. He evoked cheers and laughter. The delegates sent him on his way with an ovation." Daniel Bell thought the more portentous of Reuther's talks "vague, woolly and full of bombast," but for the less professionally skeptical—among whom were numbered the vast majority of UAW members and a good slice of the liberal public—Reuther's speeches were, to use the words of loyalist Martin Gerber, "all the same, but like a great symphony: you never got tired of it."[12]

Central to Reuther's social democratic vision was his guileless faith that the UAW remained America's most democratic and progressive trade union. "Our union was built from the bottom up," he bragged to the veteran labor journalist Mary Heaton Vorse. "No other union has such a basic rank and file structure."[13] In truth, there was much to sustain this belief. Throughout his lifetime the union's political culture remained more self-consciously pluralist than that of virtually any other institution in American life. In the postwar era all the big trade unions were one-party regimes, none more so than the industrial unions that bargained with the big firms in America's oligopolistically structured industries. But Reuther could never rule by fiat alone. Well into the 1960s many big locals and many key staff jobs were marbled with old radicals who measured the UAW and its leadership by a standard forged in the great battles of the 1930s and 1940s. The very size and activism of this cadre ensured that politics, of both the ideological and "porkchop" varieties, still motivated a broad stratum within the UAW. By one estimate, UAW locals, regions, and departments published more than four hundred newspapers—nearly half of all those printed by the labor movement in the United States. Even during the depths of the McCarthy era the UAW remained one of the few institutions in the United States in which the left could still make its voice heard. In 1951 the UAW convention resolution defending Truman administration policy on Korea came under vigorous attack from both Communists and Trotskyists; in response, Reuther reworked a section to make explicit UAW criticism of the South Korean dictator Syngman Rhee.[14]

Reuther himself positioned the UAW at the left margin of conventional politics. During the 1940s he had never been seduced by the Roosevelt cult or the frenzied expectations generated by the CIO's political action committee. Indeed, Sidney Hillman considered Reuther so unreliable a Democrat that he had never called on him for CIO-PAC work in 1944. During that election many Reuther partisans had been active in the effort to build the Michigan Commonwealth Federation, a

third party modeled after Ontario's newly emergent Canadian Commonwealth Federation. Reuther's own position was somewhat more nuanced. In the long run
Reuther favored "the formation of a new political party of all liberal, non-totalitarian,
American groups." But whether this new political vehicle would be based upon
the "realignment" of the Democratic Party—with the Texas oilmen and the Dixiecrats eliminated—or upon an entirely new labor-based party remained purposefully ambiguous. Such a party was clearly needed, but it "cannot be declared into
existence. . . . The time must be ripe, the people must be ready."[15]

That time seemed nearly right in 1947 and 1948. Even among unionists and liberals of less political sagacity than Reuther, President Truman and his brand of
Democratic Party politics held little appeal, especially when the unelected president was cast in the shadow of his increasingly mythic predecessor. The founding
in the fall of 1946 of both the anti-Communist ADA and the Communist-backed
Progressive Citizens of America testified to the manifest weakness of the Democratic Party and to the search for some political formation to its left. When C.
Wright Mills surveyed CIO leaders at that time, he found that 23 percent favored
the immediate formation of a labor party; looking ahead ten years, the proportion
jumped to over half, and among CIO national officers—the key group—it stood
at 65 percent. Within Reuther's circle such sentiment was commonplace. On the
executive board Emil Mazey and Martin Gerber were third-party activists, and
some members of the Reuther brain trust—Don Montgomery, Paul Sifton, Brendan Sexton, Victor Reuther, and Lewis Carliner—were chomping at the bit. *Life*
and *Look*, the two most widely read pictorial magazines of the era, forecast
Reuther as the presidential candidate of a new labor party.[16]

At first the Progressive Party candidacy of Henry Wallace seemed but a further
spur to such political realignment. Reuther thought Wallace little more than a
dupe of the Communists, but he knew that if the CIO merely relied upon Truman
and the Democrats, a lot of "decent guys" would end up in the Progressive Party
camp. From Washington, Don Montgomery summarized the danger: "Most progressive people are thoroughly fed up and disgusted with both major parties," he
wrote in early 1948. "They are looking for a place to go. They want leadership. . . .
Out of desperation a lot of good people will wallow with Wallace until there is
something to vote for." Reuther had to look no farther than his own family for con-
firmation: his new brother-in-law, Gene Richey, a YMCA secretary who had just
married his sister Christine, was a Progressive Party enthusiast until Reuther subjected him to a Sunday afternoon's verbal pummeling.[17]

To counter the Wallace threat and fill the vacuum left by Truman, Reuther
groped for a political alternative. Speaking to an ADA convention in February
1948, Reuther subordinated his usual denunciation of the Communists to a
tongue lashing directed at the "tired liberals" who were "fancy on promises and
short on the guts it takes to deliver on those promises." In a preview of themes that
Arthur Schlesinger would codify in his *Vital Center* of 1949, Reuther asserted that
it would take the creation of a "third force . . . an independent, positive, aggressive

force in America," to defeat the authoritarians of left and right. To a cheering audience Reuther proclaimed the ADA not as the "left wing or tail of any established party, but as the matrix from which a new movement shall arise."[18] A UAW executive board meeting the next month gave Reuther's sentiments some concreteness by calling for "the formation after the 1948 national elections of a genuine progressive political party." But this idea was hardly satisfying, even to Reuther, who briefly joined the ADA's desperate flirtation with Dwight D. Eisenhower until Conway, Montgomery, and other aides pounded home the supreme commander's limitations as a warrior for the labor-liberal camp. Thereafter, Reuther argued that the ADA should merely support an open convention.[19]

Certain that Truman would lose the general election, the UAW saw good prospects for a genuine realignment, if not an actual third-party break. In Michigan the mobilization of hundreds of UAW political activists had shifted the Democratic Party sharply to the left, enabling the G. Mennen Williams–Neil Stabler reform group to wrest control of the Democratic Party from the hands of Jimmy Hoffa and his Highway Department allies. More dramatically, the ADA's successful campaign for a strong civil rights plank at the Democratic National Convention had sparked the walkout of the most reactionary southern Democrats, thus putting realignment clearly on the agenda. Reuther offered Truman a tepid endorsement late in the fall, but only after he had taken a full page of the August *United Auto Worker* to denounce "both the Republican and Democratic parties as presently constituted and aligned." With this go-ahead, Emil Mazey told UAW local union presidents to take "concrete action in building an independent labor party of workers and farmers." Plowing this same ideological ground, Victor Reuther made plans for a blockbuster of an educational conference, scheduled for the day after Thomas Dewey's inauguration. On the speakers list were Aneurin Bevan of the British Labour government, Tommy Douglas, head of the Canadian Commonwealth Federation, and the Columbia University sociologist Robert Lynd, an organizer and advocate for a labor-based third party in the United States.[20]

Reuther was recovering from corrective surgery at the Duke University hospital when Jack Conway broke the unexpected news that Truman had been reelected. Without batting an eye, Reuther responded, "That just goes to show you what happens when you take the issues to the people."[21] From Reuther's perspective, the election results were very good. Wallace's vote had been held to 1.2 million nationwide; more important, the Communist-backed third party never made it out of single digits even in the most laborite urban centers. Meanwhile, the Democrats had recaptured control of Congress, propelling a new cohort of liberals to national prominence. Hubert Humphrey of Minnesota and Paul Douglas of Illinois joined the Senate, while Adlai Stevenson became a national figure after winning the Illinois statehouse. Most dramatically, the UAW political mobilization in hundreds of Michigan precincts had sent G. Mennen Williams to Lansing, where he would remain for twelve years as the embodiment of labor-liberal collaboration in state politics. Finally, Truman's victory had been sweet. He won without the help of the Deep South or the cadres of the old Popular Front, and although he had none of Roosevelt's broad appeal, his whistle-stop campaign had been built upon a "Fair Deal" pledge to revive much of FDR's domestic agenda. Truman's electoral support may well have been the most class-stratified of any winning president. Among autoworkers who cast a ballot, an astounding 89 percent gave him their vote. "Labor did it!" Truman acknowledged at the moment of victory.[22] After the election Reuther consigned all third-party talk to the future. Victor recast his educational conference to conform to the views Walter offered A. H. Raskin in a post-election interview: "We must make a real try to influence the old parties. If we find we cannot, then the move for a third party must come from the bottom up."[23] For a time Reuther continued to insist—especially during moments of tension with the Truman administration, such as the Korean War mobilization crisis—that "nobody owns us. . . . We don't belong to anybody and we won't be the tail of any political party kite." But short of a political earthquake, Reuther was committed to a de facto alliance with the Democrats—or more specifically, with the northern, urban, liberal wing of the party. In Michigan Reuther worked agreeably with the Industrial Union Council president Gus Scholle, a protégé of Philip Murray who policed the careful alliance between UAW radicals and statehouse Democrats. In charge of the union's national political front he put his brother Roy, who now returned to the UAW inner circle after almost a decade in the wilderness. Roy was the most mild-mannered and affable of the Reuther brothers, but he was also an organization man in politics. The last of the brothers to abandon active participation in the Socialist Party, Roy shifted allegiances to become the most committed builder of the UAW's Democratic Party political operation. By 1960, when Roy took a leave of absence from the UAW to work full-time on voter registration for the Democratic National Committee, the alliance was complete.[24]

The Reuther brothers soon found that American politics had indeed been "realigned," but hardly along the progressive lines drawn by the UAW. In Congress southern Democrats and Republicans formalized their decade-old alliance. The "Dixiegop" coalition, as the UAW called it, now strengthened the rules of the Senate—and especially Rule 22, which mandated a vote by two-thirds of all members to invoke cloture and end a Dixiecrat filibuster—in order to halt Truman's Fair Deal program in its tracks. Within little more than a year virtually all of the administration's programs were blocked: national health insurance, repeal of Taft-Hartley, a national fair employment law, and a modest program of low-income housing construction.[25]

In Detroit as well racial politics trumped UAW liberalism, making the crystallization of a social democratic current inside the urban-labor wing of the Democratic Party far more difficult than Reuther might have imagined. In the mayoral election of 1949 the UAW threw its organizational muscle behind George Edwards, Reuther's old comrade from Local 174 who had demonstrated an engaging popularity, solid competence, and sterling New Deal credentials as the chair-

Reuther surrounded himself with forceful, independent aides. In the 1930s George Edwards *(above left)*, later a federal judge, challenged Reuther's leadership among UAW socialists. As the union's Washington lobbyist in the 1950s, Don Montgomery *(above)* kept a jaundiced eye on Democratic Party affairs. Reuther made Jack Conway and Paul Schrade *(left)* administrative assistants, but both clashed with him over politics in the late 1960s. *Archives of Labor and Urban Affairs, Wayne State University.*

Jack Conway was Reuther's right-hand man during his first fifteen years in the UAW presidency. In the 1960s he became close to the Kennedys. *The George Meany Memorial Archives.*

John Kennedy flattered Reuther by making him an ambassador to the European left, but the president ignored the UAW's economic advice and deferred to George Meany when it came to trade union appointments. Kennedy spoke before the UAW convention in May 1962. *Photo no. ST171-16-62 in the John F. Kennedy Library.*

In the early 1960s social democracy seemed in the ascendent on both sides of the Atlantic. Here Reuther rows Hubert Humphrey, Willy Brandt, and Tage Eerlander back to the Swedish prime minister's summer house at Harpsund. *Archives of Labor and Urban Affairs, Wayne State University.*

Reuther often had a difficult relationship with UAW blacks. As head of the union's Fair Employment Practices Department in the 1940s, George Crockett *(left)* gave leadership to African-Americans allied with George Addes. Fifteen years later Horace Sheffield's *(right)* Trade Union Leadership Council embarrassed Reuther by demanding he put a black on the UAW executive board. *Archives of Labor and Urban Affairs, Wayne State University.*

Eleanor Roosevelt was Reuther's friend and mentor for more than twenty years. *Archives of Labor and Urban Affairs, Wayne State University.*

Martin Luther King, Jr., and Reuther meet the press just prior to the spectacularly successful "Walk to Freedom" in Detroit, June 1963. Reuther wanted to tap the social energy King had mobilized. *Archives of Labor and Urban Affairs, Wayne State University.*

left to right: Joe Rauh, Whitney Young, Roy Wilkins, A. Philip Randolph, Walter Reuther, and Matthew Ahmann in the front rank at the 1963 March on Washington. The UAW paid for the signs and a whole lot more. *Archives of Labor and Urban Affairs, Wayne State University.*

At the March on Washington, August 1963. Reuther was enormously pleased when some African-Americans called him "the white Martin Luther King." *Archives of Labor and Urban Affairs, Wayne State University*

Reuther was always well prepared when he testified before Congress. Here he complains to a Senate committee in October 1963 that unemployment has fallen too slowly during the current upturn in the business cycle. *Alexander Negative Collection, The George Meany Memorial Archives.*

Walter Reuther was an enthusiast for the Model Cities idea when he explained the concept to Lyndon Johnson in August 1965. Reuther's commitment to Great Society reformism destroyed his credibility on the left during the era of the Vietnam War. *Photo by Yoichi R. Okamoto, LBJ Library Collection.*

At the 1964 UAW convention in Atlantic City, Lisa, Linda, and May join Reuther after his re-election as union president. *Archives of Labor and Urban Affairs, Wayne State University.*

Reuther saw the UAW Family Education Center at Black Lake, designed by his friend Oskar Stonorov, as his aesthetic and pedagogical legacy, designed to "keep the stars burning brightly in the eyes of the UAW for years ahead." *Archives of Labor and Urban Affairs, Wayne State University.*

In the 1960s Douglas Fraser (*right*) eclipsed Leonard Woodcock as Reuther's heir apparent. But when the UAW executive board chose a new president in 1970, Woodcock edged out Fraser, who had to wait seven years for his turn. *Archives of Labor and Urban Affairs, Wayne State University.*

At the end of his life, Reuther saw himself as an educator of a new generation of unionists. *Archives of Labor and Urban Affairs, Wayne State University.*

man of the Detroit Common Council since 1945. The UAW and other CIO unions sent union members canvassing door to door throughout the city. Pamphlets in English, Polish, and Hungarian lambasted Edwards's opponent, the city treasurer Albert Cobo, a former business executive and bland conservative, for his connections with bankers and slumlords who "live in Grosse Pointe, Birmingham, and Bloomfield Hills." By all the usual criteria the Edwards campaign was far superior to that of Richard Frankensteen's effort four years before, and unlike the 1945 contest, Edwards had full backing from Walter Reuther and the whole UAW apparatus.[26]

But Edwards lost by even more than Frankensteen, almost two to one. His defeat encapsulated all the social tensions and ideological cross-currents that crippled labor-liberal politics at midcentury. Anti-Communism, racism, and New Deal social policy again divided working-class Detroit and broke yet another CIO effort to win the mayor's office in the Motor City. In 1949 the key issue was public housing, which had convulsed Detroit politics since the Sojourner Truth riots of 1942. Mobilized into dozens of militant neighborhood associations, thousands of working-class homeowners agreed with Albert Cobo's conflation of public housing with the "Negro invasions." White working-class Detroiters, who otherwise voted solidly Democratic, saw the Fair Deal's modest housing initiative of 1949 (the Taft-Ellender-Wagner housing bill, which called for construction of five hundred thousand new units over ten years) as a subversion of their newly acquired "right" to a racially homogeneous neighborhood. Despite much talk of embourgeoisement, white workers had a precarious hold on home ownership at midcentury, a fact that seamlessly linked their economic vulnerability to their racial identity. Edwards rapidly lost support: the Detroit Federation of Labor endorsed Cobo, as did the Teamster-dominated wing of the Wayne County Democratic Party. And "to the astonishment of secondary UAW leaders, the new homeowners in Detroit among the auto workers spoke openly in the shops against 'labor's man,'" reported B. J. Widick. Nor did Edwards's longstanding anti-Communism offer any immunity to the red-baiting that now invested so much political rhetoric. Editorialized the Detroit Free Press, "The only party [Edwards] has ever been associated with outside the Socialists is 'Americans for Democratic Action,' a heterogenous group of parlor pinks, Socialists, and other cloud kissers."[27]

Reuther was stunned by the Edwards defeat because he never understood the passions unleashed by the racialist housing controversy. Reuther saw such neighborhood social conflict as either an atavistic remnant of a more insular America or the product of racial divisions fostered by the real estate lobby. His response was one of modernistic social engineering and union-sponsored counterpropaganda. Through Oskar Stonorov, the Bauhaus School had shaped Reuther's understanding of housing reform as a terrain for social planning on the grand scale. When he testified on behalf of the Housing Act of 1949, he captured much attention with yet another "Reuther Plan": a program to convert idle airframe factories to the mass production of millions of government-financed units of prefabricated single-family housing. But such schemes went nowhere because both the left and the right saw them as largely irrelevant to the social tensions that gripped America's housing frontier. "Why the hell can't Reuther see," complained Catherine Bauer Wurster, one of the nation's foremost advocates of public housing, "that all he does . . . is hand ammunition to the boys who will ride any ostrich to delay legislation once more. . . . The curse of this country is the half-baked, technocratic romancing of the 'progressive' labor skates."[28]

After the Edwards debacle, the UAW never again seriously challenged conservative control of Detroit municipal government. Liberals took over city hall in 1962, but the victory of the young reformer Jerome Cavanagh was a product of a new civil rights insurgency, not the UAW machine, which actually endorsed Louis Miriani, the more conservative incumbent. Walter Reuther himself kept municipal politics at arm's length and left Michigan affairs to Gus Scholle, Leonard Woodcock, and Roy Reuther. Because of the political unreliability of the UAW's own constituency, Reuther and other union officers were convinced that only nonlabor liberals could finesse the racial and class issues that had proven so polarizing in the Edwards campaign. Such concerns were reinforced during the 1950 elections when, in an atmosphere of growing McCarthyite hysteria, Robert Taft demolished a CIO-backed opponent in Ohio and G. Mennen Williams barely held on to the statehouse in Lansing. The American labor movement, argued Reuther, had "to learn to work with a party without trying to capture it." Thus, when Sen. Arthur Vandenberg's death in early 1951 gave Governor Williams the chance to appoint George Edwards as a replacement, Reuther proved noticeably cool, because the former mayoral candidate seemed so polarizing a figure. Williams therefore turned to Blair Moody, the popular but politically untested columnist for the Detroit Free Press.[29]

Reuther's political difficulties in Detroit and elsewhere were also very much a function of the transformation taking place within the United Automobile Workers. Reuther's obsessive anti-Communism reinforced the pervasive industrial regimentation generated by his grand bargain with the auto corporations; unchecked, both helped to undermine his claim to the vanguard role he had staked out for his union in American politics. The forms of democracy were never abandoned within the UAW, but by 1952 Reuther had so narrowed the limits of debate and the possibility of real opposition that he had crippled his union's capacity to mobilize its forces on behalf of even the political issues the leadership fully endorsed.

Unlike Philip Murray, who had first approached the purge of the CIO's Communist-led unions with vexation and reluctance, Reuther demonstrated a self-confidence, an impatience, and a determination that resulted from his own uncompromising victory in the 1946–47 faction fight. After the collapse of the Wallace movement had revealed the isolation of the Communists in 1948, Reuther was among the first on the CIO executive board to move for the outright expulsion of the left-wing unions from the organization. Murray knew that such a divorce might have become politically necessary, but his own experience as a coalition builder in the CIO told him that the split would not come without a heavy cost. Reuther had no such doubts. The Communist-line unions would "fold up overnight" once the CIO offered workers in the electrical, farm equipment, and clerical fields "decent, clean American unions that will follow CIO policy." Reuther even believed that the CIO might launch a huge organizing campaign, in the South and elsewhere, because now its organizers would not have to spend so much time "apologizing for the Communists."[30] When Reuther's *Collier's* essay of 1948, "How to Beat the Communists," first appeared, one radical young staffer asked his boss, "How does it feel to speak to the American people as if you were [the HUAC chairman] J. Parnell Thomas?" To which Reuther shot back, "Nuts. This way they might read the thing. Then they'll find out the title should really run 'How to Build a Democratic Union.'"[31]

But Reuther's conception of democratic trade unionism was becoming highly attenuated—constrained first by the utter contempt in which he held "the comrades," and then hardened by the unexpected failure of these embattled oppositionists to simply give up. During the UAW faction fight of 1946 and 1947 Reuther's boast that he had defeated the Communists in a democratic fashion had much validity, if only because he had no alternative. But in the polemical exchanges of 1948 and 1949 any such restraints were cast aside. Indeed, Reuther's very language took on a brutality and crudeness that sustained the CIO's bureaucratic determination to simply suppress the Communist-led unions. "They have scabbed against us on the picket line and they have scabbed against us at the ballot box," declared Reuther at the 1949 CIO convention. He was for "fumigating" the labor movement and combating the "filth" printed by Communist publications. Communist trade unionists were not part of the left, argued Reuther. "They are the phoney Left, they are the corrupted Left, and they are the morally degenerated Left." At the CIO's 1949 convention Reuther was the principal author of the resolution that declared the 400,000-member United Electrical Workers to be "the Communist Party masquerading as a trade union." Argued Reuther: "The body politic has a bad case of cancer and we have . . . come here to cut out the cancer and save the body of the CIO."[32]

Reuther soon found that his effort to "clean up" the American trade union movement was a far more difficult and vexing task than he could have imagined. Sheer government repression, combined with the Communist Party's own sectarianism, repelled numerous fellow travelers and shop activists. And yet the party's battered cadre continued to function, especially as they merged their bitter anti-Reutherism into the general undercurrent of resistance to the Treaty of Detroit. When it came to the micropolitics of shop grievances, racial empowerment, and informal workshop leadership, anti-Communism often proved ineffective and awkward. The party itself could do little to capitalize on this sometimes contradictory syndicalism, but from Reuther's point of view, it seemed as if his old enemies had hardly been vanquished. Thus the *United Auto Worker* labeled a briefly influential opposition caucus of early 1949 "a strange compound of Communists,

Trotskyites and freebooting opportunists with no political ideology and no moral principles."[33]

Reuther was stymied when a UAW raid against the small, Communist-led Farm Equipment Workers' Union (FE) failed to turn these workers against their officers. At Reuther's insistence, the CIO had given the UAW virtually carte blanche to take over the union, which still represented almost half of all workers in that Midwest industry. Reuther thought that the rescue of some forty thousand workers from Stalinist bondage would prove easy: FE leaders had been Henry Wallace partisans, they had signed the Taft-Hartley affidavits more than a year after the leaders of most non-Communist unions, and their organization was dwarfed by the size and resources of the UAW, which now poured scores of organizers into the raid. "From here on out," announced UAW Vice-President John Livingston, "the UAW-CIO is going to take its appeal for unity directly to the rank and file membership of the FE locals."[34]

But aside from the capture of the big Peoria Caterpillar works—where the FE had been barred from the NLRB ballot because its officers had not yet signed the Taft-Hartley affidavits—the UAW raid made little headway among workers at either John Deere or International Harvester, where small-town solidarity, a syndicalist tradition of shop-floor militancy, and careful attention to the grievances of African-American workers generated much rank-and-file loyalty to the embattled FE leaders. The UAW-FE conflict got off on a characteristic note in February 1949 when a pitched battle erupted between a large contingent of UAW leafleteers and an even bigger phalanx of FE loyalists outside a Harvester plant in East Moline, Illinois. The latter had attacked "Reuther, the two-bit Caesar, who is trying to raid all unions who don't agree with his brand of sell-out Socialism." A dozen UAW organizers were sent to the emergency room, while Livingston and Pat Greathouse, the UAW regional director, were arrested and booked for disorderly conduct. "FE shop workers drove Reuther goons off," crowed the FE News.[35]

With the FE holding its own, Reuther vented his frustration upon those within the UAW who seemed sympathetic to the rival union. At the 1949 UAW convention the hammer fell upon two veteran unionists, Tracy Doll, the pioneer leader of the big Hudson local, and Sam Sage, a former president of the Wayne County CIO council. Neither was a Communist, but both had been Wallace partisans and were now seeking to build a new oppositional caucus within the UAW. As part of this political work, Doll and Sage had republished and distributed a confidential 1946 report to the UAW executive board that falsely linked Reuther with a gangster clique at a New Jersey aircraft local. "Reuther and Company Silent on Thuggery, Mayhem, Tire Slashing" read one bold-face headline. Reuther was incensed because the FE had also used the broadside as effective propaganda against the UAW raids that winter. To Reuther, Doll and Sage had put themselves beyond the pale, outside the bounds of honest speech: "It is a matter of people who are treasonous to this Union, people who are betraying the Union because they want to play their kind of politics, even though it means wrecking the Union."[36]

Factional debate within the UAW was now virtually illegitimate; the executive board began to screen the local newspapers put out by opposition locals, including Plymouth in Detroit and Chevrolet in Flint, for what Reuther considered slanderous and antiunion material. Scornful and impatient with his critics, Reuther sought to balance his own self-image as a radical democrat with the organizational machinery he had built to service the Treaty of Detroit. His rationale was essentially Leninist: once the CIO or the UAW had established policy on a vital issue, opponents were "morally obligated to accept the democratic will of the majority."[37] Or as he put it in 1951,

> Everybody has a right to his own opinion, but the past is dead, as far as the factional considerations are concerned; and I urge the fellows in those few remaining locals where they are still living in terms of the 1946 Convention and 1947 Convention . . . those conventions are behind us. . . . And I plead, we are not fighting on top and there is no reason why there should be a single fight on the local union level. You are going to have contests for offices. . . . But let's have democratic contests without factionalism. Let's have democracy but not factionalism.[38]

This was an absurd distinction, and it soon drove Reuther toward the most autocratic measures. He did encourage debate at union conventions, conferences, and local union meetings, if only to reveal sources of discontent and identify rank-and-file spark plugs. During the biannual conventions Reuther frequently appointed an opposition figure to the Resolutions Committee, and he made certain that his opponents had equal time on the floor microphones in debate. He wanted as large and informed a majority as possible behind his program. Defending this practice, which some executive board members thought too solicitous of a dissident minority, Reuther asserted: "The opposition does have its uses. It is like a flea on a dog. It keeps the dog in action!"[39]

But such dissent did not extend to the UAW staff, whose bureaucratization was perfectly symbolized by the opening of Solidarity House in 1951. Designed by Oskar Stonorov in a pastel-colored international style, the UAW's home on the Detroit River might well have been mistaken for a midsize corporate headquarters, but only by overlooking the courtyard statue of an autoworker cast in a heroic, social realist pose. By the mid-1950s the UAW employed about seven hundred staffers, over four hundred of whom were International representatives who directly "serviced" the membership. These were good steady jobs, paying more than twice the wages of a GM production worker, so few turned down the call from Solidarity House. The process of bureaucratic encrustation was therefore an organic one: because Reuther had lost so much of his capacity to inspire a sophisticated layer of shop politicians, the committed Reutherites on the staff were now a small minority.[40] The Socialist Frank Marquart called the rest of them "ghosts within"; *Labor Action* bemoaned the tendency of even the most capable local leaders to transform themselves into "voiceless paid employees."[41]

The case of the Local 600 militant Shelton Tappes is emblematic. Although Tappes had long been a blistering critic of Reuther at the Rouge, he was one of several fellow travelers who distanced themselves from the Communist-oriented "progressive" caucus there in 1949, in part because he simply would not join the party. The next year, when he sought a job on the previously all-white Ford Department staff, Reuther immediately acquiesced, precisely because of the great credibility Tappes carried among African-American workers. But there was a cost. As Tappes told Jack Conway, "Walter knows what my politics are, and unfortunately, all the years that I've been a delegate, I've never voted for him." To which Conway replied, "Walter's prepared to accept you as you are, with one condition, and that is, you do no politicking as an International Representative. Whatever your opinions are, you don't get on a soapbox, so to speak."[42]

Alienation soon set in among these once highly politicized staffers, whose voices and interests were often ignored by the Reutherite top leadership. In the early 1960s a movement to organize a staff union swept their ranks. Reuther was "hurt and shocked," especially when these UAW employees pointedly called him "management" at a Solidarity House meeting in October 1963. To avoid an embarrassing NLRB election, Reuther established a formal grievance procedure—with binding arbitration by a neutral outsider—and agreed to negotiate with an elected staff council.[43]

Political and organizational discipline extended to the UAW executive board as well. By 1950 none offered Reuther any overt opposition; as Martin Gerber put it, most viewed their chief with a combination of "respect, awe, and some cynicism." Reuther used the board to air the ideas and proposals developed by his brain trust and the top officers, taking periodic straw votes on the few controversial issues that did not generate an immediate consensus. Although the board gave Reuther considerable leeway when it came to collective bargaining strategy, and a truly free hand in Washington politics, not all regional directors were cut to the Reutherite pattern. Especially among those who had joined his faction in the Martin era, there was little enthusiasm for political action, ineffective administration of local contracts, and much foot dragging over implementation of the UAW Fair Employment Practices Department program. Many board members saw the brain trust around Reuther as an "alien faction," remembered Lewis Carliner of the Education Department staff. In the summer of 1949 this resentment exploded at an off-the-record session of the executive board when southern-born Vice President John Livingston denounced Brendan Sexton as one of the "obnoxious long-hairs" who used union time for Socialist activities. Sexton was an Irishman, but the whiff of anti-Semitism was unmistakable. Reuther asked his brother Victor to investigate; as for himself, his official biography had by this time suppressed all evidence of his youthful radicalism. And when Norman Thomas visited Solidarity House, Reuther was certain to be unavailable.[44]

On all the big questions, Reuther kept the absolute loyalty of the UAW executive board because he would brook no opposition to their reelection, even when it came from unionists of a more committed and effective Reutherite outlook. The "Reuther caucus" was a machine for the preservation of the status quo within the UAW. By the mid-1950s all officers and International representatives were expected to contribute to a "flower fund" for this very purpose. "Keeping it in the family, that's my job," Reuther told the executive board members who feared opposition from within their regions. Thus, in Toledo, Reuther defended Richard Gosser, whose thuggish rule and questionable outside business interests had proved a growing embarrassment, against more than a decade of attack from local union leaders with solid Reutherite credentials. In justification, Reuther pointed to Gosser's power and effectiveness as a trade unionist, as well as to his loyalty, which went all the way back to the days when the Toledo flying squadrons roared up the Dixie Highway.[45]

But of California Regional Director Cyril O'Halloran none of this could be said. A former Addes man, O'Halloran spent much time at the racetrack or in the company of Los Angeles underworld figures who could have been taken right out of Dashiell Hammett novel. From 1947 on he encountered stiff opposition from within Region 6, much of it led by Paul Schrade, whose politics had been forged when he took Harold Laski's classes in political economy at Yale. Reuther saw Schrade, who revitalized the North American Aviation local in Inglewood, as just the kind of bright young radical the UAW needed. But in California Reuther repeatedly blocked Schrade's insurgency and used his considerable influence to keep O'Halloran on as Region 6 director. In 1955 Reuther finally dumped O'Halloran in favor of a more respectable figure, but the UAW president still kept Schrade on the Region 6 sidelines, this time by enticing him to come work at Solidarity House, where Schrade later served as one of Reuther's key assistants.[46]

Violation of caucus discipline brought swift and devastating retribution. When in 1953 an International representative, Panfilo Campja, organized a surprise coup that defeated Thomas Starling for the directorship of the southern region, Reuther and the rest of the executive board determined to make an example of the upstart. Starling had been a drunkard, as well as inattentive to the racial issues then beginning to simmer in the southern assembly plants, but Campja's crime would not be forgiven. "We felt that what he did was an act of betrayal," remembered Martin Gerber. The rest of the executive board simply boycotted Campja, while Reuther sent Jack Conway and other top staffers south to organize opposition to his reelection. As Gerber succinctly put it, "We could have run a lamppost against Campja and beaten him." He was out of office and out of the UAW, but not without a few sad words at the 1955 convention bemoaning the union's "controlled democracy."[47]

Given such organizational imperatives, it is not surprising that Reuther took extreme measures when he found himself confronting the full-blown factional opposition that emerged out of Local 600. Reuther thought that he had finally neutralized the big local in 1950 when thirty-four-year-old Carl Stellato, who won election to the local's presidency as a Reutherite, put five of the local's most prominent Communists on trial for violation of the previously unenforced clause in the UAW constitution that barred Communists from holding union office. Reuther's good friend and fellow ADA activist Abe Zwerling handled the actual prosecution of the bitterly contested case. The Zwerling-Reuther strategy was not dissimilar from that of the recently completed CIO "trials," which had finally expelled some ten Communist-led unions earlier in the year. Zwerling thought it sufficient to demonstrate that the Rouge building leaders Ed Locke, Paul Boatin, John Gallo, Nelson Davis, and David Moore had held political views identical to those of the *Daily Worker* for several years. Commented B. J. Widick in *Labor Action*, "It's amazing! Walter Reuther points out a thousand times in a thousand speeches that Stalinism cannot be defeated by force alone—superior ideas and a better program for the workers is the only answer! Yet in the UAW today, the only answer to Stalinism is bureaucratic force!"[48]

Even Reuther's considerable powers could not untangle the Local 600 knot. The big Rouge local was an entire world of ethnic and ideological complexity, and its political trajectory did not always run parallel with that of Reutherite America. Ford Motor Company's effort to speed up production and decentralize operations made anti-Reuther polemics an attractive temptation, especially for essentially opportunist politicians like Carl Stellato, who had to contend with the still sizable Communist faction at the Rouge. Indeed, Locke, Davis, and others associated with the party were usually reelected to important offices in the Rouge. By early 1951 Stellato had come to the well-founded conclusion that only a break with Reuther and a de facto alliance with the Communist-oriented "progressives" could sustain his presidency.[49]

He signaled the switch at the UAW's 1951 convention, where he argued that Reuther should put the union's vexing dues increase issue to a membership referendum rather than vote it through at the convention. The UAW clearly needed the additional income, but many delegates, and not only the anti-Reuther radicals, were aware of much rumbling back in the shops. They saw the dues question as a device by which they could signal their displeasure with the five-year contract, the Korean War layoffs, and the chronic speedup problems. But this time Reuther was determined to push it through, tongue-lashing "the great Carl Stellato" and other equivocators and admonishing them to "step up to your responsibilities. . . . Don't hide behind the rank and file."[50] Reuther got his dues increase, but *Ford Facts* responded with a counteroffensive under the banner headline "BETRAYAL." Stellato wrote that a "high-powered, well-oiled political machine" was destroying a formerly "hectic, militant, truly democratic organization."[51]

Local 600 now emerged as an energetic center of opposition to virtually all elements of the Reuther program. Stellato denounced the five-year contract as a form of "entrapment" and opened a coordinated campaign to fight Korean War–era job losses with the slogan "30 hours work for 40 hours pay." Just as Reuther had once distributed the *West Side Conveyor* to all the anti-Martin activists in the UAW, now Stellato and company made *Ford Facts* a unionwide organ of Reuther's opposition.

"We used to come out weekly," remembered Walter Dorosh, a skilled-trades Communist in the early 1950s. "When I was running the paper, every local in the city was ordering hundreds of copies."[52] When Stellato invited John L. Lewis to be the featured speaker at Local 600's gala tenth anniversary celebration in June 1951, Reuther and the rest of his executive board boycotted the event. The old lion attacked Reuther as a "pseudo-intellectual nincompoop" and compared the five-year escalator contract to the sliding wage scales imposed by the coal operators in the late nineteenth century. Asserted Lewis: "These profoundly intellectual union leaders should stop dreaming dreams and start paying attention to the bread and butter problems of the members."[53]

Reuther thought Lewis little more than a bad joke, but he had to take Local 600's capacity to undermine the Treaty of Detroit far more seriously. After the 1949 speedup strike Reuther had personally assured Ford personnel director John Bugas that once Ford signed a GM-style five-year contract the UAW and the company would open "a lengthy period of stable and peaceful relations." But Ford workers were as strike-prone as ever: by one company calculation, strikes and walkouts, most in the Rouge itself, generated more than one hundred times the number of lost production hours as at GM. And given the Local 600 campaign against Reuther's bargaining strategy, Bugas had good reason to believe that Stellato and his faction were quite willing to wink at such shop militancy.[54]

If wildcat strikes and bargaining strategy had been the only issues in dispute at the Rouge, Reuther would not have had such a difficult problem. By 1952 the "labor problem" was on its way to a thorough domestication. After fifteen years in the business, Reuther knew how to contain wildcat strikes without great damage, and he also knew how to unleash shop militancy when it served his larger purposes. But Local 600's oppositional independence also raised the civil rights issue in a fashion that Reuther found far more subversive. Even at America's McCarthyite nadir, the Communists retained a certain legitimacy within the black community. There recruitment still took place, political alliances were forged with progressive ministers and local NAACP activists, and antilynching campaigns generated support reminiscent of the old Popular Front days. Local 600 blacks in and near the party took the leading role in the Detroit Negro Labor Council (NLC), a classic front organization that nevertheless had genuine resonance among hundreds of the most politically active African-American unionists. With staff support from Local 600, the NLC began a citywide petition drive to put a referendum mandating creation of a municipal fair employment practices commission (FEPC) on Detroit's 1951 ballot.[55]

Reuther also wanted an FEPC law in Michigan. Whatever the level of racism among white autoworkers, Reuther understood that by the early 1950s civil rights was one of the central questions by which liberalism defined its meaning and measured its progress. Reuther sat on the board of directors of the NAACP, and almost all of the top UAW officers were life members of that organization. In Detroit the union turned over the entire regional apparatus—offices, phone banks, and mailing lists—during the local NAACP chapter's annual membership drive. The UAW probably contributed more funds to the national NAACP than did all other trade unions combined. With Joe Rauh as his Washington counsel and friend, Reuther had one of the nation's most prominent civil rights and civil liberties attorneys on retainer. Rauh, a confidant of A. Philip Randolph and Hubert Humphrey, helped write the 1948 Democratic Party platform plank on civil rights that sparked the Dixiecrat walkout; four years later he filed for the UAW an amicus curiae brief in *Brown vs. Board of Education*. Reuther himself proved a highly visible and articulate spokesman for the UAW's civil rights agenda. He frequently testified before Congress, gave the keynote speech at almost every CIO civil rights conference, and lectured his own locals on the need to push forward the International's fair employment programs. "By delaying FEPC we are giving Communist propagandists a psychological weapon as potent as a stockpile of H-bombs," Reuther told a Michigan CIO conference late in 1951.[56]

But Reuther was willing to go only so far. In the early 1950s Reuther feared both the inflammation of popular racism and the threat that the Communists might sill capitalize upon sentiment within the black community for a more vigorous antidiscrimination program. Reuther therefore proceeded with much caution. For example, the NAACP's Emergency Civil Rights Mobilization, to which the UAW sent eighty local officials and staffers in January 1950, had a dual agenda. Convened in Washington, hundreds of Mobilization participants lobbied Congress against Rule 22 and for a national FEPC bill. Those efforts proved fruitless, but such lobbying was not the Mobilization's only function. Central to its purpose, as Walter Reuther urged upon NAACP Secretary Roy Wilkins, was the elimination of Communist and Popular Front elements from coalition with mainstream civil rights activists, a task begun with great energy by the conference's Credentials Committee and thereafter policed by Reuther, Joe Rauh, and others well into the 1960s.[57]

Given such a perspective, it is not surprising that Reuther and the UAW denounced the Local 600–NLC referendum effort as an "irresponsible, Communist-inspired approach" launched without prior consultation "with the UAW-CIO . . . or other sincere advocates of FEPC in this community." After the Edwards debacle of 1949, Reuther and other Michigan liberals feared that any effort to take racial issues to the electorate might well generate another white backlash; thus, the UAW stood aside during Albert Cobo's effortless reelection campaign of 1951, while firmly rejecting any union mobilization on behalf of the Rev. Charles Hill, the former Detroit NAACP president whose left-wing campaign for city council swept the city's African-American wards. As in Washington, the Reutherites were determined to monopolize—for themselves or their allies in the equally anti-Communist NAACP—all civil rights activity in an effort to deprive the Communists of any broader access to the black community. Here was a telling instance of the politics of anti-Communism trumping that of civil rights even on an issue of such importance to the character of midcentury liberalism. The Jewish Labor

Committee, the NAACP, and the UAW worked strenuously and successfully to counter the FEPC petition drive and keep their rivals off the ballot. As William Oliver confessed to Jack Conway after the demise of the Negro Labor Council's petition: "If they had been successful, their influence would have grown greatly and they would have made great inroads in the Negro community." The Communists were thwarted, but so too was the momentum for a Michigan FEPC, which did not get through the legislature until 1955, long after that of most other northern industrial states.[58]

Local 600 was therefore a large bone in Reuther's throat when a Detroit visit by the House Un-American Activities Committee brought the conflict to crisis proportions. The HUAC hearings of February and March 1952 contained all the now-standard elements of the McCarthyite melodrama. Much time and testimony was spent in identifying Communists who continued to hold office and wield influence within Detroit unions and civil rights organizations, but the larger theme was that of the incapacity of the UAW and the rest of the liberals to divorce themselves from these subversives. With "kids in Korea dying," Reuther feared that Washington reactionaries planned "to try to put the union in a position where we were condoning the communists and were covering up for the communists."[59]

The hearings reopened an ugly doorway to the racial and political passions that lurked just beneath the surface. Most African-American witnesses put up a magnificent show of defiance. By attacking the racist background of the several southern committee members and asserting their own civil rights patriotism, the black activists Charles Hill, Coleman Young, a veteran militant, and William Hood, an NLC leader who was recording secretary of Local 600, put their interrogators on the defensive and won near-universal approbation from the African-American press and pulpit. But if Detroit's black leadership demonstrated a remarkable immunity to the McCarthyite virus, white resistance proved almost nil within the factories, offices, and unions of the great city.

The collapse began when the Detroit newspapers gave enormous coverage to the testimony of Bernice Baldwin, an FBI informant inside the Michigan CP who reeled off the names, duties, and places of employment of scores of Communists active in the labor movement. Almost immediately a wave of violence and intimidation swept through a dozen Detroit factories. Scores of workers named as Communists were beaten up and hustled out to the street. Blacks came under particularly vicious attack: in more than one shop a symbolic lynching rope was hung from a crane or scaffolding. At Chrysler's Jefferson Avenue assembly plant, shop leaders who tried to protect one former Communist were abused, cursed, and called "Nigger-lovers" by many among the heavily southern-born workforce. Soon the purge spread well beyond the blue-collar working class. A packed meeting of the normally liberal Detroit Federation of Teachers voted two to one against defending an art teacher of twenty-three years' seniority who was accused at the hearings of being a Communist Party member, and the Musicians' Union expelled a Detroit Symphony violinist. Diego Rivera's incendiary murals of factory life at the Detroit Institute of the Arts were saved from destruction only after the city art commission found that it could find in them no trace of "ideology."[60]

For Walter Reuther, this was a moment of near-panic. He denounced the assault from the congressional reactionaries, but even more he feared "the irreparable damage" facing the UAW if rank-and-file autoworkers came to identify Communism with the UAW's brand of trade unionism. Already two thousand workers at Midland Steel had walked out when local officials defended the due process rights of a Communist there. At the Rouge, Reuther expected turmoil and fistfights. "The membership will revolt against our Union because they are revolting against Communism," Reuther warned his executive board. Organizing drives would come to a halt. "People are incensed," Reuther blurted out. "The good name of our international union has got to be protected."[61]

With Local 600 now a nationally advertised symbol of laborite Communism, Reuther moved the whole weight of the UAW directly against it. Within hours after HUAC had concluded its hearings on March 12, Reuther opened his own proceedings directed toward putting the big local in an "administratorship" directly under the control of his executive board. There was nothing subtle about this exercise in raw power. Reuther personally presented the executive board's case during a nine-hour "trial" two days later, and although he repeatedly claimed that the UAW followed democratic procedures, the whole event reflected the HUAC spirit. Reuther's brief was twofold: Local 600 President Carl Stellato had made a deal with the Rouge Communists to avoid the punishment required under the UAW constitution, and Stellato's own attack on Reuther's "political machine" was tantamount to a "betrayal" of the UAW. "[Westbrook] Pegler could not have written a more anti-union article," asserted Reuther, with a copy of Ford Facts in hand. ". . . Free speech does not permit you to stand up in a crowded theatre and yell 'Fire!'" As for the Communists, their cowardly use of the Fifth Amendment was little more than a "subterfuge." Reuther's closest confidants, including Jack Conway and Leonard Woodcock, thought the trial and subsequent administratorship an unprincipled capitulation to the HUAC. But Reuther would not delay. To "clean up" Local 600, he made himself chairman of a six-man board of administration composed of all the union's top officers. Jack Conway was put in charge of actually running the big local.[62]

At first the International's steamroller proceeded without a hitch. Conway fired twenty left-wing staffers, while the UAW administrative board stripped the five Rouge Communists of their elected offices. Ford Facts ceased its campaign against the five-year contract and the Reutherite bargaining system. Working through the Association of Catholic Trade Unionists, Reuther began to assemble a slate to oppose Stellato in the local's elections. But the takeover soon turned into a huge embarrassment after Conway reported that an explicitly Reutherite slate was doomed against Stellato and his allies. "They made martyrs of us and they knew it," crowed William Hood when the International announced that it was abandoning any effort to campaign against the Stellato group.[63]

Reuther's real problem was that his faction had lost the capacity to reproduce itself when it was not in control of the union apparatus. When Reuther's seizure of Local 600 first hit the headlines, an old partisan of the UAW leader cracked, "I can remember when we used to beat those bastards in elections." Even the ACTU complained that it had lost support in the Rouge: all its key activists had been recruited onto the International staff. "When they go to West Grand Boulevard [the regional headquarters] or Solidarity House, although it's only a few miles from Local 600, they might as well be across the ocean."[64] Thus in the September 1952 unit elections anti-Reuther candidates swept fifteen Rouge buildings and carried more than 80 percent of the delegates to the Local's general council. Stellato won reelection a few months later and consolidated his power as never before; he remained a thorn in Reuther's side for the balance of the decade.[65]

Reuther's humiliation at the Rouge proved but one index of his declining capacity to mobilize a politically coherent movement and influence American politics. When he interviewed UAW staffers at the end of the 1950s, the novelist Harvey Swados often heard them remark, "The leadership is ahead of the rank and file."[66] Indeed, social memory and historical scholarship define the 1950s as a "conservative" decade in which an affluent working class turned its back on the radical values of an earlier decade. But working-class consciousness in the 1950s seemed conservative only when measured against a somewhat mythic image of the 1930s. Neither racism, anti-Communism, nor apolitical apathy was a new phenomenon in the postwar era. The more telling comparison may well be with the nonunion 1920s (or better yet, with the 1980s and 1990s), when the political alienation, ethnic competition, and deunionization of so many blue-collar workers severed the linkage between political consciousness and class status.

That relationship was still important in the 1950s. When Arthur Kornhauser surveyed the political attitudes of Detroit autoworkers in 1952, he found that few workers opposed outright the union's extensive political engagement—in sharp contrast to the prewar era, when the slogan "Keep politics out of the union and the union out of politics" won applause at many a union meeting. Although Dwight Eisenhower won a landslide in the general election, Adlai Stevenson still won 75 percent of UAW votes, compared with only 55 percent of all unionists. Among Catholics, who were still a largely working-class group, 81 percent of UAW members voted for the Democratic presidential candidate, compared with 50.5 percent of all Catholics; among Protestants, 71 percent of the autoworkers voted for Stevenson, compared with just 36 percent of the entire group. "Detroit area auto workers are not going 'middle class,'" concluded Kornhauser, whose verdict was confirmed by a generation of sociologists who studied this well-paid proletarian social strata. Autoworkers thought business too powerful, wanted labor to have more influence in government, and trusted the electoral recommendations of their leaders.[67]

What had changed between the 1930s and the 1950s was not some abstract measure of political consciousness, but the range of opportunities for political expression and social action that confronted those same autoworkers, in the factory, in the union, and in the electoral arena. The unionization of more than one-third of all workers outside the South had given to American party politics a definite social democratic tinge; thus, in 1954 and 1958 liberal-labor forces would again make substantial headway in both the House and the Senate. But these electoral shifts never bore the fruit expected of them, for the liberal wing of the Democratic Party could not bring to bear its full weight, either within its own party or in the national legislature. At its most obvious level, the system was rigged—not unlike the Prussian Reichstag a half-century before—on behalf of a landed elite and its Republican allies. The maintenance of a racially exclusive franchise and a rigid system of congressional seniority enabled the South's white oligarchy to project its power directly into the heart of the national polity. And because of the vital role the South still played in Democratic presidential politics, even those Democrats elected from solid laborite constituencies were drawn into compromise and coalition with the right. The CIO bargained with the Democratic Party "much as it would with an employer," admitted the CIO-PAC head Jack Kroll in the early 1950s. Thus the radical disjunction between the relative solidity of the working-class vote and the weakness of its political representation contributed to the demobilization and demoralization of those very forces upon which Reuther counted.[68]

The emergence of both Adlai Stevenson and Lyndon Johnson as Democratic Party leaders demonstrated the extent to which this shift had marginalized Reuther and the UAW. Like so many liberals, Reuther was captivated by Adlai Stevenson's eloquence and genuinely impressed with his defense of civil liberties while governor of Illinois. But on the core issues of American social politics, Stevenson's candidacy represented a retreat from even Truman's equivocal brand of Fair Deal liberalism. Stevenson did not favor the repeal of Taft-Hartley, opposed national health insurance, and believed that civil rights legislation should be left to the states so that the federal government did not "put the South over a barrel." As John Kenneth Galbraith noted, "He ran for President not to rescue the downtrodden but to assume the responsibilities properly belonging to the privileged."[69]

"This man, now clearly a candidate, presents us with a problem," Don Montgomery wrote to Reuther just before the 1952 Democratic National Convention. As part of an ADA delegation, Reuther met with Stevenson for three hours on July 12, but the meeting proved a fiasco. Reuther was enthralled by Stevenson's patrician manner, but incredibly, he never raised the issue of how Stevenson stood on FEPC or other civil rights questions. "Walter was so mesmerized by this guy . . . his beautiful English and his beautiful common sense that he forgot to ask," remembered Joe Rauh with astonishment. But it was more than a lapse of memory, for neither Reuther nor the ADA was willing to draw the line on such issues.[70]

For his part, Stevenson was determined to accommodate the Democratic Party's southern wing, and to do so he was willing to keep the labor-liberals at arm's length. At the Democratic Convention, Stevenson's forces threw their weight against a loyalty pledge for southern delegates and quietly worked to weaken the party's 1948 civil rights plank. Then Stevenson went on to reject the Tennessee liberal Estes Kefauver for vice president, in favor of Alabama's orthodox John Sparkman. Franklin Roosevelt, Jr., called Stevenson the "Northern Dixiecrat," and from the other side of the political spectrum the *Wall Street Journal* asserted, "The Democratic Party itself called a halt to the militant movement that for 20 years has been known as the Fair Deal or New Deal." Six weeks later, when the Democratic candidate kicked off his campaign in Cadillac Square, he made no concessions to the UAW. "You are not my captives," Stevenson told the smallish crowd that showed up. "And I am not your captive."[71]

In the fall the UAW faced a double loss. Stevenson was swept aside in the Eisenhower landslide, but this may well have been the lesser defeat. Eisenhower had relatively short coattails, and as Reuther liked to point out, his election had been a personal one. The Republican victory had not greatly eroded labor's electoral base, nor was the Eisenhower administration about to launch an assault upon the fundamental structures of the New Deal state or the Treaty of Detroit. Eisenhower himself was curious about Reuther, and in a meeting a few weeks after the inauguration he was impressed by Reuther's dexterous mind and corporatist vision. The president even explored the possibility of convening the tripartite economic conference Reuther thought essential to deal with Korean War demobilization issues. But Eisenhower dropped the idea like a hot potato when he found out that to Republican congressional leaders any idea associated with the UAW president was political anathema.[72]

Reuther could hardly have been surprised by such a rebuff, but for labor-liberals the more serious problem was the further drift to the right of the Democratic Party's congressional leadership. The Democrats' loss of both the House and the Senate in 1952 increased the strength of the Dixiecrat wing and gave Lyndon Johnson his opportunity to make a successful push for Senate minority leader. Johnson was not the most reactionary of southern Democrats in the early 1950s, but after an early opportunistic alliance with the Roosevelt New Deal, he had rebuilt his career as a labor-baiting spokesman for the Texas establishment. Throughout the 1950s he would use his power, vastly enhanced after the Democrats rewon both chambers in 1954, to avoid conflict with the president and push the congressional liberals to the very margins of policy and politics. The resultant political stalemate simply demobilized the Democratic Party's liberal constituency. For the Reutherite liberals, Don Montgomery framed the issue with bitterness and precision: "How can we get out the vote and win in northern . . . states on a program sparked by champions of . . . tax loopholes, white supremacy and union busting?"[73]

Reuther was astute enough to understand that he had taken a political and organizational beating in 1952. He undertook no dramatic transformation in his politics, but the moment of defeat did make him realize that the greatest threat to his vision of a progressive and powerful union movement came from the political and social right, not from the tattered battalions to his left. Reuther therefore stepped back from the most autocratic measures inside the UAW and dropped much of his obsession with the remaining pockets of Communist influence within the CIO. He himself recognized that things had gotten out of hand. As he confessed to a meeting of his supporters just before opening the 1953 UAW convention: "How do you keep a union free and democratic . . . and yet prevent a small group of people . . . from tearing the guts out of the organization? It is not easy. That is how unions get bureaucratic. The easiest way to protect a union is to get bureaucratic so you can chop down anybody who raises a voice. We don't want that kind of a union."[74]

Reuther's election as president of the CIO after Philip Murray's death in the fall of 1952 had also demonstrated that he could not afford to alienate potential allies on his left. Reuther's ascendancy had long been expected, but his actual election to the office proved hardly triumphant. He defeated the CIO's longtime director of organization, Allan Haywood, by a mere 52 to 48 percent margin. Haywood was a popular figure: his constant travels had put him in contact with virtually every officeholder within the CIO, especially among the smaller unions, which required much guidance from the national office. But the surprisingly large degree of opposition to Reuther also reflected the CIO's failure to develop a distinctive postwar politics aside from that of militant anti-Communism. A stolid parochialism had advanced within the ranks of the CIO officialdom, spearheaded by David J. McDonald, Murray's vain and jealous successor at the Steel Workers, who literally hated "that no good red-headed socialist bastard Reuther." A certain cynicism toward the UAW president was evident even among his supporters. "Maybe we don't know where Reuther's going," a staffer from the Oil, Chemical, and Atomic Workers told Miriam Kolkin of the Federated Press, "but at least he's going someplace."[75]

Reuther spent most of his time in Detroit and never attempted to put his impress upon the CIO. He found the Jackson Place headquarters in Washington full of complacent steelworkers from the Murray regime. John Riffe, Reuther's ostensible second-in-command, was a McDonald man and a recent convert to Frank Buchman's "Moral Rearmament" movement, which preached a doctrine of social harmony and quasi-fascist social discipline. Because of the post–Korean War recession, which slashed CIO dues income, as well as McDonald's threat to pull the Steel Workers out of the organization, the CIO's field staff did little effective work. Reuther found that preparation for the CIO's orderly merger into the AFL was his chief order of business.[76]

Reuther took little pleasure in the merger negotiations; he saw the two-year process as one of organizational and financial necessity. By 1953 there were no coherent ideological differences between the CIO and the AFL, whose presidency had just been taken over by George Meany, a staunch anti-Communist nevertheless at ease among Reuther's generation of New Deal–Fair Deal liberals. Meany presided over an organization that was nearly twice the size of the CIO, whose smaller affiliates were threatened by constant raiding from big AFL unions such as the Teamsters and the International Brotherhood of Electrical Workers. Reuther's hand was therefore weak: the unity agreement finally worked out in February 1955 contained few of the provisions that he wanted prohibiting jurisdictional raids, racial discrimination, or corrupt practices among the AFL-CIO's more than one hundred affiliates. Reuther did win agreement for a new industrial union department from which he hoped to launch CIO-style organizing drives, but McDonald crippled the effort at the outset by insisting upon a 60 percent cut in the per capita dues tax paid by the affiliates of the old industrial union federation.[77]

Still, Reuther willed himself to believe that the merger might yet spark a new era of union activism. "We have not achieved labor unity based upon stagnation," he asserted at the founding convention of the AFL-CIO in late 1955. Reuther knew that cash-rich AFL unions put a low priority on organizing, but he hoped to "zip open those money bags" for an "organizational crusade to carry the message of unionism in the dark places of the South, into the vicious company towns, in the textile industry, in the chemical industry." When Mike Quill of the CIO Transport Workers Union charged that the merger agreement was a sellout to the "three R's" of the AFL—racism, racketeering, and raiding—Reuther responded that in the final analysis, "this is a matter of believing. . . . This is no time for doubt."[78]

Reuther needed this faith because stasis and conservatism were hardly absent even on the UAW executive board. John Livingston, who had been Reuther's point man when the UAW went to war against the FE, spoke for that large section of the union bureaucracy that was uninterested in Reuther's brand of social pioneering, resentful of his spartan values, and eager to reach an even more solid accommodation with corporate America. Reuther admired toughness, so he made Livingston head of the GM Department after Johnstone's forced departure in 1952. But Livingston actually began to assemble his own quasi-factional following, soon making it clear that he did not endorse the more ambitious elements of Walter Reuther's agenda. For example, when discussion finally turned to the union's guaranteed annual wage demand during a long bargaining session in 1955, Livingston ostentatiously pushed his chair back from the table with the disdainful remark, "This is not my issue; this is Walter Reuther's issue." Within months Reuther had eased Livingston out and into the new AFL-CIO, where he ran an ineffectual organizing department.[79]

Given the spreading influence of these conservatives, Reuther had to mend his fences with the left. At the 1953 convention Reuther let Stellato and the Local 600 militants have all the time they wanted to defend themselves. Tracy Doll and Sam Sage were readmitted to membership. Reuther even reached out to his Communist opponents to help put across his program in the shops. Walter Dorosh, who had been purged from his tool and die leadership post during the Local 600 administratorship, recalled the crisis generated by a 1955 "revolt" of the skilled trades as the occasion when Reuther and he reached a mutual accommodation.

Reuther knew that only the old radicals at the Rouge, Fisher No. 23, and the other big toolrooms retained the influence and ideological commitment necessary to counter the growth of craft separatism. "Look guys, we need your help," Reuther admitted during a tense meeting in the fall of 1955. Remembered Dorosh, "That was the first time I ever heard him say that."[80]

Reuther also called off the CIO campaign against the Communist-led unions. This first became apparent when Reuther, as president of the CIO, offered rebellious right-wingers within the United Packinghouse Workers (UPW) no comfort in their campaign to expose officials whose Popular Front associations within that union were hardly less than those in other organizations, like the UE or the FE, which had been thrown out of the CIO three years before. A CIO committee steered by Emil Mazey, impressed with the UPW's vigorous efforts to end racial discrimination even in the Deep South, found the top leadership of the Packinghouse Workers "free from communist domination or influence." Thereafter, UPW President Ralph Helstein counted Reuther a staunch ally within organized labor's higher circles.[81]

In Michigan the wheel also turned. HUAC returned to the state in the summer of 1954, this time focusing on Flint, where the committee sought to expose CP agitation in the GM factories. At Reuther's instigation, Joe Rauh immediately prepared a long and detailed denunciation of the legislative inquiry, which the UAW sent out to all its locals. By this time the televised Army-McCarthy hearings had done much to discredit the inquisitorial technique, so Reuther's indignation was hardly of a vanguard sort. Still, the UAW endorsed a rather vigorous defense of the Fifth Amendment. Communists were still ejected from the plants in Flint, but this time the UAW did not stand aside. The union pressured General Motors to give those in greatest danger leaves of absence, and it sent staffers into Flint to pacify the situation.[82]

However, Reuther was now burdened by his own history, for he was personally identified with the clause in the UAW constitution that barred Communists from holding any union office, appointive or elective. Reuther insisted that in dealings with HUAC and other government inquiries, the UAW would make a distinction between rank-and-file workers, whose right to take the Fifth Amendment was unlimited, and union staffers and officials, who were required to testify freely about their past political associations. Joe Rauh thought this distinction untenable, as did the American Civil Liberties Union, which declared that the UAW policy undermined the constitutional rights of its most active members.[83] Indeed, Reuther probably had second thoughts himself, because he knew that according to the expansive standards held by the Washington witch-hunters, virtually every UAW officer had a skeleton, if not in his or her own closet, then in that of a close comrade from the old days. Reuther told his staff that they had to testify about their own personal political history, but that the UAW would defend them if they refused to "smear some Joe Doakes who was in the Party when you were . . . and he is living a respectable life."[84]

Reuther was therefore happy to bankroll Rauh when in 1955 he took the case of the UAW staffer John T. Watkins up through the courts. Watkins had never actually been a member of the Communist Party, but he had been an FE militant with many CP contacts. He went on the UAW payroll in 1954 as a reward for finally swinging the East Moline Harvester plant into the UAW. His appointment opened the door to the even larger rapprochement between the long-suffering, but remarkably tough, FE cadre and the UAW. Consummating the long-sought merger, Reuther gave five FE leaders UAW staff jobs in return for the incorporation of the key farm equipment locals into a unified UAW Agricultural Implement Department. Meanwhile, Watkins had been convicted of contempt of Congress when, after recounting his own relationship to the party, he refused to tell HUAC whether he had known some thirty persons to be Communists. Rauh argued the case before the Supreme Court in 1957, and in one of the decade's landmark civil liberties decisions, won a reversal that imposed new judicial curbs on the investigative powers of congressional committees when they threatened individual rights guaranteed by the First Amendment.[85]

The Watkins case helped restore Reuther's reputation as a civil libertarian, but it actually created a situation in which UAW trial procedures for screening its officialdom were in some respects more stringent than those of the courts. Among union staffers and officers, there was no such thing as "taking the Fifth" inside the UAW. This generated scores of union trials involving not only the erstwhile Communists but those accused of unethical or undemocratic practices within their locals. All these internal disputes could be appealed to the UAW executive board or the biannual convention, but such quasi-judicial conflicts were time-consuming and disruptive. Given his new opening to the left, Reuther wanted to depoliticize these issues by getting them off his agenda and into the hands of an outside review board.

His opportunity came in 1957 when the Senate's new McClellan Committee investigating union corruption put issues of union democracy and racketeering in the headlines. The UAW's Public Review Board, formally endorsed at its convention in April of that year, proved a remarkably popular innovation, especially in liberal-labor circles, where it seemed further proof of Reuther's democratic and progressive instincts. Composed at most times of seven prestigious clergymen, jurists, and industrial relations academics—the last initially represented by Clark Kerr and Edwin Witte—the board held the power, upon appeal by an aggrieved party, to review any executive board decision that dealt with the union's internal, non-policy-making affairs. Reuther called this "acting as a public watchdog," but the board's function was also that of a convenient buck-passer. Reuther used the review board in just this fashion in its inaugural season when the UAW executive board happily off-loaded the cases of eleven union staffers and local officials whose complete break with their past Communist Party associations had been questioned by Sen. Barry Goldwater and other Republicans anxious to embarrass the UAW. These included two former FE staffers whose testimony before the Senate

Internal Security Subcommittee had been less than forthcoming. But the darkest of the McCarthy days were a half-decade past, and the eminent liberals on the review board gave all concerned a clean bill of health.[86]

The eclipse of the Communist issue gave the UAW's internal regime a somewhat more expansive political flavor, but the limits to Reutherite liberalism were now so deeply embedded within the political culture that the cruder sort of crackdown characteristic of the late 1940s and early 1950s was unnecessary. To his ideological left Reuther had virtually no enemies within the UAW. Guided by the party's 1955 decision to "join the mainstream of American labor," the few remaining Communists within the auto union now muted their criticism, while the Trotskyists either abandoned the auto union for posts in academe or joined the UAW staff as sophisticated defenders of Reuther's social democratic politics. The UAW's elaborate program of education and political mobilization continued, but it too reflected an increasingly narrow political orthodoxy. Guy Nunn was pulled off the air in the early 1960s, in part because his own still-radical personage had won a far higher profile in the shops than that of many regional directors. *Ammunition's* creative and radical edge was lost when the magazine was transferred from the Education Department to Public Relations; likewise, the UAW summer schools and periodic classes became increasingly inhospitable to unorthodox discourse. When during the late 1950s one young Socialist referred to the "class struggle" at a Port Huron class, Roy Reuther fumed, "Don't use that kind of sectarian Marxist crap in this school!"[87]

By the late 1950s Walter Reuther's options as a unionist and politician had been drastically reduced, within both the collective bargaining system and the world of domestic politics. Reuther was neither complacent nor conservative: he remained a whirlwind of activity and a fount of proposals, ideas, and initiatives. And yet Reuther no longer commanded a political instrument that could make its full weight felt or feared at either the bargaining table or the ballot box. Manipulation of his own constituency had for so long taken the place of mobilization that a kind of institutionalized hypocrisy became second nature. Reuther sometimes glimpsed the dual nature of the regime over which he presided, but more often he masked his own inner conflict with an asceticism that was itself a kind of indulgence. As his friend Joe Rauh put it, "Walter was lost in some fantasy that life depended on his being more virtuous than anyone else." Indeed, there was a larger hypocrisy at work, one that reflected the crisis of American liberalism itself. As Harvey Swados reflected at this time: "One cannot complain, as one might with almost any other union, of an absence of intellect, or of a lack of application of that intellect to the problems of our age. What one can say, I think with justification, is that the UAW leadership no longer takes its own demands seriously."[88]

15

REUTHER ABROAD: "PRODUCTION IS THE ANSWER"

Trade unions are at one with business men in believing that mass-production private capitalism offers the world's best answer to poverty and unrest—and believing too, that it is a progressive and revolutionary system compared with many of the backward class-ridden regimes they find in Europe and elsewhere.

—C. A. R. Crosland, "The Transition from Capitalism,"
New Fabian Essays, 1952

We cannot afford to leave foreign policy to the State Department.

—Walter Reuther, 1953

Early in the cold war years, Walter Reuther was the most famous American labor leader in the world. His name recognition was always far greater than his actual power in international trade union affairs, but in the cold war context, appearances had their own political leverage. To millions in Western Europe and Asia, the disappointments and frustrations Reuther encountered at home seemed largely inconsequential measured against his energetic appearance as the cosmopolitan representative of American liberalism, a humane and refreshing contrast to the darker shadows so often cast by cold war America and its militarized diplomacy.

With his brother Victor, who would spend more than two decades as the UAW's chief international affairs strategist, Walter Reuther began his active engagement in trade union diplomacy only after the postwar effort to reconstruct a Popular Front in Europe had been broken. By 1948 the World Federation of Trade Unions (WFTU), in which the CIO, the British Trade Union Congress, and the Soviet "trade unions" had maintained a gingerly cooperation, was well on its way to disintegration. This collapse on the left was a function not only of the growing cold war antagonism between the United States and the Soviet Union but also of the generation-long civil war between Socialists and Communists that World War II had only briefly suspended. In France and Italy, Socialist and Catholic trade unionists had virtually completed their withdrawal from the big Communist-influenced labor federations even before the Marshall Plan exacerbated these divisions within the European left. Announced by Secretary of State George Marshall in a Harvard speech of June 1947, the five-year, $17 billion aid program made certain that the reconstruction of Western Europe would take place within a context that anchored those nations receiving U.S. aid firmly within American capitalism's economic and political orbit. When the Soviet Union made rejection of the program a central tenet of its ideological counteroffensive, the cold war was well and truly launched.[1]

In this political contest the U.S. government needed the help of American unionists because even the most conservative State Department mandarins recognized the power of anticapitalist sentiment in Western Europe and the extent to which the entire political spectrum there had shifted to the left. Throughout Europe industrial elites who had collaborated with the fascists were greatly weakened, and the influence of the left—whether of social democratic or Communist orientation—was greatly enhanced. As the British intellectual A. J. P. Taylor assured his listeners in a BBC broadcast of November 1945, "Nobody in Europe believes in the American way of life—that is, in private enterprise; or rather those who believe in it are a defeated party and a party which seems to have no more future than the Jacobites in England after 1688."[2] Victor Reuther bearded a conservative audience of Detroit businessmen with the same views three years later: "Very few people in Europe give a hoot about private profits or private property," he told the Detroit Economic Club after his 1948 tour of the Continent. "That was settled after World War I."[3] In Germany, Austria, Finland, France, and Italy, trade union movements that had virtually destroyed during the 1930s came roaring back. In this atmosphere even conservatively dominated governments—such as that led by Charles de Gaulle in France—nationalized a substantial chunk of the most important and most politically tainted banks and companies. Across the war-torn continent ministers and managers took responsibility for national planning, full employment, and a higher standard of living. These were the years of the "battle for production."

American policy in the reconstruction of Western Europe was guided, there-fore, not simply by anti-Communism, and not by outright hostility to social demo-cratic industrial planning, but by what the historian Charles Maier has character-ized as "the politics of productivity." The Marshall Plan sought a long-term restructuring of Western capitalism in which economic growth would depoliticize issues of political economy into a technocratic world of output, efficiency, and modernization. Administered by such liberal capitalists as Paul Hoffman and Averell Harriman—both of whom had a good working relationship with the Reuther brothers—the European Recovery Program (ERP) sought to convince both capitalists and workers that class tensions might well dissolve in a general pro-gram of high productivity, labor-management collaboration, and raised living stan-dards. "I am here to talk to you not about ideologies, because we have no Ameri-can ideologies to export," CIO Secretary-Treasurer James Carey lectured a 1947 meeting of the World Federation of Trade Unions, "but about food and coal and fertilizers and agricultural machinery, and power plants." Europeans had to learn, Paul Hoffman wrote, that the United States was "the land of full shelves and bulging shops made possible by high productivity and good wages" and by a way of life "marked by the primacy of the person in a setting of teamwork."[4]

Here were the essential elements of a European Treaty of Detroit, but one nego-tiated on a terrain even more difficult than that of postwar America. Marshall Plan-ners knew that aside from all the technical and economic problems in the recon-struction of the Continent's obsolete and war-torn industry, even their most optimal projections for economic recovery could not contemplate an actual increase in working-class living standards until the early 1950s. Until then the sur-plus generated by greater productivity had to be reinvested and the European working class convinced that such sacrifice was necessary. "It is essential to [the] success of ERP that non-communists regain and hold control of European labor movements," wired the State Department to the American ambassador in Rome—thus the importance of American trade union support for and input into the administration of the European Recovery Program. The appearance of Secretary of State Marshall at the 1947 CIO convention made this clear, as did the subse-quent appointment of almost eighty American unionists as Economic Cooperation Administration (Marshall Plan) aides and State Department labor attachés.[5]

Like other CIO anti-Communists, Reuther offered the Marshall Plan a strong endorsement. He wanted the participation of American labor to ensure "demo-cratic methods" in the reconstruction of Europe, but Reuther was also certain that, to defeat Communism, "production is the answer, at least the biggest part of the answer."[6] With Victor he would soon become critical of the actual adminis-tration of the European Recovery Program, but in these early years the Reuther brothers were quite willing to troll for U.S. government funds on behalf of the social democratic unionists they saw as the key bulwark against Communist influ-ence within the European labor movement. With other U.S. unionists, Walter made anti-Communist radio broadcasts to Italy just before the crucial elections of

April 1948. Three months later, when Victor flew into Berlin with the airlift, he met with the American high commissioner for Germany, General Lucius Clay, and secured seven hundred thousand Reich marks for distribution to trade unionists in the eastern zone of Berlin. After the American elections that fall, Victor urged Walter to get the CIO to step up its work in Europe; moreover, Victor wanted his brother and other top CIO people to meet with Truman and secure at least five million dollars for AFL and CIO groups in Europe. Walter's younger brother recognized the potential for embarrassment: "I cannot over-emphasize the importance [that] whatever funds are sent in the name of Labor being channeled through trade-union groups. Under no circumstances should there ever be any indication that funds other than trade-union contributions are being sent to these trade union groups overseas."[7]

In December 1949 Reuther flew to London for the founding conference of the International Confederation of Free Trade Unions (ICFTU), where the CIO joined the AFL, the British Trade Union Congress, and other national labor centers in establishing the West's resolutely anti-Communist trade union front. Touring the Continent for the first time since his sojourn in the early 1930s, Reuther first traveled to Germany, where he found the situation well in hand: the social democratic unionists in Berlin were "really in the front lines in the fight against Communism." But France was a different and more dismal story. He thought the Socialist split from the Communist-led Confédération Générale du Travail (CGT) in late 1947 had been premature. The anti-Communist Force Ouvriere (FO), largely concentrated in government employment and white-collar fields, had insufficient numbers and resources to take on the CGT. The FO was virtually insolvent, and at Renault, perhaps the key production facility in all of France, Communists had just won 89 percent of the vote in the works council elections. The anti-Communist forces could not fight with "peanuts," Reuther told Assistant Secretary of State George W. Perkins. "They must have the kind of money which can match the resources of the Communists, whose sources of funds are certainly not confined to membership dues." Reuther thought that the AFL and the CIO might together raise a million dollars to aid anti-Communist unions in France and Italy, but to give U.S. unions real influence abroad, labor would need "supplementary funds" from government sources.[8]

Clearly, Reuther did not then realize the extent to which the U.S. government was already funding AFL operations in Europe, perhaps as much as two million dollars a year. But Reuther won his small funding slice as well. In what would later become a highly publicized incident, the CIA officer Thomas Braden flew to Detroit in the fall of 1951 and hand-delivered to Walter Reuther fifty thousand dollars in cash; Walter sent the money on to Victor, who was now the CIO's European representative in Paris, where the funds supported a CIO effort to strengthen the FO and consolidate an anti-Communist organizing drive in the Parisian metal working industry. From the CIA's point of view, the covert money transfer was really a gambit, part of Braden's larger effort to enlist as subsidized organs of American foreign policy a whole phalanx of ostensibly independent and liberal-left institutions, including the Congress for Culture Freedom, the British magazine *Encounter*, the National Student Association, and the World Assembly of Youth.[9]

Braden might well have expected that Walter Reuther was willing to join this effort, certainly if he took as evidence a brief essay that appeared under Reuther's byline in *Collier's* magazine for October 27, 1951. Graced with a lurid cover that portrayed atomic bombs exploding over the Soviet Union, this infamous issue may well mark the cold war's absolute ideological nadir. Apparently inspired by Arthur Koestler, who had just published *Darkness at Noon*, the entire magazine was devoted to essays by journalists and public figures—many of a decidedly liberal bent—describing their participation in "World War III" and in Russia's subsequent reconstruction. Reuther's contribution reported upon his return visit to Gorky, where he greeted workers newly freed from Stakhanovite oppression and helped put in place a UAW-style trade union.[10]

Walter was probably embarrassed by the actual appearance of the magazine; Victor thought the essay made his brother look like a Nazi *gauditer* in charge of an occupied country. Thus Braden got nowhere when he later approached Victor at an American embassy meeting in Paris to inform him of the CIA funds taken by his brother and to suggest not only that he accept additional monies but that he keep the arrangement hidden from his ostensible boss, CIO President Philip Murray. According to Victor's recollection of a quarter-century later, he was "shocked and angry" and rejected the idea on the spot. Walter was not so fastidious as his younger brother, but in this case he followed Victor's lead. Both reactions accord with the memory of no less a figure than James Jesus Angleton, the legendary chief of CIA counterespionage, who remembered the Reuther brothers as "soft and naive."[11]

The Reuther brothers were staunch anti-Communists, but they were also more willing than either the State Department or the AFL to subordinate grand strategy to the unique history and character of each national labor movement. In Latin Europe they respected the secular, Republican tradition that so often divided Socialists from Christian Democrats; moreover, they saw social democracy not as "soft" on Communism but as the most authentic and effective force defending the traditions of an independent labor movement. Thus they hectored the military occupation authorities in Germany and Austria, whose bias toward the old bourgeoisie and deflationary fiscal policy put obstacles in the path of a Keynesian democratization of society. For example, when Victor visited Germany in 1948, he became convinced that American military authorities were "lukewarm and unpredictable friends of German democracy." The U.S. military had allowed prominent Nazis to return to their important posts in industry, had vetoed a co-determination law in the state of Hesse, and had continued to dismantle steelworks and engineering factories, thereby demoralizing working-class advocates sympathetic to the West. In a widely reported speech, "Is the Marshall Plan in Danger," Victor asserted, "If we want German democracy to grow we are going to have to help it—and in order to help it we must be able to tell a democrat from a Nazi on the rebound." On the dismantlement issue Walter sent President Truman a well-documented protest, which helped end the practice. He often summed up his own outlook with the pungent, hopeful comment that "we have got to make it clear that the choice in the world is not between Stalin or Standard Oil."[12]

The CIO therefore set up its own Paris office as a way of influencing the administration of the Marshall Plan's labor program and maintaining its own independent role in European trade union affairs. Victor headed up this office from 1951 to 1953, when he returned to the United States to continue much the same work as head of the CIO International Affairs Department in Washington. Victor was happy to get out of Detroit: the unsolved assassination attempt made him feel like a hunted man, and with no substantive role in the all-important world of collective bargaining, he felt as if he would always remain Walter's kid brother if he stayed in the Motor City. In foreign affairs, as in domestic politics, Victor stood just to the left of his older brother: a tireless foe of colonialism, a friend of those favoring the denuclearization of Germany and Great Britain, and an early advocate, in Italy and elsewhere, of an "opening to the left" in coalition government. In annoyance, Walter sometimes called his younger brother "the deacon."[13]

Egged on by Victor, Walter was at loggerheads with George Meany, the AFL president after 1952, and with his chief foreign affairs specialist, Jay Lovestone, who had offered Homer Martin ideological tutelage in the 1930s. Lovestone had an utterly Manichaean view of the world: the defense of a liberal capitalist order required the most intransigent and sectarian hostility to the Communists and their allies. The spirit was entirely in keeping with that of his revolutionary youth, when Lenin and Zinoviev had used fair means and foul to split the world socialist movement. Now Lovestone continued this work, but from the other side of the divide. The AFL wanted a "free trade union movement" to combat Communism, but in southern Europe, and later in Africa, Asia, and Latin America, Lovestone and Meany were entirely willing to back the most conservative, corrupt, or state-controlled organizations to fill this role. Contemptuously, Lovestone often referred to the Reuther brothers as "the *yipsels.*" Victor replied in kind, repeatedly denouncing the AFL's "cloak and dagger operations" and the "indiscriminate white washing of the obvious shortcomings in U.S. foreign policy."[14] In the early 1950s the Reuthers channeled their international activities through the newly formed International Confederation of Free Trade Unions. The influence of British, Dutch, German, and Swedish trade unionists gave this international body a distinctly social democratic coloration. For example, in 1951 the CIO worked cooperatively with these unionists to secure ICFTU affiliation for Italy's socialist and anticlerical Unione Italiana del Lavoro, despite intense opposition from George Meany, who insisted that the Confederazione Italiana Sindacati Lavoratori, a group heavily subsidized both by the AFL and the Vatican, remain the only internationally recognized labor body. Later in the 1950s Reuther proved instrumental in securing the ICFTU presidency for his good friend Arne Geijer, a vigorous young leader of the Swedish metalworkers. Meany responded to the ICFTU's social democratic tilt by welshing on the AFL-CIO's full contribution; he considered the body tinged with neutralism and entirely unreliable in the anti-Communist battle.[15]

The 1955 merger between the AFL and CIO merely exacerbated the growing foreign policy conflict within the American house of labor. Victor Reuther thought it premature, a "shotgun wedding." Walter was more hopeful. Expecting the younger, more dynamic CIO leaders and staff to increase their influence gradually, he relinquished any claim to full-time office at the Washington headquarters. Walter Reuther would serve as merely one of the twenty-seven vice presidents on the AFL-CIO executive council, albeit *primus inter pares*.[16]

George Meany dominated the organization as its full-time president. A. H. Raskin described him in the early 1950s as a 220-pound "cross between a bull-dog and a bull." A tough, cigar-smoking, gruff-voiced man, Meany had been a full-time union official since 1923, when he became business agent for his father's plumbers local in the Bronx. He was always disdainful of the "missionary types" who saw organized labor as the core of a social movement; in later years he would boast that he had never walked a picket line or led a strike. Meany normally respected the autonomy and diversity of the individual unions joined under the AFL-CIO umbrella. He made no demands on them, so few unionists made any demands on him. In the 1930s, when he served as president of the New York State Federation of Labor, he aligned himself with the New Deal's economic and legislative agenda, but as a stolid craft unionist Meany always rejected the politics of social mobilization necessary to push this program forward in the postwar years.[17]

However, foreign affairs was another matter entirely. Here Meany was an activist who sought the centralization of power within the AFL-CIO executive council and its Free Trade Union Committee, over which Jay Lovestone held sway. During his twelve years as secretary-treasurer of the AFL, Meany had immersed himself in the struggle against Soviet-oriented trade unionism. He frequently traveled abroad and now saw himself as the central link between the U.S. government, overseas labor organizations, and the American union movement. He would set AFL-CIO policy and approve all appointments of labor personnel to government boards, agencies, and posts. Reuther soon realized that he could do nothing to curb Lovestone's influence within the merged organization or to prevent the U.S. government from funding a huge expansion of an AFL-CIO international affairs operation that functioned entirely apart from the ICFTU.

Both at home and abroad Reuther had a higher profile than Meany, but Reuther could never translate his renown into any real influence within the AFL-CIO. Meany ran the executive council in a personal fashion: during its ten-day meetings, often at resort hotels in Florida, Meany would spend plenty of time on the golf course or around the gin rummy table, but always as a kind of rolling caucus. Reuther would fly in at the last minute ready for programmatic debate. Henry Fleisher, a former CIO publicist, recalled the very first postmerger meeting: "Walter came in and said, 'Henry, do you have a copy of the agenda for the meeting?'

I said, 'No, what agenda?' And I can see a kind of wild look in Walter's eyes. He says, 'You mean there's no agenda?' I said, 'Well, none that I've ever seen or heard of.'" Within the AFL-CIO high command Reuther remained an alien presence who wanted to transform a college of cardinals into a combat organization. "Reuther was anathema to them," said Jack Barbash, who worked at the AFL-CIO's Washington headquarters just after the merger. "He never relaxed; he was always making a speech at them. You see, making a speech was almost his natural method of discourse."[18]

Reuther could barely hide his contempt for Meany, but he assumed that the AFL-CIO president, who was sixty-one at the time of the merger, would soon retire, opening the way to his own succession, or at the very least, that of a like-minded colleague. Thus Reuther could never quite decide whether to wage all-out war on Meany's leadership or to simply bide his time until the top spot in the AFL-CIO became available. Reuther's role within the merged federation therefore alternated between bouts of feverish activism and long months of neglect. When he did bring an issue to the table, Reuther often pulled back at the last moment, fearful either of revealing his own isolation or antagonizing the AFL conservatives whose support he would need if he ever hoped to win the presidency. Reuther "just washed himself out," remarked an otherwise sympathetic staffer.[19]

Meany returned Reuther's hostility with his own. He resented Reuther's fame and his independent access to so many politicians, diplomats, and leaders of the international labor movement. Meany assumed that personal ambition, not simply a more liberal ideological vision, dictated Reuther's frequent attack upon his policies. "Ideology is baloney," he once told a group of European unionists. "There can be no ideological differences among real trade-unionists." Of his young rival Meany once said, "What Reuther wants of me is to die, and I mean die."[20]

If Meany and Lovestone controlled the money, the manpower, and the files, Walter Reuther nevertheless held his own kind of international influence as a symbol and spokesman for one particularly attractive version of American life. In truth, Reuther never strayed far from the consensus that framed American foreign policy in these years, but he nevertheless saw himself as a liberal, a critic standing outside of the axis formed by the AFL, the congressional conservatives, and the Eisenhower-era State Department. Like most midcentury liberals, Reuther believed that in the long run the only way the West could win the cold war was through a dramatic and substantial rise in the standard of living among the citizens of the countries devastated by war and colonialism. In Delhi and Milan, as in Detroit and Milwaukee, Reuther believed that American production technique and organizational genius held the key to enhanced productivity and greater economic growth. In this sense, he was at one both with the Marshall Plan advocates of productivity politics and with the emerging school of modernization theorists who emphasized the linkages between bureaucratic rationality, industrial development, and democratic institutions.

At the founding conference of the ICFTU, Reuther chaired the committee that adopted Guy Nunn's ambitious draft of an economic development manifesto, "Bread, Peace, and Freedom." Six months later, after the outbreak of the Korean War, the UAW published a proposal modestly entitled "A Total Peace Offensive." This new Reuther Plan, which won considerable publicity, came in the wake of the Kremlin's own propaganda campaign for "peace." Reuther thought Asia would certainly be lost to Communism if the conflict were waged by military means alone. "They are fighting natives against us because the natives are hungry," Reuther told the UAW executive board. To wipe out "human misery and desperation," Reuther's peace plan envisioned a U.S. contribution of thirteen billion dollars annually for one hundred years to a United Nations development fund administered by a "People's World Assembly." Only such "bold action" could "win the loyalty and support of hundreds of millions of people and strip the Kremlin of its power to exploit them and sacrifice them in battles of aggression."[21] Later in the decade Reuther lectured a union audience: "We are now at a place where the struggle is not a matter of dividing up scarcity. We now have the opportunity and the new revolutionary force in the world which makes the Communists archreactionaries, the revolutionary power of economic abundance."[22]

Such views put Reuther in agreement with those who thought a central focus of U.S. foreign policy had to be the enhancement of economic growth. Accordingly, Victor Reuther served as cochairman of the Anglo-American Council on Productivity, which operated on the assumption that British trade union practice constituted one large obstacle to the Labour government's desperate export drive. In 1951 he helped put together a U.S.-funded "pilot plant" project that sought to move French firms away from the restrictive embrace of the traditional *patronat*, encourage technological change, and institute American-style collective bargaining. "The Communist union apparatus fills a vacuum created by failure of the democratic union forces to rally their own scattered ranks and provide leadership in behalf of the long-unsettled economic grievances of the French workers," argued Victor. He therefore deemed it of particular importance that non-Communist trade unions like Force Ouviere were for the first time negotiating a "productivity bonus" with individual firms. The Reuther brothers hoped these compacts would help the "democratic trade unions" win significant economic gains and "make inroads in the Communist strongholds."[23]

Walter Reuther proved a tribune of this kind of unionism, but by the time he again toured Europe in the summer of 1953 it was clear that productivity bargaining of the sort fostered by Marshall Plan diplomats had encountered obstacles barely foreseen two years before. In France and Italy the opposition came chiefly from employers who faced unions that were weak, divided, or, in the case of the Communist CGT, entirely uninterested in the kind of depoliticized bargaining required by an American-style focus on wage enhancement in a single firm or industry. In Italy the UIL had pulled out of the Marshall Plan's productivity program just as Reuther arrived in Rome for a talk with the new American ambassador, Clare Booth Luce. She appealed to Reuther to help persuade the UIL to resume its participation. Reuther found it amusing that Luce, who had baited the CIO unmercifully as a Republican congresswoman from Connecticut, now appreciated the importance of trade unionism in the anti-Communist struggle. But he turned the embassy down. "Hell, I wouldn't ask anybody to stay in this thing. . . . You show me in the whole of Europe one employer contract that spells out the guarantee that the worker who gets out more production is going to profit by higher earnings because of that greater production."[24]

In Germany and Austria employers were willing to sign such contracts, but in these countries social democratic union movements were already thinking in terms of a solidarity wage structure and corporatist bargaining scheme, symbolized in part by the German codetermination laws covering iron and steel. Such industrywide arrangements precluded the firm-specific wage negotiations that Reuther and other American unionists now took for granted as the essence of "free" collective bargaining. In Austria he told the American ambassador that unionists there would not be "sold" on greater productivity until "there could be assurances to labor that there would be sharing of benefits and safeguards against resulting unemployment." To advance this effort, Reuther favored sending a team of labor and management representatives to the United States to observe collective bargaining in Detroit and Pittsburgh.[25]

Marshall Plan efforts to implement productivity schemes often ended in failure, but the ideology of mass production and technocratic collaboration between labor and management nevertheless proved enormously attractive all across postwar Europe. As the historian Anthony Carew has demonstrated in his study of the Marshall Plan, the European Cooperation Agency put out much propaganda hailing a mythic industrial landscape across the Atlantic in which progressive employers and democratic unionists harmoniously advanced their mutual interest in high wages and technological change.[26] No figure seemed to stand more clearly for this linkage than Walter Reuther, who so effectively accommodated the language of American productivity to the values of European social democracy in the difficult years when living standards had barely risen beyond their prewar levels. When the UAW signed its first guaranteed annual wage contract with Ford in 1955, the news made the front pages all across Europe. Typical were the comments of the Parisian left-wing newspaper *Franc-Tieur*, which took Reuther's GAW at face value and then commented ruefully: "How different are things over here . . . when we look at our backward employers, our divided workers, our outmoded routines . . . and [then] we witness this forward movement in America, marked by technical progress and social justice." Two years later British unionists offered Reuther an even more rapturous reception when he addressed the annual conference of the Trades Union Congress at Blackpool. The laborite *Daily Herald* enthused:

> The spellbinder from Detroit, the Pied Piper of Hope, excited this conference today with an explosion of vitality as American as a skyscraper and as adventurous

as a covered wagon. . . . He gave us the American dream, the dawn of the era when
we have the tools of unprecedented abundance, when social justice and peace and
plenty are inseparable and are there for the taking. . . . Reuther is a 20th century
peddlar who backs his dreams with the reality of Detroit and Pittsburgh, atomic
power and automation.

"Reuther's Day" was how the conservative *Daily Express* described it. "No overseas
visitor in living memory has made such an immense impact by his personality and
his tempestuous oratory."[27]

Reuther's popularity proved most useful to the ascendant "revisionist" wing of
the Labour Party, which rejected unilateral nuclear disarmament, downplayed
industry nationalization, and celebrated technical and scientific dynamism as the
key to Great Britain's economic rejuvenation. In his efforts to transform British
industry, Harold Wilson found Reuther a particularly refreshing figure; the American's ideas helped convince the future prime minister to make "the white heat of
technological change" a key theme in the Labour Party's 1963 electoral campaign.[28] To Wilson, Reuther was an attractive salesman for the American system
whose "approach was to force the pace in industrial efficiency—the dividends of
which would accrue in full measure to his members—by a ruthless approach to
unorganized and backward employers. . . . No excuses would be accepted: if the
firm did not know how to raise productivity . . . he would put in the union's efficiency experts."[29]

For almost two decades Reuther's annual trips abroad—usually for three or four
weeks each summer—held the character of something approaching a state visit.
In each country he delivered a major speech before a trade union meeting, held
a press conference, met with the American ambassador, and often paid a courtesy
call upon the prime minister. In Germany, Sweden, Austria, Italy, and Great
Britain, Reuther held long discussions with social democratic or Labour Party par-
liamentarians, and upon his return to the United States he usually briefed State
Department officials. His *Selected Papers*, which appeared in 1961, saw publication in twelve languages.[30] Often his family came along for the vacation time
carved out between the meetings. Indeed, these were the only true vacations they
took together, although Reuther's near-celebrity status kept him in the limelight.
"I have no privacy anyplace in the world," Reuther once lamented. "It's a terrible
thing." He recalled with chagrin how a twilight gondola ride with his wife in
Venice was once interrupted by a shout from a nearby boat: "Hey, Mr. Reuther,
can I see you at the hotel in the morning?" Reuther's reaction: "I felt like going
over and upsetting his damned gondola."[31]

Reuther liked Sweden best. His appreciation of that nation's advanced welfare
state, full employment policies, and corporatist wage bargaining transcended the
merely political and entered the realm of an idealized aesthetic. To social democrats of the early postwar years, Sweden competed with the United States as a
symbol of modernity, but one that emphasized social equality, class harmony, and

generous internationalism. Reuther was an unqualified enthusiast for the "Swedish model." Certainly he must have looked on with admiration and a certain envy when Arne Geijer, chairman of the Confederation of Swedish Trade Unions and one of his few genuinely intimate friends, sat down with the director of the Employers Confederation to peacefully reforge an annual wage agreement covering virtually the entire working population. When a reporter asked Reuther and Geijer why American unions were not Socialist, the two exchanged a knowing look. "Different historical backgrounds," replied Reuther. "Our basic aims are similar." Indeed, the Swedes saw Reuther as something of an American soul mate. He was in regular contact with Prime Minister Tage Erlander and his political secretary, Olaf Palme, whose Kenyon College honors' thesis of 1948, on the UAW, endorsed Reuther's leadership in the most enthusiastic terms.[32]

Such acclaim made Reuther's influence a palpable force within Western European trade unionism, where he sought to transplant the principles at the heart of the UAW's own system of collective bargaining. By the mid-1950s the key institution in which such discussions took place was the sixty-year-old International Metalworkers Federation (IMF), based in Zurich. As early as 1946 IMF General Secretary Konrad Ilg, a staunch anti-Communist who had nursed the organization through the fascist era from neutral Switzerland, had seen Reuther and the big American industrial unions as the key to IMF revitalization. In 1949 Reuther was made chairman of a newly formed world automotive department. Here his financial and organizational clout was considerable, and in the 1950s IMF General Secretary Adolph Graebal took few important decisions without checking with the UAW president.[33]

Reuther's chief goal was to strengthen communications and build a world automobile council for all the unions representing workers laboring within a single multinational firm, GM and Ford being the key targets. To Reuther, not only did such a council seem an elementary step toward international labor solidarity but the need for it would become increasingly urgent in the late 1950s and early 1960s with the appearance in the American automobile market of the first invasion of imports from Germany and Japan. Reuther favored free trade and rejected protectionist measures as a matter of principle, but to safeguard the jobs and incomes of his members he needed some assurance that the huge wage differentials then in existence—in 1958 Ford workers in the United States earned four times as much as German autoworkers—would soon narrow. At an IMF conference in Bremen he called the German export drive "wage dumping."[34]

To solve the problem Reuther envisioned a sharp increase in wages and a rapid reduction of hours for workers in those industries—chief among them automobile manufacturing—where postwar productivity gains had outstripped improvement in wages and working conditions. To accomplish this he proposed to pace the elimination of trade restrictions then being negotiated under the General Agreement on Tariffs and Trade (GATT) with a nation's agreement to abide by an international fair labor standards treaty. To Reuther the key linkage here, between productivity growth in a particular industry and higher wages for the workers in that industry, seemed but a practical and just extension of the Treaty of Detroit. "We have to find a rational way to bring to bear the maximum power of international solidarity," he told a 1961 IMF congress in Rome, "or we will be isolated and divided, weak and defenseless in the face of the growing power of international capital to exploit us separately."[35]

European unionists hailed Reuther's confident internationalism, but even among like-minded social democrats within the IMF, Reuther encountered much resistance in his efforts to develop what he considered a practical collective bargaining program. This was especially true of the social democrats who led IG Metall, the big West German union in steel, automobiles, and electrical manufacturing. IG Metall was not a German version of the UAW. As a union for the entire metalworking sector, IG Metall was organized on a unitary basis with no special divisions for individual industries or firms. Strikes were often conducted on a regional basis by workers in a variety of companies. Because no single industry employed a majority of its membership, union leaders saw productivity bargaining as highly divisive. More important, their links to the Social Democratic Party (SDP) were qualitatively far closer and more decisive than those between union leaders and Democrats in the United States; collective bargaining and political action, therefore, were organically linked. In the 1950s and 1960s German trade unionists saw the reconstruction of industry as a national project predicated upon the maintenance of a relatively egalitarian wage structure and a labor market heavily regulated by the state. There was some opportunism here, in part based on the low-wage advantage then enjoyed by German carmakers in the international market, but IG Metall's rejection of the linkage between sectorial wages and industry-specific productivity represented a fundamental critique of one of the key elements in the Treaty of Detroit.[36]

Thus Reuther's efforts to strengthen the world automobile councils and coordinate transnational bargaining proved controversial. When Reuther stressed the need for the IMF to devote more of its resources to the auto campaign than to general organizing activities in metalworking, he met spirited resistance from IG Metall. In 1964 he pressed for the extension of such councils to cover workers at Chrysler, Fiat, and Volkswagen, but the IMF's German president, Otto Brenner, prevaricated; at a 1964 executive committee meeting in Vienna the UAW threatened to leave the organization if the program were held back. Pressing on, Reuther poured in money and manpower to make his vision a reality, and in 1966 he convened meetings in Detroit of the auto councils, which for the first time adopted a common commitment to a general set of collective bargaining goals.[37]

Reuther's brand of trade union internationalism encountered even greater difficulties in Japan. The automobile industry there was just emerging onto the export scene when Reuther made a semiofficial visit in November 1962. Although some Kyoto University radicals denounced him as an "agent of American imperialism," Reuther struck all the right notes on his two-week tour, asserting that the hydrogen bomb should be "outlawed" and "positive neutralism" encouraged. His chief purpose was to establish a UAW-funded Wage Research Center designed to encourage cooperation within Japan's highly fractionalized union movement while at the same time highlighting the low-wage competition that had already made the Japanese steel, textile, and radio industries a threat to U.S. jobs. But the labor leaders in the Japanese manufacturing sector proved reluctant to cooperate, because the very concept of an industrywide — much less an international — wage standard undermined the collaborative, enterprise unionism upon which the ultra-conservative unions in the automoble, steel, and electronics industries had staked their future. Reuther "did not understand our domestic situation," a trade union official recalled of a long discussion with the UAW president. As with West Germany's IG Metall, some exchange of information on wages and working conditions took place, but Reuther's vision of collective bargaining on an international scale was thwarted even before the competitive frenzy that engulfed the world auto industry in the 1970s subverted all such hopes.[38]

These were difficulties for the future, barely perceived in the late 1950s when Reuther's persona had reached its greatest international influence, both as symbol and diplomat for American liberalism. The first thaw in the cold war had given room for maneuver to those in the West who sought to break free of the bipolar orthodoxies that had suffocated social reform and transformed international relations into a zero-sum game. Reuther saw himself both as a critic of this dangerous standoff and as an adventuresome lieutenant scouting out the left flank of American foreign policy. He supported détente with the Soviets, neutralism in Asia, and an "opening to the left" in Europe. He stood with Eleanor Roosevelt, Adlai Stevenson, William Fulbright, and Hubert Humphrey as a voice for liberalism, committed to the essential structures of the American policy but continually frustrated by the actual diplomacy that arose out of the tensions generated by the cold war.[39]

In April 1956 Reuther made a hugely successful tour of India that served both as a semiofficial endorsement of Indian neutralism and as a clear indication that, despite the recent AFL-CIO merger, Reuther would hardly play second fiddle to George Meany when it came to staking out American labor's place in the world. Indian neutralism was highly controversial in the mid-1950s: American policy makers alternated between frosty admonition and warmer efforts at seduction. When he served as ambassador in 1952, Chester Bowles, Reuther's friend from OPA days, had urged the UAW president to visit; by mid-1954 India's ambassador to the United States, Zebun Mehta, was sending back the names of Reuther and Supreme Court Chief Justice Earl Warren as the two Americans, excepting Dwight Eisenhower, who would make the best impression in the subcontinent.[40]

Reuther put them off until late 1955, when George Meany changed his mind. The marriage of the AFL and CIO was little more than a few days old when Meany made it perfectly clear that the merger had done nothing to temper his Lovestoneite worldview. To a stunned audience of well-wishers assembled for a luncheon of the National Religion and Labor Foundation, Meany lectured "the many people in our country who call themselves liberals" for being "stone silent about the Soviet concentration camps . . . [and] the Communist imperialist destruction of the national independence and democratic rights of hundreds of millions of people in Europe and Asia." Commenting on Indian Prime Minister Jawaharal Nehru, who had just escorted the Soviet leaders Nikita Khrushchev and Nikolai Bulganin on a tour of the subcontinent, Meany lashed out, "No country, no people, no movement, can stand aloof and be neutral in this struggle. Nehru and Tito are not neutral. They are aides and allies of communism in fact and in effect."[41]

Meany's blast, front-page news in India and the United States, sent Reuther and his liberal allies into a flurry of activity. In her "My Day" newspaper column, Eleanor Roosevelt, who had attended the luncheon, wrote that it was a "sad mistake" to say Nehru was a Communist; indeed, Indian neutrality was proof that not all the world needed to divide into two hostile camps. Chester Bowles again urged Reuther to visit India, and even in the State Department of John Foster Dulles many realized that Meany's speech did great harm to Indo-American relations. John Sherman Cooper, Eisenhower's ambassador to India, personally appealed to Reuther to make his long-postponed tour of the subcontinent. For their part, the Reuther brothers feared that Meany had strengthened the hand of the congressional "die hard group who advocate a policy of aid only to military allies." And they worried that the main Indian trade union center, the Indian National Trade Union Congress, might pull out of the ICFTU. Working closely with David Burgess, a former CIO official and the American labor attaché in New Delhi, Victor Reuther soon won from Prime Minister Nehru and the Trade Union Congress formal invitations for his brother's visit.[42]

The prospective trip generated remarkable interest and controversy. Late in March Reuther released the text of a letter to Secretary of State Dulles criticizing the U.S. effort to erect an alliance system in South Asia, including military aid to Pakistan. Reuther's letter to Dulles was front-page news in India, after which the *New York Times* expressed great relief that Reuther was going on a "mission to India." Of course, Reuther's semiofficial, high-profile diplomacy irritated George Meany no end. When Victor Reuther got the Voice of America to rebroadcast one of his brother's press conferences—in which he endorsed Indian neutralism and criticized AFL-CIO policy—Meany blew up at both Reuther brothers for airing the policy dispute in public.[43]

Reuther had a wonderful time in India. From his arrival on April 4 until his departure twelve sleepless days and nights later, "Volta Rutta," as cheering crowds called him, delivered as many as sixteen short speeches a day. Endlessly garlanded with flowers, he spoke to Congress Party leaders, trade union officials, workers at factory gates, socialist intellectuals, newspaper editors, and American diplomats. Reuther's triumphant reception was based upon his ability to appeal to so many divergent elements in Indian society. To nationalists, Reuther symbolized a liberal, internationalist America that understood Indian neutrality, repudiated colonialism, and endorsed the government's five-year development plan as "a practical demonstration of democratic planning at its best." To Congress Party officials, grown irritated at the sniping they received from the U.S. State Department, Reuther's tour, during which he frequently denounced Soviet imperialism, neatly balanced the Bulganin-Khrushchev visit. Socialists opposed to the government's growing domination of the trade union movement hailed Reuther's strong defense of independent unionism and free collective bargaining.

U.S. diplomats in India were hugely pleased with Reuther's goodwill tour. By linking Indian nationalism with the values of the progressive West—including the Gandhian element in the dramatic Montgomery, Alabama, bus boycott—Reuther helped defuse much anti-Americanism within elite circles. Reuther and Nehru got on famously. In New Delhi, Reuther announced that he totally disagreed with Meany's appraisal of the prime minister, calling him "truly one of the great statesmen of the world." And after a three-hour talk, Nehru returned the compliment, telling his Congress Party executive committee, "What a remarkable, amazing, stimulating fellow he is." The Congress Party's *Hindustan Times* soon editorialized that "Mr. Reuther . . . is a most welcome whiff of fresh air. . . . [He] has revived Indian faith in American democracy." The *Washington Post* called him "Ambassador Extraordinary."[44]

Reuther's fame hardly impressed George Meany, who again denounced India's neutralist elite and dispatched Irving Brown as the AFL-CIO's official delegate to the annual convention of the Indian National Trade Union Congress. "Meany wants it clearly understood," the *Detroit Free Press* reported, that Reuther had visited India "strictly as a tourist." The two clashed repeatedly at an AFL-CIO executive council meeting shortly after Reuther's return. Reuther wanted to debate the AFL-CIO's hard line in Asia, but Meany was more preoccupied with the challenge to his leadership. The meeting degenerated into a "knock-down, drag-out affair," reported one observer, after Reuther asserted that his dispute was less with Meany than with Jay Lovestone, who really controlled AFL-CIO foreign policy. To the UAW executive board Reuther reflected: "George Meany's position really is based upon the assumption that Europe is Asia and Asia is Europe. You cannot mechanically apply a foreign policy point of view that may make sense in Europe to Asia . . . where conditions are so different."[45]

Indeed, Reuther's approach to the Soviets in Europe was almost as orthodox as that of George Meany. In 1955 the Reuther brothers had done their bit to ensure Eisenhower administration support for an Austrian peace settlement—Lovestone was against it—that neutralized that nation in return for a complete Soviet pullout. But Walter Reuther's lack of sympathy for such a formula in Germany put him at odds with the West German trade unions and much of the leadership of the Social Democratic Party. SDP Chairman Erich Ollenhauer and others of a generation once active in Weimer politics resisted efforts by Chancellor Konrad Adenauer and the governing conservative coalition to rearm West Germany and turn the nation's fate firmly toward an Atlantic alliance. Instead, they fought German membership in NATO and favored negotiations with the Soviets that looked to the reunification of a neutral, denuclearized German state.

But the SPD was being pushed in a more Atlanticist direction by younger men like Willy Brandt and Helmut Schmidt. Brandt was a particularly important figure. A left-wing militant in the early 1930s, Brandt had spent the Nazi era in Scandinavia, after which he returned to Germany and became a protégé of the legendary Ernst Reuter, Berlin's steadfast mayor during the airlift and the difficult years thereafter. The Reuther brothers came to know him well at this time. In the 1950s Brandt was among those who argued that the SPD could achieve majority status only if it abandoned both the Marxism of its founders and the neutralist tilt of its current leadership. The shift finally took place at the end of the decade when the SPD met in Bad Godesberg, where it recast itself as a cross-class party that, in the words of a leading party theoretician, sought a social market economy that would ensure "competition as far as possible, planning as far as necessary." Declaring itself in favor of a "home defense," the SPD firmly aligned itself with the main structures of Adenauer's "option for the West."

Walter Reuther was entirely in sympathy with this political evolution, and he played a small but highly symbolic part in support of Willy Brandt during the Berlin crisis of 1959. Nikita Khrushchev precipitated the new turn in the cold war late in 1958 when he demanded Western recognition of the German Democratic Republic (GDR) and the transformation of Berlin into a demilitarized "free city," perhaps as part of a general denuclearization of Central Europe. Some in the SPD, possibly a majority, wanted to use the crisis to open negotiations with the Soviets and the GDR, but Brandt, now governing mayor of Berlin, categorically opposed all concessions to the Soviets. Indeed, Brandt now emerged as the clear leader of the SPD right wing: pro-American, anti-Communist, and, like Adenauer, an advocate of the status quo in Central Europe.[46]

During the first half of 1959 Reuther echoed this line, and in the most dramatic and personal fashion. Like Brandt, Reuther thought progressives in the West must talk with the Soviets, if only to make them understand that they faced a united front. Thus, when Deputy Premier Anastas Mikoyan visited the United States early in 1959 and indicated that he wished to meet with representatives of American labor, Reuther, James Carey, and a few other union leaders quickly arranged a lunch at the International Union of Electrical Workers (IUE) headquarters across the street from the Soviet embassy. Reuther dominated the conversation, in which he challenged Mikoyan, especially over the Soviet suppression of the Hungarian uprising and Soviet intentions toward Berlin. Reuther's stance was that of Brandt, Adenauer, and the State Department: free elections first, then negotiation of German unity. When Mikoyan asserted that no difference existed between the Democratic and Republican Parties, Reuther cut him off with the observation that at the time of their split, far less separated the Bolsheviks and Mensheviks. Back in Moscow, Mikoyan reported that he had gotten along well with American businessmen and diplomats; his rudest reception had been from Walter Reuther.[47]

The exchange was widely reported, which may well have prompted Brandt to invite Reuther as the principal speaker at a giant "Freedom Rally" organized by West Berlin trade unions on May Day 1959. Reuther's presence at the Brandenberg Gate served two purposes: it demonstrated to the Soviets and the GDR that even among those most publicly critical of America's cold war mindset, no dissent existed over the Berlin question; and it reminded Brandt's Social Democratic rivals of the staunch support he enjoyed in America's most progressive circles. Whatever the political calculation, Reuther must have felt some kind of apotheosis when he stepped to the podium and heard six hundred thousand people welcome him with a hearty roar. His speech broke no new ground, but the sheer symbolism of the moment counted for enough. Speaking in German, he recalled his first visit to Berlin in the aftermath of the Reichstag fire, his experience as a worker in the Soviet Union, his efforts to forestall dismantlement of German industry, and his confrontation with Mikoyan. He was in Berlin as a representative of the "free world" and as a spokesman for its "free labor movement." "We shall stand with you in Berlin no matter how strong and cold the Soviet winds blow from the East."[48]

The cold war had a surreal quality. During the same season in which Khrushchev threatened unpredictable conflict at Europe's most sensitive flashpoint, he was pleased to accept President Eisenhower's invitation to visit Washington in September 1959 and tour the nation. He made quite an engaging appearance. On Iowa farmsteads, Hollywood production lots, and San Francisco streets, Khrushchev came across as an earthy Russian peasant ready to bargain. As he fraternized with businessmen and politicians, he kept complaining loudly, "Where are the workers?"

The State Department had hoped that the AFL-CIO might invite Khrushchev to address its annual convention in San Francisco, but George Meany would have nothing of it. Throughout his adult life he had maintained a principled opposition to virtually all intercourse with any representative of the Soviet state—including officials and diplomats visiting the United States, but above all, those claiming to represent the state-controlled "trade unions." What, he once asked, could a democratic unionist possibly find to discuss with them? "The latest innovations being used by the secret police to ensnare those who think in opposition? . . . Or perhaps, bigger and better concentration camps for political prisoners?"[49] Reuther shared none of these illusions, but he came to argue, as did Brandt and others who favored *Ostpolitik*, that debate, exchanges, and trade lowered cold war tensions, ameliorated Soviet control of the East bloc, and opened the door to political reform. Moreover, it irked Reuther that he had to remain on the sidelines while America's leading capitalists, including RCA's David Sarnoff and Tom Watson of nonunion IBM, met with Khrushchev, and that Averell Harriman could assure the Soviet dictator that "continuance of the cold war was not in the interests of American capitalism."[50]

With State Department encouragement, Walter and Victor organized a dinner for the Soviet premier in San Francisco during the AFL-CIO convention. When

Reuther asked the federation's executive council to endorse the meeting, Meany again demonstrated his authority by mobilizing twenty-two votes against. Only James Carey of the IUE and O. A. Knight of the Oil Workers offered him support. (Knight, it might be noted, was the AFL-CIO vice president in closest contact with the CIA, which used his union to gather intelligence about the refinery industry and petroleum unions in Latin America and the Middle East.) Reuther was joined at the September 20 dinner by half a dozen other union executives, including Emil Rieve of the Textile Workers, who explained, "I think it's wrong for the Executive Council to endorse a dinner with the head of the Russian state but if I want to have dinner with him, that's my business."[51]

But what could American trade unionists say to the Soviet premier? Given Meany's hostility to the whole affair, the public character of the dinner, and the potency of popular anti-Communism, demonstrated throughout Khrushchev's trip, Reuther could hardly be expected to air his critique of the Eisenhower administration's cold war posture or to advance proposals for the demilitarization of Central Europe. Indeed, the boisterous, three-hour meeting, fueled by much whiskey and cognac, soon turned into the most contentious exchange that occurred during Khrushchev's American trip. Despite many friendly toasts, Reuther and his colleagues were determined to assert their anti-Soviet credentials and to demonstrate the "irreconcilable" differences that divided American labor from the Communist system. Khrushchev met Reuther toe to toe, turning the debate into a simplistic, set-piece battle. When Reuther told Khrushchev, "You exploit the workers of East Germany," the premier replied, "Where did you dream that up?" Reuther reminded him that three million had crossed the border into West Germany, to which Khrushchev barked, "You are feverish," still later shouting, "We call what you represent—capitalist lackeys!"[52]

"He defended their system and we defended ours," concluded Reuther at a packed press conference. With reports of the confrontation circulating well inside the Soviet bloc, Reuther had clearly riled the Soviet premier; the next month Khrushchev had his revenge when *Trud*, the Soviet trade union newspaper, ran a series of uncomplimentary stories based on the memories of those who had known Reuther at Gorky a quarter-century before. Among these were Reuther's old comrade from the Rouge, John Rushton, who remembered him as stingy and self-absorbed, and Reuther's girlfriend Lucy, who offered a tale of betrayal and abandonment. For its part, *Trud* could find no difference between Meany and Reuther: "Both were trying to preserve the Cold War ice." Two years later at the Vienna summit, when Khrushchev told John Kennedy that the United States was controlled by monopolists, the U.S. president reminded him that he had met Reuther in San Francisco. "Yes," replied Khrushchev, "I met him. We hung the likes of Reuther in 1917."[53]

16

DEMOCRATIC DILEMMAS

There is nothing wrong with the American labor movement excepting that we haven't mobilized it. The rank and file are ready.

— *Walter Reuther, 1959*

The labor movement is trapped by its affiliation with the Democratic Party. . . . It has little independence of action left.

— *Hobart Rowen*, The Free Enterprisers, *1964*

A t the end of the 1950s Reuther's booming popularity overseas had fewer echoes at home. His steadfast anti-Communism in Europe and Asia had long since been discounted on the domestic political battlefield. The recession of 1957–58 demonstrated the limited capacity of the Treaty of Detroit to address structural imbalances within the economy; at the same time a more vigorous, right-wing politics at odds with Dwight Eisenhower's brand of "Modern Republicanism" came to reject the settled character of the New Deal state and the bipartisan internationalism that linked ADA liberals to State Department conservatives. Unlike Joe McCarthy, Republican Senators Barry Goldwater of Arizona and William Knowland of California were as hostile to industrywide collective bargaining and trade union political influence as they were to the tattered remnants of the old Popular Front. Such ideological combat soon gave rise to a popular conservative movement whose very first initiative put "right-to-work" referenda banning the union shop on the ballot of six states, including Ohio and California.[1]

Naturally Reuther came in for a terrific drubbing as a "labor boss." The attack hit its stride when Michigan Republicans invited Barry Goldwater to address a January 1958 fund-raising dinner in Detroit. To an audience heavily marbled with auto executives he declared Reuther and the UAW "a more dangerous menace than the Sputnik or anything Soviet Russia might do to America." Goldwater, who was then serving on the Senate's Select Committee on Improper Activities in the Labor and Management Field—the McClellan Committee—put Reuther in the same league with Dave Beck, Jimmy Hoffa, and other corrupt leaders of the Teamsters Union. Not surprisingly, Victor's Gorky letter was returned to the right-wing circuit.[2] But exhibit A in the GOP brief was the long, bitter, and sometimes bloody strike waged by the UAW against the Kohler Company, a manufacturer of bathroom fixtures in Sheboygan, Wisconsin. Kohler, which had broken strikes in the 1890s, the 1930s, and the 1950s, was but the most prominent of a remarkably large group of militantly antiunion firms that were quite unwilling to sign onto the Treaty of Detroit. Goldwater and his equally conservative Republican colleagues on the McClellan Committee, Carl Curtis of Nebraska and Karl Mundt of South Dakota, saw the UAW strike, in which at least two organizers sent from Detroit beat up Kohler scabs, as a chance to prepare the ground for a fall campaign waged against the big industrial unions and their liberal Democratic allies. They charged that the committee's Democrats, especially the presidential aspirant John F. Kennedy and the chief counsel Robert Kennedy, were thwarting a probe into UAW affairs.[3]

Reuther relished the chance to confront Goldwater and the Senate committee chaired by John McClellan of Arkansas. He rounded up a decade's worth of personal financial records and sent Jack Conway to Robert Kennedy's office with the union's complete Kohler file. Remembered Conway, "I made it very clear that we were going to be open and aboveboard and direct and that if he was the same way that we'd have no trouble." Kennedy was a thoroughly political animal who saw the UAW as a potential ally, but he nevertheless thought that UAW charges against Kohler had to be exaggerated. At Conway's urging, he visited Sheboygan—that very evening—where he found the company just as reactionary, and the town as divided and dispirited, as the union had charged. Kennedy met with the Kohler attorney Lyman Conger, who "made no secret of his deep and abiding hate for the union. It was an all-consuming hate—a thing unpleasant to see." Thereafter, Robert Kennedy and his brother did all they could to help the UAW make its case at the committee hearings. "Bobby must have had some form of communication with his brother Jack," observed the UAW counsel Joe Rauh. "Every time we were getting into trouble, Jack would enter the hearing room. . . . It got to be a joke inside our crowd as Jack walked down the aisle each time Mundt, Goldwater, or Curtis was scoring points against us." Reuther thought John Kennedy "a real saint towards the UAW," but he came to feel more rapport with Robert, sensing that the younger brother was less detached, more committed, and more of an activist.[4]

Reuther's three-day appearance before the committee late in March 1958 showcased all his virtues. He was confident, fluent, and ready to debate the conservatives on points of politics, law, and economics. In refreshing contrast to the multilayered financial complexity of a Dave Beck or Jimmy Hoffa, investigators found Reuther's family accounts as scrupulous and spare as his puritanical reputation: his one investment of $1,000 in Nash-Kelvinator stock in 1948 had earned him a total profit of $1.26 when he sold it eight years later. Reuther admitted that the UAW had made mistakes in the Kohler strike, but he defended the union's large expenditure of funds in Wisconsin and then went on to denounce Goldwater for asserting that Herbert Kohler had the "right not to have a union if he can win a strike." Even under Taft-Hartley, Reuther corrected him, only employees can make that decision.

The hearings also buried the Gorky letter of 1934, or at least its last phrase, "for a Soviet America," which most right-wing versions appended to the text. Working through Hubert Humphrey, the Reuther brothers got the committee to interrogate all of their old comrades from the early 1930s. The Republican conservatives had hoped that Melvin Bishop, to whom the letter had originally been sent, might help add depth to their attack. He was now a minor Teamsters official and no friend of Walter, but his testimony was so contradictory in its details that when Reuther appeared, neither Curtis, Goldwater, nor Mundt chose to question him about the Gorky letter. The Reuthers took this as a vindication, which they nailed down when committee chairman John McClellan signed Joe Rauh's draft of a letter to Humphrey asserting "the established unreliability of Mr. Bishop and the fact that the existence and text of the letter were so questionable, no member of the committee saw fit to ask Mr. Reuther about it."[5]

All the Reutherites thought they had come through the hearings without a scratch; Walter Reuther actually ordered a bottle of sparkling burgundy at a dinner celebration afterwards. But if Reuther's stature was confirmed within the liberal community, the McClellan committee raised still higher the walls of rhetoric and image that defined the trade unions and their leadership as a tainted interest group divorced from the popular aspirations of the American people. Under klieg lights and television cameras, the committee interrogated its witnesses in the same room where the Army-McCarthy hearings had been held four years before. Reuther easily divorced himself from the Teamster corruptionists, but like the ex-radicals of the McCarthy era, he nevertheless offered his tormentors much ideological terrain. He denied that the UAW had particular influence in the politics of the upper Midwest, downplayed the need for mass picket lines, repudiated the usefulness of flying squadrons in difficult strike situations, and reaffirmed his anti-Communist bona fides.[6]

The Republicans saw their chance and they lunged for it. Early in the summer of 1958 the GOP's national campaign committee published a 216-page handbook entitled "The Labor Bosses—America's Third Party," more than half of which was devoted to an attack on the UAW and Walter Reuther. "The dollars, manpower, and pressure [Reuther] has been able to direct into political channels has made him the greatest single power in the Democratic Party today," asserted the GOP national chairman Meade Alcorn. In Indiana, Republicans announced that the election of the Democratic Senate candidate Vance Hartke would make their state "legally annexed to Walter Reuther's socialist empire." In California the GOP put out a leaflet entitled "Know Your Opponents," in which a picture of Reuther appeared next to each of the top ten elective offices in the state.[7]

To Reuther, these unprecedentedly personal attacks made the sweeping Democratic victory in the 1958 elections sweet indeed. He felt elated. In a time of economic adversity, blue-collar voters had once again demonstrated their loyalty to the Democratic Party. Republican losses were the most massive since 1936. In the Senate the Democrats held nearly a two-thirds majority, 64 to 34; in the House they had picked up 42 districts to give the party a commanding 282 seats, with the Republicans holding but 154. Except in agrarian Kansas, all the right-to-work referenda were defeated, often by votes of two to one. The unions had mobilized their core constituency as never before. "No middle ground. You had to be counted," Reuther crowed to his executive board. "And the people chose to identify themselves with the forces of Labor. . . . I personally think this is the most significant political election in terms of the basic loyalties that has taken place in American politics in many, many years."[8]

One might say of this election, " 'Twas a famous victory," but nothing seemed to come of it. Within months Reuther found that the remobilization of the working-class electorate in 1958 generated few dividends, either within the halls of Congress or across the bargaining table. The problem was twofold: on the legislative front, liberal Democrats found that their newly swollen ranks were still too few and too disorganized to breach the procedural fortress behind which the Republican-Dixiecrat coalition held its ground. To Reuther's stunning disappointment, the liberal-labor policy agenda of 1958—civil rights, aid to "depressed areas," a big public works program, health insurance for the elderly—was soon in stalemate, bottled up in congressional committees dominated by southern Democrats or vetoed by President Eisenhower. At the bargaining table, the election of 1958 had even less of a payoff. Liberal Democrats were increasingly reluctant to identify their fate with that of organized labor. More important, the political economy generated by the Treaty of Detroit had effectively insulated the world of political struggle from that of collective bargaining. Reuther still spoke of labor's dual battles at the ballot box and the bargaining table, but for most midcentury managers, the depoliticized insularity of the American bargaining regime was precisely its greatest virtue. Thus the liberal victory of 1958, like Kennedy's election two years later and the Johnson landslide in 1964, had remarkably little impact within the industrial relations system.

For the next half-decade Reuther would hold but the weakest cards. The 1957–58 recession proved a dress rehearsal for the disasters that would befall American unionism at the end of the Vietnam War boom. After 1958 unemployment remained well above 6 percent for almost five years, and cities like Detroit, Cleveland, and Buffalo were never to boom again, except for a few brief years at the end of the 1960s. From this point on black unemployment always stood at twice the rate for whites. And each year the Labor Department labeled scores of regions as chronically distressed. These were structural weaknesses in the social economy that even the most robust recovery could barely ameliorate. However, even during the 1958 recession the Eisenhower administration was afraid to stimulate the economy for fear of generating "inflationary bottlenecks." This policy left demand soft, unemployment chronic, and the unions open to attack from once-complacent adversaries. Corporations used the recession to cut back the power of the shop stewards, stop private-sector white-collar organizing, and attack a whole set of traditional work arrangements as "featherbedding" and "restrictive work rules."[9]

In 1959 the steel industry provoked a 116-day stoppage in an effort to abolish work rules that had been in effect for almost two decades; the next year General Electric successfully propagandized for back-to-work movements during a disastrous strike that revealed the internal disarray of the rival unions in the electrical industry. Within the manufacturing sector, union growth came to an abrupt halt. Even the UAW was stymied: its efforts to organize professional and technical employees in the unionized factories of the Midwest got nowhere, and in California strikes and negotiations designed to bring aircraft wages in line with those of the auto industry generated few dividends. From its peak of one and a half million members in 1955, UAW membership dropped four hundred thousand in five years, putting Reuther's union second, behind the Teamsters, in the labor rankings.[10]

Labor looked to a more liberal Congress for relief, but it was clear from the very first hour of the new term that the congressional stalemate remained firmly in place. The majority leader Lyndon Johnson used the considerable power at his command, as well as the famous "Johnson treatment," to nullify the Senate's leftward parliamentary tilt. By adroitly parceling out committee assignments, Johnson moved a majority of the first-term liberals into his camp, behind a "reform" of Rule 22 that would still require a two-thirds vote—now of those present, rather than of the entire Senate—to invoke cloture. The Reutherites felt betrayed, their hard-won victories subverted in the Senate cloakroom. "Our people go out and ask for votes for these candidates, tell people the candidates are going to support the Democratic platform," Roy Reuther told Bobby Baker, LBJ's powerful chief-of-staff soon afterward. "Then they find the party leadership here working for just the opposite, and they're mad." The encounter turned into a noisy, public shouting match, after which Johnson phoned Walter to denounce Roy for the "controversial" role this Reuther brother had come to play in the Democratic Party.[11]

But minor eruptions of this sort were soon smothered by the organizational logic of the UAW alliance with the Democrats. Despite all their differences, Reuther never really broke ranks with LBJ; indeed, while recognizing that Johnson had to pay homage to his Texas constituency, Reuther secretly admired the majority leader's skillful exercise of legislative power. "It would be nothing short of tragic for the liberals to beat Lyndon Johnson over the head," he told his executive board in the spring of 1960. The Republicans were the enemy, "the guys that betrayed us."[12] On the key issues that divided the Democratic Party, and most especially civil rights, Reuther still saw himself as a militant, but his commitment was repeatedly confronted by a growing sense of responsibility for the Democratic Party itself. Joe Rauh called Reuther's evolution a "metamorphosis": the UAW president moved from an "independent" to an almost "straight Democratic Party position." The shift was facilitated by the death in 1957 of Don Montgomery, who had spent more than a decade dissecting for Reuther the failure and hypocrisy of Democratic officeholders. He was replaced as Reuther's confidant and political operative by men like Jack Conway and Leonard Woodcock, who prided themselves on their organizational talents. "You can't influence Democratic Party decisions from the outside," Reuther told his executive board after the 1958 elections. "You got to do it from the inside." By 1960 Reuther could write to Eleanor Roosevelt that despite all its deficiencies, the Democratic Party is "the only political instrument capable of providing America with the leadership and program" they both saw as essential to progressive politics.[13]

Reuther's drift toward such an intimate identification with the Democrats was in part compensation for his disappointment with the merger between the AFL and the CIO. The merger had created few political or organizational dividends. Reuther's Industrial Union Department (IUD) never won backing from the old AFL unions for the kind of aggressive unionization effort that the UAW had hoped to lead. "The phones never ring," complained one IUD staffer. "No one has any sense of purpose." Instead, the AFL-CIO leadership was almost immediately consumed by jurisdictional conflicts of the most divisive sort. "We merged, but we did not unite," was the way Reuther put it.[14] The Teamsters and the building trades assumed that with the merger industrial union jurisdictions were now fair game. Thus, when Reuther complained to Jimmy Hoffa that Detroit Teamsters had never picketed UAW factories when they were in separate federations, Hoffa shot back, "You're damn right. . . . We are going to treat you just like we used to treat each other in the AFL." Reuther turned livid. At the next AFL-CIO council meeting he warned Meany to hold the building trades in check. "I did not agree to become a part of this united labor movement to dissipate my time and energy in this kind of endless and senseless controversy. . . . I have never slugged a guy in my life, never intend to; but Christ I will not yield!"[15]

But Meany was not the problem. Despite all of his devotion to his old cronies in the building trades, Meany actually sided with Reuther and the industrial unionists in most of these jurisdictional disputes. The real problem was that neither Meany nor the top building trades officials themselves had the power to enforce a no-raiding agreement within the decentralized, quasi-feudal structure that stood at the heart of the building trades empire. Business agents in the building trades saw themselves as caretakers for a body of tradesmen whose militant effort to monopolize a limited set of work opportunities generated a predatory and expansionist drive. It therefore took endless meetings and hundreds of hours of talk to massage the building trades into signing a 1961 agreement enforced by outside arbitration. To Meany, this work embodied the essence of AFL-CIO politics, but to Reuther it was all existential futility. "We have seen unions come before the executive council arguing and haggling over three members," Reuther fumed. "The AFL-CIO is totally paralyzed."[16]

To Reuther, an attack on unemployment and a program for reviving the economy were the essential tasks facing the labor movement. Reuther was chairman of the AFL-CIO economic policy committee; he favored an extension and standardization of unemployment benefits, a crash program of public works, and targeted investments to aid the one-industry towns and mine villages devastated by market shifts and technological obsolescence. But Reuther was not simply a liberal Keynesian who favored social spending and budget deficits in order to stimulate the economy. As in 1945 he thought inadequate purchasing power a function of an "unbalanced economy" in which business oligopolies still "administered prices" to reach a level of profits otherwise unsustainable in a truly competitive marketplace. Such views had been in eclipse since the late New Deal, but Reuther won a national spotlight for this critique of big business during the late 1950s when Senator Estes Kefauver conducted an exhaustive series of hearings into the administered prices maintained in key industries like steel, automobiles, and electrical machinery. Reuther and Weinberg once again demonstrated the potency of GM's price leadership, denounced the company's huge profits, and argued that lower car prices would soon generate a market big enough to lower Motor City unemployment and end the inventory glut. Kefauver and other antitrust Democrats wanted to break up GM and Ford, but Reuther favored a public commission to put big business price policy in a "fishbowl."

In effect, Reuther wanted to regulate the automobile industry like a utility in which the relative profit share distributed to consumers, shareholders, and workers was subject to an open set of political negotiations, not all that different from the democratic corporatism emerging in export-oriented European states such as Austria, Sweden, and Finland. In advancing these ideas Reuther remained a moralist and a Veblenite who argued that unemployment and unused capacity represented not only human misery but an irrational and unpatriotic abdication of their responsibility by the nation's political and industrial elite. "We are wasting 25 percent of the total industrial productive potential of the American economy," Reuther lectured Kefauver's committee at the depths of the recession. "I wish that the Russian economy was operating at 25 percent below its industrial potential. Then the free world could relax."[17]

Meany and Reuther were in agreement on most economic stimulation issues, but the AFL-CIO executive shared none of Reuther's passion. He was scornful of the press, complacent in politics, and when it came to the symbolic rituals of public life, Meany struck a chord that only the faithful could hear. All these qualities were manifest at a February 1959 meeting of the AFL-CIO executive council, held at the Caribe Hilton Hotel in San Juan, Puerto Rico. The council met there because Meany had unhappily yielded to Reuther's insistence that he get the council off Miami's garish hotel strip. But instead of moving back to Washington, Meany just shifted the venue to another winter resort. Reuther was hardly amused, but he charged forward nonetheless. Seeking to reweave the banners under which the unions had once filled Cadillac Square, Reuther had begun to explore how labor might again organize the unemployed and advertise their plight. As part of a UAW "Get America Back to Work" campaign, Reuther envisioned a series of rallies and meetings that would bring together unionists, local government officials, managers from hard-hit industries, and the unemployed. Arriving in Puerto Rico a day before Meany, who was delayed by a head cold, Reuther immediately convened a meeting of his economic policy committee to build momentum for a mass march and rally of the jobless in Washington, D.C. "They are desperate," Reuther charged. The march "is the sort of thing that has got to be done to jar this government of ours out of its complacency."[18]

Meany saw Reutherite activism as little more than lèse-majesté; moreover, he knew that any demonstration of the unemployed would offer a platform to Communists and other radicals, and "we want no damned part of it." A stormy two-hour council meeting put Reuther on the verge of resignation, but the next day they both searched for a compromise. "Meany would say he didn't want Reuther to resign, and Reuther would make a conciliatory reply," observed the International Union of Electrical Workers' James Carey. "We followed the script beautifully— didn't miss a line." At the end of the day Reuther and Meany agreed there would be a big meeting on the unemployed issue, but the "marchers" would sit at tables in a National Guard armory, where those attending could be screened.[19]

President Eisenhower compounded Reuther's humiliation when, at a news conference, he derided the value of an unemployment march called by labor leaders meeting in sunny Puerto Rico. Reuther had flown coach to San Juan, had spent all day in meetings, and even marched on a picket line of electrical workers. But the imagery of Ike's jab could never be countered, no matter how unjust. "I have spent no time on the sunny beaches of Puerto Rico nor have I been with you and your many big business friends on the golf courses, the duck blinds or the quail hunts," read a defensive Reuther handout to the press. Privately Reuther fumed, "We don't have a labor movement. We have a club. It's a very exclusive club: stays in the best hotels, in the finest resorts in the western hemisphere. But it isn't doing the job."[20]

Reuther was frustrated and embittered all through the long recession months. In the spring of 1959, while AFL-CIO lobbyists devoted virtually all their energy to fending off the "reform" legislation that had emerged from the McClellan Committee (eventually passed as the Landrum-Griffith Act), a coalition of Republicans and Dixiecrats gutted the liberal-labor legislative package, turning back efforts to broaden and extend unemployment compensation, aid to depressed areas, and medical care for the retired. The Eisenhower administration, meanwhile, abandoned the mild Keynesianism of its first term, fixating instead upon the specter of inflation even as unemployment reached levels not seen since 1941.[21]

"We won a great victory in 1958," pleaded Reuther, "and we pour it down the drain in 1959. . . . The labor movement has to assume the major responsibility for that. . . . On the legislative front we failed. On the organizational front we failed. On the jurisdictional front we wage warfare on each other."[22]

Reuther's energy and honesty were among his most attractive qualities, but in defeat and disappointment he found it all too convenient to displace a large chunk of his frustration onto George Meany's argumentative and cigar-smoking personage. For the better part of a decade he kept a detailed record of all his encounters with the AFL-CIO president, documenting and indicting Meany's egotistical and maladroit leadership. To his executive board, to old CIO comrades like James Carey, and to Arne Geijer and other friends in Europe, Reuther could hardly contain his outrage and contempt. Much of it was justified, for George Meany was a singularly uninspiring trade unionist who repeatedly blocked Reutherite initiatives, often for the most petty and self-serving of reasons. But Reuther's obsession with Meany also proved self-destructive. It was a seductively satisfying hatred, for it gave Reuther a large and powerful figure upon whom to displace all the disappointments and failures that beset the union movement. Meany's stolid existence absorbed far too large a proportion of the residual radicalism and oppositional energy that Reuther might otherwise have directed toward the corporations, the White House, or the Democratic Party.

Reuther's remarkably cordial relationship with the Kennedy-era Democrats is a case in point. With Eisenhower finally ready for retirement, Reuther smelled victory in 1960 if only the party held together behind the right candidate. In the months leading up to the Democratic National Convention in Los Angeles the UAW maintained a formal neutrality, which served only to mask the heterogeneous politics that now characterized the executive board and the top layers of the UAW apparat. After the McClellan committee hearings, Jack Conway was practically a member of the Kennedy brain trust; meanwhile, Joe Rauh served as Hubert Humphrey's speech coordinator during the primaries. On the UAW board the Massachusetts senator clearly had the most support, though Humphrey enjoyed backing from the Midwest regional directors Pat Greathouse and Harvey Kitzman. Even Lyndon Johnson and Missouri Senator Stuart Symington had their regional UAW clients.[23]

Reuther at first favored Humphrey, perhaps with Kennedy at the bottom of the ticket. The autoworkers had clearly demonstrated their preference for Humphrey's passionate brand of social rhetoric when he followed Kennedy to the podium at the UAW's 1959 convention; moreover, Reuther shared the distrust felt by Eleanor Roosevelt and other Stevensonians toward Kennedy, a man they saw as too cool, too cynical, and too soft on Joe McCarthy. Finally, Reuther worried that Kennedy's Catholicism would prove an insuperable obstacle in the general election. This concern was no academic judgment, but a product of Reuther's West Virginia childhood, later confirmed by the ethno-religious fissures that exacerbated the decade-long UAW faction fight. "You just don't understand," he once told Jack

Conway, "how deep this is, the anti-Catholicism in the country. You grew up in a Catholic neighborhood as a Catholic kid, so you have a different view of this than those of us who come out of the Protestant Bible Belt."[24]

But whatever these campaign judgments, they lacked the kind of ideological bite that had driven UAW politics a decade before. "Once the Wisconsin primary was over," Jack Conway recalled, "Walter's attitude toward Jack Kennedy changed in the sense that he saw for the first time a guy who did have the potential to get nominated. . . . Hubert ran like he was running for sheriff." Reuther and Conway tried to persuade Humphrey to quit even before he was crushed by the Kennedy steamroller in West Virginia. Reuther "didn't go for Hubert," remembered Joe Rauh, "because he felt that was kind of a useless gesture and that's the kind of thing you let idealists do. . . . You don't go for a guy who is not going to win."[25]

Kennedy made Reuther's switch all the easier by tacking sharply to the left during the months leading up to the 1960 convention. He agreed to cosponsor the old-age health insurance bill developed by the AFL-CIO, and he became far more visible in his commitment to civil rights legislation. When Reuther and Conway held their first serious political discussion with Kennedy early in 1960, the senator admitted that on this issue he took his cues from Humphrey. After Reuther pressed him further, Kennedy leaned forward in his rocking chair, stood up, and asserted, "All right. There's no question. The Negroes are right." Later that spring the UAW took the lead in organizing what Jack Conway called "an informal crap game" in which representatives from the Kennedy, Humphrey, and Stevenson camps cooperated to make sure civil rights liberals took control of all the convention posts and committees. The results were very much to the UAW's liking, with Reuther's old friend Chester Bowles appointed chair of the platform committee. Bowles's committee served up a platform that incorporated virtually the entire labor-liberal agenda, not just on taxes and economic growth measures but on the divisive civil rights issues as well: rapid desegregation of the schools, an end to literacy tests and poll taxes, a federal FEPC, and a permanently funded civil rights commission. Meanwhile, Reuther put all his energy into breaking the "Stop Kennedy" campaign pushed forward by liberals like Eleanor Roosevelt and Eugene McCarthy (with Lyndon Johnson's covert backing). To this end, Reuther and Rauh thought they had won a commitment from Kennedy to nominate Hubert Humphrey or some other midwestern liberal for vice president.[26]

JFK's selection of LBJ as his running mate therefore seemed like an act of calculated cynicism, a double cross. In the Reuther suite, "people were sitting around in almost stunned silence," remembered Leonard Woodcock. May Reuther and Joe Rauh were in tears, Woodcock himself in "shock." Reuther was livid with rage, profane in his anger. But the decision had been taken, so Reuther adjusted quickly, matching Kennedy's calculation with his own. Reuther knew he could get along with Johnson; more important, the UAW leader was a team player who had internalized a sense of responsibility for the Kennedy campaign and the party's fortunes.[27]

Thus, when Reuther learned that G. Mennen Williams sought a roll call vote on the vice-presidential nomination, Reuther tackled the revolt in a methodical fashion, mobilizing his UAW aides against it. Conway wrote up LBJ's foursquare endorsement of the party's civil rights plank, Woodcock carried the ball against Williams in the Michigan delegation, and Reuther took on the AFL-CIO executive council, where hostility to the new vice-presidential candidate was unexpectedly strong. Jack Conway remembered the AFL-CIO's executive council session that evening as one of Reuther's rare victories over Meany. "Reuther did the job. . . . And all it required was two and a half hours of plain god damn hard work. What he did, in effect, was beat Meany down." To a meeting of UAW staffers two weeks later Reuther blamed "liberals going in ten directions" for the Johnson nomination. "It is the power equation in politics that is decisive," Reuther lectured his staff. "In politics you arrive at that point you arrive at in collective bargaining. You exert all your influence, fight as hard as you can, and then you have to make a decision. . . . You wind up doing something short of perfect and that is where we are in the political struggle."[28]

The UAW threw itself into the fall campaign. Roy Reuther, who became codirector of the Democratic Party's voter registration committee, helped spend the $500,000 the UAW raised for AFL-CIO "educational" activities. To deflect Protestant hostility toward Kennedy's Catholicism, the UAW devoted the entire front page of its 1.5 million–circulation newspaper to a line drawing of the Statue of Liberty with a hood over its head, beneath which a caption read, "Which do you choose, liberty or bigotry?" Reuther was again on the stump, backed up by the full-time commitment of hundreds of UAW International representatives and the voluntary labor of thousands more from the activist ranks of 1,250 local unions. Conway remembered that the campaign manager, Robert Kennedy, "used to say flatly that the UAW was the spine of the whole thing."[29]

The impressive mobilization reconfirmed the voting patterns etched into the electorate during the late New Deal era. Membership in the UAW increased Democratic Party partisanship within the working class by almost 15 percent. A remarkable 73 percent of UAW voters supported JFK; thus, African-American and Polish Catholic unionists were for all practical purposes unanimous in their choice. The pollster Louis Harris found the UAW the "anchor point for the most heavily Democratic sector of the electorate. . . . There is such a thing as a labor vote, and there is a distinguishable UAW vote as well." Kennedy carried Detroit by the largest margin of any industrial city in the nation; in Polish Hamtramck, the senator took 92 percent of the vote. "If you made it any higher," quipped Reuther, "people would think it was dishonest."[30]

Overall, Kennedy's victory was paper-thin, but Reuther had great faith that the new president would govern as a liberal, pushing an agenda long championed by the UAW: federal aid for education and the depressed areas, health insurance for the elderly, a higher minimum wage, and a new set of civil rights initiatives. "There is no question whatsoever in my mind about that," Reuther told his executive board. Reuther's earnest social engineering found little resonance within Kennedy's circle of detached and technocratic cold warriors; still, Reuther gave the new administration a long honeymoon. He found JFK bright and intelligent, like himself a quick study, and the first American president with whom he could actually hold a conversation and exchange ideas.[31]

Reuther was startled to realize that he was more than a decade older than the Kennedy set: visiting Hyannis Port on August 3, soon after the convention, Reuther flushed when Jacqueline Kennedy asked him how "his generation" handled the isolation and the dangers of public life. It may have been a moment of self-recognition: at fifty-four, Reuther was no longer part of an insurgent generation assaulting a well-suited table of automotive executives. Still, Reuther was eager to make use of the presidential power and was delighted to finally see a path through which his ideas might transform policy. At Hyannis Port that same day, Reuther did most of the talking at a discussion Kennedy had arranged with James Tobin, Seymour Harris, and other economists active in the campaign; afterwards, Reuther distributed a seven-page press release outlining the UAW's ambitious program for the new administration. "Anything that you do, just send it down to our boys and we'll fix it up for you," Reuther told the campaign economists. "Forget it," remarked Kennedy after Reuther had departed. Of course, Reuther was too important to simply brush away. When Kennedy was in the White House, Jack Conway, who had taken a top post in the Housing Administration, arranged for Reuther to meet with the president half a dozen times. These were one-on-one affairs, held late in the afternoon, in which Reuther offered his wisdom, his experience, and his program to the young man who just happened to be president. But Kennedy was often "indulging Walter," thought Conway.[32]

Kennedy proved skillfully seductive, so much so that the Reutherites often functioned as a sort of left flank just outside his administration, an advance guard for New Frontier initiatives. Arthur Schlesinger, Jr., who served as a Kennedy link to the liberals, found Reuther "always reliable." Collaboration was closest when it came to pushing a very tentative "opening to the left" in American foreign policy. From Kennedy's perspective, this new gambit in the cold war—exemplified by the Alliance for Progress in Latin America, a more accommodative approach toward Indian neutralism, and the negotiation of a nuclear test ban treaty with the Soviets—represented an effort to broaden the ideological appeal of the West and shift neutralist and social democratic forces into the American orbit. For years Reuther had crossed swords with Lovestone and the Dulles State Department toward this very end. Thus the UAW hailed the administration's new "strategy for waging peace," which "is now replacing obsolete security conceptions that rely upon total nuclear terror."[33]

Reuther had been especially pleased during the campaign when Kennedy used a midnight appearance at the University of Michigan to advocate a "peace corps" of young civilian volunteers, the very existence of which would symbolize at least a partial commitment to a demilitarization of the cold war. Although the idea was hardly new or unique, Reuther had been one of the more prominent proponents of such a voluntary assistance agency. Under Reuther's scheme, elements of which had been put forward in the UAW's "Total Peace Offensive of 1950," "technical missionaries with slide rules, with medical kits, with textbooks," would "fight Communism on a positive basis." Victor Reuther and Hubert Humphrey had periodically put forward the idea in the Eisenhower years—by 1959 they had labeled it "Volunteers for Peace"—and Reuther had urged Kennedy to do likewise in the campaign, if only to distinguish his rather hawkish foreign policy posture from that of rival Richard Nixon. The enthusiastic response elicited from a section of the student "silent generation" demonstrated that at the level of symbol and discourse, if nothing else, the Eisenhower years were on the wane.[34]

The American debacle at the Bay of Pigs in April 1961 hardly represented a reevaluation of cold war orthodoxy, but Kennedy called upon Reuther to help clean up the mess. More than twelve hundred soldiers from the anti-Castro invasion force were being held in Cuban prisons, a source of intense personal pain to the president and an embarrassing reminder of the invasion's failure. "I'm willing to make any kind of a deal with Castro to get them out," JFK told his aide Kenneth O'Donnell just days after their capture. When Fidel Castro gave a speech indicating that he wanted to exchange the prisoners for an "indemnity" of five hundred bulldozers, Robert Kennedy called up Reuther: since the administration's hard line on Cuba virtually precluded any direct negotiations with that regime, the president needed an ostensibly private group to ransom the prisoners.[35]

Reuther and his brother Victor plunged into the work, putting together a high-profile "Tractors for Freedom" committee that listed Eleanor Roosevelt and the president of Johns Hopkins University, Milton Eisenhower, on the letterhead. Reuther tapped Pat Greathouse to fly to Havana to see whether Castro would accept agricultural implements and tractors rather than the militarily useful bulldozers. Castro haggled and finally said he would settle for the dollar value of the earth-moving equipment, about $28 million, but by then Republican attacks on the deal were reaching a crescendo. Milton Eisenhower threatened to resign, the Kennedys backed off, and Reuther disbanded "Tractors for Freedom" at the end of June. It took another year and a new committee to ransom the Bay of Pigs prisoners with a huge shipment of pharmaceutical goods, but by taking the heat for a couple of months, Reuther's effort did give John Kennedy a few weeks of breathing space in which to regain his poise.[36]

A more fruitful point of cooperation between Reuther and the Kennedy circle came in the transformation of U.S. policy toward politics in Italy, where the idea of a governmental "opening to the left"—to the Socialist and Social Democratic left—had been bruited about for a decade. Eisenhower's State Department had been firmly opposed to any broadening of the conservative coalition that presided over one unstable government after another. But the Reuther brothers were convinced that the Socialists must be brought into the cabinet and their power strengthened in the trade unions in order to stabilize the regime and enact des-

perately needed social reforms. Since Kennedy was reluctant to expend the political capital necessary to put the State Department behind such a policy shift—a
messy fight might well blow up on Capitol Hill—White House liberals like Arthur
Schlesinger were happy to enlist the Reuther brothers to ease the transition.

In May 1961, when Reuther was in Rome for a congress of the International
Metalworkers Federation, he held talks with the Socialist leaders Pietro Nenni and
Giuseppe Saragat and with Amintore Fanfani, the left-leaning Christian Democratic prime minister, to assure them that a government coalition "opening to the
left" had the support of the new American president. Nenni was the key figure, an
old militant whose trade union followers maintained a working relationship with
the dominant Communist group inside the Confederazione Generale Italiana del
Lavoro. This association made him anathema to Meany, Lovestone, and the
American embassy in Rome, but Victor and Walter were convinced, especially
after the Soviet invasion of Hungary, that the Nenni Socialists had become suffi-
ciently anti-Stalinist and pro-Western in their outlook. The Reuthers discussed the
situation with Robert Kennedy, who in turn set up a meeting of the National Security Council, before which Walter made his case in persuasive detail. With
Nenni's parliamentary support, Saragat's Social Democrats entered the government in early 1962; Victor Reuther called it the "partial turn to the left."[37]

In northern Europe another opening to the left put Reuther in league with a
powerful and high-profile group of social democratic politicians. By the early
1960s Reuther's ambitions had far transcended the fractious trade union sphere;
rather, he saw himself as a spokesman for an American social democracy—almost
a part of the governing regime—whose European counterparts included the Scandinavian social democrats, the British Labour Party (which seemed increasingly
certain to oust the tired and scandal-ridden Conservatives at the next elections),
and Willy Brandt's SPD, now primed to make its weight felt after the retirement
of *Der Alte*. The Kennedy liberals saw a social democratic Europe on the rise as
well, and they were happy to see Reuther as one of their ambassadors. The president himself was intrigued by French-style "indicative" planning and impressed by
Germany's rapid economic growth. Working with Arthur Schlesinger and the well-
connected, emigré socialist Adolf Sturmthal, Reuther proposed to get a "small
group of friends together from Sweden, Germany, Great Britain and the United
States for several days of frank and friendly discussion."[38]

Beginning in July 1963, summer conferences were held for three years at Harpsund, the country home of Swedish prime minister Tage Erlander. In addition to
Reuther, who remained the driving force behind the initiative, the key Harpsund
figures included Arne Geijer of the Swedish Landsorganisationen (LO), Erich
Ollenhauer and Brandt of the SPD, Harold Wilson from the Labour Party, and
Hubert Humphrey, who was then serving on the Senate Foreign Relations Committee. Reuther was indeed among friends, functioning within a milieu both sympathetic and powerful. He always briefed John Kennedy, and later Lyndon Johnson, on the Harpsund dialogue. At the first Harpsund conference, Harold Wilson

argued for a Keynesian internationalism designed to raise living standards in the Third World and soak up unemployment in the first. This topic was meat and potatoes for Reuther, who took the lead in setting up a study group of liberal economists to devise techniques for strengthening the International Monetary Fund so as to foster economic growth without exacerbating the chronic balance-of-payments difficulties faced by Great Britain and the United States. President Kennedy had long felt particularly hamstrung—indeed, unduly so—by this problem, but such technical studies, no matter how useful, were hardly the chief purpose of Harpsund. Rather, the meetings were themselves an assertion that an influential, transatlantic left might yet play a role in reshaping the social life and economic performance of the capitalist democracies in the 1960s and beyond.[39]

Reuther found New Frontier diplomacy exciting, but he could not forget that his entrée at Hyannis Port and Harpsund rested upon the livelihood of the men and women who cut sheet steel, welded car bodies, and assembled tractors in towns like Rockport, Saginaw, Toledo, and Moline. When Kennedy took office, huge layoffs had just swept through the California aircraft industry; in the Midwest, tractor production stood at 40 percent of capacity, and in machine tools at less than 30 percent. As for auto, "the worst is yet to come," predicted Reuther. Nearly one million unsold cars in inventory made certain weeks of layoff in the spring. Unemployment stood at 8.1 percent in the nation, and above 11 percent in Michigan. "Widespread and mounting unemployment is the most urgent domestic problem with which the new Administration and the new Congress are faced," announced the UAW's *Administrative Letter* just after the inauguration.[40]

To Reuther, chronic unemployment and job insecurity spelled trouble within the UAW, where a well-organized movement for work sharing and early retirement gave political leverage to the dismal statistics. It was called "30–40–60"— thirty hours' work at forty hours' pay with retirement at age sixty. Although long-service workers were protected from layoffs by seniority, they were in a panic to get out of the shops. The decline in auto industry employment—whether a consequence of recession or automation—had shifted thousands of older workers into the "rough" work that foremen usually assigned to the under-thirty set. Meanwhile, the big cohort of younger workers hired in the mid-1950s felt the sting of short paychecks and frequent layoffs. "In a plant like our own," explained Leo Fenster, the veteran leftist from GM's Fisher Body local in Cleveland, "early retirement cut across the entire workforce and supplied everyone with a motive. . . . The middle seniority group looked forward to the promotion possibilities this would open up, and the low seniority people saw it as a hedge against perpetual layoffs." *Fortune* magazine found Reuther "squeezed between an irresistible force—the deep and widespread desire among UAW members for greater job security . . . and what may be an immovable object: a 'united front' of the auto manufacturers."[41]

Given the stagnant economy, Reuther could do little to satisfy rank-and-file demands in the 1961 round of auto industry contract negotiations. For once he had no grand strategy: at a special UAW convention in April Reuther pleaded for "flexibility" at the bargaining table. American Motors agreed to a profit-sharing plan precisely because George Romney's struggling car company could see so little black ink on the horizon. Reuther did marginally better with the Big Three — about 2.5 percent a year, including a small SUB diversion to supplement paychecks during short workweeks — but no early retirement plan was forthcoming. Even when employment grew in 1962 and 1963, the pressure from below did not cease. Leaders of the early retirement movement, like John DeVito from Local 45 in Cleveland and Jack Wagner of Buick Local 599 in Flint, were savvy political operators, many of them veterans of the Reuther opposition. Skillfully they avoided any direct challenge to Reuther's formal control of the UAW; in return, Reuther proved far more willing than a decade before to adopt as his own the bargaining agenda that emerged from this loyal opposition. "I think we all agree," he told a 1963 meeting with Flint activists, ". . . What we do at the bargaining table in '64 has got to be measured primarily by this standard: How many jobs does it create?"[42]

Reuther understood the inherent limits to this bargaining strategy. "No matter how hard you work, no matter how ingenious you may be in drafting new proposals, when there are two workers and one job, you are in trouble," Reuther had told a 1962 hearing of the Joint Economic Committee.[43] The solution had to come from Washington, where Reuther saw the president and his economic team, especially the Keynesians on the Council of Economic Advisers (CEA) and the labor-liberals in the Labor Department, as temperamentally and intellectually far more sympathetic to the UAW vision of a full-production, high-employment society than any administration since the mid-1940s. Reuther hoped for a revival of the Washington-centered social corporatism that had been cast into the shadows by the Treaty of Detroit. He approved of the president's selection of the Steel Workers' counsel, Arthur Goldberg, as the new secretary of labor, and he applauded the responsibility Goldberg immediately took for the settlement of industrial conflict, ranging all the way from a strike by Metropolitan Opera musicians to a walkout by New York tugboat pilots. Kennedy himself lobbied California aerospace executives to win for the UAW a new contract that broke industry resistance to the union shop. Reuther found the president's activist, interventionist pledge to "get the country moving again" entirely in harmony with the UAW's oft-repeated condemnation of the economic waste generated by unemployment and underutilization of so much plant and equipment.[44]

Reuther plunged into the work of the president's Labor-Management Advisory Committee, which Secretary Goldberg established as one of his first and most important initiatives. Reuther hoped that the high-profile committee, in which Henry Ford II, Thomas Watson, and other executives had agreed to participate, might well serve as but the first step toward the elaboration of the kind of corporatist bargaining structure he so admired in Sweden and Austria. In Sweden a "solidaristic" wage policy penalized inefficient producers even as it ensured that the most advanced industrial sectors could maintain stable prices and earn profits high enough to finance an aggressive export drive. To replicate elements of this system in the United States, the UAW revived proposals similar to those first put forward in the 1940s: a "national planning agency" modeled along Western European lines; a "technological clearing house" to keep track of automation trends; and a "permanent price hearings agency" to counter the "administered prices" Reuther thought largely responsible for the anemic character of the economic recovery.[45]

Reuther's radical ideas won a hearing. Willard Wirtz, who replaced Goldberg at Labor, shared much of Reuther's perspective, including his admiration for Swedish labor market institutions designed to push unemployment well below even the most optimistic projections of the Kennedy administration Keynesians. In October 1962, and again in March 1963, Reuther and Wirtz arranged for the Labor-Management Committee to interrogate high-level Swedish delegations, which outlined the operation of that country's labor market board, its price and cartel agency, and its investment reserve system, which channeled tax-free capital to those regions with high unemployment.[46]

Although Kennedy was personally intrigued with such European-style planning ideas, their translation onto the American scene proved difficult indeed. In June 1961 Kennedy aide Walt W. Rostow, the former MIT economist famous for his studies of productivity growth, asked Reuther whether he would consider a wage freeze for auto and steel in return for an employer promise to convert productivity gains into price reductions. With a twinkle in his eye Reuther immediately returned the query with his own. If he were "damn fool enough to agree," could Kennedy guarantee that the steel industry would not raise its prices? Reuther doubted whether "White House professors could handle that crowd."[47]

Whatever his skepticism, Reuther was in constant contact with Kennedy, Goldberg, and Walter Heller, chairman of the Council of Economic Advisers, as the contract negotiations in auto came to a head late in the summer of 1961. The administration took Reuther's modest agreement—which Rostow thought should have actually generated a price decline in auto—as an important precedent for the even more decisive steel industry negotiations of early 1962. Reuther was therefore pleased when Goldberg and Kennedy played handmaiden to a rock-bottom, "noninflationary" contract settlement signed by the USW and the steel industry on April 6, 1962. And he was joyfully astonished the next week when Kennedy put all of his presidential prestige on the line and mobilized a good slice of the federal bureaucracy to roll back the 3.5 percent general price increase unilaterally put into effect by the U.S. Steel Corporation. "I say thank God John Kennedy was in the White House with the moral courage to stand up to it." Reuther saw Kennedy's decisive counterstroke as the most promising step toward the public scrutiny of corporate price decisions since Truman's fact-finding panel during the General Motors strike of 1945–46.[48]

But none of these developments resolved the unemployment problem, which virtually all economists and policy makers still thought too high at nearly 6 percent, or the sluggish recovery from the depths of the 1960–61 recession. When John F. Kennedy became president, he was shackled to the ghosts of the 1950s: a Congress whose key committees were commanded by Dixiecrat conservatives; a personal obsession with the balance of payments and the gold drain, perhaps yet another dark legacy from his deeply conservative father; and a razor-thin mandate that he sought to broaden through the appointment to the Treasury of such orthodox tight-money men as the GOP aristocrat C. Douglas Dillon. On the domestic front Kennedy was therefore remarkably timid during the first two years of his administration. His failure to put forward any sort of civil rights program is well remembered, but the Kennedy rhetoric calling for more economic growth bore equally little programmatic fruit. There was some area-redevelopment legislation, an increase in the minimum wage, food stamps for the poor, and some liberalization of unemployment benefits. But social Keynesianism—government spending for housing, jobs, and education—of the sort long advocated by the unions and by ADA liberals got nowhere. There was plenty of deficit spending in the first two years of the Kennedy administration, but it was largely a function of the big military buildup that followed the Berlin crisis of August 1961, when the East Germans put up the wall.[49]

Reuther leaned over backwards to give Kennedy as much leeway as possible. "The problem in Washington is not indifference. The people there just do not realize the seriousness of the unemployment problem," he announced upon the eve of a UAW "Get America Back to Work" conference in the first months of the new administration. His aides Weinberg and Sifton kept Reuther abreast of all the New Frontier's domestic failings, but the UAW president certainly thought Kennedy was moving in the right direction. Early in 1962 Reuther told Congress that the Kennedy program "is a good beginning . . . only a beginning. I do not think it is adequate." But even such mild criticism was muffled when Kennedy spoke before the UAW convention in May 1962. At a time when both the ADA and the principal civil rights organizations berated Kennedy for his timidity on domestic issues, UAW resolutions directed all their fire at Congress and the southern segregationists. When Heller telephoned Reuther to object to a passage in his convention report calling for wages and salaries to increase faster than productivity—"at least in the immediate future"—the UAW president retreated, quickly issuing a press release announcing that the auto union "supports the efforts of the President to achieve a stable price structure."[50] The columnist Murray Kempton, whose journalistic barbs reflected the growth of liberal impatience with the New Frontier, felt betrayed by UAW leaders, who "believe that their highest duty to their country and their President is almost uncritical acceptance." Kempton found the convention "one long Loyalty Day."[51] Even in private Reuther shielded Kennedy from attack: "He is more and more willing to do what is necessary to get this economy on the move," Reuther told his executive board after a meeting with JFK in June 1962. "But I think he is up against the basic problem that we are all concerned about: How does the President of the United States take an idea and get it implemented by Congress? This is the roadblock . . . on education, on public works, on every basic issue: The Administration, who want to do the right thing, are forced to compromise and compromise and compromise and to make their program less and less adequate."[52]

Reuther was the trade union movement's most energetic player in the formulation of the administration's macroeconomic policy. Since direct legislative efforts to structure corporate pricing and investment decisions had been blocked, Keynesian tax policy seemed to be the only road toward economic growth still open. Throughout 1961 and 1962 Reuther was in frequent contact with the CEA chair, Walter Heller, who found the UAW a convenient political counterweight to the Treasury conservatives in the big debate over Kennedy's tax cut. Prepped by Nat Weinberg, Reuther denounced Treasury proposals for a 7 percent investment tax credit, which the UAW economist calculated would merely generate "pools of stagnant savings" unneeded by American corporations. Even in 1961, as *Fortune* pointed out, cash-rich General Motors could not profitably invest its existing reserves. In the absence of new purchasing power, government incentives to modernize plant and equipment would simply generate even greater levels of technological unemployment. The solution had to come on the demand side, where an enormous working-class market stood ready to power the U.S. economy out of its lethargy. Reuther therefore proposed an across-the-board tax credit of two dollars a week, which Weinberg estimated would generate an annual five billion dollars of "high velocity spending power."[53]

Reuther's aggressive commitment to demand-side Keynesianism reflected a faith in the perfectibility of mass-production–mass-consumption capitalism that was not shared by all laborites, even at the dawn of the 1960s. The unique and intractable character of "structural unemployment" had become a policy issue pushed forward both by older liberals like John Kenneth Galbraith and Senator Paul Douglas, who saw the labor market as an inherently flawed institution, and by younger radicals like Michael Harrington, whose *Other America* was about to put the persistent poverty of the nation's racial and regional minorities at the center of liberal reform. Reuther would soon join this antipoverty crusade, but in the early 1960s he was certain that geographically concentrated joblessness would "dwindle automatically to manageable numbers" under full employment. Then, in a fashion not unlike that of World War II, Reuther foresaw workers moving from depressed areas to urban centers, while companies shifted some production back to labor-surplus regions.[54]

Likewise, Reuther's faith in managerial Keynesianism put him at odds with the AFL-CIO when the federation formally endorsed the thirty-five-hour workweek late in 1962. Although AFL-CIO economists were just as committed to growth economics as Weinberg and Reuther, Meany and his building trades allies retained much of their pre–New Deal worldview, which saw competition for a limited set of jobs as a fundamental constraint faced by the labor movement. Chronic unemployment in the construction industry had generated widespread interest, sometimes successful, in share-the-work schemes, which pushed the hours of some exceptionally skilled tradesmen as low as twenty-five per week.[55] Like Kennedy, Reuther argued that "there is enough work to do in America to keep us busy," if only the economy were geared to full production. Shorter-hours schemes were vaguely unpatriotic. Reuther therefore rejected a reduction in statuary hours but publicized Nat Weinberg's concept of a "flexible work week" in which weekly work time automatically rose and fell with the unemployment level.[56]

John F. Kennedy's reluctant encounter with and ultimate embrace of Keynesian economics has been endlessly retold as a classic moment in the history of liberal statecraft. Indeed it was, but it was also a moment that marginalized the Reutherite agenda in Washington's corridors of power. Kennedy's decision to go for a tax cut came after his confrontation with big steel in April 1962 was followed by a sharp drop in the stock market and a notable sag in the recovery, convincing even the Treasury Department inflation hawks that the CEA Keynesians had to have their chance. But the $11 billion stimulation package that emerged from this generation of the best and the brightest was stunningly regressive in its determination to win back business confidence and avoid even a hint of redistributive politics. The cumbersome process of enacting the few spending measures that did pass in Kennedy's first year convinced Walter Heller and his colleagues that tax cuts were the only fiscal tool available.[57]

Kennedy parlayed this political judgment into a celebration, not only of the demise of social Keynesianism but of ideology itself. In a 1962 commencement address at Yale, the president offered Americans a technocratic guidebook to Washington policy-making. "What is at stake in our economic decisions today is not some grand warfare of rival ideologies which will sweep the country with passion but the practical management of a modern economy." Most of the problems faced by the nation, said Kennedy, "are technical problems, are administrative problems. They are the very sophisticated judgements which do not lend themselves to the great sort of 'passionate movements' which have stirred this country so often in the past." It was in this vein that a Democratic administration advocated a purely supply-side investment tax credit, on top of which came an across-the-board tax cut that delivered a lopsided stimulus to corporations and the wealthy. Our tax system, argued Kennedy late in 1962, "siphons out of the private economy too large a share of personal and business purchasing power. . . . It reduces the financial incentives for personal effort, investment and risk-taking." Such rhetoric would be heard again, for Kennedy had unleashed a most powerful conservative genie in American politics.[58]

Much as he admired Kennedy's style and statecraft, Reuther was at heart a moralist whose chest still burned with a passion for social justice and a disdain for those motivated merely by personal gain and greed. He would not defend this version of what John Kenneth Galbraith called "reactionary Keynesianism," even if it had been formulated by Ph.D. economists from the Ivy League. "This, of course, is exactly the reverse of the kind of tax reduction needed," Weinberg told Reuther when the broad outlines of the Kennedy program first become public. Even Walter Heller acknowledged labor's defeat. "With the unemployment rate stuck at 5–6 percent," he wrote Kennedy in October 1962, labor leaders "wonder if they wouldn't be better if this so-called 'anti-business' administration reversed itself and became violently 'anti-labor.'" By the time the AFL-CIO executive council met at Bal Harbour, Florida, in February 1963, Reuther was ready to attack JFK's leadership directly. The council turned a personal critique aside, but its resolution was still fairly sharp, finding the administration's tax proposals "far too conservative.... The goals it has set have been far too low, and the programs it has proposed have been too limited even to achieve those inadequate goals." To the UAW executive board Reuther argued that only in "the framework of a full employment economy lies the economic answer to our problems. Otherwise Jack Kennedy is going to be a prisoner and in 1964 the New Frontier is still not going to be off the ground."[59]

Reuther's political frustrations with the Kennedy administration and American politics were all the while reflected and refracted through another round of rivalry with George Meany. Both sought Kennedy's patronage, and in this contest Meany was absolutely determined to defend his prerogatives as titular leader of American labor. Despite an element of condescension, Kennedy found Reuther the more attractive figure, but the president had little choice but to sustain Meany's rank. The AFL-CIO president therefore blackballed Reuther's long-sought appointment as an honorary member of the U.S. delegation to the United Nations, and he would not clear the 1962 appointment of Jack Conway as undersecretary of labor because, Meany said, Reuther did not first "spend five minutes on the telephone" with him to secure the AFL-CIO endorsement.[60]

Meany undercut Reuther's capacity to influence economic policy as well. The AFL-CIO president rarely attended the meetings of the Labor-Management Advisory Committee in which Reuther put so much stock, and Meany would not let Reuther speak for the AFL-CIO during the latter's rather frequent trips to the White House. During the hectic days of June and July 1962, when Heller wanted labor's input on the tax bill, Meany was in Europe, from where he blocked Reuther's efforts to put together a team of AFL-CIO economists to meet with their Treasury and CEA counterparts. At one point AFL-CIO economist Stanley Ruttenberg had actually scheduled a meeting with Treasury Secretary Dillon only to be called by Meany from Geneva and told, "Don't do it!" "Now this teed Reuther off no end," recalled Ruttenberg. "I tried to explain to Meany on the phone there was no difference of opinion; that what Reuther proposed . . . was in line with what the executive council had already said in resolutions. But to Meany, it was a matter of protocol."[61]

Their conflict descended to a kind of uncontrollable rivalry when Reuther tried to put some limits upon Meany's petty and jealous rule at the AFL-CIO. At various council meetings Meany condemned James Carey, who was Reuther's staunchest ally, as a "psychopathic case." Meanwhile, Meany kept on the council old AFL cronies who had lost their union posts, while making it difficult for the CIO group to replace its retiring members. Reuther and Meany spent months in 1962 bickering over a replacement for L. S. Buckmaster, the former president of the United Rubber Workers (URW). Meany vetoed George Burdon, the new URW president, as a "goon," but when Reuther and the entire CIO group nominated the energetic Ralph Helstein of the Packinghouse Workers, Meany blocked him as well, on the grounds that his union was still "tainted with communism." In an August 14 shouting match with Meany, Reuther declared that he "did not see how he could in good conscience serve on the Executive Council because if [you] can veto every fellow, then there is no relationship." Meany refused to take Reuther's word that the CIO group had not put forward Helstein's name just to embarrass him. To this Reuther coldly replied, "As far as you are concerned I have no honesty or integrity." Meany said, "Yes."[62]

Two days later Reuther convened an IUD war council to consider a bolt. "Meany's utter contempt for people," asserted Reuther, "must be curbed once and for all." But the old CIO chieftains had no stomach for the fight, and they gave up entirely three months later when Meany trounced Reuther one more time. At an October meeting of the executive council Meany read a telegram from Reuther's resentful CIO nemesis, David J. McDonald, nominating John J. Grogan of the Industrial Union of Marine and Shipbuilding Workers for the post Reuther had considered it a matter of principle that Helstein would fill. Grogan was overwhelmingly elected. Only Reuther, Carey, Karl Feller, Emil Rieve, and Jacob Potofsky, all heads of former CIO unions, abstained. "The meaning of this vote," a council member later told the journalist Joseph Goulden, "was that Walter no longer could carry a majority of the CIO bloc. Dave cut him off at the knees, deliberately. No one was really unhappy about it, either."[63]

It took one humiliation after another, but Reuther finally realized that he was not about to transform the AFL-CIO. If Meany's health deteriorated—he was plagued by a painful hip that made long meetings an agony—Reuther might yet remobilize his forces, but in the meantime it was pointless to put much energy into the merged labor organization. The sterile feud with Meany, the persistent unemployment problem, the regressive tilt in the president's tax package, all were symptoms of the stalemate in American social politics. Only a new labor movement could break this up, but it had to be a revitalized unionism linked to other progressive forces in American life. For the moment Reuther would ignore the AFL-CIO and refocus his attention on the UAW itself. Already he had brought a new cohort of youthful, energetic collaborators into his inner circle. In 1961 Reuther chose the GM Department whiz Irving Bluestone to replace the departed Jack Conway as his administrative assistant, and in 1962 Paul Schrade and Douglas Fraser finally made it onto the executive board. Schrade soon became the UAW's unofficial ambassador to the farmworkers and student radicals in California; Fraser piloted a revamped UAW drive to organize engineers and white-collar professionals; while Bluestone, among his other duties, persuaded Reuther that the UAW should make available its Port Huron summer camp for a 1962 meeting of the Students for a Democratic Society (SDS).[64]

As the UAW celebrated the twenty-fifth anniversary of the sit-down strikes, Reuther found the memories more painful than nostalgic. To the delegates at the union's 1962 convention he affirmed that "there is something quite sacred about that early period" that could still be put to practical use. "A labor movement can get soft and flabby spiritually. It can make progress materially, and the soul of the union can die in the process."[65] Reuther knew he needed new ideas as well as new organizers. Early in 1963 he put Brendan Sexton in charge of a leadership study center at Solidarity House, and he funded a series of internships in Washington and Detroit for the new generation of campus radicals. In June the UAW executive board held a weeklong retreat in the Poconos, where speakers ranged from SDS president Tom Hayden to Norman Cousins of *Saturday Review*.[66]

In these same months Reuther persuaded Jack Conway to leave the government and head up the Industrial Union Department, from which Reuther sought to launch the kind of organizing drive that had eluded him since the merger. Conway, who had grown progressively frustrated with the incremental politics of the Kennedy era, welcomed the chance to spark-plug a "comprehensive, cooperative, coordinated" IUD drive largely funded by and under UAW control. Reuther did not quite see himself as another John L. Lewis, but he wanted to put his wager on a new generation of young radicals. As he told the UAW executive board, whose average age was now past fifty, "We were [once] young and we were wild and we didn't believe you couldn't organize."[67] With more than two hundred staffers in the field, there were plans on several fronts: for an assault on DuPont, where the "independent" unions were growing restless; for a multiunion campaign to organize blue-collar workers in Houston, Dallas–Fort Worth, and the new industrial suburbs of Boston, Philadelphia, and Chicago; and for the long-postponed unionization of private-sector engineers and technicians.[68]

But all this was not enough. Whatever Reuther's fervent hope, UAW money and manpower could not simply reproduce the excitement and dynamism of the 1930s on cue. The law had turned into a straitjacket, employers had recovered their self-confidence, the left-wing cadres were absent. When Sexton lectured a group of young stewards on the virtues of social unionism, he was appalled to find that far too many were wanna-be pork-choppers. And within a year of the IUD campaign launch, Conway had to report that there "is still no 'magic wand' insuring NLRB election victories." The IUD would organize a modest one hundred thousand during the boom years of the next half-decade, but these were incremental gains, with no dramatic breakthrough of the sort Reuther must have dreamed about.[69]

To the radical writer Harvey Swados, Reuther's dilemma was that of a man "eager to be at the center of a social movement, but no longer having a social movement in which to function." In the *Atlantic Monthly*, A. H. Raskin observed the same tension: "The United Automobile Workers is a union in search of a mission. . . . It has moved from lip service to action in acknowledging the necessity for a basic reassessment of labor's goals and how to reach them."[70] Of course, there was such a social movement in America, whose thunder on the near horizon had already begun to awaken the powerful and transform the language of politics. Walter Reuther eagerly embraced the new civil rights movement, but the encounter would prove one of both championship and subversion, for the political structures upon which he had staked his own fortunes put him at odds with the one force in the 1960s that could have fulfilled his social democratic vision.

17

UNEASY PARTNERS

We are getting sick and tired of the civil rights runaround practiced by the present leadership of both political parties.

—Walter Reuther, 1959

He could make excellent speeches on brotherhood, and what we need to do, and what democracy requires and so forth. But all in the context of what was best for him politically.

—George Crockett, 1970

On August 28, 1963, Walter Reuther was by far the most prominent white person to speak at the March on Washington. He deserved to be there because for nearly a generation the UAW had put more money and muscle behind the civil rights revolution than had any other trade union. It was a wonderful day: afterwards he beamed with pleasure when Irving Bluestone told him that he had overheard a pair of African-American marchers call Reuther the "white Martin Luther King."[1]

Throughout the 1950s and early 1960s Walter Reuther had proven a highly visible and articulate spokesman for American liberalism's civil rights agenda. "The United States cannot lead the world unless we are ready to fight the master race theory in Mississippi as we fought the master race theory in Germany," Reuther told a UAW civil rights conference just after the murder of Emmett Till in 1955. UAW contributions to the NAACP proved controversial among southern autoworkers, but when their grumbles reached Detroit, Reuther was defiant: "I would rather have 100,000 less members in our union than have a million more and have to compromise our position on civil rights."[2] The South African novelist and antiapartheid activist Alan Paton was impressed. "Some kind of youthful enthusiasm and sincerity shines out of Walter Reuther," he wrote after a survey of race relations in the United States. "I record his work and him as two of the best and most hopeful things I found in America."[3]

By this time Reuther had abandoned the Debsian faith that union strength and full employment alone would ameliorate white racism and integrate black workers into the larger polity. He therefore understood the need for constant education and agitation on behalf of racial equality, and he emphasized the structural character of racial discrimination, not only in the South but in the urban North as well. Government pressure to secure full and fair employment was therefore essential. As early as 1947 Reuther told Congress, "No single institution such as the CIO . . . can do more than fight a holding action until the community moves through law to guarantee basic freedoms."[4] Reuther therefore proved an activist on behalf of civil rights legislation: the push for FEPC laws at the state and national levels and, above all, the defeat of the Senate's Rule 22 in order to deprive the Dixiecrats of their chokehold over civil rights legislation.

But he remained chronically frustrated by the veto the southern Democrats exercised on all political initiatives that sought even a modest reform of American race relations. After the 1954 *Brown* decision and the Montgomery bus boycott pushed civil rights issues to the top of the liberal agenda, Reuther told an ADA audience, "If the Democratic Party tries to straddle the civil rights issue, I for one will not support it. . . . I say that no party that tries to hedge on that has a moral right to political power from the American people."[5]

Such rhetoric soon brought Reuther face to face with his own understanding of political reality. In the late 1950s virtually all the key party leaders, including liberals like Eleanor Roosevelt and Hubert Humphrey, saw a civil rights straddle as essential to Democratic Party unity and electoral success. Adlai Stevenson, whom Reuther backed for another run at the presidency in 1956, remained so committed to conciliation of the southern Democrats that he was quite willing to waffle on enforcement of the *Brown* decision. Reuther had campaigned long and hard against Stevensonian "moderation," but he too felt the tug of this accommodation. At the 1956 Democratic National Convention, Reuther came to agree with the Stevensonian liberals who feared that too much militancy would split the convention and play into the hands of Estes Kefauver or Averell Harriman, whom most thought not electable.

The crunch came late on the night of August 17 after House Speaker Sam Rayburn, then serving as an imperious convention chairman, pushed through a civil rights plank that cautioned against the use of force to implement judicial rulings in the South. In the ensuing uproar, the Michigan, Minnesota, and New York delegations had been expected to demand a roll call vote. But the Michigan delegates remained strangely passive. Working through Woodcock and Conway, the UAW forces inside the Wolverine delegation had defeated their titular leader, Governor

G. Mennen Williams, who still sought to fight for a more forceful civil rights platform. According to Joe Rauh, Reuther told Williams, "We've got all we can so let's
stop."[6]

This capitulation soon bred yet more stalemate. In 1956 Stevenson lost by an
even larger margin than in 1952, in part because the Republicans won nearly 40
percent of the black vote. When the new Congress assembled, Rule 22 remained
inviolate; indeed, the southern Democrats felt so confident by early 1957 that they
chose to emasculate rather than filibuster a voting rights bill ushered through the
Senate by Lyndon Johnson. It was the first law labeled "civil rights" to pass the
Congress in eighty-three years, so the UAW, represented by Paul Sifton and the
two-hatted Joe Rauh (he held the ADA portfolio as well), had fought for the civil
rights coalition to endorse it, if only to forestall Republican charges that the
Democrats were completely paralyzed on this issue. When the NAACP's Roy
Wilkins sided with Rauh, the Leadership Conference on Civil Rights followed, as
did the majority of Senate liberals. Reuther reported to the UAW that the 1957 law
had made "slight, but nevertheless substantial progress," yet even this description
was a stretch, for Lyndon Johnson had allowed the southerners to veto Title III,
which would have given the attorney general the power to initiate voting rights
suits in the South. Segregationist congressmen had also insisted upon a "jury trial
amendment" that made it virtually certain that no white southerner would ever be
convicted of violating a civil rights statute.[7]

Kennedy's nomination in 1960 shifted the Democrats slightly to the left on civil
rights issues, but presidential timidity and Dixiecrat intransigence did little to disturb the policy stalemate. Despite the dramatic struggle unfolding throughout the
Deep South, Reuther let the new administration off the hook. At its 1962 convention the UAW endorsed the activism of Martin Luther King, Jr., and other "heroic
Negroes"; at the same time the union hailed "the many advances made by the
Kennedy Administration in this field."[8]

If Reuther's links to the Democratic Party had been the only constraint upon his
activism, these might well have been strained as the movement reached flood tide.
But Reuther's growing identification with both John F. Kennedy and Lyndon
Johnson had its reflection, if not its actual origins, inside the UAW itself, where he
found the growth of a rights-conscious militancy an ideological and organizational
challenge of the first order. In the early 1940s the rise of a black insurgency within
the automobile and agricultural implement factories had been organically linked
to the growth of industrial unionism itself. A generation later, when a second wave
of racial militancy surged forward, it crashed with full force against a shop-floor
regime and a union structure of far greater rigidity. This was a contradiction that
Reuther could never resolve or escape.

At the end of the 1950s racial structures based on the subordination of African-
American workers had a threefold character within the automobile industry. First,
there was still outright segregation, maintained by employers and sustained by
local unionists, in many UAW-organized factories in the South. In the decade after

World War II this problem had actually become more prominent as the decentralization of Big Three auto production out of the urban North and the organization of new facilities, especially those of the aircraft and agricultural implement industries, put upwards of 10 percent of all UAW membership south of the Ohio River and the Mason-Dixon Line.

In the Atlanta, Dallas, Memphis, and Norfolk automotive assembly plants the prewar tradition barring blacks from all but janitorial work remained largely intact. "When we moved into the South," one of GM's plant managers in Atlanta explained in 1957, "we agreed to abide by local custom and not hire Negroes for production work. This is no time for social reforming . . . and we're not about to try it." Reuther was personally acquainted with the virulent racism of the Georgia workers. In 1945 he had flown to Atlanta to demand that Fisher Body Local 34 admit black sweepers to membership and upgrade them to production jobs. At a packed meeting that lasted five hours, Reuther pulled out all the stops, arguing for solidarity against the company and threatening the local with an administratorship if it failed to follow UAW policy. Soon 120 black sweepers were formally enrolled in the local, but none won production jobs. Indeed, the GM Atlanta locals remained a center of segregationist agitation, especially after the *Brown* decision, when the autoworker Elston Edwards, an Imperial Wizard of the Georgia Ku Klux Klan, recruited actively among his workmates.[9]

Memphis proved an equally intransigent bastion of Herrenvolk militancy. Management at International Harvester hired hundreds of African-Americans to help staff its new agricultural equipment factory in the late 1940s. But trench warfare immediately broke out between whites and blacks on the shop floor. As in so many factories, mills, and shipyards, not all confined to the Deep South by any means, Harvester's white workers linked a militant job control impulse with a racialist construction of the factory hierarchy. A close-knit fraternity of whiteness, skill, and union power kept Harvester Local 988 a storm center of segregationist conflict. In the late 1950s Local 988 thumbed its nose at Solidarity House when it constructed a new union hall complete with segregated rest rooms and water fountains.[10] "We belong to Reuther's union but we don't believe in Reuther's integration," announced one militant welder at a stormy meeting held between UAW officers and Local 988 whites. "When the showdown comes we'll take segregation and leave you guys up in Detroit."[11]

In fact, Solidarity House seemed without the will to intervene. As late as 1957 Reuther still maintained that, "except for isolated instances," discrimination in the matter of promotions and transfers had been eliminated. "The most glaring instance of continued discriminatory practices is discrimination by management at the hiring gate, a process over which, in most instances, we have no direct control."[12] Clearly, this was not the whole story in the South, but Pat Greathouse, the UAW vice president in charge of the Agricultural Implement Department, was himself from downstate Illinois. He had spent much of the previous decade fighting the FE Communists, whose championship of African-American demands at

Harvester made most Reutherites think twice before they leaped into the racial fray. The leader of the embattled Harvester blacks, George Holloway, found Reuther's high-profile agitation against the Dixiecrats a genuine inspiration, but by 1959 he pleaded with Detroit that his workers "felt that the UAW-CIO executive board has thrown us to the wolves and forgot their promises to correct this evil situation."[13]

Reuther and his executive board eventually moved against such blatant segregation in the southern locals, but a second racial problem, the upgrading of black workers into the skilled trades, proved even more difficult to resolve. During World War II northern blacks had broken through the caste lines that kept them confined to foundry and janitorial work, but upward mobility halted in the 1950s as job opportunities contracted and the union pushed for higher apprenticeship standards. By the end of the decade the black proportion of the skilled trades stood at minuscule levels, 2 percent or less, a proportion that was often below that of even the notoriously exclusionary building trades. Black staffers called the skilled trades "the Deep South" of the UAW. But Reuther was not about to take aggressive action here: because the skilled trades had begun a long-simmering "revolt" against industrial-style unionism, Reuther hesitated to further roil the waters with an assault upon the racial nepotism of this strategically placed section of the union.[14]

Finally, black production workers in the late 1950s and early 1960s confronted an industrial relations structure of authority that seemed increasingly intolerable. The auto industry as a whole was about 13 percent black in the early 1960s, and in Michigan upwards of 20 percent. On the semiskilled Detroit production lines, the proportion reached even higher. At Chrysler's Jefferson Avenue and Dodge Main facilities and in the Rouge assembly building about half of all production workers were nonwhite. Not unexpectedly, as black workers became more numerous and more concentrated at the point of production, they came to see the shop-floor relationships embedded in the Treaty of Detroit in specifically racial terms. Thus paragraph 63 of the UAW-GM contract, which gave foremen so much discretion in the transfer and upgrading of production workers, took on an ugly racial coloration when implemented by white supervisors still unacculturated to a multiracial workforce. Reuther had spent the better part of a decade in an unsuccessful effort to reform paragraph 63, but few black workers had any sense of this difficult prehistory. As the rights consciousness of the 1960s moved from the lunch counters of North Carolina to the production lines of Detroit, African-American workers became sharply conscious of the oppressive and hierarchical character of the factory regime. And they soon blamed Reuther—or at least their regional director—for not doing more about it.[15]

The UAW's Fair Employment Practices Department (FEPD) proved incapable of resolving these explosive pressures. It was largely "ceremonial and symbolic," in the words of F. Ray Marshall, an industrial relations expert friendly to the UAW. William Oliver, Reuther's 1946 choice as FEPD codirector, had been a foundryman in Ford's Highland Park factory. But unlike George Crockett, his predecessor in the job, or the many radical blacks who came out of the Rouge, Oliver had no large reservoir of political support in the UAW, nor did he attempt to build a constituency during the quarter-century he directed the department. Under his tenure the FEPD had a dual role: it represented the UAW to the national civil rights community, to the NAACP, the Urban League, and the more liberal federal agencies and congressmen; and it served to route, usually back to the regional directors, discrimination complaints as they percolated up from the African-American membership and the occasional UAW local. Oliver's FEPD kept tabs on African-American sentiment within the UAW but played no mobilizing role throughout the formative years of the civil rights revolution. "We are a fire station," admitted Sheldon Tappes, who periodically served in the department under Oliver, "and when the bell rings we run to put out the fire."[16]

Reuther knew he had a problem with Oliver; in 1952 he had tried to displace him with James Farmer of the Congress of Racial Equality (CORE). Farmer had all the right credentials: he was an activist, a forceful speaker, and, perhaps most important, an anti-Stalinist comfortable among old Socialists and the left-wing Reutherites. Guy Nunn frequently put him on the UAW radio show. To give Farmer the kind of credibility he would need with black workers and to prepare him for elective office, Reuther wanted him to get a job in an auto plant and then move up to Solidarity House. But the idea collapsed when it met fierce resistance on the executive board, most likely led by John Livingston, who found Farmer's marriage to a white woman even more offensive than his socialist-pacifist politics.[17]

All of Reuther's problems on the racial front were symbolized by the union's failure to elect even one African-American to serve on its 22-man executive board. By 1959 black demands for such representation had been a continuing feature of UAW debate for almost twenty years, and several national unions, including the International Longshoremen's and Warehousemen's Union, the Packinghouse Workers, and the Transport Workers had blacks on their highest governing bodies. Yet the UAW executive board remained all white (and all male). It was "embarrassing" to lobby for civil rights legislation, remembered Bill Dodds, a white liberal in the UAW Citizenship Department, "when top-level UAW blacks were so scarce."[18]

On this issue as on so many others, Reuther had become a prisoner of the institution he did so much to construct. In no UAW region did blacks command a majority of all workers, and, of course, all existing posts on the UAW executive board were already taken by Reuther loyalists. Over time Reuther expected that the steady growth of minority employment in the Detroit area would produce a black majority in one of the city's regions, but the only alternative seemed to be the creation of one or more new posts on the executive board, an option the Reutherites had steadfastly opposed as "reverse Jim Crow."

The situation was intolerable, and Reuther was soon confronted by a remarkably vibrant, independent black protest movement within the UAW itself. Founded in 1957, the Trade Union Leadership Council (TULC) linked the black union politics of the 1940s with the new militancy that would erupt after 1963. Because it was little more than a caucus of black UAW staffers, TULC would be overshadowed by the spectacular appearance of a more radical and nationalist autoworker movement organized into the Dodge Revolutionary Union Movement and similar plant-level groupings. But like so much of the history that would characterize the 1960s, the ideas and sentiments that surfaced in the early years of that memorable decade foreshadowed the explosions that would come later.

TULC activists had been politicized largely within the Reutherite orbit. Buddy Battle, the titular president of the TULC, was "the Mayor Daley of the Rouge," a consummate deal-maker and machine politician who nevertheless kept in touch with the more activist blacks in the city. His clout was given an articulate vision by Horace Sheffield, who as an NAACP youth leader had played a vital role in mobilizing black support for the great Rouge walkout of 1941. Well schooled in the Trotskyist critique of Popular Front politics, Sheffield fought the Communist-oriented blacks in Local 600 all during the 1940s and early 1950s, later working under Roy Reuther in the UAW Citizenship Department as a sort of emissary from the UAW to the civil rights movement.[19] The TULC, wrote Sheffield, must "interpret the Negro community to the labor movement. . . . Not from the outside, advising, if you can get an appointment. But from the inside, speaking up as a member of the union with all the rights and privileges that go with membership." Most important, Sheffield denounced Reutherite hypocrisy, asserting that black unionists could no longer "accept as adequate the fact that some of our international unions have a good public posture on the question of 'civil rights and fair practices' while, at the same time, they resist with every means at their disposal any effort to change the 'lily-white' character of their own international executive boards."[20]

The TULC caught Reuther off balance at the UAW convention held in October 1959. At an evening "caucus" held the day before the opening gavel, Battle and Sheffield insisted that Reuther commit himself to putting a black on the UAW executive board. The issue was urgent because just weeks before—at the annual AFL-CIO convention—George Meany had publicly admonished the veteran civil rights leader A. Philip Randolph with the taunt: "Who appointed you the guardian of all the Negroes in the United States?" This public affront had to be answered; otherwise, white unionists would continue to assume that they could speak for their black membership. But Reuther's handling of their challenge was defensive and maladroit. And not only Reuther—throughout the meeting no white participant took the floor to support Sheffield and Battle. Some were hostile, clapping and yelling "Sit down!" at the black speakers. Reuther himself hated this ambush. Unlike his brothers Victor and Roy, Walter had never cultivated a personal friendship with any African-American, and he easily mistook civil rights militancy for the racial nationalism he abhorred. "I realize that Negroes are on the march all over the world," Reuther acknowledged. But he once again asserted that "the UAW is part of America" and could do little more than reflect the racial mores of the society. When Reuther condescendingly announced, "There will come a time when a Negro will be qualified and . . . at such a time a Negro will be placed on the board," black unionists seethed with fury.[21]

TULC blacks quickly organized a "conspiracy" to offer a black vice-presidential candidate from the convention floor. "I was going to walk down that plank," remembered Sheffield. "I had made up my mind this was it. If Jesus himself had said, 'Don't do it, Shef!' I would have ignored Jesus."[22] As twenty-eight hundred delegates listened in a silence quite unusual for the vast Atlantic City hall, Sheffield reminded them that for sixteen years UAW blacks had been promised a representative on its highest governing body. In 1943 he had been one of the few African-Americans against a Negro, "as a Negro," being slotted for the international executive board, but even the UAW now insisted that blacks be represented at all levels of government. Asserted Sheffield, "The Negro people are asking, 'What about the UAW? What is wrong with the UAW?'" Then in a caustic reference to Reuther's caucus remarks, Sheffield told the convention that "Negroes are sick and tired of the matter of qualifications being raised . . . because I think it is fairly evident to everyone here that it is not necessary to be a Rhodes Scholar to sit on the International Executive Board."[23]

Yet the man Sheffield nominated for vice president was perhaps the union equivalent of a Rhodes scholar. Willouby Abner, thirty-nine years old in 1959, was a Chicago-born black who had organized thousands during the war in several South Side foundries and small manufacturing plants. Like Sheffield, Abner was a Reuther loyalist in the 1940s and 1950s who had been politically educated by the anti-Stalinist left. A law school graduate, he was an adept and forceful speaker who clashed repeatedly with Communist-oriented blacks in the Cook County Industrial Union Council and the Chicago branch of the NAACP, of which he had been president for two terms in the early 1950s. In 1962 he took on Malcolm X before a University of Chicago audience and, according to most observers, got the better of the black nationalist in open debate.[24]

Abner declined the nomination, as planned, but when Reuther downplayed TULC concerns during the remainder of the convention—he put forward a routine civil rights resolution in the conclave's last, ragged hours—Battle organized a walkout of most of the remaining African-American delegates. Reuther again found himself on the defensive, pleading from the podium, "No one can say your union has not tried hard to fight against discrimination in the shop and at the hiring gate." To which the *Pittsburgh Courier* responded, "No one in the country kowtows more frequently before the shrine of civil rights than Walter P. Reuther . . . but Negro laborites are sick and tired of having their union bosses kid them on this question. . . . Walter Reuther, George Meany and the other union moguls had better get wise, and the sooner the better."[25]

The black challenge could not be ignored. Immediately after the convention, Reuther's key political operatives, Jack Conway and Leonard Woodcock, met with the TULC group and reached an understanding: the Reuther "administration caucus" would nominate a black to the executive board at the next convention, thirty months later. Meanwhile, Reuther did what he could to bolster the UAW's bona fides among black autoworkers. In January 1960 the UAW executive board finally took decisive action against the segregationists in control of the Memphis Harvester local. Local 988 was put into an administratorship; Pat Greathouse and Douglas Fraser were sent to Tennessee to take physical possession of the local hall, repaint the offensive rest room signs, and organize a new leadership. The struggle took almost a year, but an integrationist set of officers finally took power after two hundred white supremacists, mainly welders, boycotted union affairs.[26]

Reuther also dropped the stale rhetoric blaming only the auto corporations for racial discrimination in the industry. After new surveys revealed the extent of racism within UAW-organized factories—and after much NAACP prodding and publicity—the UAW began a more vigorous effort to desegregate southern and border-state auto factories and upgrade black workers out of the janitorial ranks. Progress was hardly rapid, but in the 1961 round of contract negotiations the UAW pushed hard for an antidiscrimination clause from each of the Big Three automakers. The companies balked—they insisted upon retaining sole control over hiring—but the issue was on the table. Reuther also continued to patronize the civil rights movement, even as its tactics and rhetoric moved beyond those of his old NAACP allies. In 1961 Reuther invited Martin Luther King, Jr., to keynote the UAW's mammoth twenty-fifth anniversary dinner; his speech happily acknowledged the extent to which the civil rights movement was "proudly borrowing some of your [sit-in] techniques." And that summer the UAW rushed five thousand dollars to CORE to bail its "freedom riders" out of jail.[27]

But none of these efforts defused the white-hot politics surrounding the selection of a black executive board member. The obvious candidates were Sheffield and Abner. The latter had the solid backing of all the predominantly black unions in Chicago; moreover, his sheer talent would instantly make him a new figure on the national civil rights scene. Sheffield was not quite a union intellectual of Abner's standing, but his leadership of TULC had begun to make him a substantial force in Detroit-area civic and union politics. Therein lay the problem: both candidates symbolized the emergence of a powerful political movement, independent and in some ways counterpoised to that of the institution over which Reuther presided. They were, in the language of many UAW officials, "too controversial"; they were not "team players."[28]

Indeed, the TULC had already begun to demonstrate a powerful independence when it played a leading role in the municipal election that broke a generation-long stalemate in Detroit politics. The Motor City had become increasingly black; in the 1950s the African-American proportion of the population nearly doubled to almost 30 percent. By 1961, when the UAW and business leaders again supported a white conservative, Louis Miriani, for mayor, the union leadership had "moved well to the right of its own rank and file," concluded the political scientist J. David Greenstone.[29] Recognizing these demographic and political shifts, Sheffield and the TULC joined with the NAACP, the black churches, and municipal workers to mobilize thousands of campaign workers for the successful mayoralty bid of Jerome Cavanagh, a young, white liberal politician who campaigned heavily in the black districts. Sheffield used the Cavanagh campaign to make TULC a mass movement for the first time. With upwards of ten thousand members in 1962, the organization was now a major force in Detroit politics. Sheffield's critique of the UAW now extended well beyond the union's racial politics: he denounced the growth of a "business unionism" mentality within its leadership and saw in the sit-ins of young people in the South an inspiration for a revival of the "crusading spirit that marked the advent of the CIO in the 1930s." Thereafter, the UAW could no longer automatically dominate liberal-black politics in Detroit; by the mid-1960s George Crockett, Coleman Young, and John Conyers, Jr., whose political roots all went back to the Reuther opposition of the 1940s, had won elective office in the Motor City.[30]

Reuther was also irritated by the close links forged between TULC and the NAACP, most notably personified by Herbert Hill, the vigorous, caustic NAACP labor secretary who promoted a campaign of publicity, protest, and, in extreme circumstances, legal decertification of the unions that systematically discriminated against African-American workers. Reuther had little quarrel with Hill's exposure of auto management's capitulation to Deep South segregation or with the NAACP assault upon the building trades. But when Hill's 1961 NAACP report, "Racism within Organized Labor: A Report of Five Years of the AFL-CIO," included a blistering exposure of institutionalized discrimination in the industrial unions, especially the ILGWU and the Steel Workers, Reuther winced. In Detroit as well, Hill and the TULC kept up the pressure, in effect challenging the UAW's capacity to speak for, mobilize, and bargain for its African-American members.[31]

Reuther restrained his annoyance, but Emil Mazey exploded in the fall of 1961, denouncing the NAACP for "its criticism of labor for actions which were obviously the sins of management." The UAW secretary-treasurer still thought of himself as a proletarian radical. He therefore found formation of an independent black movement an implicit challenge not only to the union's authority but to his own left-wing conviction that the unity of the working class required it to speak with but one voice. Reuther was far more tactful. He knew that an open break with the civil rights community would rob him of the legitimacy essential to leadership of the broad progressive coalition he hoped to reconstitute. When in the fall of 1962 speculation arose that Reuther might quit the NAACP board, he squashed it quickly: "I couldn't resign if I wanted to," he told reporters at the Negro American Labor Council convention in December 1962. "I am in this fight [for civil rights] because I want to be."[32]

Thus Reuther faced the most potent internal union challenge to his leadership since the 1940s. Should he try to co-opt Sheffield and the TULC forces or excommunicate them? Many of the old radicals around Reuther, including Guy Nunn, Brendan Sexton, Leonard Woodcock, and Nat Weinberg, were covert TULC partisans, and sometime advisers, who saw the civil rights insurgency as the long-sought key to a revitalization of American labor. They wanted a man like Sheffield or Abner on the executive board as a forceful spokesperson for the new movement. But most UAW executive board members, and especially those representing the heavily black regions in the Midwest, rightly feared TULC as a threat to the racial status quo over which they had come to preside. Detroit-area directors like George Merrelli and Joseph McClusker, as well as the vice presidents Norm Matthews, Pat Greathouse, and Richard Gosser, had built ethnic political machines that were certain to clash with a politically mobilized black constituency. Emil Mazey gave these conservatives a kind of ideological leadership. "You have to be either a trade unionist or a civil rights leader," Mazey told Sheffield on more than one occasion. "As a practical matter," wrote the well-connected *Detroit Times* reporter Jack Crellin, "the feeling persists among many members of the UAW hierarchy that it would be a fatal mistake to keep on the staff a man who violates caucus rules."[33]

Thus the actual selection of a black executive board member hung fire for more than two years, finally prompting Buddy Battle to fire off a blistering challenge to Reuther late in 1961. "The UAW will have to choose between the liberal image you have projected for it and resolve this burning question or retrogress by accepting the backward leadership that seems on the increase in our union. . . . There will be no doubt in anyone's mind after the 1962 UAW convention as to which road the UAW has elected to travel."[34] Faced with this deadline, Reuther finally got down to work. He finessed the old "reverse Jim Crow" conundrum by making the new black seat part of a package of three new board members elected at large. The Reuther protégé Douglas Fraser would fill one of the seats, the Ford Department head Kenneth Bannon would get another, and the third seat was reserved for an African-American selected by the UAW executive board.

Reuther conducted the search as if the UAW were hiring an important new staffer. Résumés were checked, letters of endorsement filed, interviews held. Reuther made a point of asking every possible candidate whether he was prepared to "accept and support wholeheartedly the decisions of the [administration] caucus."[35] In the furious political lobbying that led up to the board vote, TULC made its support for Sheffield clear; if he were vetoed, the organization insisted that only a black in some way associated with their movement would be acceptable. Walter Reuther may well have favored Sheffield, who was the private choice of so many other UAW liberals. But Reuther also had to live with the rest of the executive board; he had to maintain that "teamwork in the leadership" that a man like Sheffield had the power and the will to tear asunder.[36]

This was one of those issues upon which Reuther simply could not impose his will. When the decisive vote was taken in the days just before the opening of the UAW convention in May 1962, the executive board split wide open, narrowly rejecting Sheffield by a vote of eleven to eight, with five abstentions. In his place, the UAW turned to Nelson Jack Edwards, another longtime UAW staffer; he was one of the "conspirators" at the 1959 UAW convention but, unlike Abner and

Sheffield, not a high-profile civil rights activist. Ironically, Edwards had not been a Reutherite in the 1940s, when it counted, but had switched sides after 1947. Thereafter, he worked under Joseph McClusker as a service representative on the West Side of Detroit, never seeking to rock the boat in that big region.[37]

Edwards was far from an "Uncle Tom," but his elevation to the UAW executive board did play a decisive role in limiting the influence of the TULC in Detroit politics over the next few years. Working through the UAW, Edwards created a rival black community association that successfully competed with the TULC for influence at city hall and for power within the Michigan Democratic Party. Although black appointments to the UAW staff increased markedly in the late 1960s—and Reuther used his influence to ensure the election of a second African-American to the executive board in 1968—TULC lost its authoritative capacity to speak for black autoworkers. Sheffield and Battle remained at the center of a quasi-oppositional caucus within the UAW, but by the mid-1960s they could no longer forge an organic link with the younger generation of African-Americans who were flooding into the auto shops. At the age of fifty, both Sheffield and Edwards had more in common with each other than with many angry young radicals. In 1967 the two signified a truce when Edwards appointed Sheffield his administrative assistant.[38]

Reuther's constrained sense of political practicality became clear even during the months when he aspired to the mantle of a "white Martin Luther King." Despite—or perhaps because of—his great difficulty in satisfying black demands within the UAW, Reuther turned his enormous energies toward championship of the civil rights movement when it made its most determined assault upon the bastions of southern segregation and congressional gridlock. Reuther's most spectacular intervention came at the climax of the Birmingham demonstrations in May 1963. After nearly two weeks of mass civil disobedience and brutal police attack, all televised to a worldwide audience, Martin Luther King, Jr., had finally worked out a settlement with the white businessmen and merchants of the city. However, the Birmingham jails, controlled by Eugene "Bull" Connor and his bitterly segregationist police department, still held more than eight hundred demonstrators. King appealed for help to Robert Kennedy, who immediately got in touch with Jack Conway, Joe Rauh, and then Walter Reuther. "Why do you call me about these kinds of things?" Reuther asked, perhaps in genuine curiosity. "Because we don't know anyone else that we can call," admitted the attorney general. Overnight Reuther and Rauh came up with $160,000 in bail money, fully half pledged by Reuther in his dual capacity as president of the UAW and of the AFL-CIO Industrial Union Department. Within hours the UAW staffers Irving Bluestone and William Oliver were on their way south, the cash stashed in bulging money belts around their midsections.[39]

The epic confrontation in Birmingham, followed by a wave of sit-ins, demonstrations, and near-riots throughout the South, reminded Reuther and his comrades of the heady days that followed GM's capitulation at Flint. "The American Revolution of '63" was the title of a three-hour NBC documentary on the struggle against segregation. *Time* made "the Negro Revolt" its cover story during a month when press and politicians finally recognized the primacy of civil rights within the American polity. For all his detachment and moderation, President Kennedy had to act. In a speech of June 11, he finally adopted the language and urgency of the new movement: "We are confronted primarily with a moral issue," announced the president. "A great change is at hand, and our task, our obligation, is to make that revolution, that change, peaceful and constructive for all."[40]

Reuther knew the moment had come in American politics when a legislative breakthrough was finally possible. At a meeting between trade union leaders and the president on June 13, he made an impassioned plea for inclusion of a fair employment practices title in the administration's civil rights bill. Nine days later he joined a delegation of civil rights leaders, including King, Randolph, and Wilkins, who met with Kennedy in the cabinet room. By this time the plans of Bayard Rustin and A. Philip Randolph for a new March on Washington for "Jobs and Freedom" had gained momentum, but the obstacles to the actual passage of a civil rights bill were equally clear. Since the Dixiecrats would mount an intransigent defense of the old order, the key players were the bloc of midwestern Republicans whose hostility to federal authority had sustained their generation-long alliance with the racial oligarchy of the South. "We want success in Congress, not just a big show at the Capitol," Kennedy told the civil rights leaders. "The only effect is to create an atmosphere of intimidation—and this may give some members of Congress an out." In response, Randolph tutored Kennedy in the internal dynamics of American protest. "The Negroes are already in the streets. . . . Is it not better that they be led by organizations dedicated to civil rights and disciplined by struggle rather than to leave them to other leaders who care neither about civil rights nor about non-violence?"[41]

Right after their exchange with the president, King, Randolph, and other leaders held a lunch and strategy session at Reuther's hotel suite. One purpose of the meeting was to dissuade King, who now symbolized the new militancy, from trying to deploy in the nation's capital the tactics that had proven so spectacularly impressive in Birmingham. To King, and even more so to the militant cadre in the Student Nonviolent Coordinating Committee (SNCC), the distinction between a mass march and civil disobedience had become rather blurred in recent months. As Wilkins remembered it, Reuther and he were on one side, Dr. King on the other, and Randolph in the middle. Reuther and Wilkins tended to emphasize the need for a grass-roots mobilization combined with a full-press effort to lobby Congress. Reuther's idea, which was in part a product of talks with President Kennedy and others in the administration, foresaw a "Coalition of Conscience" in which whites from labor, church, and civic groups would join with the civil rights organizations to pressure northern Republicans to back a beefed-up civil rights bill. Randolph's march therefore represented a "perfect compromise," especially if it were shaped in direct support of the administration's own civil rights bill.[42]

The very next day Reuther got a taste of the enormous power unleashed by the civil rights movement when he flew back to Detroit for a huge march down Woodward Avenue. A black ministerial alliance had organized the "Walk to Freedom" on short notice, but it proved a sensational success, the largest mass march in the United States since the Taft-Hartley demonstrations of 1947. The advance crowd, singing the old labor songs and the new civil rights hymns, spilled out of a 21-block staging area and headed downtown without Reuther, King, or other march leaders. When their motorcade finally intercepted the head of the line at Cadillac Square, people shouted out King's name and swarmed forward, knocking aside the police cordon. Crowd estimates ranged upwards from 125,000. Reuther, King, Mayor Jerome Cavanagh, and Rev. C. L. Franklin, who had coordinated the organizational work of Detroit's black churches, linked arms to keep from being swallowed up. But the tide of people pushed them forward with such force that their feet hardly touched the ground. At a packed Cobo Hall, Reuther hailed the march as "the beginning of a crusade to mobilize the moral conscience of America," after which King thrilled the audience with a version of the "I Have a Dream" speech he would make world-famous two months later.[43]

All of America's great reform movements, from the crusade against slavery to the labor upsurge in the 1930s, defined themselves as champions of a moral and patriotic nationalism, which they counterpoised to the parochial and selfish elites who stood athwart their vision of a virtuous society. Legitimacy and success are well advanced when a Lincoln, a Roosevelt, or a Kennedy links his statecraft to the growing power of an insurgent social movement. In the U.S. context, this legitimization from the ruling elite is an essential element in the movement's capacity to transform dissent and protest into a new hegemony. But a fine line has to be drawn between the rhetorical, symbolic alliance forged with the governing power and the capacity of the movement to maintain an independent, perhaps even an unpredictable, trajectory in the field. From Montgomery to Memphis, Martin Luther King, Jr., understood this imperative. As biographers Taylor Branch and David Garrow have demonstrated, King time and again resisted, if sometimes imperfectly, White House tutelage on the place and timing of his demonstrations, the resolution of his demands, the expulsion of Communists from his inner circle, and, in the last year of his life, the Vietnam imbroglio. Whatever his strategy, radical or accommodative, King guarded his freedom and the autonomy of the movement for which he spoke.

Reuther stepped over the line. He was organized labor's most vigorous and powerful champion of the civil rights insurgency, and for this he momentarily won a well-deserved place within the high councils of movement decision-making. But throughout these crucial months of 1963 and 1964, Reuther used his influence to serve that of the president within these councils. He saw no contradiction, for the UAW president had become convinced that the corridors of power were now open to labor-liberals for the first time in almost a quarter-century; a great realignment in American politics seemed in the offing. Reuther had been at the margins of power for so long that he took even Kennedy's limited accommodation as signifying an intimate collaboration. "He was close to us because I believe we understood each other and shared the same values and dreamed the same dreams," Reuther told a union conference two months after the assassination.[44] Taking into account even the bathos of the post-Dallas weeks, one senses again the powerful seduction to which Reuther had succumbed. Though he complained of Kennedy's timidity, Reuther gave his administration, and that of his successor, the kind of political trust that was certain to be broken.

Beginning in late June the Kennedys worked through Reuther, as well as the white philanthropist Stephen Currier, to make certain that the thrust of the march and that of the administration ran along parallel paths. To step up the work of the Leadership Conference on Civil Rights and move its operations from New York to Washington, Reuther funded two additional staffers and provided the office space at IUD headquarters. With strong support from Roy Wilkins, Reuther also proved instrumental in giving his "Coalition of Conscience" a broader leadership by encouraging Randolph to add the Protestant notable Rev. Eugene Carson Blake, the Jewish leader Rabbi Joachim Prinz, and the Catholic layman Matthew Ahmann to the "Big Six" civil rights leaders (King, Wilkins, Randolph, SNCC's John Lewis, the Urban League's Whitney Young, and CORE's James Farmer) who composed the March on Washington steering committee. The restructuring into a "Big Ten," including Reuther, diluted the social democratic content of the March on Washington, shifting it toward an exclusive endorsement of the administration's rather limited civil rights bill, which at this stage did not contain even an FEPC provision. Randolph and Rustin had seen a full-employment economy as central to the well-being of black America, but this demand now evaporated, as did the urgent necessity for a two-dollar minimum wage, which white religious leaders vetoed.[45]

News of the impending march brought to the surface the atavistic fears of a deeply racist society. Washington was still a southern city, and even among partisans of the Kennedy civil rights bill, few imagined that thousands of blacks could pour into town without some outbreak of violence, drunkenness, or racial conflict. Expectations were so negative that the Washington Senators postponed two night baseball games, and hotel rooms went begging because so many businessmen and tourists stayed out of town. To monitor the situation, Robert Kennedy set up a Justice Department planning group that came to play an increasingly large role in the management of the march itself. The attorney general was particularly interested in making sure the gathering was peaceful and orderly, keeping the rhetoric within bounds, and getting the focus of the demonstration turned from the Capitol to some other part of the city. The president and his brother also wanted to make sure that the gathering was impressive in size and with noticeable white participation.[46]

Reuther and Jack Conway, who represented the UAW president with both the Justice Department and the march organizers, played key roles in moving the demonstration in this direction. In several New York planning sessions for the march,

Conway argued that only a large and unobstructed area away from the Capitol could comfortably contain the two hundred thousand now expected for the rally. Downplaying the political significance of the switch, Conway convinced Randolph and other organizers that the Lincoln Memorial would work best for such a large turnout; of course, Reuther's IUD would foot the $16,600 bill for the large and expensive sound system necessary to reach an audience now awkwardly divided by the monument's reflecting pool. That was the "clincher," remembered Conway.[47]

To anchor his "Coalition of Conscience," Reuther wanted the AFL-CIO to endorse the march. But when George Meany finally convened a council meeting at the ILGWU's Pocono retreat on August 12, Reuther got nowhere. For an entire afternoon their contest was a replay of all the old fights. "George Meany was very sharp and very negative," remembered Reuther. Meany feared mass action and riot, mistrusted Reuther's activism, and held the public support of most labor chieftains. "You either were voting for him or against him," Reuther told his own executive board. "It had nothing to do with the idea." In the end Reuther got two votes, his own, and that of the march organizer A. Philip Randolph. Meany himself drafted a self-serving release that restated AFL-CIO support for a comprehensive civil rights bill and permitted individual trade unions to participate if they chose to do so. Several did, and in force, including the ILGWU, the IUE, and the American Federation of State, County, and Municipal Employees (AFSCME). But Reuther's jibe, that Meany's endorsement was "so weak that they will have to give it a blood transfusion to keep it alive long enough to mimeograph it," appeared near the top of most press accounts.[48]

By late August the UAW had shifted a sizable proportion of its entire staff to Washington in support of the march. The union rented two hundred hotel rooms, printed two thousand signs, and hired buses and trains to bring a minimum of five thousand of its own members to the march.[49] But the night before the ceremonies Reuther faced one last threat to his conception of the civil rights coalition essential for a successful March on Washington. Jack Conway had found a freshly mimeographed copy of SNCC Chairman John Lewis's speech for the Lincoln Memorial rally. Justice Department aides got their copy at almost the same moment and passed on the text to Robert Kennedy and his assistants. All were alarmed. The speech said that SNCC could *not* support the Kennedy civil rights bill because it was "too little and too late." "We are now involved in a serious revolution," read the text, which was the joint effort of several SNCC staffers, some fresh from the frustration and brutality of southwestern Georgia. Lewis's rhetoric would soon become the common coin of the New Left, but in 1963 his language was certain to outrage many of the more moderate civil rights supporters whom the Kennedys and Reuther had been so anxious to involve in the leadership of the march. "This nation is still a place of cheap political leaders who build their careers on immoral compromises and ally themselves with open forms of political, economic and social exploitation," the text declared. "We will take matters into our own hands. . . . If any radical social, political and economic changes are to take place in our society, the people, the masses, must bring them about." And Lewis vowed a transformation of the South: "We will march through the Heart of Dixie, the way Sherman did. We shall pursue our own 'scorched earth' policy and burn Jim Crow to the ground—nonviolently."[50]

"Here was the Chairman of the Student Nonviolent Coordinating Committee calling for open revolution," Reuther told his executive board a month later. "That Negroes could not get redress of their grievances within the framework of the legal structure. . . . It was really something." Apprised by Robert Kennedy of the contents of Lewis's speech, several Catholic notables threatened to issue a denunciation and pull out. Patrick Cardinal O'Boyle, the prelate of Washington, declared he would not offer the invocation or share the same platform with Lewis.[51]

Working in tandem with the Justice Department, Reuther turned his considerable powers of persuasion and organization into getting the speech modified and the leadership coalition reunified. A late-night meeting with Lewis and others in SNCC proved inconclusive, so the dispute continued on the morning of the march. It was still unresolved when Reuther, King, Randolph, and other march leaders assembled at the Lincoln Memorial. Reuther laid out the issues as if he were at a union caucus:

> Look. We have got a decision to make real quick, and there is no use debating it because we haven't got time. . . . If John Lewis feels strongly that he wants to make this speech, he can go some place else and make it, but he has no right to make it here because if he tries to make it he destroys the integrity of our coalition and he drives people out of the coalition who agree to the principles and he stays in when he doesn't agree. This is just immoral and he has no right to do it, and I demand a vote right now because I have got to call the Archbishop.

As Lewis and his comrades retyped their speech, Reuther called O'Boyle's hotel room and reached an agreement with the prelate that if the Protestant churchman Eugene Carson Blake were given a veto over the revised draft, then the Catholics would again participate. The deal struck, O'Boyle and his contingent were soon spirited to the Lincoln Memorial by a Secret Service detail and opened the ceremonies as scheduled. Lewis delivered his revised speech and was immediately followed by Reuther, who had thought he might have to "pick up the pieces in case it became necessary."[52]

At the podium Reuther first offered a well-worn but still vital query: "If we can have full employment and full production for the negative ends of war, then why can't we have a job for every American in the pursuit of peace?" He cautioned the movement to "rational and responsible action," but his seven-minute speech also contained several of the day's most radical and pointed phrases. He denounced the nation's "pious platitudes" and "high octane hypocrisy," after which he put a sharp barb in Kennedy liberalism itself: "We cannot defend freedom in Berlin so long as we deny freedom in Birmingham!" Reuther thumped the podium repeatedly and spoke loudly into the microphone, his voice easily carrying the length of the reflecting pool. Applause interrupted him time and again, even as his voice cracked with emotion. His peroration offered a prophetic warning: "If we fail, the vacuum of our failure will be filled by the Apostles of Hatred who will search for answers in the dark of night, and reason will yield to riots, and brotherhood will yield to bitterness and bloodshed and we will tear asunder the fabric of American democracy." Though his remarks were instantly overshadowed by the prose poetry of Martin Luther King, Reuther had remained faithful to the original social democratic thrust of the march, linking fair employment to full employment, jobs and freedom in equal measure.[53]

It was a good speech, but two decades of such talk had long since devalued Reuther's brand of social democratic rhetoric. Indeed, the summer of 1963 may well be taken as the moment when the discourse of American liberalism shifted decisively out of the New Deal–Fair Deal–laborite orbit and into a world in which the racial divide colored all politics. When march leaders met in the White House cabinet room at 5:00 P.M. that day, Martin Luther King knew he had given the speech of a lifetime, but one that might well evoke a large measure of jealousy from other civil rights leaders. So he deflected a presidential compliment for his "I Have a Dream" oration by asking Kennedy if he had heard the excellent speech of Walter Reuther. "Oh, I've heard him plenty of times," replied Kennedy. Both president and nation had turned their ears to another messenger and another message.[54]

Reuther may not have been the star, but he still felt immensely proud of the role played by the UAW in staging the March on Washington. Millions of TV viewers had seen Reuther marching in the front rank with King, Rauh, Randolph, Wilkins, and the other civil rights leaders. Neatly printed UAW signs calling for "FEPC, Equal Rights and Jobs NOW" were in every photo. "I think it was one of the great things in the history of American democracy," Reuther told his union executive board. "People were impressed all over the world that this many people could come together in a free society and demonstrate and not have one single incident."[55]

Of course, the march was not a civil rights law, especially not the draft that Kennedy's Justice Department sent up to Capitol Hill. With the Leadership Conference on Civil Rights, Reuther backed the strongest possible civil rights bill. Lobbying Congress and the White House all during the summer and fall of 1963, Joe Rauh and Jack Conway fought both Robert Kennedy and Assistant Attorney General Nicholas Katzenbach, who sought to strip from the bill both a fair employment practices provision and the old Title III, which gave the attorney general authority to pursue injunctive relief against civil rights violators in the South. There was a constant tug-of-war therefore between the LCCR, where Rauh and Conway were such influential figures, and the Justice Department, which thought labor-liberal efforts to add FEPC to the civil rights bill "a disaster."[56]

The trade union movement, both the AFL-CIO and the UAW, was primarily responsible for the addition of FEPC, now rechristened the Equal Employment Opportunities Commission (EEOC), to the original Kennedy bill. Meany insisted upon an EEOC to give his office a new weapon with which to force the integration of literally hundreds of still segregated southern locals. Reuther did not need such a bludgeon in the far more centralized UAW, but with TULC still an influential movement and his own reputation on the line, compromise was out of the question.[57] In late October the House Judiciary Committee voted out a beefed-up bill, and in February, after the UAW and the LCCR had mobilized hundreds of grass-roots lobbyists during a "Victory Week," the House of Representatives passed by a vote of 290 to 130 one of the most radical pieces of social legislation in American history. When scores of otherwise conservative Republicans abandoned their erstwhile allies in the South, it seemed as if Reuther's progressive realignment of American politics were finally in the offing. With action shifting to the Senate in the spring, thousands of civil rights leaders, clergy, and church-affiliated laymen, invariably tutored by veteran LCCR labor-liberals, besieged Capitol Hill. It looked as if Reuther's "Coalition of Conscience" had become a reality. Again midwestern Republicans proved the decisive minority. When the crusty Illinois conservative Everett McKinley Dirkson reached a détente with Hubert Humphrey, the Senate whip for the civil rights bill, the Dixiecrat diehards found that their only allies were limited to a handful of mountain state conservatives led by Barry Goldwater. This was not enough to avoid cloture, which the Senate voted on seventy-one to twenty-nine.[58]

By this time Lyndon Johnson was president. On the day after Kennedy's assassination, Reuther was in Washington, where he had viewed the president's body at the White House. Joe Rauh, Jack Conway, and other confidants were in Reuther's suite at the Statler mulling over the new political landscape. Then the phone rang. It was Lyndon Johnson: "My friend, I need your friendship and support now more than ever." In a few days LBJ wanted to get together with Reuther to discuss the administration's social and economic program. Reuther and his friends were impressed, at least until they learned that the new president had been calling scores of prominent liberals, labor leaders, and civil rights activists all across the nation. It was the opening shot in a presidential offensive designed to dispel skepticism from the left and assert Lyndon Johnson's intention not only to fulfill Kennedy's domestic program but to put his own expansive stamp upon it. As LBJ told Rauh in early December, "If I've done anything wrong in the past, I want you to know that's nothing now—we're going to work together."[59]

Reuther was ready for LBJ's embrace. "Detachment, understatement, irony, sophistication, coolness—those were the qualities that were seen in the manner of John F. Kennedy," observed the columnist Anthony Lewis. "The trademarks of Lyndon B. Johnson are emotion, flamboyance, folksiness." Reuther was not folksy, but he understood the down-to-earth activism of this Texan come to power. They had known each other for twenty years, ever since Reuther had slept on the Johnson sofa during his World War II visits to Washington. Reuther saw Johnson's politics as a function of the interplay between the rightward pressures that arose out of his conservative constituency in central Texas and the more liberal pull generated by his powerful ambition to rise in Washington. The players were different in the auto world, but the dynamic was much the same. During the Kennedy years Reuther had invariably used Jack Conway as his intermediary to the White House, but Conway remembered that after the assassination, "the whole thing changed. My relationship to Johnson was nil, negative as a matter of fact, and I told Walter that I simply was not an appropriate person to do this. It was much more important for him to deal directly with Lyndon Johnson."[60]

Never before had Reuther been on such close, continuous, and informal terms with an American president. Throughout 1964 and 1965 there were phone calls almost every week, dinner invitations to the White House, and the kind of open political collaboration that Reuther craved. When in December 1963 he joined an American delegation to attend independence ceremonies in Nairobi, Kenya, Reuther held the rank of "special ambassador." While in Africa, he had long political discussions with Secretary of the Interior Stewart Udall, who reported to LBJ that Reuther's support was "strong and unqualified. For him, the civil rights program is the touchstone issue. . . . Walter will be a powerhouse for you next year."[61]

Within days Johnson had solicited Reuther's ideas for his 1964 State of the Union address, in which he would declare a "War on Poverty" and thereby truly claim the presidency as his own. Working with Nat Weinberg and Jack Conway, Reuther put together a six-page memo, "An Economy of Opportunity," which repackaged in the cadence of mid-1960s liberalism key elements from the UAW's long-neglected economic program. Several thematic phrases, especially the Reutherite dichotomy between America's technologically advanced "economic abundance" and the "unmet needs of the American people," were incorporated into the president's January 8 address. Johnson made no mention of "democratic national planning" or even of the Reuther-Weinberg insistence that an "economy of opportunity requires rededication to the objectives of the Employment Act of 1946—to 'maximum employment, production and purchasing power.'" But like most American liberals, the UAW president was not yet interested in the details; it was enough that for the first time since the New Deal an American president had committed the money, power, and prestige of the federal government behind a program whose success would transform the social order. Even months later, when Reuther knew the limited character of Johnson's gambit, he nevertheless described himself as "one of your loyal soldiers in the unconditional war against poverty to which you have summoned America."[62]

Reuther put UAW money and organization behind this commitment. For nearly a year he had sought some way to institutionalize the coalition of labor, church, and African-American groups that had lobbied so effectively on behalf of the civil rights bill. Reuther therefore pushed through his executive board a proposal for a "Citizens Crusade against Poverty" (CCAP) to pull together this coalition on behalf of "an all-out crusade against poverty parallel to our crusade for civil rights." The CCAP, to which the UAW appropriated an initial one hundred thousand dollars in April 1964, offered advice, organization, and leadership to the local Community Action Programs that Johnson's new Office of Economic Opportunity (OEO) made key recipients of antipoverty funds. Over the next four years UAW expenditures would total five hundred thousand dollars, plus over one million dollars from the Ford and Stern Family Foundations. The Community Action Program (CAP) was by far the most radical innovation in the antipoverty program, for it was premised upon the idea that poverty is rooted as much in the political powerlessness of the poor as it is in their lack of jobs, education, or motivation. As Reuther put it in a resolution he drafted for the March 1964 UAW convention: "The fight against poverty must not develop along the lines of a well-intentioned social welfare program of the rich doing favors for the poor." Instead, he told a congressional committee shortly afterward, "we have to organize the poor so that they are not only visible but have a voice."[63]

Reuther organized a founding conference of the CCAP in June; leaders from 125 organizations met at the Mayflower Hotel in Washington. In addition to lobbying for Johnson's antipoverty legislation, an important function of the CCAP was to identify and train hundreds of ghetto and barrio leaders who could function within the framework of the Office of Economic Opportunity's Community Action Program. Reuther's CCAP won instant influence when Lyndon Johnson appointed Jack Conway to head the new CAP initiative. To get it rolling, Conway recruited labor educators from the Reuther circle, including Brendan Sexton and the old Socialist Judah Drob, who coined the phrase "head start" to name OEO's most widely acclaimed program. Reuther and Conway saw the CAPs, whose enabling legislation mandated "maximum feasible participation" by the poor, as the community equivalent of trade union locals. They were "political action basically." These new organizations would implement OEO programs by educating new leaders, aggregating neighborhood concerns, and, if necessary, bargaining with local political elites. "What we have really got to do is to train people in the poor neighborhoods to do in terms of their problems what we did thirty years ago," Reuther told his executive board. "John Lewis didn't go into a single General Motors plant. . . . The guys in the plants did the job and that is what has got to be done with the poverty neighborhoods."[64]

Reuther's quest for an opening to the left in American politics not only led to the podium of his union's 1964 convention in Atlantic City—at which President Lyndon Johnson reiterated his commitment to "unconditional surrender" in the poverty campaign—but could be found in the balcony, where virtually the entire leadership of the Students for a Democratic Society sat in attendance. They were there because Reuther invited them, but more important, because for this brief moment in the history of American liberalism the UAW and SDS shared an equally radical agenda. In their famous manifesto of 1962, the "Port Huron Statement," adopted at the UAW's summer education center north of Detroit, the SDS emphasis on the need to wind down the cold war, realign the Democratic Party, achieve racial justice, and above all, make work bearable and meaningful, were all common coin of the UAW leadership strata in the early 1960s. The unions had lost much of their idealism, asserted the draft prepared by Tom Hayden, who had grown up in Catholic, working-class Royal Oak just outside Detroit, but the labor movement's "numbers and potential political strength, its natural interests in the abolition of exploitation, its reach to the grass roots of American society, combine to make it the best candidate for the civil rights, peace and economic reform movements." Walter Reuther could not have phrased it more clearly.[65]

The UAW connection with SDS, whose most dynamic chapter was in Ann Arbor, was practically maternal. Irving Bluestone, then Reuther's closest assistant, and Mildred Jeffrey, in charge of community outreach, were proud to have children active in SDS organizing projects. Bluestone called them "our kind of youngsters" and easily won Reuther's support for at least ten thousand dollars in funding for the organization's Economic Research and Action Project.[66] Unlike Michael Harrington and other New York Socialists, who found SDS's "anti-anti-Communism" tendentious, Reuther saw these young people as a bridge through which the labor movement could rewin the loyalty and appreciation of young intellectuals and then energize its white-collar organizing campaigns. He authorized a series of student internships in Detroit and Washington, put SDS President Todd Gitlin on the CCAP steering committee, and urged UAW locals across the country to cooperate with SDS organizing projects. On one occasion Reuther turned down an SDS funding request, but only because he mistakenly thought too much money was earmarked for "education" and not enough for "organizing." When Reuther spoke with the New Left contingent during a break in the proceedings at the UAW's Atlantic City convention, twenty-three-year-old Frank Joyce was startled — and inspired — by the militancy of the UAW president's politics. "We just sat there stunned because we thought we were the radicals, we were the tough kids, the street fighters. And this guy comes in and blows everybody away." Reuther was not to be outflanked on the left.[67]

The effort to embrace both Lyndon Johnson and SDS within the same coalition could hardly last. The left would soon defect, but Reuther had his difficulties with LBJ's political economy even earlier. Reuther called Johnson's War on Poverty a "first small step," but for all its humane intentions, the Johnson policy was a heterogeneous jumble of education and job training programs, much of whose inspiration flowed from recent work on such disparate "structural" problems as technological displacement, juvenile delinquency, and the pathologies of the ghetto work culture. From the point of view of Reuther, Weinberg, and old New Dealers like Leon Keyserling, the War on Poverty was crippled from the start because of the government's failure to link the amelioration of poverty to the reform of the larger labor market. Above all, such a linkage required an assault upon income inequality and unemployment, an effort that was essential to reveal the true dimensions of the joblessness that supposedly arose out of the cultural or educational deficiencies of the poor. As Reuther put it early in 1964, "The argument that unemployment is largely structural is a new version of the old, discredited notion—always useful to an uneasy conscience—that unemployment is the fault of the unemployed."[68]

The UAW had a whole raft of reform programs—ranging all the way from a public employment service and a higher minimum wage to "national planning"—that it urged upon the president. Reuther's model once again was Sweden, where the Social Democratic Party's "active labor market policy" used a high level of social spending and a vigilant Keynesianism to keep labor mobile, unemployment rare, and wages egalitarian across the entire working class, both white collar and blue. Reuther's program would have therefore deracialized the War on Poverty and given Great Society job programs more of a European flavor. For all his devotion to "consensus politics" in 1964, President Johnson was not about to explore this social terrain. LBJ did set up the automation commission long urged by the UAW, but he saw targeted investment planning as anathema. Thus, after Reuther had again arranged for Hubert Humphrey to attend the Harpsund conference in Sweden, Humphrey, as a desperate vice-presidential hopeful, asked the president if he should go. A socialist summit? "My God, no!" roared Johnson, appalled to hear that the senator had gone the year before.[69]

If Lyndon Johnson's War on Poverty encapsulated but a fraction of Reuther's programmatic vision, the president's simultaneous determination to avoid a realignment crisis at the Democratic Party's Atlantic City convention that August put Reuther at odds with the most energetic and militant elements of the civil rights insurgency. The Mississippi Freedom Democratic Party (MFDP) embodied all the possibilities and perils of a genuine transformation in American politics. Spearheaded by SNCC, CORE, and a newly invigorated Mississippi NAACP, the MFDP had begun to mobilize the state's African-Americans not merely to challenge but to displace the white supremacist delegation at the Democratic Convention. If the legal standing of the new party was questionable, MFDP's moral credentials were more than solid—and well known, especially after hundreds of young, white volunteers had spent the summer of 1964 in Mississippi, where they came face to face with the murders, beatings, and church burnings sponsored by a deeply racist regime.

UAW backing for the MFDP challenge began on an informal basis at the union's convention in March when Robert Moses, SNCC's charismatic chairman, and Ella Baker, the veteran civil rights activist, met with Joe Rauh and Mildred Jeffrey. It was arranged that Rauh would handle the legal work and take charge of the MFDP brief at the convention credentials committee. UAW political operatives like Bill Dodds, Roy Reuther, Jack Conway, and Jeffrey were convinced that the challenge was a feasible and prudent one, especially if the net result turned out as Joe Rauh proposed: seat both delegations, in which case all the white regulars would walk out, much to everyone's relief. Reuther was not closely involved that spring, but there is little doubt that he supported the MFDP challenge. Indeed, he clearly held the confidence of many SNCC militants. When the FBI failed to take resolute action after Neshoba County sheriff's deputies murdered Mickey Schwerner, James Chaney, and Andrew Goodman on June 21, SNCC fired off a desperate telegram urging Reuther to put pressure on Lyndon Johnson and Robert Kennedy to send federal agents to Mississippi. Without hesitation, Reuther got the union's Washington office working on the problem. And Rauh found liberal Democrats enthusiastic for the MFDP: delegations from Michigan, California, and New York all pledged their support.[70]

But President Johnson was determined to derail this challenge. As the Atlantic City convention approached, Johnson may well have understood the centrifugal forces set in motion by the civil rights movement better than many liberals. Although the GOP's nomination of Goldwater obscured the immediate political difficulties, the MFDP challenge began a process of disintegration within the Democratic Party that would take place over the next twenty years. As Texas Governor John Connally is reported to have told Johnson, "If you seat those black buggers, the whole South will march out." But it was not just the potential defection of the white South that bothered Johnson: the inroads George Wallace had already made among northern Democratic voters stoked his fears as well. The southern segregationist had taken more than 30 percent of the 1964 Democratic primary vote in Wisconsin, Maryland, and Indiana.[71]

This white revolt could not deprive Lyndon Johnson of reelection, but it did threaten the consensual, majoritarian Democratic Party upon which he sought to build a mandate of truly Rooseveltian proportions. Johnson discussed "the Mississippi situation" with Reuther right after the Washington CCAP conference on June 24, and then again when he visited Detroit on June 26. Whatever Reuther's initial views of the challenge, he soon adopted the president's agenda. On July 29 he is reported to have "exploded" against the pro-MFDP work of his staff. Thereafter, LBJ called Reuther repeatedly and told him that Humphrey's vice-presidential nomination depended on "settling the Mississippi thing thoroughly." LBJ expected Reuther, as Rauh's ostensible employer, to order him out of the MFDP challenge. Reuther's notes of one presidential phone call record Johnson's main goals: "avoid a floor fight, unify party." On August 14, after it had become clear that Rauh was still winning delegates to the challenge, LBJ was again on the phone to Reuther. "Lyndon thinks if we seat those people, Goldwater will win," Reuther told Rauh immediately afterwards. Rauh thought such a prospect preposterous. Besides, if he pulled out the Communists in the Lawyers Guild would simply step into the void. But ironically, the anti-Communist card no longer played well in Reuther's calculations. The maintenance of LBJ's broad coalition proved of far greater import. "Look Walter," Rauh told his best and oldest client, "I am acting not as your general counsel, but as a citizen. I've got a private law practice. If you want to fire me, for Christ's sake, be my guest." Reuther was "so fucking mad," Rauh recalled, "you could fry an egg on his heart." He yelled into the phone: if Humphrey did not become vice president, "Hubert's blood" would be on Rauh's conscience for the rest of his life.[72]

MFDP prospects soared on August 22, two days before the official opening of the convention, when the earthy and charismatic Fannie Lou Hamer electrified the credentials committee with a tale of heroic perseverance at the hands of brutal sheriffs and callous landlords. Johnson called a meaningless press conference just to cut her off the air, but the TV networks replayed her testimony well into the evening. When Johnson realized the damage, he got Clark Clifford to call Reuther on August 23. The UAW president was right in the midst of GM negotiations, and he did not want to leave Detroit. But then LBJ came on the line and turned on the famous "Johnson treatment." Reuther could not have resisted for too long: he agreed that a smashing defeat of Goldwater trumped all other considerations, and he did not have to be reminded that in the president's Labor Day speech, scheduled for Cadillac Square the very next week, Reuther wanted LBJ to offer the UAW his warmest embrace.[73]

Reuther therefore broke off his Detroit talks, chartered an airplane, and rushed to Atlantic City. He arrived at 3:00 A.M. and then spent the rest of the night with Humphrey and his protégé Walter Mondale and with Johnson's key operatives on the MFDP fight, White House aides Walter Jenkins and Tom Finney. By sunrise Reuther had been thoroughly briefed on the Johnson hard line: the administration would continue to mobilize all its powers of patronage and politics to deprive the MFDP of the votes on the credentials committee necessary to launch a floor fight at the convention. Meanwhile, Reuther, Humphrey, and Bayard Rustin, who also sought Democratic Party unity, had to persuade Joe Rauh and those wavering civil rights leaders over whom they had influence—Martin Luther King, Jr., James Farmer, perhaps even Robert Moses of SNCC—to accept a White House "compromise": two at-large delegates for MFDP, Ed King, a white teacher, and Aaron Henry of the NAACP, both from the middle-class wing of the party. The Mississippi regulars also had to sign a loyalty pledge—of course they would not—and starting in 1968, all the southern delegations would be integrated.[74]

The deal might well have been acceptable to the MFDP militants if it had been part of a true set of negotiations in which the White House recognized the moral authority and political legitimacy of the Mississippi insurgents. But Johnson wanted to impose a dictate, and Reuther, who had his marching orders, was in no mood for equivocation. "Reuther always thinks he knows more than anybody else when he gets into a fight like this," remarked Joe Rauh a few years later. In an afternoon meeting with civil rights leaders, Reuther reminded Martin Luther King of how much money the UAW had provided his organization. About Rauh, his ally of twenty years and more, the UAW president was brutal: "That man worked for us, and we'll break him if we have to, destroy him. We'll fire him if he goes and keeps working for you [MFDP] people." Reuther had enough clout to recess the credentials committee hearings and get Rauh on the phone. "Here's the decision," he told Rauh, whose phone booth was surrounded with TV cameras and reporters. "I am telling you to take this deal."[75]

Rauh insisted to Reuther that at the very least he had to talk with Aaron Henry, but before the MFDP had the chance to discuss the final White House plan, Pennsylvania Governor David Lawrence, chair of the credentials committee, announced the formal acceptance of the package. Rauh shouted out a futile "No!" The news came over the TV when Reuther was still in tense discussions with Rustin, King, and the key MFDP leaders. Robert Moses got up and literally slammed the door on Hubert Humphrey. Fannie Lou Hamer told reporters: "We didn't come all this way for no two seats." The next day, after a bitter internal debate, the MFDP rejected the compromise outright, later infiltrating the convention floor to sit in the seats of the now-absent Mississippi delegation.[76]

By this time Reuther was at the White House briefing the president on his successful intervention at Atlantic City. But the legacy of this work would roll on and on. For SNCC and the generation for whom it spoke, there was an enormous sense of betrayal that extended from Johnson, Humphrey, and Reuther at the top to all those well-established civil rights advocates, like Rauh, Rustin, and Wilkins, who had advocated MFDP acquiescence in the Johnson "compromise." In the bitter debates that consumed movement circles, Reuther became the symbol of realpolitik, a liberal icon of devious power. Bayard Rustin, who sought to move civil rights forces from "protest to politics," argued for a broad Reutherite coalition that required compromise, dialogue, and discipline. "We must think of our friends in labor, Walter Reuther and the others who have gone to bat for us. If we reject this compromise we would be saying to them that we didn't want their help." But Robert Moses spoke for a far more powerful New Left sensibility that rejected coalition building as the road to hypocrisy, inaction, and moral failure. As one of his comrades remembered it, "He didn't want anyone telling him down in Mississippi about Walter Reuther needing help, Reuther hadn't come to Mississippi."[77]

There is irony as well as tragedy in Reuther's partisanship at Atlantic City. Like Reuther, most MFDP militants wanted a realigned Democratic Party—"the destruction of the awesome power of the Dixiecrats," remembered SNCC's Cleveland Sellers. Then "the way would have been clear for a wide-ranging redistribution of wealth, power and priorities." But to these cadres of the New Left, Reuther had discredited the very politics of liberal coalition building upon which such a strategy was based. "After Atlantic City," wrote Sellers, "our struggle was not for civil rights, but for liberation." Within months Joe Rauh reported sourly, "The Freedom Party is the greatest boon to the left-wing on the campuses of the nation in our generation." Perhaps the decomposition of an alliance between the UAW and the most dynamic elements of the African-American freedom movement could not have been avoided. But the costs seem clear: the political marginalization and social impoverishment of both. Joe Rauh's friendship with Walter Reuther was broken. He later reminisced: "Walter Reuther made the greatest mistake of his life in thinking that the way you run something like this is with muscle instead of with thought and care."[78]

18

A PART OF THE ESTABLISHMENT

This is the trouble with the American Labor Movement. It is becoming a part of the "Establishment."

—Walter Reuther, 1966

They are striking against us, they are striking against Walter Reuther. We are the victims of anarchy.

—General Motors official, 1967

In the mid-1960s Reuther probed, for one last time, the outer limits of the Treaty of Detroit. These years were the high noon of American capitalism in this century, a time when unemployment sank below 4 percent, wages outpaced inflation, and corporate profitability reached a postwar peak. For white workers as well as black, for skilled trades veterans as well as the most streetwise youth, this was an era of rising expectations and rising militancy. American liberalism was feeling the strain, but if ever there was a moment in which the ground that had been lost during a generation of union retreat and left-wing defeat was to be retaken, these were the years of opportunity.

As unemployment dropped, shop tensions rose. Between 1964 and 1973 all the indexes that have traditionally measured "militancy"—strikes, wildcat stoppages, per capita grievances, contract rejections—reached their postwar heights. Indeed, a stable system of collective bargaining proved increasingly incompatible with the full-employment economy generated by Great Society programs and the military Keynesianism of the Vietnam era. Rank-and-file militancy at the work site was not simply a product of the concentration of nationalist blacks in urban factories or the influx of young workers influenced by a New Left hostility to factory life. These ideological currents gave a political edge to many shop struggles, especially after 1967, but the growing shop-floor dissidence of this era was symptomatic of far larger defects in America's peculiarly firm-centered system of social regulation.

Given the grudgingly incremental expansion of social legislation, collective bargaining had been forced to assume an enormous burden — to regulate not only the wages and working conditions in the shop but the vicissitudes of an individual's entire life cycle. By the end of 1964 the Ford contract totaled 365 pages in two volumes, ten times the size of the slim booklet in use right after the Rouge strike of 1941. And this was only the national contract: each of the ninety Ford locals had its own separate agreement. Ford executives liked to point out the seemingly frivolous character of some of the four thousand local issues negotiated that year, such as the request for new parking lots or the demand that plant management supply feed for the migratory ducks settling on a nearby pond. But such issues also testify to the way in which the plant community had become a universe of meaning and struggle, in which ambitious shop politicians explored the limits of union power and management resolve.[1]

If Reuther was to challenge this well-constrained industrial relations system, the year 1964 was particularly propitious. American politics had entered a season of leftward flux at the same time that the Republican Party split asunder on the Goldwater candidacy. After years in the doldrums, the automobile industry was roaring back. All of the Big Three automakers, including once-sickly Chrysler, made more than 20 percent return on their after-tax profits in 1963; General Motors had two and a half billion dollars in cash, a reserve so large and so liquid that the *Wall Street Journal* quipped, "It's rumored in Wall Street that the General Motors Corporation is saving up to buy the United States Government." Reuther thought his union had "the most favorable economic circumstances that we have ever bargained under."[2]

Reuther saw an opportunity to win finally the measure of corporatist collaboration in the auto industry for which he had struggled so long. Johnson and his Council of Economic Advisers were pressing hard to keep an auto settlement — the key contract bargain of the year — within the 3.2 percent wage guideposts. "Whenever I go to the White House on Saturdays this is a constant pressure point with him and he doesn't let up," Reuther explained to a group of local union leaders.[3] Reuther told Johnson and top cabinet officials that the UAW was a "responsible" union; indeed, he made it clear early in 1964 that if the administration actually convinced the corporations to reduce auto prices the UAW would agree to a moderate wage package. But the White House had to make the case. Otherwise, Reuther would be accused of again trying to "run the industry."[4]

Reuther prepared the way for this deal by putting at the top of the UAW bargaining agenda the one issue that had proven so intractable over the course of his entire trade union career: working conditions, speedup, "dignity and humanity on the job." General Motors Corporation, Reuther told delegates at the 1964 convention, was the "largest, [most] glorified, gold-plated sweatshop in the world. . . . What's basically involved here . . . [is that] when a worker punches his time clock, they don't buy him body and soul. They may own the machinery, but they don't own the workers, and they'd better begin to act like it." These words were not merely rhetorical flourish: since 1961 an executive board committee under Mazey and Woodcock had been exhaustively probing the chronic production standard issue. The UAW would fight for more committeemen, longer work breaks, an end to compulsory overtime, and the salarization of blue-collar workers. The last point garnered little support among most autoworkers, whose paychecks were bulging with overtime pay. But Reuther pushed it hard. Salary status for blue-collar workers was a step toward a real guaranteed annual wage, but even more important, it touched a Jacobite nerve in Reuther's psyche. He wanted to abolish the lines of caste and status that so sharply divided employees in America's biggest corporations. With General Motors as the clear target, the UAW called its program "Justice on the Job."[5]

Reuther wanted a settlement in which GM paid, but not merely in paycheck dollars. If the Johnson administration was to establish a de facto linkage between automobile prices and wages, then the UAW would take its slice of GM profits on the shop floor itself, where the chronic battle over production standards, job assignments, and union power had never ceased to make life miserable for the committeemen and local union leaders on the firing line. In 1963 more than one-third of the top officials in UAW production locals had been denied reelection in campaigns that turned on such grievances. "There is a revolt in our plants," announced Robert Lopez of Fisher Body Tarrytown, "and we of the secondary leadership . . . are the first casualties." To a Wall Street Journal reporter, Buick Local 599 President Russ Alger asserted, "Work Standards—this is the high point—what we get from the company here is what makes or breaks you in this job." Shop activists put the bumper sticker "Humanize Working Conditions" on thousands of autoworkers' cars. These pressures, boiling up inside the UAW for years, had to be defused in a cathartic battle with GM. As the veteran leftist John DeVito put it in a Solidarity House meeting with Reuther that summer, "If we put General Motors on the back burner, they are going to say down in the plants that we are chicken. . . . Nineteen years is a long time to hang up our gloves."[6]

Veteran militants were puzzled by Reuther's ambitious shift in bargaining strategy. Since 1950 he had used the auto industry's cyclical booms to ratchet up the private welfare state the UAW had negotiated for its members. Speedup issues were traded off against the dollar. But Reuther was restless this year: he resented the critique of "big labor" offered by otherwise sympathetic writers like Paul Jacobs, Murray Kempton, and Harvey Swados, whose recent essay "The UAW:

Over the Top or Over the Hill?" sent a buzz through Solidarity House. These old radicals recognized that Reuther and the UAW were the most progressive products of the modern union movement, but that was no longer good enough. The civil rights movement had set a vastly higher standard and demonstrated that a committed few could once again put social justice at the top of the nation's political agenda. Reuther would not be shunted aside; he would demonstrate that collective bargaining was not "Old Before Its Time," as Paul Jacobs had just concluded in a 1963 study of trade unionism for the Center for the Study of Democratic Institutions. Indeed, Reuther's very language reflected the moral earnestness of the times. "The Bible is filled with this struggle," he told the autoworkers. "The end purpose of human effort is to enrich and fulfill human life . . . to assert the sovereignty of the person over the machine." Reuther could hardly match the rhetoric of a Martin Luther King, but he was reaching for it.[7]

Everybody in the UAW high command expected Reuther to finally take on General Motors, and until late June his strategy seemed on track. A cabinet-level economic team from Labor, Treasury, and the CEA recommended a set of price cuts ranging from $50 to $150 a car. Defense Secretary Robert McNamara, a former president of Ford, put out feelers to his old boss, Henry Ford II, as well as to GM. "We thought that we could strike some sort of a bargain," remembered CEA Chair Walter Heller. He told LBJ, "Now it's up to you. . . . If there's going to be a deal in which they pledge to cut car prices and you get Walter Reuther to take a modest settlement, you have to do it." But Johnson turned Heller down cold. "He didn't explode, but he was just very final and very positive about it." Shortly thereafter, the president flew to Detroit for a gala $100-a-plate Democratic fund-raiser. Along with the UAW high command, auto executives were well represented, and Henry Ford II publicly endorsed the president. There would be no automobile industry price cuts.[8]

Reuther was left holding the bag. Since even this limited sort of corporatism in the auto industry had been sacrificed to LBJ's lust for a wall-to-wall electoral front, Reuther reverted to the usual norms of auto industry collective bargaining. There was plenty of pressure to do so. Since 1961 the movement for early retirement had become a well-organized political caucus, periodically nipping at Reuther's heels. These veterans wanted to get out of the auto plants, not transform them. But the new pensions would cost real money: four hundred dollars a month at age sixty. As with the production standard work issues, their agitation had been centered in General Motors, but in late August Reuther surprised almost everyone by choosing Chrysler as the number-one strike target. The decision was pure opportunism. In a preliminary bargaining round, Chrysler Chairman Lynn Townsend virtually pleaded with Reuther that if the company had another nine months of full production, it could rewin the market share lost in the late 1950s. Within minutes Reuther, Irving Bluestone, and Doug Fraser decided to go after Chrysler; the decision itself was made in Reuther's big Packard right outside corporate headquarters. Reuther's choice to hit the weakest of the Big Three automakers first meant that

GM and Ford would have little difficulty matching Chrysler's monetary package, but it also ensured that the UAW could put no real muscle behind the effort to reform GM working conditions.[9]

Chrysler signed on September 10 with a package containing higher wages, longer vacations, more relief time, and an early retirement scheme that met almost all of the union's essential criteria. The new contract came in at nearly 5 percent a year; as for the CEA's wage-price guideposts, Reuther boasted to LBJ himself, "We bent the hell out of them."[10] Company, union, and president scrambled to downplay the breach, but Reuther's problems were far from over. A trade union leader, C. Wright Mills once observed, "mobilizes discontent and then sits on it." Reuther had taken months to raise the union's banners against GM; he could not fold them overnight. GM negotiators thought all the talk of improving local working conditions could readily be boiled down to a five-hour increase in the grievance-handling time of the nearly eighteen hundred union committeemen at the corporation. When GM Vice President Louis Seaton offered such an increase at the eleventh hour of the contract talks, Reuther eagerly accepted. But both Seaton and Reuther had miscalculated. The top negotiating team from the GM locals, whose predecessors had often played poker while Reuther cut the last-minute deal, now unanimously rejected the offer. Reuther then proposed arbitration of all the difficult shop issues, but the company immediately turned him down. GM was stuck with Chrysler's big monetary settlement, so the giant corporation, which so guarded its shop prerogatives, was not about to compromise on local work rules as well.[11]

It was September 25, 1964, almost the height of the campaign season. With much reluctance, Reuther authorized a GM strike, but unlike 1945–46, it was clearly not a showdown fight. Reuther insisted that forty-one locals, with a membership of more than eighty thousand GM workers, remain at work in order to supply the parts needed to keep the rest of the auto industry in production. "We are under great pressure in Washington," Reuther confided to a closed meeting of his executive board. Johnson was hectoring the UAW president to avoid a serious shutdown. Within a week all national contract issues were cleared up, but more than ninety local unions were still stubbornly on strike, in search of their own plant-level agreements. Reuther wanted these ended, and quickly: "Every regional director has to see that his staff members go into these locals and make a real effort to settle. . . . There's a bunch of punks in the locals who hit the bricks because they don't know what's really going on."[12]

However, Reuther had neither the moral authority nor the raw power to simply halt the first big strike at General Motors since the end of World War II. In 1946 he had commanded a strike against GM that polarized the nation. A generation later he again presided over a work stoppage in the nation's largest corporation, but few outside the industry seemed to notice. For weeks Solidarity House held itself aloof from the local disputes, allowing each union to "slug it out" with management. The GM work stoppages therefore ended in piecemeal fashion, with

Reuther prodding the most steadfast militants into settlements just before the election. He told reporters then that "no strike . . . in the history of the American labor movement has yielded the kind of meaningful results . . . as this strike." But even Leonard Woodcock, head of the UAW's GM Department, admitted that the top leadership had made no systematic evaluation of the local union agreements signed at scores of work sites. Thus Louis Seaton was certain that his corporation had again held the line on what was most essential: "We haven't agreed to anything that is going to impair our responsibility to our shareholders to run an efficient business . . . and that's what this strike has been about."[13]

In fact, neither GM nor Reuther could declare victory, for the final settlement was a ragged affair. From August through December strikes, confrontations, and all-night bargaining sessions had deprived the industry of the one thing the Treaty of Detroit had promised it: a predictable and stable production environment, so essential to the nation's highly integrated corporations. Louis Seaton had been "mystified and amazed" that rank-and-file pressures had forced Reuther to reject the GM national contract on September 25; at Ford, Malcolm Denise also saw the union's collective bargaining strategy as "increasingly disorganized," its policy of postsettlement bargaining as "chaos in local negotiations."[14] Corporate officials respected Walter Reuther, but some now suspected that under conditions of high employment and rising social expectations, he might no longer command the authority to ensure the kind of union discipline upon which the Treaty of Detroit had for so long been grounded.

Reuther himself was sure that Lyndon Johnson's smashing election victory that fall vindicated his strategic moderation and the president's consensual, coalition-building strategy. With congressional majorities of a scope and quality not seen since the New Deal heyday, Reuther thought the political gateway finally open to a Rooseveltian era of social reform and popular mobilization. The labor movement could subordinate its immediate interests to the president and his party because all were carried forward by the same powerfully progressive current. In December 1964 Reuther was in Ford Hospital for surgery to remove a growth on his lower right lung; from there he joked that his mechanical bed was so comfortable and convenient that "to build the Great Society, we must insist that they become standard equipment in every home."[15] His legislative ambitions were hardly less expansive. "We are at that place in history," Reuther told IUD colleagues, "where we do have . . . the most exciting possibility of making legislative progress."[16]

Reuther believed that the realignment of the American political system was in the works. With May, Roy, and a large contingent of UAW officials, he flew to Selma, Alabama, for Martin Luther King's march to Montgomery in March 1965. Within weeks King's effort to win a federal voting rights law won a ringing endorsement from President Johnson, and by midsummer the 1965 Voting Rights Act had swept through Congress on a wave of liberal votes. The new black voters would revolutionize the "balance of political power in the Southern states," Reuther informed Willy Brandt. "The congressional elections in the near future will send to Washington the most progressive congressional delegations from a region of the United States which historically has been represented by the most reactionary and socially backward forces." But it was not only black workers who had realigned their politics. Outside of the South the white "backlash" had failed to move work-ing-class voters. Johnson's sweeping victory was sustained by a huge vote for the Democratic Party: 70 percent throughout the entire working class, 80 percent among white UAW members, nearly 100 percent from black America. To British Prime Minister Harold Wilson, Reuther bragged, "This I think you will agree is a high percentage of working class solidarity, considering that the American worker is not considered to be as ideologically and politically sophisticated as his Euro-pean counterpart."[17]

Reuther plunged into the work of building the Great Society, especially the work of revitalizing urban America. From his days as an advocate of Bomber City, Reuther had seen the transformation of the built environment as but another form of moral exhortation and social reform. In his home at Paint Creek each new room and new bookcase had embodied his own therapeutic regeneration, of both hand and mind. Likewise, Reuther saw the transformation of Detroit urban life as a form of moral engineering. In the mid-1950s, after scores of East Side housing blocks had been leveled by the Cobo administration, Reuther sparked the formation of an elite coalition, the Citizens Redevelopment Committee, which erected a set of glass and steel skyscrapers designed by Ludwig Mies van der Rohe. They obliter-ated the old cityscape and housed chiefly middle-class Detroiters, but Reuther remained a steadfast advocate of urban redevelopment to "rebuild the whole inner cores of our great cities and produce in those inner cores an attractive, healthy, wholesome living environment that will be so exciting that everyone will want to live there."[18]

By the mid-1960s such schemes had already come under attack by planners and theorists like Jane Jacobs and William White, but their appreciation of an organic and complex urban synthesis evoked little sympathy from the UAW president. Brendan Sexton, who hailed from working-class New York City, debated the issue with Reuther time and again. He thought Reuther's aesthetic sensibility essen-tially "rural, with farm boy values." With his imagination still fired by the promise of new building technologies, Reuther rejected rehabilitation of the existing housing stock. To use the words of one LBJ aide, Reuther was for "bull-dozing and rebuilding."[19]

After a campaign of memos and meetings that began in May 1965, Reuther convinced Lyndon Johnson to set up a small planning committee that would lay the groundwork for a program to select a set of "demonstration" cities where the federal government could put the Great Society on graphic display. Developed with his architect friend Oskar Stonorov, Reuther's original proposal perfectly tar-geted LBJ's Rooseveltian ambitions. This "urban TVA" would build "total com-munities" on huge urban parcels, seven hundred to a thousand acres, where new technologies of housing construction and prefabrication, new types of schools, old-age centers, and recreational facilities would set the standards for a "physically beautiful and socially sound America." Reuther's vision "captured the President's imagination," recalled the presidential assistant Joseph Califano, especially after the upheaval in Watts, when political necessity and private sentiment were briefly merged.[20] Reuther helped choose the task force members, who met almost every weekend from October through December 1965. Aside from Reuther, the key players were Benjamin Heineman, the socially progressive CEO of the Chicago and Northwestern Railway; Edgar Kaiser, an industrialist who shared Reuther's interest in new housing technologies; Kermit Gordon, a former director of the Bureau of the Budget; and the urban planners Robert Wood, Charles Haar, and William Rafsky. LBJ was enormously pleased; in his own words, he was proud of "this here best group of experts" working on city problems. His aide Harry McPherson told the president that "Reuther has supplied the vision, drive, and sometimes mere rhetoric that has kept us moving."[21]

The costs were manageable—$2.3 billion over five years—and the politics seemed attractive, so Johnson gave Reuther's "Demonstration Cities" scheme his blessing. Initially Reuther proposed a "competition" to determine which of six big cities would share the bulk of the available funds. Johnson doubted whether he could win legislative support without spreading the money around, so he expanded the list more than tenfold. To make certain Detroit got its share, Reuther spearheaded the organization of yet another nonprofit, elite-run corporation, the Metropolitan Detroit Citizens Redevelopment Authority, to channel the Demonstration Cities funds that were soon to flow from Washington. As chair, Reuther saw his job as nothing less than "rebuilding the inner core of Detroit . . . so that people now living in a slum can move into neighborhoods worthy of citizens of the Great Society."[22]

Reuther never felt closer to power nor more loyal to Johnson; he was proud to be "a devoted member of your working crew." In December 1965, when Ben Heineman and Harry McPherson asked whether he would be available to take over the new Department of Housing and Urban Development, Reuther replied that if the president asked him, he would do it. To make the cabinet post even more of a social action agency, Reuther wanted to transfer Conway's Community Action Program out of OEO and oversee it himself in HUD. Most in the urban task force favored the switch; although mortgage bankers and builders were sure to oppose Reuther, McPherson thought that "it should not be difficult . . . to generate considerable business support."[23] For HUD secretary Johnson finally settled on Robert Weaver, a low-profile black administrator, but Reuther's commitment to the president remained steadfast. "Walter enjoys the relationship with Johnson," one observer noted. "Walter loves power. He loves people who know how to exercise power, and he sees Johnson as one who exercises power in the public interest." At the UAW's Long Beach convention of May 1966, Reuther presented President Johnson with the union's Social Justice Award.[24]

But Reuther had hitched his fate to a falling star. Within eighteen months after the landslide election of 1964, Johnson's Great Society was in trouble, its momentum broken by the racial conflicts it could not resolve and by the fiscal drain that sucked its lifeblood into Vietnam. Liberalism's increasingly sour prospects were encapsulated in the fate of the Demonstration Cities legislation itself. With characteristic ambition, Johnson introduced the program as a step toward making the nation's urban areas "masterpieces of our civilization," but his vision had few enthusiasts in Congress. Urban liberals scoffed at what they considered the legislation's paltry funding, while a reborn coalition of southern Democrats and Republicans took the title "Demonstration Cities" and threw it back in Johnson's face as bowing to black demonstrators and rioters. They also objected, both North and South, to the bill's desegregation requirements. By the time the renamed "Model Cities" bill scraped through Congress just before the 1966 elections, its funding had been slashed by more than 60 percent.[25]

Never had the collapse of liberal ideology and liberal power been more precipitous. At the UAW's Los Angeles convention in May 1966, Secretary of Labor Willard Wirtz found that "the one thing on everybody's mind is Vietnam." Delegates jeered antiwar demonstrators in the balcony, but their anger translated into precious little enthusiasm for the Johnson administration. "Vietnam is the biggest single issue," Reuther admitted to IUD colleagues in July 1966. "This is what is eating away at the security and the sense of solidarity of the American people."[26] Reuther's instincts were dovish, but he had forged his links with the president and he was not about to move the UAW into opposition. During the years of escalation, especially 1965 and 1966, when Reuther's influence reached its apogee, the UAW president calculated that the advancement of the Great Society domestic agenda still outweighed the political and social divisiveness generated by the war. He remained clearly in Johnson's camp even as the nation's polarization over Vietnam made such an alliance one of dubious remuneration.

Johnson assiduously cultivated Reuther's loyalty. The president forwarded Reuther an advance text of his 1965 Johns Hopkins speech—in which he sought to disarm liberal critics by pledging "unconditional" negotiations with the North Vietnamese—and he personally reassured Reuther that he had taken great care to ensure the selection of "purely military targets" in North Vietnam. Arthur Goldberg, who was now Lyndon Johnson's ambassador to the United Nations, made Reuther a "senior adviser" on his delegation. Convinced that the United States was searching for a genuinely negotiated settlement, Reuther defended the American policy to European social democrats, among whom his influence was unique and powerful. In July 1965 Reuther put all his prestige on the line to forestall a stormy Vietnam debate at the Amsterdam conference of the International Confederation of Free Trade Unions (ICFTU); later that same month at Harpsund, Reuther again defended American conduct of the war to Swedish social democrats, who were beginning to find the antiwar views of their new foreign minister, Olof Palme, far more attractive.[27]

Reuther played the same role in Detroit, where he faced a growing revulsion against the war from his closest friends and colleagues. Among his old comrades the war rekindled all the pacifist, anti-imperialist passions that had been so long smothered during the struggles against European fascism and Soviet Communism. At a New Year's Eve party in 1965 his daughter Lisa remembered an "unrelenting" argument between Reuther and Katherine Lowery, a Hull House veteran and SP comrade from the 1930s. Nat Weinberg, Brendan Sexton, Jack Conway, Guy Nunn, and his brother Victor (but not Roy) were dovish to begin with and became increasingly militant opponents of the war over the years. On the executive board Reuther still got his pro-LBJ Vietnam resolutions passed, but only after some of the liveliest debate since the factional warfare of two decades before. Martin Gerber argued that "the Vietnam War is a war of the people of Vietnam against the landowners," while Emil Mazey, who soon emerged as one of the most vocal and highly placed trade union opponents of the war, considered the Johnson administration claim that bombing would strengthen its negotiating position "the most ridiculous and asinine argument I've ever seen."[28]

Within such a milieu, Reuther rationalized his support for the administration in the most tortured and shifting fashion. First, he tried his best to define Johnson himself as a dove: the president was substituting a carefully controlled escalation of the war for the hawkish strategy demanded by the Republican right. In a letter to Harold Wilson, Reuther blamed John Foster Dulles for initiating America's Vietnam entanglement and then went on to describe the Johnson administration's war policy as hardly different from that of J. William Fulbright, the skeptical chairman of the Senate Foreign Relations Committee. Reuther was convinced that U.S. conduct of the Vietnam War did not mean "unlimited escalation and indiscriminate bombing." Toward Johnson himself Reuther's self-deception was uncharacteristically softheaded. "I know the president of the United States," he told a meeting of labor chieftains late in 1966, at a time when the administration had begun a radical shift of funds from domestic reform to Vietnam. "I have known him a long time. . . . I do not share the view that Lyndon Johnson doesn't care about the problems of the poor, or about the problems of our minority groups. . . . I think that basically, he is a man of compassion."[29]

Second, Reuther chose to assume that a majority of rank-and-file workers endorsed the war; open debate would split the union and inject into its body politic the kind of ideological fissures that had once factionalized its internal life. There were a few hawks on the executive board, and among white workers widespread distrust of antiwar demonstrators, but blue-collar workers, and union workers in particular, remained considerably more "dovish" than the college-educated middle class. Throughout the late 1960s the most explosive fissure within the white working class was not Vietnam but race relations, and on this issue Reuther did not hesitate to champion racial liberalism, even when it provoked rank-and-file resentment.

Finally, George Meany's AFL-CIO remained a convenient foil against which

Reuther measured his own liberalism. To Meany and Jay Lovestone, the U.S. fight against the Vietnamese Communists required the same passion and commitment as that devoted to the defense of Western Europe two decades before. Against their militancy, Reuther saw himself as an advocate of Johnsonian moderation. Thus he worked with Arthur Goldberg to ensure that a 1965 AFL-CIO resolution on the war avoided the kind of bellicose language that foreclosed a negotiated settlement; nine months later Reuther decried a particularly offensive executive council statement attacking antiwar dissent as "intemperate, hysterical, jingoistic." Reuther thought of George Meany as a "hawk" who was ready to sacrifice domestic reform for an aggressive prosecution of the war.[30] But this characterization was all too convenient, for it seems almost certain that his renewed frustration with Meany's leadership in 1966 and 1967 represented not only a genuine clash of social ideologies but Reuther's sublimated struggle against the political constraints that now held him so tightly within Lyndon Johnson's suffocating embrace.

In the mid-1960s Reuther and Meany had almost enjoyed a truce when the onrush of domestic reform dissipated their mutual rancor in an optimistic and productive legislative season. But the détente could not last. Their breach came over foreign affairs—not Vietnam per se, but Meany's determination to run AFL-CIO foreign operations in what Reuther thought a reactionary and sectarian fashion. Meany treated the ICFTU (whose president was Reuther's Swedish friend Arne Geijer) with contempt: crippling its operations by withholding hundreds of thousands of dollars in dues, denouncing its politics as insufficiently anti-Communist, and insulting its staff as an "ineffective bureaucracy right down to the fairies." By the early 1960s the AFL-CIO was constructing its own international affairs apparatus—for Latin America, setting up the American Institute for Free Labor Development (AIFLD) in 1961, and three years later the African-American Labor Center. Its murky finances obscured the fact that more than 90 percent of the AIFLD's multimillion-dollar budget came out of U.S. government funds. Reuther answered Meany's unilateral trade union diplomacy with the UAW's own well-financed international affairs program. In 1962 the UAW established the Free World Labor Defense Fund, financed by the interest generated each year from the union's multimillion-dollar strike fund. Working closely with their social democratic comrades in Europe, the Reuther brothers used the money for projects unlikely to win Jay Lovestone's blessing, including aid to leftist trade unions in Greece, Spain, and Turkey.[31]

Reuther had served, inattentively, on the AIFLD board, but it was clearly not his kind of operation. Among the AIFLD directors were businessmen with extensive holdings in Latin America, including its chair, J. Peter Grace, whose company operated steamship lines and mining operations throughout Central America, Venezuela, and Peru. AIFLD-trained unionists had been active in the coup that brought down the Goulart regime in Brazil in 1964 and in political activities designed to undercut the leftist government of Juan Bosh in the Dominican Republic. Victor denounced these operations to his brother, but Walter did not quit the AIFLD board until 1965 when management at Airmold Products, a Grace subsidiary in Tonawanda, New York, defeated a UAW organizing drive there by handing out leaflets that traded on the UAW's indirect AIFLD connection: "Do you want to pay dues to help finance foreign unions in foreign countries? Ask the paid organizer about this private foreign aid program."[32]

"This is shocking," reported Reuther. "Dis-Grace-ful," interjected Leonard Woodcock. Reuther could hardly continue to sit on the same board with a man like Peter Grace, whose subordinates used the AIFLD itself to attack the UAW. Reuther knew, in a general way, that the taxpayers were funding AIFLD, but he attacked Meany for the corporate rather than the government influence in the Latin American institute. "A trade union movement ought to train its own leadership," asserted Reuther. The UAW was certainly prepared to "fight against Communism and all kinds of totalitarianism in Latin America . . . but this is not the way to do it."[33]

This dispute had been kept within the house of labor, but AIFLD funding and control became a major public issue in May 1966 when Victor Reuther, then attending the UAW convention in Long Beach, gave *Los Angeles Times* reporter Harry Bernstein an extensive interview suggesting CIA ties with the AFL-CIO's foreign affairs operation. "Mr. Lovestone seems to have brought into the labor movement the working habits and undercover techniques that he learned when he was in the highest echelons of the Communist Party," charged Victor. Such revelations would have once been considered bizarre, if not unpatriotic, but in 1966 Victor's exposé won instant credibility as but another item in a catalog of government duplicities. Congressional committees soon confirmed the CIA's extensive program to subsidize AIFLD and other ostensibly independent organizations, but the AFL-CIO conceded nothing. The Communications Workers' Joseph Beirne, who headed up the AIFLD for Meany, labeled Victor's remarks "a damned lie," and Meany called Walter to ask whether it would be necessary in the future for him to first consult Victor "to ascertain the views of the UAW on international concerns."[34]

The feud escalated a few days later when Reuther opened yet another front in his war against George Meany's intransigent anti-Communism. As with the ICFTU, AFL-CIO relations with the Geneva-based International Labor Organization (ILO) had been deteriorating for years. The ILO was little more than a talk shop, but in a cold war world it remained one of the few institutions in which East and West could discuss international labor issues. Western European social democrats dominated the organization, but in June 1966 Asian and African delegates voted with the Communist bloc to elect a Polish government official as ILO president. Rudy Faupl, the AFL-CIO delegate, immediately walked out, offering in explanation the orthodox Meany-Lovestone line: "I could not, in good conscience, sit in the conference presided over by a representative of a totalitarian country."[35]

Reuther was outraged when he learned, in the Detroit papers, of the AFL-CIO's abrupt departure. It was "unfair, undemocratic and contrary to established AFL-CIO policy," charged the UAW in a long press release authored by Victor Reuther and Irving Bluestone. Walter Reuther demanded that the AFL-CIO discuss the issue at its next executive council meeting. Again, Reuther did not take issue with Meany's denunciation of Communist-bloc unionism, but he asserted that such a walkout, which violated the spirit of what Lyndon Johnson called his "bridge-building" efforts in Eastern Europe, should not have been taken so precipitously.[36]

But why this Reuther blowup, and over so distant and miniscule an issue? Consider the moment. After an abortive bombing pause ended on January 31, Johnson had again ratcheted up the Vietnam War's intensity. Operation Rolling Thunder's bombing campaign extended all the way to the Chinese border, and the number of American ground troops was headed toward four hundred thousand. At home the Great Society was in trouble, the ideological lines hardening. Reuther's entire defense of Johnson's war policy had been based upon its pragmatic, limited character, its divorce from the cold war's stark polarities. The vigor of Reuther's attack upon Meany's hard line therefore arose out of his desperate effort to preserve this distinction, to maintain some ideological space for Reutherite liberalism.[37]

Naturally Reuther's blast got nowhere inside the AFL-CIO executive council. When it met on June 16, Reuther tried to raise the big issues: the need for international dialogue and negotiation, the specter of nuclear conflagration, and the necessity for a thorough review of the Federation's "rigid, frozen" foreign affairs posture. Meany and other union chiefs pounded away, however, both at Victor Reuther's AIFLD revelations and at Walter's propensity to make his critique of AFL-CIO policy in the public press. After trading insults for three hours, the council voted eighteen to six to support the ILO walkout.[38]

Reuther had been promised a thorough discussion of the AFL-CIO's Latin American operations at the council's next meeting in August. At the very least he hoped to ventilate AIFLD finances and get men like Grace off the AIFLD board. But it was not only the labor conservatives who feared letting the CIA cat out of the bag. Cord Meyer, the Agency's top labor and cultural affairs specialist, told Jack Conway, "Something has got to be done to stop this. It's doing a lot of damage." Soon Hubert Humphrey and Robert Kennedy made calls to Walter, who beat a hasty retreat. Reuther did not doubt the veracity of his brother's charges, but he feared to open simultaneous battlefronts with both Meany and the U.S. government. He gave Victor a dressing-down, later admitting to his AFL-CIO council critics that his brother's interview with the Los Angeles Times had been a "mistake . . . as the CIA is something which you do not discuss publicly."[39]

But Reuther's usual pattern, of attack and then conciliation, had been played out once too often. Reuther thought he had a solid agreement, brokered through Jack Conway and Lane Kirkland, Meany's top assistant, to keep AIFLD off the agenda when the AFL-CIO met in Chicago that August. But he was again pelted with abuse, led by AIFLD Director Joseph Beirne, who compared Victor Reuther's exposé to the "slanderous line of the Commies." Reuther considered the verbal onslaught a double cross. He was again in isolation, on the defensive, with but one other council member, Joe Curran of the Maritime Union, objecting to a resolution denouncing "the campaign of vilification that has been waged against AIFLD." Conway remembered this as the defining moment when Reuther convinced himself that the UAW had to go it alone. "That's it!" Reuther shouted when he stormed out of the council meeting. "I'm through. When it gets to the point that two men make an agreement in a face-to-face meeting, and it isn't carried out, what's the use?"[40]

The divorce proved awkward and lengthy. Unlike John L. Lewis, who had simply scrawled, "We disaffiliate," on a 1948 note to AFL President William Green, Reuther wanted to use the breakup as a vehicle to define his trade union program and mobilize his supporters. But the whole process was bedeviled by tactical indecision. In February 1967 he resigned from the AFL-CIO executive council, after which Irving Bluestone authored a series of UAW administrative letters outlining a program of demands for far-reaching reform within the Federation. These emphasized not the foreign affairs issues that had blown up in the previous year, but Reuther's old frustrations with the AFL-CIO: its failure to launch a big organizing program, establish a joint defense fund for embattled strikers, or align itself with progressive movements outside the house of labor. Reuther proposed to make his case at the Federation's next convention, but in November 1967, just days before the start of the meeting, his executive board announced that a set of uncompleted negotiations with General Motors precluded UAW attendance. Reuther then demanded the convocation of a special AFL-CIO meeting after the 1968 elections; to his chagrin, Meany acceded, but only if the UAW were bound by the convention mandates. The UAW rejected this gambit, refused to pay its dues, and was suspended from participation in AFL-CIO affairs in May 1968. Formal disaffiliation followed two months later.[41]

This entire episode reflected the ambivalence and ambition at the heart of Reuther's politics. As the Great Society faltered and the AFL-CIO set its face firmly against the new social currents that disrupted the American body politic, Reuther sensed that the time might well be ripe for the kind of breakthrough that had enabled John L. Lewis and Sidney Hillman to seize an analogous opportunity thirty years before. Reuther did not see himself as a latter-day Lewis—his contempt was too deep-seated for that—but like the master, he did seek to patronize the social movements of the day and channel their energies into new institutions that could again sustain Reutherite claims upon the polity. Since the early 1960s Reuther's IUD had come through with almost one million dollars to advance the explosive growth of teacher unionism in the urban North, and in Los Angeles, Regional Director Paul Schrade devoted much time and money to the establishment of a "community union" that channeled Labor Department training funds into Watts following the 1965 riot. Reuther wanted to set up UAW citizenship councils and a youth department to link the union to the activist students and leftward-drifting intellectuals whose energy and élan he sought to capture. The old Chicago radical Sidney Lens thought that "Reuther may very well be the bridge, the man who forges a labor-liberal-radical coalition" that could fill the great vacuum Meany's AFL-CIO had generated between the unions and the New Left.[42]

Reuther's championship of the farmworkers' movement led by Cesar Chavez perfectly encapsulated the mentoring role he was so anxious to play. In the fall of 1965 Paul Schrade and Roy Reuther had first alerted him to the dramatic struggle taking place in Delano, California. By the time Reuther flew there just after the AFL-CIO's San Francisco convention in December, Chavez's three-month-old grape strike displayed all the moral dichotomies of Depression-era labor at its most desperate moment. After years of struggle, Chavez had discovered the near-mystical formula that enabled a generation of Filipino and Chicano farmworkers to stand against the Central Valley's Anglo-Armenian elite. The AFL-CIO funded a small organizing committee, but Chavez and his independent union had won outside support only from campus radicals and scattered elements of the Catholic church.

Meany would later dismiss Reuther's two-day Delano appearance as "press agentry," but like the equally brief visits of John L. Lewis to the CIO's midwestern flash points thirty years before, Reuther's simple presence legitimized the struggle in a fashion essential to that of even the most vigorous local insurgency. When Walter, May, and their party got off the plane, the scene in Delano was electric. The authorities had banned farmworker marches, even the use of Spanish in their strike calls, but Chavez and Reuther nevertheless led a cheering column of thousands through the town. "Viva Reuther!" they shouted. "Viva la Huelga!" At a packed rally Reuther exulted, "You are leading history," and then pledged five thousand dollars a month to sustain the strike. The UAW had beaten Ford, he told Delano's mayor a few hours later. "You tell the growers that sooner or later these guys are going to win. . . . Why not talk now and avoid all the bitterness?" By putting Delano in the national spotlight, Chavez thought Reuther's visit "the turning point in our strike." Shortly afterwards, Reuther and Conway persuaded Robert Kennedy, now a senator from New York, to attend a Migratory Labor Committee hearing in Delano; Kennedy proved an instant convert, and Chavez had won a new and even more powerful patron. In August 1966 the AFL-CIO made Chavez and his Farm Workers Organizing Committee a formal affiliate, and in 1967 the Federation stepped up its funding. Nevertheless, Reuther long counted Meany's early parsimony a signal indictment of his rival.[43]

The farmworkers and their remarkable grape boycott soon captured the imagination of American liberals; still later the African-American sanitation workers of Memphis and the female hospital workers of Charleston, South Carolina, would prove themselves lasting symbols of the excitement generated by this rights-conscious trade unionism. Reuther's identification with these insurgencies was profound, arising out of the humanism and solidarity still lodged deep within his Debsian soul. Thus he walked on their picket lines at the same time that his rivalry with George Meany kept the cash flowing from the treasuries of both their organizations. Indeed, Reuther was never more eloquent than when he linked the fortunes of the autoworkers to their struggling brethren. After Reuther had flown to Memphis in April 1968 to give striking sanitation workers the largest check they would receive from any outside source, even some UAW officials in the North raised their eyebrows. But Reuther forged ahead, offering an impassioned defense of interracial solidarity: "We laid $50,000 on the line to demonstrate we meant business," he told three thousand delegates to the 1968 UAW convention. "Who helped *us* back in 1936 and 1937 when we were being beaten up and shot at, when our offices and our cars were being blown up by the gangsters hired by the corporations? Who helped us? The Coal Miners . . . the Clothing Workers . . . as long as I am identified with the leadership of this great union we are going to extent a hand of solidarity to every group of workers who are struggling for justice."[44]

Reuther's impulse was heartfelt, but not without its own irony, for it was in Detroit itself that the nation's most explosive social forces were at work, among both urban blacks and well-employed whites. By 1966 the biracial liberalism of the early 1960s, symbolized in the massive "Walk for Freedom" down Woodward Avenue, had given way to an assertive, sometimes nationalist current within African-American thought and politics. In Detroit a dozen nationalist groups were started: the Rev. Albert Cleage, the most dynamic new voice, drew large audiences to his Shrine of the Black Madonna, where he rejected nonviolence and denounced both the white power structure (including the UAW) and the Trade Union Leadership Council, which now functioned as a federally funded job training institution and political club.

Reuther disdained black nationalism and thought it a dead-end impulse—"just common sense would say that you would want to belong to a broad coalition"— but he also recognized that the UAW had to step warily lest it become embroiled in a self-defeating ideological battle with the most self-confident elements of the black community.[45] Horace Sheffield was hardly counted a black radical in 1966, but when the UAW tried to transfer him from Detroit, where he operated as a political activist virtually independent of the union, to Washington, D.C., Reuther faced an embarrassing protest from much of the city's black community. Surprised that the TULC saw the staff reassignment as an effort to "exile" an important black leader, Reuther retreated as gracefully as he could and rotated Sheffield back to the Motor City within a year.[46]

Reuther was equally tactful five months later when Stokely Carmichael and other SNCC militants popularized the "Black Power" slogan during the Mississippi march of James Meredith in June 1966. Emil Mazey thought "somebody ought to really muzzle this guy Carmichael," but as Reuther prepared to fly to Jackson for the final stage of Meredith's march against fear, he was far more circumspect. "It is one thing for Roy Wilkins to be critical of SNCC personally. It is another thing for us to be. We have got to handle this with great care."[47] But Reuther was not simply a white liberal incapable of standing up to the new militancy. When a group of "young turks" on the NAACP's national board dropped Reuther's name from the organization's reelection slate late in 1966, Reuther fought back as if his very honor were at stake. Mobilizing the union's potent resources within the national community of NAACP loyalists, Reuther's black staff waged a vigorous, successful campaign for an "independent slate" of Association veterans. Reuther felt entirely vindicated when his name came in at the very top of the NAACP ballot.[48]

Reuther's faith in the power of coalition politics remained intact even after Detroit's catastrophic rebellion of July 1967, in which forty-three were killed, seventy-two hundred arrested, and a quarter-billion dollars in property damage incurred. Between Gratiot Avenue on the East Side and Twelfth Street in the West, more than a thousand buildings were gutted and twenty-five hundred looted. Detroit's inner city "look[ed] like Berlin in 1945," mourned Mayor Jerome Cavanagh. Reuther was in suburban Rochester during the worst of the rioting, but he was constantly on the phone with Cavanagh and the White House brokering the politically sensitive dispatch of federal troops to the riot zone.[49] To Reuther, the riots demonstrated once again the necessity for economic development, urban renewal, and biracial cooperation. But by late 1967 the Johnson administration was not about to advocate more money for ghetto rehabilitation, so Reuther put his greatest effort into the 39-member New Detroit Committee, which Mayor Cavanagh and Governor Romney pulled together even before the last fires had ended. Here was a true assemblage of Detroit's power elite: Henry Ford II, Lynn Townsend of Chrysler, James Roche of GM, Walter Cisler of Detroit Edison, Max Fisher of Marathon Oil, Joseph Hudson, Jr., of Hudson Department Stores, plus Reuther, city politicians, educators, and a token delegation from the ghetto itself. To Reuther, New Detroit was not a lobbying operation for more federal dollars but a corporatist embodiment of the urban power structure with the resources, and perhaps even the will, to rebuild the ghetto. Roche pledged the "facilities, skills, resources, and people" of General Motors to "insure the prompt and effective rebuilding of Detroit." "I thought I was aware," admitted Henry Ford II at the inaugural meeting on July 27, "but I guess I wasn't. This thing has to wake us up." Reuther had waited a lifetime for this kind of corporate cooperation. Exuberantly he pledged the volunteer labor of six hundred thousand UAW members in "removing the scars" of the riot.[50]

Despite all its clout, New Detroit was programmed to fail. Over two years it put about ten million dollars into the inner city, largely in low-cost housing—this was Reuther's specialty—and in studies of economic development, urban education, and the police. Both Ford and GM set up community hiring halls in the black ghetto, through which they recruited about ten thousand "hard core unemployed." And several hundred thousand dollars went to black community groups, including that of the Rev. Cleage, an investment most thought of as "riot insurance." Though it had all started with a burst of energy, New Detroit announced its efforts "hopelessly inadequate" within a year. Reuther's impulsive cleanup offer went nowhere after it met resistance from the building trades and city workers, who wanted the jobs, and the UAW rank and file, who valued their leisure. Corporate lobbying on behalf of an open housing law endorsed by Governor Romney collapsed in the face of opposition from legislators representing Detroit's white suburban collar. Most important, the revitalization campaign championed by New Detroit's corporate executives stood counterposed to yet another round in the structural decentralization of the city's most important employers. Chrysler, Ford, Budd, and K-Mart moved factories or offices to Troy and Dearborn during the very same months when their chief executives pondered job creation schemes for the ghetto. Most of the new, post-riot jobs in the auto industry evaporated during the mild recession that began in 1969, and when Reuther proposed that layoffs be scheduled according to a voluntary system of inverse seniority—"juniority," the UAW called it—the corporations argued that older employees were far more disciplined and productive than their new hires.[51]

The Detroit riot was the most costly and bloody of the 1960s. Neither Detroit, Walter Reuther, nor American liberalism ever recovered. With its high level of wages, home ownership, and political organization, with its liberal mayor, productive industry, and ambitious UAW, Detroit had been the "model city" in which Great Society liberalism saw its brightest prospect. "Detroit is a symbol of UAW power," the ILGWU's Evelyn Dubrow told an interviewer in 1968. ". . . So you say, all right, here was a chance where the programs were Walter's and he had a chance to make decisions there. Yet even he with all his thinking ahead is not able to conceive that this would happen." In the city and its suburbs, racial polarization took a quantum leap upward, even as Reuther personally committed the UAW to endorse Richard Austin, an African-American professional, in Detroit's next mayoralty election. The city was now 45 percent black, but when the returns were counted in the fall of 1969, the Wayne County sheriff Roman Gribbs edged out the labor-black candidate in an election that mirrored the stark racial polarities of the George Edwards defeat twenty years before. If Reutherite liberalism was spurned by metropolitan whites, it came under merciless attack from Detroit nationalists, who found the "fat cats" on the New Detroit Committee an easy target. Even Democratic Congressman John Conyers ridiculed the UAW leader. When, during a 1968 campaign stop in Detroit, Hubert Humphrey defended Reuther's work on behalf of the "Negro cause," Conyers shot back: "Reuther doesn't understand the black problem any more than you do."[52] Here was the ideological ground from which would soon spring a new wave of black radicalism, this time centered not in the streets of Detroit but in the auto factories, where the UAW seemed such an integral part of the establishment.

If ghetto riots and antiwar demonstrations have long defined our image of social turmoil in the late 1960s, these were also years of industrial militancy among well-paid white workers, whose blue-collar rebellion posed an even more powerful challenge to the corporate structures that had for so long circumscribed union power and thwarted the Reutherite agenda. During every year from 1966 to 1973 work stoppages reached levels not seen since the end of World War II, and throughout unionized industry more than 10 percent of the contracts negotiated by labor leaders were rejected by the membership, an unprecedented proportion. Thus all the primal conflicts and structural grievances left unresolved by the Treaty of Detroit again moved onto the agenda.

The bargaining system could not quite contain the new energy. Wildcat strikes proliferated, not only in auto and coal mining but in trucking and municipal services, at AT&T, even in the post office and among suburban schoolteachers. *Fortune* magazine called it a "shift from the familiar faces to the facelessness of the rank and file." Several of the old CIO unions saw an abrupt change of leadership, instigated by fellow officers who rode to power on a wave of membership discontent. Reuther's old friend James Carey was deposed in the IUE, and in AFSCME and the Oil, Chemical, and Atomic Workers, union presidents who had made their organizations conduits for the CIA were replaced by more aggressive trade unionists. Finally, in the once-monolithic USW, the veteran officeholder I. W. Abel deposed David J. McDonald by championing the resentment of a generation of solid unionists who rejected McDonald's ostentatious collaboration with the industry's top executives.[53]

Reuther's regime did not totter, but the new militancy made him scramble to keep one step ahead of the turmoil. In the decade after 1958 a huge generational shift transformed automobile industry factories. Richer pensions and better medical insurance lured tens of thousands of older workers out of the shops just as the auto boom of the 1960s sucked in a multiracial workforce that was far younger than at any time since the 1920s. The new workers were not intrinsically more rebellious than their elders, but the rights consciousness engendered by the new social movements of the era quickly filtered down to the shop floor, where it gave a new sharpness to the raw power that had suddenly devolved upon a working population now almost fully employed for the first time since World War II.

"Nowadays," remarked Ford's Malcolm Denise in 1969, "employees are less willing to put up with dirty and uncomfortable working conditions.... Large numbers of those we hire find factory life so distasteful that they quit after only a brief exposure." Daily absenteeism doubled during the decade, and grievance filings over health and safety, work assignments, discipline, and countless other issues rose even more quickly. These workers still valued the union as a wage-setting and welfare-insurance institution; however, when asked in a UAW membership survey whether they thought their committeeman was a "stand up guy who protects the workers," only 16 percent answered in the affirmative in 1967, down from 26 percent six years earlier. This generated a mood of sourness and cynicism: UAW members were far more approving of locally initiated job control strikes than of those called by the national leadership, but they also believed that the conduct of such shop struggles was "only fair" or "poor."[54]

The skilled workers who composed about 15 percent of the UAW were Reuther's most vexing constituency. As in his youth, they were still a powerful vanguard within the entire metalworking population, whose episodic fluctuation between class militancy and parochialism reflected a precisely calibrated social opportunism. Although well represented at every level of the union, the skilled trades had grown increasingly disenchanted with the Reutherite brand of industrial unionism. Since their talents were normally in high demand, much that Reuther hailed as the UAW's most important bargaining achievements, including supplemental unemployment benefits (SUB) and the early retirement scheme of 1964, had little effect on their work life. Instead, the craft pride and social consciousness that had once made them such union pioneers now fed a hundred prickly resentments. UAW tradesmen envied their more highly paid brethren in the building trades and resented the increasingly narrow wage advantage they held against a production workforce of multiethnic hues.

Above all, UAW tradesmen feared the dilution of their skills by the technological transformation of their labor, by the permanent promotion into their ranks of thousands of "upgraders," and by corporate outsourcing of their most challenging work. Unlike production workers, whose very lack of skill made them adaptable to any factory technology, the specialized skills of the craftsmen were their Achilles' heel. Thus they adopted one of two strategies: allying themselves with production workers in a general assault on management's prerogatives, or erecting defensive barriers—rigid lines of demarcation and racially exclusive apprenticeship rules—in order to fortify their relatively privileged position against management's continual shift of production technology. In a confidential 1967 survey for the UAW, Oliver Quayle confirmed that the "UAW now has a serious problem with those in the skilled trades."[55]

Given the postwar weakness of Reutherite unionism on the shop floor, it is not surprising that a skilled trades "revolt" in the UAW tilted toward parochialism and craft separatism. In the mid-1950s a genuinely rank-and-file movement, calling itself the International Society of Skilled Trades (ISST), signed up thousands of workers who found little use for the fringe benefits and egalitarian wage structures to which UAW bargainers had given first priority. Drifting toward the Goldwater wing of the Republican Party, the ISST railed against "monopoly unionism" and denounced Reuther as a socialist who "must play the masses like the strings of a lute." The ISST revealed the fault lines that lay beneath the seemingly solid industrial union monolith, but as an organization it disintegrated in 1957 when the NLRB ruled for the UAW and the auto companies against its effort to carve craft units out of the unionized workforce.[56]

The recessionary years after 1957 kept craft separatism in eclipse, but by the mid-1960s the Vietnam-era demand for skilled labor of all types provided an extraordinary opportunity for the ISST to come roaring back. When Detroit-area building tradesmen won a wage increase of almost a dollar an hour in 1965, UAW craftsmen were furious, especially when they worked side by side with outside maintenance and construction workers contracted into their factories. Led by the ISST founder Joseph Dunnebeck, who had sharpened his political skills in the Republican campaign of 1964, the dissident ISST put more than a score of organizers in the field, and by early 1966 it could fill the largest auditorium in Flint on a Saturday night. Reuther was frightened, and with good reason. Reported *Detroit Free Press* correspondent Patrick Owens, "In several Detroit plants the ISST has so much support that UAW skilled trades leaders have found themselves out manned and on the defensive."[57]

Here was a threat that Reuther had to counter or accommodate. He denounced the ISST as "financed by the most reactionary political forces in this country," and he put Douglas Fraser, who had eclipsed Leonard Woodcock as the presidential heir apparent, in charge of the newly aggressive Skilled Trades Department. Reuther had little sympathy for the demands of skilled tradesmen, whose motivation seemed so crudely invidious, so difficult to square with the broader social program to which he so often linked the union's collective bargaining agenda. Still, Reuther met with pro-UAW leaders of the skilled trades at the union's May 1966 Long Beach convention, where he urged them to "mobilize their army" in order to reopen the contract that summer, a full year before its termination in the fall of 1967. To lend credibility to this big push, Reuther amended the union's constitution to give skilled workers an absolute veto over the entire contract settlement. Within weeks skilled tradesmen loyal to the UAW had launched a powerful, popular "$1 an Hour Now" campaign that channeled discontent back into the union and knocked much wind out of ISST sails.[58]

All this was a typically sophisticated Reuther maneuver, but the UAW president turned out to be too clever by half. The corporations were hardly happy with this effort to breach a solemn contractual obligation, and as Reuther must have half expected, they rejected the gambit in August 1966. Leaders of the "$1 an Hour Now" movement had meanwhile organized a series of mass demonstrations that Solidarity House found highly embarrassing. When Reuther and Fraser told them to wait until the next year for the big wage push, thousands of skilled tradesmen balked, and their movement came under the leadership of anti-Reuther leftists from such traditionally dissident strongholds as the GM tech center and the Rouge toolroom.[59] Meanwhile, the ISST was far from dead. Early in 1967 an explosive set of wildcat strikes, touched off by skilled workers at GM's Mansfield, Ohio, stamping plant, forced the layoff of two hundred thousand workers and an executive board seizure of the local, after which the shop chairman quit and went on the ISST payroll as an organizer. GM saw the Mansfield work stoppage, which lasted almost three weeks, as one of the most serious challenges to UAW leadership in two decades; if Reuther had not squashed this rebellion, the corporation was ready to go to court to seize the UAW's $70 million strike fund.[60]

"The only way Walter can get out of this one is to get everybody a raise," reported the *Detroit Free Press*. The money was there, of course. Automobile profits were "fantastic," reported CEA Chairman Gardner Ackley: in 1965 GM had earned about the same return as a "newly opened gold mine." But auto wages were negotiated in a national spotlight. Given the tight labor market and the inflationary pressures generated by Vietnam War spending, Johnson administration Keynesians like Ackley feared that if the government again failed to force the auto companies to cut their prices, Reuther would "go after their profits with a huge wage demand. And he will get it. Workers in other industries will surely try to follow him, touching off a massive wage-price spiral."[61]

Reuther actually agreed with this analysis: he rejected the old 3.2 percent wage guideposts, which put the entire anti-inflation burden on minimum-wage employees and union labor. And he also played an outspoken role rejecting a tax increase, which the orthodox Keynesians advocated in order to soak up excess demand and "soften" the labor market. As long as youth unemployment among blacks stood at more than 25 percent, Reuther saw any economic slowdown as a recipe for a new round of urban riots. When he spent an afternoon at Johnson's Texas ranch early in December 1966, Reuther urged LBJ to keep Great Society spending programs intact. When the president asked him where he should go for the money without a tax increase, Reuther shot back, "Cut it out of the space program," because there was nothing the United States could do by that time to match the "psychological impact of the Sputnik."[62]

Out of this conundrum Reuther and Weinberg still hoped that a corporatist initiative might yet arise to forestall the impending inflationary surge. To replace the guideposts, Reuther wanted a price-wage review board that would investigate and expose big price increases in the corporate sector and open the door to an American version of the "incomes policy" just implemented by Wilson's Labour government. Here was an echo of the World War II "equality of sacrifice" idea: state controls would bear equally on all forms of income, wages, salaries, profits, dividends, and interest. CEA Chairman Ackley, along with numerous economists and labor relations practitioners from the old War Labor Board fraternity, favored the idea as well. "If equity is neglected," wrote Reuther to Johnson, "stabilization policy in a free society will sooner or later break down—as the guideposts have broken down."[63]

But Vietnam evoked none of the social patriotism of World War II. As Lyndon Johnson himself understood all too well, sacrifice and equity had radically different meanings within a polity increasingly polarized over race, war, and social reform. He rejected the incomes policy idea and long delayed his war tax legislation, because he rightly feared that an effort to make explicit the linkages between domestic social policy and the Vietnam escalation promised to further inflame his opposition, from hawks and doves alike. The best that Johnson could do was a kind of jawboning and ad hoc arm-twisting, much of it directed toward Reuther, whose 1967 bargaining round seemed fraught with inflationary dangers. As *Business Week* put it in June 1967, "The architects of the Administration's wage-price policies are holding their breaths ... pondering alternatives to simple persuasion if 'the big one'—auto bargaining—blows."[64]

Reuther had spent more than twenty years seeking to tame the wage-price spiral. But this was no time for statesmanship. Reflecting what he called "the pressure of priority" within his union, he felt he had little choice but to accommodate the Hobbesian mood. Even Henry Ford II admitted that, although he favored the guidelines, "when we sit down with Walter and the UAW, they are not going to mean a damn thing."[65] Thus by mid-1967 Reuther had abandoned a big push for the salarization of the hourly workforce in return for a new emphasis on a "substantial" wage increase. For this, Reuther wanted no CEA admonitions or special invitations to the White House. Indeed, Reuther sought to have his cake and eat it. Given his rivalry with Meany, he wanted not only Johnson's neutrality but his approbation in order to demonstrate that his effectiveness had been curbed neither by his split with the AFL-CIO nor by his mildly dovish views on the war.[66]

The strategy seemed to pay off in June 1967 when a UAW local in Bridgeport, Connecticut, marbled with skilled machinists, stood on the verge of a renewed strike against the Lycoming Division of AVCO, the army's sole supplier of helicopter engines used in Vietnam. Cornering Reuther after a White House meeting on the Model Cities program, LBJ himself pleaded with the UAW president to do something to avoid a work stoppage when the Taft-Hartley eighty-day cooling-off period expired two weeks later. Reuther replied, "I will do my best . . . [but] I have some other ones coming up that are very important." Then, as Reuther proudly recounted the incident to his executive board, the president put his arm around the UAW president and assured him, "You put this one to bed and as far as I am concerned you've got a green light to strike these others for the rest of the summer." "I shook his hand," remembered Reuther. "I said 'We have an understanding.'"[67]

Meeting at the Pentagon with Secretary of Defense Cyrus Vance, University of California President Clark Kerr (a longtime mediator and arbitrator), and top AVCO executives, Reuther worked out a warfare state wage deal of classic proportions. The company agreed to double its last monetary offer in return for Vance's sub-rosa assurance that the army would pay considerably more for its Huey engines when the old contract expired. Using the government's threat to seize the factory for its persuasive effect, Reuther and other UAW officials then sold the settlement to the restive Bridgeport workers. Reuther called this "free collective bargaining," but whatever the nomenclature, he moved into the Big Three negotiations with a precedent-setting wage increase and renewed confidence that the White House would not intervene to dampen an auto pay hike.[68]

Despite Johnson's benevolent neutrality, a strike that fall was inevitable. "If we could work out a settlement with Walter that he would buy right now, he couldn't take it back to his people yet," an industrial relations executive told Fortune. "He's got to walk that last mile for them."[69] Still wary of GM, where even a short strike would quickly drain the union treasury, Reuther targeted Ford and struck the company for forty-seven days, making it the longest UAW work stoppage since the three-month Chrysler strike in 1950. Reuther got enough new money to placate the skilled tradesmen. The settlement came in at well above 6 percent: fifty cents an hour for skilled workers, twenty cents an hour for production workers, and an employer contribution large enough to bring SUB payments up to 95 percent of take-home pay. In addition, the union won two more holidays and another big increase in relief time for assembly-line workers. Most important, the long work stoppage tempered the centrifugal forces at work within the union. Skilled trades agitation continued throughout the strike, but as Al Gardner of the Rouge tool-room remembered, "They put you out on strike, not to weaken the company but to weaken the people on strike. After seven weeks people are hurting."[70]

But the stoppage also demonstrated the extent to which the Treaty of Detroit was about to come unstuck. Henry Ford II called the negotiations "the most diffi-cult in our 26-year relationship with the UAW." Reuther too had a rough fall sea-son, spending scores of hours bickering over contract details in several all-night negotiating sessions. Indeed, the entire bargaining round lasted more than six months, with some GM locals still on strike in April 1968. And Reuther had made a huge blunder. He took at face value Lyndon Johnson's assurances that there was light at the end of the Vietnam tunnel. He gambled that inflationary pressures would soon ease once a negotiated settlement in the war led to cutbacks in mili-tary spending. Reuther therefore paid for the big wage increase by agreeing to a "cap" of sixteen cents an hour on the cost-of-living adjustment during the three-year life of the contract. In a televised speech designed to sell the agreement, Reuther declared that the new contract "preserved the basic integrity" of the COLA clause. But Reuther was a knave if not a fool, for the inflationary surge of the next three years cost the average UAW worker more than eight hundred dol-lars. Before the UAW could rectify the debilitating miscalculation, Reuther was dead, and it was left to his successors to rewin the money in the long GM strike of the autumn of 1970.[71]

This was the least of the UAW's problems. By early 1968, when Reuther and his subordinates were cleaning up the contract details, collective bargaining in heavy industry was about the last thing on the minds of most Americans. With the coun-try coming apart along so many fracture zones, the very insulation of the triannual bargaining ritual from the larger social currents sweeping through the body politic was one of the most notable, if unseen, features of the social landscape. But this isolation was a source of weakness rather than strength. Reuther was desperate to bridge the gulf that separated American unions from the political ferment that swept across the nation in these years, but his role was an utterly schizophrenic one: his linkage to the White House and his responsibilities as a trade union leader were at war with his championship of an insurgent liberalism. He would now be forced to choose.

19

FROM 1968 TO BLACK LAKE

It is hard to change institutions fundamentally. That is why there are revolutions in the world.

—Walter Reuther, 1968

euther had begun the 1960s as one of the figures who defined the left wing of social and economic liberalism. By 1967 he had influence and access in Washington, London, and Bonn, but on the most vexing issue of the day he let "history" pass him by. His dilemma and his pain were summed up on an April evening that year when Walter, May, and their youngest daughter, Lisa, attended a Seder with some of their closest friends—among them, Roy Reuther and his wife Faina, and their hosts Irving and Thelma Bluestone. Present also were twenty-two-year-old Barry Bluestone and his girlfriend of that time, Leslie Woodcock, daughter of the UAW vice president. It had taken some special persuasion on the part of the elder Bluestones to secure their son's attendance, because Barry and Leslie were furious with Walter Reuther.

At the University of Michigan the young couple were antiwar activists, riding the cusp of a movement that was finally bursting off the campuses and into the mainstream of American politics. On April 4, in a forceful and radical sermon delivered at Riverside Cathedral in New York, Martin Luther King, Jr., had put his great prestige on the line to declare that "this madness must cease." Ten days later antiwar marches filled the streets of San Francisco and New York, the largest demonstrations in U.S. history up to that time. Each Sunday the *New York Times* carried yet another antiwar manifesto to which thousands of clergy, writers, faculty, and student leaders put their names. On the college circuit administration liberals like Hubert Humphrey and Arthur Goldberg were given icy receptions, and for fear of outright disruption, President Johnson's public appearances were now confined almost exclusively to military bases. Within left-liberal circles, including those in Solidarity House, the war had become the touchstone of political rectitude.[1]

If Barry and Leslie were going to attend the Seder, they were determined to make Walter Reuther confront the war issue. As part of the service, they offered a twenty-minute reading, with stanzas from the embittered antiwar poetry of Wilfred Owen and passages from King's recent speech. When they were done, May Reuther was highly irritated, but Walter was bemused. "I take it, that's all aimed at me," he countered. Barry Bluestone later remembered that in the furious debate that followed,

> I explained how important we thought it was that Walter make a national state-ment, like King had made, and get the support of the UAW behind the end-the-war movement. Walter said that to be honest, he agreed that the war was wrong, but he added that he couldn't do it now while they were entering negotiations. "It was no time to split the union on this kind of ideological issue."
>
> Leslie was taking all of this in. She turned to Walter and said, "You really said that, didn't you?" And Walter said, "What did I say?" And Leslie just became as angry as I ever saw her. Her face was flushed with anger. "You really said that, you really said that." And Walter, frustrated, again asked, "What did I say?" Leslie turned to him and said, "What are you trying to do, maybe get eighty cents an hour in the pay envelope, five cents here, five cents there? You're telling me that you are unwilling to make a statement that may save fifty thousand lives or one hundred thousand lives or maybe a million lives because you want to get fifty more cents in your God-damn fucking contract. . . . That's the most inhumane thing I have ever heard of in my life."[2]

Reuther was unquestionably pained by this exchange—and arguments no less acrimonious with his daughters Linda and Lisa—but the UAW president's dovish instincts were trapped within what Jack Conway called an "institutional personal-ity" that Reuther thought mandated a publicly cordial relationship with the administration. There were the politically sensitive negotiations for a 1967 auto contract, the effort to keep LBJ neutral during the feud with George Meany, and the realization that the government played hardball when it came to national secu-rity issues. This became clear just two weeks later when the ex-CIA official Thomas Braden published in the *Saturday Evening Post* a long defense of the Agency's covert operations, "I'm Glad the CIA Is Immoral." Braden justified CIA funding of labor, student, and cultural groups in order to counter the "enormous naivete" of those who thought the nation could avoid secret operations. Although Braden admitted that the CIA had funded the AFL's postwar activities in Europe, his most sensational disclosure—and the only one involving names, places, and specific cash figures—involved the Agency's 1952 transfer of fifty thousand dollars to Walter and Victor Reuther. "Victor Reuther ought to be ashamed of himself," charged Braden, who had followed the UAW's recent campaign against AFL-CIO links to the CIA.[3] Walter Reuther took Braden's exposé as a warning shot over the bow. In February, when Walter read an uncritical report on one of Victor's anti-CIA speeches in the *Daily Worker*, he slashed "Vic should *stop*" across the margin; he also gave his younger brother a vicious tongue-lashing for putting them both so far out on the political limb. And the UAW president took the very same line toward Paul Schrade, the West Coast regional director whose increasing identification with the New Left paralleled his growing revulsion with the war. After Schrade appeared as the principal labor spokesman at the April 15, 1967, antiwar demonstration in San Francisco, Reuther called him on the carpet, lecturing Schrade "not to get too far ahead of the membership on Vietnam."[4]

As the tempo of antiwar sentiment rose, Reuther put his influence firmly against those who were searching for an alternative to LBJ in the crucial months leading up to the 1968 presidential campaign season. Appearing on "Meet the Press" late in September 1967, Reuther still argued that it "is much easier to criticize the President than it is to come up with a workable alternative." Reuther said he favored a bombing halt over North Vietnam, then the minimal requirement of the doves, but he would not be part of any "Dump Johnson" movement. Instead, he joined University of California President Clark Kerr and Norman Cousins of the *Saturday Review* in the mildly dovish "Negotiations Now!" group. Kerr and Reuther visited LBJ several times in the fall of 1967, urging that the military extend its annual Christmas cease-fire into the Tet holidays, thus preparing the ground for negotiations, even with the National Liberation Front. These private meetings had no influence with the war planners; indeed, an increasingly suspicious White House now considered Reuther unreliable, if not an actual emissary for Robert Kennedy's government in exile.[5]

But the president and his men were mistaken. As late as February 1968 Victor Reuther himself carried his brother's personal assurances to Hubert Humphrey: "The UAW is for President Johnson all the way."[6] And Walter stood against his own, increasingly aroused labor-liberal constituency to demonstrate his loyalty. In the fall of 1967 he blocked Emil Mazey's effort to win official UAW endorsement of the Labor Assembly for Peace, which brought over five hundred trade union leaders to Chicago that November. Attending as individuals, not UAW spokesmen, Mazey and Victor Reuther gave uncompromising speeches whose enthusiastic reception demonstrated that a Reutherite critique of AFL-CIO complacency could enlist plenty of foot soldiers when linked to a repudiation of the Vietnam War. Walter Reuther might well have stepped forward as their leader, but two months later he again stood against political insurgency by mobilizing UAW influence within the Americans for Democratic Action to reject the antiwar presidential candidacy of Eugene McCarthy when his old comrade Joe Rauh pushed the organization for an endorsement during the winter of 1967–68. As in the MFDP fight nearly four years earlier, Rauh thought mainstream liberals had to shift leftward in order to retain influence upon the insurgent forces of the 1960s. When the ADA governing board met for a climactic meeting on February 10, 1968, however, Reuther—who was in contact with the White House on this issue—instructed Jack Conway and the rest of the UAW contingent to cast its four votes against the McCarthy endorsement. It nevertheless passed, sixty-five to forty-seven, after which Reuther stated that he "sympathized completely" with those AFL-CIO hawks who resigned from the liberal organization, although Jack Conway and other UAW liberals would remain inside in order to "refashion the labor-liberal coalition."[7] Even after McCarthy's stunning campaign in New Hampshire, Reuther did not budge. He discounted the significance of the McCarthy vote, and in early March, while Johnson's entire presidency hung in the balance, Reuther declared that he would certainly continue to support him: "No one on the horizon is remotely more entitled to my vote than he is. He has made a tremendous contribution on domestic programs."[8]

Reuther's stubborn commitment to the Johnson camp remains virtually inexplicable. The death of his father, Valentine, in November 1967, followed two months later by that of his brother Roy, who suffered a massive heart attack, certainly left Reuther shaken. Roy may have been the only Reuther brother who could get along with George Meany, and on the war issue he was almost as hawkish. But Roy Reuther was also a shrewd political operative who knew when to cut his losses.[9] Walter could have used such advice, because by March 1968 Reuther's vision of American politics and society was apocalyptic. In Vietnam he saw "a real disaster." In the cities he prophesied guerrilla warfare leading to martial law, perhaps even a civil war. Within the labor movement Reuther excoriated the conservatives, and not just George Meany but also his erstwhile CIO comrades who failed to recognize the need for a radical break with stand-pat policies. "It is hard to change institutions. That is why there are revolutions in the world," he tutored his executive board. The labor movement "has to have the youth. It has to have the student movement . . . the kind of forces that motivated guys to go to Mississippi to start the Civil Rights movement."[10]

The crunch came at an executive board meeting on March 19 just after Robert Kennedy had announced his presidential candidacy. Except for Reuther, virtually all the key players in the UAW high command were pro-Kennedy. Indeed, Paul Schrade and Jack Conway were part of the Kennedy campaign's inner circle. Reuther was not about to defect to RFK, but the White House kept an impatient tab on the UAW president. In Michigan and elsewhere, noted one Humphrey aide, "the great question is what Walter Reuther and the auto workers will do." Throughout the day Reuther refused to take Humphrey's phone calls. "This means trouble," wrote Jim Rowe, who implored LBJ to get on the line to Reuther. To his board the UAW president admitted that RFK's candidacy created "a whole new ball game," but he thought the challenge would fail, though not before it split the Democratic Party and opened the door to a Nixon victory in the fall. On the other hand, Reuther still valued LBJ's clout as a domestic policy fixer. "We cannot wage a war against Johnson and then ask for his support [in the aerospace negoti-ations]," warned Reuther. With party realignment a long-abandoned dream, Reuther wanted the UAW to be in a position to "knit together the warring factions in the Democratic Party when the primaries are behind us." Thus he favored adher-ence to the UAW's tradition of "neutrality" during the primary season, a position that the White House counted as a significant brake on Kennedy's momentum.[11]

But Paul Schrade was determined to carry Kennedy's banner in California, where he was putting together a powerful primary slate that extended from Cesar Chavez on the left to Jesse Unruh's Democratic Party stalwarts on the right. "Wal-ter fought Paul on it," remembered Conway. "It became very divisive." The dead-lock finally broke when Leonard Woodcock, whom Schrade had long considered the "spiritual and intellectual leader of the hawks," offered a carefully measured but very firm condemnation of Lyndon Johnson and his war. "You could have heard a pin drop," remembered one observer. When the vote finally came at 9:00 P.M., Schrade's political activities remained unencumbered by UAW policy. Reuther's defeat was confirmed the next day after the Kennedy forces filed their slate in California. As Jack Conway put it, "Holy christ everything broke loose in the UAW board room because both Lyndon Johnson and Hubert Humphrey called Walter Reuther and really read the riot act to him." Reuther tried to get the board to reverse its policy, but "Paul really hung tight." Reuther found himself opposed by his closest associates: all the old socialist staffers—Weinberg, Sexton, Conway, and Victor Reuther—plus the board heavyweights Woodcock, Fraser, Mazey, Ken Bannon, Martin Gerber, Nelson Jack Edwards, Ed Grey, and Ray Berndt. Reuther had to give in: UAW members, he conceded, could now support any candidate they wished.[12]

Reuther borrowed the title of John Reed's most famous book to describe the events that then convulsed the nation: "Ten Days That Shook the World." He was stunned by Lyndon Johnson's decision to renounce another run for the presidency and doubly shamed five days later, first, when Martin Luther King, Jr., was gunned down in Memphis, and then, just hours later, when some Nashville UAW workers protested the lowering of their plant's flag to half-mast. The riots that scarred nearly one hundred American cities confirmed the nation's racial polarization and sus-tained Reuther's apocalyptic mood: "The hour is later than we think and the urgency is deeper than we appreciate." To such trauma Reuther's response was always a flurry of activity. After King's assassination, he rushed to Memphis, where he upstaged the AFL-CIO with the UAW's donation of fifty thousand dollars to the city's striking sanitation workers. Immediately afterwards, he flew to Atlanta for King's huge funeral march and then on to Washington, where a long political talk with Hubert Humphrey took place in a city occupied by twelve thousand National Guardsmen. Reuther wanted the administration to take advantage of the "psycho-logical opportunity" generated by King's death to revive Great Society liberalism and make the government the employer of last resort.[13] To this end Reuther pushed his executive board to endorse Martin Luther King's last initiative, the

Poor People's Campaign, which encapsulated King's recent turn toward a class analysis of America's social crisis. The UAW contributed fifty-five thousand dollars to help underwrite the Campaign's "Resurrection City" encampment near the Washington Monument, but the ineffectually led enterprise literally bogged down in the capital's mud and rain. Reuther gave a short, militant speech at the Campaign's large rally on June 19, to which the UAW bussed three thousand members, but in the chaos that had engulfed the political world after Robert Kennedy's assassination, few were listening.[14]

The spring of 1968 was the last moment in the twentieth century when the most decisive issues facing the nation would be fought out within the house of American liberalism. At a moment of extraordinary political plasticity, the Democratic presidential primaries mobilized the electorate in a contest that encapsulated many of the political choices and social dilemmas that faced postwar liberalism at its moment of greatest crisis. Once Lyndon Johnson had renounced the presidency, George Meany's AFL-CIO became the rock upon which Hubert Humphrey grounded his loyalist candidacy. Despite his quarter-century career as liberal tribune, he now relied upon the most conservative elements in the Democratic Party and organized labor to sustain his campaign. Meanwhile, his opponents, within the Democratic Party and out, tapped into the wellsprings of energy unleashed by the New Left at the very moment when American radicalism stood poised between self-destruction and self-reliance.

Among all the major trade unions, only the UAW stood apart, and in two states, California and Indiana, Reuther's union played a key role in energizing a multiracial, working-class vote for Robert Kennedy. In California, where the farmworkers' union provided the backbone of the campaign throughout the Central Valley, Paul Schrade's energetic role earned him lasting fame on the night of June 4 when he was wounded in the same gunfire that killed Robert Kennedy in the kitchen of the Ambassador Hotel. But for all its political weight, California may not have been the most telling battle of that campaign season. This had come a month earlier in Indiana, where UAW Regional Director Ray Berndt helped Kennedy defeat the Steel Workers and the AFL-CIO on their home turf. As expected, Kennedy carried black working-class wards in Gary and Indianapolis by huge margins, but Kennedy and and his rival, Eugene McCarthy, also overwhelmed the entire Democratic Party establishment, which was backing Hubert Humphrey's stand-in, Governor Roger Branigin. The Kennedy-McCarthy margins were particularly notable in the Slavic, Hungarian, Italian, and Polish wards, since George Wallace had won the votes of many of these same ethnic voters in the 1964 Democratic primary.[15]

One might have expected Walter Reuther to play a central role in all this, crystallizing anew a progressive, labor-liberal agenda linked to the insurgent forces mobilized on behalf of the antiwar candidates. But Reuther's role was a muted one. Although the most active elements in the UAW apparat were passionately pro-Kennedy, Reuther was careful to maintain good relations with the White

House; when he visited there on April 29, he informed LBJ that he favored Humphrey, although Jack Conway told reporters later that same year that Reuther really "couldn't choose between these two guys." Reuther had lost control of UAW political operations that spring, however, so his opinion made little difference in the 1968 primary battle, except in Michigan, where his abdication was probably responsible for a Democratic Convention delegation split between Kennedy and Humphrey.[16]

But in the larger sense, Reuther's persistent failure to divorce his person and his union from the administration's war program squandered a real chance to link at least one important institution of the working class to the thousands of men and women energized by the movement against the war. In 1966, 1967, or even in early 1968, a UAW break with Johnson might well have legitimized political opposition on an even wider scale and provided, in the words of ADA Chairman John Kenneth Galbraith, "the political strength, disciplined troops and stability" that the new politics sorely lacked. Reuther's caution meant that he had abdicated any meaningful role for himself or for his union in shaping the American New Left he so earnestly sought to build. "If Reuther had marched with King against the war, it would have made all the difference in the world," mused one Berkeley activist. Thus the UAW's final break with the AFL-CIO in 1968 passed with hardly a ripple in liberal or New Left circles; after all, both Meany and Reuther backed the same candidate for the Democratic nomination, and on the strategy for ending the Vietnam War their differences were not significant.[17]

Reuther's equivocation continued after Robert Kennedy's death, when Reuther stepped up to cochair Clark Kerr's peace organization, now renamed the National Committee for a Political Settlement in Vietnam. Funded almost entirely by the UAW, the Kerr-Reuther group took Humphrey's nomination as a given but sought to nudge him toward dovish moderation, including a "stand-still cease-fire." On June 16, Reuther met with Humphrey for six hours at his home in Waverly, Minnesota, and came away under the impression that Humphrey was no longer a "prisoner" of the administration's war policy. Reuther immediately put UAW staffers to work drafting a speech for the vice president that committed him to the unilateral bombing halt so often rejected by Lyndon Johnson. However, the draft went nowhere, for as the divisive Democratic Convention loomed ever closer, Humphrey remained a political and psychological vassal of his president. Stymied, Reuther and Kerr did not opt for the peace Democrats and a break with the vice president. Instead, they were determined to find a formula upon which Humphrey and his party opponents could agree. Conway remembered Reuther's state of mind as, "There's no reason why the Democratic Party should tear itself up on this peace plank." So Reuther and Kerr spent hours on the phone with the vice president, hammering out a compromise in which Humphrey moved toward an immediate bombing pause but the United States reserved the right to renew air attacks on North Vietnam at any time. When the man from Texas vetoed even this formulation, Kerr and Reuther secured a meeting with George McGovern, a leader of the dove forces, and vainly urged him to water down his minority peace plank to the point where Humphrey could run on it.[18]

All the frantic matchmaking came to nought. At Chicago the fault lines within the party of the New Deal coalition were etched in blood. At the very moment when Hubert Humphrey was being nominated, thousands of police were pummeling antiwar demonstrators in the streets and parks of Chicago. Reuther came away from the convention miserable, unhappy with the young protesters, and appalled at the reign of police violence. The UAW quickly put out a statement denouncing the "naked brutality and savage beatings by those charged with the maintenance of order," but when Reuther learned that 70 percent of the American people applauded the repression, he feared the country might be drifting toward fascism and a "police state."[19]

This was not an uncommon sentiment among American liberals in the convention's aftermath. Humphrey could not escape Chicago's violent taint, so his campaign got off to a wretched start. For the first time in twenty years the Democratic candidate for president did not launch his campaign in Cadillac Square. And because of poor participation, the UAW canceled a mid-September political convention to endorse Hubert Humphrey. But Reuther remained unshaken. "The choice is clear and simple," he told the UAW executive board on September 10: it was Humphrey or Nixon for president, and he wanted an emphatic UAW endorsement of the Democrat. "This is no time for people on the left to be dividing our political forces because they don't like exactly the way Hubert Humphrey puts his position on Vietnam. I don't like it, either, but the future of America cannot hinge upon one thing." Predictably, Reuther's only opposition came from Paul Schrade, but his New Left skepticism won no second in the UAW board room.[20]

The antiwar liberals came around after Humphrey finally endorsed a bombing halt at the end of September, but to Reuther and the rest of the Democratic Party's labor wing, the Wallace phenomenon posed the greater challenge by far. By late September a Gallup poll gave George Wallace 21 percent of the national vote. Most of this backing was concentrated in the Deep South; in the North white-collar workers and middle-class suburbanites gave Wallace at least half of his support. But he could also draw lines of class feeling with exquisite skill. Indeed, Wallace's rhetoric moved beyond the postwar norm: for the first time in a generation, a national political figure offered the white working class an identity both combative and virtuous. It had been years since even Reuther deployed the vocabulary of class conflict. The labor leader's language was that of liberal humanitarianism or technopolitical bargaining: the UAW, as a voice for "the whole man, the whole human being and all his needs," sought "equity . . . our rightful share of the increased productivity and the increased profitability made possible by a revolutionary technological development." In contrast, Wallace counterpoised "top politicians," "bureaucrats with beards," and "federal judges playing God" to a gritty working class: "This man in the textile mill, this man in the steel mill, this barber, the beautician, the policeman on the beat."[21]

All through the summer reports of intense Wallace partisanship poured into Solidarity House. Regional officials and local union officers were for Humphrey 90 percent, but Wallace won straw polls and union meeting endorsements at Ternstedt in Flint, Fisher Body in Willow Spring, Illinois, and GM in Linden, New Jersey. Reuther was embarrassed and alarmed, especially when the elected leadership at the huge Chevy Local 659 in Flint refused to endorse Humphrey for fear of alienating the Wallace partisans in the rank and file. Wallace attracted support from two kinds of northern workers: older skilled workers, often of Polish or Italian extraction, who feared African-American encroachment in their schools and neighborhoods; and young production workers attracted to Wallace's populist, antiestablishment denunciation of liberal elites. "If Reuther was for Wallace, we'd be for Humphrey" was the way some put it. Reuther got a taste of this alienation when he was heckled by a Wallace contingent during a UAW meeting in St. Louis. "If sister will sit down, I'll explain that," Reuther said at one point. "Don't you call me a sister!" came the reply, a deeply shocking one to a man who had dedicated his life to the idea of social solidarity.[22]

The national media interpreted the Wallace phenomenon as a political upheaval of the first order, a subversion within liberalism's most veteran regiment. As the *Washington Post*'s Joseph Kraft reported after a swing through the heartland, "A great many workers in Flint resent the union leadership. In particular, they resent union stands being taken on behalf of political candidates and social issues without what they feel is adequate consultation of the rank and file." To Reuther, this was an enormous challenge, not just to the Humphrey campaign but to his very credibility as the progressive spokesman for American labor. UAW leaders tended to discount all but the racist and authoritarian elements in the Wallace appeal. "Listen," an unnamed UAW official told journalists in September, "the men in the plants want to zap the Negroes by voting for Wallace. It's as simple as that." Reuther thought the Wallace campaign mendaciously simpleminded: "Let's smash the people who dare to demonstrate. Let's forget about the problems in the ghettos. Let's just suppress the forces of revolt."[23]

Whatever the analysis, the UAW threw its resources into blocking the Wallace phenomenon. The effort was unquestionably the union's finest hour in 1968, a last hurrah for Reutherite labor-liberalism. Solidarity House set up a "Wallace Desk" and poured half a million dollars and upwards of six hundred full-time staffers into a nationwide campaign that successfully counterpoised racial pluralism and social democracy to the racially charged populism of the Wallace movement. Reuther stumped the industrial heartland, denouncing the "Wallace strategy of divide-and-rule" as a "formula for national disaster." In tandem with the AFL-CIO, Reuther's union advertised all of Alabama's social pathologies and lay the blame for the state's history of low wages and antiunionism squarely on the Deep South's legacy of racism.

Such propaganda proved remarkably effective, for American autoworkers were neither so racist nor so affluent that they could ignore an appeal directed to their class interest. By election day a New Deal–ish and somewhat more dovish Hubert Humphrey had rewon the confidence of a solid majority of blue-collar workers in the North, while the Wallace vote shrank to about 9 percent of manual workers there. Despite Nixon's slim victory overall, Reuther felt relieved and vindicated when he heard that Humphrey had taken Michigan by a margin substantially greater than that won by John Kennedy eight years before. In 1968 the standard of living built by a quarter-century of New Deal social programs and union bargaining contracts remained intact. When in the next two decades these institutions failed to defend blue-collar Democrats, the political liberalism of the white working class would decline as well.[24]

With the 1968 elections out of the way, Walter Reuther seemed ready to strike out on his own, to test his new freedom with neither Lyndon Johnson nor George Meany looking over his shoulder. Since the Democrats were out of power, Reuther had no difficulty shifting to the left on Vietnam and other foreign policy issues. The UAW proved a staunch opponent of both the Nixon administration's antiballistic missile program and its support for the military junta that had recently seized power in Greece. On Vietnam, Reuther now saw continuation of the war as incompatible with domestic reform, a clear if unacknowledged switch from his guns-and-butter perspective during the heyday of the Johnson administration. Thus he finally endorsed an antiwar demonstration, the quasi-liberal "moratoriums" of October and November 1969, to which the UAW donated five thousand dollars. Reuther was wary of the inflammatory rhetoric and National Liberation Front flags that now gave so many public protests an "anti-American" coloration, but he was persuaded—by Woodstock, among other phenomena—that there were "revolutionary forces at work among the youth of the world." His daughters Lisa and Linda both took part in the demonstrations, the younger in Washington, the older in San Francisco. So once again Reuther seized upon a rival social movement with envy and calculation. "I think we ought to get in there and take it over," Reuther told his executive board in October 1969; vainly, he hoped to marginalize the radicals and capture for the labor progressives at least some portion of the energy and moral authority flowing out of the peace movement.[25]

The UAW was not about to step into the vanguard of the peace movement, but Reuther did seek to turn his definitive break with Meany and the AFL-CIO into a new opportunity for progressive politics abroad. Despite Moscow's destruction of Prague's "socialism with a human face," the UAW forged ahead with its own version of *Ost Politic*, including extensive contacts with Communist trade unions in Yugoslavia, Romania, Poland, even Czechoslovakia, where the metalworkers' union fought the hard-line regime for many months after the Warsaw Pact invasion. Like Willy Brandt, who would soon assume the chancellorship in Bonn, the Reuther brothers favored détente as a strategy to reduce East-West military tensions, but they also thought that bridges to Eastern Europe, "both psychological and economic," might well accelerate a process of internal reform and nationalist self-assertion. This process seemed most advanced in Yugoslavia, which Walter

Reuther visited in December 1968. Accompanied by Guy Nunn, who had fought with Tito's partisans during the war, Reuther delighted his trade union hosts by the aggressive interest he took in the semiautonomous workers' councils they had organized in many heavy industry workplaces. Plans were laid for more trade union exchanges and a series of UAW-Yugoslav training projects in the developing world.[26]

Such internationalism met with the hearty approval of his social democratic colleagues in the ICFTU, so Reuther expected a sympathetic hearing when the UAW applied for its own membership, independent of the AFL-CIO. Such direct ICFTU affiliation was not without precedent, and more important, Reuther actively supported the work of the international labor body, while Meany made no secret of his contempt for its policies and personnel. However, Reuther had put his European colleagues in "a delicate situation," to use the diplomatic phrase of one embarrassed friend. Meany bitterly opposed Reuther's independent participation in the ICFTU; if the UAW kept its seat, the AFL-CIO, still the largest and wealthiest ICFTU affiliate, was sure to quit. The ICFTU executive board therefore stripped Reuther of his vice presidency in November 1968. Eight months later the Confederation Congress, despite months of hard European lobbying by his brother Victor, refused to reverse the decision. Meany compounded Reuther's humiliation when, in the midst of these transatlantic maneuvers, he announced the suspension of all AFL-CIO relations with the ICFTU, while still managing to exercise an effective veto on Reuther's membership. Reuther called this "blackmail" and feared his erstwhile comrades in the ICFTU were forfeiting their "integrity, autonomy and self-respect."[27]

At home Reuther poured even more of his remarkable energy into a strangely intriguing alliance with the Teamsters Union. Reuther's turn toward this unlikely partner came even before his definitive break with the AFL-CIO, when he finally realized that he could win not the slightest support on the executive council, even from the reformist officers of the Steel Workers or the Machinists, the second- and third-largest unions in the Federation. For a time in the spring of 1968 Reuther had hoped to postpone a final rupture and make the IUD his semiautonomous base of operations, but Meany would have none of that. Thus the USW's I. W. Abel commiserated with Reuther in the privacy of his Pittsburgh office but gave Meany no offense when it came to this bitter feud.

Meanwhile, the Teamsters were looking for respectability. By 1967 Jimmy Hoffa was in Lewisburg Federal Prison, serving an eight-year sentence for jury tampering. As a caretaker for the union, he had handpicked his old sidekick Frank Fitzsimmons, from whom Hoffa expected merely a titular presidency. But Fitzsimmons began to strike out on his own. Within the Teamsters he made himself indispensable by letting the barons who controlled the regional conferences and big locals retake firm control over the pension funds and contract bargaining Hoffa had been so anxious to consolidate in his own hands. Meanwhile, Fitzsimmons raised his personal profile by tacking to the left on many of the big public issues, like civil rights and Vietnam, for which Hoffa had such disdain. Reuther was particularly impressed that Fitzsimmons was the only other important trade union official present at Martin Luther King's funeral in Atlanta.[28]

Thus their Alliance for Labor Action (ALA) was a convenient liaison for the top leadership of both outcast trade unions. Exploratory meetings in the spring of 1968 went extremely well. "Their attitude on all sorts of questions was excellent. It was basic," reported Leonard Woodcock after a session late in June. The Reutherites were particularly pleased that Fitzsimmons had chosen the lone radical on the Teamster executive board, the ex-Socialist Harold Gibbons of St. Louis, to play a leading role within the ALA. Carried away with the program outlined by Gibbons and Reuther, Fitzsimmons enthused, "By God, I predict within six months the AFL-CIO will be coming to us asking how to restructure the American labor movement."[29]

To Reuther, the prospects were indeed intoxicating. "This could be a powerful force for good in American society," he told his executive board, "and would have a profound impact upon the attitude of the American labor movement generally." With a total of more than three and a half million dues payers, the ALA was far larger and richer than the CIO at its founding thirty-three years before. The "ALA links two of the country's most important activist unions, together about one-fourth the size of the AFL-CIO: powerful separately—much more together," *Business Week* observed. Reuther hoped that if the strategically located power of the Teamsters—in interstate trucking and warehousing—were linked to the social vision of the UAW, the combination might just spark the great postwar organizing drive for which he had long sought the magic formula. The new organization would therefore divide its $4.5 million annual income on both union organizing—this was the prime responsibility of the Teamsters—and on community and social action projects, where Reuther's liberalism set the agenda. By the fall of 1969, when the ALA finally got into high gear, almost fifty staffers were put to work in a targeted organizing drive covering the Atlanta region, home of almost half a million nonunion blue-collar workers. The campaign was energetic and intelligent: organizers pounded the college lecture circuit, and telephone inquiries were answered almost immediately with personal visits. "We've never seen more sophisticated techniques," a local management lawyer remarked. But the results were only modest. Although black workers proved most responsive, merely seventy-five hundred new workers had been organized when the campaign ended late in 1971. Reuther had still not found the key to a reborn labor movement.[30]

George Meany did not help. He denounced the "UAW-Teamster combine" in virtually the same language the AFL had once hurled against the CIO of John L. Lewis: the ALA was "a dual organization, rival to the AFL-CIO." Reuther proposed a "universal no-raiding agreement" to signify his virtuous intentions, but Meany was right. As early as July 1968, when the Teamsters and the UAW announced the formation of their joint organization, Reuther had already targeted the progressive unions he wanted to recruit: the American Federation of State, County, and

Municipal Employees, the United Farm Workers, and the American Federation of Teachers (which had all received much financial support from the UAW), ex-Communist unions like the United Electrical Workers, the International Longshoremen's and Warehousemen's Union, Hospital Workers Local 1199, and District 65 of the Retail and Distributive Workers, plus the 85,000-member International Chemical Workers and the even larger Oil, Chemical, and Atomic Workers. Reuther had a spectacular chance to demonstrate his commitment to a union movement revitalized in struggle when on May 10, 1969, he cut short his stay at an International Metalworkers Federation meeting in Copenhagen to fly all night to Charleston, South Carolina. There the Southern Christian Leadership Conference and the largely black and female membership of Local 1199B were in the midst of an epic strike battle against arrogant hospital administrators and the city's white elite. Still groggy from jet lag, Reuther marched with Ralph Abernathy, Andrew Young, and the local firebrand, Mary Moultrie, through streets lined with hundreds of National Guardsmen. For the ALA Reuther contributed ten thousand dollars to Charleston's Hospital Workers local, prompting William Kirchner, the personal representative of George Meany, to show up with a check for twenty-five thousand dollars—which the ALA soon matched. "If the labor movement would only split two more ways, we'll make a profit here," quipped Local 1199's Moe Foner to Andrew Young.[31]

Reuther entered discreet negotiations with the friendly officers of several of these smaller unions, but except for New York City's District 65, where black and Puerto Rican workers wanted to install their own leaders, and the financially hardpressed Chemical Workers, Reuther picked up no new affiliates. Still, the ALA looked very much like a rival federation at its founding conference in Washington late in May 1969. Teamster leaders were more cautious than Reuther, but they were nevertheless willing to sign on to his liberal social agenda, including a new legislative initiative in support of national health insurance and the formation of what Reuther envisioned as "community unions" in Watts, Norfolk, and elsewhere. In addition to Senators George McGovern and Charles Percy, Nixon's labor secretary, George Shultz, felt it politically useful to address the conclave.[32]

Reuther's faith and energy sustained the ALA, so its collapse after his death in 1970 surprised almost no one. The improbable alliance was one of oil and water. Whatever the intentions of Gibbons and Fitzsimmons on the top, the Teamster barons at the local and regional levels were antithetical to almost everything for which the Reutherites stood. In New Jersey, Martin Gerber thought the Teamsters "had no concept of trade unionism." In a meeting with officials from locals controlled by the mobster Anthony Provenzano, Gerber remembered them "leaning back, filing their finger nails," virtually smirking at the UAW social agenda. Likewise, Douglas Fraser thought the ALA a "disaster," which was amply demonstrated in the California lettuce fields when Fitzsimmons could do nothing to prevent Hoffa allies in the Western Conference from signing sweetheart contracts with the growers in July 1970, after which both waged war against Cesar Chavez and his struggling union. The Teamster endorsement of Nixon's reelection in 1972—part of Fitzsimmons's White House deal to keep Hoffa out of the union—seemed merely to confirm that Reuther's ALA had been a "sad mistake."[33]

But Reuther's failure in the last years of his life arose out of far more than a misbegotten alliance with Teamster thuggery. Like the CIO, whose treasury was long sustained by the autocratic leadership of the Mineworkers, the ALA might have had a chance had it been able to capture even a slice of the social energy erupting out of the body politic at the very moment of its birth. Reuther was desperate to do so, but by 1969 he was his own prisoner, entrapped within a set of institutions that cut him off from the movement-building forces all about him. As they privately conceded, the Reutherites themselves were devoid of the young cadre "with stars in their eyes." Thus, when it came to the distribution of its two and a half million dollars, Reuther's Community and Social Action Division of the ALA functioned like a philanthropic committee. Many worthwhile grants supported job training and community action, but these projects held no organic link to the unions and differed little from programs funded by the Ford Foundation. Indeed, the methodology proved so compatible that the billion-dollar foundation agreed to take over the complete funding of Reuther's Citizen's Crusade against Poverty when the UAW spun it off early in 1969.[34]

The UAW was not a foundation, however. The radical cadre Reuther sought were already present in UAW-organized shops, but he found their politics alien and divisive. The black militancy that flared so brightly at the end of the 1960s was part of a transatlantic surge that challenged workplace hierarchies in France, Italy, Great Britain, Quebec, and Poland. In the United States this insurgency emerged out of the demographic revolution that had transformed the auto industry's urban factories. By 1970 blacks comprised almost one-quarter of all autoworkers in the Detroit region; on many assembly operations they constituted an outright majority. At the aging Dodge Main complex, for example, the final assembly plant was 60 percent black in 1970, and in the body shop and trim department the number was even higher. A new color line therefore split the industry: virtually all foremen at Chrysler and General Motors were white, often older ethnics who had finally made the leap to supervision after decades on the line, while in Detroit's big UAW locals, including Dodge Local 3, Chrysler Local 7, Ford Local 600, and Chevy Gear and Axle Local 235, black unionists were still without real power. Thus during the 1967 riot no UAW officer thought it odd when hundreds of National Guardsmen used the halls of Locals 3 and 7 as their temporary headquarters.[35]

Reuther saw the birth of the Dodge Revolutionary Union Movement (DRUM) as a nationalist threat to UAW unity that had to be suppressed where it could not be co-opted. DRUM's inflammatory rhetoric replicated the nationalist bravado so common in the late 1960s, but its industrial militancy targeted shop issues virtually identical to those that had animated UAW radicals from one generation to the next. The auto corporations had used the dip in the economy in 1967 as a chance to tighten up on production standards, so low-seniority workers—virtually all black—felt the brunt of the new speedup. Indeed, DRUM had its origins in April 1968 when Chrysler fired more black workers than white in the aftermath of a speedup strike instigated by a group of older Polish women. Black militants then captured the national spotlight when a "community" picket line in July crippled Dodge Main production for two days; three months later widespread support for DRUM among black workers seemed to be confirmed when Ron March, one of its leading militants, finished first among twenty-seven candidates in a preliminary election for Local 3 trustee.

DRUM and its several factory offshoots—including FRUM (Ford Revolutionary Union Movement), ELRUM (Eldon, Chrysler's gear and axle plant), and JARUM (Jefferson Avenue)—remained a self-conscious vanguard in which working-class students from Wayne State University played a leading role. They embraced a racially charged Marxist-Leninism, sometimes informed by the anti-imperialist idiom of the Caribbean Trotskyist C. L. R. James. But whatever their politics, DRUM's founding cohort constituted the same species of ideologically motivated cadre who had animated the UAW in its heroic youth. However, in 1968 and 1969 these young radicals faced a dual enemy. They attacked the auto capitalists as "the main adversary" but reserved their sharpest invective for "the racist, tyrannical and unrepresentative UAW." DRUM denounced Local 3 officials as "Polish pigs" and demanded that blacks take half the seats on the UAW executive board. To raise funds, DRUM raffled off an M-1 rifle. "Behead the Redhead," screamed one of their leaflets.[36]

This nationalist militancy sent the union's Detroit leadership into a frenzy of opposition. Many regional officials now routinely packed guns. Though the DRUM phenomenon had less support within the shops than many of the other anti-Reuther insurgencies, it struck an ideological chord that resonated across the larger black community, where the Black Panther Party and community control politics had undermined liberal integrationism. Reuther was appalled: "You have no moral right to destroy something unless you're fighting to put something better in its place," he told radical students on his campus visits. The UAW therefore responded with a full-bore countermobilization. Reuther thought DRUM a "terrorist" group, and in an *Administrative Letter* sent to 350,000 Detroit-area unionists in March 1969, the UAW labeled the Revolutionary Union Movement an organization of "extremists . . . whose goals are the complete separation of races in the shop and the destruction of our Union through the tactics of violence, fear and intimidation." Tipping its hand to the corporations, the UAW announced that it would not protect workers who struck "with the conscious purpose of dividing our union along racial lines."[37]

DRUM was beaten within the year. Chrysler and other corporations with inner-city factories took a hard line against the militants, while simultaneously rushing hundreds of blacks into supervisory jobs. Likewise, UAW staffers broke the picket lines of DRUM-instigated wildcat strikes and mobilized the white retiree vote against the black radicals, even as top officers like Douglas Fraser, now head of the

Chrysler Department, encouraged blacks loyal to Solidarity House to take power from the generation of Polish and Italian unionists who controlled the big production locals and the regional directorships in Detroit. Faced with a choice between DRUM's racial nihilism and the UAW's stolid reformism, most African-American workers plunked for the tried and true. By August 1969 Reuther thought the threat had "tapered off to the point where it's very unimportant."[38]

DRUM nevertheless left a troubling legacy. By the difficult standards of 1969, neither Reuther nor his principal collaborators were racist, but with the UAW's structural incapacity to accommodate the new wave of shop activism, militancy quickly turned to cynicism. At the very moment Reuther sought to revitalize the labor movement and champion the insurgencies sweeping America, he faced the scorn of a newly politicized generation. "Put Walter in a halter," they chanted. Vainly did Reuther assert himself in a "state of continuous revolt against the status quo ... the Establishment," but his widely reported appearances at each flash point of the civil rights battlefront had "not fooled black workers," charged the African-American Marxist Charles Denby. "When they see him marching on a picket line in Charleston or Selma ... they know that he hasn't been on a picket line with his own UAW workers for so many years he's forgotten what it's like." This charge was factually inaccurate, but it contained a mythic truth that was devastating in New Left circles, both white and black.[39]

Approaching the 1970 round of contract negotiations, Reuther also faced a seismic shift in the economics of the automobile industry. He still declared the Big Three a "golden goose" of "fantastic" profitability, but the great automotive boom of the postwar years was growing stale. To curb inflation, the Nixon administration had programmed a recession—it would turn into "stagflation"—that generated layoffs and short workweeks from Flint to Framingham. Meanwhile, German and Japanese imports were rising sharply, on their way to 20 percent of the U.S. market. Most ominously of all, the productivity of American automobile factories had taken a sudden plunge, from an annual average of 3.5 percent during the first two postwar decades to little more than 1 percent in the years after 1967. The corporations blamed the new breed of younger, blacker workers, as well as the UAW for its failure to keep them in line. GM managers observed an alarming increase in "tardiness, loitering, failure to follow instructions, and abuse of employee facilities." Grievance filings jumped 50 percent per employee in the late 1960s, while time lost to strikes shot up more than threefold over the start of the decade. In truth, the great productivity slowdown of this era remains something of a mystery, for the revival of a rights-conscious militancy within the working class explains but a fraction of the problem. Reuther agreed that absenteeism rates were "shocking," but he remained convinced that productivity was chiefly a function of capacity utilization—Fordism at full throttle—combined with a renewed investment in technology and a more cooperative management attitude.[40]

On April 20, 1970, when Reuther gaveled open his last UAW convention, he faced both a fractious membership and a tough bargaining season. The union

political pot was on high boil. In five regions candidates of the administration caucus confronted serious challenges, and in Ohio an insurgent actually defeated a
Reutherite executive board member. Reuther himself faced an articulate, ideologically driven opposition—largely Trotskyist and skilled-trades—that made him
endure his first presidential roll call vote in twenty-one years. He trounced it easily, but Reuther's days were numbered. He was sixty-two years old, just four years
away from mandatory retirement. He was growing bored with the rituals of collective bargaining and frustrated with his political marginalization under the
Nixon administration. Increasingly Reuther saw himself as an "educator" of the
next generation of unionists. During the previous year he had poured his energy
and intellect into building the UAW's family education center at Black Lake in
northern Michigan. After retirement, he wanted to preside there, or perhaps get a
position on a campus, "teaching or something."[41]

At the podium Reuther remained near the top of his form. The well-worn phrasing of his zealous, evangelistic keynote address bored the working press, but it still
brought more than three thousand delegates to their feet time and again. And
Reuther easily finessed his critics. "One should encourage enough opposition to
make it interesting but not enough to make it dangerous," he wrote an admirer.
"My opposition at the Convention met neither of these standards." Reuther admitted that he had made a mistake in 1967 in permitting the Big Three to cap their
COLA costs, but he stole leftist thunder by vowing to inflation-proof UAW paychecks once again, while accommodating the insistent rank-and-file demand for
an early pension ("30 and out"). Reuther would therefore have to go for a big monetary settlement, and that meant taking on General Motors. To demonstrate its
seriousness, the UAW had amassed a strike fund that would soon hit $120 million;
for the first time in twenty-four years it looked as if Reuther would again test his
leadership in a strike at the world's largest corporation.[42]

Reuther would face that battle in the fall. In the meantime, his preoccupation
with the planning and construction of the UAW education center on the wooded
shores of Black Lake, 260 miles north of Detroit, had become a consuming passion. For years Reuther had considered the UAW summer camp at Port Huron little more than a "recreational slum"; in its place the union needed one or more
year-round education and recreation centers, modeled after Swedish labor's network of training facilities and vacation hostels. Black Lake, a summer refuge for
the Detroit elite, was just the place. Reuther saw the project as a key to the reinte-
gration of the union with its increasingly young, increasingly disaffected membership. Here the UAW would offer shop leaders a dose of Reutherite social unionism, as well as a first-class family vacation. Black Lake would train a new
generation to "keep the stars burning brightly in the eyes of the UAW for years
ahead."[43]

As usual, Reuther chose Oskar Stonorov as architect. His elegant design preserved the natural contours of the site's one thousand acres with a stunning set of
Scandinavian buildings in Douglas fir, Wisconsin stone, glass, and teak. But few

on the UAW executive board shared Reuther's enthusiasm for Black Lake. It was remote even from Detroit, and its cost soon spiraled out of control, to more than twenty million dollars, four times the original estimate. But this was Reuther's indulgence, his monument, his fantasy. Flying there on the UAW's leased Lear jet, he visited Black Lake at least a dozen times in 1969 and 1970. Fastidiously Reuther pored over the blueprints, busied himself with construction details, and tangled with the fractious building trades. By the spring of 1970, when he proudly showed it off to visiting unionists, Reuther declared Black Lake "a thing of beauty where man and nature can live in harmony." His ecological consciousness was genuine. Since the late 1950s he had been a nuclear power skeptic; in Rochester he organized his Paint Creek neighbors to stop the county's efforts to run a sewer line through the bubbling watercourse; he spoke at Earth Day meetings that April; and he began planning for an international conference of ecologists to meet at Black Lake in the summer.[44]

The last ten days of Reuther's life were tumultuous for the nation. On April 30, Richard Nixon announced a massive expansion of the Vietnam War into neighboring Cambodia. The campuses exploded in a wave of protest, which turned into a kind of general student strike after National Guardsmen shot into a crowd at Kent State University, killing four. Watching the evening news that Monday, May 4, Reuther flew into a rage, left the dinner table, and called Victor. Over the next two days they drafted a telegram to the president that denounced the "needless and inexcusable use of military force" at home and the expansion of the war as "a moral defeat beyond measure among the people of the world." Two more students were killed at Jackson State in Mississippi by the time the UAW wired Reuther's message to the White House on Thursday, May 7. The next day the country's polarization deepened as hundreds of helmeted construction workers assaulted antiwar demonstrators in New York City's financial district.[45]

Reuther was sickened by the attack; still, the weekend would be more pleasant. He arose early Saturday morning to plant trees for his Japanese garden overlooking Paint Creek. Late that afternoon he drove with May to the Detroit Metro Airport for a flight to the Pelston airstrip near Black Lake. There Oskar Stonorov and he would make an inspection before the center's dedication in June. "Just a short trip to check last-minute details," he told Lisa. Stonorov's flight from Philadelphia arrived late, so the twin-engine Lear jet did not lift off until 8:44 P.M. On board were May, Walter, Stonorov, and William Wolfman, Reuther's nephew and bodyguard. As the jet approached the small airport in darkness, low clouds, and drizzle, the otherwise experienced pilots undershot their glide path, probably because of a faulty altimeter. At 9:33 P.M. the jet slammed into a stand of trees, sheered off both wings, and burst into a huge fireball. No one escaped from the flaming wreckage, which burned the bodies of May and Walter beyond recognition.[46]

Reuther's death was front-page news. At his memorial service on May 13, thirty-four hundred jammed into Detroit's Ford auditorium, thirty thousand autoworkers remained away from work, and the big automakers silenced their assembly lines for three costly minutes. Condolences came in from both left and right: from Richard Nixon, from GM's James Roche, as well as from old friends like Willy Brandt, Harold Wilson, Golda Meir, Cesar Chavez, and Senators Philip Hart and Edward Kennedy. Even his enemies, in the Soviet trade union apparat and on the AFL-CIO executive council, recognized that Reuther's death required a moment of reflection. For two days thousands of workers, stopping by before or after their shift, filed silently past the oak caskets of May and Walter. Reuther was eulogized, as he would have wished, for his social vision and broad humanitarianism as well as for his effective trade unionism.[47] *Business Week* called him labor's "most potent personification of socially-oriented unionism," and in a long obituary the *New York Times* summed up Reuther as "a crusader for a better world." Coretta Scott King remembered him as "the most respected white labor leader in the nation," because "he was there when the storm clouds were thick." To the United Farm Workers, Reuther was a "man who thirsted for justice and freedom"; to Henry Ford II, "a central figure in the development of modern industrial history." Irving Bluestone, Reuther's closest friend at the time of his death, praised him as a man of "human dignity and human brotherhood" who had "practical goals to be achieved, dreams to be made real. . . . He never wavered, never faltered in this faith."[48]

Many commented that Reuther's death deprived liberalism of yet another powerful tribune; few could guess how closely his passing would coincide with the end of American capitalism's long postwar boom. Reuther's self-confident engagement with all the world's problems remained his greatest virtue. "You can't opt out of life," he reflected late in 1968. "You've got to make up your mind whether you're willing to accept things as they are, or whether you're willing to try to change them.

"Well I believe in the things I believe; and so if that means you have to get pushed around and roughed up and even maybe have your life taken away, that's the price one has to be willing to pay . . . if you believe. And I believe! It's that simple. I don't have to debate myself on this. It's a very simple thing with me. I just believe, and I do what I believe."[49]

Epilogue
"WHAT WOULD WALTER DO?"

In the quarter-century since the death of Walter Reuther, the fortunes of the American trade union movement have fallen more sharply and more continuously than at any time since late in the nineteenth century. The proportion of wage earners enrolled in organizations that claim to bargain for their members has declined from 30 percent to less than 17 percent, and in the Rust Belt industries where the CIO once claimed supremacy, a wave of layoffs, plant closures, and outright deunionizations has stripped millions of workers from labor's roll. The UAW lost six hundred thousand in the years after 1979, and like many other trade unions, it negotiated a series of concessionary labor contracts that actually reduced wages and benefits to its members and the millions more whose incomes were linked with the union sector. For the vast majority of Americans, real wages have been flat and good jobs hard to find during the last two decades.[1]

In these difficult times, veteran autoworkers have been wont to ask, "What would Walter do?" His soul cannot be queried, but the complex and powerful legacy of his leadership remains a tangible presence not only within the UAW's high councils but for all who see the labor movement, as Reuther did, as an essential lever with which to reshape society. For a dozen years after his death, top UAW leaders were men who had worked with Reuther on the most intimate terms; thereafter, the new generation who took command were quick to proclaim themselves part of the Reuther tradition.[2]

The UAW executive board elevated Leonard Woodcock, Reuther's old SP comrade, to the union presidency in May 1970. The vote was close, thirteen to twelve, for it was an open secret around Solidarity House that Reuther had tapped Douglas Fraser, the popular vice president, as heir apparent. But now Woodcock had his unexpected chance. He was often cold and remote, but his leadership was Reutherite to a fault. Like his predecessor, Woodcock consolidated his presidency by conducting a long strike at General Motors, during which he won back the COLA protection Reuther had sacrificed in 1967. Although Woodcock was as much an advocate of industrial self-discipline as Reuther, he let the auto companies know that the UAW could still fight. He authorized a celebrated speedup strike by youthful militants in GM's state-of-the-art Lordstown, Ohio, assembly plant in 1972, then backed Irving Bluestone, the new GM director, when he coordinated a series of short but crippling stoppages that convinced the giant automaker to abandon efforts to build a union-free set of southern supplier plants. Meanwhile, the UAW refurbished its reputation for political liberalism by mobilizing its resources on behalf of George McGovern during the same campaign season when George Meany bludgeoned the AFL-CIO into a hawkish "neutrality."[3]

But the years of Woodcock's tenure, which ended in 1977, now seem like an Indian summer that ended abruptly in a series of fierce winter storms. Until 1979 UAW membership rolls stood near their all-time high, 1.6 million, while each new collective bargaining contract was marginally better than the last. But the economic foundations upon which the Treaty of Detroit had been built were ready to crumble. During the 1970s cheap, low-mileage Japanese cars won one-quarter of the American market at the very moment when the two "oil shocks" of that decade rendered obsolete much of the U.S. industrial plant, thereby making it impossible for manufacturers to reverse the productivity decline begun in the late 1960s. Meanwhile, the rise of worldwide economic competition had its domestic counterpart in the growth of manufacturing by low-wage, nonunion labor in Alabama, Tennessee, and other Sun Belt states.[4]

When Chrysler almost went bankrupt in 1979, Douglas Fraser, then the UAW president, deployed the rhetoric of Reuther's World War II "equality of sacrifice" campaign to convince skeptical autoworkers that the survival of the company depended on UAW agreement to a new labor contract that cut wages and benefits well below those of its competitors. In return for a loan guarantee, the Carter administration scrutinized every move by Chrysler management, and the company even put the UAW's Fraser on its board of directors. But if this auto bargain temporarily breached management's well-guarded "prerogatives," it also generated a wave of "concession" bargaining, even among profitable companies. In the ensuing scramble the Treaty of Detroit collapsed as individual firms abandoned pattern bargaining, cost-of-living protection, and employment security. Soon managers in trucking, airlines, mining, meatpacking, steel, rubber, municipal government, and retail trade discovered the virtues of an aggressive attack on their unions and their labor costs. To millions of workers, trade unionism became a synonym for wage reductions, plant closures, and lost strikes. By the 1990s the UAW found that it could not organize the new Japanese and German transplants, shut down big firms like Caterpillar, or halt the deunionization of almost the entire auto parts sector.[5]

It is easy to blame the rise of a world market in goods and services for this debacle, but market pressures alone were insufficient to generate the collapse of union strength and the stagnation in living standards so characteristic of the years after 1979. The same competitive conditions were felt in all the industrialized democracies, but in most countries union movements weathered the storm with far less damage than in the United States. In Germany, Canada, and Sweden conservative governments often nipped at the welfare state, but after two full decades of heightened competition, real wages remained intact and the trade unions potent. Reuther was right to admire German social democracy and the "active labor policy" sustained by Swedish corporatism, for these institutions shielded wage earners and promoted industrial productivity far better than did the ad hoc and tattered system in the United States.

Canada offers a nearby case in point. Because of the unified character of the North American auto industry, Reuther had always thought autoworkers in the UAW's Canadian region would naturally follow in the wake of his big Detroit-based union. In 1965, when Reuther helped President Lyndon Johnson push the free-trade "auto pact" though Congress, he expected the fate of these two sections of the union to grow even more alike. But over the next thirty years a growing political divergence generated two union movements with quite dissimilar outlooks. Although Canada has often had higher unemployment than the United States, a legal environment less hostile to labor, a higher social wage, and an independent party of labor and the left have created conditions that have enabled UAW membership there to double, tracking the twofold rise in union density for the working population as a whole. Thus the Canadian UAW successfully resisted corporate demands for wage concessions early in the 1980s, leading to the region's 1984 secession from the International.[6]

Unions are weak in the United States because of a larger fragmentation in the character of American liberalism. In almost every one of his speeches, Reuther warned that "labor must make what progress it can with the community and not at the expense of the community." This was an echo of his Socialist youth, when leftists of all persuasions saw the trade unions as the vanguard of social reconstruction. He advanced this argument most forcefully during the 1945–46 General Motors strike when he sought not only to buttress his case for a big wage increase but to deflect the potential anger of middle-class consumers who would blame big labor for postwar inflation. But half a century later trade unionism's greatest danger comes from an explosive division within the working population itself. As unionized labor has become but an island of well-being in a sea of resentful, low-wage aspirants, income inequality within the working class has reached levels unseen for more than two generations. It is not surprising therefore that one employer after another has opted for a policy of radical deunionization and brutal wage reductions. When Caterpillar took on the UAW in the early 1990s, managers found that years of deindustrialization and wage stagnation had generated a huge reservoir of eager "replacement workers" whose residual commitment to their working-class neighbors had long since been extinguished in their desperate scramble to hold on to their houses, cars, and dignity.[7]

Reuther became a prisoner of the institutions he did so much to build. In seeking to link collective bargaining to the interests of the larger community, Reuther was battling against an entire structure of industrial relations law and praxis. The Wagner Act itself was premised upon the idea that higher wages and industrial democracy could flow from agreements worked out between workers and managers at a single firm or work site. Reuther knew that an effective program had to encompass a far larger slice of the economy; the working class had to advance together or not at all. But as the UAW itself cut deals with marginal companies, Reuther realized that only a larger government-structured arrangement could avoid the debilitating inequities that were bound to arise through the normal give-and-take of collective bargaining. In the mid-1940s and the early 1960s he probed these possibilities, but when it came to the crunch, Reuther commanded neither the power nor the will to generate a political crisis of sufficient impact to break with the insular bargaining patterns championed by state and industry.

A realignment of American politics offered the only way out. Until the last few years of his life Reuther knew that the Democrats were a poor substitute for the kind of political party that could speak for labor and the liberals. Reuther had three chances to give his politics a more forceful expression: in 1937, 1948, and 1964. In the municipal elections of prewar Detroit, victory eluded the CIO because of the deep political and racial antagonisms that still divided the working population; after World War II the unions were never stronger, but the cold war and the Reutherite assault upon the Communists foreclosed an independent initiative when it offered the greatest advantage; and in 1964 liberalism had its moment of glory, but by then Reuther had wedded himself to Lyndon Johnson, subordinating both a breakthrough at General Motors and a realignment of the Democrats to LBJ's presidential agenda. By 1967 and 1968, when Reuther had one last chance to make the UAW's weight felt on the left side of the political equation, his fixation with the gamesmanship of auto industry bargaining blinded him to the stakes that had been raised by Lyndon Johnson's commitment in the Vietnam War.

But even if Reuther had been attuned to these possibilities, the racial polarization that began in the late 1960s was eroding the electoral constituency that for more than a generation had given his voice potent amplification. The greatest difficulty facing progressive America has been its failure to find the strategy that can bridge the gap between white and black. Industrial unions themselves flourished only during that middle third of the century when the fortunes of the movement for workers' rights and civil rights were linked in progressive and fruitful synthesis. Reuther's understanding of this linkage had many limitations, but he never doubted that it was an absolute precondition to the advance of his agenda. As it turned out, his death coincided almost precisely with the moment at which American liberalism lost the natural allegiance of the white working class. Although the UAW had turned back George Wallace's northern invasion in 1968, the Alabamian's social politics took hold with a vengeance in the American body politic. In white working-class Macomb County, just north of Detroit, opposition to school busing and neighborhood integration transformed a classically liberal, Democratic bastion into one of the North's more reliably Republican districts.

Had Reuther's postwar planning initiatives made it onto the social agenda, Detroit and other industrial cities might have forestalled the wave of plant closures and relocations that turned them into urban Bantustans. And if the economic chasm between the city and its white suburbs had been smaller, so too might the racial polarization have been muted as well. Indeed, the Reagan Democrats of the 1980s were not themselves hostile to trade unionism, public education, social security, or many of the other transfer payments that constitute the modern American welfare state. But the racialization of their vote in counties like Macomb put into place a new governing order that, at best, was indifferent to all the liberal institutions and policies that had once sustained the incomes of working families. The politicians who pandered to suburban racial fears did little to defend the livelihoods of these same constituents when they faced a wave of economic insecurity in the 1980s and 1990s.[8]

No matter how farsighted the men and women of Reuther's generation, their capacity to thwart American racism, limit the impact of the world market, and fight the corporations was always constrained by time and circumstance. But Reuther and his heirs did have the freedom to define the very meaning of the trade unionism they preached. And this is a part of Reuther's legacy that has become enormously contentious. During most of Reuther's life American managers emphasized hierarchy, obedience, and the precise division of labor within their workplaces. They drew a hard line between the prerogatives of management and the responsibilities of labor, between the authority of the foremen and the rights of their subordinates. But managerial rhetoric has transformed itself dramatically in the last dozen years. Faced with lagging productivity, the competitive challenge from Japan, and the need for a more "flexible" work environment, American managers now offer workers "quality circles," "employee involvement," "teamwork," and a "nonadversarial relationship." As a General Motors advertisement of the late 1980s asserted, the corporation wants to correct the "great flaw in the assembly line concept [that] tends to exclude the creative and managerial skills of the people who work on the line." No longer would its plants employ workers and bosses, just "associates" and "advisers."[9]

Most of Reuther's heirs within the UAW leadership welcomed this management initiative. At General Motors' new Saturn factory in Spring Hill, Tennessee, a joint union-management committee rewrote the entire labor contract, substituting for the hallowed management rights clause a commitment to a "consensus decision-making process." Instead of committee men and women, industrial relations at this flagship factory would now be conducted on labor's behalf by a set of "team leaders" whose "cooperative problem-solving relationship" with management was predicated upon a "Saturn culture" that guaranteed salaried jobs for at least 80 percent of the workforce. Irving Bluestone, Douglas Fraser, and other UAW elders thought the Saturn experiment a progressive fulfillment of Walter Reuther's vision: because "the union plays a key role in all aspects of the decision-making process," Saturn was "a milestone in the advance of the UAW toward industrial democracy." The UAW's regional director in California gushed over a similar "jointness" program in his state: "The workers revolution has finally come to the shop floor. The people who work on the assembly line have taken control and have the power to make management do their jobs right."[10]

This Panglossian interpretation of the new industrial relations soon faced much dissent, and from an unexpected source. Victor Reuther had resigned from the UAW International Affairs Department in 1972 to write his memoirs. During the next decade he offered no objection to the strategy followed by UAW leaders, even backing the union during the difficult years of concession bargaining in the early 1980s. But Victor Reuther found the Saturn contract a rebuke to everything for which he thought his brother Walter had stood. The eclipse of the union system of shop representation, along with the abolition of most work rules, deprived workers of the ability to resist a new and subtle form of speedup. "Team production" schemes were but a return to the preunion days in which straw bosses mercilessly drove their workmates to ever-higher levels of production. Most important, Victor, and the sizable slice of labor opinion for which he spoke, objected to the whole philosophy of "jointness" and the "enterprise unionism" upon which it is predicated. "I wonder how many people who helped organize the UAW in the thirties would be called team players?" he asked shortly after the Saturn project was announced. "Walter would be spinning in his grave," Victor later asserted, "at the thought of the UAW supporting a corporate agenda based on competitiveness and all that."[11]

Victor charged that the Saturn contract, along with the UAW's entire approach to the new management strategy, had not been democratically debated. He allied himself with a new UAW insurgency that was attacking concession bargaining and "jointness" projects while mounting campaigns for regional director and the UAW presidency itself. This challenge reached its height in the early 1990s, but UAW officers easily turned it back, often with the same organizational tools so well forged by Walter Reuther during his long tenure at the UAW helm.[12]

But Victor Reuther's claim that his brother would have resisted the new industrial relations could not be dismissed so easily. From his earliest days as president of Local 174, Reuther emphasized that a sense of justice and solidarity underlies the very essence of the union idea. If this is lost, a trade union's entire raison d'être vanishes with it. Of this he was certain: between management and labor, between first-line supervisors and their crew, tension and conflict inevitably arise out of the very nature of ownership and authority in the modern enterprise. Walter Reuther's actual record fighting speedup issues was always a mixed one, as his opponents in Flint and Dearborn never let him forget. But when it came to the very purpose of trade unionism, Reuther's voice was clear. "Experience has shown that there is no end to the variety and ingenuity of the methods management invents . . . to quicken the work pace at the expense of the workers' health and safety," read a UAW resolution of the 1950s. The union's job, first and foremost, was "eternal vigilance and militant resistance." Whatever the union's other projects, Reuther asserted toward the end of his life, the worker "has every right to say, 'Damn it, my union has to do something about that problem I've got; and I've got it right now, today—not tomorrow, right now.'"[13]

NOTES

CHAPTER 1: FATHER AND SONS

1. *Wheeling [W.V.] Daily Intelligencer*, December 10, 1903, quoted in Paul Douglass, "The Reuther Family and the Rewarding Society, 1972," file 20, box 68, Victor G. Reuther Collection (hereafter cited as VGR Collection).

2. *Daily Intelligencer*, December 24, 1903, quoted in Victor G. Reuther, *The Brothers Reuther and the Story of the UAW* (Boston: Houghton Mifflin, 1976), 25.

3. David T. Javersak, "One Place on This Great Green Planet Where Andrew Carnegie Can't Get a Monument to His Money," *West Virginia History* 44 (1981): 15–17.

4. See, for example, Leon Fink, *Workingmen's Democracy: The Knights of Labor and American Politics* (Urbana: University of Illinois Press, 1983); Nick Salvatore, *Eugene V. Debs: Citizen and Socialist* (Urbana: University of Illinois Press, 1984); Roy Rosenzweig, *Eight Hours for What We Will: Workers and Leisure in an Industrial City* (New York: Cambridge University Press, 1983).

5. Javersak, "One Place on This Great Green Planet," 19.

6. Douglass, "Reuther Family," 11.

7. The world of steelworkers and steel masters is discussed in two classic works: David Brody, *Steelworkers in America: The Non-Union Era* (New York: Harper & Row, 1960); and David Montgomery, *The Fall of the House of Labor: The Workplace, the State, and American Labor Activism, 1865–1925* (New York: Cambridge University Press, 1987).

8. Reuther, *Brothers Reuther*, 12–14; see also Dorothee Schneider, *Trade Unions and Community: The German Working Class in New York City, 1870–1900* (Urbana: University of Illinois Press, 1994), 130–36, 172–76, 207–17; John Laslett, *Labor and the Left: A Study of Socialist and Radical Influences in the American Labor Movement, 1889–1924* (New York: Basic Books, 1970), 32–43.

9. Hartmut Keil, "German Working-class Radicalism in the United States from the 1870s to World War I," in *"Struggle a Hard Battle": Essays on Working-Class Immigrants*, ed. Dirk Hoerder (DeKalb: Northern Illinois University Press, 1986), 71–94; Salvatore, *Debs*, 222–26; Irving Howe, *Socialism and America* (San Diego: Harcourt

Brace Jovanovich, 1985), 30–45; James Weinstein, *The Decline of Socialism in America, 1912–1925* (New York: Monthly Review Press, 1967).

10. Frederick A. Barkey, "The Socialist Party in West Virginia from 1898 to 1920: A Study in Working-class Radicalism" (Ph.D. diss., University of Pittsburgh, 1971), 24–31.

11. Dirk Hoerder, "German Immigrant Workers' Views of 'America' in the 1880s," and Hartmut Keil, "An Ambivalent Identity: The Attitude of German Socialist Immigrants toward American Political Institutions and American Citizenship," both in Marianne Dubouzy, ed., *In the Shadow of the Statue of Liberty: Immigrants, Workers, and Citizens in the American Republic, 1880–1920* (Paris: Presses Universitaires de Vincennes, 1988), 17–33, 247–63 (the quote from the *Sozialdemokrat* of 1881 is on p. 22).

12. Reuther, *Brothers Reuther*, 17–18; Valentine Reuther, interview with VGR, Wheeling, W.V., January 11, 1963, file 3, box 17, VGR Collection.

13. Salvatore, *Debs*, 256–57; Barkey, "Socialist Party in West Virginia," 150.

14. Christine Richey, interview with the author, Reading, Mass., July 18, 1993; Elisabeth Logan Davis, *Mothers of America: The Lasting Influence of the Christian Home* (Westwood, N.J.: Fleming H. Revell Co., 1954), 145–54.

15. Reuther, *Brothers Reuther*, 36–37; Marie Tyler McGraw, interview with the author, Charlottesville, Va., December 1, 1992.

16. Salvatore, *Debs*, 291–302, 308; Reuther, *Brothers Reuther*, 21.

17. Reuther, *Brothers Reuther*, 27–28; Laslett, *Labor and the Left*, 32–43.

18. McGraw, interview with the author; Reuther, *Brothers Reuther*, 22–23; Barkey, "Socialist Party in West Virginia," 200–202.

19. Barkey, "Socialist Party in West Virginia," 224–35; Melvyn Dubofsky and Warren Van Tine, *John L. Lewis: A Biography* (New York: Quadrangle, 1977); Socialist Party report, file 13, box 14, Herman Wolf Collection.

20. Douglass, "Reuther Family," 16; Jean Gould and Lorena Hickok, *Walter Reuther: Labor's Rugged Individualist* (New York: Dodd, Mead and Co., 1972), 51; Reuther, *Brothers Reuther*, 64.

21. Reuther, *Brothers Reuther*, 38–40.

22. Robert Ihlenfeld, telephone interview with the author, July 2, 1986; Richey, interview with the author; WPR quoted in Fred J. Cook, *Walter Reuther* (Chicago: Encyclopedia Britannica Press, 1963), 24.

23. Cook, *Walter Reuther*, 22.

24. Richey, interview with the author; Cook, *Walter Reuther*, 21–23.

25. VGR, interview with Harry J. Grubler, Wheeling, W.V., November 10, 1972, file 6, box 2, VGR Collection.

26. VGR, interview with Grubler; Cook, *Reuther*, 30.

27. VGR, interview with Leo Hores, Elmgrove, W.V., November 10, 1972, file 7, box 2, VGR Collection.

28. Cook, *Reuther*, 30–33.

CHAPTER 2: LIFE AT THE ROUGE

1. Quoted in Mary Jane Jacob, *The Rouge: The Image of Industry in the Art of Charles Sheeler and Diego Rivera* (Detroit: Detroit Institute of the Arts, 1978), 14.

2. Stephen Meyer, "The Persistence of Fordism: Workers and Technology in the American Automobile Industry, 1900–1960," in *On the Line: Essays in the History of Auto Work*, ed. Nelson Lichtenstein and Stephen Meyer (Urbana: University of Illinois Press, 1989), 73–99; Steve Babson, "Class, Craft, and Culture: Tool and Die Makers

and the Organization of the UAW," *Michigan Historical Review* 14 (Spring 1988): 33–55.

3. Frank Cormier and William J. Eaton, *Reuther* (Englewood Cliffs, N.J.: Prentice-Hall, 1970), 11; VGR, interview with Leo Hores, Elmgrove, W.V., November 10, 1972, file 7, box 2, VGR Collection.

4. WPR, interview with Frank Cormier and William J. Eaton, Detroit, July 1, 1968, Frank Cormier and William J. Eaton Collection, John F. Kennedy Library.

5. Fred J. Cook, *Walter Reuther* (Chicago: Encyclopedia Britannica Press, 1963), 35; Allan Nevins, *Ford: Expansion and Challenge, 1915–1933* (New York: Charles Scribner's Sons, 1957), 455–56; VGR, interview with Hores. Leo Hores returned to Wheeling shortly thereafter.

6. Donald Finlay Davis, *Conspicuous Production: Automobiles and Elites in Detroit, 1899–1933* (Philadelphia: Temple University Press, 1988), 206–14; David Hounshell, *From the American System to Mass Production, 1800–1932: The Development of Manufacturing Technology in the United States* (Baltimore: Johns Hopkins University Press, 1984), 284–89. See also David L. Lewis and Laurence Goldstein, eds., *The Automobile and American Culture* (Ann Arbor: University of Michigan Press, 1983).

7. Stephen Meyer, *The Five Dollar Day: Labor Management and Social Control in the Ford Motor Company, 1908–1921* (Albany: State University of New York Press, 1981), 9–36; William J. Abernathy, *The Productivity Dilemma: Roadblock to Innovation in the Automobile Industry* (Baltimore: Johns Hopkins University Press, 1978), 3–9; Meyer, "Persistence of Fordism," 78–83.

8. As quoted in Hounshell, *American System to Mass Production*, 288.

9. Ibid., 286–87. For a world-historical critique of the mass-production model, see Michael Piore and Charles Sabel, *The Second Industrial Divide: Possibilities for Prosperity* (New York: Basic Books, 1984).

10. Victor G. Reuther, *The Brothers Reuther and the Story of the UAW* (Boston: Houghton Mifflin, 1976), 46; WPR, interview with Cormier and Eaton.

11. WPR, interview with Cormier and Eaton.

12. Reuther, *Brothers Reuther*, 47–48.

13. Nevins, *Ford: Expansion and Challenge*, 288, 200–216; Jacob, *The Rouge: The Image of Industry*, 7–10.

14. "Walter P. Reuther," Ford Motor Company personnel records, Ford Industrial Archive, Redmond, Mich.; Reuther, *Brothers Reuther*, 67; Frank X. Braun, interview with the author, Ann Arbor, Mich., June 25, 1987; Sorenson quoted in Hounshell, *American System to Mass Production*, 290.

15. Steve Babson, *Skilled Workers and Anglo-Gaelic Immigrants in the Rise of the UAW* (New Brunswick, N.J.: Rutgers University Press, 1991), 39–43; Russell Leach, interview with Jack Skeels, July 23, 1963.

16. WPR, "Time," October 24, 1929, file 2, box 10, VGR Collection; Braun, interview with the author.

17. Leach, interview with Skeels; Babson, *Building the Union*, 43–49; Harley Shaiken, *Automation and Labor in the Computer Age* (New York: Holt, Rinehart, 1984), 34–35.

18. Cook, *Reuther*, 42; Reuther, *Brothers Reuther*, 46–48; WPR, interview with Cormier and Eaton.

19. Nelson Lichtenstein, "'The Man in the Middle': A Social History of Automobile Industry Foremen," in Lichtenstein and Meyer, *On the Line*, 158–63.

20. Braun, interview with the author.

21. Jeffery Haydu, *Between Craft and Class* (Berkeley: University of California Press, 1988), chap. 3; Ronald Schatz, *American Electrical Workers* (Urbana: University of

Illinois Press, 1983), 34–38; David Montgomery, *The Fall of the House of Labor: The Workplace, the State, and American Labor Activism, 1865–1925* (New York: Cambridge University Press, 1987), 310–29; Walter Dorach (a Rouge toolmaker and union pioneer), interview with the author, Dearborn, Mich., October 12, 1983.

22. Babson, *Building the Union*, 48–49; Peter Drucker, *Adventures of a Bystander* (New York: Harper & Row, 1978), 275.

23. WPR, interview with Cormier and Eaton; VGR, interview with the author, Washington, D.C., December 10, 1989; Nevins, *Ford: Expansion and Challenge*, 245–47.

24. Fordson High School librarian, telephone interview with the author, December 5, 1989; Donald Baut (Dearborn Historical Museum), telephone interview with the author, December 5, 1989.

25. Merlin Bishop, interview with William J. Eaton, Atlantic City, N.J., May 5, 1968, in Cormier and Eaton Collection; Reuther, *Brothers Reuther*, 50–51.

26. WPR, "Time."

27. "Four-C Club," file 2, box 8, VGR Collection; Bishop, interview with Eaton.

28. Four-C applications, file 3, box 8, VGR Collection; Merlin Bishop, telephone interview with the author, January 10, 1986.

29. "Four-C Club."

30. Reuther, *Brothers Reuther*, 50–51; Bishop, interview with Eaton.

31. Reuther application, file 3, box 8, VGR Collection; Braun, interview with the author.

32. WPR, "Thomas Paine," "Prohibition," and "Success" (1929–1930), file 2, box 10, VGR Collection.

33. WPR to Paul Ritterskamp, August 20, 1932, reel 34, letter no. 515, Norman Thomas–Socialist Party Collection (microfilm edition); WPR to Cecil Halbert, undated [1932?], file 1, box 1, Small Collections.

CHAPTER 3: TOOLING AT GORKY

1. Merlin Bishop, interview with William J. Eaton, Atlantic City, N.J., May 5, 1968, in Cormier and Eaton Collection.

2. Christine Richey, interview with the author, Reading, Mass., July 18, 1993; Victor G. Reuther, *The Brothers Reuther and the Story of the UAW* (Boston: Houghton Mifflin, 1976), 40–41; Paul Douglass, "The Reuther Family and the Rewarding Society, 1972," file 20, box 68, VGR Collection; "The Blessings of Citizenship," file 1, box 2, VGR Collection.

3. Reuther, *Brothers Reuther*, 55–56.

4. Ibid., 57, 65; Frank X. Braun, interview with the author, Ann Arbor, Mich., June 25, 1987.

5. Robert Conot, *American Odyssey* (Detroit: Wayne State University Press, 1986), 258–90.

6. Reuther, *Brothers Reuther*, 61–64; Braun, interview with the author; WPR to Cecil Halbert [1932?], file 1, box 1, Small Collections.

7. "Student, Faculty Vote GOP," *Detroit Collegian*, October 20, 1932; "Victor Reuther Represents Socialists in Student Poll," *Detroit Collegian*, November 3, 1932.

8. Reuther, *Brothers Reuther*, 61; Braun, interview with the author.

9. Milton Cantor, *The Divided Left: American Radicalism, 1900–1975* (New York: Hill and Wang, 1978), 44–45; Bernard K. Johnpoll, *Pacifist's Progress: Norman Thomas and the Decline of American Socialism* (Chicago: Quadrangle, 1970), 88.

10. Christopher Johnson, *Maurice Sugar: Law, Labor, and the Left in Detroit, 1912–1950* (Detroit: Wayne State University Press, 1988), 63-69, 92-97. "Membership Report by

State, 1937," reel 54, Norman Thomas–SP Collection (Chadwyck Healey, Inc., microfilm edition).

11. W. A. Swanberg, *Norman Thomas: The Last Idealist* (New York: Charles Scribner's Sons, 1976), 128; Irving Howe, *Socialism and America* (San Diego: Harcourt Brace Jovanovich, 1985), 53–56; Johnpoll, *Pacifist's Progress*, 88.

12. Johnpoll, *Pacifist's Progress*, 89; Reuther, *Brothers Reuther*, 68; Thomas quoted in Gary Gerstle, "The Politics of Patriotism: Americanization and the Formation of the CIO," *Dissent* (Spring 1986): 89; "L.I.D. Organizes Speakers Bureau," *Detroit Collegian*, November 19, 1931.

13. Eileen Eagan, *Class, Culture, and the Classroom: The Student Peace Movement of the 1930s* (Philadelphia: Temple University Press, 1981), 42–71 passim; Robert Cohen, *When the Old Left Was Young: Student Radicals and America's First Mass Student Movement, 1929–1941* (New York: Oxford University Press, 1993), 79–91.

14. Jeffrey Mirel, "Out of the Cloister of the Classroom: Political Activity and the Teachers of Detroit, 1929–39," *Journal of the Midwest History of Education Society* 11 (1983): 57–62.

15. "Dr. Bergman Exonerated," *Detroit Collegian*, December 10, 1931; Mirel, "Out of the Cloister," 59.

16. Mirel, "Out of the Cloister," 63–74.

17. Fred J. Cook, *Walter Reuther* (Chicago: Encyclopedia Britannica Press, 1963), 47–50.

18. VGR, interview with Loren Walters, Black Lake, Mich., August 17, 1972, file 11, box 3, VGR Collection.

19. Frank Cormier and William J. Eaton, *Reuther* (Englewood Cliffs, N.J.: Prentice-Hall, 1970), 19–20; David Shannon, *The Socialist Party of America: A History* (New York: Macmillan, 1955), 222–23.

20. On the AWU, see Roger Keeran, *The Communist Party and the Auto Workers Unions* (Bloomington: Indiana University Press, 1980), 45–59; Rushton quoted in Osgood Caruthers, "Four Soviets Label Reuther Traitor," *New York Times*, October 31, 1959.

21. Johnson, *Maurice Sugar*, 120–22; VGR, interview with the author, Washington, D.C., December 10, 1989.

22. Kurt S. Schultz, "Building the 'Soviet Detroit': The Construction of the Nizhnii-Novgorod Automobile Factory, 1927–1932," *Slavic Review* 49 (Summer 1990): 200–212; Mira Wilkins and Frank Ernest Hill, *American Business Abroad: Ford on Six Continents* (Detroit: Wayne State University Press, 1964), 208–27.

23. WPR, interview with Frank Cormier and William J. Eaton, Detroit, July 1, 1968, Frank Cormier and William J. Eaton Collection, John F. Kennedy Library; Reuther, *Brothers Reuther*, 66–67.

24. Jean Benson, "Guiding the Revolution," *LID Monthly* 10 (January 1932): 8–9, 16. Of course, Soviet "planning," especially during the First Five-Year Plan, more closely resembled a mad scramble for resources among feudal baronies than it did a bureaucratically structured command economy. See Sheila Fitzpatrick, "New Perspectives on Stalinism," *Russian Review* 45 (October 1986): 357–413; and Schultz, "Building the 'Soviet Detroit.'"

25. Shannon, *Socialist Party of America*, 215.

26. U.S. Federal Bureau of Investigation, "Walter P. Reuther" file, January 15, 1941, record designation 61–9556–13. Reuther's Ford employment record is part of this FBI file.

27. Reuther, *Brothers Reuther*, 67–68.

28. Maurice Sugar, "My Visit to the Soviet Union" [chapter manuscript, n.d.], "Supplement" box, Maurice Sugar Collection; Reuther, *Brothers Reuther*, 67. Communists

were the key leaders of the bitter, unsuccessful Briggs strike, but Socialists and Wobblies gave it staunch backing as well. Keeran, *Communist Party*, 87–95.

29. VGR, "Gathering Forces," file 6, box 71, VGR Collection; "The Briggs Strike," *Student Outlook* (March 1933): 4–5.

30. VGR, "Germany," file 5, box 71, VGR Collection; VGR, "Germany 1959," file 4, box 92, UAW International Affairs Department Collection.

31. This account of their stay in western Europe is based on Reuther, *Brothers Reuther*, 72–87.

32. Johnpoll, *Pacifist's Progress*, 116–17; "Conference of the Labor and Socialist International: Report of the Majority," file 3, box 14, Herman Wolf Collection.

33. Reuther, *Brothers Reuther*, 81–82.

34. VGR, "Germany."

35. Reuther, *Brothers Reuther*, 87.

36. Cormier and Eaton, *Reuther*, 30–31; Reuther, *Brothers Reuther*, 95.

37. Andrea Graziosi, "Foreign Workers in Soviet Russia, 1920–40: Their Experience and Their Legacy," *International Labor and Working-class History* 33 (Spring 1988): 39.

38. Ibid., 38–47.

39. Sheila Fitzpatrick, *The Russian Revolution, 1917–1932* (New York: Oxford University Press, 1984), 128; Moshe Lewin, *The Making of the Soviet System: Essays in the Social History of Innerwar Russia* (New York: Pantheon, 1985), 218–20. For the argument that the collectivization of agriculture retarded industrialization, see Robert Conquest, *The Harvest of Sorrow: Soviet Collectivization and the Terror-Famine* (New York: Oxford University Press, 1986).

40. Kendall Bailes, *Technology and Society under Lenin and Stalin: Origins of the Soviet Technical Intelligentsia, 1917–1941* (Princeton, N.J.: Princeton University Press, 1978), 265–83; Lewin, *Making of the Soviet System*, 249–50.

41. Lewin, *Making of the Soviet System*, 218.

42. VGR, "Tooling at Gorky," file 7, box 71, VGR Collection.

43. VGR and WPR to Melvin and Gladys Bishop, January 20, 1934, quoted in Cormier and Eaton, *Reuther*, 135; hereafter referred to as "the Gorky letter." This famous letter was reproduced in virtually all of Walter Reuther's FBI files and in numerous publications over the next thirty years.

44. "Gorki Americans Ask Greater Efficiency in Shops," *Moscow Daily News*, May 4, 1934. For the increase in production figures, see also "Gorki Auto Plant's 100,000th Automobile," *Moscow Daily News*, April 17, 1935.

45. Quoted in Reuther, *Brothers Reuther*, 94.

46. Victor Herman, *Coming out of the Ice: An Unexpected Life* (New York: Harcourt Brace, 1979), 69; Anatoli Ilyashov, "Victor Reuther on the Soviet Experience, 1933–35: An Interview," *International Review of Social History*, 31 (1986), 298–323; Reuther, *Brothers Reuther*, 106–8.

47. Gorky letter, quoted in Cormier and Eaton, *Reuther*, 133–34.

48. Bailes, *Technology and Society*, 279–81; Reuther, *Brothers Reuther*, 98–99; see also "Moscow and Leningrad Plant Foreigners Organize Socialist Competition," *Moscow Daily News*, April 17, 1935.

49. Gorky letter, quoted in Cormier and Eaton, *Reuther*, 133–34.

50. Vad Andrle, "The Management of Labour in Soviet Industry: Objectives, Methods, and Conflicts in the 1930s" (paper presented at the Soviet Industrialization Project Seminar, University of Birmingham, March 1986); Fitzpatrick, *Russian Revolution*, 129–34; Lewin, *Making of the Soviet System*, 209–57 passim.

51. Bailes, *Technology and Society*, 273–79; Graziosi, "Foreign Workers in Soviet Russia," 44–45.

52. Anna Louise Strong, *I Change Worlds* (New York: Henry Holt and Co., 1935), 301–3.

53. "Says Management Holds Main Key to Efficiency," *Moscow Daily News*, January 9, 1934. Reuther was not alone in making technical administrative criticisms: they constituted the common complaint of foreign specialists, including those most politically committed to the Soviet regime. John Rushton thought maintenance appalling and wasteful, while the American Communist John Smith, who worked at the Elektrozavod factory in Moscow, found production managers technically incompetent and heavy-handed; "Supports Idea of Liquid Cooling," January 15, 1934, and "Gorki Americans Ask Greater Efficiency in Shops," both in *Moscow Daily News*, May 4, 1935. See also Andrew Smith, *I Was a Soviet Worker* (London: Robert Hale & Co., 1937), 57–69; and Robert Robinson, *Black on Red: My Forty-four Years inside the Soviet Union* (Washington, D.C.: Acropolis Books, 1988), 75–124. Robinson, a black toolmaker from the Rouge, was elected to the Moscow Soviet in the mid-1930s but soon became entirely disillusioned, in part because of the pervasive racism he encountered at all ranks of Soviet society.

54. "Tooling at Gorky," file 7, box 71, VGR Collection; Graziosi, "Foreign Workers in Soviet Russia," 47–49.

55. Gorky letter, quoted in Cormier and Eaton, *Reuther*, 133.

56. VGR to "Everyone," August 6, 1934, Proletarian Tourist Base, Moscow, letter in possession of Jon Bloom. Conditions were not so rosy; see Fred C. Koch, *The Volga Germans: In Russia and America* (University Park: Pennsylvania State University Press, 1977).

57. Cook, *Reuther*, 60; Reuther, *Brothers Reuther*, 109–10.

58. WPR and VGR to Maurice Sugar, June 20, 1935, Samarkand, Central Asia, file 1, box 65, Maurice Sugar Collection.

59. Graziosi, "Foreign Workers in Soviet Russia," 50–52.

60. FBI, "Walter Reuther" file; B. J. Widick, interview with the author, Detroit, October 22, 1988; Genora Johnson (Los Angeles), telephone interview with the author, December 10, 1989.

61. Reuther, *Brothers Reuther*, 102–3.

62. Ibid., 116–23.

CHAPTER 4: RADICAL CADRE AND NEW DEAL UNION

1. Victor G. Reuther, *The Brothers Reuther and the Story of the UAW* (Boston: Houghton Mifflin, 1976), 124–26.

2. An excellent literature exists on the political economy of the New Deal. See, for example, Melvyn Dubofsky, *The State and Labor in Modern America* (Chapel Hill: University of North Carolina Press, 1994), 119–31; Steve Fraser, *Labor Will Rule: Sidney Hillman and the Rise of American Labor* (New York: Free Press, 1991), 289–323 passim; Colin Gordon, *New Deals: Business, Labor, and Politics in America, 1920–1935* (New York: Cambridge University Press, 1994), 166–203 passim.

3. Steve Babson, *Building the Union: Skilled Workers and Anglo-Gaelic Immigrants in the Rise of the UAW* (New Brunswick, N.J.: Rutgers University Press, 1991), 116–26, 163–68; Henry Kraus, *Heroes of Unwritten Story: The UAW, 1934–1939* (Urbana: University of Illinois Press, 1993), 99–106; Sidney Fine, *Sit-down: The General Motors Strike of 1936–1937* (Ann Arbor: University of Michigan Press, 1969), 48–51.

4. Steve Jefferys, *Management and Managed: Fifty Years of Crisis at Chrysler* (New York: Cambridge University Press, 1986), 49–67.

5. Collins quoted in American Social History Project, *Who Built America*, vol. 2 (New

York: Pantheon, 1992), 378; Gallagher quoted in Babson, *Building the Union*, 136; see also Kraus, *Heroes of Unwritten Story*, 107–29.

6. For accounts of these two conventions, see Melvyn Dubofsky and Warren Van Tine, *John L. Lewis: A Biography* (New York: Quadrangle, 1977), 217–21; Robert Cohen, *When the Old Left Was Young: Student Radicals and America's First Mass Student Movement, 1929–1941* (New York: Oxford University Press, 1993), 140–47.

7. Reuther, *Brothers Reuther*, 124–26; WPR, excerpts from daily activities calendar, 1935–36, file 25, box 6, VGR Collection; WPR to May Wolf, February 25, 1936, letter in possession of Linda Reuther.

8. Richard J. Altenbaugh, *Education for Struggle: The American Labor Colleges of the 1920s and 1930s* (Philadelphia: Temple University Press, 1990), 205–19; Merlin Bishop, telephone interview with the author, January 10, 1986. In the 1920s Brookwood's guiding spirit had been A. J. Muste, but he lost control after the AFL repudiated his increasingly radical leadership. See also JoAnn Robinson, *Abraham Went Out: A Biography of A. J. Muste* (Philadelphia: Temple University Press, 1982), 228–90.

9. Jonathan Bloom, "Brookwood Labor College: The Final Years, 1933–1937," *Labor's Heritage*, 2 (April 1990), 24–43; Larry Rogin, interview with the author, Washington, D.C., January 5, 1987; Thomas R. Brooks, *Clint: A Biography of a Labor Intellectual* (New York: Atheneum, 1978), 65–127 passim.

10. Quoted in Altenbaugh, *Education for Struggle*, 140.

11. Characteristically, Goodlavich learned of Brookwood not through a union but from a Brown University student turned shipyard organizer, Philip Van Gelder. The Emergency Peace Campaign was well funded and briefly linked radical pacifists, mainstream churches, and conservative advocates of the World Court and the League of Nations. Charles Chatfield, *For Peace and Justice: Pacifism in America, 1914–1941* (Knoxville: University of Tennessee Press, 1971), 256–86 passim; VGR, interview with the author; Rogin, interview with the author; Frank Winn, telephone interview with the author, June 17, 1985.

12. Roy Reuther to Tucker Smith, October 27, 1934, and March 3, 1935; "Reuther Likes Flint Workers," *Flint Weekly Review*; all in file 11, box 90, Brookwood Labor Collection; Altenbaugh, *Education for Struggle*, 225; Genora Dollinger, interview with Jack Skeels, July 31, 1960, 5–7; Rogin, interview with the author.

13. Reuther, *Brothers Reuther*, 126–27; WPR to Tucker Smith, January 29, 1936, Tucker Smith to WPR, February 6, 1936, WPR to Tucker Smith, February 22, 1936, all in file 18, box 3, VGR Collection; VGR, interview with the author, Washington, D.C., June 12, 1986.

14. Reuther, *Brothers Reuther*, 127; Linda Reuther, interview with the author, San Anselmo, Cal., March 23, 1988; Eleanor Wolf, telephone interview with the author, April 11, 1988; on the Proletarian Party, see Margaret Collingwood Nowak, *Two Who Were There: A Biography of Stanley Nowak* (Detroit: Wayne State University Press, 1989), 15–16, 70.

15. WPR, excerpts from daily activities calendar; Christine Richey, interview with the author, Reading, Mass., July 18, 1993; Eleanor Wolf, telephone interview with the author.

16. WPR to May Wolf, May 26, 1936; April 22 and April 29, 1937; June 13 and November 10, 1938; letters in possession of Linda Reuther; Linda Reuther, interview with the author.

17. W. A. Swanberg, *Norman Thomas: The Last Idealist* (New York: Charles Scribner's Sons, 1976), 166–73; Murray Seidler, *Norman Thomas: Respectable Rebel* (Syracuse, N.Y.: Syracuse University Press, 1961), 104–70; Frank Warren, *An Alternative Vision:*

The Socialist Party in the 1930s (Bloomington: Indiana University Press, 1974), 21–34; Christopher Johnson, *Maurice Sugar: Law, Labor, and the Left in Detroit, 1912–1950* (Detroit: Wayne State University Press, 1988), 63–69, 92–97; "Membership Report by State, 1937," reel 54, Norman Thomas–SP Collection.

18. Alan Strachan, interview with the author, Washington, D.C., September 10, 1987; Wolf, interview with the author; "Minutes of the Labor Committee," November 19, 1936, file 13, box 3, VGR Collection; "Trade Unionists" (Socialist Party—1936), file 14, box 3, VGR Collection. The SP still had German, Yugo-Slav, Jewish, Bohemian, and Polish sections, but these were ingrown social clubs divorced from the emerging union movement. Fifteen SP members were in the AFT, seventeen in MESA, and eleven were listed simply as "auto workers."

19. Dollinger, interview with Skeels, 11; VGR FBI file, "Walter Reuther," January 4, 1951 (1014) vol. 30, Reading Room, J. Edgar Hoover Building, Washington, D.C. To an FBI informant in this Protestant town, the most sensational part of Reuther's Flint talk came when he was asked whether the Soviets believed in God. Reuther replied, "We do not believe in God, but that man is God."

20. "Minutes of the Socialist Party Labor Committee," October 3, 6, 31, 1936; November 11, 19, 1936; file 13, box 3, VGR Collection.

21. "After the AF of L Convention—What?" file 13, box 3, VGR Collection.

22. Roger Keeran, *The Communist Party and the Auto Workers Unions* (Bloomington: Indiana University Press, 1980), 96–147; Paul Boatin, interview with the author, Dearborn, Mich., October 23, 1982; Saul Wellman, interview with the author, Washington, D.C., October 12, 1985.

23. Johnson, *Maurice Sugar*, 178–80; VGR FBI file, "Walter Reuther."

24. Phillip Bonosky, *Brother Bill McKie* (New York: Pioneer Publishers, 1953), 66–71; Martin Glaberman, "A Note on Walter Reuther," *Radical America* 7 (November-December 1973): 113–17; Johnson, *Maurice Sugar*, 315; Lincoln Fairley, "A Few Facts about Walter Reuther," March 30, 1949, file 4–13, box 4, Wyndham Mortimer Collection; WPR, daily activities calendar (1936).

25. WPR, interview with Frank Cormier and William J. Eaton, Detroit, July 1, 1968, in Frank Cormier and William J. Eaton Collection, John F. Kennedy Library.

26. Keeran, *Communist Party*, 141; Frank Cormier and William J. Eaton, *Reuther* (Englewood Cliffs, N.J.: Prentice-Hall, 1970), 60–62.

27. Johnson, *Maurice Sugar*, 180; WPR to VGR and Roy Reuther, May 2, 1936, quoted in Kevin Boyle, "Building the Vanguard: Walter Reuther and Radical Politics in 1936," *Labor History* 30 (Summer 1989): 442.

28. WPR, daily activities calendar (1936).

29. Quoted in Cormier and Eaton, *Reuther*, 61.

30. Keeran, *Communist Party*, 141–42; Murray Kempton, *Part of Our Time: Some Ruins and Monuments of the 1930s* (New York: Simon & Schuster, 1955), 279.

31. John Barnard, *Walter Reuther and the Rise of the Auto Workers* (Boston: Little, Brown, 1983), 38–39; UAW, "Proceedings of the Second Constitutional Convention," South Bend, Ind., May 6–12, 1936, 26–30.

32. Ronald Edsforth, *Class Conflict and Cultural Consensus: The Making of a Mass Consumer Society in Flint, Michigan* (New Brunswick, N.J.: Rutgers University Press, 1987), 97–126; Peter Friedlander, *The Emergence of a UAW Local, 1936–1939: A Study in Class and Culture* (Pittsburgh: University of Pittsburgh Pres, 1975).

33. Keeran, *Communist Party*, 145–46.

34. WPR to May Reuther, May 6, 1936, letter in Linda Reuther's possession; Marvin Persky, "Walter Reuther, the UAW-CIO, and Third Party Politics" (Ph.D. diss., Michigan State University, 1974), 42.

35. Boyle, "Building the Vanguard," 441; Kraus, *Heroes of Unwritten Story*, 170; Barnard, *Reuther*, 39.

36. UAW, "Proceedings of the Second Constitutional Convention," 64, 76; WPR to May Reuther, May 6, 1936. In taking this first step up the UAW ladder, Reuther edged out his Socialist comrade Alan Strachan, who was head of a citywide district council of autoworkers. Because of Strachan's anti-Stalinism, the Communists may have favored Reuther, but Strachan himself admitted that he was simply not as rhetorically effective as his younger rival. Henry Kraus, "The Remarkable Rise of Walter Reuther," *National Guardian*, May 17, 1950, in Reuther biography file, Solidarity House, Detroit; Fairley, "A Few Facts about Reuther"; Alan Strachan, interview with the author, Washington, D.C., August 26, 1987; B. J. Widick, telephone interview with the author, June 10, 1993.

37. UAW, "Proceedings of the Second Constitutional Convention," 112–14. Reuther in turn selected his old roommate and Socialist comrade, the Brookwood instructor Merlin Bishop, as the UAW's full-time education director. Bishop's salary was partially paid by Brookwood. "Bishop Chosen Education Department Temporary Head," *United Auto Worker* (July 1936).

38. Widick, interview with the author; Frank A. Warren, *An Alternative Vision: The Socialist Party in the 1930s* (Bloomington: Indiana University Press, 1974), 77–87.

39. Quoted in Boyle, "Building the Vanguard," 444–47.

40. WPR to May Reuther, May 25, 1936, letter in Linda Reuther's possession; WPR, daily activities calendar (1936). As the Roosevelt landslide gathered momentum in the summer, both the SP and the FLP political efforts fell apart.

41. Cormier and Eaton, *Reuther*, 67–68; "Fired, Builds Union," *United Auto Worker* (July 1936): 7. Again Reuther exaggerated, for he enrolled a probable majority of the plant only after outside organizing activity by other unionists, including himself.

42. Barnard, *Reuther*, 40; Olivier Zunz, *The Changing Face of Inequality: Urbanization, Industrial Development, and Immigrants in Detroit, 1880–1920* (Chicago: University of Chicago Press, 1982), 292–309.

43. "28 Attend First Institute Held by International," *United Auto Worker* (September 1936), 6; Barnard, *Reuther*, 40; John Anderson, "My Battle against Reuther: The Story of a Rank and File Autoworker" (manuscript in author's possession, 1985), 74–80.

44. Strachan, interview with the author; Alan Strachan, "Draft for Organizational Drive in the Auto Industry" [1936?], file 20, box 36, Adolph Germer Collection, State Historical Society of Wisconsin. The idea originated with Strachan, who adapted it from the British tradition of craft amalgamation.

45. Bonosky, *McKie*, 135–45; Anderson, "My Battle against Reuther," 81–88; "Minutes of the City Wide Organizational Meeting Held October 12, 1936," file 45, box 1, WPR Collection.

46. Alice Dodge (secretary, "Labor League for Thomas and Nelson") to Roy Reuther, October 28, 1936, reel 54, Norman Thomas–SP Collection; "Report on Labor Committee Supper," October 30, 1936, file 13, box 3, VGR Collection; Persky, "Reuther," 52–53.

47. Arthur Schlesinger, Jr., *The Politics of Upheaval* (Boston: Houghton Mifflin, 1960), 638–39.

48. Quoted in Fine, *Sit-down*, 96.

49. Kraus, *Heroes of Unwritten Story*, 204.

50. Richard M. Scammon, *America at the Polls* (Pittsburgh: University of Pittsburgh Press, 1965), 220, 222.

51. Thaddeus Radzialowski, "Polish Americans in Detroit Politics," in *Ethnic Politics in*

Urban America, ed. Angela Pienkos (Chicago: Polish Historical Society, 1980), 52–53; Thomas Gobel, "Becoming American: Ethnic Workers and the Rise of the CIO," *Labor History*, 29 (Spring 1988), 173–98; Edward Jennings, "Ethnicity and Class: Detroit's Polish Workers in the CIO Era" (Ph.D. diss., Northern Illinois University, 1981), 72–74; Nowak, *Two Who Were There*, 75–96.

52. Babson, *Building the Union*, 171–79; Kraus, *Heroes of Unwritten Story*, 205–20; "Growth of Union in Detroit Leaps up by Thousands," *United Auto Worker* (December 1936): 1.

53. Barnard, *Reuther*, 41; Michael Manning, interview with Jack Skeels, July 6, 1960, 12; Frank Manfried, interview with Jack Skeels, June 26, 1960, 19; "Michigan's Newest Foundry," *Michigan Manufacturer and Financial Record*, August 17, 1935, and "Special Union Meeting," both in file "1935," box 1, Michael Manning Collection. Ford was worried about supplier plant strikes; for a detailed listing, see "Major Purchased Items on Which We Would Have Trouble Maintaining Production in Case of Strike at Supplier," December 4, 1936, file AA-Z, box 88, accession no. 390, Henry Ford Museum.

54. For discussions of union cadre in heavy industry, see Ronald Schatz, *The American Electrical Workers: A History of Labor at General Electric and Westinghouse, 1923–1960* (Urbana: University of Illinois Press, 1983), 80–101; Babson, *Building the Union*, 95–133; Friedlander, *Emergence of a UAW Local*, 78–90; VGR, interview with author, Washington, D.C., August 26, 1986.

55. Irving Bernstein, *Turbulent Years: A History of the American Worker, 1933–1941* (Boston: Houghton Mifflin, 1969), 374; Manning, interview with Skeels, 7–11.

56. Manning, interview with Skeels, 13; Michael Manning to Detroit District Council, UAW, December 8, 1934, file "1934," box 1, Michael Manning Collection.

57. Manfried, interview with Skeels, 1–9.

58. National Labor Relations Board (NLRB), "UAW Federal Labor Union 18677 for Election at Kelsey-Hayes," hearings, docket no. 264, Detroit, March 9, 1935, 29–41, 55, and "Report of Proceedings before NLRB, Case VII-R-195, Kelsey-Hayes and Local 174, UAW," Detroit, September 15, 1939, 54–65; both in box 2032, RG 25, National Archives.

59. Manning, interview with Skeels, 38; George Kennedy to NLRB, February 27, 1935, and "NLRB Case No. 380 in the Matter of Kelsey-Hayes Wheel Company and UAW Federal Labor Union No. 18677," September 15, 1939, docket no. 264; both in box 2032, RG 25, National Archives.

60. Manfried, interview with Skeels, 16.

61. Robert Kanter, interview with Jack Skeels, April 26, 1963, 1–9; Anderson, "My Battle against Reuther," 73–75; "Robert Kanter," in vertical file; Merlin Bishop, interview with Jack Skeels, March 29, 1963, 30–41; Sophia and Victor Reuther to Myra [last name unknown], December 20, 1936, file 14, box 6, VGR Collection.

62. Bishop, interview with Skeels, 30–41; Winn, interview with the author; VGR, interview with the author, Washington, D.C., August 25, 1986; Sophia and Victor Reuther to Myra [last name unknown], December 20, 1936.

63. Winn, telephone interview with the author; George Edwards, telephone interview with the author, September 5, 1986; Frank Winn to George Edwards, October 3, 1936, file 13, box 1, George Edwards, Jr., Collection; George Edwards, interview with Clinton Fair, Detroit, August 10, 1979, George Meany Center for Labor Studies, Silver Spring, Md.; George Edwards, *Pioneer at Law: George Edwards* (New York: W. W. Norton, 1974), 11–148 passim.

64. Strachan, interview with the author.

65. Cohen, *When the Old Left Was Young*, 134–76.
66. Edwards, interview with the author; Harvey Klehr, *The Heyday of American Communism: The Depression Decade* (New York: Basic Books, 1984), 316–18.
67. Reuther, *Brothers Reuther*, 132–33; WPR and Roy Reuther, telegram to Victor Reuther, November 28, 1936, file 28, box 6, VGR Collection; Kraus, *Heroes of Unwritten Story*, 226–31.
68. Merlin Bishop, "The Kelsey-Hayes Sit-in Strike," box 1, file 30, WPR Collection; Frank Boles, "Walter Reuther and the Kelsey-Hayes Strike of 1936," *Detroit in Perspective* 4 (Winter 1980): 78–80; Reuther, *Brothers Reuther*, 134.
69. Boles, "Walter Reuther and Kelsey-Hayes Strike," 77–79; Local 174 press releases and leaflets, file 14, box 6, VGR Collection; Kelsey-Hayes Wheel Company clippings, box 22, Joe Brown Collection.
70. Bishop, "Kelsey-Hayes Sit-in Strike"; Boles, "Walter Reuther and Kelsey-Hayes Strike," 79–80.
71. Reuther, *Brothers Reuther*, 135–36; Sophia and Victor Reuther to Myra [last name unknown], December 20, 1936.
72. Bishop, "Kelsey-Hayes Sit-in Strike"; Boles, "Walter Reuther and Kelsey-Hayes Strike," 80–83.
73. Bishop, "Kelsey-Hayes Sit-in Strike"; Cormier and Eaton, *Reuther*, 72; Boles, "Walter Reuther and Kelsey-Hayes Strike," 82–85; "Kelsey-Hayes Signs Peace," *Detroit News*, December 23, 1936, in vol. 4, p. 84, Joe Brown Collection.
74. Boles, "Walter Reuther and Kelsey-Hayes Strike," 84–85; Kraus, *Heroes of Unwritten Story*, 231–35; VGR, interview with the author. According to Kraus, Frank Manfried and Sophie Goodlavich may also have considered the settlement a sellout.
75. Reuther, *Brothers Reuther*, 139.
76. "Kelsey-Hayes, Aluminum Co. Strikes End," *Detroit Times*, December 24, 1936, in vol. 4, p. 85, Joe Brown Collection.
77. Edwards, interview with the author; George Edwards, "New World at Kelsey," *United Auto Worker*, January 22, 1937, 5.
78. George Blackwood, "The United Automobile Workers of America, 1935–1951" (Ph.D. diss., University of Chicago, 1951), 447–48; "NLRB Case No. 380," 51–65.
79. Kanter, interview with Skeels; May Reuther, interview with Jack Skeels, May 29, 1963; Reuther, *Brothers Reuther*, 141.

CHAPTER 5: THE WEST SIDE LOCAL

1. Arthur Miller, *Timebends: A Life* (New York: Grove Press, 1987), 267.
2. This summary and assessment of the GM strike is based on Sidney Fine, *Sit-down: The General Motors Strike of 1936–1937* (Ann Arbor: University of Michigan Press, 1969), 121–265 passim; Henry Kraus, *Heroes of Unwritten Story: The UAW, 1934–1939* (Urbana: University of Illinois Press, 1993), 236–73 passim; Christopher Johnson, *Maurice Sugar: Law, Labor, and the Left in Detroit, 1912–1950* (Detroit: Wayne State University Press, 1988), 191–206; Roger Keeran, *The Communist Party and the Auto Workers Unions* (Bloomington: Indiana University Press, 1980), 148–85 passim; Bert Cochran, *Labor and Communism: The Conflict That Shaped American Unions* (Princeton, N.J.: Princeton University Press, 1977), 114–26; and Ronald Edsforth, *Class Conflict and Cultural Consensus: The Making of a Mass Consumer Society in Flint, Michigan* (New Brunswick, N.J.: Rutgers University Press, 1987), 157–89.
3. Fine, *Sit-down*, 133–48; WPR, interview with Henry Kraus, Detroit, 1938, in author's possession. Ironically, Homer Martin, Fred Pieper, and other executive board con-

servatives agitated for an immediate companywide strike. As Reuther put it to Kraus, "Pieper had a strike on his own hands [in Atlanta], and if a general strike would be called his own problem would be absorbed by a bigger problem."

4. Stewart Strachan, telephone interview with the author, September 21, 1987.

5. John Anderson, "My Battle against Reuther: The Story of a Rank and File Autoworker" (manuscript in author's possession, 1986), 84. Like Michael Manning at Kelsey-Hayes, Tribeau had been the leader of the AFL federal local in the plant. In 1936 he ran for Congress on Father Coughlin's Union Party ticket. (There were two politically active John Andersons in the UAW. "Little" John Anderson, the author of "My Battle against Reuther," was a Trotskyist at Fleetwood. "Big" John Anderson was a Communist and president of the East Side Skilled Trades Local 155.)

6. Victor G. Reuther, *The Brothers Reuther and the Story of the UAW* (Boston: Houghton Mifflin, 1976), 152–57; Henry Kraus, *The Many and the Few: A Chronicle of the Dynamic Auto Workers* 2d ed. (Urbana: University of Illinois Press, 1985), 125–45; Albert Maltz quoted in Fine, *Sit-down*, 5.

7. Fine, *Sit-down*, 251–53; Reuther, *Brothers Reuther*, 160–61.

8. "Cadillac-Fleetwood Men Prove Their Mettle," *United Auto Worker*, February 25, 1937, 17.

9. Reuther, *Brothers Reuther*, 163–64; Fine, *Sit-down*, 262–63.

10. On the scheme to take over Chevy No. 4, see Kraus, *The Many and the Few*, 189–226; Fine, *Sit-down*, 266–69; Genora Dollinger, interview with Jack Skeels, July 31, 1960, 31–32; Genora Dollinger, telephone interview with the author, December 19, 1989.

11. Dollinger, interview with Skeels, 33. Trager was also an ideological leader of the uncompromising "clarity" group within the Socialist Party, with which most of the Michigan labor activists were then aligned. According to Dollinger (whose name was Johnson in 1937), "Reuther . . . would have been very embarrassed if he had refused to cooperate with Trager." See also Frank Warren, *An Alternative Vision: The Socialist Party in the 1930s* (Bloomington: Indiana University Press, 1974), 84–88.

12. WPR, interview with Kraus, 1938; "Cadillac-Fleetwood Men Prove Their Mettle," 17; Kraus, *The Many and the Few*, 206–22.

13. Fine, *Sit-down*, 303–7.

14. "Roy Reuther Remembers the Great Sit-Down Strike," *Detroit Free Press*, February 10, 1967.

15. Robert Zieger, *The CIO, 1935–1955* (Chapel Hill: University of North Carolina Press, 1995), 54–89 passim; and for a still useful and exciting account, see Irving Bernstein, *Turbulent Years: A History of the American Worker, 1933–1941* (Boston: Houghton Mifflin, 1970), 551–634 passim; Robert Kanter, interview with Jack Skeels, August 31, 1961, 11.

16. Steve Babson, *Working Detroit* (New York: Adama Books, 1984), 84–85; Steve Jefferys, *Management and Managed: Fifty Years of Crisis at Chrysler* (New York: Cambridge University Press, 1986), 71–77.

17. George Edwards, telephone interview with the author, September 5, 1986; Kraus, *Heroes of Unwritten Story*, 284–86; Babson, *Working Detroit*, 86.

18. "Report on Condition of Plants in the West Side Local 174," February 24, 1938, file 45, box 1, WPR Collection; "Big Delegation," *West Side Conveyor*, July 20, 1937; "Appendix I: Roll of Delegates," in UAW, "Proceedings of the Third Annual Convention," Milwaukee, Wisc., August 23–28, 1937, 15–16.

19. Edwards, telephone interview with the author; "Strike Rioters Face Court," *Detroit Times*, April 15, 1937; "They Did Their Duty," *Detroit News*, April 16, 1937; "120 Convicted in Sit-down at Yale & Towne," *Detroit Free Press*, April 29, 1937; "Yale and

Towne Announces Closing Plant Here," *United Auto Worker*, May 22, 1937; Sidney Fine, *Frank Murphy and the New Deal Years* (Chicago: University of Chicago Press, 1979), 341.

20. Keith Sward, *The Legend of Henry Ford* (New York: Rinehart, 1948), 275–313; Babson, *Working Detroit*, 92; August Meier and Elliott Rudwick, *Black Detroit and the Rise of the UAW* (New York: Oxford University Press, 1980), 3–33; Paul Boatin, interview with the author, Dearborn, Mich., October 3, 1982; Walter Dorosh, interview with the author, Dearborn, Mich., October 14, 1982; Theodore Bonaventura, interview with the author, Washington, D.C., February 12, 1982; Ed Lock, interview with Peter Friedlander, Detroit, 1976; "Ford Man Tells of Job Selling," *United Auto Worker*, November 15, 1940; Ford Motor Company, "Place of Birth and Citizenship of Persons at Present Employed," April 22, 1940, box 37, Martindale Collection, Henry Ford Museum. See also C. L. R. James, *State Capitalism and World Revolution* (Detroit: Facing Reality, 1963), 40.

21. Lock, interview with Friedlander; Ford quoted in Frank Cormier and William J. Eaton, *Reuther* (Englewood Cliffs, N.J.: Prentice-Hall, 1970), 98; Johnson, *Maurice Sugar*, 223–24; Sward, *Legend of Henry Ford*, 370–80; Allan Nevins, *Ford: Decline and Rebirth, 1933–1962* (New York: Scribners, 1963), 159–64.

22. Reuther quoted in Johnson, *Maurice Sugar*, 223.

23. Cormier and Eaton, *Reuther*, 97–99; Reuther, *Brothers Reuther*, 199–200.

24. Frank Manfried, interview with Jack Skeels, June 26, 1960, 46–47; Victor Reuther, "Battle of the Ford Overpass" [draft manuscript], file 9, box 71, VGR Collection; Cormier and Eaton, *Reuther*, 100–103; Sward, *Legend of Henry Ford*, 389–96.

25. "Walter Reuther Statement," May 26, 1937, file 5, box 22, VGR Collection.

26. "Ford Motor Co. versus UAW," *Decisions and Orders of the National Labor Relations Board*, vol. 6 (August 1–30, 1939), 629–30.

27. Cormier and Eaton, *Reuther*, 105.

28. Reuther, *Brothers Reuther*, 202–4; May Reuther, interview with Jack Skeels, May 29, 1963. Reuther recovered quickly. The next day George Edwards found him "somewhat lumpy and blue but grinning and planning to be back on the job tomorrow." Edwards to "Darlings" [parents], May 27, 1937, file 5, box 11, George Edwards, Sr., Collection.

29. Margaret Collingwood Nowak, *Two Who Were There: A Biography of Stanley Nowak* (Detroit: Wayne State University Press, 1989), 115; Catherine Gelles, interview with Jack Skeels, July 7, 1961; "Ford Motor Co. versus UAW," 631–32.

30. Both the *Detroit News* and the *Detroit Free Press* published full-page pictorials on the Battle of the Overpass. See, for example, "UAW Organizers Are Beaten and Thrown off Ford Property," *Detroit Free Press*, May 27, 1937.

31. Cormier and Eaton, *Reuther*, 107; Johnson, *Maurice Sugar*, 224; Sward, *Legend of Henry Ford*, 380–88; Lock, interview with Friedlander; Richard Frankensteen, "Tactics, Strategy, Conditions of the Ford Organizing Drive," January 12, 1938, file 7, box 8, WPR Collection.

32. "Labor," *Time*, June 7, 1937, 13.

33. "35,000 Attend Rally of UAW," *Detroit Free Press*, June 6, 1937; Kraus, *Heroes of Unwritten Story*, 308–9.

34. Johnson, *Maurice Sugar*, 224; Cormier and Eaton, *Reuther*, 109.

35. "Reuther's Statement on Ford," *West Side Conveyor*, August 17, 1937; UAW, "Proceedings of the Fourth Constitutional Convention," Cleveland, Ohio, March 31–April 5, 1939, 102–3; WPR, interview with Kraus, 1938.

36. My history of the labor slate campaign relies heavily upon Bruce Nelson, "Auto Work-

ers and Electoral Politics: The Detroit Municipal Election of 1937" (paper delivered at the North American Labor History Conference, Detroit, October 1989).

37. "AFL Drafts a Primary Slate," *Detroit News*, September 16, 1937; "AFL to Combat CIO Candidates for Political Office," *New York Times*, October 12, 1937; Johnson, *Maurice Sugar*, 228–30.

38. "The Five Conspirators," *Detroit Free Press*, October 29, 1937, file 24, box 4, VGR Collection.

39. WPR speech [undated transcript], file 28, box 3, VGR Collection.

40. Hugh T. Lovin, "CIO Innovators, Labor Party Ideologues, and Organized Labor's Muddles in the 1937 Detroit Elections," *Old Northwest* 8 (Fall 1982): 223–43. See also Nelson, "Auto Workers and Electoral Politics"; Gary Gerstle, *Working-class Americanism: The Politics of Labor in a Textile City, 1914–1960* (New York: Cambridge University Press, 1989), 232–47; Steve Fraser, *Labor Will Rule: Sidney Hillman and the Rise of American Labor* (New York: Free Press, 1991), 363–70; and Eric Davin, "The Littlest New Deal: How Democracy and the Union Came to Western Pennsylvania" (paper delivered at the Annual Meeting of the Organization of American Historians, Chicago, April 1992).

41. "What We Stand For," "Labor Slate" file, box 12, Henry Kraus Collection; Lovin, "CIO Innovators, Labor Party Ideologues," 237.

42. "Contributions from Locals to Political Action Committee," "Labor Slate" file, box 12, Henry Kraus Collection; Johnson, *Maurice Sugar*, 228–30; *West Side Conveyor*, November 10, 1937.

43. Nelson, "Auto Workers and Electoral Politics"; *New York Times* quoted in Lovin, "CIO Innovators, Labor Party Ideologues," 232; "CIO Gets Two of Its Slate in the First Nine," *Detroit Free Press*, October 5, 1937; "CIO Builds Hopes Here: Detroit Vote Takes on National Import," *Detroit News*, October 8, 1937.

44. "A Big Vote Will Scare GM," *West Side Conveyor*, October 30, 1937.

45. "Safety in a Big Vote Only," *Detroit Free Press*, October 29, 1937; "CIO's Slate Denounced by Coughlin," *Detroit News*, October 8, 1937.

46. "AFL Endorses Reading after a Stormy Session," *Detroit Free Press*, October 21, 1937; "The Issue," *Detroit Free Press*, October 18, 1937.

47. WPR radio speech, file 3, box 28, VGR Collection.

48. "The Bosses' Game," *Ternstedt Flash* (November 1937). See also Johnson, *Maurice Sugar*, 266–68.

49. Alan Strachan, "Analysis of Vote—November 2, 1937 Elections," "Labor Slate" file, box 12, Henry Kraus Collection.

50. Meier and Rudwick, *Black Detroit*, 3–22; Alan Strachan, "A History of the Work of the Political Action Committee in the Detroit Municipal Elections," "Labor Slate" file, box 12, Henry Kraus Collection.

51. Strachan, "History of the Work of the PAC"; Nelson, "Auto Workers and Electoral Politics."

52. George Edwards to "Family," February 1937, file 2, box 11, George Edwards, Sr., Collection; Carl Haessler, interview with Jack Skeels, November 27, 1959; Manfried, interview with Skeels; May Reuther, interview with Jack Skeels, May 29, 1963; "Don't Miss Your Meeting," *West Side Conveyor*, August 3, 1937.

53. For more description, see Ruth Meyerowitz, "Organizing and Building the UAW: Women at the Ternstedt General Motors Parts Plant, 1936–1950" (manuscript in author's possession, 1979); "Lecture Series: Democracy in Action," *West Side Conveyor*, September 7, 1937.

54. WPR to May Wolf, November 7, 1938, in Linda Reuther's possession.

55. Alan Strachan, interview with the author, Washington, D.C., September 10, 1987; Frank Winn, telephone interview with the author, June 17, 1986.

56. Stewart Strachan, telephone interview with the author, September 21, 1987; Adolph Germer to John L. Lewis, October 30, 1937, file 27, box 4, VGR Collection.

57. "Report on Condition of Plants in the West Side Local 174," February 24, 1938, file 1, box 45, WPR Collection; Lock, interview with Friedlander; George Edwards, interview with the author.

58. George Edwards, interview with the author; Meyerowitz, "Organizing the UAW"; Nowak, *Two Who Were There*, 129–60. Reuther quoted in Nowak, *Two Who Were There*, 116.

59. George Edwards, to "Darlings" [parents], January 2, 1937, file 1, box 10, George Edwards, Sr., Collection.

60. Anderson, "My Battle against Reuther," 110–33; Margaret Edwards, telephone interview with the author, November 7, 1994; Dollinger, interview with the author; George Edwards, interview with Clinton Fair, Detroit, August 10, 1979, George Meany Center for Labor Studies.

61. *West Side Conveyor*, July 20, 1937; Carl Haessler, interview with Jack Skeels, July 1, 1960.

62. Margaret Edwards, interview with the author.

63. WPR to "Mayichka" [May Wolf], March 14, 1937, in Linda Reuther's possession.

64. Reuther, *Brothers Reuther*, 194.

65. WPR to May Wolf, June 13, 1937, in Linda Reuther's possession.

66. Reuther, *Brothers Reuther*, 195.

67. VGR, interview with the author, Washington, D.C., August 25, 1986; Margaret Edwards, interview with the author; John Anderson, telephone interview with the author, July 27, 1987; Meyerowitz, "Organizing the UAW."

68. Anderson, "My Battle against Reuther," 103. Tribeau also favored a relatively more cooperative relationship with plant management, a plausible program at Fleetwood where speedup grievances were few.

69. Edsforth, *Class Conflict and Cultural Consensus*, 185–86; "Against Splitting Local," *West Side Conveyor*, August 13, 1938; "For a Cadillac UAW Charter" [1939?], file 21, box 6, VGR Collection.

70. "Big Delegation," *West Side Conveyor*, July 20, 1937; Anderson, "My Battle against Reuther," 115–25. Actually, Briggs Local 212, with 133 votes, was the largest local represented at the UAW's 1937 convention in Milwaukee.

71. "Women Take a Hand in Rent Strike," file 11, box 1, Dorothy Kraus Collection; George Edwards, interview with the author; James Lorence, "Controlling the Reserve Army: Organizing the Unemployed in Michigan, 1929–1942" (New Brunswick, N.J.: Rutgers University Press, forthcoming), 238–45. See also Elizabeth Faue, *Community of Suffering and Struggle: Women, Men, and the Labor Movement in Minneapolis, 1915–1945* (Chapel Hill: University of North Carolina Press, 1991), 100–141.

72. Meyerowitz, "Organizing the UAW"; Nowak, *Two Who Were There*, 114.

73. Nancy Gabin, *Feminism in the Labor Movement: Women and the United Auto Workers, 1935–1975* (Ithaca, N.Y.: Cornell University Press, 1990), 33–37; Meyerowitz, "Organizing the UAW"; "Joint Council Delegates," July 5, 1938, file 29, box 1, WPR Collection; "Women in Auto," May 1938, file 17, box 1, Dorothy Kraus Collection. The large Ternstedt delegation was a bit more than one-fifth female.

74. "Why West Side Is Strong," *West Side Conveyor*, April 10, 1940; see also "Organizing Parts Plants," *United Auto Worker* (March 1939).

75. "Report on Condition of Plants"; Kraus, *Heroes of Unwritten Story*, 366–67.

76. "No More Illusions," *West Side Conveyor*, February 8, 1938; "Resist Wage Cuts," *West Side Conveyor*, February 22, 1938.

77. Nowak, *Two Who Were There*, 121. Job setters adjusted the production machinery for unskilled workers.

78. "In the Matter of Federal Screw Works and Local 174, United Automobile Workers of America," *Decisions and Orders of the National Labor Relations Board*, vol. 21 (March 1–22, 1940), 100–107; "Report on Condition of Plants."

79. "Background of Federal Screw Works Strike," March 30, 1938, file 44, box 1, WPR Collection.

80. "Everybody out Monday to Picket Federal Screw," *West Side Conveyor*, March 29, 1938.

81. "Cops Fail to Smash Strike," *West Side Conveyor*, April 5, 1938.

82. Daniel Gallagher, interview with Jack Skeels, January 23, 1960, 47; "Forty Injured in Strike Riot," *Detroit News*, March 31, 1938; "Forty-eight Persons Hurt in Two Strike Riots," *New York Times*, March 31, 1938; WPR, interview with Kraus.

83. Nowak, *Two Who Were There*, 125.

84. "Kelsey-Hayes Picket," *West Side Conveyor*, April 5, 1938.

85. Lorraine Majka, "Organizational Linkages, Networks, and Social Change in Detroit" (Ph.D. diss., Wayne State University, 1981), 103–8. Police Commissioner Heinrich Pickert, prominently identified with the American Legion and the more conservative elements of the German community, made Detroit's Special Investigations Bureau, "the red squad," a scourge of picket lines of all kinds. Frank Donner, *Protectors of Privilege: Red Squads and Police Repression in Urban America* (Berkeley: University of California Press, 1990), 55.

86. "Cops Fail to Smash Strike"; "Statement by President Reuther on Police Savagery," March 31, 1938, "Federal Screw" file, box 12, Henry Kraus Collection.

87. "Federal Screw Pact Restores Old Pay Rates," *West Side Conveyor*, April 12, 1938.

88. Reuther, *Brothers Reuther*, 206–9; "Attack Staged at Home While Guests Watch," *Detroit Free Press*, April 11, 1937.

89. VGR, "Battle of the Overpass," file 9, box 71, VGR Collection.

90. VGR, "Battle of the Overpass"; "UAW Investigation of Shooting of Walter and Victor Reuther," May 18, 1950, VGR file, vol. 38, FBI Reading Room, Washington, D.C.; see also the UAW summary of Willard Holt's career in UAW to FBI, May 18, 1950, FBI-VGR file, vol. 38, 16–19. By denying that he had ever met Holt, Reuther made a tactical mistake at the trial: Holt's attorney then supplied a stream of witnesses who truthfully asserted that they had seen both Reuther and George Edwards at bargaining conferences with Gillespie and Holt. After his acquittal, the Ford Motor Company flew Holt to New York, where he helped construct the company's World's Fair exhibition.

91. WPR, "A Program to Organize Competitive Shops," May 1938, file 7, box 1, WPR Collection.

CHAPTER 6: GENERAL MOTORS AND GENERAL MAYHEM

1. "Conference of GM Delegates," November 14–15, 1937, box 11, Henry Kraus Collection, 1, 56, 79.

2. "General Motors," *Fortune* (December 1938): 41. After tracking the New Deal leftward, *Fortune*'s utterly respectful yet meticulously researched four-part series on the giant corporation signaled publisher Henry Luce's determination to once again celebrate managerial capitalism. See also Joseph Thorndike, "The Liberal and Salutary

Path: *Fortune Magazine* and the New Deal" (M.A. thesis, University of Virginia, 1992).

3. From *Detroit News*, April 2, 1937, as quoted in Paul Sifton, "The Record," in "UAW Pre-1945" file, box 29, Paul Sifton Papers, Library of Congress.

4. "General Motors IV: A Unit in Society," *Fortune* (March 1939): 45, 150–52; Ed Cray, *Chrome Colossus: General Motors and Its Times* (New York: McGraw-Hill, 1980); John B. Rae, "Alfred Pritchard Sloan, Jr.," in *Encyclopedia of American Business History and Biography: The Automobile Industry, 1920–1980* (New York: Facts on File, 1989), 402–13.

5. Alfred Chandler, Jr., *Strategy and Structure: Chapters in the History of American Industrial Enterprise* (Garden City, N.Y.: Doubleday, 1962), 158–99 passim; Louis Galambos and Joseph Pratt, *The Rise of the Corporate Commonwealth* (New York: Basic Books, 1988), 167–69; "General Motors," 178; Peter Drucker, *The Concept of the Corporation* (New York: McGraw-Hill, 1946), 46.

6. Colin Gordon, *New Deals: Business, Labor, and Politics in America, 1920–1935* (New York: Cambridge University Press, 1994), 35–45; James Fink, "William Knudsen," in *Encyclopedia of American Business*, 268.

7. "General Motors Plans Expansion to Cost $50,000,000," *New York Times*, August 12, 1935; Sloan as quoted in Doug Reynolds, "Engines of Struggle: Technology, Skill and Unionization at General Motors, 1930–1940," *Michigan Historical Review*, 15 (Spring 1989), 69–85.

8. "GM and Ford Are Moving Out," *Business Week*, April 3, 1937, 16; Reynolds, "Engines of Struggle," 71–80.

9. Alfred Sloan, *My Years with General Motors* (New York: Doubleday, 1964), 406; Steve Jefferys, *Management and Managed: Fifty Years of Crisis at Chrysler* (New York: Cambridge University Press, 1986), 68–87.

10. Robert Travis to Henry Kraus, March 17, 1937, box 10, Henry Kraus Collection; Ted LaDuke quoted in Doug Reynolds, "We Exploit Tools, Not Men: The Speed-up and Militance at General Motors, 1930–1940," in *Work, Recreation and Culture: Selected Essays in U.S. Labor History*, ed. Martin Blatt and Martha Norkunas (New York: Garland, forthcoming); UAW Education Department, *How to Win for the Union* (Detroit: UAW, 1940).

11. Ronald Edsforth, *Class Conflict and Cultural Consensus: The Making of a Mass Consumer Society in Flint, Michigan* (New Brunswick, N.J.: Rutgers University Press, 1987), 176–85; Robert Travis to Adolph Germer, May 17, 1937, box 11, Henry Kraus Collection.

12. Neil Herring and Sue Thrasher, "UAW Sit-down: Atlanta, 1936," in *Working Lives*, ed. Mark Miller (New York: Pantheon, 1980), 172–83; Sidney Fine, *Sit-down: The General Motors Strike of 1936–1937* (Ann Arbor: University of Michigan Press, 1969), 320–28; Reynolds, "We Exploit Tools, Not Men."

13. Margaret Collingwood Nowak, *Two Who Were There: A Biography of Stanley Nowak* (Detroit: Wayne State University Press, 1989), 110–16; "Slowdown on in a GM Plant," *Detroit Free Press*, April 16, 1937; Ruth Meyerowitz, "Organizing and Building the UAW: Women at the Ternstedt General Motors Part Plant, 1936–1950" (manuscript in author's possession, 1979).

14. Jefferys, *Management and Managed*, 3–24, 68–87. As Jefferys emphasizes, additional reasons for the relatively greater power of the union at Chrysler included management's early recognition of the shop-steward system that grew out of the company union there. At GM, by contrast, the NRA-era works council scheme was a purposefully sketchy affair, involving a maximum of six or seven employee representatives per plant.

15. Albert Sobey to Mssrs. Coquillette, Cowing, Good, Magee, et al., "Objectives as Outlined by Mr. Knudsen, March 27, 1934," vertical file, General Motors Institute of Technology, Flint, Mich.; see also Reynolds, "Foremen on the Line: Management and Labor at General Motors, 1925–1937" (manuscript in author's possession, 1989).

16. Jefferys, *Management and Managed*, 77–86; "Supplementary Agreement," April 12, 1937 [copy], box 1, WPR Collection; Reuther quoted in Reynolds, "We Exploit Tools, Not Men."

17. Quoted in Reynolds, "Foremen on the Line."

18. Stephen DuBrul to Alexander Sacks, January 1938, "Automobile Industry, 1936–1945" file, box 92, Alexander Sacks Papers, Franklin D. Roosevelt Library.

19. "Move to Condemn Sit-ins: Storm in the Senate," *New York Times*, April 2, 1937; "GMC Demands Halt in Sit-Downs," *New York Times*, April 3, 1937; Fine, *Sit-down*, 334.

20. Sidney Fine, *Frank Murphy: The New Deal Years* (Chicago: University of Chicago Press, 1979), 342–48; Henry Kraus, *Heroes of Unwritten Story: The UAW, 1934–1939* (Urbana: University of Illinois Press, 1993), 303.

21. John L. Lewis, address, April 7, 1937, "Chrysler Strike" file, box 11, Henry Kraus Collection.

22. Adolph Germer to John L. Lewis, April 14, 1937, reel 11, Papers of John L. Lewis, Microfilming Corporation of America.

23. Mortimer and Kraus quoted in Roger Keeran, *The Communist Party and the Auto Workers Unions* (Bloomington: Indiana University Press, 1980), 190.

24. George Edwards, "The Shop Steward System and Industrial Democracy" [notes], "April-May, 1937" file, box 4, George Edwards, Jr., Collection; Henry Kraus, *Heroes of Unwritten Story*, 297–98.

25. WPR, speech at Unity Caucus meeting, August 1937, file 22, box 4, VGR Collection; see also Eric Chester, *Socialists at the Ballot Box* (New York: Praeger, 1985), 70–73.

26. "Biographical Sketch of Homer Martin, 1937," vertical file. Martin may have briefly joined the Socialist Party at this time.

27. Irving Howe and B. J. Widick, *The UAW and Walter Reuther* (1949; reprint, New York: Random House, 1973), 51.

28. Stewart Strachan, telephone interview with the author, September 21, 1987; Kraus, *Heroes of Unwritten Story*, 288–89. This perception may well have crystallized in March 1937 when Martin and Richard Frankensteen were seeking to evacuate the Chrysler plants and encountered sometimes vituperative resistance among the sit-downers.

29. Peter Friedlander, "The Social Bases of Politics in a UAW Local: Midland Steel, 1933–1941" (paper delivered at the Annual Meeting of the Organization of American Historians, New York, April 1977); Alan Brinkley, *Voices of Protest: Huey Long, Father Coughlin, and the Great Depression* (New York: Oxford University Press, 1982); Steve Fraser, *Labor Will Rule: Sidney Hillman and the Rise of American Labor* (New York: Free Press, 1991), 416–18.

30. Kraus, *Heroes of Unwritten Story*, 319–20; Russell Merrill, interview with Jack Skeels, August 27, 1960; Fine, *Sit-down*, 77, 94; George Blackwood, "The United Automobile Workers of America, 1935–1951" (Ph.D. diss., University of Chicago, 1951), 53. As the UAW exploded in size, Martin found support among many autoworkers who might ordinarily have been hostile to the union, including Black Legionnaires in Flint. See Martin Hayden, "Hint Red Plot to Kill Faction-Torn UAW," *Detroit News*, November 19, 1937.

31. Keeran, *Communist Party*, 190–91; Victor Reuther, *The Brothers Reuther and the*

Story of the UAW (Boston: Houghton Mifflin, 1976), 184–85; WPR, interview with Henry Kraus, Detroit, 1938, copy in author's possession.

32. Jay Lovestone to W. Jett Lauck, October 4, 1937, box 47, W. Jett Lauck Collection, Alderman Library, University of Virginia. See also Larry Klein to Will Herberg, June 22, 1936; Klein to Sasha Zimmerman, July 19, 1936; Andrew Bishop to Zimmerman, August 9, 1936; all in ILGWU-UAW correspondence file, ILGWU headquarters, New York City. The Lovestoneites seem to have had one substantial base in the auto industry, in Lansing, where Lester Washburn, a CPO member, had built an effective and militant local at Reo Motor Car Company.

33. Jay Lovestone to W. Jett Lauck, September 17, 1937, and Lovestone to Lauck, October 4, 1937, both in file 4, box 33, VGR Collection; Morris Field, "Bad Times, Your Union and You," *United Auto Worker*, December 25, 1937. Of course, this industrial relations strategy was framed in pseudo-Bolshevik terms. Thus, William Munger, Martin's Lovestoneite editor of the *United Auto Worker*, justified UAW conciliation of General Motors by comparing the union's concessions there with Lenin's decision to sign the humiliating treaty of Brest-Litovsk with the Germans in 1918. To which George Edwards, equally at ease with the history of the Russian revolution, shot back, "If we had no ammunition, and no men and no arms, I'd be willing to give GM Poland too!" Keeran, *Communist Party*, 195.

34. WPR, "Purpose of Caucus and Report of Steering Committee," July 1937, file 17, box 5, VGR Collection; WPR to May Wolf, April 22, 1937 (courtesy of Linda Reuther); WPR to Wolf, April 25, 1937 (courtesy of Linda Reuther); Eric Chester, *Socialists and the Ballot Box* (New York: Praeger, 1985), 77.

35. WPR to May Wolf, April 22, 1937 (courtesy of Linda Reuther).

36. Ibid.; WPR, speech at Unity Caucus meeting. To the *Daily Worker* the Reuther brothers were "Socialists who were not infected with the poison of Trotskyism or influenced to any large extent by the sectarianism of the militant Socialists." Quoted in Chester, *Socialists and the Ballot Box*, 77.

37. WPR, speech at Unity Caucus meeting. As long as George Addes, Edward Hall, and Wyndham Mortimer were kept on the executive board, the Unity Caucus was willing to see Martin increase his strength by adding two Progressives: Richard Frankensteen and R. J. Thomas, the latter a leader at Local 7, which represented workers in Chrysler's second-largest Detroit factory.

38. Quoted in Jack Skeels, "The Development of Political Stability within the UAW" (Ph.D. diss., University of Wisconsin, 1957), 48.

39. Kraus, *Heroes of Unwritten Story*, 324.

40. UAW, "Proceedings of the Second Annual Convention," Milwaukee, Wisc., August 23–29, 1937, 156–57.

41. Ibid., 164–65; Kraus, *Heroes of Unwritten Story*, 334–36.

42. UAW, "Proceedings of the Second Annual Convention," 206 passim; Kraus, *Heroes of Unwritten Story*, 342–46.

43. Frank Cormier and William J. Eaton, *Reuther* (Englewood Cliffs, N.J.: Prentice-Hall, 1970), 118; "UAW Convention Ends in Unity," *Daily Worker*, August 27, 1937; UAW, "Proceedings of the Second Annual Convention," 282, 285–86. Afterwards, Walter quipped to his comrades: "One Reuther is enough." Indeed, there would never be more than one Reuther holding elective office in the UAW. Roy lost his bid for the presidency of the Flint's big amalgamated local in early 1938 when factionalism and layoffs generated a sharp backlash against union radicals. Thereafter, Roy lost his "base" in the UAW; thus, his work as an organizer and International representative in the 1930s and 1940s remained tentative and episodic. Roy Reuther to George Addes,

June 5, 1939, and Roy Reuther to Addes, March 5, 1940, both in file 32, box 6, VGR Collection.

44. Homer Martin to William Knudsen, September 16, 1937, box 10, Henry Kraus Collection; Keeran, *Communist Party*, 193–94.

45. "Ask President Martin to Retract Charge," *West Side Conveyor*, October 19, 1937; Carl Haessler, interview with Jack Skeels, July 1, 1960.

46. "West Side Well Represented," *West Side Conveyor*, November 3, 1937.

47. "Ternstedt and Fleetwood Divisions Have Instructed Their Delegates as Follows," November 13, 1937, file 6, box 18, WPR Collection.

48. "General Motors Delegate Conference" [transcript], Detroit, November 14–15, 1937, box 3, Henry Kraus Collection, 27.

49. "GM Delegate Conference," 31; WPR, radio script, March 3, 1939, "Factionalism" file, box 1, WPR Collection. According to Henry Kraus, Reuther and a West Side delegation spoke with Martin for three hours on the afternoon of the first day of the conference, convincing the UAW president to repudiate the agreement. "Go back and plague GM," Martin told Reuther. WPR, interview with Kraus.

50. "GM Delegate Conference," 79, 90; Stewart Strachan, telephone interview with the author, November 17, 1987.

51. *Pontiac Auto Worker* quoted in Paul Sifton, "The Record," "UAW-CIO Pre-1945" file, box 29, Paul Sifton Collection.

52. Martin Hayden, "Fisher Scores New Strikers," *Detroit Times*, November 18, 1937, and "GM Issues Warning to Auto Union," *Detroit News*, November 19, 1937, both in scrapbooks, Joe Brown Collection.

53. Chester, *Socialists and the Ballot Box*, 80; "Call National UAW Chiefs Here in Strike Crisis," *Detroit Times*, November 20, 1937, and "GM Strikers Defy Own Union Leaders," *New York Times*, November 20, 1937, in scrapbooks, Joe Brown Collection.

54. "Strikers Warned by Martin," *Detroit News*, November 21, 1937, and "Martin's Plea Ends Pontiac Strike," *Detroit Times*, November 22, 1937, in scrapbooks, Joe Brown Collection; editorial, *Socialist Call*, December 2, 1937.

55. "Knudsen Sees Future Peril to Collective Bargaining," *Detroit Free Press*, November 20, 1937.

56. Stewart Strachan, interview with the author, November 17, 1987.

57. Carl Rudow, "Governor Murphy Warns Labor," *Detroit News*, November 24, 1937, scrapbooks, Joe Brown Collection; Chester, *Socialists and the Ballot Box*, 80–81.

58. Louis Stark, "Reds in Auto Union Try to Oust Martin," *New York Times*, November 27, 1937, and "Auto Labor Peace Again in Balance," *New York Times*, November 28, 1937.

59. Frank Winn to Louis Stark, December 5, 1937, box 12, Henry Kraus Collection.

60. Harvey Klehr, "American Communism and the United Auto Workers: New Evidence in an Old Controversy," *Labor History* 24 (Summer 1983): 404–13; Chester, *Socialists and the Ballot Box*, 82; "Michigan CP Leader Praises Union Stand on Wildcat Strikes," *Daily Worker*, December 2, 1937. William Weinstone, the CP's leading functionary in Michigan, gave the new line definitive shape: endorsing the UAW condemnation of the Pontiac strike, he asserted "unequivocally and emphatically that the Communists and the Communist Party have never in the past and do not now in any shape, manner or form advocate or support unauthorized and wildcat actions" ("Michigan CP Leader," *Daily Worker*, December 2, 1937).

61. "Ternstedt Unionists Debate Short Hours," *West Side Conveyor*, March 10, 1938; "Local 174 Dues Record," file 9, box 1, WPR Collection.

62. United Auto Workers–International Executive Board minutes, January 17, 1938,

UAW-IEB Collection, 22; Ben Fischer, "Auto Union Maps Plans for Jobless," *Socialist Call*, January 29, 1938; William Dowell to all UAW executive board members, March 5, 1938, "March 1938-January 1939" file, box 1, UAW-GM Collection.

63. "Carl Haessler's Analysis of 7th March 1938 GM Pact," "GM" file, box 31, Joe Brown Collection, 7; "Draft Letter to Martin on GM Agreement" [WPR's notations in margin], "Reuther to Martin" file, box 1, UAW-GM Collection.

64. William Dowell to "All General Motors Locals," April 19, 1938, and Dowell to "Chairmen of Bargaining Committees in All General Motors Locals," April 29, 1938, "March 1938-January 1939" file, box 1, UAW-GM Collection.

65. Henry Kraus, "A Pastor Losing His Flock," March 24, 1938, box 12, Henry Kraus Collection; WPR, interview with Joe Brown, Detroit, June 16, 1938, "UAW Factionalism" file, box 28, Joe Brown Collection.

66. "West Side Cheers Martin," *Detroit News*, December 13, 1937; "Bob's Report of First 'Peace Meeting,'" December 15, 1937, "Factionalism" file, box 12, Henry Kraus Collection; Robert Kanter, interview with Joe Brown, Detroit, December 22, 1937; Joe Brown to Edward Wieck, December 28, 1937, "Joe Brown correspondence" file, box 10, Edward Wieck Collection.

67. George Edwards, interview with Henry Kraus, Detroit, 1938; Ben Fischer to Gus Tyler, March 23, 1938, box 10, Daniel Bell Collection, Tamiment Library, New York University; Benjamin Stolberg, *The Story of the CIO* (New York: Viking, 1938), 132–34. Though a partisan of the Old Guard, Stolberg's description of the SP national trade union policy was accurate: "The Socialist Party has been wobbling all over the lot. Norman Thomas exercises a largely nominal authority over it. Well-meaning and vague, he temperamentally cannot give cohesion to a movement, and since 1936 various wings in the party have been pulling in different directions. . . . Its policies are determined in different places by the temperament of local leaders."

68. George Edwards to "Family," October 5, 1939, file 6, box 3, George Edwards, Sr., Collection; Frank Marquart, *An Auto Worker's Journal: The UAW from Crusade to One-Party Union* (University Park: Pennsylvania State University Press, 1975), 82–83.

69. "Labor," *Time*, April 4, 1938, 14.

70. Ben Fisher to Gus Tyler, November 2, 1937, box 10, Daniel Bell Collection, Tamiment Library, New York University.

71. Ben Fischer, "Auto Bulletins," November 1937–August 1938, box 10, Daniel Bell Collection, Tamiment Library, New York University. At age twenty, Fischer's perspective was not precisely that of the Local 174 auto group: he was part of the Trotskyist-tinged Clarity faction within the SP.

72. Ben Fischer to Gus Tyler, July 28, 1938, box 10, Daniel Bell Collection, Tamiment Library, New York University.

73. Tucker Smith to "Comrades," July 22, 1938, reel 36, Socialist Party of America Collection, Library of Congress. In the spring of 1938 Tucker Smith easily defeated Roy Reuther for the chairmanship of the Michigan Socialist Party. Smith made Martin chairman of the SP's "Keep America Out of War" Committee, and he was determined to swing the party auto comrades into an alliance with the UAW president.

74. Ben Fischer to "Comrades," September 26, 1938, box 10, Daniel Bell Collection, Tamiment Library, New York University.

75. Norman Thomas to Ben Fischer, March 31, 1938, "January-March 1938" file, box 5, George Edwards, Jr., Collection.

76. Francis Henson to Norman Thomas, January 10, 1938, reel 7, Socialist Party of American Collection, Library of Congress; Tucker Smith and Homer Martin ("Detroit Committee to Keep America Out of War") to "Dear Brother," April 12, 1938, file 11,

box 1, WPR Collection; Tucker Smith to George Edwards, July 1938, "Undated 1930s" file, box 5, George Edwards, Jr., Collection; Norman Thomas to Ben Fischer, March 31, 1938, box 1, Daniel Bell Collection, Tamiment Library, New York University.

77. "Report on the CIO of Michigan and the UAWA," April 28, 1938, box 10, Daniel Bell Collection, Tamiment Library, New York University.

78. Keeran, *Communist Party*, 195–97; Kraus, *Heroes of Unwritten Story*, 370–75.

79. Victor Reuther recounts this conversation in *Brothers Reuther*, 189–90; its gist is corroborated in "Report on the CIO of Michigan and the UAWA," April 28, 1938. Weinstone's bargain with Frankensteen split the CP auto faction. Both Wyndham Mortimer and John Anderson (the CP leader of Local 155) continued to oppose Richard Leonard for the CIO secretary-treasurer job. See also Klehr, "American Communism and the United Auto Workers," 410–11.

80. Klehr, "American Communism and the United Auto Workers," 410–11. In the aftermath of the Lansing CIO convention, Weinstone lost his post as Michigan party secretary.

81. Keeran, *Communist Party*, 197. In the aftermath of the Lansing fight, Martin had briefly tried to make the auto Socialist group an ally, appointing Edwards to head WPA organizing work and again putting Reuther in charge of the Ford drive. But the suspensions destroyed the tentative rapprochement. See "Confidential Report of the Socialist Party on the Inner Situation in the Auto Union," June 7, 1938, "Socialist Party" file, box 16, Henry Kraus Collection; "Reuther Back in High Favor," *Detroit News*, May 25, 1938.

82. WPR to May Wolf, June 13, 1938 (courtesy of Linda Reuther).

83. Louis Stark, "Auto Union Splits on Red Tactics; Martin Suspends Five High Officials," *New York Times*, June 14, 1938; Christopher Johnson, *Maurice Sugar: Law, Labor, and the Left in Detroit, 1912–1950* (Detroit: Wayne State University Press, 1988), 230–33.

84. Ben Fischer to Art McDowell, June 16, 1938, and Fischer to Tucker Smith, June 16, 1938, both in box 10, Daniel Bell Collection, Tamiment Library, New York University; George Edwards to "Darlings" [parents], July 9, 1938, file 16, box 11, George Edwards, Sr., Collection.

85. Quoted in Frank Winn, "The Record," "UAW-CIO Pre-1945" file, box 29, Paul Sifton Collection.

86. Joe Brown to Edward Wieck, June 17, 1938, "UAW factionalism" file, box 28, Joe Brown Collection; Ben Fischer to Gerry [last name unknown], June 18, 1938, Daniel Bell Collection, Tamiment Library, New York University.

87. "The Auto Union Struggle" and "Heads UAWA Peace Efforts," *Socialist Call*, July 23, 1938, file 26, box 4, VGR Collection; Ben Fischer, "Auto Bulletin," July 23, 1938, box 10, Daniel Bell Collection, Tamiment Library, New York University. Even Tucker Smith admitted that the article was a "perfect weapon in the hands of the CP who are trying to discredit us by saying we have made a deal with Martin" (Ben Fischer, "Auto Bulletin").

88. Nowak, *Two Who Were There*, 129–41; Fine, *Frank Murphy*, 490–94; Ben Fischer to Bob [Kanter], August 29, 1938, Daniel Bell Collection, Tamiment Library, New York University.

89. Tucker Smith to "Comrades," August 11, 1938, reel 35, Socialist Party of America Collection, Library of Congress; Ben Fischer to Norman Thomas, August 16, 1938, and Fischer to Bob [Kanter], August 29, 1938, both in box 10, Daniel Bell Collection, Tamiment Library, New York University. Thereafter Reuther was careful to keep Nor-

man Thomas at arm's length, though relations thawed in the 1950s when both men came to lend something of the same critical support toward U.S. foreign policy. In 1960 Reuther finally invited the seventy-six-year-old Thomas to speak at Solidarity House, where, despite Thomas's sharp comments on several aspects of UAW domestic policy, he was enthusiastically received by a room packed with UAW staff and union officials. But the occasion was nostalgic, not political. Murray Siedler, *Norman Thomas: Respectable Rebel* (Syracuse, N.Y. Syracuse University Press, 1961), 98–100.

90. But not Victor, Roy, and George Edwards. Victor Reuther refused to wear a Murphy button, and he angered the Communists by failing to distribute Ternstedt's share of the Murphy election flyers. Edwards, interview with Kraus.

91. "Joint Council Minutes," December 3, 1938, "Local 174" file, box 31, Joe Brown Collection; Meyerowitz, "Organizing the UAW," 228. Nowak, just elected to the Michigan Senate, did not run for organizer, but his substitute, Percy Keys, a black Communist from Cadillac's foundry, was defeated by Robert Kanter.

92. WPR to John L. Lewis, July 28, 1938, file 12, box 4, VGR Collection.

93. "What the CIO Leaders Are Calling Each Other," *Detroit Free Press*, August 7, 1938; Johnson, *Maurice Sugar*, 231–32.

94. Robert Kanter to Frank Winn, August 17, 1938, box 10, Daniel Bell Collection, Tamiment Library, New York University.

95. WPR to John L. Lewis, July 26, 1938, file 12, box 4, VGR Collection; Arthur G. McDowell to "Socialist Comrades in the Auto Industry," August 22, 1938, box 10, Daniel Bell Collection, Tamiment Library, New York University.

96. Philip Murray to John L. Lewis, September 1, 1938, file 27, box 4, VGR Collection.

97. "We Must Use Both Fists," *West Side Conveyor*, October 8, 1938.

98. WPR radio address, March 3, 1939, file 25, box 47, Maurice Sugar Collection; WPR to May Reuther, November 7, 1938 (courtesy of Linda Reuther).

99. "Ford Local President Tells Inside Story," "Factionalism 1939" file, box 30, Joe Brown Collection.

100. Martin Halpern, "The 1939 UAW Convention: Turning Point for Communist Power in the Auto Union?" *Labor History* 33 (Spring 1992): 196–99. Martin's desertion of the CIO cost him heavily with the UAW activists who dominated the delegate selection process: he chartered scores of rump locals, but his real strength, about one-tenth of the union, came from Flint and the heavily Protestant locals scattered along the union's mid-South borderland. Delegates attending the Cleveland convention represented about 180,000 members, several times the number even Martin claimed as his, but the UAW-CIO was still on shaky ground. Dues-paying membership was less than 50,000, and Martin loyalists posed a disruptive danger in virtually every workplace.

101. Halpern, "1939 UAW Convention," 200–208.

102. In the contest for one of the Detroit executive board seats, Reuther ran against Local 155's John Anderson, a self-acknowledged Communist. According to the calculations of Henry Kraus, Anderson received support from delegates in nine of the ten Unity locals in that region, while Reuther found votes in only half of these locals. Reuther's margin of victory may well have come from former Martin supporters in Dodge Local 3, as well as from Hudson Local 154, West Side Local 174, and Briggs Local 212. Kraus, *Heroes of Unwritten Story*, 411–13; Hillman quoted in Ben Fischer to "Comrades," April 3, 1939, box 10, Daniel Bell Collection, Tamiment Library, New York University.

103. Larry Rogin, interview with the author, Washington, D.C., January 6, 1986; Ben Fischer to Art McDowell, January 26, 1939, reel 36, Socialist Party of America Collection, Library of Congress. Mortimer reportedly told Hillman that "Eddie would be

nothing but a stooge for Walt, so Sidney replied that might be a good thing" (Fischer to McDowell, January 26, 1939).

104. Halpern, "1939 UAW Convention," 208–10; Louis Stark, "Ex-Chiefs Demand Auto Union Posts," *New York Times*, April 3, 1939.

105. WPR, interview with Frank Cormier and William J. Eaton, Detroit, August 27, 1967; Ed Hall, interview with Jack Skeels, August 10, 1959. Vice President Ed Hall wanted the job, but even Reuther's opponents were not enthusiastic about this truculent and undistinguished Wisconsin unionist.

CHAPTER 7: POWER UNDER CONTROL

1. R. J. Thomas, "History of the GM Department of the UAW-CIO," file 4, box 20, WPR Collection. The report was printed under UAW President R. J. Thomas's name, but Reuther almost certainly wrote or dictated it.

2. Thomas, "History of GM Department," 8. GM's stance represented a complete reversal of its union recognition policy before Flint. Then the company had asserted its willingness to negotiate with any group of workers, but without giving exclusive recognition to any one of them.

3. WPR to "All General Motors Locals," May 16, 1939, "January 7 to September 30, 1939" file, box 1, UAW-GM Collection. An executive committee, chosen by the national GM council, would formulate policy and conduct negotiations.

4. "Highlights of the Report of Walter P. Reuther, June 10, 1939," file 7, box 26, WPR Collection.

5. Ibid.

6. Clayton Fountain, *Union Guy* (New York: Viking Press, 1949), 99; George Merrilli, interview with Jack Skeels, February 21, 1963.

7. John W. Livingston, interview with Paul Addes (AFL-CIO Oral History Project), Fort Myers, Fla., September 28, 1979.

8. VGR, interview with the author, Washington, D.C., August 25, 1986; Irving Bluestone, interview with the author, Detroit, October 25, 1987; Ben Blackwood to WPR, February 8, 1940, file 7, box 18, WPR Collection; see also Peter Friedlander, *The Emergence of a UAW Local* (Pittsburgh: University of Pittsburgh Press, 1975).

9. Edward Levinson, *Labor on the March* (New York: University Books, 1956), 326; Fountain, *Union Guy*, 110–11.

10. Eddie Levinson to Herman Wolf, June 19, 1939, file 17, box 1, Herman Wolf Collection.

11. WPR, introduction to Levinson, *Labor on the March*, xi–xii; Brendan Sexton, telephone interview with the author, October 18, 1985; Frank Winn, telephone interview with the author, June 17, 1986.

12. General Motors, "Thirty-first Annual Report of General Motors Corporation for Year Ended December 31, 1939," 7, 32.

13. "Fair Visitors 'Fly' over U.S. of 1960," *New York Times*, April 19, 1939; "Futurama Is Voted the Most Popular," *New York Times*, May 17, 1939; "Big Crowds at Fair," *New York Times*, July 4, 1939.

14. "Minutes of the GM International Council," June 10–11, 1939, file 18, box 9, Charles Beckman Collection; "GM Declines to Recognize UAW Groups," *Detroit News*, June 10, 1939; "GM Still Neutral, Knudsen Tells Both UAW Divisions," *Detroit Free Press*, June 11, 1939.

15. WPR quoted in Steve Babson, *Building the Union: Skilled Workers and Anglo-Gaelic*

Immigrants in the Rise of the UAW (New Brunswick, N.J.: Rutgers University Press, 1991), 220.

16. John Barnard, "Rebirth of the United Automobile Workers: The General Motors Tool and Diemakers' Strike of 1939," *Labor History* 27 (Spring 1986): 173–77.

17. Babson, *Building the Union*, 219–21; WPR, interview with Frank Cormier and William J. Eaton, Detroit, July 1, 1968, Frank Cormier and William J. Eaton Collection, John F. Kennedy Library.

18. *Time* quoted in Kevin Boyle, "Rite of Passage: The 1939 General Motors Tool and Die Strike," *Labor History* 27 (Spring 1986): 192.

19. Spencer Fullerton, "On the Labor Front," *Cleveland Plain Dealer*, July 16, 1939.

20. Boyle, "Rite of Passage," 192–93; Barnard, "Rebirth of the UAW," 180.

21. UAW leaflet quoted in Barnard, "Rebirth of the UAW," 181.

22. Ed Cray, *Chrome Colossus: General Motors and Its Times* (New York: McGraw-Hill, 1980), 212.

23. James F. Dewey to John R. Steelman, July 13, 1939, Federal Mediation and Conciliation Service Collection, file 3975, RG 199, National Archives.

24. Knudsen quoted in "Production: A Plan for Planes," *Time*, January 9, 1941, 13.

25. Barnard, "Rebirth of the UAW," 185; "Victory for Skilled Men," *United Auto Worker* (September 1939).

26. John W. Livingston, interview with Frank Cormier and William J. Eaton, Washington, D.C., February 13, 1969.

27. WPR to May [Reuther], October 13, 1939; May to WPR, October 11 1939, and October 12, 1939; WPR to May, February 19, 1940; copies in Linda Reuther's possession.

28. "CIO Program for GM Workers," *GM Facts*, March 1, 1940; "Record Rallies to Greet Lewis, Hillman, Murray," *United Auto Worker*, March 27, 1940.

29. "CIO and AFL Ballots Cast in GM Election," *Detroit News*, April 19, 1940.

30. WPR, GM conference speech, February 9, 1941, file 23, box 1, Charles Beckman Collection.

31. "GM Mediation Goes Forward," *Detroit Free Press*, June 8, 1940; "GM Parley Faces Crisis: Pay Raise and Steward Issues Threaten," *Detroit News*, June 10, 1940; "UAW-CIO Fearful of Public's Reaction to Strike at GM," *Wall Street Journal*, June 14, 1940; John R. Steelman to James F. Dewey, memorandum of telephone call, June 10, 1940, "UAW-GM" file, RG 199, National Archives.

32. Beverly Smith, "Secretary Wilson's Year of Trial," *Saturday Evening Post* 226 (May 1, 1954): 113.

33. Knudsen quoted in E. Bruce Geelhoed, "Charles Erwin Wilson," in *The Automobile Industry, 1920–1980*, ed. George S. May (New York: Facts on File, 1989), 483.

34. National Defense Mediation Board, "UAW-GM," May 6, 1941 [transcript], p. 653, RG 202, National Archives.

35. Peter Drucker, *Adventures of a Bystander* (New York: Harper & Row, 1978), 275; Cray, *Chrome Colossus*, 335.

36. GM-UAW contract, June 24, 1940 [copy], "General Motors" file, RG 202, National Archives; Frederick Harrison and Robert Dublin, *Patterns of Union-Management Relations* (Chicago: Science Research Associates, 1947), 80.

37. "Concessions Won in New GM Agreement," file 17, box 26, WPR Collection.

38. WPR, GM conference speech.

39. Robert Macdonald, *Collective Bargaining in the Automobile Industry: A Study of Wage Structure and Competitive Relations* (New Haven, Conn.: Yale University Press, 1963), 134–59 passim; Ruth Milkman, *Gender at Work: The Dynamics of Job Segregation by Sex during World War II* (Urbana: University of Illinois Press, 1986), 1–11, 42–48.

40. Thomas A. Johnstone, interview with George Heliker, Detroit, February 19, 1954,

ACC 940.5, Allan Nevins Collection, Henry Ford Museum; WPR to Sidney Hillman, September 9, 1939, ACWA (Amalgamated Clothing Workers of America) Papers, Cornell University (unprocessed at time of research). For example, in October 1939 Reuther spent a brutal week in the San Francisco area, where R. J. Thomas and he argued, cajoled, and threatened Local 76, representing GM workers in Oakland, out of a potentially disastrous work stoppage. WPR to May [Reuther], October 13, 1939, in Linda Reuther's possession.

41. UAW Education Department, "How to Win for the Union" (1940), 4–11.

42. UAW brief before National War Labor Board, June 15, 1942, file 8, box 27, WPR Collection.

43. WPR, GM conference speech. The shop-steward system did function at some GM plants, but without official recognition. See UAW, "How to Win for the Union," 11.

44. Steve Jefferys, *Management and Managed: Fifty Years of Crisis at Chrysler* (New York: Cambridge University Press, 1986), 68–87; Nelson Lichtenstein, "'The Man in the Middle': A Social History of Automobile Industry Foremen," in *On the Line: Essays in the History of Auto Work*, ed. Nelson Lichtenstein and Stephen Meyer (Urbana: University of Illinois Press, 1989), 163–77.

45. Alfred Sloan, *My Years with General Motors* (New York: Doubleday, 1964), 406; Charles Wilson to William Davis, May 9, 1941, "UAW-GM" file, RG 202, National Archives.

46. GM agreement, June 24, 1940, "May-August 1940" file, box 1, UAW-GM Collection.

47. "Production Standards," file 12, box 17, Ken Bannon Collection. The designation "Paragraph 78" first appeared in the 1941 UAW-GM contract, but the same wording is present in the 1940 contract section titled "Timing Operations."

48. John Anderson, *Fifty Years of the UAW: From Sit-down to Concessions: An Autobiographical Account* (Chicago: International Socialist Organization, 1985), 32. Paragraphs 8, 78, and 117 remained virtually unchanged in the UAW-GM contract for more than fifty years.

49. Drucker, *Adventures of a Bystander*, 266–67; Sloan, *My Years with GM*, 446; Howell John Harris, *The Right to Manage: Industrial Relations Policies of American Business in the 1940s* (Madison: University of Wisconsin Press, 1982), 29.

50. WPR, GM conference speech.

51. "Concessions Won in the New GM Agreement," file 2, box 19, WPR Collection; "UAW Brief before NWLB," June 15, 1942, file 8, box 27, WPR Collection.

52. John Anderson, "My Battle against Reuther: The Story of a Rank and File Autoworker" (manuscript in author's possession, 1986), 133.

53. On GM's management outlook, see Doug Reynolds, "We Exploit Tools, Not Men: The Speed-up and Militance at General Motors, 1930–1940" in *Work, Recreation and Culture: Selected Essays in U.S. Labor History*, ed. Martin Blatt and Martha Norkunas (New York: Garland, forthcoming); and Harris, *The Right to Manage*, 27–29. Studies of UAW-organized firms in which the union exercised more shop power include Jefferys, *Management and Managed*, 68–126 passim; Stephen Amberg, "The Triumph of Industrial Orthodoxy: The Collapse of Studebaker-Packard," in Lichtenstein and Meyer, *On the Line*, 190–96; and Stephen Meyer, *"Stalin over Wisconsin": The Making and Unmaking of Militant Unionism, 1900–1950* (New Brunswick, N.J.: Rutgers University Press, 1992), 105–36 passim.

54. Boyle, "Rite of Passage," 202.

55. WPR, GM conference speech; Gabriel Alexander, "The General Motors–UAW Experience," in *Arbitration and the Law: Proceedings of the Twelfth Annual Meeting, National Academy of Arbitrators*, ed. Jean McKelvey (Washington, D.C.: BNA, 1959), 113.

56. National Defense Mediation Board, "UAW-GM" [transcript], May 6, 1941, p. 636, RG 202, National Archives.

57. Christopher Tomlins, "The New Deal, Collective Bargaining, and the Triumph of Industrial Pluralism," *Industrial and Labor Relations Review* 39 (October 1985): 19–34; Katherine Stone, "The Post-War Paradigm in American Labor Law," *Yale Law Journal* 90 (June 1981): 1509–80.

58. Steve Fraser, *Labor Will Rule: Sidney Hillman and the Rise of American Labor* (New York: Free Press, 1991), 40–145 passim.

59. Ibid., 114–45 passim; Thomas Kennedy, *Effective Labor Arbitration: The Impartial Chairmanship of the Full-Fashioned Hosiery Industry* (Philadelphia: University of Pennsylvania Press, 1948), 4–19; George W. Taylor, "Hosiery," in *How Collective Bargaining Works*, ed. Harry A. Millis (New York: Twentieth Century Fund, 1942), 450–72.

60. Sumner H. Slichter, *Union Policies and Industrial Management* (Washington, D.C.: Brookings Institution, 1941), 1–2; William Leiserson, "Constitutional Government in American Industries," *American Economic Review* 12 (March 1922): 62.

61. Fraser, *Sidney Hillman*, 209–12; Taylor, "Hosiery," 473–507; Kennedy, *Effective Labor Arbitration*, 20–25. For an excellent survey of the economic conditions and ideological mindset that gave rise to collaborations such as those in hosiery, see Sanford Jacoby, "Union-Management Cooperation in the United States: Lessons from the 1920s," *Industrial and Labor Relations Review* 57 (October 1983): 18–33.

62. WPR, "Plan for Organizing Competitive Shops," May 1938, file 13, box 3, WPR Collection; "Collective Bargaining: The Evolution of the Process," *United Auto Worker*, March 20, 1940; "Practical Labor Union Problems," *United Auto Worker*, April 10, 1940.

63. Edward Levinson, interview with Edward Wieck, Detroit, October 25, 1939; Robert Kanter, interview with Edward Wieck, Detroit, November 2, 1939; both in box 10, Edward Wieck Collection.

64. C. O. Skinner, interview with Edward Wieck, Detroit, October 31, 1939, box 10, Edward Wieck Collection.

65. WPR, interview with Edward Wieck, Detroit, October 30, 1939, box 10, Edward Wieck Collection.

66. National Defense Mediation Board, "UAW-GM" [transcript], May 5, 1941, p. 436; May 6, 1941, p. 636; both in RG 202, National Archives.

67. "Re: 17 Suspended Men, Members Local 581," December 7, 1940, "GM Department 1941" file, box 1, WPR Collection; Ronald Edsforth, *Class Conflict and Cultural Consensus: The Making of a Mass Consumer Society in Flint, Michigan* (New Brunswick, N.J.: Rutgers University Press, 1987), 194–95.

68. Quoted in Edsforth, *Class Conflict*, 195.

69. United Auto Workers–International Executive Board minutes, October 7, 1940, UAW-IEB Collection, 1–6; "Victory Won by Reuther," *Detroit News*, October 10, 1940.

70. "Report of International GM Executive Committee," December 7, 1940, UAW-IEB Collection; UAW-IEB minutes, December 17, 1940, UAW-IEB Collection, 23–25, 48–51; William Allen, "Auto Union to Hold GM Contract Revision Parley," *Daily Worker*, January 23, 1941; R. J. Thomas, GM conference speech, February 9, 1941, file 1, box 1, UAW-GM Collection.

71. WPR, GM conference speech.

72. Ibid.; "Auto Delegates Battle for a Militant Policy," *Daily Worker*, March 17, 1941.

73. Edsforth, *Class Conflict and Cultural Consensus*, 191–97.

74. "Management's Future in Labor Relations," "Walter Reuther—Unused Articles, 1948" file, box 23, UAW Research Department Collection.

75. UAW, "How to Win for the Union," 14.

76. George Heliker, "Grievance Arbitration in the Automobile Industry: A Comparative Analysis of Its History and Results in the Big Three" (Ph.D. diss., University of Michigan, 1954), 118–30.

77. Tomlins, "The New Deal, Collective Bargaining," 28–32; Thomas Johnstone, interview with George Heliker, Detroit, March 1954, Allan Nevins Collection, Henry Ford Museum.

78. G. Allan Dash, interview with Clare McDermott, Washington, D.C., February 13, 1978, in National Academy of Arbitrators (NAA), *Oral History Project* (Washington, D.C.: National Academy of Arbitrators, 1982), 3–15.

79. WPR, GM conference speech; Harry Millis, "General Motors Decision A-2," October 28, 1940, "Decision A-6," November 15, 1940, and "Decision A-7," November 22, 1940; all in "UAW-GM Decisions," National Defense Mediation Board, box 21, RG 202, National Archives. For example, both Millis and Taylor ruled that management had no right to unilaterally abrogate "past work practices" if they had long been an uncontested part of the factory work regime.

80. WPR, GM conference speech.

81. George Taylor, "General Motors Decision A-13," February 7, 1941, and "Decision B-52," June 22, 1941; both in "UAW-GM Decisions," National Defense Mediation Board, box 21, RG 202, National Archives. See also Heliker, "Grievance Arbitration," 156–64, 301–3.

82. Carl Gersuny and Gladis Kaufman, "Seniority and the Moral Economy of the U.S. Automobile Workers, 1934–1946," *Journal of Social History* 18 (Spring 1985): 467.

83. UAW-GM agreement, June 24, 1940, paragraph 8, p. 22 "UAW-GM," NDMB case files, National Archives.

84. National War Labor Board, UAW-GM case no. 111-4665-D [transcript], January 4, 1944, RG 202, National Archives; see also "GM Presentation on Paragraph 63," "Negotiations with the UAW—1955" vertical file, General Motors Institute, Flint, Mich.

85. George Taylor, "Umpire Decision A-19," February 11, 1941, in "UAW-GM Umpire Decisions," "UAW-GM" file, RG 21, National Archives; Dash, interview with McDermott, in NAA, *Oral History Project*, 15–16.

86. Donaldson Brown to William Harrington, January 7, 1941, box 35, accession no. 1813, Harrington Collection, Hagley Museum and Library, Wilmington, Del.; National Defense Mediation Board, "UAW-GM" [transcript], May 6, 1941, p. 629, RG 202, National Archives. Even DuPont's Brown endorsed grievance arbitration as a vehicle to dispose of disputes that might generate "continuing friction and annoyance" (Brown to Harrington, January 7, 1941).

87. Heliker, "Grievance Arbitration," 102.

88. Heliker, "Grievance Arbitration," 339–41; Johnstone, interview with Heliker; Bluestone, interview with the author.

89. Heliker, "Grievance Arbitration," 172; Dash, interview with McDermott, in NAA, *Oral History Project*, 4; "Workers Call Parley on GM Attack on Union," *Daily Worker*, October 7, 1940. GM's narrowly defined construction of the arbitrator's duties delayed selection of the first umpire by four months. Reuther wanted James F. Dewey, the U.S. Conciliation Service's chief mediator in Detroit. But Dewey rejected the lucrative offer because he saw the umpire post as essentially powerless compared with the range of issues he had mediated during the recent Chrysler and GM negotiations with tool and die makers.

90. James Atleson, "Wartime Labor Regulation, the Industrial Pluralists, and the Law of Collective Bargaining," in *Industrial Democracy in America: The Ambiguous Promise*, ed. Nelson Lichtenstein and Howell John Harris (New York: Cambridge University Press, 1993), 142–75.

91. Frederick Harbison and Robert Dublin, *Patterns of Union-Management Relations* (Chicago: Science Research Associates, 1947), 85; Ralph Seward, interview with Richard Mittenthal, in NAA, *Oral History Project*, 22–27.

92. Johnstone, interview with Heliker.

93. James Dunne, interview with George Heliker, Detroit, February 25, 1954, Henry Ford Museum; Heliker, "Grievance Arbitration," 114–16; Walter Jason, "It Looks Like He's the Fall Guy," *Labor Action*, February 18, 1952, 2.

94. Harbison and Dublin, *Patterns of Union-Management Relations*, 82; B. J. Widick, interview with George Heliker, Detroit, March 6, 1954, Henry Ford Museum. See also Heliker, "Grievance Arbitration," 343.

CHAPTER 8: 500 PLANES A DAY

1. On Reutherism, see Irving Howe and B. J. Widick, *The UAW and Walter Reuther* (1949; reprint, New York: Random House, 1973), 193–97; and Bert Cochran, *Labor and Communism: The Conflict That Shaped American Unions* (Princeton, N.J.: Princeton University Press, 1977), 189–91.

2. The literature is voluminous. See, most recently, Leo Ribuffo, "The Complexity of American Communism," in *Right, Center, Left: Essays in American History*, ed. Leo Ribuffo (New Brunswick, N.J.: Rutgers University Press, 1992), 129–60; Alan Wald, *The New York Intellectuals: The Rise and Decline of the Anti-Stalinist Left from the 1930s to the 1980s* (Chapel Hill: University of North Carolina Press, 1987), 128–225; William O'Neill, *The Great Schism: Stalinism and the American Intellectuals* (New York: Simon & Schuster, 1982), 13–97.

3. See, for example, the purge of Elizabeth Gurley Flynn from the leadership of the American Civil Liberties Union (ACLU). Samuel Walker, *In Defense of American Liberties: A History of the ACLU* (New York: Oxford University Press, 1990), 130–34; W. A. Swanberg, *Norman Thomas: The Last Idealist* (New York: Charles Scribner's Sons, 1976), 235–38.

4. Thompson quoted in Swanberg, *Norman Thomas*, 246. Norman Thomas burned his bridges to the generation of radicals he had once tutored when in May 1941 he shared a platform with Charles Lindbergh and Burton K. Wheeler of the America First Committee. See also Murray Seidler, *Norman Thomas: Respectable Rebel* (Syracuse, N.Y.: Syracuse University Press, 1961), 210.

5. WPR quoted in CIO, "Proceedings of the Third Constitutional Convention," Atlantic City, N.J., November 21, 1940, 25; Robert Clayton Pierce, "Liberals and the Cold War: Union for Democratic Action and Americans for Democratic Action, 1940–1949" (Ph.D. diss., University of Wisconsin, 1979), 11–37 passim. UDA showcased Reuther in one of its first public events, a New York luncheon presided over by Freda Kirchway of the *Nation*. WPR, "How Labor Would Win the War," December 13, 1941, file 256, reel 14, ADA microfilm, Library of Congress.

6. Peter H. Irons, "'The Test Is Poland': Polish Americans and the Origins of the Cold War," *Polish American Studies* (Summer 1974): 5–63; Donald E. Pienkos, "The Polish American Congress—An Appraisal," *Polish American Studies* 36 (1979): 6–43; Lorraine M. Lees, "National Security and Ethnicity: Contrasting Views during World War II," *Diplomatic History* (Winter 1987): 113–25. On the eve of the big NLRB elec-

tions at General Motors, during which Martin called the CIO "Communist," Reuther issued a press release (March 2, 1940) condemning the Soviet invasion of Finland, terming it no different than Hitler's invasion of Poland and Czechoslovakia. See Marvin Persky, "Walter Reuther, the UAW-CIO, and Third Party Politics" (Ph.D. diss., Michigan State University, 1974), 105.

7. UAW, "Proceedings of the Fifth Annual Convention," St. Louis, Mo., July 29–August 6, 1940, 293–303. For accounts of the 1940 convention, see Cochran, *Labor and Communism*, 151–55; Jack Skeels, "The Development of Political Stability within the UAW" (Ph.D. diss., University of Wisconsin, 1957), 132–35; Roger Keeran, *The Communist Party and the Auto Workers Unions* (Bloomington: Indiana University Press, 1980), 211.

8. UAW, "Proceedings of the Fifth Annual Convention," 112; on Lewis's defense-era politics, see Melvyn Dubofsky and Warren Van Tine, *John L. Lewis: A Biography* (New York: Quadrangle, 1977), 339–70 passim.

9. UAW, "Proceedings of the Fifth Annual Convention," 438–39; John Barnard, *Walter Reuther and the Rise of the Auto Workers* (Boston: Little, Brown, 1983), 72–73; Keeran, *Communist Party*, 211; Victor Reuther, *The Brothers Reuther and the Story of the UAW* (Boston: Houghton Mifflin, 1976), 221; Frank Cormier and William J. Eaton, *Reuther* (Englewood Cliffs, N.J.: Prentice-Hall, 1970), 167–68; Leonard Woodcock, interview with Frank Cormier and William J. Eaton, Atlantic City, May 5, 1968.

10. "Rebellious Michigan UAW Maps Intensified Roosevelt Drive," *Detroit News*, October 27, 1940; Lewis quoted in Persky, "Walter Reuther, the UAW-CIO," 115.

11. WPR, radio address, October 31, 1940, file 13, box 539, WPR Collection.

12. Quoted in Studs Terkel, *"The Good War": An Oral History of World War Two* (New York: Pantheon, 1984), 318.

13. John M. Blum, *V Was for Victory: Politics and American Culture during World War II* (New York: Harcourt Brace, 1976), 120; see also Steven Fraser, *Labor Will Rule: Sidney Hillman and the Rise of American Labor* (New York: Free Press, 1991), 454–58; Paul A. C. Koistinen, "Mobilizing the World War II Economy: Labor and the Military-Industrial Alliance," *Pacific Historical Review* 42 (1973): 443–78.

14. *CIO Economic Outlook* (March 1941): 2; Alan Clive, *State of War: Michigan in World War II* (Ann Arbor: University of Michigan Press, 1979), 19; Richard Polenberg, *War and Society: The United States, 1941–1945* (New York: J. B. Lippincott, 1972), 5–36.

15. I. F. Stone, *Business as Usual* (New York: Modern Age Books, 1941), 23–45, 65–79.

16. Campbell quoted in ibid., 228. I. F. Stone proved a brilliant publicist for the Reuther Plan; see Stone, "Labor Formulates Plane Speed-Up Plan to Help President End Defense Log Jam," *PM*, December 22, 1940; Stone, "Auto-Factory Planes? Why Not, British Ask after Own Tryout," *PM*, December 26, 1940; Stone, "Booming Aircraft Firms Fear Reuther Plan May Curb Profits," *PM*, January, 13, 1941; see also Stone's collection, *The War Years, 1939–1945* (Boston: Little, Brown, 1988), 17–23, 42–68; Barton Bernstein, "The Automobile Industry and the Coming of the Second World War," *Southwestern Social Science Quarterly* 47 (1966): 22–33.

17. Stone, *Business as Usual*, 187, 193.

18. I. F. Stone, interview with the author, Washington, D.C., February 2, 1979; Jacob Vander Meulen, *The Politics of Aircraft: Building an American Military Industry* (Lawrence: University of Kansas Press, 1991), 182–220 passim.

19. WPR, "500 Planes a Day: A Program for the Utilization of the Automobile Industry for Mass Production of Defense Planes," in *Walter P. Reuther: Selected Papers*, ed.

Henry Christian (New York: Macmillan, 1961), 2; Cormier and Eaton, *Reuther*, 185–87.

20. Stone, *Business as Usual*, 230–32.

21. WPR, "500 Planes a Day," 2–12. Reuther did not propose a particular fighter for mass production, but he may well have favored the Curtiss-Wright P-40 Warhawk, built in Buffalo. It was an inferior fighter whose design would have been frozen for long production runs had the Reuther Plan been put into effect. In fact, the Ford organization was nearly discredited by the enormous investment at Willow Run, which turned out so many lumbering B-24s. Jacob Vander Meulen to author, April 5, 1993.

22. Fraser, *Sidney Hillman*, 470–76; John Edgar Hoover to Attorney General [Robert Jackson], January 8, 1941, FBI FOIA file 61–9556-6, FBI Reading Room; Frank C. Broadbent to Colonel Lester, "Reuther Plan," January 24, 1941, box 3114, RG 165, National Archives; George R. Clark, "Strange Story of the Reuther Plan," *Harper's* 184 (1942): 645–54.

23. See Thorstein Veblen, *Engineers and the Price System* (New Brunswick, N.J.: Transaction, [1921] 1983); WPR, "500 Planes a Day," 1–2; I. F. Stone, telephone interview with the author, May 29, 1985.

24. Fraser, *Sidney Hillman*, 453.

25. Vander Meulen, *Politics of Aircraft*, 216; Eliott Janeway, *The Struggle for Survival* (New Haven, Conn.: Yale University Press, 1951), 220–24; Jacob Vander Meulen, "West Coast Aircraft Workers and the Early Warfare State, 1935–1941" (unpublished paper in author's possession, 1991).

26. Cormier and Eaton, *Reuther*, 186.

27. Paul A. C. Koistinen, "The Hammer and the Sword: Labor and the Military during World War II" (Ph.D. diss., University of California at Berkeley, 1964), 554–73; Fraser, *Sidney Hillman*, 473–74; John Brophy to "All Industrial Union Councils," February 17, 1941, "CIO Defense Plan" file, box 3, John Brophy Papers, Catholic University of America; see also Merton W. Ertell, "The CIO Industry Council Plan: Its Background and Implications" (Ph.D. diss., University of Chicago, 1955).

28. Quoted in Cormier and Eaton, *Reuther*, 191; Jerome Frank to "the President" [Franklin D. Roosevelt], December 30, 1940, "Reuther Plan" file, box 591, WPR Collection.

29. Joseph Rauh, interview with William J. Eaton, Washington, D.C., December 11, 1967.

30. Stone, *Business as Usual*, 221.

31. "Production," *Time*, January 7, 1941, 13; "Awaiting the President," *Washington Post*, December 29, 1940; Walter Lippmann, "Plan for Holding Gains of Labor," *Detroit Free Press*, January 10, 1941; Blair Moody, "Reuther's Plan Acts as a Spur," *Detroit News*, January 7, 1941.

32. Henry Stimson diaries (New Haven: Yale University Photographic Service, 1974), reel 6, October 1, 4, 7, and 16, 1940.

33. Joseph Alsop and Robert Kintner, "Reuther 500-Planes-Daily Plan Raises Critical Defense Query," *New York Herald Tribune*, January 19, 1941; Vander Meulen, *Politics of Aircraft*, 190; Jonathan Fanton, "Robert A. Lovett: The War Years" (Ph.D. diss., Yale University, 1978), 66–67.

34. H. H. Arnold to Robert Patterson, January 29, 1941, file 3, box 142, Robert Patterson Papers, Library of Congress; WPR, GM conference speech, February 9, 1941, file 23, box 1, Charles Beckman Collection. Patterson may well have offered Reuther a job on his industrial services staff, but Reuther would have rejected the offer because acceptance would have substantiated the accusations, from his enemies on the right

and left, that his interest in defense production amounted to little more than a campaign for a government job.

35. Janeway, *Struggle for Survival* 231. This is Janeway's paraphrase of Wilson's oft-expressed sentiments.

36. Clark, "Strange Story of the Reuther Plan," 649–50.

37. Vander Meulen, *Politics of Aircraft,* 186; Jonathan Zeitlin, "Flexibility and Mass Production at War: Aircraft Manufacture in Britain, the United States, and Germany, 1939–1945" (unpublished manuscript in author's possession, 1993). Reuther soon realized the difficulties of mass production of aircraft. Maj. Gen. Hap Arnold reported that "Mr. Reuther's comments after the Martin plant indicated that he was not too confident that airplane parts or sub-assemblies could be made with greater speed or efficiency in automobile factories. However, he re-affirmed his opinion that aircraft engine parts could be very efficiently constructed." Arnold to Patterson, January 29, 1941.

38. Quoted in Bill Goode, "Espionage in the Early Days of the UAW: A Case Study" (unpublished manuscript in author's possession, 1985). John Frey of the AFL Metal Trades Council also thought Reuther was a "communist" whose interest in boosting aircraft production was but a cover for gaining a subversive knowledge of military production facilities. Frey may have been G-2's original source for this interpretation of the Reuther Plan. Robert Patterson to [Edward] McGrady, January 31, 1941, file 3, box 142, Robert Patterson Papers, Library of Congress.

39. Custodial detention cards, "Walter Reuther" file, FBI-FOIA 61–9556–20, and "Victor Reuther" file, FBI-FOIA 61–7556–26, FBI Reading Room.

40. John Edgar Hoover to William S. Knudsen and Edwin M. Watson, January 8, 1941, "Walter Reuther" file, FBI-FOIA 61–9556–10, FBI Reading Room, 11; Richard Gid Powers, *Secrecy and Power: The Life of J. Edgar Hoover* (New York: Free Press, 1987), 233, 238. The Reuther brothers were dropped from the custodial detention list in November 1941, two months after they had won national publicity for again attacking the UAW Communists at the Buffalo convention. Urging their dismissal from the list was the Detroit Special Agent in Charge John Bugas, a sophisticated observer of the labor scene who would take over personnel and industrial relations responsibilities for the Ford Motor Company in 1943. John Bugas to [FBI] Director [J. Edgar Hoover], September 9, 1941, FBI Reading Room; John Edgar Hoover to SAC [Special Agent in Charge] Detroit, November 1, 1941, "Walter Reuther" file, 61–9556–28, FBI Reading Room.

41. Quoted in "Reuther Assailed in House as a Red," *Detroit Free Press,* January 17, 1941.

42. Reuther, *Brothers Reuther,* 714–19; the letter is reprinted in Cormier and Eaton, *Reuther,* 132–36.

43. "Dr. J. B. Matthews Discusses Walter Reuther," radio broadcast, April 23, 1958, file 6, box 594, WPR Collection; Paul Sifton, "Appendix A: The Letter from Russia: A Study in the Cynical Art of Character Assassination" [1958?], "UAW CIO Pre 1945" file, box 29, Paul Sifton Collection, Library of Congress. Matthews (who would soon become a prominent right-wing anti-Communist) remembered that Roy used this phrase in a conversation of February 20, 1934, in Flint, when Matthews stopped to lecture on behalf of the League for Industrial Democracy.

44. "Reuther's Plane Speed-up Plan Not OK'd by Workers," *Sunday Worker,* December 29, 1940.

45. Blair Moody, "A Communist? Reuther Gives His Side of the Story," *Detroit News,* May 19, 1941. Moody changed Reuther's phrase "stupid peasants" to "uneducated peasants." See Blair Moody to Fred Gaertner [undated], file 2, box 11, WPR Collection.

46. WPR, "Statement for *Detroit News*," May 20, 1941, file 2, box 11, WPR Collection; Moody to Gaertner [undated]; Reuther, *Brothers Reuther*, 216.

47. Cormier and Eaton, *Reuther*, 174–75; Eldorous Dayton, *Walter Reuther: The Autocrat of the Bargaining Table* (New York: Devin-Adair, 1958), 255–66.

48. Dayton, *Reuther*, 257.

49. "Reuther Case up Thursday," *Detroit News*, May 5, 1941; "Reuther Draft Case Returns to Board," *Detroit News*, May 20, 1941; Linda Reuther, interview with the author, San Anselmo, Calif., August 16, 1988.

50. UAW, "Proceedings of the 1941 Convention," Buffalo, N.Y., August 4–16, 1941, 702; Cormier and Eaton, *Reuther*, 175.

51. Alan Clive, *State of War: Michigan in World War II* (Ann Arbor: University of Michigan Press, 1979), 28; "Joint Meeting of Labor and Industry Subcommittees on General Automotive Problems" [verbatim transcript], January 6, 1942, reel 10, Amalgamated Clothing Workers Microfilm, University Publications of America, 26; U.S. Senate, Special Committee to Investigate the National Defense Program, "Manpower Problems in Detroit," 79th cong., 1st sess., March 9–11, 1945, pt. 28, 13648.

52. "Joint Meeting of Labor and Industry," 29.

53. Ibid., 108, 118; Blair Moody, "Advisory Role Given to Labor," *Detroit News*, January 8, 1942.

54. "OPM Flops Again," *Time*, January 19, 1942, 10–11; David Brody, "The New Deal and World War II," in *The New Deal: The National Level*, ed. John Braeman, Robert Bremner, and David Brody (Columbus: Ohio State University Press, 1975), 284–85; Reuther, *Brothers Reuther*, 230; Irving Briton Holly, Jr., "A Detroit Dream of Mass-produced Fighter Aircraft: The XP-75 Fiasco," *Technology and History* 28 (July 1987): 578–93. GM executives themselves may have been seduced by the mass-production vision, but their effort to build a new model with off-the-shelf parts and subassemblies ended in costly and embarrassing failure.

55. "Joint Meeting of Labor and Industry," 29. This meeting may have represented the high point of labor efforts to win some real representation within the wartime production agencies. Though Reuther's plan for tripartite administration of a converted auto industry was rejected, labor did win a compromise: a tripartite subcommittee. But when the idea was sent back to the OPM itself, it was watered down and scrapped in the reorganization that turned OPM into the War Production Board. See Koistinen, "Hammer and the Sword," 613–14.

56. Vander Meulen, *Politics of Aircraft*, 218–19; Fraser, *Sidney Hillman*, 480–94; Polenberg, *War and Society*, 12–16.

57. "The Gas-Engine Union," *Fortune* 24 (November 1941): 73; "Reuther of the Reuther Plan," *Business Week*, January 17, 1942, 60; WPR, "Labor's Place in the War Pattern," *New York Times Magazine*, December 13, 1942, 8, 36–37; Cormier and Eaton, *Reuther*, 194–95; Davis Wells, "GM-CIO Debaters Give Unity Pledge," *Detroit Free Press*, April 1, 1942; Carl Haessler, "GM-UAW Debate Ends on Win-the-War Note," April 1, 1942, Federated Press Microfilm Collection. Charles Wilson saw the debate as part of GM's public relations–industrial relations offensive against the UAW, and he was backed up by two executives from the corporate labor relations staff, Harry Anderson and Harry Coen.

58. Cormier and Eaton, *Reuther*, 198–99; VGR, interview with the author, Washington, D.C., August 25, 1986; Joe Rauh, interview with the author, March 10, 1989.

59. "Standardization of Tank Engine by U.S. Army First Urged by UAW-CIO Leader a Year Ago: Reuther Suggests Ford Engine Be Used," December 23, 1942, file 21, box 5, WPR Collection.

60. "Tooling Pools," April 11, 1944; Kenneth Cole to WPR, April 22, 1944; "Program to Expedite Tooling and Maintain High Levels of War Production" [undated press release]; all in file 3, box 33, WPR Collection.

61. Eric Sandeen, "The Design of Public Housing in the New Deal: Oskar Stonorov and the Carl Mackley Houses," *American Quarterly* 37, no. 5 (Winter 1985): 645–67; Ursula Cliff, "Oskar Stonorov: Public Housing Pioneer," *Design and Environment* 2 (Fall 1971): 50–54. With a partner, Stonorov won second prize in the Soviet Union's 1931 competition to design a Moscow "Palace of the Soviets." First prize went to Stalin's son-in-law.

62. Oskar Stonorov to WPR, October 29, 1941; Stonorov to John A. Kingsbury, November 6, 1941; Stonorov to WPR, November 7, 1941; Sidney Hillman to FDR, November 6, 1941; Stonorov to WPR, February 14, 1942; Stonorov to Leon Henderson, March 10, 1942; all in "Walter Reuther" file, Oskar Stonorov Papers, American Heritage Center, University of Wyoming.

63. Alan Mather, "The Battle of Willow Run," *Common Sense* 12 (February 1943): 39–42.

64. Herman Wolf, "Dymaxion Dwelling Machines," "Correspondence, 1944" file, box 7, Edward Levinson Collection.

65. "Now, Mrs. Roosevelt!" *Time*, January 19, 1942, 11; Cormier and Eaton, *Reuther*, 211; Jean Gould and Lorena Hickok, *Walter Reuther: Labor's Rugged Individualist* (New York: Dodd, Mead, 1972), 204–41; WPR to Mrs. Franklin Roosevelt, August 13, 1943, and Malvania Thompson to WPR, November 13, 1943, both in file 5, box 14, WPR Collection; WPR to Mrs. Franklin Roosevelt, July 11, 1944, Eleanor Roosevelt to WPR, July 13, 1944, WPR to Mrs. Franklin Roosevelt, October 13, 1944, all in file 6, box 14, WPR Collection.

66. Koistinen, "Hammer and the Sword," 63–64. Undersecretary of War Patterson may also have asked Reuther to be his special assistant at about this time.

67. CIO, "Proceedings of the Fifth Constitutional Convention," Atlantic City, N.J., November 7–11, 1942.

68. Roy Reuther to WPR [undated, but probably February to April 1943], file 3, box 14, WPR Collection; Koistinen, "Hammer and the Sword," 676.

69. Jeffery Dorwart, *Eberstadt and Forrestal: A National Security Partnership, 1909–1949* (College Station: Texas A&M University Press, 1991), 49–68; Polenberg, *War and Society*, 14; "Labor Production Division, Minutes of the Labor Policy Committee Meeting," October 1, 1942, file 7, box 33, WPR Collection; WPR to Ferdinand Eberstadt, October 16, 1942, file 7, box 33, WPR Collection; Cormier and Eaton, *Reuther*, 204.

70. WPR to Philip Murray, October 29, 1942, file 6, box 33, WPR Collection; Koistinen, "Hammer and the Sword," 670–90.

71. Roy Reuther to WPR [undated, but probably February to April 1943], file 3, box 14, WPR Collection.

CHAPTER 9: FAUSTIAN BARGAIN

1. Paul Sultan, *Labor Economics* (New York: Holt, 1957), 48; Daniel Bell, *The Coming of Post-Industrial Society: A Venture in Social Forecasting* (New York: Basic Books, 1973), 129–39.

2. Alan Clive, *State of War: Michigan in World War II* (Ann Arbor: University of Michigan Press, 1979), 170–74; Henry Shryock and Hope Eldridge, "Internal Migration in Peace and War," *American Sociological Review* 12 (February 1947): 27–39.

3. "Money and Real Weekly Earnings during Defense, War, and Reconversion Periods," *Monthly Labor Review* 64 (June 1947): 987–89; "New Rich, New Poor," *Time*, May 4, 1942, 16.

4. Sultan, *Labor Economics*, 71; Paul Blumberg, *Inequality in an Age of Decline* (New York: Oxford University Press, 1980), 65–84; H. M. Douty, "Review of Basic American Labor Conditions," in *Labor in Postwar America*, ed. Colston E. Warne (New York: Scholarly Resources, 1949), 124–27; Geoffrey Perrett, *Days of Sadness, Years of Triumph: The American People, 1939–1945* (Madison: University of Wisconsin Press, 1973), 335, 355.

5. See, for example, "The Gas-Engine Union," *Fortune* 24 (November 1941): 75.

6. Henry Stimson and Frank Knox to FDR, May 29, 1941, "Labor-1941" file, box 141, Robert Patterson Papers, Library of Congress.

7. Joel Seidman, *American Labor from Defense to Reconversion* (Chicago: University of Chicago Press, 1953), 67–73; James A. Gross, *The Reshaping of the National Labor Relations Board: National Labor Policy in Transition, 1937–1947* (Albany: State University of New York Press, 1981), 213–40.

8. John L. Lewis, telegram to Harold Christoffel [n.d.], quoted in UAW, "Proceedings of the 1941 Convention," Buffalo, N.Y., August 4–16, 1941, 96. This summary of the Allis-Chalmers strike is based on Stephen Meyer, *"Stalin over Wisconsin": The Making and Unmaking of Militant Unionism, 1900–1950* (New Brunswick, N.J.: Rutgers University Press, 1992), 63–104; and Steven Fraser, *Labor Will Rule: Sidney Hillman and the Rise of American Labor* (New York: Free Press, 1991), 463–65.

9. Bert Cochran, *Labor and Communism: The Conflict That Shaped American Unions* (Princeton, N.J.: Princeton University Press, 1977), 163; "The Right to Strike—Keystone of Liberty," *United Auto Worker*, April 30, 1941. On the formation of the NDMB, see Sidney Hillman's testimony in U.S. Senate, "Hearings before a Special Committee Investigating the National Defense Program," 77th cong., 1st sess., April 21, 1941, 125–28; and Nelson Lichtenstein, *Labor's War at Home: The CIO in World War II* (New York: Cambridge University Press, 1982), 47–53.

10. Quoted in Frank Cormier and William J. Eaton, *Reuther* (Englewood Cliffs, N.J.: Prentice-Hall, 1970), 160.

11. Keith Sward, *The Legend of Henry Ford* (New York: Rinehart, 1949), 406–7; Irving Howe and B. J. Widick, *The UAW and Walter Reuther* (1949; reprint, New York: Random House, 1973), 104.

12. The literature on the organization of the Ford Motor Company is large: August Meier and Elliott Rudwick, *Black Detroit and the Rise of the UAW* (New York: Oxford University Press, 1980), 82–107; Christopher Johnson, *Maurice Sugar: Law, Labor, and the Left in Detroit, 1912–1950* (Detroit: Wayne State University Press, 1988), 233–49; Allan Nevins and Frank Ernest Hill, *Ford: Decline and Rebirth, 1933–1962* (New York: Charles Scribner's Sons, 1964), 159–64; Sward, *Legend of Henry Ford*, 398–408; Nelson Lichtenstein, "Life at the Rouge: A Cycle of Workers' Control," in *Life and Labor: Dimensions of American Working-class History*, ed. Charles Stephenson and Robert Asher (Albany: State University of New York Press, 1986), 237–59; and Martin Halpern, "The Rouge Is Down" (manuscript in author's possession, 1992).

13. "GM Negotiations," *West Side Conveyor*, May 1, 1941, 1; Joe Brown, memo, July 17, 1941, "Factionalism, 1940–41" file, box 30, Joe Brown Collection.

14. Ronald Edsforth, *Class Conflict and Cultural Consensus: The Making of a Mass Consumer Society in Flint, Michigan* (New Brunswick, N.J.: Rutgers University Press, 1987), 196.

15. United Auto Workers–International Executive Board minutes, April 27, 1941, UAW-IEB Collection, 17–21.

16. NDMB, "General Motors Corporation and the United Automobile Workers-CIO, Recommendations" [press release], May 16, 1941, "GM-UAW" file, RG 202, National Archives. See also James Atleson, "Wartime Labor Regulation, the Industrial Pluralists, and the Law of Collective Bargaining," in *Industrial Democracy in America: The Ambiguous Promise*, ed. Nelson Lichtenstein and Howell John Harris (New York: Cambridge University Press, 1993), 142–75; and Katherine Von Wezel Stone, "The Post-War Paradigm in American Labor Law," *Yale Law Journal* 90 (1981): 1509–80.

17. National Defense Mediation Board, "General Motors Corporation" [transcript], May 8, 1941, 111–4665-D, RG 202, National Archives, 789–90. See also U.S. Senate, Special Committee to Investigate the National Defense Program, "Manpower Problems in Detroit," 79th cong., 1st sess., March 9–11, 1945, pt. 28, 13182, 13201.

18. Osgood Nichols to William H. Davis, "Publicity Procedure—General Motors," May 8, 1941, "National Defense Mediation Board" file, box 40, CIO Secretary-Treasurer's Office Collection.

19. Wyndham Mortimer, *Organize! My Life as a Union Man* (Boston: Beacon Press, 1971), 157.

20. Lew Michener, "Report of Activities for Region Six," in UAW-IEB minutes, December 16, 1940, UAW-IEB Collection.

21. Nelson Lichtenstein, *Labor's War at Home: The CIO in World War II* (New York: Cambridge University Press, 1982), 60–62; Elting E. Morison, *Turmoil and Tradition: The Life and Times of Henry L. Stimson* (New York: Atheneum, 1964), 426; Henry Stimson Diaries (New Haven: Yale University Photographic Service, 1974), reel 6, June 6, 1941.

22. "Responsible Unionism Wins at Inglewood," UAW *American Aircraft Builder*, July 12, 1941. This section on the North American Aviation strike is based largely on the author's *Labor's War at Home*, 56–66; see also Fraser, *Sidney Hillman*, 465–67.

23. Cochran, *Labor and Communism*, 128, 184; WPR, radio address, June 12, 1941, "1941-WPR" file, box 23, UAW Research Collection.

24. "Nazi Jab at Soviet Lands Flush on Plymouth Local," *Detroit News* [undated], and "The Line Has Changed Again" [undated leaflet], both in file 19, box 9, WPR Collection; WPR to May [Reuther], July 7, 1941 (courtesy of Linda Reuther).

25. Richard Deverall to FBI, August 3, 1943, in Richard Deverall Notebooks, vol. 2, Catholic University of America; "Gas-Engine Union," *Fortune* 24 (November 1941): 171; Johnson, *Maurice Sugar*, 263–67; "UAW Officers, Staff, 4–11–41," "Officers and Staff" file, box 31, Joe Brown Collection; Edward Levinson, "1941 Convention Document," file 4, box 17, WPR Collection; Cormier and Eaton, *Reuther*, 176; Edsforth, *Class Conflict and Cultural Consensus*, 204–5. Reuther staffers frequently complained of the close scrutiny Addes gave their field expenses. Others, and not only Reuther partisans, believed that Addes took kickbacks from the company that printed the *United Auto Worker*.

26. Howe and Widick, *UAW and Reuther*, 200; John R. Steelman, *Who's Who in Labor* (New York: Dryden Press, 1946), 295.

27. Len De Caux, *Labor Radical: From the Wobblies to the CIO* (Boston: Beacon Press, 1970), 413; Cochran, *Labor and Communism*, 190; Elizabeth Hawes, *Hurry up Please: It's Time* (New York: Reynal & Hitchcock, 1946), 143.

28. Brendan Sexton, telephone interview with the author, October 12, 1985; Jean Gould and Lorena Hickok, *Walter Reuther: Labor's Rugged Individualist* (New York: Doubleday, 1972), 186–87, 195–96.

29. Linda Reuther, interview with the author, San Anselmo, Calif., March 23, 1988; Gould and Hickok, *Reuther*, 195–96. Hickok was a confidant of Eleanor Roosevelt,

and her biography may well have been partially inspired by the former First Lady's friendship with Reuther. The work is uniformly enthusiastic toward the UAW leader, except on one point: May Wolf Reuther's enforced departure from work for the union.

30. WPR to "Mayichka Darling" [May Wolf], [November 1942?], courtesy of Linda Reuther; WPR to May [Reuther], February 8, 1944, January 24, 1945, January 25, 1945, courtesy of Linda Reuther.

31. William C. Pratt, "The Socialist Party, Socialist Unionists, and Organized Labor, 1936–1950," in *Political Power and Social Theory*, vol. 4, ed. Maurice Zeitlin (New York: JAI Press, 1984), 71; Larry Rogin, interview with the author, Washington, D.C., August 2, 1986; Brendan Sexton, telephone interviews with the author, October 12 and 18, 1985. Robert Kanter and Victor Reuther were still organizers for Local 174, and Roy Reuther was an International representative based in Pontiac and Flint. But Roy's failure to build his own political base in the region meant that his employment was subject to the vicissitudes of UAW factional politics there. When in 1942 a director hostile to the Reuthers won election there, Roy lost his job.

32. Michael Whitty, "Emil Mazey: Radical as Liberal: The Evolution of Labor Radicalism in the UAW" (Ph.D. diss., Syracuse University, 1968), 35–62; Frank Marquart, *An Auto Worker's Journal: The UAW from Crusade to One-Party Union* (University Park: Pennsylvania State University Press, 1975), 103–4; Ernest Mazey quoted in Marco Trbovich, "The Fighting Mazey Boys: What Happens When a Couple of Firebrands Grow Old," *Detroit Free Press*, March 31, 1974. Reuther labeled Mazey a "screwball" in spring 1941. "We hardly ever agree. Mazey's position on war is more nearly that of the Communist Party." See Barney Crump, "Notarized Statement," June 12, 1941, file 19, box 9, WRP Collection; this is an account of a Reuther caucus meeting crashed by unionists loyal to the Communist-line leadership of Plymouth Local 51.

33. Frank Boles, "A History of Local 212 UAW-CIO, 1937–1949: The Briggs Manufacturing Company, Detroit, Michigan" (Ph.D. diss., University of Michigan, 1990), 1–36; Roger Keeran, *The Communist Party and the Auto Workers Unions* (Bloomington: Indiana University Press, 1980), 77–95; Milton Derber, *Labor in Illinois: The Affluent Years* (Chicago: University of Illinois Press, 1989), 108–13; Al Nash, "A Unionist Remembers," *Dissent* (Fall 1977): 181–89.

34. See especially Joshua Freeman, *In Transit: The Transport Workers Union in New York City, 1933–1966* (New York: Oxford University Press, 1989), 104–5; and Steven Rosswurm, "The Catholic Church and the Left-Led Unions: Labor Priests, Labor Schools, and the ACTU," in *The CIO's Left-Led Unions*, ed. Steven Rosswurm (New Brunswick, N.J.: Rutgers University Press, 1992), 119–37.

35. "Catholic Lashes Red-Baiters," *United Auto Worker*, February 11, 1939; "Father Clancy Fought for Labor," *Detroit News*, June 29, 1961; Carl Haessler, interview with Jack Skeels, November 27, 1959: ACTU minutes, July 27, 1939, "General Meeting Minutes, 1939–40" file, box 3, ACTU Collection; Neil Betten, *Catholic Activism and the Industrial Worker* (Gainesville: University of Florida Press, 1976), 131–32. Meanwhile, Mooney undercut Father Coughlin's influence by ending syndication of his broadcasts. The ACTU role here cannot be overestimated. As late as 1941 UAW leaders of both factions opposed referendum election of national officers for fear that an open vote would give Coughlin a chance to demonstrate his influence within the union.

36. Betten, *Catholic Activism*, 129; Abe Zwerling, interview with the author, Washington, D.C., August 27, 1987; Bill Goode, telephone interview with the author, November 4, 1994.

37. Deverall quoted in ACTU minutes, July 27, 1939, "General Meeting Minutes,

1939–1940" file, box 3, ACTU Collection; Thomas Linton, "A Historical Examination of the Purposes and Practices of the Education Program of the UAW, 1936–1959" (Ph.D. diss., University of Michigan, 1960), 156–58; Richard Deverall to George Creel, February 10, 1949, Richard Deverall Notebooks, vol. 5, Catholic University of America.

38. Paul Weber quoted in Dennis A. Deslippe, "'A Revolution of Its Own': The Social Doctrine of the Association of Catholic Trade Unionists in Detroit, 1939–1950," *Records of the American Catholic Historical Society of Philadelphia* 102 (Winter 1991): 31; "What Is It?" *Michigan Labor Leader*, October 18, 1940. "Corporatism," announced the ACTU, "is a system of economic democracy" ("What Is It?" *Michigan Labor Leader*, October 18, 1940).

39. ACTU quoted in Rosswurm, *CIO's Left-Led Unions*, 127.

40. Haessler interview with Skeels, 264; Joe Brown to Edward Wieck, September 29, 1940, "UAW Factionalism" file, box 28, Joe Brown Collection.

41. Harvey A. Levenstein, *Communism, Anticommunism, and the CIO* (Westport, Conn.: Greenwood Press, 1981), 120; Gary Gerstle, *Working-class Americanism: The Politics of Labor in a Textile City, 1914–1960* (New York: Cambridge University Press, 1989), 279–89; Freeman, *In Transit*, 104–5, 148–51.

42. UAW, "Proceedings of the Eighth Convention," Buffalo, N.Y., October 4–10, 1943, 248–56; Martin Gerber, interview with the author, Bradley Beach, N.J., November 15, 1988; Henry Kraus, interview with the author, Washington, D.C., May 22, 1992; WPR to May Reuther, January 25, 1945 (courtesy of Linda Reuther); board data taken from Steelman, *Who's Who in Labor*, and from "Biography" vertical file.

   Representation closely followed the industrial geography of the automobile and aircraft industries. Detroit elected four regional directors, Cleveland/Akron two, Flint, Pontiac, Toledo, and Muskegon/Lansing/Saginaw one apiece. Unionized workers in the rest of the industry were combined into larger geographical regions: Indiana; St. Louis, Texas, and Kansas City; the South (Baltimore and Atlanta); Chicago and Wisconsin (soon split into two regions); California; Canada; and a large eastern region stretching from Pennsylvania to New England that elected two directors.

   Votes were weighted according to the size of each region, and the four general officers of the UAW (two vice presidents were added in 1942) cast individual ballots equal to that of the most powerful regional director. Meanwhile, the four Detroit directors were elected at large, almost always ensuring that the Reuther caucus and the Addes group would each win two. Outside Detroit, the regional directors Paul Miley and Richard Reisinger (Cleveland), Lew Michener (California), and George Burt (Canada) had been politicized in the Communist orbit and always voted with Addes. Reuther had the support of Richard Gosser (Toledo), Thomas Starling (Atlanta), Harvey Kitsman or George Nordstrom (Wisconsin Socialists), Jack Livingston (St. Louis), and Martin Gerber (a Socialist from Linden, New Jersey, elected in 1944 and the only Jew on the World War II executive board). The regional directors from Pontiac, Flint, Indiana, and the rest of Michigan frequently shifted their allegiances and their seats.

43. Edwin A. Lahey, "UAW Control Kept in Rank and File," *Buffalo Evening News*, quoted in UAW, "Proceedings of the 1941 Convention," 493–94. Delegate participation is also tallied from the index in "Proceedings," 827–32.

44. "Meeting Notes," June 16, 1941, file 15, box 4, WPR Collection. Typical attendees of Reuther caucus meetings that summer were seven members of the International executive board, key men from the ACTU, several old Socialists from the Reuther circle, and members of the anti-Communist opposition at Packard and Plymouth.

45. UAW, "Proceedings of the 1941 Convention," 19; Cormier and Eaton, *Reuther*, 177; Cochran, *Labor and Communism*, 184.

46. UAW, "Proceedings of the 1941 Convention," 82, 88, 95–96, 772.

47. Cormier and Eaton, *Reuther*, 178; Cochran, *Labor and Communism*, 189–93; Jack Skeels, "The Development of Political Stability within the UAW" (Ph.D. diss., University of Wisconsin, 1957).

48. UAW, "Proceedings of the 1941 Convention," 412, 420, 438; Michener quoted on p. 440.

49. Cochran, *Labor and Communism*, 192; Cormier and Eaton, *Reuther*, 180; UAW, "Proceedings of the 1941 Convention," 772 passim. The roll call was remarkable for splitting up a number of large locals that had been considered solidly lined up on the Reuther-Hillman side of the fence. For example, where Frankensteen still had much influence, at Locals 3 and 7 (Dodge Main and Chrysler Jefferson Avenue), the Reuther forces lost 105 votes. Reuther also found support for a harsher penalty for Michener erode at Local 154 (Hudson) and Local 235 (Chevy Gear and Axle), both of which had been solidly opposed to seating the Allis-Chalmers delegates two days before.

50. UAW, "Proceedings of the 1941 Convention," 308–11, 574; Cochran, *Labor and Communism*, 189. Christoffel also presented evidence that George Norstrum, the Reutherite regional director from Wisconsin, had used union money to fund leaflets and newspapers for an opposition group in Local 248.

51. UAW, "Proceedings of the 1941 Convention," 692–95.

52. Leonard Woodcock, interview with Frank Cormier and William J. Eaton, Atlantic City, N.J., May 5, 1968.

53. UAW, "Proceedings of the 1941 Convention," 702, 772 passim.

CHAPTER 10: PATRIOTISM AND POLITICS IN WORLD WAR II

1. Quoted in Alan Clive, *State of War: Michigan in World War II* (Ann Arbor: University of Michigan Press, 1979), 61.

2. Ibid., 60; Frank Cormier and William J. Eaton, *Reuther* (Englewood Cliffs, N.J.: Prentice-Hall, 1970), 205–6.

3. Earl S. Hawk (bargaining committee chairman, Buick Local 599) to WPR, July 22, 1942, and Walter Henderson (plant chairman, GM Diesel Engine Division, Local 174) to WPR, 1942, both in file 2, box 27, WPR Collection; "UAW Research Department Survey," February 1943, courtesy of Robert Korstad.

4. Galbraith quoted in Mark Leff, "The Politics of Sacrifice on the American Home Front in World War II," *Journal of American History* 77 (March 1991): 1301.

5. Paul A. C. Koistinen, "The Hammer and the Sword: Labor and the Military during World War II" (Ph.D. diss., University of California at Berkeley, 1964), 185–86; WPR quoted in Cormier and Eaton, *Reuther*, 199.

6. The background to the premium pay issue is discussed more fully in Nelson Lichtenstein, *Labor's War at Home: The CIO in World War II* (New York: Cambridge University Press, 1982), 96–101; Murray reported Roosevelt's understanding in CIO executive board minutes (microfilm edition), March 24, 1942, 8–9.

7. *CIO News*, March 30, 1942.

8. Discussion of the "Victory through Equality of Sacrifice" program is found in United Auto Workers–International Executive Board minutes, March 24, 1942, UAW-IEB Collection; and UAW "Proceedings of the War Emergency Conference," Detroit,

April 7–8, 1942, Detroit, 6–10. The UAW also bought $50,000 worth of radio time and newspaper ads to publicize the "Equality of Sacrifice" idea.

9. Leff, "Politics of Sacrifice," 1302–6; Lichtenstein, *Labor's War at Home*, 99–104.

10. "Report on CIO Aviation Drive since February 1941," box A7–23, John Brophy Collection, Catholic University of America; Nicholas Dragon to FDR, July 27, 1942, and IAM quotes from special Curtiss Aircraft edition, *American Aircraft Builder* (UAW-CIO), July 24, 1942, both in Franklin D. Roosevelt Papers, Official File 142.

11. Lichtenstein, *Labor's War at Home*, 103–7.

12. UAW, "Proceedings of the Seventh Annual Convention," Chicago, August 3–9, 1942, 297, 301.

13. Dwight Macdonald, "The World's Biggest Union: How Are the Auto Workers Facing the Future?" *Common Sense* (November 1943): 411.

14. UAW-IEB minutes, August 24–31, 1942, UAW-IEB Collection; UAW, "Proceedings of the Seventh Annual Convention," 92.

15. UAW, "Proceedings of the Seventh Annual Convention," 96, 98, 534–79.

16. "General Motors Hits Back," *Business Week*, April 4, 1942, 70–71.

17. Sanford Jacoby, "Labor-Management Cooperation in World II," in *Technological Change and Workers' Movements*, ed. Melvyn Dubofsky (Beverly Hills, Calif.: Sage Publications, 1985), 100–29; H. W. Anderson to WPR, March 20, 1942, and WPR to C. E. Wilson, March 23, 1942, both in box 1, UAW-GM Collection.

18. Richard Deverall to Philleo Nash, "McNutt Manpower Regulations Arouse Widespread Opposition from Top Labor Leaders," April 19, 1943, Richard Deverall Notebooks, Catholic University of America.

19. WPR, "Program on Production and Manpower Submitted to the War Manpower Commission," January 16, 1943, file 2, box 21, WPR Collection.

20. Nancy Gabin, *Feminism in the Labor Movement: Women and the United Auto Workers, 1935–1975* (Ithaca, N.Y.: Cornell University Press, 1990), 50–51. Even Ternstedt's Irene Young feared an influx of women "from bakeries, beauty shops, restaurants and all other kinds of employment, where rates are very, very low." See UAW, "Proceedings of the Seventh Annual Convention," 357.

21. UAW, "Proceedings of the Seventh Annual Convention," 357.

22. Gabin, *Feminism in the Labor Movement*, 63.

23. Mary Anderson, "Milestone in Fight for Rights of Women Workers," *United Auto Worker*, October 1, 1942; Gabin, *Feminism in the Labor Movement*, 65–69.

24. U.S. Department of Labor, *Termination Report of the National War Labor Board*, vol. 1 (Washington, D.C.: Government Printing Office, 1946), 229–33; WPR, "Contributing Factors Leading to Dissatisfaction and Unrest in the Automobile Industry," June 22, 1944, and WPR, testimony, both in U.S. Senate, Special Committee to Investigate the National Defense Program, "Manpower Problems in Detroit," 79th cong., 1st sess., March 9–11, 1945, pt. 28, 13224–40, 13679–86; Robert Macdonald, *Collective Bargaining in the Automobile Industry: A Study of Wage Structure and Competitive Relations* (New Haven, Conn.: Yale University Press, 1963), 208–10.

25. Department of Labor, *Termination Report of the NWLB*, 1134–36; *United Auto Worker* ["Tool, Die, and Engineering" edition], April 1, 1941, January 1, 1942, and March 1, 1942; *Wage Earner*, October 13, 1942, November 13, 1942; *Labor Action*, September 23, 1942; UAW-IEB minutes, December 7–11, 1942, UAW-IEB Collection; Joseph Ferris to R. J. Thomas, October 26, 1942, box 7, Local 212 Collection.

26. Howell John Harris, *The Right to Manage: Industrial Relations Policies of American Business in the 1940s* (Madison: University of Wisconsin Press, 1982), 63–87 passim; Nelson Lichtenstein, "'The Man in the Middle': A Social History of Automobile

Industry Foremen," in *On the Line: Essays in the History of Auto Work,* ed. Nelson Lichtenstein and Stephen Meyer (Urbana: University of Illinois Press, 1989), 153–89.

27. Harry W. Anderson, testimony before U.S. Senate, "Manpower Problems in Detroit," 79th cong., 1st sess., March 9–11, 1945, pt. 28, 13782–84; "Wage Structure of the Motor Vehicle Industry," *Monthly Labor Review* 54 (February 1942): 300–301; see also Nelson Lichtenstein, "Auto Worker Militancy and the Structure of Factory Life, 1937–1955," *Journal of American History* 67 (September 1980): 335–53.

28. Exhibit no. 1435, "Detroit Manpower Problems," U.S. Senate, "Manpower Problems in Detroit," 79th cong., 1st sess., March 9–11, 1945, pt. 28, 13563–609; see also Lichtenstein, "Auto Worker Militancy," 342–47.

29. William McAulay (administrator of Local 50, Willow Run), report, June 3, 1942, box 7, R. J. Thomas Papers. For a detailed statistical survey of the social and geographical origins of the Willow Run workforce, see Lowell Julliard Carr and James Edson Stermer, *Willow Run: A Study of Industrialization and Cultural Inadequacy* (New York: Harper and Brothers, 1952), 359; Richard Deverall to Office of War Information (OWI), April 27, 1943, Richard Deverall Notebooks, Catholic University of America.

30. August Meier and Elliott Rudwick, *Black Detroit and the Rise of the UAW* (New York: Oxford University Press, 1980), 162–74; Joshua Freeman, "Delivering the Goods: Industrial Unionism during World War II," *Labor History* 19 (Fall 1978): 574–91. For an excellent analysis of the problems with this sort of "fractional bargaining," see James W. Kuhn, *Bargaining in Grievance Settlement: The Power of Industrial Work Groups* (New York: Columbia University Press, 1961), 111–43, 167–90.

31. VGR to R. J. Thomas, February 2, 1943, box 13, VGR Collection.

32. Ibid.; Philleo Nash to A. H. Feller (OWI deputy director), February 11, 1943, and Richard Deverall to Philleo Nash, March 13, 1943, both in Richard Deverall Notebooks, vol. 2, Catholic University of America.

33. Frankensteen quoted in CIO, "Proceedings of the Fifth Constitutional Convention," Boston, November 9–13, 1942, 336–37.

34. "More Pay = More Production: Murray Corporation of America Proves It at the Ecorse Plant," *Fortune* 28 (September 1943): 138–160; Walter Wiess, "What Is Incentive Pay?" *New International* (June 1943): 168–71; Steven Tolliday and Jonathan Zeitlin, "Shop Floor Bargaining, Contract Unionism, and Job Control: An Anglo-American Comparison," in Lichtenstein and Meyer, *On the Line,* 219–44; see also Lichtenstein, *Labor's War at Home,* 136–56 passim. In the British engineering industry, piecework proved the linchpin to a system of craft autonomy and workers' control harkening back to the producer ethos that sustained the nineteenth-century workshop tradition.

35. Murray's endorsement of the Roosevelt administration stabilization policy was influenced by the CIO counsel Lee Pressman and the publicist Len De Caux, both of whom advocated the accommodationist Communist Party line at this time. And having spent his life negotiating for coal miners and steelworkers, Murray had no objections to piecework pay systems, both of which were deeply entrenched in these industries. Richard Deverall to Clarence Glick, "A Study of the Incentive Pay Issue as It Has Developed in the CIO during the Past Year," July 19, 1943, Richard Deverall Notebooks, Catholic University of America; Frederick Harbison, "Steel," in *How Collective Bargaining Works,* ed. Harry A. Millis (New York: Twentieth Century Fund, 1942), 53–57.

36. Quoted in Deverall to Glick, "Study of the Incentive Pay Issue."

37. CIO, "Proceedings of the Special Meeting of the CIO Executive Board," Hotel Statler, Cleveland, Ohio, May 14–15, 1943, file 23, box 7, WPR Collection; UAW,

"Proceedings of the Eighth Convention," Buffalo, N.Y., October 4–10, 1943, 182; Deverall to Glick, "Study of the Incentive Pay Issue."

38. "Incentive Pay Denounced," *United Auto Worker*, May 15, 1943.

39. Thomas quoted in CIO, executive board minutes (microfilm edition), May 14–15, 1943, 62–63; Isador Lubin to Harry Hopkins, May 27, 1943, box 145, president's personal file, Franklin D. Roosevelt Library, Hyde Park, N.Y.; Jack Webb, "'The Whole Set-up Has to Be Changed'—Dodge Worker," *Labor Action*, May 31, 1943; see also Lichtenstein, *Labor's War at Home*, 157–65, and Steve Jefferys, *Management and Managed: Fifty Years of Crisis at Chrysler* (New York: Cambridge University Press, 1986), 91–97.

40. Earl Browder, "The Strike Wave Conspiracy," *Communist* 22 (1943): 489–92; UAW-IEB minutes, June 7–11, 1943, UAW-IEB Collection; Jefferys, *Management and Managed*, 94.

41. *Wage Earner*, May 28, 1943; *Dodge Main News*, June 1, 1943; UAW-IEB minutes, June 12, 1943, UAW-IEB Collection.

42. Quoted in Irving Howe and B. J. Widick, *The UAW and Walter Reuther* (1949; reprint, New York: Random House, 1973), 117; *Labor Action*, May 17, 1943; *Aero Notes*, May 17, 1943.

43. Quoted in Cormier and Eaton, *Reuther*, 209. The jingle may well have been the most famous, and possibly most effective, bit of factional propaganda in the history of twentieth-century labor. Fifty years later, Reutherite veterans and their opponents could still remember its verses. Martin Gerber, a Socialist delegate from GM's assembly plant in Linden, New Jersey, claims authorship. He would join the UAW executive board in 1944. Martin Gerber, interview with the author, Bradley Beach, N.J., November 8, 1988.

44. Quoted in Roger Keeran, *The Communist Party and the Auto Workers Unions* (Bloomington: Indiana University Press, 1980), 240.

45. Edward Levinson, "Must Labor Surrender Its Rights and Standards in Order to Win the War? Issues before the UAW-CIO Convention," file 23, box 7, WPR Collection.

46. Robert Korstad and Nelson Lichtenstein, "Opportunities Found and Lost: Labor, Radicals, and the Early Civil Rights Movement," *Journal of American History* 75 (December 1988): 786–811; George Lipsitz, *Rainbow at Midnight: Labor and Culture in the 1940s* (Urbana: University of Illinois Press, 1994), 69–95.

47. B. J. Widick, *Detroit: City of Race and Class Violence* (Detroit: Wayne State University Press, 1989), 99–112; Meier and Rudwick, *Black Detroit*, 192–94.

48. Richard Polenberg, *One Nation Divisible: Class, Race, and Ethnicity in the United States since 1938* (New York: Viking, 1980), 54–61; Philip Gleason, "Americans All: World War II and the Shaping of American Identity," *Review of Politics* 43 (October 1981): 483–518; Robert Conot, *American Odyssey* (Detroit: Wayne State University Press, 1986), 378.

49. Dominic J. Capeci, Jr., *Race Relations in Wartime Detroit: The Sojourner Truth Housing Controversy of 1942* (Philadelphia: Temple University Press, 1984), 78–82, 164–70; Richard Deverall to Clarence Glick, "UAW-CIO Local 190 Wildcat Strike at Plant of Packard Motor Company," Richard Deverall Notebooks, Catholic University of America; "Negro Workers Strike to Protest 'Hate Strike,'" *Michigan Chronicle*, November 18, 1944, Fair Employment Practices Dept., vertical file; WPR quoted in Meier and Rudwick, *Black Detroit*, 164; Clayton Fountain, *Union Guy* (New York: Viking, 1949), 166–69.

50. McKinney quoted in Eric Chester, *Socialists and the Ballot Box* (New York: Praeger, 1985), 108; Martin Halpern, *UAW Politics in the Cold War Era* (Albany: State Uni-

versity of New York Press, 1988), 121–32, 211–16; George Crockett, "Labor Looks Ahead," *Michigan Chronicle*, January 19, 1946, box 1, George Crockett Collection.

51. Local 174 Foundry Workers to George Addes, February 5, 1941, file 23, box 9, WPR Collection. According to Victor Reuther, many of the Kelsey militants, including Chester "Moon" Mullins and James Hindle, were "Hillbillies." They greeted African-American efforts to move out of the foundry with harassment: several put cork on their faces. Walter Reuther's responsibility for and response to this incident is cloudy. In early 1941 he no longer controlled the Kelsey-Hayes unit of Local 174. Mullins and Hindle were in charge, and they were doing everything in their power to win for Kelsey its own charter. Nevertheless, Reuther resisted their effort to pull Kelsey out of the amalgamated local, so the responsibility remained with the Local 174 Reutherites.

52. Saul Wellman, interview with the author, Washington, D.C., November 10, 1983; Sheldon Tappes, interview with Herbert Hill, Detroit, October 27, 1967, and February 10, 1968; see also Nelson Lichtenstein, "Life at the Rouge: A Cycle of Workers' Control," in *Life and Labor: Dimensions of Working-class History*, ed. Charles Stephenson and Robert Asher (Albany: State University of New York Press, 1986), 237–59.

53. Marshall Stevenson, "Points of Departure, Acts of Resolve: Black-Jewish Relations in Detroit, 1937–1962" (Ph.D. diss., University of Michigan, 1988), 204–12; Ed Lock, interview with Peter Friedlander, Detroit, 1976; Wellman, interview with the author; Walter Dorosh, interview with the author, Dearborn, Mich., October 12, 1982. The Communist-oriented coalition was heavily weighted toward Italians as well as African-Americans, especially in the foundry, stamping plant, and motor building, huge workplaces where semiskilled labor predominated.

54. WPR, "Tolerance Is Not Enough," *Michigan Chronicle*, December 19, 1945, box 1, George Crockett Collection; WPR, "The Negro Worker's Future," *Opportunity* 23 (Fall 1945): 205–6.

55. WPR, "How to Beat the Communists," *Collier's* (May 1948): 72; UAW, "Proceedings of the Eighth Annual Convention," 383. Hodges Mason, in 1943 the only black president of a UAW local, was told by Reuther that there were no blacks in the UAW "qualified" to be a member of the executive board. Hodges Mason, interview with Herbert Hill, Detroit, 1968; see also Horace Sheffield, interview with Herbert Hill, Detroit, July 24, 1968.

56. Sheffield, interview with Hill. Sheffield, an NAACP activist whose politics had been influenced by Socialists and Trotskyists of the anti-Communist left, met with Reuther before the convention in an effort to win what he thought was an agreement from the UAW vice president to support the black seat on the union executive board.

57. "Slaps Addes for Stand on Race Issues," *Michigan Chronicle*, October 2, 1943; Meier and Rudwick, *Black Detroit*, 209–12; Stevenson, "Points of Departure," 213–17; UAW, "Proceedings of the Eighth Annual Convention," 373.

58. Herbert Hill, interview with the author, Madison, Wisc., June 19, 1987; UAW, "Proceedings of the Eighth Annual Convention," 370–89, 416; Bert Cochran, *Labor and Communism: The Conflict That Shaped American Unions* (Princeton, N.J.: Princeton University Press, 1977), 223–26.

59. UAW, "Proceedings of the Ninth Convention," Grand Rapids, Mich., September 11–17, 1944, 102, 106.

60. CIO, "Proceedings of the Special Meeting of the CIO Executive Board."

61. "Meeting of the International Executive Board, UAW-CIO, for the Purpose of Requiring Officers of Local 91 to Show Cause Why They Should Not Comply with the Pro-

visions of Article 12 of the Constitution," Cleveland, Ohio, July 27, 1944, UAW-IEB Collection, 16–18.

62. Lichtenstein, *Labor's War at Home*, 152–56.

63. Victor Gary Devinatz, " A History of UAW Local 6, 1941–1981: A Study in the Development of Trade Union Bureaucratization" (Ph.D. diss., University of Minnesota, 1990), 76–92; Milton Derber, *Labor in Illinois: The Affluent Years, 1945–1980* (Urbana: University of Illinois Press, 1989), 108–12; Jack Conway, interview with Frank Cormier and William J. Eaton, Washington, D.C., October 2, 1967. In addition to Conway, key "worker-intellectuals" in the Local 6 leadership included the university students Ralph Showalter and William Dodds, the journalist Robert Stack, and Carl Shier, an activist in the Socialist Workers Party. All became UAW staffers after Reuther took control of the union, Shier a decade later than the rest. Local 6 radicals faced few wildcat strikes themselves because GM managers made little effort to tighten production standards in the government-owned Melrose Park war plant.

64. Conway, interview with Cormier and Eaton.

65. Ibid.; VGR, "Labor in the War—and After," *Antioch Review* 3 (Fall 1943): 313; Hawes, *Hurry up Please: It's Time*, 116. Not unexpectedly, Victor still kept a picture of Norman Thomas over his desk.

66. Lichtenstein, *Labor's War at Home*, 152.

67. WPR, testimony before U.S. Senate, "Manpower Problems in Detroit," March 9–11, 1945, pt. 28, 13165.

68. "Paralyze Five Units of Chevrolet," *Detroit News*, July 31, 1944; "Seven Fired at Chevrolet," *Detroit Free Press*, August 8, 1944; UAW-CIO press release, August 8, 1944, file 8, box 27, WPR Collection.

69. "WLB Orders End of Strike," *Detroit Free Press*, August 11, 1944; "GM Back to Work Rally Tonight," *Detroit News*, August 11, 1944.

70. UAW, "Proceedings of the Ninth Convention," 147–225 passim; Lichtenstein, *Labor's War at Home*, 195–96; Howe and Widick, *UAW and Reuther*, 120–23.

71. UAW, "Proceedings of the Ninth Convention," 105–7, 177–79; Lichtenstein, *Labor's War at Home*, 195. For example, in April 1944 Swell Avery, the reactionary president of Montgomery Ward, had precipitated a strike by refusing to abide by a WLB directive ordering his firm to administer a maintenance-of-membership union security clause. The CIO backed the strike, at least until the government took over the Ward headquarters, arguing that no distinction existed between military and civilian production in a fully mobilized economy.

72. Richard Polenberg, *War and Society: The United States, 1941–1945* (New York: J. B. Lippincott, 1972), 227–37; Koistinen, "Hammer and Sword," 700–802 passim; Barton J. Bernstein, "The Debate on Industrial Reconversion: The Protection of Oligopoly and Military Control of the Economy," *American Journal of Economics and Sociology* 26 (1967): 159–72.

73. UAW, "Proceedings of the Ninth Convention," 13, 101–7, 138–42, 236–43; Joseph Shaplen, "Roosevelt Urges UAW Strike Curb," *New York Times*, September 13, 1944, 13.

74. UAW, "Proceedings of the Ninth Convention," 178.

75. Ibid., 105–7, 177–99.

76. Ibid., 193–225, passim. See also Max Shachtman, "Politics among the Auto Workers," *New International* 10 (1944): 310–12; and *Labor Action*, September 25, 1944.

77. Conway, interview with Cormier and Eaton.

78. Hawes, *Hurry up Please*, 118–19.

79. Ibid., 121; Joseph Shaplen, "Balance of Power Is to Fore in UAW," *New York Times*,

September 16, 1944; Joseph Shaplen, "UAW Strife, Reelects Thomas," *New York Times*, September 17, 1; Touhey quoted in Cormier and Eaton, *Reuther*, 214–15. When the final tally was announced in the early morning hours of September 16, Reuther had won 6,176 votes, Leonard 3,477, and John McGill, a Rank-and-File candidate from Flint, 364. Reuther won 732 more votes running against Leonard and McGill than had Frankensteen in opposing Reuther and Leonard. Among the locals that shifted their votes from Frankensteen to Reuther were Fleetwood Aircraft in Bristol, Connecticut, Brewster Aviation on Long Island, Glen L. Martin in Baltimore, North American Aviation in Grand Prairie, Texas, and Vought-Sikorsky in Bridgeport, Connecticut. Moreover, two locals traditionally associated with the Addes-Communist faction, Fisher Body in Cleveland and Packard in Detroit, also shifted their votes from Frankensteen to Reuther on the second vice-presidential ballot. Thus Frankensteen's boast to the interviewers Cormier and Eaton, "I kept Walter in this union," may well have had some validity.

80. UAW-IEB minutes, March 5–8, 1945, 61–62, and July 16–23, 1945, 54–58, UAW-IEB Collection; *Wage Earner*, June 22, 1945; "Detroit UAW Asks National Strike Vote," *Labor Action*, June 25, 1945; Nat Ganley, "R. J. Thomas Plan in Auto," box 2, Nat Ganley Collection.

81. *Labor Action*, May 7, 1945; *PM*, May 19, 1945; *Wage Earner*, June 22, 1945; *United Auto Worker*, May 1 and July 1, 1945; UAW-IEB minutes, July 16–23, 1945, UAW-IEB Collection, 22–23, 54–61; "Campaign for Mayor to Start Labor Day," *Detroit Free Press*, August 26, 1945; Art Preis, *Labor's Giant Step: Twenty Years of the CIO* (New York: Pathfinder Press, 1972), 262. Widespread uneasiness in Detroit UAW ranks was also reflected in the defeat of numerous incumbent local union officers. At Willow Run, now threatened with virtual abandonment, candidates close to the Rank-and-File Caucus ousted incumbent officers loyal to R. J. Thomas. In the strategic Ford Local 600, partisans of Walter Reuther gained control of the general council and took several top posts there. *Wage Earner*, March 30, 1945; *Rank and Filer* (April 1945); *Militant*, May 5, 1945. Burt, Bishop, and Reisinger had been close to the Communist Party, whose shift to a more militant postwar line may also have accounted for their executive board vote against the no-strike pledge.

82. Rosa Lee Swafford, *Wartime Record of Strikes and Lockouts, 1940–1945* (Washington, D.C.: Government Printing Office, 1946), 20–21; UAW-IEB minutes, September 10–18, 1945, UAW-IEB Collection, 19–23; Kay O'Brien, "Workers Show Fighting Mood in Walkouts," *Militant*, September 29, 1945.

83. George Kennedy, testimony before U.S. House, "Bills to Amend and Repeal the National Labor Relations Act," 80th cong., 1st sess., February 20, 1947, pt. 3, 1016–19; Harris, *Right to Manage*, 47–74; UAW-IEB minutes, September 10–18, 1945, 21; "Strike Still Continues at Kelsey Company," *Labor Action*, October 1, 1945.

84. Anderson, testimony before U.S. Senate, "Manpower Problems in Detroit," March 9–11, 1945, pt. 28, 13563.

85. Mark McCulloch, *White Collar Workers in Transition: The Boom Years, 1940–1970* (Westport, Conn.: Greenwood, 1983), 9–65; Lichtenstein, "'Man in the Middle,'" 172–82; Hawes, *Hurry up Please*, 22.

86. UAW-IEB minutes, September 13, 1945, 46; WPR notes, "Flint Board Meeting," file "10th Constitutional Convention," box 1, WPR Collection. For a discussion of Philip Murray's postwar strategy, see Lichtenstein, *Labor's War at Home*, 216–23; and Irving Richter, *Labor's Struggles, 1945–1950: A Participant's View* (New York: Cambridge University Press, 1994), 19–29.

87. WPR quoted in UAW-IEB minutes, September 13, 1945, 47.

88. UAW-IEB minutes, September 13, 1945, 48, 54, 59–62; Gerber, interview with the author. Martin Gerber's recollection that Reuther decided to challenge R. J. Thomas for the UAW presidency at the next convention is substantiated by the extensive year-long file Reuther had begun to keep noting the failures and weaknesses of Thomas's presidency; WPR notes, "Flint Board Meeting," "Milwaukee Board Meeting," "Memorandum on R. J. Thomas," file "10th Constitutional Convention," box 1, WPR Collection.

CHAPTER 11: ON STRIKE AT GENERAL MOTORS

1. WPR, "Reuther Challenges 'Our Fear of Abundance,'" *New York Times Magazine*, September 16, 1945, 8.
2. Alan Brinkley, "The New Deal and the Idea of the State," in *The Rise and Fall of the New Deal Order, 1930–1980*, ed. Steve Fraser and Gary Gerstle (Princeton, N.J.: Princeton University Press, 1989), 105–8; Robert Collins, *The Business Response to Keynes, 1929–1964* (New York: Columbia University Press, 1981), 81–103; see also Seymour E. Harris, ed., *Saving American Capitalism: A Liberal Economic Program* (New York: Alfred A. Knopf, 1948), especially the essays by Leon Keyserling, Alvin Hansen, Chester Bowles, and Seymour Harris.
3. WPR, "GM versus the Rest of Us," *New Republic*, January 14, 1946, 42.
4. Nelson Lichtenstein, *Labor's War at Home: The CIO in World War II* (New York: Cambridge University Press, 1982), 204; Al Nash, "A Unionist Remembers," *Dissent* (Fall 1977): 188–89; *CIO Economic Outlook* (June 1945), quoted in Joel Seidman, *American Labor from Defense to Reconversion* (Chicago: University of Chicago Press, 1953), 215.
5. WPR, "Let's Use the War Plants," *Antioch Review* (Fall 1945): 351–58; WPR, "Conversion without Depression," *Mill and Factory* (1944), in "Walter P. Reuther" vertical file.
6. Quoted in Frank Cormier and William J. Eaton, *Reuther* (Englewood Cliffs, N.J.: Prentice-Hall, 1970), 218.
7. Pat Sexton to author, February 10, 1988; Victor Reuther, *The Brothers Reuther and the Story of the UAW* (Boston: Houghton Mifflin, 1976), 248; Donald Montgomery, "Rationing Is Not Enough," *Survey Graphic* 32 (February 1943): 37–40; D. E. Montgomery, "Consumers Underway," and Montgomery to John McCormack, December 30, 1942, both in file 2, box 5, Donald Montgomery Collection; "Washington Bureau of UAW to Fight on National Front," *United Auto Worker*, March 1, 1943; Donald Montgomery, "Canners Win Fight against Grade Labels; Rent Control Menaced," *United Auto Worker*, June 1, 1943. Not coincidentally, Victor Reuther first discussed with Montgomery the possibility that he might take a job with the UAW at a dinner honoring the old Progressive George Norris, who was swept from office in the disastrous 1942 elections.
8. "Don Montgomery Dies Soon after Wife; Union Mourns," *United Auto Worker* (November 1957).
9. WPR to William H. Davis, "How to Raise Wages without Increasing Prices," June 30, 1945, file 8, box 23, WPR Collection.
10. Ronald Schatz, "Philip Murray and the Subordination of the Industrial Unions to the United States Government," in *Labor Leaders in America*, ed. Melvyn Dubofsky and Warren Van Tine (Urbana: University of Illinois Press, 1987), 234–57; Melvyn Dubofsky, "Labor's Odd Couple: Philip Murray and John L. Lewis," in *Forging a Union of Steel*, ed. Paul F. Clark, Peter Gottlieb, and Donald Kennedy (Ithaca, N.Y.: ILR Press,

1987), 30–44; Murray quoted in CIO, "Proceedings of the Seventh Constitutional Convention," Chicago, November 20–24, 1944, 39.

11. Irving Richter, *Labor's Struggles, 1945–1950: A Participant's View* (New York: Cambridge University Press, 1994), 22–29; "It's Industrial Peace for the Postwar Period," *CIO News*, April 1, 1945; *Chester Wright's Labor Letter*, March 31, 1945; Joseph Loftus, "Business, Labor Frame Peace Code," *New York Times*, March 29, 1945.

12. Barton Bernstein, "The Truman Administration and Its Reconversion Wage Policy," *Labor History* 4 (1965): 216–25; Chester Bowles, *Promises to Keep: My Years in Public Life, 1941–1969* (New York: Harper & Row, 1971), 130. The CIO–AFL–Chamber of Commerce agreement collapsed when the new secretary of labor, Lewis B. Schwellenbach, failed to recommend that Truman go ahead with Bowles's 10 percent plan. Like many of Truman's new appointees, he was persuaded that the danger of inflation was exaggerated. According to Bowles, Reuther also endorsed the August wage-price agreement, although his commitment to a postwar no-strike pledge is highly questionable.

13. Though now in common usage, the term *corporatism* would not have been used in the 1940s to describe these structural arrangements because of the word's close identification with fascist ideology. For contemporary scholarship, see the work of Philippe Schmitter, "Still the Century of Corporatism?" in *Trends toward Corporatist Intermediation*, ed. Philip Schmitter and Gerhard Lehmbruch (Beverly Hills, Calif.: Sage, 1982); Wyn Grant, ed., *The Political Economy of Corporatism* (New York: Cambridge University Press, 1983); Leo Panitch, *Working-class Politics in Crisis: Essays on Labor and the State* (London: Verso, 1986), 132–86; Ellis Hawley, "Techno-Corporatist Formulas in the Liberal State, 1920–1960: A Neglected Aspect of America's Search for a New Order" (manuscript in author's possession); Margaret Weir and Theda Skocpol, "State Structures and the Possibilities for a 'Keynesian' Response to the Great Depression in Sweden, Britain, and the United States," in *Bringing the State Back In*, ed. Peter B. Evans, Dietrich Rueschemeyer, and Theda Skocpol (New York: Cambridge University Press, 1984), 132–49. See also Ronald Schatz, "From Commons to Dunlop: Rethinking the Field and Theory of Industrial Relations," in *Industrial Democracy in America: The Ambiguous Promise*, ed. Nelson Lichtenstein and Howell John Harris (New York: Cambridge University Press, 1993), 87–112.

14. U.S. Department of Labor, *The President's National Labor-Management Conference*, bulletin 77 (Washington, D.C.: Government Printing Office, 1945), 18–19; Christopher L. Tomlins, "AFL Unions in the 1930s: Their Performance in Historical Perspective," *Journal of American History* 65 (March 1979): 1021–42.

15. Quoted in Melvyn Dubofsky and Warren Van Tine, *John L. Lewis: A Biography* (New York: Quadrangle, 1978), 456–57.

16. Samuel Lubell, *The Future of American Politics* (New York: Doubleday, 1956), 10.

17. Alan Wolfe, *America's Impasse: The Rise and Fall of the Politics of Growth* (Boston: South End Press, 1981), 18–19; Grafton quoted in Alonzo Hamby, *Beyond the New Deal: Harry S. Truman and American Liberalism* (New York: Columbia University Press, 1973), 70.

18. Quoted in Bert Cochran, *Harry S. Truman and the Crisis Presidency* (New York: Funk & Wagnalls, 1973), 208.

19. Howell John Harris, *The Right to Manage: Industrial Relations Policies of American Business in the 1940s* (Madison: University of Wisconsin Press, 1982), 111–18; Robert M. C. Littler, "Managers Must Manage," *Harvard Business Review* 24 (1946): 366–76; Ronald Schatz, *The Electrical Workers: A History of Labor at General Electric and Westinghouse, 1923–1960* (Urbana: University of Illinois Press, 1983), 167–71; Don-

aldson Brown to "Post-War Planning Policy Group," January 11, 1943, box 1, accession no. 1334, Hagley Museum and Library, Wilmington, Del.

20. Jasper E. Crane, "So-called 'Unity Code' or 'Labor Management Charter for Industrial Peace,'" April 6, 1945, file 12, box 827, accession no. 542, Hagley Museum and Library.

21. Department of Labor, *President's Labor-Management Conference*, 12–24; Louis Stark, "Lewis and Murray Clash over Wages at Labor Meeting," *New York Times*, November 9, 1945; *CIO News*, November 26, 1945. For a larger analysis of the postwar corporate offensive, see Robert Griffith, "Forging America's Postwar Order: Domestic Politics and Political Economy in the Age of Truman," in *The Truman Presidency*, ed. Michael Lacy (New York: Cambridge University Press, 1989), 57–88.

22. VGR, "Look Forward Labor," *Common Sense* 14 (1945): 8–9; United Auto Workers–International Executive Board minutes, September 10–18, 1945, UAW-IEB Collection, 47–48.

23. "Get out the 'Yes' Vote October 24th!" October 18, 1945, file 6, box 21, WPR Collection. Reuther may have first proposed that all the auto corporations bargain with the UAW as a group, but once it became clear that such a proposal would get nowhere, he settled on GM as the target.

24. Wilson quoted in UAW-GM Department press release, October 22, 1945, file 6, box 21, WPR Collection; WPR quoted in Martin Halpern, *UAW Politics in the Cold War Era* (Albany: State University of New York Press, 1988), 55.

25. H. Thomas Johnson, "Management Accounting in an Early Multidivisional Organization: General Motors in the 1920s," *Business History Review* 52 (1978): 490–517; Donaldson Brown, "Pricing Policy in Relation to Financial Control," in *Managerial Innovation at General Motors*, ed. Alfred Chandler (New York: Arno Press, 1979), 283–86; George S. May, "Donaldson Brown," in *The Automobile Industry, 1920–1980*, ed. George S. May (New York: Facts on File, 1989), 39–42; E. E. Lincoln to W. S. Carpenter, Jr., September 23, 1944, file 33d, box 837, accession no. 542, Hagley Museum and Library.

26. W. F. Harrington to W. S. Carpenter, November 9, 1945, file 33c, box 837, accession no. 542, Hagley Museum and Library.

27. Alfred Sloan to Walter S. Carpenter, Jr., November 16, 1945, file 33c, box 837, accession no. 542, Hagley Museum and Library; *Here Is the Issue* (Detroit, General Motors, 1945), file "UAW-CIO 1945," box 63, Paul Sifton Collection; "Danger on the Production Front" [advertisement], *New York Times*, November 15, 1945; "Statements by GM and UAW on Issues," *New York Times*, December 30, 1945; Romney quoted in "Reuther: F.O.B. Detroit," *Fortune* 33 (December 1945): 288.

28. Paul Sifton, "Biographical Note," in guide to Paul Sifton Papers, Library of Congress; press release on Paul Sifton, file 4, box 143, WPR Collection; Abe Zwerling, interview with the author, Washington, D.C., June 6, 1985; Joseph Rauh, interview with the author, Washington, D.C., March 10, 1989.

29. "Purchasing Power for Prosperity: The Case of the General Motors Workers for Maintaining Take-Home Pay," "UAW-CIO 1945" file, box 63, Paul Sifton Collection.

30. "Summaries of Meeting of Top GM Negotiating Committee," file 7, box 35, VGR Collection.

31. UAW-GM negotiations [transcript], October 23, 1945, file 9, box 8, WPR Collection.

32. "Chronology: 1945–1946 Contract Negotiations," box 1, Frank Cormier and William J. Eaton Collection, John F. Kennedy Library; CIO, executive board minutes, Washington, D.C., November 2–3, 1945, George Meany Memorial Archives, Silver Spring, Md., 17; Van Bittner quoted in Halpern, *UAW Politics*, 56.

33. "Chronology: 1945–1946 Negotiations"; "Labor," *Time*, December 3, 1945, 19.

34. UAW executive board minutes, November 26–28, 1945, UAW-IEB Collection; Halpern, *UAW Politics*, 57.

35. Barton Bernstein, "Walter Reuther and the General Motors Strike of 1945–46," *Michigan History* 49 (September 1965): 265–66; WPR, speech, Buffalo, N.Y., December 4, 1945, "UAW-CIO 1945" file, box 29, Paul Sifton Collection; Halpern, *UAW Politics*, 62. Reuther's one-at-a-time strike tactic stood in partial contradiction to the necessity for a work stoppage of enormous mass and impact. But if the UAW shut down the entire industry, Reuther's high-profile role would have been diminished and the ideological sharpness of his GM strike program diluted.

36. Fenster quoted in Halpern, *UAW Politics*, 63; Ronald Edsforth, *Class Conflict and Cultural Consensus: The Making of a Mass Consumer Society in Flint, Michigan* (New Brunswick, N.J.: Rutgers University Press, 1987), 204; Irving Howe and B. J. Widick, *The UAW and Walter Reuther* (1949; New York: Random House, 1973), 127; Edwin Lahey, "How One Penny Can Bar Path to Pact," *Detroit Free Press*, March 6, 1946; Jack Palmer, interview with Jack Skeels, July 23, 1960.

37. John Anderson, "My Battle against Reuther: The Story of a Rank and File Autoworker" (manuscript in author's possession, 1986), 157–58; Arthur O'Shea, "GM Strike May Make 500,000 Jobless," *Detroit Free Press*, November 26, 1945; "7 Percent of GM Strikers in Detroit Seek Aid," *New York Times*, March 10, 1946.

38. WPR, "GM versus the Rest of Us," 42.

39. Hedda Garza, "'Bring the Boys Home' Movement," in *Encyclopedia of the American Left*, ed. Mary Jo Buhle, Paul Buhle, and Dan Georgakas (Urbana: University of Illinois Press, 1990), 107–8; Art Preis, *Labor's Giant Step: Twenty Years of the CIO* (New York: Pathfinder Press, 1972), 273.

40. WPR, "GM versus the Rest of Us," 42; "Remarks by Walter Reuther before the President's Fact Finding Board" [transcript], December 28, 1945, "UAW-CIO 1945" file, box 29, Paul Sifton Collection.

41. Edwin Lahey, "Strikebound Flint Unlike City of '37," *Detroit Free Press*, November 28, 1945, 12. Judge Paul V. Gadola, who in 1937 had enjoined UAW occupation of GM's factories in Flint, now favored the union with somewhat more respect. When General Motors asked his court to declare UAW picketing directed at white-collar workers illegal, the conservative judge refused to grant the corporation's injunction. "Panel Will Hear Cases of GM and Union Today," *Detroit Free Press*, December 20, 1945.

42. Robert Conot, *American Odyssey* (Detroit: Wayne State University Press, 1986), 396; Halpern, *UAW Politics*, 42–43. In the municipal elections, Frankensteen won 44 percent of the total ballot, somewhat more than the labor slate won in 1937. He took 61 percent in Polish working-class neighborhoods and 75 percent in Italian precincts. But the relative decline in their loyalty proved the margin of defeat for the CIO, which had never won more than half the votes of those who lived in Irish or southern white sectors of the city.

43. Quoted in *Detroit Free Press*, December 2, 1945; Halpern, *UAW Politics*, 64–65.

44. Paul Sifton, "Reuther: The Master of the 'Wiggle'" [April 1946?], "UAW-CIO 1945" file, box 29, Paul Sifton Collection.

45. "Truman Plan Draws Fire of Reuther," *Detroit Free Press*, December 5, 1945; "Report of the National Citizens Committee, December 1945," "UAW-CIO—1945" file, box 29, Paul Sifton Collection; and "National Committee to Aid the Families of General Motors Strikers," "Labor Union Contributions" file, box A336, NAACP Papers, Library of Congress.

46. Editorial, *Detroit Free Press*, November 22, 1945.

47. James Baughman, *Henry Luce and the Rise of the American News Media* (Boston: Twayne Publishers, 1987), 136–37.

48. Herbert Brean, "Walter Reuther," *Life*, November 26, 1945, 113, 124; "Reuther: F.O.B. Detroit," *Fortune* (December 1945): 149–50.

49. Another indication of Luce's pro-Reuther attitude: one of the publisher's most trusted confidants was Eliot Janeway, who worked directly for Luce during the years 1944–48. Janeway was a journalist and political economist whose hostility to midcentury oligopoly was matched only by his enthusiastic appreciation of the UAW leader. See Kenneth Gilpin, "Eliot Janeway, Economist and Author, Dies at 80," *New York Times*, February 9, 1993; and Eliot Janeway, *The Struggle for Survival* (New Haven, Conn.: Yale University Press, 1951).

50. Steven K. Ashby, "Shattered Dreams: The American Working Class and the Origins of the Cold War, 1945–1949" (Ph.d. diss., University of Chicago, 1993), chap. 8; Harris, *Right to Manage*, 140–41.

51. Bernstein, "Reuther and the GM Strike," 267; Halpern, *UAW Politics*, 65.

52. Alfred Sloan, *My Years With General Motors* (New York: Doubleday, 1964), 405–6; Harris, *Right to Manage*, 141.

53. Harris, *Right to Manage*, 142–43; Alfred Friendly, "American Industry's Grand Strategy," *Nation*, January 19, 1946, 62–63; "Official Report of the Proceedings before the National Labor Relations Board" [excerpts], file 17, box 72, UAW–Donald Montgomery Collection, 8.

54. "17.5 Percent GM Pay Rise Urged by Board," *New York Times*, January 11, 1946.

55. WPR, "GM versus the Rest of Us," 41; "GM Panel Will Take Pay Plan to Truman," *Detroit Free Press*, December 30, 1945.

56. General Motors press release, December 28, 1945, file 33c, box 837, accession no. 542, Hagley Museum and Library; Sloan quoted in American Social History Project, *Who Built America?: Working People and the Nation's Economy, Politics, Culture and Society* (New York: Pantheon, 1992), 472.

57. "GM Panel Will Take Pay Plan to Truman"; Frank Winn to Frank Cormier and William J. Eaton [1969], file 6, box 2, Cormier and Eaton Collection.

58. "Editorial," *New Republic*, January 7, 1946, quoted in Cormier and Eaton, *Reuther*, 226.

59. Chesly Manly, "Truman Urges GM Grant Raise of 17½ Per Cent," *Chicago Tribune*, January 11, 1946.

60. Bernstein, "Reuther and the GM Strike," 273; Halpern, *UAW Politics*, 81; UAW-IEB minutes, January 12, 1946, UAW-IEB Collection. Reuther's worry that the GM award would be cut to help reach a settlement in the steel strike proved justified. After the conclusion of the basic steel negotiations, GM's Charles Wilson told Reuther that the GM fact-finding board had lowered its recommendation from 24 percent to 17.5 percent at the instigation of Murray himself. Murray denied the charge, but in the last month of the strike it was spread throughout the UAW by Reuther partisans.

61. Wilson quoted in "CIO Acts after Parley Collapses, Entire Auto Panel Plan Rejected," *Chicago Tribune*, January 12, 1946; Donaldson Brown to Alfred Sloan, January 14, 1946, "W. S. Carpenter, 1946" file, box 1, accession no. 1334, Hagley Museum and Library.

62. Paul A. Tiffany, *The Decline of American Steel: How Management, Labor, and Government Went Wrong* (New York: Oxford University Press, 1988), 5–41; Ronald Schatz, "Battling over Government's Role," in Clark, Gottlieb, and Kennedy, *Forging a Union of Steel*, 87–102.

63. Barton Bernstein, "The Truman Administration and the Steel Strike of 1946," *Journal of American History* 52 (March 1966): 974.

64. Ibid., 975; Thomas R. Brooks, *Clint: A Biography of a Labor Intellectual* (New York: Atheneum, 1978), 227–29. UAW strategists were frustrated by the shift in White House focus; see Paul Sifton to WPR, January 16, 1946, "UAW-CIO 1946" file, box 29, Paul Sifton Collection; Murray quoted in Halpern, *UAW Politics*, 75.

65. Seidman, *American Labor*, 228–29.

66. Bowles, *Promises to Keep*, 796; Bernstein, "Truman Administration and Steel Strike," 977–80; OPA report quoted in Bert Cochran, *Labor and Communism: The Conflict That Shaped American Unions* (Princeton, N.J.: Princeton University Press, 1977), 252.

67. WPR quoted in "18½-Cent Settlement by UE Shocks UAW," *Wage Earner*, February 15, 1946. Addes was also shocked: "I don't know where the CP is going after that one," he told the *Wage Earner*. For other accounts, see Howe and Widick, *UAW and Reuther*, 142; Clayton Fountain, *Union Guy* (New York: Viking, 1949), 184; and Cochran, *Labor and Communism*, 253. From the UE's perspective, the settlement with GM was merely the lever with which they hoped to win key agreements with General Electric and Westinghouse, where more than 175,000 workers were on strike. Because of the high proportion of women workers, the high level of labor content in their products, and the large number of nonstriking white-collar workers, the UE faced far more resistance to its wage demands than did leaders of the steel, auto, oil, and rubber unions—thus their ready acceptance of GM's February 9 offer. Albert Fitzgerald to R. J. Thomas, February 22, 1946, box 62, Office of CIO Secretary-Treasurer Collection; Schatz, *Electrical Workers*, 167–74.

68. "Whither Reuther?" *Time*, February 25, 1946.

69. Truman quoted in Ashby, "Shattered Dreams," chap. 8; "Chronology: 1945–1946 Negotiations"; Halpern, *UAW Politics*, 84.

70. "GM National Strike Bulletin," February 13, 1946, file 9, box 10, WPR Collection; Halpern, *UAW Politics*, 71.

71. Donaldson Brown to Walter S. Carpenter, August 9, 1947, "W. S. Carpenter—1946" file, box 1, accession no. 1334, Hagley Museum and Library. See also Brown to C. E. Wilson, January 31, 1946, Brown to Policy Committee, February 4, 1946, and Brown to Carpenter, May 15, 1946, all in "W. S. Carpenter—1946" file, box 1, accession no. 1334, Hagley Museum and Library; "Meeting with GM Corporation," February 18, 1946, file 10, box 23, WPR Collection; UAW-IEB minutes, February 22, 1946, UAW-IEB Collection, 4; Halpern, *UAW Politics*, 82–83. Brown, who had been scheduled to take over the GM chairmanship from Sloan, proved far more hawkish than Wilson in seeking a thorough revision of all the contract clauses imposed by the WLB. Wilson's forestalling of Brown's militancy was but one indication that Detroit had finally "liberated" itself from New York. When this became clear, Brown resigned from the corporation and Sloan continued as chairman, albeit as a far more disengaged executive.

72. The War Labor Board had muddied the waters in April 1945 when it divided paragraph 63 into two sections. Part A, covering the advancement of employees to higher-paid jobs, generated little controversy, but part B, which set guidelines for transfers to new positions or vacancies within a department, proved bitterly controversial, especially when it came to the "temporary" day-to-day assignment of work, which GM saw as the essence of a foreman's authority. "UAW-GM Contract," October 19, 1942, file 8, box 23, WPR Collection; "General Motors Reply to Union Demand to Amend Paragraph 63 on Transfers" [1955], in vertical file, General Motors Institute, Flint,

Mich.; Ralph Seward, *Decisions of the Impartial Umpire, under the March 19, 1946 Agreement between GM and the UAW* (Detroit: UAW, 1950), 93–94; "Minutes of Top GM Negotiating Committee," file 7, box 35, VGR Collection; see also Nelson Lichtenstein, "The Union's Early Days: Shop Stewards and Seniority Rights," in *Choosing Sides: Unions and the Team Concept*, ed. Mike Parker and Jane Slaughter (Boston: South End Press, 1988), 65–73.

73. WPR quoted in "An Explanation of Major Sections Which the Corporation Proposes to Delete from the April 16, 1945 GM Agreement," February 12, 1946, file 9, box 23, WPR Collection; "Meeting with GM Organization," February 18, 1946, and "Points Discussed at Meeting of February 22, 1946," both in file 10, box 23, WPR Collection.

74. "Meeting of February 17, 1946," file 7, box 37, VGR Collection. Reuther was quite sensitive to the push from his negotiating committee on paragraph 63: "I want our locals to understand that it is this important part of the contract [paragraph 63] which is the stumbling block, rather than a mere one cent difference over wages." Quoted in Halpern, *UAW Politics*, 85–86.

75. Halpern, *UAW Politics*, 89–90; Lichtenstein, "Union's Early Days," 71–72.

76. "Chronology: 1945–1946 Negotiations"; Bernstein, "Reuther and the GM Strike," 269; Halpern, *UAW Politics*, 88–90.

77. Seidman, *American Labor*, 239.

78. Meg Jacobs, "'Planning in Place of Restraint': Leon H. Keyserling and the Evolution of Economic Policy Making, 1933–1946" (master's thesis, University of Virginia, 1992); Ashby, "Shattered Dreams," chap. 8; Seidman, *American Labor*, 233–44.

CHAPTER 12: "UAW AMERICANISM FOR US"

1. UAW, "Proceedings of the Tenth Convention," March 23–31, 1946, Atlantic City, N.J., 217, 336. Delegate votes were proportional to the size of their local, so fractional totals were common.

2. Steven M. Gillon, *Politics and Vision: The ADA and American Liberalism, 1947–1985* (New York: Oxford University Press, 1987), 3–9; James Boylan, *The New Deal Coalition and the Election of 1946* (New York: Garland, 1981), 11–28; Mary Sperling McAuliffe, *Crisis on the Left: Cold War Politics and American Liberals, 1947–1954* (Amherst: University of Massachusetts Press, 1978), 3–12. Both Reuther and his factional opponents inside the UAW considered themselves part of the same post-Roosevelt coalition. But among those who did favor a third party in 1946, anti-Communist radicals like Victor Reuther, C. Wright Mills, Daniel Bell, and Lewis Corey were far more active than any partisan of Commerce Secretary Henry Wallace.

3. Martin Halpern, *UAW Politics in the Cold War Era* (Albany: State University of New York Press, 1988), 101.

4. John Barnard, *Walter Reuther and the Rise of the Auto Workers* (Boston: Little, Brown, 1983), 112.

5. Clayton Fountain, *Union Guy* (New York: Viking, 1949), 187–92; Halpern, *UAW Politics*, 95–98. David Dubinsky's ILGWU subsidized some Reutherite delegates, but an effort by R. J. Thomas and the Communists to equate Reuther and Homer Martin proved largely ineffective. UAW, "Proceedings of the Tenth Convention," 7; FBI, "Communist Infiltration of the United Automobile, Aircraft and Agricultural Workers of America," May 27, 1946, file 100–26844 22932–48, FBI Reading Room, Washington, D.C.

6. Edwin Lahey, "Reuther Takes Over," *New Republic*, April 8, 1946, 469.

7. Quoted in Frank Cormier and William J. Eaton, *Reuther* (Englewood Cliffs, N.J.: Prentice-Hall, 1970), 235.

8. Jack Conway, interview with Frank Cormier and William J. Eaton, Washington, D.C., October 2, 1967; UAW, "Proceedings of the Tenth Convention," 93–94.

9. Halpern, *UAW Politics*, 106–10; Irving Howe and B. J. Widick, *The UAW and Walter Reuther* (1949; reprint, New York: Random House, 1973), 155–63; UAW, "Proceedings of the Tenth Convention," Atlantic City, March 23–31, 1946, 336–463.

10. Halpern, *UAW Politics*, 111–12. Even before his election, Reuther's campaign had sought some sort of arrangement with Addes and his non-Communist supporters. Thus there was no Reutherite challenge to Addes's reelection. But Addes stuck with the status quo, calling for the reelection of all officers to their current positions.

11. FBI, "Communist Infiltration of the UAW."

12. At Murray's behest, Haywood offered Thomas the post of CIO representative to the newly formed World Federation of Trade Unions; FBI, "Communist Infiltration of the UAW." Thomas even refused to vacant his presidential office at the UAW headquarters, until Reuther and several key aides made a ruckus. Abe Zwerling, interview with the author, Washington, D.C., August 26, 1987.

13. Halpern, *UAW Politics*, 110–11; Walter Ruch, "Leonard Vice President, Defeats Livingston by Small Margin," *New York Times*, March 30, 1946. Thomas won a substantial sympathy vote, but the Bishop candidacy also reflected the heterogeneous character of the Reuther forces at this stage of the faction fight. Although Reuther and Bishop had been housemates in their Detroit City College years, Bishop was known as a "tough character" who ran the UAW's biggest region with plenty of muscle to keep the wildcatters at Briggs and Chrysler in line. If Reuther saw Bishop as a bridge to the Addes forces, he made a blunder, because dozens of Reutherite radicals switched their votes to R. J. Thomas on the vice-presidential ballot. The West Side losses were also particularly disappointing because Reuther had placed two of his strongest supporters, Ed Cote of Local 174 and Matthew Hammond of Local 157, in opposition to William Stevenson and Percy Llewellyn.

14. Walter Ruch, "Addes, Thomas, and Leonard Issue Wage-Profit Statement as Policy for the UAW," *New York Times*, April 19, 1946. Reuther felt betrayed by the opposition's gambit because he had just spent the previous day in perfectly harmonious discussions with the Addes-Thomas-Leonard bloc. Walter Ruch, "Reuther Friendly, Setting UAW Goals," *New York Times*, April 18, 1946.

15. "New Educational Programs Lead UAW Forward," *United Auto Worker* (February 1947); Thomas Edward Linton, "A Historical Examination of the Purposes and Practices of the Education Program of the United Automobile Workers of America, 1936–1959" (Ph.D. diss., University of Michigan, 1960), 328–36; Victor Reuther, *The Brothers Reuther and the Story of the UAW* (Boston: Houghton Mifflin, 1976), 260; Conway, interview with Cormier and Eaton.

16. WPR, "Statement to the Subcommittee on Anti-Discrimination Legislation of the United States Senate Committee on Labor and Public Welfare, March 24, 1947," reprinted as the pamphlet "Justice on the Job Front" (Detroit: UAW Fair Practices Department, 1947); "Reuther Urges Support of NAACP Membership Campaign," *Detroit Tribune*, June 1, 1946; "Murray Gives Reuther Fair Practices Award," *United Auto Worker* (October 1947); William H. Oliver to WPR, November 19, 1947, file 5, box 65, WPR Collection. Oliver kept close tabs on the voting patterns of the black delegates at the 1947 convention and reported every defection. The Reuther caucus won 60 percent of the black vote.

17. Leonard Woodcock, interview with Frank Cormier and William J. Eaton, Atlantic

City, May 5, 1968; Conway, interview with Cormier and Eaton; Nat Weinberg, interview with the author, Washington, D.C., November 11, 1982; William Dodds, interview with the author, Washington, D.C., June 12, 1987.

18. Labor Press Associates, news release, March 30, 1946, "UAW-CIO 1946" file, box 29, Paul Sifton Collection; "VP Leaflet at Ford Parley Brings Blast from Reuther," *Wage Earner*, April 4, 1947.

19. WPR, "How to Beat the Communists," *Collier's*, February 28, 1948, 45. Reuther undoubtedly structured the key arguments in this famous essay, but several formulations seem close to those of the Trotskyist-influenced Jack Conway, Reuther's executive assistant.

20. Reuther was certain of a new depression as late as November 1947. See UAW, "Proceedings of the Eleventh Annual Convention," Atlantic City, N.J., November 9–14, 1947, 9; see also Ben Hall, "UAW: The Issues and Factions in the Pre-Convention Struggle," *New International* (September 1947): 195–200; C. Wright Mills, *The New Men of Power: America's Labor Leaders* (New York: Harcourt, Brace and Co., 1948), 27–30. Reuther may have read Mills: he sometimes used the author's terminology for the next depression, "the slump." Mills wrote: "Under the impact of slump, power may shift toward those who are ideologically prepared for it. Then the ideas of minor political groups, now unimportant in size and strength, may become politically relevant and their roles may become decisive in the shaping of events."

21. Roger Keeran, *The Communist Party and the Auto Workers Unions* (Bloomington: Indiana University Press, 1980), 261; Halpern, *UAW Politics*, 118.

22. Sidney Lens, *Left, Right, and Center: Conflicting Forces in American Labor* (Hinsdale, Ill.: Henry Regnery, 1949), 370–74; see also Mills, *New Men of Power*, on the "practical right" (23–25). Since R. J. Thomas was in charge of the Thompson Products campaign, his failure became a factional football, but under the brass-hat leadership of Fred Crawford, the family firm used a combination of charismatic leadership, outright repression, and "enterprise unionism" to stave off the UAW. Sanford Jacoby, "Reckoning with Company Unions: The Case of Thompson Products, 1934–1964," *Industrial and Labor Relations Review* 43 (October 1989): 19–40.

23. Peter Drucker, "What to Do about Strikes," *Collier's*, January 18, 1947, 13.

24. George Lipsitz, *Class and Culture in Cold War America: "A Rainbow at Midnight"* (South Hadley, Mass.: J. F. Bergin, 1982), 65–86; Stephen Meyer, *"Stalin over Wisconsin": The Making and Unmaking of Militant Unionism, 1900–1950* (New Brunswick, N.J.: Rutgers University Press, 1992), 147–64; United Auto Workers–International Executive Board minutes, December 12, 1946, UAW-IEB Collection, 11–12.

25. Barton Bernstein, "Clash of Interests: The Postwar Battle between the Office of Price Administration and the Department of Agriculture," *Agricultural History* 41 (January 1967): 45–57; Ira Katzhelson and Bruce Pietrykoski, "Rebuilding the American State: Evidence from the 1940s," *Studies in American Political Development* 5 (Fall 1991): 301–39.

26. WPR, "How to Smash Inflation," *Ammunition* 4 (August 1946): 4–8; "How to Organize a Cooperative in Your Community," *Ammunition* 4 (December 1946): 4–11; Halpern, *UAW Politics*, 186–87; William Serrin, "Working for the Union: An Interview with Douglas A. Fraser," *American Heritage* 36 (February–March 1985): 59.

27. For Reuther and his circle, Swedish social democracy was beginning to look like the promised land, a concrete demonstration of a society in which a powerful union movement worked cooperatively with farmers, consumers, and the state. Reuther was therefore delighted when Olof Palme, in the United States for his senior year at

Kenyon College, paid a call on the UAW president in Detroit. Palme, the future prime minister of Sweden, wrote his senior thesis on the UAW. Hendrick Hertzberg, "Death of a Patriot: Olof Palme, American," *New Republic*, March 31, 1986, 12.

28. "Flint Rehearses for the Future," *Ammunition* 5 (November 1947): 3–9; Mildred Jeffrey, interview with the author, Detroit, March 16, 1990; Saul Wellman, telephone interview with the author, June 19, 1993.

29. "Reuther Offers Help to Spur Auto Output," *New York Times*, July 28, 1946; Mrs. David W. Geer to WPR, July 29, 1946, S. Roy Remar to WPR, July 26, 1946, and G. D. Gurley to George T. Christopher [copy to WPR], August 3, 1946, all in box A7, Philip Murray Papers, Catholic University of America.

30. Abe Zwerling to WPR, "Reason for Shortage of Copper," August 1, 1946; WPR to J. W. Frazer, July 26, 1946; Henry Ford II to WPR, July 31, 1946; Herman Weckler to WPR, August 1, 1946; Paul Hoffman to WPR, August 1, 1946; WPR to Harry S. Truman, August 3, 1946; WPR to James M. Mead, August 3, 1946; "Union Labels Lack a Deliberate Policy," *Detroit Free Press*, August 2, 1946; UAW press release, August 4, 1946; all in "Postwar 1946" file, box 29, Paul Sifton Collection.

31. Halpern, *UAW Politics*, 186–87; James Boylan, *The New Deal Coalition and the Election of 1946* (New York: Garland, 1981), 47–48; UAW-IEB minutes, August 16, 1946, UAW-IEB Collection, 201–2.

32. Boylan, *New Deal Coalition and 1946 Election*, 151–67; Steven K. Ashby, "Shattered Dreams: The American Working Class and the Origins of the Cold War, 1945–1949" (Ph.D. diss., University of Chicago, 1993), chap. 8; Joel Seidman, *American Labor from Defense to Reconversion* (Chicago: University of Chicago Press, 1953), 233–44; Hamby, *Beyond the New Deal*, 121–40; WPR, "Election of GOP Congress Confirms Need for Labor Political Action," *United Auto Worker* (November 1946). Reuther attacked the "cult of FDR" and hinted at the need for a new labor-based party.

33. McAuliffe, *Crisis on the Left*, 15.

34. Joseph Loftus, "CIO Shaping Pledge of U.S. Allegiance," *New York Times*, November 17, 1946; CIO, "Proceedings of the Eighth Constitutional Convention," Atlantic City, November 19–22, 1946, 112, 114. In addition to Reuther, the members of the hastily appointed committee were, on the right, Emil Rieve of the Textile Workers and Milton Murray of the Newspaper Guild; on the left, Abe Flaxer of the United Public Workers, Ben Gold of the Fur and Leather Workers, and Mike Quill of the Transport Workers. Reuther also insisted that their resolution endorse FDR's Four Freedoms "everywhere," but the best the Communist-oriented leaders could do to embarrass Reuther and his circle of ex-Socialists was to include with the CP "other political parties and their adherents" among those the CIO sought to exclude from its affairs.

35. Meyer, "*Stalin over Wisconsin*," 178–210; WPR to R. J. Thomas [February 1947?], file 13, box 36, WPR Collection.

36. Meyer, "*Stalin over Wisconsin*," 198.

37. Ensworth Reisner to WPR, February 4, 1947, file 9, box 36, WPR Collection; WPR to R. J. Thomas [February 1947?].

38. R. J. Thomas to WPR, January 26, 1947, and John Brophy to WPR, January 31, 1947, both in file 13, box 36, WPR Collection; Walter Ruch, "Reuther, Thomas Renew UAW Fight," *New York Times*, January 29, 1947.

39. Meyer, "*Stalin over Wisconsin*," 197–213.

40. WPR to Thomas [February 1947?]. Reuther also clashed with Thomas over the latter's failure to make effective use of his large organizing department. See WPR to Thomas, March 8, 1947, and WPR to Thomas, July 2, 1947, both in file 11, box 64, WPR Collection.

41. Quoted in Howe and Widick, *UAW and Reuther*, 166; Meyer, "Stalin over Wisconsin," 213.

42. WPR, testimony before U.S. Senate, Committee on Labor and Public Welfare, 80th cong., 1st sess., February 21, 1947, 1287.

43. UAW-IEB minutes, March 18, 1947, UAW-IEB Collection, 159–60; M. J. Heale, *American Anti-Communism: Combating the Enemy Within, 1830–1970* (Baltimore: Johns Hopkins University Press, 1990), 137.

44. Halpern, *UAW Politics*, 142. At various moments the Addes-Thomas-Leonard group also recognized the political costs of their alliance with the Communists. In June 1946, after the Reuther forces swept the Michigan CIO convention, a caucus of Addes-Leonard men actually voted to exclude UAW Communists from their meetings. But such a formal disengagement had no teeth, for even anti-Communists like Leonard needed Communist support in their death struggle with the Reutherites.

45. UAW-IEB minutes, March 18, 1947, 155–59; Keeran, *Communist Party*, 261–65; Irving Richter, interview with the author, Washington, D.C., March 19, 1989.

46. UAW-IEB minutes, March 18, 1947, 162–64; Keeran, *Communist Party*, 264–65; Irving Richter, *Labor's Struggles, 1945–1950: A Participant's View* (New York: Cambridge University Press, 1994), 134–41. In fact, Richter still had support from important senators, including Democrats Claude Pepper of Florida and Glen Taylor of Idaho.

47. Quoted in R. Alton Lee, *Truman and Taft-Hartley* (Lexington: University of Kentucky Press, 1968), 83.

48. See Christopher Tomlins, *The State and the Unions: Labor Relations, Law, and the Organized Labor Movement in America, 1880–1960* (New York: Cambridge University Press, 1985), 247–316; and James B. Atleson, "Wartime Labor Regulation, the Industrial Pluralists, and the Law of Collective Bargaining," in *Industrial Democracy in America: The Ambiguous Promise*, ed. Nelson Lichtenstein and Howell John Harris (New York: Cambridge University Press, 1993), 142–75.

49. Mills, *New Men of Power*, 230–38. Along with many Schactmanite Trotskyists, Mills emphasized the statification of the unions; in fact, the state's power did prove decisive, but toward the enforced privatization and parochialization of the collective bargaining function.

50. WPR, "Are We Moving toward a Government Controlled Economy?" May 30, 1946, and UAW press release, December 7, 1946, both in file 8, box 542, WPR Collection; Lester Velie, *Labor, U.S.A.* (New York: Random House, 1958), 64.

51. UAW-IEB minutes, April 22, 1947, UAW-IEB Collection, 22.

52. Alfred Sloan, *My Years with General Motors* (New York: Doubleday, 1964), 294; UAW-IEB minutes, April 22, 1947, 4–6, 21.

53. "250,000 Detroit Workers Quit Factories to Protest Anti-Labor Bills at Rally," *New York Times*, April 25, 1947; John Anderson, "How the Left Was Defeated by Walter Reuther and His Allies in Local 15," John Anderson, vertical file. Among the GM factories, only Chevy Gear and Axle and Fleetwood closed down. Meanwhile, Reuther was in the midst of a nine-hour final bargaining session with General Motors.

54. Anderson, "My Battle against Walter Reuther," 168–70.

55. UAW-IEB minutes, April 27, 1947, UAW Collection, 153–54; A. L. Zwerling to WPR, "Reinstatement of Discharged and Disciplined Employees," May 6, 1947; "Memorandum of Understanding: General Motors and UAW-CIO," May 8, 1947, both in file 16, box 10, WPR Collection; Sloan quoted in Sloan, *My Years with GM*, 395.

56. Nelson Lichtenstein, "'The Man in the Middle': A Social History of Automobile Industry Foremen," in *On the Line: Essays in the History of Auto Work*, ed. Nelson Lichtenstein and Stephen Meyer (Urbana: University of Illinois Press, 1989), 169–81.

57. UAW-IEB minutes, June 9, 1947, UAW-IEB Collection, 8.

58. Robert Keys to WPR, June 17, 1947, and Keys to WPR, June 24, 1947, both in file 12, box 96, WPR Collection; UAW-IEB minutes, July 1, 1947, UAW-IEB Collection, 3–14.

59. WPR to "All UAW-CIO Local Unions," "Merger Proposal of UAW-CIO and FE-CIO," June 23, 1947, file 11, box 93, WPR Collection; "Before the National CIO Jurisdictional Committee: In the Matter of UAW versus FE," April 1945, file 10, box 93, WPR Collection; UAW-IEB minutes, June 20, 1947, UAW-IEB Collection, 9. As conceived by the Addes-Thomas bloc, the UAW-FE merger was clearly unconstitutional: the new UAW Farm Equipment Department would elect its own director, hire its own staff, and swallow up existing UAW farm equipment locals, most of whom were bitterly hostile to the Communists.

60. Halpern, *UAW Politics*, 206; Conway, interview with Cormier and Eaton; Keeran, *Communist Party*, 278–79; Bert Cochran, *Labor and Communism: The Conflict That Shaped American Unions* (Princeton, N.J.: Princeton University Press, 1977), 276; Clancy Sigal, *Going Away* (New York: Dell, 1961), 330.

61. Conway, interview with Cormier and Eaton; Harvey Levenstein, *Communism, Anticommunism, and the CIO* (Westport, Conn.: Greenwood Press, 1981), 204; "Mechanical Majority in FE Merger Defeat," *Wage Earner*, July 18, 1947.

62. Philip Murray quoted in UAW, "Proceedings of the Eleventh Convention," 81.

63. UAW-IEB minutes, September 8–12, 1947, UAW-IEB Collection, 28.

64. Ibid., 137, 171, 177. Reuther lost the first skirmish—the board voted thirteen to nine against compliance—but even before the UAW convention assembled in November he had won this war. In September Philip Murray announced that compliance with Taft-Hartley was a matter to be decided by each CIO affiliate. Reuther immediately polled his executive board, which now gave him a large majority. Only five Addes supporters voted fully against compliance—Addes, Thomas, Stevenson, Llewellyn, and Kenneth Forbes. Halpern, *UAW Politics*, 208–9.

65. WPR, "Report to the Membership," *United Auto Worker* (September 1947).

66. WPR, "How to Beat the Communists," *Collier's*, February 28, 1948, 11, 44.

67. "The Bosses' Boy: A Documentary Record of Walter Reuther" (in author's possession, 1947), 3–5, 22–23; WPR, "Report to the Membership." Irving Richter and Sigmund Diamond wrote most of "The Bosses' Boy." By all accounts, the publication enraged Walter Reuther: stretching their evidence, the authors accused Reuther of favoring speedup, maintaining an alliance with Robert Taft, and failing to fight discrimination against African-Americans in the UAW. Wellman, interview with the author.

68. WPR, "Report to the Membership"; Scott quoted in Halpern, *UAW Politics*, 233.

69. Samuel Lubell, *The Future of American Politics* (New York: Doubleday, 1951), 191.

70. "No 'Deal' in UAW, Reuther Says," *Wage Earner*, October 24, 1947, 8.

71. Conway, interview with Cormier and Eaton.

72. Halpern, *UAW Politics*, 229–33; "Reuther's Auto Workers," *Newsweek*, November 17, 1947, 28. Reuther ran with only token opposition from John DeVito, a Cleveland unionist close to the Communist Party.

73. John Anderson, "My Battle against Walter Reuther"; "Biography of Joseph McCusker," September 28, 1953, "Thomas Starling" (n.d.), "Biographical Sketch of Raymond Berndt," February 1966, and "Biography of Pat Greathouse," January 9, 1956; all in vertical file.

74. Asher Lauren, "UAW Purge in Full Swing," *Detroit News*, November 18, 1947; "CIO Shakeup Felt in East," *Detroit News*, December 6, 1947; "UAW Signs Legal Chief," *Detroit News*, January 8, 1948; Abe Zwerling, interview with the author, Washington,

D.C., June 6, 1985; Joseph Rauh, interview with the author, Washington, D.C., October 22, 1990; Christopher Johnson, *Maurice Sugar: Law, Labor, and the Left in Detroit, 1912–1950* (Detroit: Wayne State University Press, 1988), 296–97; Halpern, *UAW Politics*, 237–42.

75. Dorothy Healey and Maurice Isserman, *Dorothy Healey Remembers: A Life in the American Communist Party* (New York: Oxford University Press, 1990), 107; Selig Harrison, "A Political Program for the UAW" (master's thesis, Harvard University, 1949), 34.

76. "Reuther Hits Wallace, ADA Warns of Third Party Danger," December 13, 1947, Federated Press Microfilm Collection, George Meany Memorial Archives, Silver Spring, Md.; CIO executive board minutes, January 22, 1948, 69, 71–72.

77. James A. Wechsler, "Labor's Bright Young Man," *Harper's* 196 (March 1948): 265.

78. UAW, "Proceedings of the Eleventh Convention," 203, 205.

CHAPTER 13: THE TREATY OF DETROIT

1. United Auto Workers–International Executive Board minutes, April 20, 1948, UAW-IEB Collection; Reuther quoted in "Reuther Is Shot, Badly Wounded," *New York Times*, April 21, 1948; Frank Cormier and William J. Eaton, *Reuther* (Englewood Cliffs, N.J.: Prentice-Hall, 1970), 255–59; "Who Shot Walter?" *Time*, May 3, 1948, 19; Thomas Johnstone, interview with the FBI, January 12, 1952, file 1292, vol. 38, VGR-FOIA, FBI Reading Room, Washington, D.C.

2. Cormier and Eaton, *Reuther*, 261.

3. Ibid., 259–62; Victor Reuther, *The Brothers Reuther and the Story of the UAW* (Boston: Houghton Mifflin, 1976), 284–87; "Who's after the Reuthers?" *Business Week*, January 7, 1950; "'Yule' Bomb Found at UAW Offices," *CIO News*, December 26, 1949.

4. John Hutchinson, *The Imperfect Union: A History of Corruption in American Trade Unions* (New York: Dutton, 1970); Vernon H. Jensen, *Strife on the Waterfront: The Port of New York since 1945* (Ithaca, N.Y.: Cornell University Press, 1974); Walter Sheridan, *The Fall and Rise of Jimmy Hoffa* (New York: Saturday Review Press, 1972). In Detroit Jimmy Hoffa's rise to power in Teamster Local 299 generated a tangle of mutually beneficial arrangements that he worked out with tavern owners and trucking operators, as well as the Detroit police and the conservative, Greek-Italian wing of the Wayne County Democratic Party.

5. Bill Sunday Farnum, interview with Frank Cormier and William J. Eaton, Washington, D.C., October 16, 1967, box 1, Frank Cormier and William J. Eaton Collection, John F. Kennedy Library; UAW Research Department, "Untitled Summary of Gang Activity in Detroit," May 18, 1950, "Summary of Richard Gosser Testimony," January 12, 1952, and "Attempted Bombing of UAW-CIO International Headquarters," all in file 1292, vol. 38, VGR-FOIA, FBI Reading Room.

6. In 1941 Reuther had played an inadvertent role in Santo Perrone's rise to power. The CIO effort to organize Ford's car haul drivers was under the control of John L. Lewis and his brother Denny, who headed a UMW-financed Motor Transport Workers organizing drive in Detroit. As street battles flared between the Teamsters and the CIO, Denny Lewis appealed to the UAW for support. Reuther led the opposition on the UAW executive board: not only did Reuther mistrust John L. Lewis, but he agreed with Sidney Hillman that CIO "raids" on traditional AFL jurisdictions were harmful to the defense effort. With the UAW on the sidelines, Perrone forged a successful and profitable alliance with Hoffa and the Teamsters. Arthur A. Sloane, *Hoffa* (Boston:

MIT Press, 1991), 31–33; Dan E. Moldea, *The Hoffa Wars: Teamsters, Rebels, Politicians, and the Mob* (New York: Paddington Press, 1978), 35–39; UAW-IEB minutes, Chicago, September 17, 1941, UAW-IEB Collection; Kenneth F. Silver, "The Dead End Kids: A History of Local 212 UAW-CIO" (honors thesis, University of Michigan, 1980), 50–68; Genora Dollinger, "I Warned Reuther!" *American Socialist* (February 1954): 19–25.

7. Reutherite histories of the assassination hint strongly that underworld figures such as the Perrones had formed a "strange coalition" of gangsters, Communists, and Addes partisans. Communist strength in the union — in the Ford factories and among African-Americans and first-generation eastern European immigrants — offers some support to these charges. Rouge politics in particular were always a complex brew of ideological commitment and ethno-fraternal calculation. But Reuther himself had cut his deals with unsavory union politicians. He long maintained a rather calculating alliance with Melvin Bishop, whose efforts to discipline the Briggs local complemented Reuther's own defense of the no-strike pledge. Reuther, *Brothers Reuther*, 270–76; John Herling, "Personal and Private," "Reuther" file, box 32, president's office files, John F. Kennedy Library.

8. "Summary of Jack Conway testimony," September 13, 1951, and UAW Research Department, "Attempted Bombing of UAW-CIO International Headquarters," both in file 1320, vol. 38, VGR-FOIA, FBI Reading Room; WPR testimony, in "Manpower Problems in Detroit," 79th cong., 1st sess., March 9, 1945, pt. 28, 13166. The UAW-Ford umpire later reinstated all of those fired by Bugas. Harry Shulman ruled that if Ford were to discipline the gamblers, all had to suffer equally. Naturally Ford retreated, for such a massive disciplinary effort might well have crippled production.

9. Hoffa's relationship to several of the principals in the Reuther assassination attempts remains most intriguing. Hoffa dominated Teamster Local 299, which had close links with many of the elements of the Detroit polity that were hostile to Reuther-style social unionism. By early 1948 Hoffa and the UAW-CIO were bitter antagonists in a war for influence within the Michigan Democratic Party. In the 1950s Teamster attorneys represented Perrone gangsters in their legal difficulties with Canadian and U.S. law enforcement officials. Hoffa also proved instrumental in securing Melvin Bishop a job as a Teamster organizer in the East. Dudley W. Buffa, *Union Power and American Democracy: The UAW and the Democratic Party, 1935–1972* (Ann Arbor: University of Michigan Press, 1984), 14–21; Herling, "Personal and Private," 15–36.

10. Hoover quoted in Reuther, *Brothers Reuther*, 281. Joe Rauh also remembered Attorney General Joseph Clark repeating Hoover's reply to requests that the FBI enter the case. After the attempted bombing of the union's headquarters, Hoover finally moved, but like the Detroit police, the FBI theory of the crime took the wrong track: toward an investigation of Reuther's political rivals inside the UAW. The Detroit FBI office thought that the attempted bombing of the UAW headquarters was a hoax, instigated by two of Reuther's most trusted aides, Frank Winn and Guy Nunn, who successfully used the bomb scare to bring the FBI into the case; [first name unknown] O'Conner to Director [J. Edgar Hoover] re: WALREU, January 31, 1951, file 1031, vol. 31, VGR-FOIA, FBI Reading Room. Perhaps as a result of their skepticism, the FBI closed the case on the Reuther shootings and the UAW headquarters bombing in May 1952, less than seventeen months after they had entered it. Legal counsel to J. B. Adams, October 9, 1974, file 1451, vol. 41, VGR-FOIA.

11. The UAW conducted its own extensive investigation (headed by Jack Conway) of the Reuther shootings and discovered that the triggerman in both assassination attempts was Clarence Jacobs, who had worked at the Stove Works for several years. Carl

Renda's attorney in his suit against the UAW was Joseph Louisell, a Teamster attorney and Hoffa business associate who also played a key role in bribing Donald Ritchie, who had assisted Jacobs in the assassination attempt, to withdraw a 1953 confession he had made to the Wayne County prosecutor. Herling, "Personal and Private," 32–37; Cormier and Eaton, *Reuther*, 269–72.

12. WPR, "Our Union . . . Its Ideas and Ideals Can Never Be Murdered," *United Auto Worker* (July 1948): 3; WPR to Anna Reuther, quoted in Cormier and Eaton, *Reuther*, 257.

13. "Who Shot Walter?" 19; Jack Crellin, "Reds Suspected in Reuther Case," *Detroit Times*, May 26, 1949; Carl Haessler, interview with Jack Skeels, October 24, 1960. For example, at the 1949 UAW convention both William Hood, a leading Rouge Communist, and Paul Silver, another longtime opponent, went out of their way to condemn the shootings and praise Reuther as a symbol of union strength and integrity; UAW, "Proceedings of the Twelfth Constitutional Convention," Milwaukee, Wisc., July 10–15, 1949, 67–68; see also "Report of Interviews with Walter Reuther," January 21, 1950, FBI file 44–2925–468, FBI Reading Room. Hoover finally authorized an FBI investigation of the Reuther shootings after the attempted bombing of the UAW headquarters, but only after unanimous resolutions from the Detroit Common Council and the U.S. Senate.

14. Elisabeth Reuther Dickmeyer, *Reuther: A Daughter Strikes* (Southfield, Mich.: Spelman Publishers, 1989), 12, 226; Linda Reuther, interview with the author, San Anselmo, Calif., August 15, 1988. According to her autobiography, Lisa's relationship to her father was one of devotion and respect, alternating with moments of estrangement not unlike that felt by her older sister.

15. Brendan Sexton, telephone interview with the author, October 18, 1985; Abe Zwerling, interview with the author, Washington, D.C., June 6, 1985; William Manchester, "Walter Reuther," in *Controversy* (Boston: Little, Brown, 1976), 362–63; Irving Howe and B. J. Widick, *The UAW and Walter Reuther* (1949; reprint, New York: Random House, 1973), 200–201.

16. For general discussions of a postwar "settlement," see Alan Wolfe, *America's Impasse: The Rise and Fall of the Politics of Growth* (New York: Pantheon, 1981), 1–40; Samuel Bowles, David Gordon, and Thomas Weisskopf, *Beyond the Wasteland: A Democratic Alternative to Economic Decline* (Garden City, N.Y.: Anchor Press, 1983), 70–75; Charles Maier, *In Search of Stability: Explorations in Historical Political Economy* (New York: Cambridge University Press, 1987).

17. Robert Nathan Associates, *A National Wage Policy for 1947* (Washington, D.C.: U.S. Department of Labor Library, December 1946), 14.

18. John Loftus, "U.S. Steel Slashes Prices $25,000,000; Bars Pay Increase," *New York Times*, April 23, 1948; "Check to Inflation Discerned in Trend to Bar Wage Rises," *New York Times*, April 25, 1948; "Ford Asks Cut for Auto Workers to Win Goal of 'Public Security,'" *New York Times*, May 16, 1948.

19. Kathyanne Groehn El-Messidi, "Sure Principles Midst Uncertainties: The Story of the 1948 GM-UAW Contract" (Ph.D. diss., University of Oklahoma, 1976), 58–61; Jack Palmer, interview with Jack Skeels, August 23, 1959.

20. UAW-IEB minutes, March 1, 1948, UAW-IEB Collection, 43–51. Even after the UAW-GM contract was signed, a 1948 survey conducted by the National Industrial Conference Board found that more than 85 percent of all big-business executives were unwilling to adopt the COLA formula. Henry Lowenstern, "Adjusting Wages to Living Costs: A Historical Note," *Monthly Labor Review* 97 (July 1974): 24.

21. Wilson quoted in Frederick Harbison, "The UAW-General Motors Agreement of

1950," *Journal of Political Economy* 58 (October 1950): 402; Howell John Harris, *The Right to Manage: Industrial Relations Policies of American Business in the 1940s* (Madison: University of Wisconsin, 1982), 150.

22. Harry W. Anderson, *Behind the General Motors Wage Program* (San Francisco: California Personnel Management Association, 1950), 5–6; El-Messidi, "Sure Principles," 84; Harris, *Right to Manage*, 148–51; UAW, "Proceedings of the Twelfth Constitutional Convention," 12, 16–17; Ed Cray, *Chrome Colossus: General Motors and Its Times* (New York: McGraw-Hill, 1980), 485. GM lore holds that Wilson first thought up the COLA idea during a long hospital stay in 1942 when he was recovering from a skating accident. Wilson quoted in Peter Drucker, *Adventures of a Bystander* (New York: Harper and Row, 1978), 266.

23. "UMT Truce Said to Be Backed in Aims by Truman," *New York Times*, April 29, 1948; "Eighty Group Air Force Plan Is Approved by Senators; Move to Arm Europe Likely," *New York Times*, April 30, 1948.

24. Stephen Amberg, *The Union Inspiration in American Politics: The Autoworkers and the Making of a Liberal Industrial Order* (Philadelphia: Temple University Press, 1994), 165.

25. Ibid., 158–59; El-Messidi, "Sure Principles," 88–91; Daniel Bell, "The Subversion of Collective Bargaining: Labor in the 1950s," *Commentary* (March 1960): 697–713. In the 1948 agreement GM pledged to increase wages one cent an hour for each 1.14-point increase in the BLS cost-of-living index. If the BLS index declined, autoworkers were protected by a 5 percent cap on any wage reductions over the life of the contract. "GM Raises Wages Eleven Cents an Hour; Ties Pay to Living Costs," *New York Times*, May 26, 1948.

26. W. S. Woytinsky, *Labor and Management Look at Collective Bargaining: A Canvas of Leaders' Views* (New York: Twentieth Century Fund, 1949), 105–9; El-Messidi, "Sure Principles," 60; "UAW Press Release on GM Contract," May 25, 1948, file 5, box 72, UAW-Montgomery Collection. The final quotation is taken from T. A. Johnstone's press release of August 25, 1948, which announced a three-cent wage increase under the contract's new COLA formula. See also WPR to Agnes Meyer, August 6, 1948, file 15, box 101, WPR Collection; Reuther wrote that "the settlement finally reached can be regarded only with moderate enthusiasm."

27. "Speakers' Notes for General Motors Area Conferences," February 1949, file 6, box 56, WPR Collection; Charles E. Wilson, *Five Years of Industrial Peace* (Detroit: n.p., 1950), 21–23; Anderson, *Behind the General Motors Wage Program*, 5; Anderson quoted in Harris, *Right to Manage*, 151.

28. General Motors, "Chronology: 1950 Contract Negotiations," "Contract Negotiations" file, box 1, Frank Cormier and William J. Eaton Collection; press commentary is from "GM: Comments on GM's Five-Year Contract," vertical file.

29. "Tobin, Ching Praise New GM Compact," *New York Times*, May 24, 1950; Walter Ruch, "Reuther's Stock Goes Up; What Next? Detroit Asks," *New York Times*, May 28, 1950.

30. Quoted in Harbison, "GM-UAW Agreement of 1950," 403; Lowenstern, "Adjusting Wages to Living Costs," 24–25.

31. Daniel Bell, "The Treaty of Detroit," *Fortune* (July 1950): 53.

32. Harold Enarson, "Notes on Some Contrasts in the Wage Stabilization Problem: World War II and the Present Emergency," November 11, 1950, "Wage Stabilization 1950–52" file, box 6, Harold L. Enarson Collection, Harry S. Truman Library; "Credit Controls: Regulations W and X," *UAW-CIO Administrative Letter*, October 23, 1950; UAW-IEB minutes, November 17, 1950, UAW-IEB Collection, 7–16; Seth

Wigderson, "The UAW in the 1950s" (Ph.D. diss., Wayne State University, 1989), 154.

33. *UAW-CIO Administrative Letter*, December 23, 1950; Walter Jason, "Truman Orders Peril Auto Workers' Gains," *Labor Action*, December 25, 1950; Daniel Bell, "Walter Reuther Marches On," *Fortune* (July 1951): 41–42; Walter Jason, "It's Reuther versus Reuther," *Labor Action*, January 28, 1952; B. J. Widick, "Politics of the Auto Settlement," *Nation*, October 25, 1958, 291.

34. Monte M. Poem, *Harry S. Truman versus the Medical Lobby* (Columbia: University of Missouri Press, 1979), 29–43; Woytinsky, *Labor and Management*, 128–40.

35. Vivian Vale, *Labour in American Politics* (London: Barnes and Noble, 1971), 97; Harold Wilensky, *The Welfare State and Equality* (Berkeley: University of California Press, 1975), 24–26.

36. See Sumner Slichter, James J. Healy, and E. Robert Livernash, *The Impact of Collective Bargaining on Management* (Washington, D.C.: Brookings Institution, 1960), 372–76; Donna Allen, *Fringe Benefits: Wages or Social Obligation?* (Ithaca, N.Y.: Cornell University Press, 1964), 99–152; and Beth Stevens, "Blurring the Boundaries: How the Federal Government Has Influenced Welfare Benefits in the Private Sector," in *The Politics of Social Policy in the United States*, ed. Margaret Weir, Ann Shola Orloff, and Theda Skocpol (Princeton, N.J.: Princeton University Press, 1988), 123–48.

37. CIO, "Proceedings of the Eighth Convention," Atlantic City, N.J., November 18–22, 1946, 186-87.

38. Stevens, "Blurring the Boundaries," 141.

39. Benjamin M. Selekman, *Problems in Labor Relations* (New York: Academic Publishing, 1950), 298–309; Cormier and Eaton, *Reuther*, 294–96.

40. WPR quoted in UAW, "Proceedings of the Twelfth Constitutional Convention," Milwaukee, July 10–15, 1949, 13; Alan Derickson, "Health Security for All? Social Unionism and Universal Health Insurance, 1935–1958," *Journal of American History* 80 (March 1994): 1333–56; Cray, *Chrome Colossus*, 336; Barnard, *Walter Reuther*, 150–53. Because of Reuther's intense dissatisfaction with the insurance company–dominated Blue Cross/Blue Shield system, the UAW played a key role in founding Michigan's Community Health Association, a prepaid health maintenance organization modeled on the Kaiser plan in California.

41. Walter Ruch, "100 Day Chrysler Strike Ends in a Bitter Mood of Futility," *New York Times*, May 1, 1950; Steve Jefferys, *Management and Managed: Fifty Years of Crisis at Chrysler* (New York: Cambridge University Press, 1986), 116. Chrysler was willing to pay the $100 a month pension, but not to fund it according to UAW standards. President T. K. Keller refused to provide the union's Research Department with the relevant actuarial data, on the grounds that such costs were none of the union's business. The strike ended when Chrysler put $30 million in its pension fund. Doing so did not fulfill Reuther's definition of an "actuarially sound" pension scheme, but when GM conceded the concept to the UAW just a few weeks later, Keller was forced out of his job. For the next twenty-nine years, Chrysler adhered to the pattern bargaining system.

42. "Reuther to Seek Annual Wage through an Industry Council," *Wage Earner*, March 29, 1946; Nat Weinberg, interview with the author, Washington, D.C., November 11, 1982; WPR, report to the Fourteenth Constitutional Convention, Atlantic City, N.J., March 22–27, 1953, 9.

43. Nat Weinberg to Don Montgomery, December 31, 1952, "GAW-Finance" file, box 70, UAW Research Department Collection; WPR, report to the Fifteenth Constitu-

tional Convention, Cleveland, Ohio, March 27–April 1, 1955, 13–15; minutes, National Ford Council, May 9, 1955, "Ford Motor Company" box, Ken Bannon Collection, 50.

44. "The GAW Man," *Time*, June 20, 1993, 20.

45. William Serrin, *The Company and the Union: The "Civilized Relationship" of the General Motors Corporation and the United Automobile Workers* (New York: Random House, 1973), 180–81.

46. WPR quoted in Cormier and Eaton, *Reuther*, 332.

47. Malcolm Denise (labor relations, Ford Motor Co.), interview with the author, Detroit, October 21, 1982; Cormier and Eaton, *Reuther*, 328; David Brody, *Workers in Industrial America* (New York: Oxford University Press, 1980), 193–95.

48. All press commentary quoted in "Judgments and Prophecies," *Time*, June 20, 1955, 23.

49. WPR, speech before the Society of Business Magazine Editors, September 19, 1958, "1958 April-September" file, box 591, WPR Collection; Henry Brandon, "A Conversation with Walter Reuther: 'How Do We Live with Bigness?' " *New Republic*, July 21, 1958, 15.

50. UAW-IEB minutes, Detroit, October 3–7, 1955, UAW-IEB Collection, 301; Brendan Sexton, telephone interview with the author, December 24, 1985.

51. Richard Lester, *As Unions Mature* (Princeton, N.J.: Princeton University Press, 1958), 115–26; Christopher Tomlins, *The State and the Unions: Labor Relations, Law, and the Organized Labor Movement in America, 1880–1960* (New York: Cambridge University Press, 1985), xi–xii; U.S. Department of Commerce, *Statistical Abstract of the United States* (Washington, D.C.: Government Printing Office, 1975), 286.

52. UAW, "Proceedings of the Thirteenth Constitutional Convention," Cleveland, Ohio, April 1–6, 1951, 10; Marjorie Thines Stanley, "The Amalgamation of Collective Bargaining and Political Activity," *Industrial and Labor Relations Review* 10 (October 1956): 40–47.

53. UAW, "Proceedings of the Thirteenth Constitutional Convention," 10.

54. Roger Davenport, *USA: The Permanent Revolution* (New York: Time-Life, 1951); for a critique of the worker embourgeoisement thesis, see the classic work by Ely Chinoy, *Automobile Workers and the American Dream* (1955; Urbana: University of Illinois Press, 1992); Paul Blumberg, *Inequality in an Age of Decline* (New York: Oxford University Press, 1980), 9–64, summarizes the literature.

55. "89,000 Votes Bury a 40-year-old Lie," *Ammunition* (August 1948): 4–6. A sizable number of Ford workers actually interrupted their vacations and drove hundreds of miles to cast their ballot for the union.

56. Leo Fenster, "The 1964 Contract Struggle" (manuscript in author's possession, n.d.).

57. Barnard, *Walter Reuther*, 154; Kevin Boyle, " 'A Class Apart': The National Political Behavior of American Automobile Workers, 1960–1968" (paper presented at North American Labor History Conference, Detroit, October 1989).

58. "What Does a UAW Member Look Like?" *Ammunition* (August 1948): 30–33; Louis Harris and Associates, "The Mandate of the UAW Rank and File for Contract Negotiations in 1961," box 10, Ken Bannon Collection; Jack Stieber, *Governing the UAW* (New York: John Wiley and Sons, 1962), 157.

59. Johnstone quoted in Harbison, "GM-UAW Agreement of 1950," 405; Anderson quoted in Brody, *Workers in Industrial America*, 185.

60. Stephen Amberg, "The Triumph of Industrial Orthodoxy: The Collapse of Studebaker-Packard," in *On the Line: Essays in the History of Auto Work*, ed. Nelson Lichtenstein and Stephen Meyer (Urbana: University of Illinois Press, 1989), 190–218;

Mike Davis, *Prisoners of the American Dream* (London: Verso, 1986), 121–24; George Strauss, "The Shifting Power Balance in the Plant," *Industrial Relations* 1 (May 1962): 81–83.

61. UAW-IEB minutes, September 13, 1948, UAW-IEB Collection, 329; UAW, "Proceedings of the Twelfth Constitutional Convention," 12, 16–17.

62. "Automation: A Report to the UAW-CIO Economic and Collective Bargaining Conference," November 12–13, 1954, file 15, box 55, WPR Collection; Robert C. Hendon, "The Challenge of Tomorrow's Industrial Relations," in American Management Association, *Personnel Series* 164 (1955): 7; Nat Weinberg, "Labor on the Hook," *Saturday Review*, January 22, 1955, 19, 38–40.

63. Stephen Meyer, "The Persistence of Fordism: Workers and Technology in the American Automobile Industry, 1900–1960," in Lichtenstein and Meyer, *On the Line*, 86–91; Norbert Wiener to WPR, August 13, 1949, "Norbert Wiener" file, box 1, Small Collections.

64. UAW, "Proceedings of the Fourteenth Constitutional Convention," 150; Jack Conway, "Preliminary Report of the UAW-CIO Committee on Automation" (1955), "Automation" file, box 44, UAW Research Department Collection.

65. Martin Halpern, *UAW Politics in the Cold War Era* (Albany: State University of New York Press, 1988), 257; UAW, "Proceedings of the Fourteenth Convention," 150–51; Julius Rezler, *Automation and Industrial Labor* (New York: Random House, 1969), 81–91; Jack Conway, "Labor Looks at Automation," April 13, 1955, "Automation Reports" file, unprocessed box, Ken Bannon Collection. The Reuther exchange is now part of labor lore; this phrasing comes from the author's interviews with Malcolm Denise and Douglas Fraser, Detroit, October 21, 1982, and April 17, 1990. For a contemporary critique of Reuther's views on technological progress and productivity, see Ben Hall, "Conservative Mood in Ranks," *Labor Action*, April 6, 1953.

66. Chester Myslicki, "Report on Productivity Increase in the Auto Industry," *Monthly Labor Review* 92 (March 1969): 37–39; Charles P. Larrowe, *Harry Bridges: The Rise and Fall of Radical Labor in the United States* (New York: Lawrence Hill, 1972), 352–55; David Noble, *Forces of Production* (New York: Alfred A. Knopf, 1984); Robert Howard, *Brave New Workplace* (New York: Oxford University Press, 1985).

67. M. A. Williams (UAW Local 560) to Tom Bladen and Jeff Washington (National Ford Department), July 24, 1964, box 17, Ken Bannon Collection.

68. UAW-GM negotiations [transcript], September 9, 1958, file 3, box 102, WPR Collection, 2; Oliver Quayle and Co., "A Study in Depth of the Rank and File of the UAW: May 1967," box 147, WPR Collection; Louis Harris and Associates, "The Mandate of the UAW Rank and File for Contract Negotiation in 1961," box 10, Ken Bannon Collection. For a longer discussion of this subject, see Nelson Lichtenstein, "UAW Bargaining Strategy and Shop-Floor Conflict: 1946–1970," *Industrial Relations* 24 (Fall 1985): 369–79.

69. Chinoy, *Automobile Workers*, 70; Richard Herding, *Job Control and Union Structure* (Rotterdam: Rotterdam University Press, 1972), 147–50.

70. The work-rule issue has become a highly contentious one. For part of the debate, see Harry Katz, *Shifting Gears: Changing Labor Relations in the U.S. Automobile Industry* (Cambridge, Mass.: MIT Press, 1987), 30–71; Steven Tolliday and Jonathan Zeitlin, "Shop Floor Bargaining, Contract Unionism, and Job Control: An Anglo-American Comparison," in Lichtenstein and Meyer, *On the Line*, 219–44; and Mike Parker, "Industrial Relations Myth and Shop-Floor Reality: The 'Team Concept' in the Auto Industry," in *Industrial Democracy in America: The Ambiguous Promise*, ed.

Nelson Lichtenstein and Howell John Harris (New York: Cambridge University Press, 1993), 249–74.

71. National Ford Council, "Proceedings of Special Meeting," Detroit, May 9, 1955, "Ford Motor Company" box, Ken Bannon Collection, 44; Harbison, "GM-UAW Agreement of 1950," 408.

72. UAW-IEB minutes, April 28, 1949, UAW-IEB Collection, 95.

73. Ford Motor Co., "Executive Communication," March 4, 1948, box 12, UAW Research Department Collection; Al Commons, "The 1949 Ford Strike—Beginning of an Era" (seminar paper, Department of History, Wayne State University, 1978); "Ford Provoked Strike: Reuther Faces Hard Test," *Labor Action*, May 10, 1949; "Reuther on the Run?" *Detroit Free Press*, May 7, 1949.

74. Ford Motor Co., "Study on Work Stoppages" (1955), "Ford Department" box, Ken Bannon Collection, 5. For a larger history of Rouge politics and industrial relations in this era, see Nelson Lichtenstein, "Life at the Rouge: A Cycle of Workers' Control," in *Life and Labor: Dimensions of American Working-class History*, ed. Charles Stephenson and Robert Asher (Albany: State University of New York Press, 1986), 237–59.

75. Shulman ruled that Ford had no right to run its lines faster than 100 percent of "standard," but the decision did nothing to resolve the problem because the speedup issue had always involved not only line speed but work assignments, manning schedules, production mix, and evaluation of new technology—all of which remained largely the prerogative of management. Ford Motor Co. and UAW-CIO, "Arbitration Award," 1949, "FMC" box, Ken Bannon Collection; Ford Motor Co., "Collective Bargaining Review and Proposals," July 16, 1961, box 18, Ken Bannon Collection, 21; Local 600, "Strike Betrayal" [leaflet], Local 600 vertical file; Commons, "1949 Ford Strike."

76. UAW, "Proceedings of the Fourteenth Constitutional Convention," 318; UAW, "Proceedings of the Eighteenth Constitutional Convention," Atlantic City, N.J., May 4–10, 1962, 519.

77. "Revolt of the Victors," *Detroit Free Press*, June 8, 1955; Walter Dorosh (former president of UAW Local 600), interview with the author, Dearborn, Mich., October 21, 1982.

78. Walter Jason, "It Looks Like He's the Fall Guy," *Labor Action*, February 18, 1952, 2; Thomas A. Johnstone, interview with George Heliker, Detroit, February 19, 1954; James Dunne, interview with George Heliker, Detroit, February 25, 1954; both in accession no. 940.5, Ford Motor Company Archives, Henry Ford Museum; Weinberg, interview with the author; Irving Bluestone, interview with the author, Detroit, October 25, 1987. Unlike Johnstone, the UAW president understood the usefulness of rhetorical militancy. At the GM Council meeting that voted in the five-year contract, Johnstone, who negotiated virtually every clause in the new agreement, had been ecstatic. "We are no longer the burr under management's saddle," he announced to a skeptical assembly of veteran unionists. When Leo Fenster met Roy Reuther on the floor a few minutes later, he sarcastically quoted Johnstone's remark. "In the afternoon," recalled Fenster, "Walter spoke. He ripped into GM. We had won the concessions because of our solidarity and our readiness to strike. . . . The corporation would never give up its greed for higher and higher profits. . . . We would have to fight them during every minute of the five year contract. Roy Reuther sought me out. 'There you are,' he said. 'Walter has just put the burr back under the saddle.'" Fenster, "1964 Contract Struggle," 10.

79. Ford Motor Co., "Study on Work Stoppages," "Ford Department" box, Bannon Collection, 19–21; Elie Abel, "Ford to Lay off 85,000 in Strike," *New York Times*, May 21,

1953; "GM Lifts Pay, Rewrites Pact Though It Had Two Years to Run," *New York Times*, May 23, 1953; Jack Conway, interview with Frank Cormier and William J. Eaton, Washington, D.C., November 20, 1967. The duel between GM and Ford for supremacy in the low-cost auto market may also have played a role in sustaining Reuther's "living document" gambit. During the five-week Canton strike—"the Canton Can Opener"—Ford lost production of one hundred thousand cars, but the number-two automaker was prepared to hang tough until GM unexpectedly reopened its contract with the UAW. The Big Three incorporated nineteen cents of the cost-of-living increase into each worker's base pay and gave skilled workers a ten-cent raise. William Harris, "The Trouble in Detroit," *Fortune* 57 (March 1958): 106.

80. Edwin Lahey, interview with Donald Shaughnessy, Detroit, August 28, 1957, Columbia University Oral History Collection, 57; Rauh quoted in "Business Looks at Walter Reuther," *Nation's Business* (October 1957): 125.

81. Davis, *Prisoners of the American Dream*, 122–23;"Romney Asks Congress to Split GM, Ford, and the Auto Union," *New York Times*, February 8, 1958; Joseph A. Loftus, "Reuther Declares Charge by Goldwater Is a 'Smear,'" *New York Times*, March 29, 1958; "Head of Chamber Asks Labor Curb," *New York Times*, September 22, 1958; John Herling, "Old Ford Union-Hater Tries to Take GM for a Spin Now," *Washington Daily News*, September 22, 1958. Among the individuals sponsoring a revival of the most right-wing, antilabor polemics were a roll call of entrepreneurial industrialists, including Charles Hook of American Rolling Mills, J. J. Woodhall of Woodhall Industries, Harry Bradley of Allen-Bradley, and Charles M. White of Republic Steel.

82. Royal E. Montgomery, Irwin Stelzer, and Rosalin Roth, "Collective Bargaining over Profit Sharing: The Automobile Union's Effort to Extend Its Frontier of Control," *Journal of Business of the University of Chicago* 31 (October 1958): 318–34; General Motors, "Chronology: 1958 Contract Negotiations," "Contract Negotiations" file, box 1, Frank Cormier and William J. Eaton Collection; UAW, "Proceedings of the Special Constitutional Convention," Detroit, January 22–24, 1958, 21. In the past both Reuther and Weinberg had been eloquent opponents of profit sharing: the scheme ensured the destruction of standardized wage rates across the entire industry and it put wages at the mercy of management financial decisions over which the union had no control. A hostile but accurate critique is offered in Chamber of Commerce of the United States, *Reuther's Profit-Sharing Demand* (Washington, D.C.: Chamber of Commerce, 1958), 1–22.

83. Jefferys, *Management and Managed*, 127–45; Everett Martin, "Reuther's Undefeated Union versus an Unprecedented Alliance," *The Reporter*, August 7, 1958, 28.

84. Dan Cordtz, "Reuther's Strategy: Auto Union Chief Plays Waiting Game, Figures Time Is on His Side," *Wall Street Journal*, June 3, 1958; "How to Operate a Local Union without a Contract," file 11, box 45, Leonard Woodcock Collection.

85. Charles Obertance, "Work-Standards Issues to Play Big Part in Auto Contract Talks," *Wall Street Journal*, April 7, 1958; Edward Breslin, "Revolt at Chrylser," *Detroit Times*, October 2, 1958; UAW, "Proceedings of the Eighteenth Constitutional Convention," Atlantic City, May 4–10, 1962, 522. In 1957 and 1958 there were more than 450 unauthorized stoppages at Chrysler plants each year. When Chrysler reported but twenty-three largely insignificant wildcats in the first half of 1959, Jack Conway attributed the reversal to "the change which we brought about." Jack Conway to WPR, August 3, 1959, file 12, box 50, WPR Collection.

86. Walter Ruch, "Reuther Promises to Be 'Reasonable,'" *New York Times*, May 25, 1950; Harold Levinson, "Pattern Bargaining: A Case Study of the Automobile Workers,"

Quarterly Journal of Economics (Spring 1959): 299; Paul Blumberg, *Inequality in an Age of Decline* (New York: Oxford University Press, 1980), 65–107.

87. Thomas Segrue, "The Structures of Urban Poverty: The Reorganization of Space and Work in Three Periods of American History," in *The "Underclass" Debate: Views from History*, ed. Michael Katz (Princeton, N.J.: Princeton University Press, 1993), 85–117.

88. John DeMotte, "The 1955 Ford-UAW Contract," *Addresses on Industrial Relations*, bulletin no. 24 (Ann Arbor: University of Michigan School of Business, 1956), 2. Even before negotiation of the 1955 SUB agreement, critics on both the right and the left had attacked the "experience rating" idea, which made employer contributions to the unemployment compensation system dependent upon fluctuations in the payroll of an individual firm. Trade unionists had disparaged experience rating for decades on the grounds that unemployment was a systemic, national problem. See Emerson P. Schmidt, "Private Guaranteed Wages and Unemployment Compensation Supplementation," *Proceedings, Industrial Relations Research Association* (1953), 96–112; Murray W. Latimer, *Guaranteed Wages* (Washington, D.C.: Government Printing Office, 1947).

89. Nelson Cruikshank, telephone interview with the author, July 18, 1984; David Jacobs, "The UAW and the Committee for National Health Insurance: The Contours of Social Unionism," *Advances in Industrial and Labor Relations* 4 (1987): 119–40; Hugh Mosley, "Corporate Benefits and the Underdevelopment of the American Welfare State," *Contemporary Crisis* 5 (1981): 130–54; Stevens, "Blurring the Boundaries," 145–48. UAW-negotiated fringe benefits were also implicitly patriarchal. Pension benefits were linked to unbroken seniority standing at a single firm. Because of the failure of the UAW to modify its seniority-based pension rules to take into account the discontinuous work history of many women workers (itself the result not only of their reproductive role but of outright discrimination), female autoworkers received benefits proportionately far lower than those of men when they left the workforce. Jill Quadagno, "Women's Access to Pensions and the Structure of Eligibility Rules: Systems of Production and Reproduction," in *Sociological Quarterly* 29 (1988): 541–58.

CHAPTER 14: AN AMERICAN SOCIAL DEMOCRACY

1. Daniel Bell, "Labor's New Men of Power," *Fortune* 47 (June 1953): 148.

2. Ibid., 150; B. J. Widick, *Labor Today: The Triumphs and Failures of Unionism in the United States* (Boston: Houghton Mifflin, 1964), 182–83.

3. Selig Harrison, "A Political Program for the UAW" (senior thesis, Harvard University, 1949), 34.

4. WPR quoted in Ben Hall, "Reutherism Marks Time on the Main Issues at UAW Convention," *Labor Action*, April 6, 1953; Mazey quoted in Harvey Swados, "The UAW: Over the Top or Over the Hill?" in Swados, *A Radical at Large: American Essays* (London: Rupert Hart-Davis, 1968), 71.

5. Quoted in Arthur Kornhauser, Albert Mayer, and Harold L. Sheppard, *When Labor Votes: A Study of Auto Workers* (New York: University Books, 1956), 15.

6. Alan Raucher, "Employee Relations at General Motors: The 'My Job Contest,' 1947," *Labor History* 28 (Spring 1987): 28, 221–32.

7. Howell John Harris, *The Right to Manage: Industrial Relations Policies of American Business in the 1940s* (Madison: University of Wisconsin Press, 1982), 177–204; Raucher, "Employee Relations at General Motors," 221–32; Elizabeth Fones-Wolf,

Selling Free Enterprise: The Business Assault on Labor and Liberalism, 1945–1960 (Urbana: University of Illinois Press, 1994), 67–96; Frederick quoted in ibid., 95.

8. Fones-Wolf, *Selling Free Enterprise*, 120; "Dedicate Flint Co-op to Unity," *United Auto Worker* (September 1948); Jack Stieber, *Governing the UAW* (New York: John Wiley and Sons, 1962), 117; United Auto Workers–International Executive Board minutes, Detroit, December 5, 1951, UAW-IEB Collection, 89; *Ammunition* (July 1948): 48.

9. "What Does the UAW-CIO Education Department Do?" *Ammunition* (April 1951): 27–29.

10. Brendan Sexton, "Deep Therapy on the Assembly Line," *Ammunition* (April 1949): 47–53. His attacks upon Peter Drucker and Lillian Gilbreth were equally acute; "Confessions of a Valet," *Ammunition* (June 1950): 21–22; and "They Served Therbligs," *Ammunition* (July 1950): 26–27.

11. Andy Wilson, "Guy Nunn, UAW Voice, Irritates, Soothes Listeners," *Detroit Times*, June 2, 1957; Robert Hoyt, [untitled news clipping], *Detroit Free Press*, June 6, 1965; both in vertical file; [Guy Nunn?], "Radio," file 21, box 12, UAW Citizenship Collection.

12. Cathy Hennen, "Campaign against Communism: The Rhetoric of Walter Reuther" (Ph.D. diss., University of Pittsburgh, 1986), 39–40; Stanley Levey, "The Rhetoric of Walter Reuther," *Reporter*, March 14, 1963, 27; Bell, "Labor's New Men of Power," 47, 149; Martin Gerber, interview with the author, Bradley Beach, N.J., November 15, 1988.

13. Mary Heaton Vorse, "The Union That Grew Up," *Harper's* (July 1954): 85, in "Walter Reuther," vertical file.

14. UAW, "Proceedings of the Thirteenth Constitutional Convention," Cleveland, Ohio, April 1–6, 1951, 77–85; John Anderson, "My Battle against Walter Reuther," (manuscript in author's possession, 1986), 189–219 passim.

15. CIO executive board minutes, March 14, 1947, George Meany Memorial Archives, Silver Spring, Md., 403; Marvin Persky, "Walter Reuther, the UAW-CIO, and Third Party Politics" (PhD. diss., Michigan State University, 1974), 167.

16. David Brody, *Workers in Industrial America* (New York: Oxford University Press,1980), 221; Emil Mazey "Looking Forward," *United Auto Worker* (January 1948): 5; "List of Signers for Statement of Principles for NECNP [National Educational Committee for a New Party], [1946?], "New Party" file, box 4, Lewis Corey Papers, Columbia University; Jack Alexander, "What Does Walter Reuther Want?" *Saturday Evening Post*, August 14, 1948, 48–64.

17. Don Montgomery to WPR, "PAC Meeting and Outlook," January 26, 1948, file 13, box 64, UAW Washington Office Collection; Christine Richey, interview with the author, Reading, Mass., July 18, 1993.

18. "Address by Walter Reuther to the First Annual Convention, Americans for Democratic Action" [transcript], Philadelphia, February 22, 1948; and UAW press release, February 22, 1948; both in file 13, box 542, WPR Collection; Arthur Schlesinger, Jr., *The Vital Center* (Boston: Houghton Mifflin, 1949), 223–24. Reuther's actual speech should be compared with the draft prepared by Don Montgomery and Frank Winn. The latter was an even tougher denunciation of liberal equivocation on the domestic scene.

19. "Board Backs CIO-PAC Vote Drive, Pledges New Party Drive in '49," *United Auto Worker* (April 1948); Kevin Boyle, "Politics and Principle: The United Automobile Workers and American Labor-Liberalism, 1948–1968" (Ph.D. diss., University of Michigan, 1990), 64.

20. Dudley W. Buffa, *Union Power and American Democracy: The UAW and the Democratic Party, 1935–1972* (Ann Arbor: University of Michigan Press, 1984), 12–21; Emil Mazey, "Looking Forward," *United Auto Worker* (October 1948): 5; Boyle, "Politics and Principle," 56–74.

21. Quoted in Frank Cormier and William J. Eaton, *Reuther* (Englewood Cliffs, N.J.: Prentice-Hall, 1970), 284.

22. Fay Calkins, *The CIO and the Democratic Party* (Chicago: University of Chicago Press, 1952), 112–33; Alanzo Hamby, *Beyond the New Deal: Harry S. Truman and American Liberalism* (New York: Columbia University Press, 1973), 247–65; Allen Yarnell, *Democrats and Progressives* (Berkeley: University of California Press, 1974), 87–107.

23. Quoted in Anthony Carew, *Walter Reuther* (Manchester: Manchester University Press, 1993), 67.

24. UAW, "Proceedings of the Thirteenth Constitutional Convention," 14; Buffa, *Union Power*, 26–51; Calkins, *CIO and the Democratic Party*, 112–30; J. David Greenstone, *Labor in American Politics* (New York: Alfred A. Knopf, 1969), 120–29; "Roy Reuther," vertical file.

25. John Frederick Martin, *Civil Rights and the Crisis of Liberalism* (Boulder, Colo.: Westview Press, 1979), 89–91; Hamby, *Beyond the New Deal*, 330–51 passim; Boyle, "Politics and Principle," 89–93.

26. CIO pamphlets quoted in Carl Haessler, "Why George Edwards Didn't Become Mayor of Detroit," December 4, 1949, Federated Press Microfilm Collection, George Meany Memorial Archives, Silver Spring, Md.

27. "Cobo Backed by Rebel Democrats," *Detroit Free Press*, November 1, 1949; "AFL Backing of Cobo Is Reiterated," *Detroit Free Press*, October 27, 1949; B.J. Widick, *Detroit: City of Race and Class Violence* (Detroit: Wayne State University Press, 1989), 154; Greenstone, *Labor in American Politics*, 121; Thomas Sugrue, "The Origins of the Urban Crisis: Race, Industrial Decline, and Housing in Detroit, 1940–1960" (Ph.D. diss., Harvard University, 1992), 208–78 passim; *Detroit Free Press* editorial, October 25, 1949, quoted in Boyle, "Politics and Principle," 96.

28. Brendan Sexton, telephone interview with the author, December 24, 1985; Wurster quoted in Boyle, "Politics and Principle," 88.

29. Buffa, *Union Power*, 39; Greenstone, *Labor in American Politics*, 138–40.

30. Harvey Levenstein, *Communism, Anticommunism, and the CIO* (Westport, Conn.: Greenwood Press, 1981), 208–32, 269–78; CIO executive board minutes, November 17, 1948, George Meany Memorial Archives, Silver Spring, Md., 80–81.

31. WPR quoted in Harrison, "UAW Politics," 70.

32. CIO executive board minutes, January 22, 1948, George Meany Memorial Archives, Silver Spring, Md., 68; CIO, "Proceedings of the Twelfth Constitutional Convention," Cleveland, Ohio, November 1949, 266–69, 302.

33. Maurice Isserman, *If I Had a Hammer: The Death of the Old Left and the Birth of the New Left* (New York: Basic Books, 1987), 3–17; Steve Rosswurm, ed., *The CIO's Left-Led Unions* (New Brunswick, N.J.: Rutgers University Press, 1992), 1–17; Saul Wellman, interview with the author, Greenbelt, Md., March 14, 1989; "Committee for a Militant and Democratic Union," file 7, box 56, WPR Collection; Stieber, *Governing the UAW*, 139. At the UAW's 1949 convention the executive board's proposal for a dues increase proved so polarizing that Reuther simply abandoned the issue.

34. Toni Gilpin, "Left by Themselves: A History of the United Farm Equipment and Metal Workers Union, 1938–1955" (Ph.D. diss., Yale University, 1992), 216–52; Livingston quoted on p. 237.

35. *FE News* quoted in UAW-IEB minutes, March 15, 1949, UAW-IEB Collection, 267; Gilpin, "Left by Themselves," 167–215.

36. UAW, "Report of the President to the Twelfth Constitutional Convention," Milwaukee, Wisc., July 10, 1949, 63–67; Persky, "Walter Reuther, UAW-CIO, and Third Party Politics," 199.

37. CIO executive board minutes, November 17, 1948, George Meany Archives, Silver Spring, Md., 76. As early as March 1949 Reuther had gone after Plymouth Local 51 when its newspaper denounced the "phoney GM formula." FE propagandists then picked up the critique and hurled it back at UAW organizers. UAW-IEB minutes, March 15, 1949, UAW-IEB Collection, 262; UAW, "Proceedings of the Thirteenth Constitutional Convention," 352–55; Ben Hall, "The UAW Convention," *Labor Action*, April 10, 1951.

38. UAW, Proceedings of the Thirteenth Constitutional Convention," 167.

39. Quoted in Walter Jason, "Attack on Civil Liberties," *Labor Action*, March 31, 1952.

40. "Comparison of Income: UAW International Representative and GM Worker," file 3, box 167, WPR Collection; "Comparison of Number of Staff Members by Departments," file 14, box 11, UAW Citizenship Department.

41. Frank Marquart, *An Auto Worker's Journal: The UAW from Crusade to One-Party Union* (University Park: Pennsylvania Sate University Press, 1975), 131–32; Ben Hall, "Conservative Mood in the Ranks," *Labor Action*, April 6, 1953.

42. Sheldon Tappes, interview with the author, Detroit, March 16, 1982; Tappes quoted in Judith Stepan-Norris and Maurice Zeitlin, "The Organizer" (manuscript in author's possession, 1991), 84–85.

43. John Pomfret, "Auto Workers' Staff Sets Up Own Union; Reuther Fights Step," *New York Times*, October 2, 1963; John Pomfret, "Reuther Settles Dispute in UAW," *New York Times*, October 14, 1963; UAW-IEB minutes, September 14, 1963, UAW-IEB Collection, 169–79.

44. Lewis Carliner, telephone interview with the author, February 18, 1988; WPR notes, file 4, box 103, WPR Collection; Stieber, *Governing the UAW*, 73–77; Boyle, "Politics and Principle," 108–9; Morris Weisz, "The UAW as a Business Union" (manuscript in author's possession, 1952). As a result of Livingston's attack, Sexton may well have reneged on plans to review *The UAW and Walter Reuther* in *Ammunition*. Howe and Widick gave Reuther a largely sympathetic portrait but skewered Livingston as a "conservative and unimaginative red baiter," 183.

45. Stieber, *Governing the UAW*, 72–73; "UAW-CIO Minimizes Toledo 'Revolt,'" May 20, 1950, Federated Press Microfilm Collection, George Meany Memorial Archives, Silver Spring, Md.; Walter Jason, "Charges against Gosser Create Scandal in UAW," *Labor Action*, May 29, 1950; "Rebellion against Gosser Spurred by Plan to Form Steering Group for Action," *Toledo Blade*, May 22, 1950; Frank Sido to WPR, January 2, 1951, Richard Gosser to WPR, February 19, 1951, both in file 2, box 82, WPR Collection; WPR notes, file 4, box 103, WPR Collection. The plea of the Toledo unionist Frank Sido was typical: "Walter, you can ill-afford to barter the respect and good will of our Union Members and the general public that you have won in past years, for the support of Gosser and his fanatic ex-convicts, thugs and gutter bums." Reuther referred the letter back to Gosser himself.

After an embarrassing congressional hearing in 1959, Reuther finally stripped Gosser of some of his UAW offices, but the Toledo unionist was reelected twice more as a UAW vice president, until in early 1963 he was actually convicted of stealing IRS documents that bore upon a government investigation of his income tax returns. Reuther forced him to resign, but only over the bitter objections of his old comrades

Emil Mazey and Martin Gerber, who were as cynical as Jimmy Hoffa about American justice. U.S. Senate Select Committee, *Investigation of Improper Activities in the Labor or Management Field*, 86th cong., 1st sess., August 11–13, 1959; UAW-IEB minutes, March 6, 1963, UAW-IEB Collection, 88–118 passim; Murray Kempton, "The Gosser Case," *New York Post*, November 16, 1962, file 13, box 82, WPR Collection.

46. Paul Schrade to WPR, February 6, 1951, file 7, Schrade to WPR, March 5, 1954, file 10, both in box 215, WPR Collection; Paul Schrade, interview with the author, Los Angeles, August 19, 1987; Paul Schrade, interview with Frank Cormier and William J. Eaton, Atlantic City, N.J., May 3, 1968.

47. Stieber, *Governing the UAW*, 64–66; Martin Gerber, interview with the author, Detroit, October 28, 1987; UAW, "Proceedings of the Fifteenth Constitutional Convention," Cleveland, Ohio, March 27–April 1, 1955, 193. Campja's challenge did not turn on racial issues, but he was a liberal who later took a job with the American Federation of State County and Municipal Employees. In 1968 he helped organize the Memphis sanitation strike in support of which Martin Luther King, Jr., met his death.

48. John McManis "UAW's Stellato Emerges as Coming Strong Man," *Detroit News*, June 7, 1955; "Most Ford Local 600 Officials Sign Loyalty Pledges," July 15, 1950, Federated Press Microfilm Collection, George Meany Memorial Archives, Silver Spring, Md.; Walter Jason [B. J. Widick], "Union Democracy under Attack in UAW-Ford Trial," *Labor Action*, October 16, 1950. Davis, Moore, Gallo, and Locke were Communists, but Boatin had been expelled from the party in August 1949 after he objected to CP efforts to micromanage politics in the Motor Building, where he was president. Joseph Rauh to VGR, "Paul Boatin Statement," May 13, 1957, file 17, box 250, WPR Collection.

49. "Left Wing Keep Control of '600' Executive Board," *Wage Earner* (April 1950); Carl Stellato, "My Differences with Walter P. Reuther," September 4, 1951, file 4, box 97, WPR Collection; William D. Andrew, "Factionalism and Anti-Communism: Ford Local 600," *Labor History* 20 (Spring 1979): 242–45.

50. UAW, "Proceedings of the Thirteenth Constitutional Convention," 119.

51. Quoted in Andrew, "Factionalism and Anti-Communism," 244.

52. Stellato, "My Differences with Reuther"; Walter Dorosh, interview with the author, Dearborn, Mich., October 14, 1982. Dorosh claimed that Local 600 printed 150,000 copies of *Ford Facts* weekly at the height of the anti-Reuther campaign.

53. "UAW Controversy over Ford Local Bid to Lewis Sharpens," June 14, 1951, Federated Press Microfilm Collection, George Meany Memorial Archives, Silver Spring, Md.; Elie Abel, "Foes of Reuther Praised by Lewis," *New York Times*, June 24, 1951; Andrews, "Factionalism and Anti-Communism," 244–45. See also Robert Zieger, "Showdown at the Rouge," *History Today*, 40 (January 1990), 49–56.

54. John S. Bugas to WPR, September 5, 1950, and John S. Bugas telegram to WPR, October 18, 1950; both in file 4, box 96, WPR Collection. In the fall of 1951 Reuther was forced to defend the five-year contract all over again; "Reuther on the Stump," *New York Times*, October 28, 1951.

55. Lou Arkles, "Negro Group Set for FEPC Fight," *Detroit Times*, October 2, 1951; "Wayne County CIO Debates Detroit FEPC Issues: Delegates Ask Action," *Militant*, August 12, 1951; Gerald Horne, *Communist Front? The Civil Rights Congress, 1946–1956* (Rutherford, Penn.: Fairleigh Dickinson University Press, 1988), 289–92.

56. Herbert Hill, interview with the author, Madison, Wisc., June 20, 1987; William Oliver to Roy Reuther, "Status of UAW Officers and NAACP Memberships," February 21, 1961, file 24, box 9, UAW Citizenship Department Collection; Joseph Rauh

to WPR, March 4, 1959, box 36, Joseph Rauh Collection, Library of Congress; UAW, "Report of UAW-CIO President Walter Reuther to the Fifteenth Constitutional Convention," 82D–93D; WPR quoted in "UAW Adopts Five Point Program," *Michigan CIO News*, November 26, 1951.

57. Seth Wigderson, "The UAW in the 1950s" (Ph.D. diss., Wayne State University, 1989), 330–54; Boyle, "Politics and Principle," 103–4.

58. Oliver quoted in Marshall Stevenson, "Points of Departure, Acts of Resolve: Black-Jewish Relations in Detroit, 1937–1962" (Ph.D. diss., University of Michigan, 1988), 299–300; "Local 600 Officials Urge Enactment of FEPC Ordinance," *Ford Facts*, May 5, 1951; "FEPC Urged to Foil Reds," *Detroit News*, June 27, 1951; "Wayne County CIO Debates Detroit FEPC Issues: Delegates Ask Action," *Militant*, August 12, 1951; "Job Democracy Comes to Michigan as FEPC Swings into Operation," *Michigan CIO News*, October 10, 1955.

59. UAW-IEB minutes, March 12, 1952, UAW-IEB Collection, 36, 33; Wellman, interview with the author.

60. B. J. Widick's reportage in *Labor Action* is excellent: see "The Circus Comes to Detroit; Un-Americans to Probe UAW," February 4, 1952; "Un-American Probers Try to Whip up Detroit," February 29, 1952; "Witchhunt, Labor-Baiting, Jim Crow, Anti-Semitism," March 17, 1952; "Detroit Becomes Salem: Probe Looses Hysteria," March 10, 1952; "Attack Continues on Civil Liberties," March 31, 1952. Much of his reportage is collected in B. J. Widick, *Detroit: City of Race and Class Violence* (Detroit: Wayne State University Press, 1989), 113–36.

61. UAW-IEB minutes, Detroit, March 12, 1952, UAW-IEB Collection, 37–41, 44.

62. Ibid., 43; UAW-IEB minutes, March 14, 1952, UAW-IEB Collection, 29–38; Gerber, interview with the author; Stieber, *Governing the UAW*, 147–48.

63. "Ford Local Electioneering Begins," May 16, 1952, Federated Press Microfilm Collection, Gerorge Meany Memorial Archives, Silver Spring, Md.; "Ford Local Clash with UAW Eases," *New York Times*, August 31, 1952.

64. Jack Wilson, "UAW Exec Takes over Ford Local," *Labor Action*, March 24, 1952, 1; "Local 600 Starving for Pirated Leaders," *Wage Earner* (March 1952); "Ford Local Electioneering Begins," May 16, 1952, Federated Press Microfilm Collection, George Meany Memorial Archives, Silver Spring, Md. Until abandoned at the last moment, Solidarity House's candidate against Stellato had been the former ACTU activist and Local 600 education director Edgar Lee, now on the International payroll.

65. "Opponents of Reuther Favorites in Ford Election," August 22, 1952, Federated Press Microfilm Collection, George Meany Memorial Archives, Silver Spring, Md.

66. Swados, "UAW: Over the Top or Over the Hill?" 80.

67. Kornhauser et al., *When Labor Votes*, 19, 42, 281–82; Harold Sheppard and Nicholas Masters, "The Political Attitudes and Preferences of Union Members," *American Political Science Review* (June 1959): 437–47; Bennett Berger, *Working Class Suburb* (Berkeley: University of California Press, 1963); Boyle, "Politics and Principle," 160–62. In contrast to much popular literature, Berger found suburbanization relatively inconsequential in shaping political consciousness.

68. Kroll quoted in James Foster, *The Union Politic: The CIO Political Action Committee* (Columbia: University of Missouri Press, 1975), 199; Davis, *Prisoners of the American Dream*, 97–100. In recent years the decline in working-class voting has been the most visible manifestation of this depoliticization process; see Thomas Edsall, *The New Politics of Inequality* (New York: W. W. Norton, 1984), 141–201; and Thomas Ferguson and Joel Rodgers, *Right Turn: The Decline of the Democrats and the Future of American Politics* (New York: Hill and Wang, 1986), 61–67.

69. Galbraith quoted in Steven M. Gillon, *Politics and Vision: The ADA and American Liberalism, 1947–1985* (New York: Oxford University Press, 1987), 83–85.

70. Don Montgomery to WPR, July 2, 1952, file 21, and Robert Nathan to ADA executive board members, August 8, 1952, file 22, both in box 430, WPR Collection; Joseph Rauh, interview with the author, Washington, D.C., March 10, 1989; Rauh quoted in Boyle, "Politics and Principle," 153. In August the ADA voted fifty-five to zero to endorse Stevenson, with but four abstentions, only one of which sought a clarification of the candidate's position on civil rights issues.

71. Roosevelt and *Wall Street Journal* quoted in Gillon, *Politics and Vision*, 88–89; Wigderson, "UAW in the 1950s," 191.

72. "Reuther Asks Eisenhower for National Conference on Peacetime Production," April 7, 1953, Federated Press Microfilm Collection, George Meany Memorial Archives, Silver Spring, Md.; Sherman Adams, *Firsthand Report: The Story of the Eisenhower Administration* (New York: Harper and Brothers, 1963), 6.

73. Robert Dallek, *Lone Star Rising: Lyndon Johnson and His Times, 1908–1960* (New York: Oxford University Press, 1991), 159–224, 314, 467–508 passim; Montgomery quoted in Boyle, "Politics and Principle," 163. Reuther tried to get the CIO to support Johnson in his famous, controversial 1948 senatorial primary fight against Coke Stevenson.

74. Ben Hall, "Reutherism Marks Time on the Main Issues at UAW Convention," *Labor Action*, April 6, 1953.

75. McDonald quoted in Robert Zieger, "Leadership and Bureaucracy in the Late CIO," *Labor History*, 31 (Summer 1990), 256; Miriam Kolkin, "Reuther Elected CIO President, Defeats Haywood," December 4, 1952; Oil, Chemical, and Atomic Workers staffer quoted in Miriam Kolkin, "Compromise on Officers Forecasts Uneasy Year for the CIO," December 8, 1952, Federated Press Microfilm Collection, George Meany Memorial Archives, Silver Spring, Md.

76. Zieger, "Leadership and Bureaucracy in the Late CIO," 256–70.

77. Robert Zieger, *The CIO, 1935–1955* (Chapel Hill: University of North Carolina Press, 1995), 360–64; Henry Fleisher, interview with Don Kennedy, Washington, D.C., May 4, 1979, AFL-CIO Oral History Project, George Meany Memorial Archives, Silver Spring, Md.

78. Reuther's AFL-CIO speech quoted in AFL-CIO, *Proceedings of the First Constitutional Convention*, New York, December 5–8, 1955, 146; Reuther otherwise quoted in Zieger, *The CIO*, 363, 370; Joshua Freeman, *In Transit: The Transport Workers Union in New York City, 1933–1966* (New York: Oxford University Press, 1989), 333.

79. Schrade, interview with Cormier and Eaton. Livingston also blundered when he ordered back to work scores of GM locals immediately after the UAW and GM signed their 1955 agreement. Local negotiations were still in progress, and several key locals insisted on staying out. Irving Bluestone, interview with the author, Detroit, March 26, 1987.

80. Dorosh, interview with the author.

81. WPR to Ralph Helstein, June 25, 1953, file 14; Helstein to WPR, August 6, 1953, file 15; Joseph Colaneri to WPR, August 16, 1953, file 16; David Burgess to Jack Conway, September 17, 1953, file 18; "In the Matter of United Packinghouse Workers of America, CIO," October 16, 1953, file 20; WPR to Helstein, October 30, 1953, file 21; all in box 292, WPR Collection.

82. UAW, "Proceedings of the Fifteenth Constitutional Convention," 307–18. Many of these Communists were "colonizers" from New York who falsified their employment applications by failing to list college degrees, white-collar work, etc. When HUAC revealed their backgrounds, General Motors fired them.

83. Joseph Rauh, interview with the author, Washington, D.C., March 10, 1989; Damon Stetson, "Civil Liberty Unit Condemns UAW," *New York Times*, October 13, 1957.

84. UAW-IEB minutes, August 1957, "UAW Public Review Board" file, box 55, Edwin Witte Collection, Wisconsin State Historical Society.

85. "UAW Beats UE-FE Rival at Harvester," *Labor Action*, June 14, 1954; James Reston, "Judiciary Seen as Setting Limit on Other Branches," *New York Times*, June 18, 1957; WPR, "The United Automobile Workers: Past, Present, and Future," *Virginia Law Review* 50, no. 58 (1964): 96.

86. Jack Stieber, "The UAW Public Review Board: An Examination and Evaluation," and Michael Harrington, "What Union Members Think of Public Review," both in *A Report: Democracy and Public Review*, ed. Jack Stieber (Santa Barbara, Calif.: Center for the Study of Democratic Institutions, 1960), file 11, box 274, WPR Collection; "Nine Senate Witnesses to Go before UAW Review Board," *Detroit News*, August 29, 1957; "UAW's Watchdogs Try Their Teeth," *Business Week*, July 12, 1958. In later years the board functioned primarily as "a small claims court," to use Paul Schrade's phrase. Paul Schrade, interview with the author, Los Angeles, August 19, 1987.

87. Wellman, interview with the author; Roy Reuther quoted in Marquart, *Auto Worker's Journal*, 123. Nunn's firing came after he debated George Romney on his show during the 1962 Michigan gubernatorial race. Romney got the better of him, but Nunn's real crime was that he was far better known and more outspokenly left-wing than any regional director. B. J. Widick, interview with the author, Ann Arbor, Mich., July 22, 1989.

88. Rauh, interview with the author; Swados, "UAW: Over the Top or Over the Hill?" 88–89.

CHAPTER 15: REUTHER ABROAD:
"PRODUCTION IS THE ANSWER"

1. Denis MacShane, *International Labour and the Origins of the Cold War* (Oxford: Clarendon Press, 1992), 79–186, 238–77 passim; Michael Hogan, *The Marshall Plan: America, Britain, and the Reconstruction of Western Europe, 1947–1952* (New York: Cambridge University Press, 1987), 26–134 passim.

2. Quoted in Charles S. Maier, "The Two Postwar Eras and the Conditions for Stability in Twentieth-Century Western Europe," in Maier, *In Search of Stability: Explorations in Historical Political Economy* (New York: Cambridge University Press, 1987), 153.

3. "Marshall Plan Will Fail Unless U.S. Works with European Unions," October 22, 1948, Federated Press Microfilm Collection, George Meany Memorial Archives, Silver Spring, Md.

4. Charles Maier, "Politics of Productivity: Foundations of American International Economic Policy after World War II," in Maier, *In Search of Stability*, 121–52; Carey quoted in Anthony Carew, *Labour under the Marshall Plan: The Politics of Productivity and the Marketing of Management Science* (Detroit: Wayne State University Press, 1987), 252; Hoffman quoted in Hogan, *Marshall Plan*, 143. Ironically, Hoffman was himself a former executive of Studebaker, the American car firm whose production regime was among the most "European" and least Fordist in the United States. When the company's fortunes took a nosedive in the mid-1950s, he returned to more active control and tried to recast both its labor relations and product line along the orthodox General Motors pattern. Labor relations became embittered, quality deteriorated, and the firm when bankrupt. See Stephen Amberg, "The Triumph of Industrial Orthodoxy: The Collapse of Studebaker-Packard," in *On the Line: Essays*

in the History of Auto Work, ed. Nelson Lichtenstein and Stephen Meyer (Urbana: University of Illinois Press, 1989), 190–218.

5. Peter Weiler, "The United States, International Labor, and the Cold War: The Breakup of the World Federation of Trade Unions," *Diplomatic History* 5 (Winter 1981): 12–14.

6. "Reuther Statement on European Recovery Program," February 1948, file 3, box 101, WPR Collection.

7. Ronald Filippelli, *American Labor and Postwar Italy, 1943–1953* (Stanford, Calif.: Stanford University Press, 1989), 133; VGR quoted in MacShane, *International Labour,* 139; "Victor George Reuther, Interview of December 31, 1949," file 468, vol. 38, FBI-FOIA.

8. Henry A. Byroade, "Department of State, Memorandum of Conversation," January 18, 1950, box 4409, RG 59, National Archives; United Auto Workers–International Executive Board minutes, September 8, 1953, UAW-IEB Collection, 78.

9. Thomas Braden, "I'm Glad the CIA Is Immoral," *Saturday Evening Post,* May 20, 1967, 10–14; "Ex-CIA Aide Lists Big Grants to Unions," *New York Times,* May 8, 1967; "CIA Man Who Told: Thomas Wardell Braden," *New York Times,* May 8, 1967; Victor Reuther, *The Brothers Reuther and the Story of the UAW* (Boston: Houghton Mifflin, 1976), 424–26.

10. WPR, "Free Men at Work," *Collier's,* October 27, 1951, 37, 108; John B. Stone, "Government Policy, Group Hysteria, or Circulation Stunt?" October 24, 1951, Federated Press Microfilm Collection, George Meany Memorial Archives, Silver Spring, Md. Among the other contributors were Edward R. Morrow, Hanson W. Baldwin, J. B. Priestley, Bill Mauldin, Stuart Chase, Allan Nevins, and Robert E. Sherwood. Baldwin, the *New York Times* military correspondent, projected a war of thirty-two months' duration, but in his contribution Reuther speculated that a general strike in the Soviet Union would end the fighting within weeks.

11. Reuther, *Brothers Reuther,* 424–26; VGR, interview with the author, Washington, D.C., August 25, 1986; James Jesus Angleton, interview with the author, Washington, D.C., June 13, 1982. Angleton was well informed as to Lovestone's activities in Europe.

12. VGR, "Is the Marshall Plan in Danger?" *Vital Speeches* (December 1, 1948), 109–11; Arthur O'Shea, "Unionist Rips Policy in Reich," *Detroit Free Press,* [undated—August 1948], file 19, box 63, UAW Washington Office Collection; WPR to Harry S. Truman, May 10, 1949, James E. Webb (acting secretary of state) to WPR, June 14, 1949, and Paul Hoffman to WPR, June 10, 1949, all in file 10, box 449, WPR Collection; CIO, "Proceedings of the Twelfth Constitutional Convention," Chicago, November 21, 1950, 297.

13. VGR, interview with the author, August 25, 1986; Abe Zwerling, interview with the author, June 6, 1985; "Vic Reuther Will Remain Abroad," December 12, 1950, Federated Press Microfilm Collection, George Meany Memorial Archives, Silver Spring, Md.

14. MacShane, *International Labour,* 85–89; VGR, "CIO Report from Europe," March 31, 1952, file 8, box 294, and VGR, "CIO Report from Europe," December 1952, file "Vic Reuther, 1952" box 1, both in WPR Collection.

15. VGR to WPR, April 28, 1952, and VGR to WPR, May 29, 1952, both in file 9, box 294, WPR Collection; VGR to "Members of CIO Committee of International Affairs," December 8, 1952, file 7, box 294, WPR Collection; VGR to "All CIO Delegates to ICFTU Congress," "Strengthening the ICFTU Secretariat," February 1955, "ICFTU" file, box 3, WPR Collection; VGR, "Subject: American Labor and the

ICFTU" (1955), "UAW-CIO, 1955" file, box 30, Paul Sifton Collection, Library of Congress; "Meany's Attitude toward the ICFTU," in *John Herling's Labor Letter*, June 14, 1957; Filippelli, *American Labor and Postwar Italy*, 194. When Meany asked for a recount during the 1951 UIL affiliation debate, the ICFTU's British president, Vincent Tewson, snapped, "What for? Maybe you want to make note of who didn't support you in order to stop financing them?" (Filippelli, *American Labor and Postwar Italy*).

16. Robert Zieger, *American Workers, American Unions, 1920–1985* (Baltimore: Johns Hopkins University Press, 1986), 158–58; Reuther, *Brothers Reuther*, 362–63. Among the AFL-CIO vice presidents, Reuther's name was listed first on the new organization's letterhead. Jack Barbash, interview with Jim Cavanaugh, Washington, D.C., February 2, 1979, AFL-CIO Oral History Project, George Meany Memorial Archives, Silver Spring, Md., 5.

17. A. H. Raskin, "The New Labor Leaders—A Dual Portrait," *New York Times Magazine*, December 21, 1952, 13; Robert Zieger, "George Meany: Labor's Organization Man," in *Labor Leaders in America*, ed. Melvyn Dubofsky and Warren Van Tine (Urbana: University of Illinois Press, 1987), 328–29. Barbash, interview with Cavanaugh. Meany was a founder of the New York State American Labor Party in 1936.

18. Joseph Goulden, *Meany: The Unchallenged Strong Man of American Labor* (New York: Atheneum, 1972), 271–83; Henry Fleisher, interview with Don Kennedy, Washington, D.C., May 4, 1979, 21–28, AFL-CIO Oral History Project, George Meany Memorial Archives, Silver Spring, Md.; Barbash interview with Cavanaugh, 9. When he reprinted the CIO songbook in 1956, Fleisher was careful to put "The Star-Spangled Banner" well before the Joe Hill ballads, but this editorial choice hardly bridged the cultural divide between the AFL and the CIO. When Virginia Tehas, George Meany's private secretary, saw a copy, she demanded of Fleisher, "What are you trying to do, make fools out of us? . . . They don't sing at union meetings." Fleisher told her union singing built morale on the picket line, but Tehas replied, "Well, I've never heard of anything so ridiculous in my life" (Fleisher interview with Kennedy).

19. Stanley Ruttenberg, interview with Don Kennedy, Washington, D.C., July 20, 1979, 28, AFL-CIO Oral History Project, George Meany Memorial Archives, Silver Spring, Md.

20. Daniel Bell, "Labor's New Men of Power," *Fortune* 47 (June 1953): 151; Goulden, *Meany*, 402.

21. Adolf Sturmthal, "The International Confederation of Free Trade Unions," *Industrial and Labor Relations Review*, 3 (April 1950), 375–82; Kevin Boyle, "Politics and Principle: The United Automobile Workers and American Labor-Liberalism, 1948–1968" (Ph.D. diss., University of Michigan, 1990), 112–14; Walter Rush, "Trillion for Peace Urged by Reuther," *New York Times*, July 19, 1950. Truman aides quickly buried Reuther's proposal as impractical and politically awkward in these early months of the Korean War. The AFL's Irving Brown dismissed Reuther's emphasis on economic development and productivity as a naive "belly Communism" irrelevant to the more direct ideological struggle. See Carew, *Labour under the Marshall Plan*, 123.

22. UAW, "Proceedings of the Fifteenth Constitutional Convention," Cleveland, March 27–April 1, 1955, 10.

23. Carew, *Labour under the Marshall Plan*, 172–73; Hogan, *Marshall Plan*, 140; VGR to Jacob Potofsky, August 22, 1951, file 6, box 294, and VGR to WPR, "Action Projects in French Labor," December 1951, file 7, box 294, both in WPR Collection. By this point the Reuther brothers were extremely disappointed with "the passivity and lack of dynamism" of the FO leadership. The CIO and, in this instance, its CIA-

funded organizing drive in the Paris region was therefore also designed to build an opposition caucus within the FO. Victor called it "looking towards building some new leadership" (VGR to WPR, "Action Projects in French Labor").

24. Carew, *Labour under the Marshall Plan*, 178; UAW-IEB minutes, September 8, 1953, UAW-IEB Collection, 77.

25. Ben Thibedeaux, "Memorandum of Conversation," July 31, 1953, box 5270, 863.062/8–1453, XR 032, RG 59, National Archives; VGR, interview with Eugene R. Sensenig, Washington, D.C., May 25, 1988 (in author's possession).

26. Carew, *Labor under the Marshall Plan*, 131–223 passim.

27. "Judgements and Prophecies: Guaranteed Annual Wage," *Time*, June 20, 1955, 23; British press quoted in Anthony Carew, *Walter Reuther* (Manchester: Manchester University Press, 1993), 96–97.

28. Geoffrey Foote, *The Labour Party's Political Thought: A History* (London: Croom Helm, 1985), 207–41 passim; Harold Wilson, *The Labour Government, 1964–1970: A Personal Record* (London: Weidenfeld and Nicolson, 1971), 8–9, 194.

29. Wilson, *Labour Government*, 194. Reuther claimed to have "170 industrial consultants at Ph.D level on his staff," an obvious exaggeration.

30. "Itinerary and Time Table, Walter Reuther and Party," June 26–August 4, 1953," file 1, box 462, WPR Collection; "CIO Histadrut Open Culture House at Eilat," *Jerusalem Post*, September 6, 1955, file 13, box 462, WPR Collection; "Reuther Sees Bonn Ministers," *New York Times*, May 7, 1959; Carew, *Reuther*, 147.

31. Linda Reuther, interview with the author, San Anselmo, Calif., March 23, 1988; Frank Cormier and William J. Eaton, *Reuther* (Englewood Cliffs, N.J.: Prentice-Hall, 1970), 362. This incident probably took place in 1961 after an International Metalworkers Federation conference in Milan.

32. Arne Ruth, "The Second New Nation: The Mythology of Modern Sweden," in *Norden: The Passion for Equality* (Oslo: Norwegian University Press, 1986), 240–82; "How Sweden Creates Full Employment to Avoid Slump" (1963), file 12, and "Swedish Press Reports: Walter Reuther's Visit to Stockholm" (1959), file 1, both box 461, WPR Collection; VGR, interview with the author, August 25, 1986. Geijer was also chairman of the Social Democratic Party's foreign affairs committee. Reuther must have been envious.

33. Reuther, *Brothers Reuther*, 402–4; MacShane, *International Labour*, 71.

34. Carew, *Reuther*, 119; see also "IMF Report on International Fair Labour Standards," 1959, file 1193, IMF Collection, Friederick Ebert Foundation, Bonn.

35. UAW, "Report of President Walter P. Reuther to the Seventeenth Constitutional Convention," Atlantic City, N.J., October 9–16, 1959; Fritz Opel, *Seventy-five Years of the Iron International, 1893–1968* (Geneva: International Metalworkers Federation, 1968), 172.

36. Otto Jacobi and Walter Muller-Jentsch, "West Germany: Continuity and Structural Change," in *European Industrial Relations: The Challenge of Flexibility*, ed. Guido Baglioni and Colin Crouch (London: Sage Publications, 1990), 127–53; Alexis Marion, "Neo-Corporatism and Industrial Relations: The Case of German Trade Unions," *West European Politics* 6 (1983): 75–92; Andrei Markovits, *The Politics of West German Trade Unions: Strategies of Class and Interest Representation in Growth and Crisis* (Cambridge: Cambridge University Press, 1986).

37. Carew, *Reuther*, 123–24; and see remarks of West German trade unionists in "Fifth World Automobile Conference," Frankfurt, November 16, 1964, file 1173, IMF Collection, Friederick Ebert Foundation, Bonn.

38. The left-wing labor federation Sohyo was Japan's largest and was also quite sympa-

thetic to Reuther and the UAW, but its four million workers were concentrated in government service and the railroads. Japanese manufacturing unions pulled out of the Wage Research Center in 1968 after the first wage surveys proved embarrassing. UAW, *Report of President Walter P. Reuther to the 20th Constitutional Convention* (Long Beach, May 16–21, 1966), 134; Boyle, "Politics and Principle," 289–303; Carew, *Reuther*, 120–22; Michael Cusumano, *The Japanese Automobile Industry: Technology and Management at Nissan and Toyota* (Cambridge: Harvard University Press, 1985), 165–85.

39. John B. Martin, *Adlai Stevenson and the World* (Garden City, N.Y.: Doubleday, 1977); Robert A. Packenham, *Liberal America and the Third World* (Princeton, N.J.: Princeton University Press, 1973).

40. William Barnds, *India, Pakistan, and the Great Powers* (New York: Praeger, 1972); James Hitchman, "Parry and Thrust: Eisenhower, the Soviet Union, and India, 1953–1961," *World Review* 24 (April 1985): 11–24; Selig Harrison, "Reuther in India," *New Republic*, May 21, 1956, 9.

41. Goulden, *Meany*, 272.

42. VGR to David Burgess, February 1, 1956; Burgess to VGR, February 27, 1956; VGR to Burgess, March 21, 1957; Burgess to VGR, April 18, 1957; all in file 1, box 105, UAW Washington Office Collection (International Affairs Department); Roosevelt quoted in Goulden, *Meany*, 272.

43. VGR to WPR, March 12, 1956, file 12, box 105, and "Walter Reuther Press Conference" [transcript], March 28, 1956, file 13, box 105, both UAW Washington Office Collection (International Affairs Department); Reuther, *Brothers Reuther*, 387; Harrison, "Reuther in India," 9–11. The trip was indeed virtually a state visit: Victor spent hours with State Department officials putting together his brother's itinerary.

44. Reuther, *Brothers Reuther*, 387–88; Arthur Bonner, "Through India with Walter Reuther," *Reporter*, May 17, 1956, 31–34, 32; Harrison, "Reuther in India," 9; "Ambassador Extraordinary," *Washington Post*, April 26, 1956.

45. UAW-IEB minutes, May 3, 1956, UAW-IEB Collection, 105–15; *Detroit Free Press*, April 3, 1956, quoted in Boyle, "Politics and Principle," 209–12.

46. Jack M. Schick, *The Berlin Crisis: 1958–1962* (Philadelphia: University of Pennsylvania Press, 1971), 3–68 passim; Dennis L. Bark and David R. Gress, *A History of West Germany: From Shadow to Substance, 1945–1963* (Cambridge: Blackwell Publishers, 1988), 437–39; VGR to "All CIO Delegates to ICFTU Congress," "German Rearmament" (1955), ICFTU folder, box 3, WPR Collection; John A. Calhoun, "Memorandum for Brig. Gen. A. J. Goodpaster; Subject: Willy Brandt's Views on Berlin," December 11, 1958, 762.00\12–1158, RG59, National Archives; American Embassy, Bonn, to Department of State, "Basic Attitudes of German Political Leaders to the German Question," December 22, 1958, 762.00\12–2258, RG 59, National Archives; VGR, interview with Eugene R. Sensenig. Brandt's views were similar to Adenauer's; indeed, he was the only other politician besides the foreign minister who accompanied Adenauer to a January 1959 NATO meeting in Paris.

47. John Herling, "U.S. Labor versus Mikoyan," *New Leader*, February 2, 1959; "Statement by the AFL-CIO Executive Council on the Berlin Crisis" (1958), file 1, box 450, WPR Collection.

48. "West Berlin Affirms Freedom in Record Rally," *New York Times*, May 2, 1959; U.S. Information Service, "Berlin's Free Workers Stand Firm," *Labour News from the United States*, May 22, 1959, in "Walter Reuther" vertical file.

49. "Meany Not Reuther Named to UN Post," *New York Times*, August 22, 1959; Reuther, *Brothers Reuther*, 394; Meany quoted in Zieger, "George Meany," 332.

50. Reuther, *Brothers Reuther*, 392–97; "Business Leaders Meet with Khrushchev," *New York Times*, September 18, 1959.

51. Rieve quoted in Cormier and Eaton, *Reuther*, 363–64.

52. "Khrushchev Greeted by Cheers in San Francisco, Won't Cut Trip, Debates Sharply with Unionists," *New York Times*, September 21, 1959; "Summary of Dinner Debate between U.S. Union Leaders and Khrushchev," *New York Times*, September 22, 1959; Cormier and Eaton, *Reuther*, 363–66; Reuther, *Brothers Reuther*, 394–97.

53. "Khrushchev Greeted by Cheers in San Francisco"; Osgood Caruthers, "Four Soviets Label Reuther Traitor," *New York Times*, October 30, 1959; Osgood Caruthers, "Soviets Continue Reuther Attack," *New York Times*, October 31, 1959; Reuther, *Brothers Reuther*, 398.

CHAPTER 16: DEMOCRATIC DILEMMAS

1. David Reinhard, *The Republican Right since 1945* (Lexington: University Press of Kentucky, 1983), 138–45; Michael Miles, *The Odyssey of the American Right* (New York: Oxford University Press, 1980); and Mike Davis, *Prisoners of the American Dream* (London: Verso, 1986), 166–70.

2. Goldwater quoted in Arthur Schlesinger, *Robert Kennedy and His Times* (Boston: Houghton Mifflin, 1978), 175; Herbert Parmet, *Jack: The Struggles of John F. Kennedy* (New York: Dial Press, 1980), 422; J. B. Matthews, "The Truth about Reuther," *Human Events* 14 (June 8, 1957); see also "Goldwater Stooges for Auto Firms," *UAW Administrative Letter*, February 3, 1958.

3. Schlesinger, *Robert Kennedy*, 174; Parmet, *Jack*, 422; Frank Cormier and William J. Eaton, *Reuther* (Englewood Cliffs, N.J.: Prentice-Hall, 1970), 341–46; Walter Uphoff, *Kohler on Strike: Thirty Years of Conflict* (Boston: Beacon Press, 1966). Emil Mazey, in charge of the strike, turned to his old Briggs local for militants when it became clear that the Kohler local was disintegrating in the summer of 1954. William Vinson spent thirteen months in prison for beating up a scab, but the other UAW organizer, John Gunaca, fled the state after a similar altercation. When Michigan Governor G. Mennen Williams refused to extradite Gunaca, on the grounds that he could not get a fair trial in Sheboygan, Republicans charged that Reuther controlled both the governor and the state Democratic Party. Their view was seemingly sustained when, after Reuther told the McClellan Committee that Gunaca should stand trial in Wisconsin, Williams sent him back. See Frank McNaughton, *Mennen Williams of Michigan* (New York: Oceana Publications, 1960), 155–60.

4. Robert Kennedy, *The Enemy Within* (New York: Popular Library, 1960), 274–75; Schlesinger, *Robert Kennedy*, 175–79; Parmet, *Jack*, 423. The key favor the Kennedys offered Reuther was a chance to testify. By the time the Kohler phase of the hearings actually began, in February 1958, Goldwater and the Republicans were unwilling to give Reuther the platform he demanded, but the Kennedy brothers had Chairman John McClellan's confidence, so Reuther was given his day in court.

5. McClellan letter quoted in Victor Reuther, *The Brothers Reuther and the Story of the UAW* (Boston: Houghton Mifflin, 1976), 218–19; Cormier and Eaton, *Reuther*, 348; Joseph Rauh, interview with the author, Washington, D.C., March 10, 1989.

6. Rauh, interview with the author; U.S. Senate Select Committee, *Investigation of Improper Activities in the Labor or Management Field*, 85th cong., 2d sess., March 27–28, 1958, 10068–95, 10111–14; Uphoff, *Kohler on Strike*, 268–69.

7. Rauh, interview with the author; "The Labor Bosses" cited in Harry Kraus to WPR, July 18, 1958, file 17, box 11, UAW Citizenship Department Collection; "Know Your

Opponent," file 6, box 432, WPR Collection; Alan Otten and Lester Tanzer, "GOP versus Reuther," *Wall Street Journal*, October 20, 1958; Kevin Boyle, "Politics and Principle: The United Automobile Workers and American Labor-Liberalism, 1948–1968" (Ph.D. diss., University of Michigan, 1990), 251–52. Only in Michigan did the UAW wield the kind of influence attributed to it by the Republicans. There the auto union mustered about one-third of the state convention delegates, giving the UAW an effective veto over the party's candidates. But Leonard Woodcock, Gus Scholle, and a set of local union leaders were far more active than Reuther. Leslie Veite, *Labor U.S.A.* (New York: Random House, 1958), 74; J. David Greenstone, *Labor in American Politics* (New York: Alfred A. Knopf, 1969), 112–14. The first and only hostile biography of Reuther appeared in 1958: Eldorous Dayton, *Walter Reuther: The Autocrat of the Bargaining Table* (New York: Devin-Adair, 1958).

8. Reinhard, *Republican Right*, 145; United Auto Workers–International Executive Board minutes, November 10, 1958, UAW-IEB Collection.

9. John W. Sloan, *Eisenhower and the Management of Prosperity* (Lawrence: University of Kansas Press, 1991), 90–132 passim; Stephen Amberg, *The Union Inspiration in American Politics: The Autoworkers and the Making of a Liberal Industrial Order* (Philadelphia: Temple University Press, 1994), 1–5; Thomas Sugrue, "The Structures of Urban Poverty: The Reorganization of Space and Work in Three Periods of American History," in *The "Underclass" Debate: Views from History*, ed. Michael Katz (Princeton, N.J.: Princeton University Press, 1993), 98–117 passim; George Strauss, "The Shifting Power Balance in the Plant," *Industrial Relations* (Fall 1959): 22–41; Sumner Slichter, James Healy, and E. Robert Livernash, *The Impact of Collective Bargaining on Management* (Washington, D.C.: Brookings Institution, 1960).

10. Davis, *Prisoners of the American Dream*, 121–24; Carl Dean Snyder, *White-Collar Workers and the UAW* (Urbana: University of Illinois Press, 1973), 57–77; UAW, "Proceedings of the Eighteenth Constitutional Convention," Atlantic City, N.J., May 4–10, 1962, 97–107 passim.

11. Robert Dallek, *Lone Star Rising: Lyndon Johnson and His Times, 1908–1960* (New York: Oxford University Press, 1991), 547–48; Reuther, *Brothers Reuther*, 450–51; Boyle, "Politics and Principle," 257–58; UAW, "Report of Walter Reuther to the Seventeenth Constitutional Convention," Atlantic City, N.J., October 9–16, 1959, 353.

12. Joseph Rauh, interview with William J. Eaton, Washington, D.C., December 11, 1967; UAW-IEB minutes, April 11, 1960, UAW-IEB Collection, 62; see also Rowland Evans and Robert Novak, *Lyndon B. Johnson: The Exercise of Power* (New York: New American Library, 1966), 250.

13. "Don Montgomery," vertical file; Joseph Rauh, interview with Frank Cormier and William J. Eaton, Washington, D.C., December 11, 1967; UAW-IEB minutes, November 10, 1958, UAW-IEB Collection, 38; WPR to Eleanor Roosevelt, June 16, 1960, "Reuther" file, box 4429, Eleanor Roosevelt Papers, FDR Presidential Library. Montgomery committed suicide shortly after his wife died.

14. A. H. Raskin, "Walter Reuther's Great Big Union," *Atlantic Monthly* (October 1963): 92; Reuther quoted in Cormier and Eaton, *Reuther*, 408.

15. Joseph Goulden, *Meany: The Unchallenged Strong Man of American Labor* (New York: Atheneum, 1972), 282–83.

16. UAW-IEB minutes, April 11, 1960, UAW-IEB Collection, 88; Goulden, *Meany*, 287–89. For a good study of the craft union mentality in the Progressive era, still evident forty years later, see Michael Kazin, *Barons of Labor: The San Francisco Building Trades and Union Power in the Progressive Era* (Urbana: University of Illinois Press, 1987).

17. Joseph Bruce Gorman, *Kefauver: A Political Biography* (New York: Oxford University Press, 1971), 298–313; Reuther quoted in U.S. Senate, Committee on Judiciary, Subcommittee on Antitrust and Monopoly, *Administered Prices*, 85th cong., 2d sess., January 29, 1958, 2175–89, 2241, 2250; Jonas Pontusson, *The Limits of Social Democracy: Investment Politics in Sweden* (Ithaca, N.Y.: Cornell University Press, 1992), 57–96 passim.

18. Goulden, *Meany*, 270; "Staff Meeting," January 26, 1959, file 11, box 24, Roy Reuther–UAW Citizenship Department.

19. Boyle, "Politics and Principle," 258; Carey quoted in Goulden, *Meany*, 270–71.

20. Richard Mooney, "President Fights Move to Continue U.S. Jobless Plan," *New York Times*, February 19, 1959; Jack Crellin, "Picket Line Anywhere—Reuther Can't Resist It," *Detroit Times*, February 22, 1959; Boyle, "Politics and Principle," 259.

21. Parmet, *Jack*, 489–96; R. Alton Lee, *Eisenhower and Landrum-Griffin: A Study in Labor-Management Politics* (Lexington: University Press of Kentucky, 1990), 138–59; Herbert Stein, *The Fiscal Revolution in America* (Washington, D.C.: AEI Press, 1990), 346–71; Sundquist, *Politics and Policy: The Eisenhower, Kennedy, and Johnson Years* (Washington, D.C.: Brookings Institution, 1968), 60–71, 296–308.

22. UAW-IEB minutes, April 11, 1960, UAW-IEB Collection, 88.

23. Cormier and Eaton, *Reuther*, 369–71; Jack Conway, interview with Larry Hackman, Washington, D.C., April 10, 1972, 21–22, 26–27. Reuther also wanted to keep his links open to Johnson and the congressional conservatives. When G. Mennen Williams endorsed Kennedy in June 1960, Reuther remained silent because he hoped for LBJ's help in winning congressional passage of the Forand Bill, providing medical care to the elderly. Victor Riesel, "The Story behind Reuther versus Williams," *Detroit Free Press*, July 3, 1960.

24. Parmet, *Jack*, 497–98; Conway, interview with Hackman, 21; Jack Conway, interview with Alice Hoffman, Silver Spring, Md., May 23, 1979, 29, AFL-CIO Oral History Project, George Meany Memorial Archives, Silver Spring, Md.

25. Conway, interview with Hackman, 27; Joseph Rauh, interview with Frank Cormier and William J. Eaton, December 11, 1967. Reuther no longer stood with the Democratic liberals. In an ADA straw poll of its members just before the West Virginia primary, Humphrey took 50 percent, and Kennedy something less than 10 percent. Joseph Rauh, interview with Paige Mulhollan, Washington, D.C., August 1, 1969, LBJ Library, 12.

26. Conway, interview with Hackman, 38; Cormier and Eaton, *Reuther*, 369–70; Ray Courage, "'Neutral' Reuther Quietly Directing All-out Battle for Kennedy," *Detroit Free Press*, July 7, 1960; Parmet, *Jack*, 460–78 passim.

27. Conway, interview with Hackman, 39. On JFK's selection of LBJ, see Dallek, *Lone Star Rising*, 574–81; Schlesinger, *Robert Kennedy*, 202–11.

28. Jack Conway, interview with Frank Cormier and William J. Eaton, Washington, D.C., January 10, 1968; "Special Meeting," July 30, 1960, file 17, box 11, UAW Citizenship Department Collection.

29. Conway, interview with Hackman, 50; Boyle, "Politics and Principle," 272–73; *Solidarity*, September 26, 1960.

30. Louis Harris and Associates, "The Mandate of the UAW Rank and File for Contract Negotiations in 1961," box 10, Ken Bannon Collection; Boyle, "Politics and Principle," 273–74; UAW-IEB minutes, December 13, 1960, UAW-IEB Collection, 9.

31. UAW-IEB minutes, December 13, 1960, 13; Conway, interview with Hackman, 67.

32. Victor Lasky, *JFK: The Man and the Myth* (New York: Macmillan, 1963), 414; Boyle, "Politics and Principle," 271; James Tobin, interview with Joseph Pechman, Wash-

ington, D.C., August 1, 1964, John F. Kennedy Library, 43–44; Conway, interview with Hackman, 67.

33. Schlesinger, *Robert Kennedy*, 468; UAW, "Proceedings of the Eighteenth Constitutional Convention," 309.

34. John Barnard, *Walter Reuther and the Rise of the Auto Workers* (Boston: Little, Brown, 1983), 174–75; UAW, "Proceedings of the Seventeenth Constitutional Convention," 645.

35. JFK quoted in Schlesinger, *Robert Kennedy*, 468; Conway, interview with Hackman, 67.

36. According to Schlesinger, Reuther won no gratitude from Castro for the ransom effort. He explained to a committee of the prisoners that Mrs. Roosevelt was a *vieja chocha* (a silly old lady), and Reuther a "labor baron." Kennedy labeled the "Tractors for Freedom" gambit a "major propaganda victory." Schlesinger, *Robert Kennedy*, 469; JFK to VGR, September 5, 1961, CO55/CM 1604, John F. Kennedy Library.

37. Adolf Sturmthal, *Left of Center: European Labor since World War II* (Urbana: University of Illinois Press, 1983), 85–100; Anthony Carew, *Walter Reuther* (Manchester: Manchester University Press, 1993), 115–17; Reuther, *Brothers Reuther*, 350–53; Conway, interview with Hackman, 70. Thereafter both Reuther brothers spent much time and money to enable Nenni to win a majority within the Partito Socialista Italiano for a policy of formal coalition with the Christian Democrats. When finally structured late in 1963, Nenni became deputy prime minister in a center-left government. But reform remained elusive, for the entry of the Socialists and Social Democrats into a government dominated by the corrupt and complacent Christian Democrats merely undermined the integrity and distinctiveness of the non-Communist left in Italian politics. The increasingly reformist Parti Communista Italiano soon marginalized the Socialists.

38. WPR to Harold Wilson, May 13, 1963, file 5, box 463, WPR Collection.

39. WPR to Willy Brandt, April 3, 1963, Landsorganisationen (LO), "Information to Foreign Countries," August 1963, all in file 5, box 463, WPR Collection; Carew, *Reuther*, 113–15; Arthur Schlesinger, Jr., *A Thousand Days: John F. Kennedy in the White House* (Boston: Houghton Mifflin, 1965), 646. Humphrey was a particularly enthusiastic Harpsund conferee. See Carl Solberg, *Hubert Humphrey: A Biography* (New York: W. W. Norton, 1984), 219–21; but also see Adolf Sturmthal, *Democracy under Fire: Memoirs of a European Socialist* (Durham, N.C.: Duke University Press, 1989), 191–95. Sturmthal started the Harpsund ball rolling when he proposed the idea to his friends in the SPD, but he broke with the program when he was told, after a White House meeting, that a young Johns Hopkins professor assigned to aid him in the work was actually employed by the CIA.

40. UAW-IEB minutes, December 13, 1960, UAW-IEB Collection, 16–17; *UAW Administrative Letter*, February 1, 1961, 1110; Asher Lauren, "UAW Task Force on Jobless Planned," *Detroit News*, March 2, 1961; Frank Marquart, "Trouble in Auto," *Dissent* 7 (Spring 1961): 112–15.

41. Leo Fenster, "The 1964 Contract Struggle" (manuscript in author's possession, [n.d.]), 51; "Labor: How Hard Will Reuther Push?" *Fortune* (May 1961): 231–32; "UAW Here Backs Thirty Hour Week," *Pittsburgh Press*, March 20, 1961; Rank James to "GM Department Staff Members," April 12, 1961, file 11, box 47, UAW-VP Leonard Woodcock Collection. Many Flint unionists argued for a "service-based pension" modeled after the twenty-years-and-out retirement system these ex-GIs had become familiar with in the military.

42. UAW, "Workers' Problems Are Democracy's Problems: Report of President Walter

Reuther to the Special Constitutional Convention," Detroit, April 21, 1961; Nat Weinberg, interview with the author, Rockville, Md., November 11, 1982; Reuther quoted in Fenster, "The 1964 Contract Struggle," 45–46.

43. U.S. Congress, Joint Economic Committee, *Hearings*, 87th cong., 2d sess., February 6, 1962 (Washington, D.C.: Government Printing Office, 1962), 789. "You can't solve the problems of unemployment at the bargaining table," Reuther had lectured delegates at the 1962 UAW convention. See UAW, "Proceedings of the Eighteenth Constitutional Convention," 64.

44. U.S. Congress, Joint Economic Committee, *Hearings*, February 6, 1962, 772–83; Leonard Woodcock, interview with William Moss, Detroit, January 27, 1970, 21–22, John F. Kennedy Library; UAW, "Report of Walter P. Reuther to the Nineteenth Constitutional Convention," Atlantic City, N.J., March 20–27, 1964, 5–8; see also Amberg, *Union Inspiration in American Politics*, 228–41.

45. UAW, *Proceedings of the Eighteenth Constitutional Convention*, 289–97; Jack Stieber, "The President's Committee on Labor-Management Policy," *Industrial Relations* 5 (February 1966): 1–19; for the Swedish model, see Gary Mucciaroni, *The Political Failure of Employment Policy, 1945–1982* (Pittsburgh: University of Pittsburgh Press, 1990), 224–54; Jonas Pontusson, "Labor, Corporatism, and Industrial Policy: The Swedish Case in Comparative Perspective," *Comparative Politics* (January 1991): 163–79; and Gosta Esping-Andersen, *Politics against Markets* (Princeton, N.J.: Princeton University Press, 1985).

46. "President's Advisory Committee on Labor-Management Policy," October 2, 1962, and March 25, 1963, "PACL-MP" file, box 61, RG 174, National Archives; Amberg, *Union Inspiration in American Politics*, 239–40.

47. Walter Heller, *New Dimensions of Political Economy* (Cambridge, Mass.: Harvard University Press, 1966), 42–47; Irving Bernstein, *Promises Kept: John F. Kennedy's New Frontier* (New York: Oxford University Press, 1991), 133–37; W. W. Rostow, *The Diffusion of Power* (New York: Macmillan, 1972), 140.

48. Rostow, *Diffusion of Power*, 138–43; Bernstein, *Promises Kept*, 135; UAW, "Proceedings of the Eighteenth Constitutional Convention," 63. In the 1961 bargaining round, Reuther and Weinberg were convinced that the auto corporations did not raise car prices because Kennedy administration "jawboning" reinforced the UAW's own bargaining campaign on the issue. U.S. Congress, Joint Economic Committee, *Hearings*, February 6, 1962, 744.

49. See virtually any passage on Kennedy in Taylor Branch, *Parting the Waters: America in the King Years, 1954–1963* (New York: Simon & Schuster, 1988); Sundquist, *Politics and Policy*, 296–317, 83–110 passim; Bernstein, *Promises Kept*, 160–258 passim.

50. UAW-IEB minutes, February 24, 1961, UAW-IEB Collection; U.S. Congress, Joint Economic Committee, *Hearings*, February 8, 1962, 773; UAW, "Proceedings of the Eighteenth Constitutional Convention," 267–71; Roy Hoopes, *The Steel Crisis* (New York: John Day Co., 1963), 240–41.

51. Murray Kempton, *America Comes of Middle Age: Columns 1950–1962* (Boston: Little, Brown, 1963), 123. In compensation, Kennedy was loyal to the UAW as well. The UAW convention of May 1962 was the only convention of a single trade union that JFK addressed after he became president. "Address by Walter Reuther, Tenth Annual International Skilled Trades Conference," Chicago, January 23, 1964, file 10, box 522, WPR Collection.

52. UAW-IEB minutes, June 19, 1962, UAW-IEB Collection.

53. U.S. Congress, Joint Economic Committee, *Hearings*, February 6, 1962, 718–24.

54. Mucciaroni, *Political Failure of Employment Policy*, 32–45; U.S. Congress, Joint Eco-

nomic Committee, *Hearings*, "Economic Report of the President," February 8, 1962, 757.

55. John Berry, "The Pressure Builds for Shorter Workweeks," *AFL-CIO News* (November 1961); "Labor Leaders Disagree on Work Week Cut," *Minneapolis Morning Tribune*, February 27, 1963.

56. U.S. Congress, Joint Economic Committee, *Hearings*, February 6, 1962, 790.

57. Edward Flash, *Economic Advice and Presidential Leadership: The Council of Economic Advisers* (New York: Columbia University Press, 1965), 219–75; Schlesinger, *Thousand Days*, 645–51; Jim F. Heath, *John F. Kennedy and the Business Community* (Chicago: University of Chicago Press, 1969), 42–47, 114–22; Bernstein, *Promises Kept*, 118–59 passim.

58. Allen J. Matusow, *The Unraveling of America: A History of Liberalism in the 1960s* (New York: Harper & Row, 1984), 50–51; Kim McQuaid, *Uneasy Partners: Big Business in American Politics, 1945–1990* (Baltimore: Johns Hopkins University Press, 1994), 120–24.

59. Weinberg and Heller quoted in Boyle, "Politics and Principle," 330; "Labor Demands Kennedy Revamp Economic Policy," *New York Times*, February 16, 1963; UAW-IEB minutes, March 7, 1963, UAW-IEB Collection, 255.

60. Cormier and Eaton, *Reuther*, 410. Reuther's failure to win the coveted but largely honorary spot on the U.S. U.N. delegation truly rankled, for Meany knew how much Reuther would have enjoyed the world spotlight. Since 1957, when the Eisenhower administration had created the slot, Meany had either put forward himself or some other AFL place-server to keep Reuther on the sidelines.

61. "WPR Note for George Meany File," March 8, 1962, June 20, 1962, and July 11, 1962, file 15, box 38, WPR Collection; Stanley Ruttenberg, interview with Don Kennedy, Washington, D.C., July 20, 1979, 29, in AFL-CIO Oral History Project, George Meany Memorial Archives, Silver Spring, Md.; Goulden, *Meany*, 375. AFL-CIO Secretary-Treasurer William Schnitzler did meet with Heller, but Reuther thought it hardly "the meaningful meeting that could have been held" ("WPR Note for George Meany File," July 11, 1962).

62. Goulden, *Meany*, 372; "WPR Note for George Meany file," August 14, 1962, file 15, box 38, WPR Collection. Meany refused to reappoint Carey to an ICFTU post he had held for years.

63. "Minutes of Special IUD Meeting," Sheraton-Chicago Hotel, Chicago, August 16, 1962, file 4, box 338, WPR Collection; Goulden, *Meany*, 373.

64. Conway, interview with Hackman, 87; Irving Bluestone, interview with the author, Detroit, October 25, 1987; Douglas Fraser, interview with the author, Detroit, April 17, 1990; Paul Schrade, interview with the author, Los Angeles, August 19, 1987. Reuther even talked to Kennedy about pulling out of the AFL-CIO; JFK listened sympathetically, but the president persuaded him, as Reuther himself undoubtedly understood, that a split would damage the "cause."

65. UAW, "Proceedings of the Eighteenth Constitutional Convention," 57.

66. A. H. Raskin, "Walter Reuther's Great Big Union," *Atlantic Monthly* (October 1963): 85–86.

67. UAW-IEB minutes, December 5, 1962, UAW-IEB Collection, 113.

68. "Union to Start Organizing Drive," *New York Times*, February 20, 1963; Lee Dirks, "Reuther Moves Again to Revive Militancy, Rebuild Own Power," *National Observer*, February 4, 1963; Jack Conway to Albert J. Hayes, April 29, 1963, and "A Cooperative Program for DuPont," April 30, 1963, both in file 1, box 326, WPR Collection; UAW-IEB minutes, March 7, 1963, UAW-IEB Collection, 265–70; AFL-CIO, "Pro-

ceedings of the Fifth Constitutional Convention," New York, November 14–20, 1963, vol. 2, 302–6.

69. AFL-CIO, "Proceedings of the Fifth Constitutional Convention," 306.

70. Harvey Swados, "The UAW: Over the Top or Over the Hill?" in Swados, *A Radical at Large: American Essays* (London: Rupert Hart-Davis, 1968), 88; Raskin, "Reuther's Great Big Union," 85.

CHAPTER 17: UNEASY PARTNERS

1. Irving Bluestone, interview with the author, Detroit, October 25, 1987.

2. "UAW Conference Calls for Action in Civil Rights Field," *Michigan Chronicle*, January 26, 1956.

3. Paton quoted in UAW, "Report of President Walter P. Reuther to the Fifteenth Constitutional Convention," Cleveland, Ohio, March 27–April 1, 1955, 84D.

4. "Justice on the Job Front: Statement Submitted by Walter P. Reuther to the Subcommittee on Anti-Discrimination Legislation of the United States Senate Committee on Labor and Public Welfare," March 24, 1947, "FEPC," vertical file, 23–29.

5. WPR, "The Challenge of Leadership," *New York Post*, May 20, 1956, Daniel Bell Collection, Tamiment Library, New York University.

6. John Frederick Martin, *Civil Rights and the Crisis of Liberalism: The Democratic Party, 1945–1976* (Boulder, Colo.: Westview Press, 1979), 151; Steven M. Gillon, *Politics and Vision: The ADA and American Liberalism, 1947–1985* (New York: Oxford University Press, 1987), 101.

7. Joe Rauh to WPR, "Recent Discussion with Senator Johnson," March 4, 1959, file 2, box 106, WPR Collection; Roy Wilkins, *Standing Fast: The Autobiography of Roy Wilkins* (New York: Viking Press, 1982), 244–46; Robert Frederick Burk, *The Eisenhower Administration and Black Civil Rights* (Knoxville: University of Tennessee Press, 1984), 204–26; Martin, *Civil Rights and the Crisis of Liberalism*, 160–63; UAW, "Report of Walter P. Reuther to the Seventeenth Constitutional Convention," Atlantic City, N.J., October 9–16, 1959, 347.

8. UAW, "Proceedings of the Eighteenth Constitutional Convention," Atlantic City, N.J., May 4–10, 1962, 267–69.

9. "Reuther Tells Union in South of UAW-CIO's Non-Discrimination Rules," *Detroit Tribune*, March 3, 1945, file 10, box 621, WPR Collection; Dan Wakefield, "Eye of the Storm," *Nation*, May 7, 1960, 402.

10. John Hope, "Industrial Integration of Negroes: The Upgrading Process," *Human Organization* 11 (Winter 1952): 5–14; Robert Ozanne, *The Negro in the Farm Equipment and Construction Machinery Industry* (Philadelphia: University of Pennsylvania Press, 1972), 27–43; John Bateman to Emil Mazey, December 22, 1955, from the personal papers of Herbert Hill, used with his permission.

11. Paul Molly, "Local UAW, Detroit Clash on Race Issue," *Memphis Commercial Appeal*, March 14, 1956.

12. "UAW Signs Agreement with Urban League," *Voice of Labor* 212 (July 1957), in "FEPC," vertical file.

13. Seth Wigderson, "The UAW in the 1950s" (Ph.D. diss., Wayne State University, 1989), 421; William Dodds, interview with the author, Washington, D.C., June 12, 1987; George Holloway to Emil Mazey, June 29, 1959; see also Holloway to WPR, January 20, 1955, Holloway to William Oliver, July 14, 1955, and Holloway to Emil Mazey, January 28, 1957, all letters from the personal papers of Herbert Hill, used with his permission.

14. Herbert Northrup, Carl King, and Richard Rowen, *Negro Employment in Basic Industry* (Philadelphia: University of Pennsylvania, 1970), 61–85; William Gould, *Black Workers in White Unions* (Ithaca, N.Y.: Cornell University Press, 1977), 371–75; General Services Administration, "Compliance Survey Analysis, Chrysler, Ford and General Motors Assembly Plants," February 26, 1958, file 6, box 102, and "UAW Fair Practices Survey—1963," file 12, box 90, both in WPR Collection; B. J. Widick, interview with the author, Ann Arbor, Mich., July 22, 1989; Oscar Pascal, interview with the author, Detroit, October 27, 1985; Martin Gerber, interview with the author, Bradley Beach, N.J., November 15, 1987. The chair of the Skilled Trades Department, Richard Gosser, was no help either: by 1959 he was preoccupied with a congressional probe of his finances.

15. William Oliver to Leonard Woodcock, "Suggested Proposals for the Elimination of Practices of Promotional Discrimination in GM Southern Plants," July 6, 1961, file 6, box 102, and Irving Bluestone to WPR, "Survey of Negro Employment in Companies under UAW Contract," January 21, 1964, file 12, box 90, both in WPR Collection. See also "General Motors Reply to Union Demand to Amend Paragraph 63 on Transfers" (1955), "UAW-GM," vertical file, GM Technical Institute, Flint, Mich.; and George Holloway to WPR, January 20, 1955, from the personal papers of Herbert Hill, used with his permission. At Memphis, white union officials conspired with foremen to keep black workers off the main assembly lines by classifying all subassembly jobs the same as jobs on the hay bailer and cotton picker lines. Since foremen had the right to assign jobs within the same classification—this was the power the UAW had unsuccessfully fought for a decade—black workers at Harvester were kept in de facto segregation.

16. F. Ray Marshall, *The Negro and Organized Labor* (New York: Wiley, 1965), 69; Sheldon Tappes, interview with Herbert Hill, Detroit, October 27, 1967, and February 10, 1968, used by permission of Herbert Hill; Herbert Hill, interview with the author, Madison, Wisc., June 19, 1987; William Oliver to Roy Reuther, "Ford Plant, Indianapolis," December 20, 1957, file 29, box 8, UAW Citizenship Department; Oliver to Jackie Robinson, January 3, 1958, file 30, box 8, and Oliver to WPR, "Preliminary Analysis of Allegations Made against UAW by the NAACP Labor Secretary Which Were Unfounded," November 1, 1962, file 10, box 90, both in WPR Collection. In 1959 Oliver could proudly claim that "representatives of the union have testified at every Congressional hearing on every bill relating to civil rights and fair employment practices since 1946" (Oliver to WPR, "UAW Reply to Survey at Big Three Auto Companies Conducted by General Services Administration," February 26, 1959, file 14, box 9, UAW Citizenship Department). A critique of the union movement's black staff is found in William Kornhauser, "The Negro Union Official: A Study of Sponsorship and Control," *American Journal of Sociology* 34 (March 1952): 447–61.

17. James Farmer, *Lay Bare the Heart: An Autobiography of the Civil Rights Movement* (New York: New American Library, 1985), 177–78.

18. William Dodds, interview with the author.

19. Horace Sheffield, interview with Herbert Hill, Detroit, July 24, 1968, used by permission of Herbert Hill; Horace Sheffield résumé, April 18, 1962, file 6, box 69, WPR Collection; Allan Blanchard, "Sheffield Digs in Heels on 'Exile,'" *Detroit News*, January 18, 1966.

20. TULC, Inc., "Do You Have the Time?" "TULC," vertical file.

21. Jack Stieber, *Governing the UAW* (New York: John Wiley and Sons, 1962), 42–43; "UAW 'Adjusts' to New Labor Law: Bars Negro in Top Post," *National Guardian*,

November 2, 1959; Herbert Hill, interview with the author, Madison, Wisc., June 19, 1987.

22. Sheffield, interview with Hill; Willouby Abner, interview with Herbert Hill, Detroit, June 9, 1966; Nelson Jack Edwards and Willouby Abner, "How a Negro Won Top UAW Post," *Detroit Courier*, April 4, 1964.

23. UAW "Proceedings of the Seventeenth Constitutional Convention," 362–63.

24. Willouby Abner résumé, file 6, box 69, WPR Collection; Abner, interview with Hill; "Bill Abner, I Want to Shake Your Hand," *Ammunition* (December 1947): 13–16; Daniel Miller to WPR, April 3, 1962, file 4, box 69, WPR Collection; Ofield Dukes, "UAW's Newest 'Import' Was a Foe of Dawson," *Michigan Chronicle*, August 24, 1963. Abner's greatest service to the Reuther forces came at the 1947 UAW convention when he delivered a dramatic and effective speech advocating union compliance with the Taft-Hartley law. But Abner was not a right-winger. As an organizer of UAW-PAC forces in Chicago during the late 1940s, he tried to build a counterorganization to the Democratic machine. In 1950 he ran a vigorous laborite campaign against a white Democratic Party regular. He lost badly, but as citizenship director of region 4, Abner sustained an aggressive, left-wing political posture that put him in conflict with Pat Greathouse and other midwestern UAW officials. He would also help organize a UAW staff union.

25. "Walter Couldn't Find Time," *Pittsburgh Courier*, October 31, 1959.

26. Jack Crellin, "UAW Won't Tolerate Segregation in Any Local," *Detroit News*, February 14, 1960.

27. "Negro Fight against Segregation Finds Inspiration in Labor's Past," *AFL-CIO News*, May 6, 1961; Charles Wartman, "Largest Dinner Ever Hears King Address," *Michigan Chronicle*, May 6, 1961. Of all the newly militant civil rights organizations, CORE stood closest to the socialist-pacifist heritage of the Reuther circle. CORE Secretary James Farmer had worked for several unions in the 1950s, and Walter Bergman, with whom Reuther had denounced compulsory ROTC in the early 1930s, had been severely beaten at Birmingham during the "freedom rides" of 1961.

28. Dodds, interview with the author; Gerber, interview with the author.

29. Blanchard, "Sheffield Digs in Heels," 11; Dudley W. Buffa, *Union Power and American Democracy: The UAW and the Democratic Party, 1935–1972* (Ann Arbor: University of Michigan Press, 1984), 133–73; B. J. Widick, *Detroit: City of Race and Class Violence* (Detroit: Wayne State University Press, 1989), 151–55; J. David Greenstone, *Labor in American Politics* (New York: Alfred A. Knopf, 1969), 120–25.

30. Horace Sheffield, "Bitter Frustration Gave Added Impetus to Trade Union Leadership Council," *Michigan Chronicle*, May 28, 1960; B. J. Widick, interview with the author, Ann Arbor, Mich., August 6, 1986.

31. NAACP, *Racism within Organized Labor: A Report of Five Years of the AFL-CIO, 1955–1960* (New York: NAACP, 1961); Herbert Hill, interview with the author.

32. Roy Wilkins to Herbert Hill, November 22, 1961, and Herbert Hill to Roy Wilkins, "Draft Letter to Emil Mazey," January 21, 1962, both from the personal papers of Herbert Hill, used with his permission; "Emil Mazey, UAW Spokesman, Unfairly Attacks NAACP," *Vanguard* (July 1962), in "TULC," vertical file; Stanley Levey, "Negro Labor Unit Backs NAACP," *New York Times*, November 12, 1962; William Oliver to WPR, "Preliminary Analysis of Allegations Made against UAW by NAACP Labor Secretary," November 1, 1962, file 10, box 90, WPR Collection; Ralph Katz, "Reuther Visions Equality in Labor," *New York Times*, November 11, 1962. In 1964 Hill organized a series of demonstrations against GM plants and office buildings in Detroit. Although formally directed against GM, they offered an implicit critique of the UAW as well. In response, the UAW's FEPD again sought to induce the NAACP to "coop-

erate" more closely with the UAW and route its grievances and investigations through union channels. See Damon Stetson, "Negroes Picket UAW and GM," *New York Times*, August 8, 1963; NAACP Plans a GM Job Drive," *New York Times*, April 9, 1964; David Jones, "Negroes Picket General Motors," *New York Times*, May 5, 1964; William Oliver to Roy Wilkins, "Re: Proposed NAACP Labor Advisory Committee," June 3, 1959, and Oliver to Roy Reuther, "Status of UAW Officers and NAACP Memberships," February 21, 1961, both in file 16, box 9, UAW Citizenship Department; Oliver to WPR, "Meeting with Herbert Hill," July 20, 1964, "FEPC," vertical file.

33. Gerber, interview with the author; Jack Crellin, "Racial Row Splits Ford Local," *Detroit Times*, January 20, 1960.

34. Robert Battle to WPR, December 28, 1961, file 25, box 250, WPR Collection.

35. WPR notes, file 5, box 69, WPR Collection; Stieber, *Governing the UAW*, 44.

36. Harold Keith, "'We Will Not Accept Uncle Toms,' Negroes Tell Walter Reuther," *Michigan Courier*, February 10, 1962; Sheffield, interview with Hill; Gerber, interview with the author.

37. Nelson Jack Edwards résumé, file 6, box 69, WPR Collection; Horace Sheffield, [untitled column], *Michigan Chronicle*, May 19, 1962.

38. Robert Hoyt, "How Negro Leadership Shifts," *Detroit Free Press*, December 27, 1964. Late in 1965 Reuther tried to transfer Sheffield to another staff job in Washington, but the opposition from Detroit blacks, both inside the union and out, forced him to back down. See "Reuther Outlines UAW Position on Sheffield Assignment," January 14, 1966, file 9, box 157, WPR Collection; Patrick Owens, "Sheffield and UAW Make Up," *Detroit Free Press*, January 25, 1966; "Edwards Appoints Sheffield Administrative Assistant," "TULC," vertical file, Solidarity House.

39. Taylor Branch, *Parting the Waters: America in the King Years, 1954–1963* (New York: Simon & Schuster, 1988), 774–91; Irving Bluestone, interview with the author, Detroit, October 25, 1987; Jack Conway, interview with Larry Hackman, Washington, D.C., April 10, 1972, John F. Kennedy Presidential Library, 71; WPR, interview with Jean Stein, Detroit, October 24, 1968 (in author's possession); Phil Meyer and James Robinson, "Labor Backs Negro Civil Rights Revolution with Cash, Knowhow," *Detroit News*, April 1, 1965.

40. Richard Reeves, *President Kennedy: Profile of Power* (New York: Simon & Schuster, 1993), 500, 522; Carl M. Brauer, *John F. Kennedy and the Second Reconstruction* (New York: Columbia University Press, 1977), 265–79.

41. Brauer, *Second Reconstruction*, 274; Arthur Schlesinger, Jr., *A Thousand Days: John F. Kennedy in the White House* (Boston: Houghton Mifflin, 1965), 969.

42. Wilkins, *Standing Fast*, 291–92; Kevin Boyle, "Politics and Principle: The United Automobile Workers and American Labor-Liberalism, 1948–1968" (Ph.D. diss., University of Michigan, 1990), 366–71.

43. Branch, *Parting the Waters*, 842–43; UAW, "Report of President Walter P. Reuther to the Nineteenth Constitutional Convention," Atlantic City, N.J., March 20–27, 1964, 91.

44. "Address by Walter Reuther," Tenth Annual Skilled Trades Conference, Chicago, January 23–25, 1964, file 10, box 552, WPR Collection.

45. David Garrow, *Bearing the Cross: Martin Luther King, Jr., and the Southern Christian Leadership Conference* (New York: William Morrow, 1986), 280; Paula F. Pfeffer, *A. Philip Randolph: Pioneer of the Civil Rights Movement* (Baton Rouge: Louisiana State University Press, 1990), 246–47.

46. Thomas Gentile, *March on Washington: August 28, 1963* (Washington, D.C.: New Day Publications, 1983), 126–29, 146–51; Pfeffer, *Randolph*, 259–61.

47. Schlesinger, *Robert Kennedy and His Times* (Boston: Houghton Mifflin, 1978), 350;

Jack Conway, interview with Larry Hackman, Washington, D.C., April 10, 1972, 79–81. The Justice Department liaison with the march committee, John Douglas, insisted upon a sound system that would be large enough to rivet attention upon the podium, thus avoiding crowd dispersal, and one that could be controlled by government people in an emergency. Throughout all the speeches, Jerry Bruno, Kennedy's legendary "advance man," sat behind Lincoln's statue with the cutoff switch in his hand. Irving Bernstein, *Promises Kept: John F. Kennedy's New Frontier* (New York: Oxford University Press, 1991), 115.

48. United Auto Workers–International Executive Board minutes, September 25, 1963, UAW-IEB Collection, 47–50; AFL-CIO executive council minutes, August 12–15, 1963, George Meany Memorial Archives, Silver Spring, Md. James Carey would have voted with Reuther, but he was out of the room when the council acted.

49. William Oliver to Irving Bluestone, July 25, 1963, file 4, box 2, VGR Collection.

50. Conway, interview with Hackman; UAW-IEB minutes, September 25, 1963, UAW-IEB Collection, 56; Garrow, *Bearing the Cross*, 281–82; Branch, *Parting the Waters*, 873–74.

51. UAW-IEB minutes, September 25, 1963, 56; Garrow, *Bearing the Cross*, 282.

52. UAW-IEB minutes, September 25, 1963, 59–61.

53. "Remarks by Walter P. Reuther" [transcript], August 28, 1963, file 6, box 552, WPR Collection; Gentile, *March on Washington*, 227–28.

54. Branch, *Parting the Waters*, 883.

55. William Oliver to Irving Bluestone, July 25, 1963, file 4, box 2, VGR Collection; "Remarks by Walter P. Reuther," August 28, 1963; UAW-IEB minutes, September 25, 1963, 50.

56. Schlesinger, *Robert Kennedy*, 365; Conway, interview with Hackman, 72.

57. U.S. House of Representatives, Judiciary Committee, Subcommittee No. 5, *Civil Rights: Hearings*, 88th cong., 1st sess., July 17, 1963, 1790–95, 1951–54; Joseph Goulden, *Meany: The Unchallenged Strong Man of American Labor* (New York: Atheneum, 1972), 319–22; Hugh Davis Graham, *The Civil Rights Era: Origins and Development of National Policy* (New York: Oxford University Press, 1990), 95–104, 129–34.

58. UAW, "WPR Report to the Nineteenth Constitutional Convention," 92–93; James Findlay, "Religion and Politics in the Sixties: The Churches and the Civil Rights Act of 1964," *Journal of American History* 77 (June 1990): 71–86; Carl Stolberg, *Hubert Humphrey: A Biography* (New York: W. W. Norton, 1984), 221–27.

59. "WPR Note," December 3, 1963, file 8, box 368, WPR Collection; Joseph Rauh, interview with Paige Mulhollan, Washington, D.C., August 8, 1969, 1–2, LBJ Library; Rowland Evans and Robert Novak, *Lyndon B. Johnson: The Exercise of Power* (New York: New American Library, 1966), 339–42; Boyle, "Politics and Principle," 386–89.

60. Lewis quoted in Gillon, *Politics and Vision*, 155; Jack Conway, interview with Alice Hoffman, Silver Spring, Md., May 23, 1979, AFL-CIO Oral History Project, George Meany Memorial Archives, Silver Spring, Md., 15.

61. WPR thanks the president for his hospitality during "several recent White House dinners" in WPR to LBJ, June 25, 1964, file 9, box 368, WPR Collection; "Walter Reuther," White House daily diary card file, lists thirty-one individual phone calls and meetings between WPR and LBJ in 1964 alone; "Political Memorandum for the President," December 16, 1963, "Walter P. Reuther" file, White House Central File, LBJ Library.

62. "An Economy of Opportunity" [drafts], December 30, 1963, and January 2, 1964, WPR to LBJ, January 8, 1964, and WPR to LBJ, June 26, 1964; all in file 9, box 368, WPR Collection.

63. Stephen Amberg, *The Union Inspiration in American Politics: The Autoworkers and the Making of a Liberal Industrial Order* (Philadelphia: Temple University Press, 1994), 253; UAW, "Resolutions of the Nineteenth Constitutional Convention—'Full Mobilization for a Total War on Poverty,'" 1–9; U.S. House, Committee on Education and Labor, Subcommittee on the War on Poverty Program, *Hearings*, 88th cong., 2d sess., "Economic Opportunity Act of 1964," April 9, 1964, 426.

64. Jack Conway, interview with Michael Gillette, Washington, D.C., August 13, 1980, LBJ Library, 16–17; Judah Drob, interview with the author, Washington, D.C., July 12, 1985; Boyle, "Politics and Principle," 403–4; Reuther quoted in UAW-IEB minutes, January 12, 1966, UAW-IEB Collection, 200.

65. UAW, "Proceedings of the Nineteenth Constitutional Convention," 255, 545–46; Rennie Davis to Mildred Jeffrey, February 17, 1964, file 1, box 29, Students for a Democratic Society Collection, Wisconsin State Historical Society, Madison. See also James Miller, *Democracy Is in the Streets: From Port Huron to the Siege of Chicago* (New York: Simon & Schuster, 1987), 29–32; and Peter Levy, *The New Left and Labor in the 1960s* (Urbana: University of Illinois Press, 1994), 11–15. Among the SDS activists attending the 1964 convention were Barry Bluestone, Paul Booth, Rennie Davis, Nancy Hollander, Doug Ireland, Sharon Jeffrey, Frank Joyce, Steve Max, Paul Potter, and Michael Zweig.

66. Irving Bluestone to Paul Schrade, February 11, 1964, file 8, box 216, WPR Collection; Barry Bluestone, interview with Bret Eynon, Ann Arbor, Mich., August 15, 1978; WPR to Tom Hayden, July 31, 1963, Al Haber to Irving Bluestone, December 19, 1963, and Irving Bluestone to Todd Gitlin, March 16, 1964, all in file 1, box 29, SDS Collection, WSHS.

67. Rennie Davis to Jack Conway, December 18, 1963, Davis to Carroll Hutton, March 3, 1964, Davis to Irving Bluestone, June 7, 1964, WPR to Todd Gitlin, June 9, 1964, and Bluestone to Pat O'Malley, July 29, 1964, all in file 1, box 29, SDS Collection, WSHS; Mildred Jeffrey to WPR, December 22, 1963, and Lewis Carliner to Bluestone, July 17, 1962, both in file 12, box 523, WPR Collection; Bluestone to VGR, April 26, 1963, file 4, box 25, Victor Reuther International Affairs Collection; Frank Joyce, telephone interview with the author, September 13, 1994. For a discussion of Harrington's perspective, see Maurice Isserman, *If I Had a Hammer: The Death of the Old Left and the Birth of the New Left* (New York: Basic Books, 1987), 211–15.

68. Gillon, *Politics and Vision*, 165; UAW, "Resolutions of the Nineteenth Constitutional Convention," 76. See also Margaret Weir, *Politics and Jobs: The Boundaries of Employment Policy in the United States* (Princeton, N.J.: Princeton University Press, 1992), 67–98 passim.

69. UAW, "Resolutions of the Nineteenth Constitutional Convention," 61–67; Gary Mucciaroni, *The Political Failure of Employment Policy, 1945–1982* (Pittsburgh: University of Pittsburgh Press, 1990), 224–54 passim; LBJ quoted in Stolberg, *Humphrey*, 220–21.

70. Joe Rauh, "Memorandum on the Mississippi Freedom Democratic Party," "MFDP, 1965" file, box 85, Joseph Rauh Collection; Dodds, interview with the author; Mary King, *Freedom Song* (New York: William Morrow, 1987), 386–87.

71. Godfrey Hodgson, *America in Our Time* (New York: Random House, 1976), 215; Evans and Novak, *Johnson*, 451; Connally quoted in John Dittmer, *Local People: The Struggle for Civil Rights in Mississippi* (Urbana: University of Illinois Press, 1994), 290.

72. Rauh quoted in Todd Gitlin, *The Sixties: Years of Hope, Days of Rage* (New York: Bantam, 1987), 154; and Anne Cooke Romaine, "The Mississippi Freedom Democratic Party through August, 1964" (master's thesis, University of Virginia, 1970), 313–17;

WPR, "Meeting with President Johnson," June 29, 1964, file 9, box 368, WPR Collection; "Walter Reuther," Name File, White House Central Files (WHCF), LBJ Library.

73. Kay Mills, *This Little Light of Mine: The Life of Fannie Lou Hamer* (New York: Dutton, 1993), 117–21; "Reuther to Use President's Rally as Weapon in Contract Talks," *New York Times*, September 3, 1964; "Walter Reuther," Name File, WHCF, LBJ Library.

74. Evans and Novak, *Johnson*, 453–54; Adam Fairclough, *To Redeem the Soul of America: The Southern Christian Leadership Conference and Martin Luther King, Jr.* (Athens: University of Georgia Press, 1987), 202–5.

75. Joseph Rauh, interview with William J. Eaton, Washington, D.C., December 11, 1967; Romaine, "MFDP," 341–42.

76. Romaine, "MFDP," 166–82; Mills, *This Little Light*, 132.

77. Gitlin, *Sixties*, 161; James Foreman, *The Making of Black Revolutionaries* (New York: Macmillan, 1972), 392–94.

78. Cleveland Sellers, *The River of No Return: The Autobiography of a Black Militant and the Life and Death of SNCC* (New York: William Morrow, 1973), 108–9, 111; Gitlin, *Sixties*, 161; Joe Rauh, "Memorandum for the Vice-President Elect," December 24, 1964, box 36, Joseph Rauh Collection; Rauh, interview with Eaton; see also "Mississippi Project Lawyers Honored by Detroit Chapter of Lawyers Guild," *Detroit Courier*, November 28, 1964; Stephen Schlossberg, interview with the author, Washington, D.C., December 3, 1994.

CHAPTER 18: A PART OF THE ESTABLISHMENT

1. "Text of Remarks by Malcolm Denise, Ford Motor Company Labor Relations," Notre Dame University, February 27, 1965, file 12, box 98, WPR Collection.

2. *Wall Street Journal* quoted in UAW, "Proceedings of the Nineteenth Constitutional Convention," Atlantic City, N.J., March 20–27, 1964, 46; United Auto Workers–International Executive Board minutes, May 7, 1964, UAW-IEB Collection, 104.

3. Leo Fenster, "The 1964 Contract Struggle" (manuscript in author's possession, [n.d.]), 99; see also David Jones, "Johnson Urges Restraint on Pay in Talk to UAW," *New York Times*, March 24, 1964.

4. WPR to LBJ, January 28, 1964, file 9, box 369, WPR Collection; Walter Heller to LBJ, "Meeting with Walter Reuther," April 9, 1964, and W. Willard Wirtz to LBJ, "Automobile Case," April 13, 1964, both in "BE4/Automobiles" file, box 9, White House Central Files (WHCF), LBJ Library.

5. UAW, "Proceedings of the Nineteenth Convention," 48, 305–23; see also "What Walter Reuther Wants Now from the Auto Industry," *U.S. News and World Report*, April 6, 1964, 87–89; UAW-GM National Conference, "Justice on the Job," Detroit, May 20–22, 1964, Vertical File, Institute of Industrial Relations, University of California, Berkeley; "Work Conditions Pushed by UAW," *New York Times*, May 24, 1964.

6. Gene Roberts, "Officials Ousted in Many States," *Detroit Free Press*, July 28, 1963; "UAW Target: Tedium on the Line," *Detroit Free Press*, June 21, 1964; Norman Miller, "Auto Union Ferment," *Wall Street Journal*, September 24, 1964; Stan Weir, "Forces behind the Reuther-Meany Split," *New Politics* (Spring 1967): 15; UAW-IEB minutes, August 20, 1964, UAW-IEB Collection, 8; UAW, "Proceedings of the Nineteenth Convention," 336; see also Oliver Quayle and Co., "A Study in Depth of the Rank and File of the UAW: May 1967," box 147, WPR Collection.

7. Fenster, "The 1964 Contract Struggle," 72–73; UAW, "Proceedings of the Nineteenth Convention," 48–49. See especially Paul Jacobs, "Old before Its Time: Collective Bargaining at Twenty-Eight," in Jacobs, *The State of the Unions* (New York: Atheneum, 1963), 257–93. Reuther had attended seminars at the Santa Barbara Center for the Study of Democratic Institutions in the early 1960s and gotten a feel for the growing critique of trade unionism in those circles.

8. Gardner Ackley to LBJ, "The Case for Auto Price Cuts," May 29, 1964, "Automobiles November 22, 1963 to May 29, 1964" file EX BE4/Aluminum, box 9; Walter Heller, interview with David McComb, Minneapolis, December 21, 1971, LBJ Library, 53–54; James Cochrane, "The Johnson Administration: Moral Suasion Goes to War," in *Exhortation and Controls: The Search for a Wage-Price Policy, 1945–1971*, ed. Craufurd Goodwin (Washington, D.C.: Brookings Institution, 1975), 199–214.

9. Frederick Taylor, "Possibility of Auto Strike Dwindles as UAW Names Chrysler as Target," *Wall Street Journal*, August 28, 1964; Douglas Fraser, interview with the author, Detroit, April 17, 1990. The decision to switch targets tells us something about the centralization of power in the UAW. Bluestone, Reuther, and Fraser made the final choice. GM secondary leaders were furious, and the UAW executive board sullen. It ratified the switch, but by a "majority" of two: Reuther and Fraser.

10. UAW-IEB minutes, March 1, 1968, UAW-IEB Collection, 40.

11. C. Wright Mills, *The New Man of Power* (New York: Harcourt Brace, 1948), 9; David Jones, "UAW Wins Gains in Chrysler Pact; Auto Peace Seen," *New York Times*, September 10, 1964; Norman Miller, "Surprise Strike," *Wall Street Journal*, October 5, 1964; B. J. Widick, "GM Strike: Prototype for More Conflict," *Nation*, November 16, 1964. Worried about the impact of the GM strike on LBJ's campaign, Reuther called Secretary of Labor Willard Wirtz twice on the eve of the work stoppage; Wirtz to LBJ, "Autos: General Motors and UAW," September 24, 1964, "Walter Reuther," Name File, WHCF, LBJ Library; WPR to Louis G. Seaton, September 24, 1964, file 16, box 48, UAW-VP (Leonard Woodcock) Collection.

12. "Notes of Special Meeting," October 5, 1964, box 14, UAW-IEB Collection.

13. Unlike 1945–46, Reuther ordered about one-third of all GM locals to remain at work, in order to supply Ford, Chrysler, and other companies with parts; Frederick Taylor, "Reuther Turns to Bargaining at GM, Hoping to Top Chrysler, Ford Pacts," *Wall Street Journal*, September 21, 1964; David Jones, "General Motors Struck by UAW; 260,000 Walk Out," *New York Times*, September 26, 1964; Norman Miller, "What Was Won in GM Strike," *Wall Street Journal*, November 3, 1964; UAW press releases, October 5 and October 21, 1964, file 6, box 49, UAW-VP (Leonard Woodcock) Collection.

14. Louis G. Seaton, [press conference transcript], September 25, 1964, "UAW-GM Contracts," vertical file, GM Institute, Flint, Mich.; "Text of Remarks by Malcolm Denise," February 27, 1965, 1, 17.

15. WPR to Paul Schrade, December 4, 1964, file 9, box 216, WPR Collection.

16. IUD executive board minutes, November 23, 1964, file 10, box 323, WPR Collection, 2.

17. WPR to Willy Brandt, June 18, 1965, and WPR to Harold Wilson, June 18, 1965, both in file 6, box 463, WPR Collection; Kevin Boyle, "Politics and Principle: The United Autoworkers and American Labor-Liberalism, 1948–1968" (Ph.D. diss., University of Michigan, 1990), 417.

18. Robert Conot, *American Odyssey* (Detroit: Wayne State University Press, 1986), 408, 444; Brendan Sexton, telephone interview with the author, October 18, 1985; Reuther quoted in Boyle, "Politics and Principle," 428.

19. Sexton, interview with the author; Harry McPherson to LBJ, December 9, 1965, WHCF, LBJ Library.

20. Joseph Califano, Jr., *The Triumph and Tragedy of Lyndon Johnson: The White House Years* (New York: Simon & Schuster, 1991), 130; Charles M. Haar, *Between the Idea and the Reality: A Study in the Origin, Fate, and Legacy of the Model Cities Program* (Boston: Little, Brown, 1975), 4–37, 289–91.

21. Haar, *Between Idea and Reality*, 38–39; WPR to LBJ, May 13, 1965, WPR to Richard Goodwin, June 4, 1965, and Charles Haar to Goodwin, June 9, 1965, all in "Early Origins" file, box 1, Model Cities Collection; Califano to LBJ, October 9, 1965, "Walter Reuther" file, and Harry McPherson to LBJ, December 9, 1965, both in WHCF, LBJ Library.

22. Joseph Califano, Jr., to LBJ, October 9, 1965, and "A Framework for Center City Demonstration Projects," December 8, 1965, both in WHCF, LBJ Library; Conot, *American Odyssey*, 499–501; Harry Golden, "Reuther, Mayor Plug 'Model City,'" *Detroit Free Press*, February 9, 1966.

23. WPR to LBJ, October 18, 1965, file 13, box 368, WPR Collection; Haar, *Between Idea and Reality*, 41; Harry McPherson to LBJ, December 13, 1965, "Walter Reuther" file, WHCF, LBJ Library.

24. Stanley Brown, "Walter Reuther: He's Got to Walk That Last Mile," *Fortune* 76 (July 1967): 149; UAW, "Proceedings of the Twentieth Constitutional Convention," Long Beach, Calif., May 16–21, 1966, 366.

25. Califano, *Triumph and Tragedy*, 131–35; Norman Miller, "Demonstration Cities," *Wall Street Journal*, July 28, 1966; Haar, *Between Idea and Reality*, 59.

26. W. Willard Wirtz to LBJ, May 25, 1966, "Unions" file, LA-61, WHCF, LBJ Library; IUD executive board minutes, July 7, 1966, file 2, box 324, WPR Collection. LBJ's unpopularity became clear even in Detroit when only five thousand turned up for the president's 1966 Labor Day speech. Reuther had promised to fill Cobo Hall, but neither the UAW, the Wayne County Democrats, nor the TULC mobilized their cadre to turn out the crowd. In his limousine to the airport, LBJ lectured his most important Michigan allies: "You fellows better get off your seats and work, because if they elect a Republican House of Representatives . . . Walter, you'll be in Norway, but Jerry [Cavanagh] you won't get that trillion dollars for Detroit." Bud Vestal, "Johnson Upset with Detroit Reception," *Jackson Citizen Patriot*, September 9, 1966, file 2, box 369, WPR Collection.

27. WPR to Harold Wilson, June 18, 1965, file 6, box 463, WPR Collection; WPR to Arthur Dean, April 1, 1966, and U.S. Foreign Service, "Incoming Telegram," August 4, 1965, both in file 4, box 463, WPR Collection; WPR–Arthur Goldberg correspondence, August 31, September 14, November 23, November 27, and December 28, 1965, file 13, box 463, WPR Collection; UAW-IEB minutes, October 14, 1965, UAW-IEB Collection, 185–86. Reuther also played a key role in persuading the United Nations Association of the United States to back Johnson administration policy on the war.

28. Elisabeth Reuther, interview with the author, Lake Orion, Mich., September 24, 1994; Gerber and Mazey quoted in Kevin Boyle, "Politics and Principle," 444–45. See also the anti-imperialist "Remarks of Emil Mazey on Vietnam and the Dominican Republic," Unitarian-Universalist Fellowship, May 15, 1965, copy in author's possession.

29. WPR to Harold Wilson, June 18, 1965, file 6, box 463, WPR Collection; IUD executive board minutes, December 15, 1966, file 3, box 324, WPR Collection, 24.

30. WPR to Arthur Goldberg, December 28, 1965, file 13, box 463, WPR Collection;

Reuther quoted in John Barnard, *Walter Reuther and the Rise of the Auto Workers* (Boston: Little, Brown, 1983), 191; UAW-IEB minutes, February 2, 1967, UAW-IEB Collection, 202.

31. David Langley, "The Colonization of the International Trade Union Movement," *New Politics* 5 (Winter 1966): 52–56; Henry W. Berger, "American Labor Overseas," *Nation*, January 16, 1967, 80–84; Anthony Carew, *Walter Reuther* (Manchester: Manchester University Press, 1993), 108–9; Charles Kassman, *Arne Geijer och hans tid, 1957–1979* [Arne Geijer and his times] (Stockholm: Tidens Forlag, 1991), 220–40; Victor Reuther, *The Brothers Reuther and the Story of the UAW* (Boston: Houghton Mifflin, 1976), 409–15, 488–90.

32. Reuther, *Brothers Reuther*, 414–22; UAW-IEB minutes, May 25, 1965, UAW-IEB Collection, 67–71.

33. UAW-IEB minutes, May 25, 1965, 68, 72.

34. Harry Bernstein, "AFL-CIO Unit Accused of 'Snooping' Abroad," *Los Angeles Times*, May 22, 1966; Max Frankel, "Ex-CIA Aide Lists Big Grants to Unions," *New York Times*, May 8, 1967; Reuther, *Brothers Reuther*, 423–24; Joseph Goulden, *Meany: The Unchallenged Strong Man of American Labor* (New York: Atheneum, 1972), 377–78.

35. VGR to WPR, "Current AFL-CIO Controversy with ILO," April 6, 1965, file 8, box 38, WPR Collection; "AFL-CIO Set to Quit ILO over Red Tactics, Meany Says," *New York Times*, April 9, 1965; Goulden, *Meany*, 379–81; "U.S. Labor Shuns ILO Conference," *New York Times*, June 4, 1966. As in the ICFTU, Meany's real problem in the ILO was the growing influence of the Western European social democrats and the new bloc of African-Asian unionists, both of which groups resisted the AFL-CIO's anti-Communism.

36. WPR to George Meany, June 9, 1966, and "Statement by UAW President Walter Reuther," *UAW Administrative Letter*, June 17, 1966, 4–6; both in file 8, box 38, WPR Collection.

37. The State Department also bowed to Lovestoneite pressure and denied visas to a delegation of Soviet trade unionists whose schedules the UAW had arranged in New York, Washington, and Detroit. Stephen S. Rosenfeld, "Reds' Visas Blocked by AFL-CIO," *Washington Post*, June 11, 1966.

38. "AFL-CIO Body Backs Meany over Reuther in Vote on Walkout of Geneva Delegation," *Wall Street Journal*, June 17, 1966; AFL-CIO executive council minutes, June 16, 1966, George Meany Memorial Archives, Silver Spring, Md., 4–8; Goulden, *Meany*, 382–84.

39. Goulden, *Meany*, 386–87; Jack Conway, interview with Alice Hoffman, AFL-CIO Oral History Project, George Meany Memorial Archives, Silver Spring, Md., May 23, 1979, 19–20; VGR, interview with the author, Washington, D.C., September 18, 1986.

40. Goulden, *Meany*, 387; Conway, interview with Hoffman; see also Jack Conway, interview with Frank Cormier and William J. Eaton, Washington, D.C., December 27, 1968; AFL-CIO executive council minutes, August 22–24, 1966, George Meany Memorial Archives, Silver Spring, Md., 1–3.

41. Carew, *Reuther*, 132–33; "Program for a National Organizing Crusade for the American Labor Movement," and "A Program to Strengthen and Modernize Collective Bargaining," *UAW Administrative Letters*, April 5 and 20, 1967.

42. "UAW Program for National Organizing," *UAW Administrative Letters*, April 5, 1967; UAW-IEB minutes, March 20, 1968, UAW-IEB Collection; Sidney Lens, "Reuther versus Meany," *Commonweal*, February 17, 1967, 559.

43. Dick Meister and Anne Loftis, *A Long Time Coming* (New York: Macmillan, 1977), 138–39; Jacques Levy, *Cesar Chavez: Autobiography of La Causa* (New York: W. W. Norton, 1975), 202–3; J. Craig Jenkins, *The Politics of Insurgency: The Farm Workers Movement in the 1960s* (New York: Columbia University Press, 1985), 142–43; Arthur Schlesinger, Jr., *Robert F. Kennedy and His Times* (Boston: Houghton Mifflin, 1978), 790–92; UAW, "Proceedings of the Twentieth Constitutional Convention," 230.

44. UAW, "Proceedings of the Twenty-first Constitutional Convention," Atlantic City, N.J., May 4–10, 1968, 26; Peter Levy, *The New Left and Labor in the 1960s* (Urbana: University of Illinois Press, 1994), 145. P. J. Ciampi, the southern regional director deposed by Reuther in 1955, accepted the check from Reuther as AFSCME representative. Reuther's big contribution soon generated a financial counterattack from the AFL-CIO.

45. UAW-IEB minutes, Detroit, June 8, 1966, UAW-IEB Collection, 11.

46. Joseph Strickland, "Rally Jeers Transfer of Sheffield," *Detroit News*, January 16, 1966; Patrick Owens, "Sheffield versus Mighty UAW: A Gifted Leader's Dilemma," *Detroit Free Press*, January 17, 1966; Robert Battle, "United We Won Another Battle," *TULC Vanguard* (February 1966); WPR to Horace Sheffield, January 14, 1966, file 9, box 157, WPR Collection. Walter Reuther did not instigate the transfer; it may have been the work of Emil Mazey, Nelson Jack Edwards, and Roy Reuther, who wanted Sheffield on his Washington civil rights staff.

47. UAW-IEB minutes, Detroit, June 8, 1966, UAW-IEB Collection, 13–14.

48. "NAACP Committee Selects Six for Board; Drops Four Veterans," NAACP press release, September 19, 1966, and Horace Sheffield to WPR, October 11, 1966, both in file 10, Box 504, WPR Collection; "Comprehensive Analysis—NAACP Board of Directors Election," January 3, 1967, file 11, box 504, WPR Collection; Herbert Hill, interview with the author, Madison, Wisc., June 19, 1987.

49. "WPR Note," July 31, 1967, file 5, box 369, WPR Collection; B. J. Widick, *Detroit: City of Race and Class Violence* (Detroit: Wayne State University Press, 1989), 186; Conot, *American Odyssey*, 533–43.

50. Sidney Fine, *Violence in the Model City: The Cavanagh Administration, Race Relations, and the Detroit Riot of 1967* (Ann Arbor: University of Michigan Press, 1989), 320–23; Conot, *American Odyssey*, 541, 602; Bill Davidson, "If We Can't Solve the Problems of the Ghetto, God Help Our Country," *Saturday Evening Post*, October 5, 1968, 40–46; Boyle, "Politics and Principle," 490–96.

51. Fine, *Model City*, 323; Conot, *American Odyssey*, 604; Widick, *Detroit*, 192–98, 216; Frank Cormier and William J. Eaton, *Reuther* (Englewood Cliffs, N.J.: Prentice-Hall, 1970), 402–3.

52. Dubrow quoted in Boyle, "Politics and Principle," 484; Wilbur Rich, *Coleman Young and Detroit Politics* (Detroit: Wayne State University Press, 1989), 94–96; Dudley W. Buffa, *Union Power and American Democracy: The UAW and the Democratic Party, 1935–1972* (Ann Arbor: University of Michigan Press, 1984), 156–71; Conyers quoted in Carl Solberg, *Hubert Humphrey: A Biography* (New York: W. W. Norton, 1984), 343.

53. *Fortune* (November 1966) quoted in Stanley Weir, "Forces behind the Reuther-Meany Split," *New Politics* (Spring 1967): 14; Robert Zieger, *American Workers, American Unions, 1920–1985* (Baltimore: Johns Hopkins University Press, 1986), 165–70; Kim Moody, *An Injury to All* (New York: Verso, 1988), 83–90. The most thorough account of a union leadership turnover based upon long pent-up grievances is John Herling, *Right to Challenge: People and Power in the Steelworkers' Union* (New York: Harper & Row, 1972).

54. Steve Babson, *Working Detroit* (New York: Adama Books, 1984), 180–83; Oliver Quayle and Co., "A Study in Depth of the Rank and File of the UAW: May 1967," box 147, WPR Collection; Louis Harris and Associates, "The Mandate of the UAW Rank and File for Contract Negotiations in 1961," in box 10, Ken Bannon Collection.

55. Stephen Amberg, *The Union Inspiration in American Politics: The Autoworkers and the Making of a Liberal Industrial Order* (Philadelphia: Temple University Press, 1994), 171–206 passim; Charles Sabel, *Work and Politics: The Division of Labor in Industry* (New York: Cambridge University Press, 1982), 175–79; Quayle and Co., "Study in Depth of the UAW Rank and File," 180.

56. Oscar Pascal, interview with the author, Detroit, November 1, 1984; Joseph Dunnebeck, interview with Carol Isen, Detroit, January 25, 1982 (copy in author's possession); Bill Goode, "The Skilled Trades: Reflections," in *Auto Work and Its Discontents*, ed. B. J. Widick (Baltimore: Johns Hopkins University Press, 1976), 34–44; Muriel Beach, "The Problems of the Skilled Worker in an Industrial Union" (masters' thesis, Cornell University, 1959), 72–96; UAW-IEB minutes, October 3–7, 1955, UAW-IEB Collection, 211–301 passim. To demonstrate his own concern, Reuther even applied for his UAW journeyman's card, scrupulously noting the twenty months he spent tooling at Gorky.

57. Douglas Fraser, interview with the author, Detroit, April 17, 1990; Douglas Fraser to "All Officers, Regional Directors . . . ," April 11, 1967, file 16, box 81, WPR Collection; Jim Crellin, "Mansfield Striker Aids Rival Union," *Detroit News*, April 7, 1967; Patrick Owens, "Wait Till '67, Reuther Tells Skilled Trades," *Detroit Free Press*, August 6, 1966.

58. UAW, "Proceedings of the Twentieth Convention," 404–13; Carol Isen, "Solidarity Forever?" (manuscript in author's possession, 1982), 22–31; Paul Hoffman, "UAW Craftsmen in Militant Mood," *New York Times*, March 17, 1967; "UAW Skilled Trades Members Show Little Interest in Guaranteed Pay, AFL-CIO Fight," *Daily Labor Report*, March 20, 1967. At a March 1967 skilled trades conference, delegates were profoundly uninterested in the UAW's impending split with the AFL-CIO, but they spent hours debating the definition of a new, nonapprenticed job classification called WEMR (welding machine and welder fixture repair).

59. Owens, "Wait Till '67,"; Patrick Owens, "Skilled Workers' Walkout Cripples Two Auto Plants," *Detroit Free Press*, August 18, 1966; Carol Isen, "Solidarity Forever?" 22–31.

60. Douglas Fraser to "All Officers, Regional Directors . . . ," April 12, 1967, "Skilled Trades" vertical file; UAW-IEB minutes [off-the-record notes], February 22, 1967, UAW-IEB Collection.

61. Patrick Owens, "Big Three and UAW Ready for Scrap over Pay Hikes," *Detroit Free Press*, August 22, 1966; "Rough Road Ahead," *Wall Street Journal*, August 23, 1967; Gardner Ackley to LBJ, "Subject: Solid Gold Cadillac," March 6, 1966, "Automobiles, July 22, 1965–August 15, 1966" file Ex BE4, box 9, LBJ Library.

62. UAW-IEB minutes, February 2, 1967, UAW-IEB Collection, 172.

63. James Cochrane, "The Johnson Administration: Moral Suasion Goes to War," in *Exhortation and Controls: The Search for a Wage-Price Policy, 1945–1971*, ed. Craufurd Goodwin (Washington, D.C.: Brookings Institution, 1975), 263–72; Nat Weinberg to WPR, "Council of Economic Advisers Statement of Guideposts," September 22, 1966, file 8, box 391, WPR Collection; WPR to "All Members of the President's Advisory Committee on Labor-Management Policy," "Proposal for a New Approach to Price Stabilization," November 28, 1966, pricing files, box 9, Robson-Ross Collection, LBJ Library.

64. Goodwin, *Exhortation and Controls*, 272–82; "Labor Outlook," *Business Week*, June 24, 1967, 146.

65. UAW-IEB minutes, September 8, 1966, UAW-IEB Collection, 142; UAW-IEB minutes, February 2, 1967, UAW-IEB Collection, 178.

66. Paul Hoffmann, "Reuther Says He Seeks Labor Revival," *New York Times*, March 11, 1967; "Labor Outlook," *Business Week*, June 24, 1967, 146; Bernard Rosenberg, "The UAW: An Aura of Hope," *Dissent* 14 (July-August 1967): 393; UAW-IEB minutes, March 1, 1968, UAW-IEB Collection, 41–42; A. H. Raskin, "The Impatient Reuther versus Immovable Meany," *New York Times*, February 5, 1967. Wrote Raskin, "The way things look now in the auto industry, Walter will probably need the White House to pull out a good settlement."

67. "AVCO Strike Heats up Pressure for a Law," *Business Week*, July 1, 1967, 114; UAW-IEB minutes, March 1, 1968, UAW-IEB Collection, 41-42.

68. Joseph Califano, Jr., to LBJ, June 22, 1967, and Califano to LBJ, June 26, 1967, both in "Strikes—Work Stoppages," WHCF, LBJ Library; Philip Wagner, "How U.S. Decisions on Wages, Prices Affect Economy," *Detroit News*, July 18, 1967; Reuther to "Officers," "Contract Settlement at AVCO," July 14, 1967, file 9, box 267, WPR Collection.

69. Stanley Brown, "Walter Reuther: He's Got to Walk That Last Mile," *Fortune* 76 (July 1967): 88–89.

70. Amberg, *Union Inspiration*, 258–59; Gardner quoted in Isen, "Solidarity Forever?" 66.

71. Ford Motor Co., "Third Quarter Report to Stockholders," November 1967, "July-December 1967" file, box 14, Nat Weinberg Collection; Laurence G. O'Donnell, "UAW Will Delay Rest of Auto Negotiations until Early '68 Following GM National Pact," *Wall Street Journal*, December 18, 1967; news bulletin for GM management, January 19, February 2, and April 11, 1968, vertical file, GM Institute, Flint, Mich.; Isen, "Solidarity Forever?" 50–51; Reuther quoted in "Acceptance Speech by Art Fox," file 5, box 1, Frank Cormier and William J. Eaton Collection, John F. Kennedy Library.

CHAPTER 19: FROM 1968 TO BLACK LAKE

1. Thomas Powers, *The War at Home: Vietnam and the American People, 1964–1968* (New York: Grossman, 1973), 161, 183; Melvin Small, *Johnson, Nixon, and the Doves* (New Brunswick, N.J.: Rutgers University Press, 1988), 92–110.

2. Bret Eynon, ed., *Something Exploded in My Mind: Voices of the Ann Arbor Anti-War Movement: An Oral History Sampler* (Ann Arbor: Contemporary History Project, 1981), 15–17 (Eynon's complete interview with Barry Bluestone, August 15, 1978, is on deposit at the Bentley Library, University of Michigan, Ann Arbor); Elisabeth Reuther Dickmeyer, interview with the author, Lake Orion, Mich., September 24, 1994.

3. Conway quoted in "Walter Reuther: He's Got to Walk That Last Mile," *Fortune*, 76 (July 1967), 149; Pat Sexton, telephone interview with the author, November 6, 1994. Thomas Braden's article, "I'm Glad the CIA Is Immoral," appeared in the May 20, 1967, *Saturday Evening Post*, but the news was out ten days earlier; see Max Frankel, "Ex-CIA Aide Lists Big Grants to Unions," and "Statement by Reuther on Link to CIA," *New York Times*, May 8, 1967.

4. William Allen, "Victor Reuther Assails Meany's Cold-War Policy," *Daily Worker*, February 7, 1967, file 3, box 217, WPR Collection; Victor Reuther, *The Brothers Reuther*

and the Story of the UAW (Boston: Houghton Mifflin, 1976), 424–25; Abe Zwerling, interview with the author, Washington, D.C., June 6, 1985; Paul Schrade, interview with the author, Los Angeles, August 19, 1987.

5. "Walter Reuther Meets the Press," September 24, 1967, file 11, box 1, Frank Cormier and William J. Eaton Collection, John F. Kennedy Library; Lawrence E. Davies, "Clark Kerr Takes a Key Role in Urging Talks," *New York Times*, February 11, 1968; VGR to United Auto Workers–International Executive Board members, February 12, 1968, file 13, box 4, UAW International Affairs Collection; Clark Kerr to WPR, November 26, 1967, file 3, box 511, WPR Collection; Clark Kerr, interview with Janet Kerr-Tener, Berkeley, Cal., August 12, 1985, LBJ Library, 34–39.

6. Hubert Humphrey to LBJ, February 16, 1968, "Victor Reuther" file, box 111, White House Central Files (WHCF), LBJ Library.

7. VGR to WPR, January 25, 1968, and "Americans for Democratic Action" [draft statement], both in file 1, box 472, WPR Collection; Joseph L. Rauh to Bill Dodds, "ADA," February 28, 1968, file 4, box 435, WPR Collection; Steven M. Gillon, *Politics and Vision: The ADA and American Liberalism, 1947–1985* (New York: Oxford University Press, 1987), 211–13.

8. Industrial Union Department, press conference, March 12, 1968, file 11, box 326, WPR Collection.

9. John P. Roche to LBJ, February 16, 1968, "PL2 Election Campaign" file, box 77, WHCF, LBJ Library; Reuther, *Brothers Reuther*, 455–56; William Dodds, interview with the author, Washington, D.C., June 12, 1987.

10. UAW-IEB minutes, March 1, 1968, UAW-IEB Collection, 49–50, 55.

11. UAW-IEB minutes, March 19, 1968, UAW-IEB Collection, 1–6; Jack Conway, interview with Larry Hackman, Washington, D.C., April 10, 1972; Jim Rowe to Marvin Watson, March 19, 1968, "Labor" file, box 26, and William Connell to Hubert Humphrey, March 19, 1968, "Michigan" file, box 9, both in Marvin Watson Collection, LBJ Library; Jim Rowe to LBJ, March 19, 1968, "Reuther" file, WHCF, LBJ Library.

12. UAW-IEB minutes, March 19–20, 1968, UAW-IEB Collection, 12–16; Jack Conway, interview with Larry Hackman, Washington, D.C., April 10, 1972, 95–96; Schrade, interview with the author; Stephen Schlossberg, interview with the author, Washington, D.C., December 4, 1994. LBJ finally reached WPR in Rochester, Michigan, on the morning of March 20; "Walter Reuther" file, daily diary cards, LBJ Library; Lewis Chester, Godfrey Hodgon, and Bruce Page, *An American Melodrama: The Presidential Campaign of 1968* (New York: Viking Press, 1969), 313–19.

13. UAW-IEB minutes, April 10, 1968, UAW-IEB Collection, [off the record] 5, 19–28; Jack Conway, interview with Frank Cormier and William J. Eaton, Washington, D.C., December 27, 1968.

14. Kevin Boyle, "Politics and Principle: The United Autoworkers and American Labor-Liberalism, 1948–1968" (Ph.D. diss., University of Michigan, 1990), 524–32; Bill Dodds to WPR, April 26, 1968, file 20, box 517, WPR Collection; UAW-IEB minutes, June 24, 1968, UAW-IEB Collection, 45–47; Ben Franklin, "Poor Campaign Scales down Its Goals," *New York Times*, June 13, 1968; Adam Fairclough, *To Redeem the Soul of America: The Southern Christian Leadership Conference and Martin Luther King, Jr.* (Athens: University of Georgia, 1987), 357–88 passim. In return for its support, the UAW insisted that Bayard Rustin play a major role in organizing the rally. But Rustin had been an early opponent of the Campaign, with its broad but vague demands, so he resigned after only two weeks' real work. Reuther thought his resignation was a mistake, so he spoke anyway.

15. Dan [last name unknown] to Sam Fishman, June 12, 1968, file 6, box 435, WPR Collection; Chester et al., *American Melodrama*, 156–79.

16. Conway, interview with Cormier and Eaton. The UAW controlled about half the Michigan delegation in 1968, and within that half Humphrey had considerable support, both among African-Americans and an older cohort of white unionists. Two key figures, AFL-CIO State Chairman Gus Scholle and UAW Community Action Program Director Sam Fishman, were hawks on Vietnam. Abram Chayes to Edward Kennedy, April 8, 1968, David Lebenbom to Ted Sorenson, April 25, 1968, and Lebenbom to Sorenson, May 15, 1968, all in "Michigan—1968 Presidential Campaign" file, Robert F. Kennedy Collection, John F. Kennedy Library; Dudley W. Buffa, *Union Power and American Democracy: The UAW and the Democratic Party, 1935–1972* (Ann Arbor: University of Michigan Press, 1984), 107–10.

17. John Kenneth Galbraith to WPR, March 15, 1968, file 2, box 472, WPR Collection; Dennis Creek, telephone interview with the author, December 3, 1994.

18. Conway, interview with Cormier and Eaton; David English, *Divided They Stand* (Englewood Cliffs, N.J.: Prentice-Hall, 1969), 315–17; Kerr, interview with Kerr-Tener, 34–38; UAW-IEB minutes, June 24, 1968, UAW-IEB Collection, 69–70; "National Committee for a Political Settlement in Vietnam" [news release], August 19, 1968, file 11, box 435, WPR Collection; Boyle, "Politics and Principle," 541–45.

19. Conway, interview with Cormier and Eaton; UAW-IEB minutes, September 10, 1968, UAW-IEB Collection, 14–15; Boyle, "Politics and Principle," 547.

20. Judd Arnett, "Why Hubert's Absent," *Detroit Free Press*, September 2, 1968; "UAW Changes Political Plans," *Detroit Free Press*, September 7, 1968; UAW-IEB minutes, September 10, 1968, UAW-IEB Collection, 12–13.

21. UAW, "Proceedings of the Twenty-first Constitutional Convention," Atlantic City, N.J., May 4–10, 1968, 18–19; Chester et al., *American Melodrama*, 280–81. See also Michael Kazin, *The Populist Persuasion: An American History* (New York: Basic Books, 1995), 221–42.

22. Kim Moody, *The American Working Class in Transition* (New York: International Socialists, 1969), 17; WPR, interview with Jean Stein, Detroit, October 24, 1968, 19 (copy in author's possession), 19.

23. Chester et al., *American Melodrama*, 705–6; UAW-IEB minutes, September 10, 1968, UAW-IEB Collection, 15. The high UAW official was probably Leonard Woodcock.

24. Chester et al., *American Melodrama*, 707–10; UAW-IEB minutes, November 20, 1968, UAW-IEB Collection, 36–37; "The Wallace Candidacy," file 2, box 436, WPR Collection; Boyle, "Politics and Principle," 560–65. Boyle points out that Humphrey's dramatic surge in October, especially among working-class voters in the North, was a product not simply of the trade union mobilization but of these voters' disproportionate dovishness on Vietnam, to which Humphrey finally appealed in his Salt Lake City speech of September 30.

25. UAW-IEB minutes, October 9, 1969, UAW-IEB Collection, 438–39, 441; UAW-IEB minutes, November 7, 1969, UAW-IEB Collection, 17–26; Philip Foner, *U.S. Labor and the Vietnam War* (New York: International Publishers, 1989), 85–89, 166–67; Elisabeth Reuther Dickmeyer, interview with the author.

26. VGR to Dusan Petrovic, September 25, 1968, and Guy Nunn to VGR, December 19, 1968, both in file 17, box 461, WPR Collection; UAW, "Proceedings of the Twenty-first Constitutional Convention," 334–35; Anthony Carew, *Walter Reuther* (Manchester: Manchester University Press, 1993), 135–36.

27. Guy Nunn to VGR, December 19, 1968, Otto Brenner to WPR, January 2, 1969, and WPR to Brenner, January 31, 1969, all in file 11, box 451, WPR Collection; UAW-

IEB minutes, April 12, 1969, UAW-IEB Collection, 8–14; Stephen Fay, "Brothers Fall Out," *London Sunday Times*, September 2, 1969.

28. Arthur A. Sloane, *Hoffa* (Cambridge, Mass.: MIT Press, 1991), 320–23, 341–42.

29. UAW-IEB minutes, June 24, 1968, UAW-IEB Collection, 40; Martin Gerber, interview with the author, Bradley Beach, N.J., November 15, 1987.

30. UAW-IEB minutes, June 24, 1968, UAW-IEB Collection, 41; Matt Bates, "The Alliance for Labor Action: An Example for All Unions," *Labor Center Review* (May 1984): 54–56; Edward Clayton Johnson, Jr., "An Analysis of the Origins and Programs of the Alliance for Labor Action," *Dissertation Abstracts International* (1973), 34–1A.

31. WPR, interview with William J. Eaton, Detroit, August 20, 1969; Leon Fink and Brian Greenberg, *Upheaval in the Quiet Zone: A History of Hospital Workers' Union, Local 1199* (Urbana: University of Illinois Press, 1989), 146; Alliance for Labor Action, "Disbursements Analysis," September 30, 1969, file 15, box 338, WPR Collection.

32. Bates, "Alliance for Labor Action," 55; Boyle, "Politics and Principle," 535; Joseph Hill, "Walter Reuther's Gamble," *Commonweal* 90 (May 16, 1969): 261–62; UAW-IEB minutes, April 13, 1969, UAW-IEB Collection, 92–95; "Reuther's 'Grand Alliance': Meaning to Business and Labor," *U.S. News and World Report*, June 9, 1969, 70–71; "ALA Conference Agenda," May 26, 1969, file 4, box 339, WPR Collection; Moe Foner, telephone interview with the author, October 18, 1989.

33. Martin Gerber, interview with the author; Douglas Fraser, interview with the author, Detroit, April 17, 1990; Schlossberg, interview with the author; Sloane, *Hoffa*, 350–53; J. Craig Jenkins, *The Politics of Insurgency: The Farm Workers Movement in the 1960s* (New York: Columbia University Press, 1985), 176–81.

34. Wiley Branton, "Grant Proposals for Community and Social Action," November 18, 1969, file 16, box 338, WPR Collection; Harry Bernstein, "Unions Chart New Political, Social Courses," *Los Angeles Times*, October 25, 1969; UAW-IEB minutes, November 16, 1968, UAW-IEB Collection, 148–51.

35. Steve Jefferys, *Management and Managed: Fifty Years of Crisis at Chrysler* (New York: Cambridge University Press, 1986), 166–69; James Geschwender, *Class, Race, and Worker Insurgency: The League of Revolutionary Black Workers* (New York: Cambridge University Press, 1977), 45.

36. Jefferys, *Management and Managed*, 168–74; "Labor: Black Rage on the Auto Lines," *Time*, April 11, 1969, 54; John Barnard, *Walter Reuther and the Rise of the Auto Workers* (Boston: Little, Brown, 1983), 209; see also Dan Georgakas and Marvin Surkin, *Detroit: I Do Mind Dying* (New York: St. Martin's Press, 1975), 15–62 passim.

37. WPR, interview with Eaton; *Administrative Letter* quoted in Geschwender, *Class, Race, and Worker Insurgency*, 111–13. Reuther's good friend Abe Zwerling, now president of the Detroit Board of Education, faced a similar uprising from nationalist advocates of a decentralized system. His liberal defense of bussing and integration soon cost him his post. See Jeffrey Mirel, *The Rise and Fall of an Urban School System: Detroit, 1907–1981* (Ann Arbor: University of Michigan Press, 1993), 326–45 passim.

38. Jefferys, *Management and Managed*, 181–87; Geschwender, *Class, Race, and Worker Insurgency*, 114–22; WPR, interview with Eaton.

39. John Bracey, interview with the author, Alexandria, Va., November 6, 1994; WPR, interview with Eaton; Denby quoted in Robert Zieger, *American Workers, American Unions, 1920–1985* (Baltimore: Johns Hopkins University Press, 1986), 1980.

40. UAW, "Proceedings of the Twenty-second Constitutional Convention," Atlantic City, N.J., April 20–24, 1970, 26; "GM, Roche Puts Blame on Auto Workers for Industry

Woes," *Wall Street Journal*, February 24, 1970; Jerry Flint, "Reuther Calls Pay and Pensions Major Issues in '70 Auto Talks," *New York Times*, March 13, 1970; "Auto Industry Struggling to Stop Lag in Productivity," *New York Times*, August 8, 1970; Emma Rothschild, *Paradise Lost: The Decline of the Auto-Industrial Age* (New York: Random House, 1973), 125; Harry Katz, *Shifting Gears: Changing Labor Relations in the U.S. Automobile Industry* (Cambridge, Mass.: MIT Press, 1985), 43; Barry Bluestone and Irving Bluestone, *Negotiating the Future: A Labor Perspective on American Business* (New York: Basic Books, 1992), 99.

41. Laurence O'Donnell, "UAW's Reuther Faces Pressures from Firms, Members as Talks Near," *Wall Street Journal*, April 17, 1970; Elisabeth Reuther Dickmeyer, *Reuther: A Daughter Strikes* (Southfield, Mich.: Spelman, 1989), 340; Lloyd Ulman, interview with the author, Berkeley, Calif., April 12, 1982.

42. Jerry Flint, "UAW Convention to Outline Goals," *New York Times*, April 19, 1970; "Open Politics in UAW," *Detroit Free Press*, April 25, 1970; "GM Likely Focus of Auto Workers," *Detroit Free Press*, April 26, 1970; Ralph Orr, "Reuther Step Down? He's Not Ready Yet," *Detroit Free Press*, May 3, 1970; "Acceptance Speech by Art Fox," file 5, box 1, Cormier and Eaton Collection, John F. Kennedy Library; WPR to York Langton, May 7, 1970, "Walter Reuther Personal" file, box 41, Joseph Rauh Collection.

43. UAW-IEB minutes, June 15, 1967, UAW-IEB Collection, 63; UAW, "Proceedings of the Twenty-second Constitutional Convention," 20. Reuther had been particularly impressed with the lakeside educational facility of the Swedish Metal Workers Federation at Skogaholm, which he visited in the mid-1960s. To be the first director at Black Lake, Reuther chose an old Socialist, Brendan Sexton, whose innovative programs did make those attending the school more active in the UAW, as well as more critical of the UAW's top leadership. Sune Ahlen, telephone interview with the author, February 2, 1995; Bill Goode, telephone interview with the author, November 26, 1994.

44. Gerber, interview with the author; Goode, interview with the author; UAW, "Proceedings of the Twenty-second Constitutional Convention," 20; "Minutes: Conversation Meeting Concerning the Sewer and Paint Creek," file 13, box 517, WPR Collection; Dickmeyer, *A Daughter Strikes*, 337; James Warren, "Rustic Retreat for Rank-and-Filers Is One Only a Millionaire Could Afford," *Chicago Tribune*, November 7, 1989. The UAW began chartering a five-passenger Lear jet in June 1966 when Reuther flew to Jackson, Mississippi, to take part in the Meredith march. Jim [last name unknown] to Irving Bluestone, July 1, 1966, file 1, box 157, WPR Collection.

45. Small, *Johnson, Nixon, and the Doves*, 201–9; Dickmeyer, *A Daughter Strikes*, 345; Reuther, *Brothers Reuther*, 462; Foner, *U.S. Labor and the Vietnam War*, 167.

46. Dickmeyer, *A Daughter Strikes*, 343–46; Edwin Pipp, "Three Factors Weighed in Reuther Jet Crash," *Detroit News*, May 31, 1970; National Transportation Safety Board, "Aircraft Accident Report: Executive Jet Aviation, Inc., May 9, 1970," report no. NTSB-AAR–71–3.

47. "Memorial Issue,' *Solidarity* (June 1970); Frank Cormier and William J. Eaton, *Reuther* (Englewood Cliffs, N.J.: Prentice-Hall, 1970), 424–27; A. H. Raskin, "Reuther's Legacy for Social Stability," *New York Times*, May 18, 1970.

48. "Reuther's Death Creates a Vacuum," *Business Week*, May 16, 1970, 106; Damon Stetson, "Walter Reuther: Union Pioneer with Broad Influence Far Beyond the Field of Labor," *New York Times*, May 11, 1970; "Eulogies," *Solidarity* (June 1970): 14–15.

49. WPR, interview with Stein, 20.

EPILOGUE: "WHAT WOULD WALTER DO?"

1. Louis Uchitelle, "Auto Union Seeks to Deter Detroit from New Layoffs," *New York Times*, May 2, 1993; see also Robert Zieger, *American Workers, American Unions, 1920–1985* (Baltimore: Johns Hopkins University Press, 1995), 201–11; Kim Moody, *An Injury to All: The Decline of American Unionism* (London: Verso, 1988), 95–126.

2. See, for example, Keith Naughton, "What Would Walter Do?" *Detroit News*, May 7, 1990.

3. William Serrin, *The Company and the Union: The "Civilized Relationship" of the General Motors Corporation and the United Automobile Workers* (New York: Random House, 1973), 242–306 passim; Heather Ann Thompson, "Lordstown Revisited" (manuscript in author's possession, 1988); Brendan Sexton to Leonard Woodcock, August 19, 1970, file 12, box 4, Brendan Sexton Collection; Stephen Schlossberg, interview with the author, Washington, D.C., December 4, 1994. Walter Reuther's closest confidants resigned during his tenure, including Nat Weinberg, Victor Reuther, and Brendan Sexton. And Paul Schrade lost his seat on the executive board when Woodcock abandoned him to a more conservative clique among the secondary officers within the California region.

4. Robert Reich and John Donahue, *New Deals: The Chrysler Revival and the American System* (New York: Times Books, 1985), 10–46; Harry Katz, *Shifting Gears: Changing Labor Relations in the U.S. Automobile Industry* (Cambridge, Mass.: MIT Press, 1985), 51; Moody, *Injury to All*, 127–46.

5. Reich and Donahue, *New Deals*, 160–237 passim; Moody, *Injury to All*, 165–91.

6. David Brody, "The Breakdown of Labor's Social Contract," *Dissent* (Winter 1992): 32–36; for Germany, see Lowell Turner, *Democracy at Work: Changing World Markets and the Future of Labor Unions* (Ithaca, N.Y.: Cornell University Press, 1991), 1–37, 153–71; for Sweden, see Jonas Pontusson, *The Limits of Social Democracy: Investment Politics in Sweden* (Ithaca, N.Y.: Cornell University Press, 1992); for Canada, see Charlotte A. B. Yates, *From Plant to Politics: The Autoworkers Union in Postwar Canada* (Philadelphia: Temple University Press, 1993), 192–252 passim.

7. Kevin Kelly, "For Now, the UAW Can't Keep Cat from Purring," *Business Week* (October 3, 1994), 57; Robert L. Rose, "Temporary Heaven: A Job at Struck Caterpillar," *Wall Street Journal*, November 29, 1994; Aaron Bernstein, "Inequality: How the Gap Between Rich and Poor Hurts the Economy," *Business Week* (August 15, 1994), 78–83; Deith Bradsher, "Productivity Is All, but It Doesn't Pay Well," *New York Times*, June 25, 1995; James Bennet, "UAW, Ranks Thinning, Elects a Fighter as President," *New York Times*, June 15, 1995.

8. Thomas Byrne Edsall and Mary Edsall, *Chain Reaction: The Impact of Race, Rights, and Taxes on American Politics* (New York: W. W Norton, 1991), 27; Dudley W. Buffa, *Union Power and American Democracy: The UAW and the Democratic Party, 1935–1972* (Ann Arbor: University of Michigan Press, 1984), 176–77.

9. Stephen Waring, *Taylorism Transformed: Scientific Management Theory since 1945* (Chapel Hill: University of North Carolina Press, 1991), 160–86; GM advertisements, *Business Week*, April 27, 1987, 127; May 4, 1987, 115.

10. Barry Bluestone and Irving Bluestone, *Negotiating the Future: A Labor Perspective on American Business* (New York: Basic Books, 1992), 191–201; Leonard Woodcock, Douglas Fraser, et al., "An Open Response to Victor Reuther" (unpublished circular letter in author's possession, February 1989); Bruce Lee quoted in Jane Slaughter, "Management by Stress," *Multinational Monitor* (January 1990): 12.

11. "Saturn Labor Pact Assailed by UAW Founder," *New York Times*, October 28, 1985; "Victor Reuther on Today's Labor Movement," *Labor Notes* (December 1985): 10; John Lippert, "Factions Grasp for Walter Reuther's Legacy," *Detroit Free Press*, May 5, 1990; Mike Parker, "Industrial Relations Myth and Shop Floor Reality," in *Industrial Democracy in America: The Ambiguous Promise*, ed. Nelson Lichtenstein and Howell John Harris (New York: Cambridge University Press, 1993), 249–74.

12. William Serrin, "Disputed Election Is Embarrassing UAW," *New York Times*, August 25, 1986; Barbara Koeppel, "Victor Reuther: 'We Need a Union That Acts like a Union Again,'" *The Progressive* (December 1989), 25–28.

13. UAW, "Proceedings of the Fourteenth Constitutional Convention," Atlantic City, N.J., March 22–27, 1953, 317; WPR, interview with Frank Cormier and William J. Eaton, Detroit, August 20, 1969, Frank Cormier and William J. Eaton Collection, John F. Kennedy Library.

INDEX

Abner, Willouby, 377, 534n24

Ackley, Gardner, 416–17

Addes, George, 56; anti-Communist purge of Allis-Chalmers local, 258; factional war with WPR, 191–93, 208–9, 251, 267; Flint wildcat strike, 147–48; on GM strike of 1945–46, 233; premium pay issue, 197; pro-Communist position, 128–30, 157, 184; Unity Caucus appeal for sanity, 117; Yale and Towne strike, 81

Addes-Frankensteen Caucus, UAW factional struggle, 210–11, 216–19

Addes-Thomas Caucus, UAW factional struggle, 250, 253–54, 503n44

Adenauer, Konrad, 342–43

administered prices by auto industry, 352

Aeronautical Chamber of Commerce, 182

aeronautics, WPR's experience in, 20–21

AFL. *See* American Federation of Labor

AFL-CIO: ALA challenge, 431–32; base of Humphrey support, 425; foreign programs conflict with UAW, 406–9; jurisdictional conflicts with UAW, 351–52; lack of support for civil rights, 385; LBJ's vice presidential nomination, 355–56; shortened workweek conflict, 364; Viet-

nam War position, 405–6; withdrawal from European union organization, 430; WPR-Meany feud, 366–67

African-Americans: auto industry subordination of, 372–75; lack of union involvement, 91, 179; left out of corporate welfare state, 297; militancy in late 1960s, 411–12, 433; wartime militancy in UAW, 202, 206–11; WPR's attempts to gain support, 252, 315–17. *See also* civil rights movement; racial politics

aircraft industry: Ford Tri-Motor, 21; postwar plight of, 222; unionization drive, 182–83, 198; wage increase attempt, 350; war mobilization, 160–70, 176, 479n37

Alcorn, Meade, 348

Alliance for Labor Action (ALA), 431–33

Allis-Chalmers strikes, 178, 191–92, 258–59

Alter, Victor, 35

Amalgamated Association of Iron, Steel and Tin Workers, 2–4

Amalgamated Clothing Workers of America (ACWA), 145

amalgamation among UAW locals, 60

America First Committee, 159

551